2nd Edition

CHILDHOOD PSYCHOPATHOLOGY

a developmental approach

Irwin Jay Knopf
Emory University

Prentice-Hall, Inc. Englewood Cliffs, New Jersey 07632

Library of Congress Cataloging in Publication Data

KNOPF, IRWIN J.
Childhood psychopathology.

Bibliography: p.
Includes index.
1. Child psychopathology. I. Title. [DNLM: 1. Mental Disorders—In infancy and childhood. 2. Psychopathology—In infancy and childhood. W S 350 k72e]
RJ499.K568 1984 618.92′8907 83-22945
ISBN 0-13-130444-5

Editorial/production supervision: Helen Maertens and Linda Benson
Cover design: Judy Knopf
Manufacturing buyer: Ron Chapman

Printed in the United States of America

10 9 8 7 6 5 4 3 2 1

ISBN 0-13-130444-5

Prentice-Hall International, Inc., *London*
Prentice-Hall of Australia Pty. Limited, *Sydney*
Editora Prentice-Hall do Brasil, Ltda., *Rio de Janeiro*
Prentice-Hall Canada Inc., *Toronto*
Prentice-Hall of India Private Limited, *New Delhi*
Prentice-Hall of Japan, Inc., *Tokyo*
Prentice-Hall of Southeast Asia Pte. Ltd., *Singapore*
Whitehall Books Limited, *Wellington, New Zealand*

Dedicated to Bobbie,
our children,
and our grandchildren

CONTENTS

PREFACE

TO THE FIRST EDITION

Throughout its history, the field of psychopathology has been concerned almost exclusively with disorders of the adult years while little, if any, attention has been directed toward childhood psychopathology. One only needs to examine the traditional college course offerings and the many published textbooks in the area for ample support of this observation. And yet, the primary emphasis on adult aberrations is understandable since it reflects the relative availability of clinical and research findings on these populations.

However, our society's recent fascination with youth has stimulated the strong need to identify quick and easy child-rearing formulae and to establish special child-centered programs that promote normal development. Deviant behavioral patterns of youngsters, especially disruptive ones, have become matters of public concern because they have become too difficult to manage through society's existing institutions. Problems arising from mental retardation, learning disabilities, drug abuse, delinquency, and changing sexual mores, among others, cry out for social action. In turn, these issues have generated interest in the creation of programs of prevention, early identification, and remediation. The relatively new child subspecialists in the fields of medicine, psychology, education, social work, and nursing have responded to this challenge by training a growing number of professionals who are prepared to study and work with abnormal behaviors in children. Their efforts already have furthered our understanding of the causes, treatment, and management of many childhood disorders. But we merely have explored the tip of the iceberg with so much more to be discovered!

This heightened public interest and the growing involvement of students in child-oriented professional careers are sufficient reasons for writing a textbook devoted entirely to childhood psychopathology. However, in the final analysis, my long-time enthusiasm and fascination with the field became the dominant motivational force. My intention was to bring together in a single presentation as much as is currently known about childhood psychopathology without strict allegiance to either a particular theoretical viewpoint or a single source of data. Because too often our current knowledge is inconsistent and incomplete, I approached the writing with a conceptual openness and with the freedom to include the best available information from both the clinical and research literatures. However, extensiveness in reporting without direction and interpretation runs the risk of poor pedagogy, especially for beginning students. Consequently, I have tried to go beyond a compilation of what is currently known to include critical evaluations and limitations in our knowledge, interpretations of the accumulated data, and inferences about future directions.

As a scientist, I have a penchant for quantitative data that are obtained under controlled conditions. As a practicing clinician, I also have acquired a healthy respect for the contributions that even a single, but carefully observed, case can make. I believe that investigative endeavors can be sharpened appreciably by sound clinical insights, and that effective clinical work can be enhanced by a solid grasp of research methodology. Therefore, the book draws from the empirical, experimental, and clinical findings to provide students with a blend of information that hopefully will further their interest in both research and practice. In addition, excerpts from clinical cases and samples of research studies are included to illustrate various abnormal conditions, different treatment approaches, and methodological issues and problems.

Equally important to the substance and organization of the book is its emphasis on development which involves sequential and orderly changes over time in the organism's structure and function, and which is affected by the complex interplay of biological and sociopsychological factors. Behavior cannot be viewed as a static event that occurs simply "out of the blue." Instead, behavior can be understood more reasonably as a dynamic occurrence that has been influenced by prior conditions that interact in complex ways. Moreover, all behaviors lead to some consequences that, in turn, may trigger off other responses. In order to increase the student's appreciation of the dynamic and multidimensional nature of behavior in the growing child, a developmental perspective is taken as a major theme that is reflected in specific chapters as well as generally throughout the book. I also have tried (albeit imperfectly) to organize the chapters dealing with the various clinical syndromes within a broad developmental outline. While this developmental progression provides the student with an age perspective by which frequent and common abnormal behaviors may be viewed, the developmental progression should not be regarded as fixed or distinct time periods in which other forms of psychopathology cannot occur.

The book consists of fourteen chapters that are divided into four parts. The four chapters of Part I deal with introductory material and the basic issues of: Childhood Psychopathology: Past and Present; The Nature of Psychopathology;

Normal Personality Development; and Conceptual Models of Psychopathology. Part II covers methods of assessment and treatment in two chapters, while Part III consists of seven chapters dealing with the full range of clinical syndromes from infancy through late adolescence and the college years. These clinical chapters discuss the behaviors manifested (symptoms), factors associated with the clinical picture, differential diagnostic problems, incidence estimates, etiological considerations (genetic, biological, and psychological), and the most frequently used and promising treatment approaches for each disorder. The final part of the book consists of a single chapter dealing with outcome implications and prevention.

Childhood Psychopathology was written as a comprehensive but beginning text primarily for undergraduates majoring in psychology, education, or sociology, or for those who are preparing for child-oriented careers in these areas or in medicine, dentistry, nursing, social work, counseling, juvenile justice, or corrections. Although a specific undergraduate course of this type is not yet commonplace, I am persuaded that the situation will change rapidly over the next several years. Childhood psychopathology is simply too important, too alive and productive, and too relevant to college students to be omitted much longer from the usual course offerings. Until the change occurs at the college level, the book also should be useful to beginning graduate and professional students in a variety of child-related programs as both a source of study and reference.

Completing an undertaking of this magnitude could not have been possible without the help, advice, and encouragement from so many giving people. I want to express my deep feelings of affection and gratitude to my wife, Bobbie, whose unfaltering love, understanding, and friendship for more than twenty-seven years have been a significant influence and a source of strength in my life. Her collaboration on this project was evident in so many ways, but especially in her genuine willingness to read the entire manuscript almost as many times as I did, and in her professional appraisal of the book's organization, contents, and readability. I also am proud of and grateful to our children, David, Bill, and Randy for their encouragement and assistance with the manuscript, and particularly to our daughter, Judy, for her artistic talents in creating the cover for the book. I have been fortunate to be associated with helpful colleagues and loyal and dedicated graduate students who helped search the literature, evaluated various chapters, and checked the accuracy of references. I am grateful for their efforts and particularly those of Dr. Philip H. Dreyer, Nancy Hayim, June Kaufman, Richard Rosenberg, and Andrew Schiff. I also am indebted to the many anonymous reviewers whose criticisms and suggestions improved the manuscript, and to Jeffrey Bogart, John Isley, and Marina Harrison for their confidence and technical assistance. Finally, I owe a debt of gratitude to Margaret Madgett and Marcia Rice for their secretarial expertise and care with which they prepared the many drafts and the final manuscript.

TO THE SECOND EDITION

In many ways the revision of one's book begins even before the first edition appears in press with an almost incessant search for new references and information and an active regard for better ways of presenting the relevant and appropriate materials. Valuable assistance comes from reactions, comments, and suggestions of colleagues and interested readers who have been kind enough to take the time to share their thoughts, and from students, who, after all, are the primary group to whom the book is directed. The intent to bring together in one comprehensive volume what is known currently about childhood psychopathology from a developmental perspective, and with a critical openness to a variety of theoretical views and sources of data, has not changed from the first edition. In fact, I am more convinced than ever that there is not a single existing theoretical position that can adequately account for the diverse forms of abnormal behaviors observed in children and adolescents, or one conceptual view that could not be more effectively studied if the other views were known and understood. In this sense, the book continues to be eclectic in its exposition of theory, and inclusive in reporting empirical, experimental, and clinical findings. Consequently, the intent of this revision is to strengthen the book by including new and significant data, conclusions, and directions found in the literature since the original manuscript first appeared.

In general, the organizational structure of the book remains essentially the same, although some chapters have been drastically or almost totally revised, a new chapter has been added, and one of the old ones has been dropped. Because of the field's increasing emphasis on the relation between the brain and abnormal behaviors, a new chapter was written dealing with brain damage, its nature, its etiological factors, and its clinical manifestations in the discussion of such conditions as the epilepsies, aphasia, and other language disorders. In addition, the concept of minimal brain dysfunction has been more extensively covered and discussed in another chapter which also more fully presents the major categories of learning disabilities and the hyperkinetic syndrome. With these and other additions, it became necessary to reassess the relative importance of the material to be included in this edition in order to provide the reader with the most comprehensive and appropriate coverage of the field, and without substantially lengthening it beyond the scope of what reasonably could be studied within the time period of a quarter or a semester. The decision was made to exclude the chapter on the college years because it focused primarily on sources of stress and potential problem areas for a specific group about whom generalizations cannot be drawn readily for other groups of young people of the same age. However, the section of this chapter dealing with suicide (a serious problem of youth) was revised and incorporated into a broadened chapter now dealing with adolescence and youth.

In the relatively few years between editions, the field of childhood psychopathology has continued to attract growing numbers of scientists and practitioners to the various related disciplines. One can sense the excitement and the increasing significance of the field in the quality and the quantity of new research, in its impact on other disciplines and public awareness, and the considerable interest expressed in it by many of our best students.

Although I take full responsibility for the contents of this volume, I could not have undertaken or completed it without the help and generosity of so many people. I am grateful for the encouragement, love, and professional contributions of my wife, Bobbie, who has together with our children and grandchildren filled my life with purpose, pride in their accomplishments, and the joys of sharing. I especially thank our daughter, Judy, for creating an attractive and fitting cover, and for enhancing the book with her artistic skills and talent. I am fortunate also to have so many loyal and helpful colleagues and students who assisted in the completion of the revision by reading parts of the manuscript and offering their valuable suggestions and/or who searched the literature, found references, and proofread the text. My appreciation goes to June Kaufman, Craig Rich, Andrew Schiff, Ronda Shiff, Larry Tupler, David Patterson, Donna Colglazier, Pamela Epps, Mark Hartigan, Jane Nofer, Joseph Schwartz, and Daniel Wojnilower. My thanks also to John Isley, Linda Benson, and other members of the staff of Prentice-Hall for their patience and their professionalism. But after all is said and done, the typing and final preparation of the manuscript was the most laborious and taxing job. For this, I am grateful to Gail Hudson, Mary Campbell, Monica Simpson, and especially to Linda McLeod and Jayne Zaloba who took charge with amazing efficiency and organization to complete the book and get it to the publisher on time.

Irwin Jay Knopf
Emory University
Atlanta, Georgia

Part 1 BASIC ISSUES

1

CHILDHOOD PSYCHOPATHOLOGY: Past and Present

PROLOGUE

Tommy W., a four-year-old only child, was referred for psychological evaluation because of his peculiar motor patterns and his slow emotional and social development. In spite of repeated urgings by his pediatrician, who recognized that Tommy was suffering from some serious psychological disorder, his parents were reluctant to seek specialized help. In fact, Mr. and Mrs. W. fortified their resistance with the belief that their son's difficulties stemmed from his premature birth and that, in time, he would experience a sudden growth spurt that would bring his developmental level up to normal.

Although Mrs. W. had some difficulty conceiving Tommy, her pregnancy was uneventful. Tommy weighed slightly over four pounds at birth and needed to remain in an incubator for about two weeks. During the first few months he slept in short bursts and cried much of the time he was awake. He was bottle fed, but because he would take only several ounces at a single feeding, Mrs. W. tended to feed him at frequent intervals. A few months later Mrs. W. noticed that Tommy failed to show any anticipatory response to being picked up, and he seemed stiff and unresponsive when held by her or his father. His unresponsiveness to social stimuli continued, although he did show an early interest in toys. In addition, his motor and language development were slow. He did not stand alone until he was fourteen months old or walk unaided until he reached twenty months. He spoke his first word on his first birthday, but within the next six months he spoke only two or three short sentences which were difficult to understand. At about age two Tommy stopped speaking except for saying his name and making funny vocal noises to himself.

Because of his unresponsiveness to people and his slow language development, Mr. and Mrs. W. thought Tommy might be hard of hearing, but medical tests revealed no auditory defect. He was toilet trained before his second birthday, but by the age of three he began soiling his pants and smearing feces on the walls and on the furniture. At about this time he also began to rock back and forth while sitting, to whirl on his toes in little circles, and to bang his head against the wall at bedtime. He engaged in these strange motor patterns for long periods while he vocalized incomprehensible sounds to himself. His disinterest in people continued, although he was fascinated and content when playing with his toys.

On examination, Tommy appeared to be frail, thin, and small for his age. He was neatly attired and tidy, but he seemed to have a glazed and vacuous look on his face. He took the psychologist's hand and went with him to the playroom without any show of concern about separating from his mother. During the evaluation session Tommy spent much of the time either whirling or sitting in a corner, rocking and banging his head against the wall. He rejected the examiner's overtures but became interested in playing with blocks. Except for his apparent interest in and preference for inanimate objects, he was virtually unapproachable. During the several subsequent sessions his peculiar motor patterns persisted. However, he did evidence interest in the playroom and a need to rearrange the furniture and toys as he had previously left them. Each time he entered the playroom and found it changed, he screamed, whirled, and rocked for a short while and then began to put everything back the way it was before. Tommy was later diagnosed as a psychotic child (see Chapter 8) who required immediate and prolonged professional care.

One could reasonably assume that the strange and peculiar behaviors of children like Tommy have long been matters of public concern and professional inquiry. However, abnormal behaviors of children have been virtually ignored until recently, while interest in either the possessed, the lunatic, or the mentally ill adult has been evident since the beginning of recorded history. The reasons for this dichotomy can be traced to the way Western civilization differentiated the responsibilities of adults and children, the high mortality rate of children in ancient and medieval times, and the failure of early societies to distinguish childhood from adult life.

Adults always have been expected to meet certain social and economic obligations for themselves, and as society developed, for others as well (family and community). Because abnormal conditions often impair one's ability to meet these obligations, the afflicted adult can be a potential source of danger, an economic liability, and a community management problem. In severe cases the community is left with no choice but to take some remedial action to preserve its own integrity. Ancient societies dealt with deranged adults through persuasion or brutal torture. Later societies tried either to isolate them through institutionalization (prisons or asylums) or to treat the sickness. Currently we deal with the problem through more humane private and public diagnostic and treatment facilities. For those who cannot afford the regular fees of practitioners or the cost of private-pay hospital care and low-cost treatment, hospitalization is provided through government subsidies as well as through public welfare and family subsistence programs.

In contrast to the responsibilities culturally attributed to adults, contemporary society views children as minors who are dependent on adults for their care and well-being. Since society assumes that children need supervision, it assigns this function to the family and holds parents accountable for any disruption, danger, or economic loss their children create. Rarely, and only when parents fail to adequately manage their children, does the community become involved. Under these cultural guidelines the problems of disordered adults are handled by the adults themselves, by other adult members of the family, or by the community; those of children are generally considered the responsibility of the family. Moreover, while society regards adults as more stable, more resistant to change, and more fixed in their behavioral patterns, it tends to view children as growing and ever-changing organisms. Although this optimistic outlook regarding human development has important implications for prevention programs, it has been obscured for too long by society's emphasis on the immediate problems of the abnormal adult, as well as by the common "do nothing, wait and see" attitude parents (such as Mr. and Mrs. W.) readily adopt toward their children.

Yet children have not always been viewed in this light, and many of our current ideas about them are of relatively recent vintage. Therefore, we will begin with a historical review that traces the evolution of the ideas and forces that have led to the scientific inquiry of childhood psychopathology. Not only will this approach enable us to show how and where childhood psychopathology began, but it will also provide a broader context in which to view the field's present and future directions.

THE HISTORY OF CHILDHOOD

Prior to the Seventeenth Century

Ancient Abuses. Contrary to our own experiences as children, the history of childhood had been described as "... a nightmare from which we have only recently begun to awaken. The further back in history one goes, the lower the level of child care, and the more likely children are to be killed, abandoned, beaten, terrorized, and sexually abused" (de Mause, 1974, p. 1). In ancient times infanticide was a common and accepted practice used to do away with babies who evidenced imperfection of any sort. It was also used for a variety of other purposes, such as religious sacrifice, the purging of evil, economic circumstances, or even personal convenience. It was also commonplace for children to be abandoned, used as political hostages, sold into slavery, castrated, and sexually abused by older men. In addition, de Mause describes brutal and severe beatings as a continuous and regular part of the life of children born prior to the eighteenth century.

The Absence of Childhood. As shocking and life-endangering as these practices were, it may be even more difficult for us to conceive of a world without children as we know them today. But in antiquity the period of childhood was not known, since children were considered little adults or *homunculi* (little men) without personalities of their own (Aries, 1962). In all likelihood this view could be attributed to the extremely high incidence of infant mortality and to the short life expectancy of everyone in those days (Greenleaf, 1978). Under environmental conditions that argued against survival, it was safer and surely less painful for adults to remain aloof from and uninvolved with their young children.

From studying old paintings, sculptures, figures on tombstones, diaries, and autobiographies Aries (1962) (recommended for fascinating reading) arrived at the conclusion that the medieval world lacked awareness of the unique state of childhood. He observed that except for later characterizations of the Infant Jesus, art forms rarely portrayed children as anything other than miniature adults. Children dressed as adults in clothes that were differentiated only by social class. Similarly, he found no special play activities, games, or literature for children, or any particular topic—including sexual matters—that could not be discussed openly in their presence. Even the word *child* was not used in the restricted way we use it now, since it referred to a state of dependence in adults who were of lower and more submissive rank to others.

Childhood was neither of interest nor of significance to the medieval world—it was a brief period that passed quickly for those few who survived. Children belonged to adult society just as soon as they could live without the constant care of their mothers or wet nurses. Although children of all ages mingled freely with adults, they were viewed as weaker and more fragile than their elders and were used as economic pawns. Marriage contracts arranged for them often were consummated by age twelve (Brown, 1939). For the privileged, school life and apprenticeships began after infancy (age six or seven) in a setting where the young and the old intermingled and where strict discipline was maintained by corporal punishment (the birch stick) and—in rare cases—by imprisonment. Further, in medieval times the family existed solely in a formal sense for the transmission of life, property, and names.

Notwithstanding opposition from the Church and the legal abolition of infanticide, abortion, and the abandonment or sale of children, these abusive practices persisted for more than a thousand years (Lyman, 1974; McLaughlin, 1974). In fact, the medieval belief that children were unimportant continued unabated through the sixteenth century, when some signs began to emerge indicating a new awareness of childhood. Adults seemed more inclined than ever before to recognize children as human beings with special developmental problems and to attend more to their youngsters' physical and emotional needs (Tucker, 1974).

Beyond the Seventeenth Century

The Discovery of Childhood. According to Aries (1962), more definitive changes began to appear in the seventeenth century, especially in the upper socioeconomic classes. Aries noted that adults more openly expressed affection and amusement at children's endearing qualities of simplicity, humor, and tenderness. Themes of childhood emerged in family portraits showing parents coddling, holding hands, and playing with their children. In addition, portraits showed groups of boys and girls at play for the first time. Notice was also taken of childhood jargon and of children's games and play activities. As adults became more openly attached to and interested in children, they began to stress the need to understand them in order to correct their behavior, develop their reasoning ability, and turn them into "good Christians." Aries further noted that ideas about morality changed too; the concept of the "innocence" of the child surfaced in sharp contrast to the previously held notion of immodesty. For example, the sexual ribaldries of adults were no longer permitted for children. Instead, children were taught to exercise control over the social behaviors that now were considered indecent. For some, this shift in morality carried over to the kinds of material children were allowed to read, giving rise to a separate literature for children and adults. But most important, the innocence of children was affirmed by the Church in the seventeenth century; the first communion ceremony was introduced at that time and has since become an important religious festival of childhood.

The Family. The family, which originated in the fifteenth century, changed from a rather impersonal contract to legitimize the transmission of property to heirs to a more meaningful relationship between parents and children. Children became an integral part of everyday life, and their parents showed an increasing concern for their education, career, and future welfare. The emergence of childhood and parental involvement also was linked to the religious idea that children were the living images of their parents, an inspiring belief that further enhanced the family bond.

During the Colonial Period American families were held together by strict, rigid, and austere religious codes of morality. Further, rural economic conditions required every family member (including young children) to share fully in the workload. Because children were needed to ensure the family's economic survival, they were given home training and kept in tow by harsh disciplinary measures (Abramovitz, 1976). Later, during the Industrial Revolution, the American family assumed particular importance, providing its members the social stability and support needed to withstand the unsettling forces of economic growth and social change of that era (Lomax, Kagan, and Rosenkrantz, 1978).

Education. During this period education ceased being mere instruction in basic skills; instead, it developed a larger concern for the physical, mental, and spiritual welfare of the student. Two opposing views emerged: one favoring a protective and coddling approach, the other representing a more moralistic, authoritarian attitude. However, both views recognized the weakness of children and the fact that they were developing organisms who required special instruction and moral training. In fact, by the eighteenth century Rousseau, the father of modern educational philosophy, underscored the idea of childhood when he wrote:

> We expect to find the man in the child without thinking of what the child is before he is a man. . . Childhood has ways of seeing, thinking, feeling peculiar to itself; nothing is more absurd than to wish to substitute ours in their place. (Brown, 1939, p. 11)

Largely through the writings of philosophers such as Locke and Pestalozzi, children were seen as unformed and malleable in character, with inclinations for evil and virtue that could be checked and shaped through the influence of parents and teachers (Strickland, 1970). More than a century later Horace Mann promoted this idea in America, fighting successfully for compulsory schooling on the grounds that early education and conscientious parenting together would result in the development of worthy citizens.

After so many centuries of indifference, ignorance, and neglect, childhood was finally recognized as a valuable and distinct period of life. But this struggle for recognition was paralleled by a much stormier battle, which has raged for as many years: Who controls children? Who holds the ultimate responsibility for what children may do and what is done to them? And who has the final say about matters concerning their life and death? As we shall see in the next section, the issue of who has the authority to direct the child's activities has aroused bitter controversy throughout history among parents, the Church, and the State.

THE CONTROL OF CHILDREN

It may seem sinister to suggest—but nonetheless it is true—that the perennial struggle for the control of children stemmed from their special value as a labor force, as a source of military strength in defending or extending the State, and as spiritual recruits for increasing the influence of the Church. As rich resources leading to economic, political, and religious gains, children have been exploited and abused for centuries, without regard for their person or welfare. However, with the discovery of childhood there has been an increasing trend for one group or another to intercede on behalf of children who are abused excessively.

Children as a Labor Force

In primitive times, when the concept of paternity was unknown, children were linked closely to their mothers, who were their obvious source of survival. However, youngsters were put to work as soon as possible, first as aids to women and later as either hunters or tillers of the soil. In ancient Sparta children (both boys and girls) were wards of the State. A council of elders held the authority to decide whether they would live or die (Brown, 1939). Similarly, the children of Thebes were taken care of initially by public funds, although they were required to repay the debt through work as soon as they were able. As

Christianity emerged and grew, parents became the supreme authority over children. This authority continued without question until the sixteenth century, when the Church issued strict injunctions regulating children, and the State (for example, England) tried to take control by legislating an apprenticeship system and compulsory military training.

The battle between Church and State also was evident in the field of education, as both forces tried to exert influence on the developing child through directives concerning working children. In 1912 the Federal Children's Bureau was established in the United States, extending the State's jurisdiction and responsibility for the welfare of children to the areas of child labor, child health and recreation, child education, and the care of the atypical child. In this country the Wages and Hours Bill of 1938 prohibited the employment of children under sixteen years of age in hazardous occupations (manufacturing and mining). Since the early part of the twentieth century, mechanization, labor unions, and the need to find enough jobs for adults have all contributed significantly to the declining use of children as a labor force in our society.

Child Abuse

As we have seen, children often were abused, severely treated, brutally punished, and immorally exploited until the end of the nineteenth century. They were dealt with in many different ways by various people or institutions who held absolute authority over their fate. In western society children were put to death for stealing a loaf of bread or were imprisoned for other trivial offenses; and often in prison they became the prey of hardened and seasoned criminals (Wilkerson, 1973). In the nineteenth century Illinois and Colorado established separate juvenile courts to provide children with less harsh treatment and to deal with the special problem of juvenile delinquency. Unfortunately, this new view of justice for children was not fully realized, since the correctional and remedial personnel and facilities needed to implement an effective program simply were not made available. Even today the existence of separate courts and detention facilities for children has done little to reduce the incidence of juvenile delinquency or to decrease the recidivism rate for these youngsters (see Chapter 13).

Child abuse was first noted as a contemporary problem in 1946; in 1961 it was named the Battered Child Syndrome (Shepherd, 1973). The term refers to regular physical assaults on a child by a parent with fists, sticks, hot irons, cigarettes, or other harmful objects. Often these assaults result in lacerations, burns, broken bones, internal bleeding, and sometimes death. In a broader context child abuse also refers to sexual molestation or serious neglect which deprives the child of the necessary ingredients for survival. In 1959 the United Nations Assembly adopted a declaration affirming its belief in human rights for children as well as adults. In addition, the Assembly resolved to enact more effective child abuse laws and to improve juvenile courts and child welfare services (Coughlin, 1973). More recent recognition of this problem (which some experts say was much more serious one hundred years ago) is found in the many state statutes requiring physicians to report instances of child abuse. At the federal level Congress enacted the 1974 Child Abuse and Prevention Act, which allocated 85 million dollars to treat these youngsters and their parents ("The Battered Children," 1977).

Child abusers tend to be suspicious of others, to be socially isolated, and to have low frustration tolerance. They are not easily identified by their sex, economic status, race, religious preference, or distinctive personality traits. Their most frequently shared characteristic is a common history of being battered or neglected children (Spinetta and Rigler, 1972). In addition, it is extremely difficult to prove child abuse, since parents may take their battered children to different hospitals to avoid detection, and the police are prevented by law from intruding into family affairs unless there are ample grounds for suspicion. Doctors also are placed in the difficult position of interpreting their medical findings on the basis of indirect evidence and of challenging the parents' accounts of the injury.

In this country the courts have held two different views concerning the boundaries of parental discipline. One view makes the parent the sole arbiter in punishing the child as long as the punishment "does not result in disfigurement or permanent injury, or is not inflicted maliciously" (Shepherd, 1973, p. 177). The other position states that "the parent has a right to punish a child within the bounds of moderation and reason so long as he does it for the welfare of the child; but that if he exceeds due moderation, he becomes criminally liable" (Shepherd, 1973, p. 177). Under either interpretation the interests of the State clearly are more potent than those of the parents in protecting the welfare of children. The fact that child abuse or neglect now ranks fifth as the leading cause of death among young children in the United States (following accidents, cancer, congenital abnormalities, and pneumonia) is sufficient justification for the intrusion of society into the activities of abusive parents ("Battered Children," 1977).

Child Welfare

Child welfare refers to a social and legislative movement which became influential in the latter part of the nineteenth century as a humanitarian reaction to the inhumane treatment of children. The movement has provided the impetus for a good deal of regulatory legislation as well as for the creation of specialized agencies for the care and protection of children. During the 1700s the only services available to needy children were harsh and punitive institutions (almshouses and orphanages), while in the following century services were expanded to include financial aid to families to support their children at home, maternity homes, day care centers, adoption procedures, and services for child abuse victims (Kadushin, 1976). During the nineteenth and twentieth centuries laws were enacted dealing with almost every aspect of child welfare, including mandatory immunization, care of the physically and mentally handicapped, the protection and care of the neglected and the homeless, and the medical examination of preschool children. In addition, special facilities and programs were established and publicly funded to ensure that every child had access to some of the most important ingredients for normal development. Among these were maternal and baby clinics, residential treatment centers, community health centers, services for homebound children, playgrounds and parks for recreation, compulsory education, and free school lunches to prevent malnutrition (Kadushin, 1976).

The child welfare movement involved almost all levels and branches of government in child care and was influential in decreasing the supreme authority of parents to act on behalf of their children. Moreover, the movement reflected a growing change in society's attitude toward children, who were now seen as individuals with rights of their own.

Children's Rights

According to Takanishi (1978), developments in the children's rights movement were associated with the socioeconomic changes brought about by industrialization and urbanization, as well as by the changing views on the nature of childhood, especially as interpreted by social reformers. These reformers sought social justice for children through governmental intervention, subsidies, and judicial actions. To these they attached ". . . new concepts of what a child is, what a child needs, and what a child deserves" (Kiesler, 1979, p. 1014). In fact, Stier (1978) contends that society's failure to provide the basic necessities to educate and maintain the health of its children has prompted many reformers to insist that these ingredients are the "legal imperatives" of children.

Indeed, decisions rendered by the courts for more than the last hundred years have given added credence and importance to the legal rights of children. In the case of *Fletcher* v. *Illinois* (1869)[1] the Court restricted parental authority over children to actions that are within the boundary of reason and humanity, and held further that children must be protected by the law from depraved parents who commit wanton and needlessly cruel acts. In *Haley* v. *Ohio* (1948)[2] the Court took the clear position that rights guaranteed to adults apply to children as well. Other judicial decisions have established children's rights to equal access to educational opportunities *(Brown* v. *Board of Education,* 1954)[3]; due process for those charged with delinquency (*In re Gault,* 1967)[4]; fair procedures in classifying the mentally retarded (*Mills* v. *State Board of Education,* 1969)[5]; and humane treatment for the institutionalized mentally retarded (*Wyatt* v. *Stickney,* 1972)[6].

In addition to court decisions, social legislation and policy positions taken by various national and international organizations have advanced the children's rights movement. For example, in 1912 Congress established the Children's Bureau "to investigate and report upon all matters pertaining to the welfare of children and child life among all classes of our people" (cited in Kiesler, 1979, p. 1014). More recent agencies and commissions created by Congress to protect the rights of children include the President's Panel on Mental Retardation (1961), to consider the needs of mentally retarded children; the National Institute of Child Health and Human Development (1963), mandated to investigate child health broadly in a developmental context rather than to deal with specific problems or conditions of childhood; the Joint Commission on Mental Health of Children (1965), to serve as an advocate of children's needs; the Office of Child Development (1967), to administer programs such as Head Start; the Developmental Disabilities Program (1970), to develop programs to aid special groups of disabled children; and the Juvenile Justice and Delinquency Prevention Office (1974), to establish prevention programs and promote research in the area of juvenile delinquency (Kiesler, 1979; Sobel, 1979).

In its most sweeping action for special groups of children, Congress enacted legislation in 1975 (PL 94–142) which provided financial aid to the states for education of handicapped children. This new law assures free and appropriate public education for *all* handicapped children and guarantees their right to maximal educational opportunities. In addition, the law requires the assessment of school programs designed to meet these special needs. The legislation is inclusive with respect to the definition of handicapped children and assures professional attention to the education and remediation of many previously neglected youngsters.

In addition to issuing a declaration concerning the rights of children, the United Nations General Assembly designated 1979 as the International Year of the Child, both to promote child advocacy and to encourage actions that would meet the various needs of children. In this country the Joint Commission on the Mental Health of Children published in 1970 a very strong statement about the rights of children, which included the following: to be born healthy, to live in a healthy environment, to live in a family whose basic needs are met, to receive continuous and loving care at home and in school, to acquire intellectual and emotional skills for effective citizenship, to receive meaningful employment, to receive appropriate care in treatment facilities which meet children's needs and which are kept as closely as possible within the child's normal social setting, to enjoy a racial and ethnic identity and share a real and functional equality of opportunity, and to participate in the political process (Berlin, 1975).

[1] Fletcher v. The People of the State of Illinois, 1869
[2] Haley v. Ohio, 332 U. S. 596 (1948)
[3] Brown v. Board of Education, 347 U. S. 483 (1954)
[4] In re Gault, 387 U. S. 1 (1967)
[5] Mills v. State, 256 A.2d 752 (Del., 1969)
[6] Wyatt v. Stickney, 344 F. Supp. 373 (M.D. Ala., 1972)

Yet with all the progress made to date, contemporary society still faces a number of controversial questions about the rights of children. We are currently confronted with heated and conflicting arguments about abortion which pit the rights of the pregnant woman against those of the unborn child. Further, we must deal with the question of the legitimacy of children born by artificial insemination as well as with the current practice of disregarding children's rights either to consent to or reject various medical procedures.

The way future generations of children develop may well depend on the final outcome of this persistent battle for their control.

THE DEVELOPMENT OF CHILDHOOD PSYCHOPATHOLOGY AS A FIELD

Up to this point we have given a general account of the past and present status of children. We now consider the more specific, but divergent, forces that have contributed to the development of childhood psychopathology as an area of scientific inquiry and clinical practice. Obviously, the history of this field has neither a fixed beginning nor a single antecedent condition. Many factors have interacted in some unique way, although the task of tracing these events and of assessing their relative impact is especially difficult, since it requires the sorting out of happenings that occurred within a relatively brief time span. While we have organized the material in this section around several major factors, we recognize that later historians, with a longer time perspective, may choose to interpret the past in a different light, with different emphases.

Early Views of Adult Psychopathology

The history of ideas about psychopathology has been tied largely to adult behaviors that have historically aroused public attention. The oldest etiological view, *demonology*, assumed that abnormal behaviors were the product of evil spirits that inhabited objects, animals, and people (Zilboorg and Henry, 1941). Early Greek civilization embellished this view by suggesting that the gods had the dual power to cause and cure possession. During the Dark Ages demonology was revitalized and used by the Church to investigate and eliminate witchcraft. Throughout these years the underlying philosophy for treating demonology remained the same, although the specific methods employed often changed. Demons were either mollified or removed, although a decided preference for punitive methods was evident.

The concept of organic disease was first introduced by Hippocrates, who spoke of humors and corresponding personality temperaments. However, this etiological position only became viable and dominant in the eighteenth century, when significant advances occurred in the fields of anatomy, physiology, neurology, chemistry, and general medicine (Zilboorg and Henry, 1941). These advances made possible the demonstration of organic pathology as the basis of many physical ailments and buoyed the expectations that abnormal behavior would have a similar cause. Early in the twentieth century the discovery of a specific organic etiology (syphilitic infection) for a disorder known as General Paresis provided confirmation for the previously assumed causal link between brain pathology and psychopathology. Gall's theory of phrenology further emphasized that the brain was the principal organ underlying personality aberrations. He proposed that character traits were localized in some thirty-seven different areas of the brain and that psychopathology was tied to the overdevelopment of these areas.

The German psychiatrist Wilhelm Griesinger—an even more respected influence (or a less controversial one)—held a similar view about brain disease and abnormal behavior. Griesinger is credited with writing the first modern textbook in psychiatry as well as with emphasizing the organic viewpoint as an exclusive cause of mental illness. However, Emil Kraepelin (1856–1926), a follower of Griesinger, played a singularly important role in perpetuating the organic view (Zilboorg and Henry, 1941). Kraepelin not only recognized the significance of brain pathology in abnormal behavior, but he also developed a classification system that is the basis of the one largely used today. Kraepelin observed that certain groups of symptoms in hospitalized patients occurred together often enough to be considered specific types of mental diseases. Each type was regarded as distinct and followed its own fixed course. His early classification focused on two prominent types of mental diseases—manic-depressive psychosis and dementia praecox (now known as schizophrenia). He regarded the excited and euphoric symptoms of mania and the melancholic and despondent states of depression as one disorder, noting that these different mood symptoms generally succeeded each other in the same individual. He suggested that the cause of manic-depression was an irregularity of metabolic functioning attributable to some kind of hereditary defect. Dementia praecox was caused by malfunctioning glands which produced an unhealthy chemical state that adversely affected the central nervous system.

During the nineteenth century psychiatry contributed little to child psychopathology, with a few notable exceptions. Benjamin Rush, the founder of American psychiatry; Esquirol, who was associated with the hospital reform movement in France; and Griesinger all made isolated references to specific forms of childhood disorders in their extensive writings on adult psychopathology (Rie, 1971, pp. 3–50). In addition, Walk (1964) described some interest by pediatric medicine in childhood disorders, while Harms (1967) noted that there were at least three books published during this period which were primarily devoted to the mental disorders of children. However, there were few facilities and programs designed especially for disordered children, except in the area of mental retardation.

Mental Retardation

The first childhood disorder to arouse public attention was mental retardation, which was seen even in ancient Greece and Rome and was treated with contempt and persecution. With the rise of Christianity, the public attitude shifted from disdain to pity. During the Dark Ages the mentally retarded either served as fools (jesters) for the amusement of others or were abandoned to fend for themselves (Rosen, Clark, and Kivitz, 1976). The enlightenment of the Renaissance provided an impetus for scientific inquiry into mental retardation. In 1672 Sir Thomas Willis labeled the condition *feeblemindedness* and gave the first detailed description of its varying degrees. The terms *mental deficiency* and *mental retardation*, both referring to the same condition, were introduced in the 1920s and 1950s, respectively (Potter, 1972).

However, the first real stirrings of sustained interest in treating mental retardation occurred at the close of the eighteenth century, when Jean Itard made a valiant attempt to educate the Wild Boy of Aveyron. The boy was discovered by peasants as he ran naked through a forest in the south of France (Lane, 1976). Victor, as he was later named by Itard, quickly became the object of considerable curiosity, fear, and a determined hunt that ended in his capture. He was put on display in the village square, but he soon escaped, only to return to the village two years later. Itard stood almost alone in his conviction that Victor was educable and that the boy's strange and retarded development was the result of prolonged sensory deprivation and isolation from human contact. Itard undertook the enormous task of bringing the boy (who was then about seventeen years old) "to a civilized state." After five laborious years of intensive tutoring, Itard abandoned the project because Victor remained mute and showed little progress. However, the publicity surrounding the case stimulated a good deal of interest in the possibility of training the mentally retarded. Although a few schools for the retarded already had been founded, additional ones were established in Europe and America following Itard's celebrated experiment (Rosen, Clark, and Kivitz, 1976).

Itard's work on mental retardation was carried forth first in Europe and then in the United States by Edward Seguin (1812–1880), who became a leader in educating both the legislature and the public about the problems of this disorder (Rie, 1971). Seguin shared Itard's belief that retardates were educable and could be cured by physiological training of sensory functions, especially perception. However, this optimistic outlook soon gave way to pessimism. Professional workers and the public showed renewed interest in Mendelian genetics and were influenced by the findings of pedigree studies suggesting that mental retardation was an inherited disease (and thus unmodifiable) leading to delinquency and crime. This pessimistic climate made possible the enactment of eugenic laws for the sterilization of retardates and also justified their isolation in prison and pauper homes (Rosen, Clark, and Kivitz, 1976). Although newer and more specialized facilities (residential schools) began to appear during the early part of the twentieth century, segregation of the mentally retarded persisted. Many of these institutions, still in existence today, were constructed in remote geographical areas as a way of protecting the public. However, their inaccessibility also served to deter parents from maintaining close ties with their institutionalized youngsters.

During the course of this century considerable progress has been made in the area of mental retardation. This can be attributed to many factors. Some, such as the development of intelligence tests, the founding of child guidance clinics, and the emergence of child psychology as a field of study, will be discussed later in this chapter. Other factors, such as advances in genetics, improved pre- and postnatal care, better health and nutrition for mothers and infants, and the development of training programs for educational specialists, will be included in Chapters 11 and 14. However, we need to acknowledge the special and influential role that parents have played in successfully pressuring for facilities and programs. In 1950 parents and other interested citizens founded the National Association of Parents and Friends of Mentally Retarded Children, which later became the National Association for Retarded Citizens (Blain, 1975). This association serves as an advocate for mentally retarded citizens at the national, state, and local levels. The association is involved in such varied activities as sponsoring research, mounting public educational programs, providing the documentation necessary for the preparation of new legislation, and delivering direct management and training services. It also worked with other groups under the sponsorship of President John F. Kennedy to bring about in 1962 the President's Panel on Mental Retardation. This group later called for new legal concepts, research, preventive measures, improved facilities, and emphasis on the home and local care of retardates. These efforts led to the passage in 1963 of the Mental Retardation Facilities and Community Mental Health Centers Construction Act, which funded new facilities and programs (Blain, 1975).

Unlike the early interest shown in mental retardation, most of the major forces that influenced the field of child psychopathology did not emerge until the latter part of the nineteenth century or the first two decades of this century. Many of these developments occurred concurrently, suggesting a zeitgeist that was conducive to ferment and change and an interaction that promoted progress. Which of these parallel forces made others possible, or which are most important, are questions we cannot readily answer. We simply can note surface relationships when they are apparent and encourage the readers to make their own judgments about the matter of significance.

Intelligence Tests

As an outgrowth of interest in mental retardation, the mental testing movement began in 1904, when the French Minister of Education created a commission to assure the best training possible for all retarded children and to construct a test that would identify feebleminded youngsters (Goodenough, 1949; Anastasi, 1965). A psychologist by the name of Alfred Binet was asked to develop the measuring device. He completed it in 1905 with the aid of his collaborator, Theophile Simon. Revising the scale in 1908 and 1911, Binet introduced the concept of *mental age*, by grouping test items according to the chronological age at which children usually answered such items correctly. Children whose test performance (mental age) matched their chronological age were considered average. Those who exceeded their chronological age were considered brighter than average, while those with a mental age lower than their chronological age were labeled below average in intelligence. In this way Binet found a procedure that provided a frame of reference (relative to chronological norms) for the interpretation of his intelligence test. A year later William Stern improved on Binet's idea by suggesting the idea of an *intelligence quotient* (now better known as the IQ) to express the relationship between the child's mental age and chronological age in quantitative terms. In this country Lewis Terman and his associates restandardized and modified the original Binet-Simon scales, and they popularized the IQ in a new test version called the Stanford-Binet Intelligence Scale, which was published in 1916. The new test and its subsequent revisions became the most widely used individual intelligence test for children until the Wechsler scales appeared (see Chapter 5).

During World War I it became necessary to construct new tests of intelligence to help the military select mentally able candidates from a large number of illiterate recruits (Anastasi, 1965). The new tests were designed with economy in mind, since they could be administered to groups of people (group intelligence tests) by a proctor. The cost of group-administered tests is low when contrasted to the Binet-type scales, where one person at a time is tested by a trained psychologist. In addition, the test items were completely nonverbal (performance tests) and were therefore independent of the academic skills in which the illiterate subjects were deficient. In the course of time test constructors and users became increasingly aware of factors other than intelligence that could influence IQ scores. These factors included education, culture, the skill of the examiner, and so forth. In addition, they gave more attention to the important issues of reliability, validity, and standardization procedures, as well as to other problems and limitations of these tests.

Public acceptance of mental tests encouraged the development of newer measuring devices purporting to assess academic achievement, personality, special aptitudes, abilities, interests, and brain damage. As school attendance became mandatory and the period of education was lengthened for children, the need for some of these tests became more apparent. The availability of intelligence tests and other psychological tests opened the way for the more objective and accurate assessment of children's abilities, the more effective preparation of remedial programs, and the empirical investigation of many important questions associated with the intellect, personality, and social functioning of children and adults.

Early Conceptualizations and Influences

Psychoanalysis. As psychopathology came to be viewed predominantly as an organic disease (from the eighteenth century on), a new line of thinking emerged that proposed psychological factors as the cause of abnormal behavior. This view focused almost exclusively on the frustrations and emotional conflicts of early childhood and daily living as the origins of mental illness.

Curiously enough, the beginnings of this development can be traced to the highly dramatic work of Anton Mesmer (1734–1815), a physician who was eventually banned from practicing in France and was denounced as a charlatan. He died in obscurity in Switzerland (Zilboorg and Henry, 1941; Deutsch, 1949; Mora, 1967). Mesmer believed that the stars influenced people through magnetic forces and that an imbalance of magnetic forces within an individual could cause illness. He therefore reasoned that magnetic powers could be used to cure his patients. Mesmer was a flamboyant showman with a bag of props and a staging know-how equal to that of a P.T. Barnum or a Cecil B. DeMille. He sat patients around a large tub that had iron rods protruding from it and in which he put various chemicals. He darkened the room, played appropriate music, and made his appearance dressed in a purple robe with a wand in his hand, which he used to touch each person, thereby effecting a dramatic cure. Mesmer called his magnetic power *animal magnetism* and erroneously attributed his success to this factor rather than to the effect of suggestion or hypnosis, or both. In 1784 the French Academy of Science appointed a distinguished committee to investigate the curative powers of magnetism. Their investigation failed to confirm that animal magnetism was responsible for Mesmer's results. The importance of Mesmer's contributions lies in the fact that he unknowingly focused attention on psychological processes (hypnosis and suggestion) as potent variables in the acquisition and elimination of abnormal behaviors, and his work stimulated others to develop this concept further.

At about the same time two French physicians, Liebeault (1823–1904) and Bernheim (1837–1919), were impressed with the curative effects of suggestion after successfully using mesmerism to treat their rather unsophisticated peasant patients. Further study led them to observe that hypnosis could remove many of the physical symptoms in perfectly normal individuals. Thus, they concluded that hysteria and hypnosis were closely related and that hysteria was a form of self-hypnosis (Zilboorg and Henry, 1941; Deutsch, 1949).

Their view was refuted initially by Jean Charcot (1825–1893), who was then head of Salpetriere, a mental hospital in France. However, Charcot could neither provide adequate evidence to support his organic view of hysteria as microscopic lesions from trauma nor could he successfully challenge the evidence presented by Bernheim and Liebeault. Charcot not only accepted his defeat gracefully but also used his influence to facilitate the study of the role of psychological factors in the production of mental illness.

Soon thereafter Charcot brought to Salpetriere a young scientist by the name of Pierre Janet (1859–1947), who described a phenomenon called *dissociation,* which he claimed was central to hysteria. Janet believed that the normal personality consisted of systems of organized ideas and actions that interacted with each other. He used dissociation to describe a separation among the systems of the personality and the isolation of certain systems from the rest of the personality. The distinguishing characteristic of this isolation was amnesia, a failure of the hysterical patient to remember relationships between critical events and systems of ideas. This was illustrated in the case of Irene, a young woman who periodically went into a sleepy state and then reenacted the upsetting scene of her mother's death. After Irene completed the reenactment, she returned to her prior normal state and carried on with whatever she was doing without any apparent effects and without memory of what transpired during the dissociated state. Janet called attention to the power of the personality to block out unpleasant events and experiences.

During this period a young neurologist by the name of Sigmund Freud (1856–1939) began to collaborate with a more senior physician, Joseph Breuer (1856–1925), who used hypnosis successfully in the removal of hysterical symptoms. In treating one of his hysterical patients, Breuer noted a peculiar periodic state in which the patient appeared confused and mumbled thoughts that were not readily understandable. He called this condition *absence,* and he found that the patient could reveal the fantasies that were present during her period of absence while under hypnosis. Breuer later encouraged the patient during hypnotic sessions to talk freely about her problems and to fully express the emotional states associated with them. This procedure permitted the patient to release emotional tensions and to uncover the difficulties that gave rise to her hysterical symptoms.

Breuer and Freud noted, however, that the patient could not see the relationship between her problems and her hysterical symptoms, although it was readily apparent to both of them. This led them to propose the notion of the *unconscious* and to ascribe to it a most important role in the determination of behavior (Freud and Breuer, 1959). Their continued work permitted observations that highlighted certain difficulties and limitations in their procedures. They found that symptom removal cures under hypnosis lasted only a relatively short period of time (a few months) before other hysterical symptoms (symptom substitution) appeared in the patient.

The discovery that not all his patients could be hypnotized led Freud to conclude that some patients could not be permanently cured through hypnosis alone. Instead, Freud began to use a method he later called *free association,* which did away with the induction of a hypnotic trance. He encouraged the patient to relax and to say anything and everything that came to mind without conscious direction, censure, or regard for logic. In effect, free association opened the door to past unconscious memories that troubled the patient and caused hysterical symptoms. The technique proved to be more than a method for releasing suppressed emotions and for revealing unconscious problems; it led Freud to other significant discoveries.

Freud observed that his patients could not comply consistently with the rules of free association. This led him to formulate the notion of defense mechanisms and the ideas of resistance and repression (banishment of unacceptable impulses to the unconscious), which protect the personality from unbearable and unacceptable thoughts and impulses. Freud also sought to identify those impulses that were so discrepant with societal standards and so repugnant to the individual that they fell under the rule of repression, and yet were so strong that they would seek expression even through a neurotic illness. Because of the Victorian attitude toward sex and Freud's observation that many of his female patients used neurotic behavior to avoid sexual relationships, he concluded that the strangulation of sexual impulses was the basic source of neuroses.

By the beginning of the twentieth century Freud had formulated many of the basic ingredients of his psychoanalytic theory, which emphasized the importance of early childhood experiences for later personality development. He focused on the sexual drive as the basic source of anxiety and neuroses and described stages of development in which problems in dealing with sexuality at various ages had implications for later personal adjustment and the formation of neuroses. Although we shall present a more detailed discussion of Freud's psychoanalytic theory in Chapters 3 and 4, we should note that Freud continued to refine and elaborate his theory until he died.

Psychoanalytic theory greatly influenced the fields of child psychology and child psychopathology through its emphasis on the critical role of early childhood experiences for both normal and abnormal personality development. Freud established the significance of past experiences for the understanding of present behavior and promoted the importance of childhood. Although he constructed psychoanalysis as a theory and a treatment method intended primarily for neurotic adults, Freud demonstrated in the famous case of Little Hans that the notions he inferred from adult patients about infantile sexuality and psychosexual stages of development in particular were directly revealed in the child (Freud, 1959). Little Hans, a five-year-old boy suffering from a horse phobia, was treated for it by his father under Freud's supervision. The father provided Freud with detailed information about the boy's past history and current behaviors, from which Freud was able to confirm some aspects of his theory as well as to formulate the nature of Hans's unconscious conflicts. In Hans, Freud found evidence of sexuality as early as age two, of castration anxiety at age three, and of sexual desires toward the mother accompanied by fear and hostility toward the father between the ages of four and five. In addition, Freud showed that psychoanalysis could be effectively used in treating a phobic reaction (intense fear) in a young child.

Child Psychology. Late in the nineteenth century child psychology developed as a field of scientific inquiry mainly because of the pioneering efforts of G. Stanley Hall and the development of several research techniques to systematically observe children's behavior (Dennis, 1949). Although no longer used as a research tool because of problems of observer error and reliability, the baby biography was an early scientific method of studying the child and was the basis for the development of more adequate investigative techniques.

G. Stanley Hall ushered in the child-study movement by improving the questionnaire as a method of obtaining information about children. He sent large numbers of questionnaires to parents, teachers, and children as a way of accumulating data about child development in such diverse areas as motor abilities, fears, dreams, appetites, prayers, and emotional expressions (Watson, 1959). Hall's intense interest in learning about children marked the beginning of the scientific study of the child, per se, in America. It also represented the conviction that this area of study was important in understanding human behavior. Moreover, the child-study movement was essential to the development of the field of child psychopathology, since it provided the necessary developmental norms by which abnormality could be judged. Further, it generated the basic data for a better understanding of how abnormal behaviors occur.

Classical conditioning. A major contributor to the field of learning and child psychology was Ivan Pavlov (1849–1936), a Russian physiologist who developed the experimental method of classical conditioning (Pavlov, 1928). Although Pavlov's work influenced the scientific study of learning at all levels of human development, its major impact on child psychology was to provide an experimental procedure that made infants and young children suitable subjects for psychological study. Pavlov showed that learning can occur if a previously neutral stimulus is paired successively with a stimulus already known to elicit the response in question. His experiments showed that hungry dogs learned to salivate at the sound of a bell alone after repeated pairings of the sound and food were presented in close temporal order. In 1920 Watson and Rayner (1920) used the Pavlovian paradigm to demonstrate the acquisition of a fear response in an eleven-month-old boy named Albert. Prior observations of Albert indicated that he was not afraid of a white rat but that he showed fear of loud noises. Therefore, the experimenters arranged repeated presentations of a white rat followed closely by a loud noise; in time Albert evidenced a fear reaction to the presentation of the rat alone.

Behaviorism. In 1913 the American investigator, John B. Watson (1878–1958) introduced behaviorism as a reaction against the study of consciousness, which was psychology's chief interest at that time. Watson questioned the latter's use of methods designed to provide information about what was going on inside the individual (Watson, 1913). Instead, he adopted the view that psychology as a science need only concern itself with behaviors that can be directly observed and measured. According to Watson, through the analysis of stimulus-response (S-R) connections, the more complex forms of human behavior eventually can be understood. He argued that environmental forces play a dominant role in influencing and shaping personality, and he intended that child psychology be the focus of his behavioral studies (White, 1970). Watson established an infant laboratory, and on the basis of his research on emotional conditioning, he wrote a book dealing with the psychological care of infants. The book greatly influenced child care and training practices (Watson, 1928). Watson's own words best convey his position and the optimism he felt:

> Give me a dozen healthy infants, well-formed, and my own specialized world to bring [them] up in, and I'll guarantee to take any one at random and train him to be any type of specialist. I might select doctor, lawyer, artist, merchant, chief, yes, even beggarman and thief, regardless of his talents, penchants, tendencies, abilities, vocation and race of his ancestors. . . . Please note that when this experiment is made I am allowed to specify the way the children are brought up and the type of world they have to live in. (1925, p. 82)

Watson's behaviorism was carried forth by B. F. Skinner, whose work in operant conditioning provided another important experimental paradigm for learning. Not only has his systematic research (primarily with pigeons) contributed significantly to the understanding and prediction of human behavior but it has also had widespread application to education as well as to the treatment of abnormal conditions. Skinner's operant conditioning involves the strengthening of a stimulus-response bond by reinforcing (rewarding) the response when it occurs and by making the reinforcement contingent on the emission of the proper response. It is this procedure we use to teach a dog a new trick, or a child to do his or her homework. It is, like Watson's behaviorism, totally focused on the discovery of principles that govern behavior and is unconcerned with what goes on inside the organism.

Children's abilities and maturational stages. With the addition of the experimental method to the earlier research techniques of baby biographies and the Hall-type questionnaires, it became possible to study a wider range of factors (including abilities, achievement, interests, emotional reactions, drawings, and cognitive processes) in children of various ages. New knowledge was gained about children's abilities and the orderly changes in their behavior that come with maturity. The founding of university-sponsored nursery schools in the 1920s permitted longitudinal behavioral studies that extended over periods of months and sometimes years. Developmental norms and the role of maturation with respect to the child's readiness to learn was highlighted in the 1930s and 1940s in the observational research of Arnold Gesell (1880–1961), a student of Hall (Gesell, 1928; Dennis, 1935; Gesell, Thompson, and Amatruda, 1938). Although not very clearly articulated, human development was viewed until the 1950s as an orderly series of maturational stages that are described by developmental norms and their potential for the adjustment of the child (White, 1970).

Other research in child psychology. As an outgrowth of the testing movement and of heightened interest in the area of intelligence, the age old nature-nurture controversy reappeared. The belief that intelligence was a fixed and inborn characteristic was given support by the well-known pedigree studies of Galton, Dugdale, and Goddard, while studies showing similarities between parent and child, and twins and siblings, argued for the genetic transmission of intelligence (Sears, 1975). On the other side, environmental studies showing the effects on intelligence of various external factors, such as parental education, socioeconomic level, and urban versus rural living conditions, argued for the powerful influence of the environment in shaping human behavior. Later studies, especially those carried out by psychologists at the University of Iowa, investigated the adverse effects of institutionalization on intelligence to demonstrate the significance of environmental conditions on human behavior (Sears, 1975). Although the controversy continues to the present, new advances in both genetics and research paradigms have moved most researchers away from an extreme position. Many observers now view human behavior as the product of some interaction between nature and nurture (more extensively discussed in Chapter 4).

Finally, during the 1920s and the latter part of the 1930s, a number of important longitudinal studies were published which provided valuable information about child development. The longitudinal approach involves the periodic but repeated assessment of the same children over the course of many years. It was in this way that Terman (1921) studied intellectually "gifted" children and accumulated much needed data about their physical, emotional, social, and vocational growth. Employing this method, Macfarlane (1928), Jones and Stolz (1932), and Sontag (1929), respectively, studied the effects of parental guidance on development, the relationship between physical and physiological measures on social development, and the relationship between parental behaviors and personality development (cited in Sears, 1975).

Emotional and behavioral disorders. According to Kanner (1972), it was not until the 1930s that attempts were made to study children with severe emotional disturbances, and it was not until the next decade that two discernible schools of thought were evident. One school, led by Beata Rank, introduced the idea of the "atypical child," intending by this term to disregard any distinctions between forms of disturbances in early childhood. Those who held this position considered problems in the mother-child relationship as the critical—but common—etiological factor in atypical children. Others argued strongly for heterogeneity and the search for various distinct clinical entities. Kanner himself was a proponent of this latter view and is identified with the first clinical description of a disorder he labeled *Early Infantile Autism* in 1943. The disorder referred to as Symbiotic Infantile Psychosis was introduced in the literature by Margaret Mahler in 1949, while Bergman and Escalona in 1949 and Bender in 1954 described children with unusual sensitivity to sensory stimulation and subtypes of Childhood Schizophrenia, respectively (Kanner, 1972).

MENTAL HYGIENE MOVEMENT

At the turn of the twentieth century, the most important figure in American psychiatry was Adolph Meyer (1866–1950), who exerted influence not as a theoretician but as a teacher and integrator of information. Meyer, a Swiss psychiatrist, came to this country in 1893 to work as a pathologist in a state hospital (Lief, 1948). Faced with the almost impossible task of examining pathological tissues without life-history information, Meyer pressed for a program that would carefully study the patient's full life course. He accumulated large amounts of data that led him to emphasize psychological processes and variables, since the autopsies performed on mental patients rarely demonstrated organic pathology. He became interested in the antecedent conditions of mental illness, and he saw the importance of gathering statistical data about childhood disorders. One of Meyer's students, Leo Kanner, later became the founder of child psychiatry in the United States. With the cooperation of the departments of pediatrics and psychiatry at Johns Hopkins University Medical School, Kanner formed a clinic where he and his students evaluated and treated a wide variety of abnormal conditions in children. He accumulated basic data on the incidence of various childhood abnormalities, and as noted earlier, he was the first to identify and describe Early Infantile Autism (Chapter 8).

Meyer viewed psychopathology as faulty

reactions of a psychobiological organism (the mind and the body) that can be understood only through a careful and chronological analysis of the individual's past history and corrected through the acquisition of new reactions (habits). He preferred the concept of *reaction type* to the prevaling psychiatric assumption of disease and favored *forms of unsuccessful adjustment* to the legal and popular term *insanity*. Perhaps most important for the field of child psychopathology was his interest in prevention and his willingness to lend his influence and support to the mental hygiene movement, a project started by a former mental patient named Clifford Beers.

Beers, a graduate of Yale University, became obsessed with the fear that he, too, would be a victim of epilepsy soon after his older brother evidenced the disease. Beers became depressed and attempted suicide; he was hospitalized in several mental institutions for about three years. In 1908, after he had recovered in the home of an attendant, Beers wrote *A Mind That Found Itself*. There he described his own experiences as a mental patient and the cruel and horrible treatment he and others received in the institutions (Beers, 1908). Beers successfully aroused the interest and concern of some highly influential citizens and professionals. Together with Meyers and others, in 1909 Beers organized the National Committee for Mental Hygiene. Intended as an organization to encourage the prevention and early identification of mental illness, to dissipate the public's pervasive attitudes of fear about such illness, and to improve the prevailing conditions in mental hospitals, the National Committee exerted considerable influence. It was a guiding force in establishing the first training program for psychiatric social workers at Smith College in 1918 and in arousing public interest in developing facilities to treat children's disorders.

Child Guidance Clinics

Lightner Witmer established the first psychological clinic for children in 1896 at the University of Pennsylvania. Although interested in school-age children who were educationally retarded and/or handicapped, Witmer did not ignore those with emotional or nonacademic problems. Two years later Illinois and Colorado created separate juvenile courts to deal with the special problems of juvenile delinquency and to provide legal consideration for juvenile offenders apart from adults. Experience with the juvenile court led to the conclusion that delinquent children frequently evidenced abnormal behaviors that were modifiable. In 1909 William Healy founded the first child guidance clinic in Chicago (named the Juvenile Psychopathic Institute) as a clinical treatment facility for delinquent youths. Aided by the National Committee for Mental Hygiene, other child guidance clinics were established to handle a broader range of psychological disorders in children (Kanner, 1972). In 1921 Thom founded the prototype of the modern child guidance clinic in Boston. Staffed by a team consisting of a psychiatrist, a psychologist, and a social worker, the clinic treated the undesirable habits of preschoolers in order to minimize the risk of the children later developing more serious difficulties. Intervention was broadened to include work with parents, siblings, teachers, and others who may have contributed to the children's problems.

THE DEVELOPMENT OF SPECIALISTS

As we have seen, progress for the mentally retarded and handicapped child was fostered by the emergence of psychological tests to measure intelligence and other abilities and by the research on normal child development. In addition, interested parent groups awakened the public to the special needs of impaired and disordered children by advocating community and legislative involvement. Further, teacher training programs for *special education* (started in 1914) achieved substantial growth and effective quality after World War II. Formal training programs provided competent professionals in the areas of mental retardation, social and emotional maladjustment, sensory and speech deficits, and learning disabilities.

The need to train other child specialists was dramatized both by the mental hygiene movement and by the burgeoning of child guidance clinics throughout the United States. In the past *psychiatric social workers* functioned as the primary clinic contact for parents, families, and schools and as the professional member of the clinic team who interpreted information for and worked therapeutically with the child's parents (most often with the mother). In addition to these traditional functions, social workers today assume the role of child therapist, family therapist, and liaison with other agencies in the community. Guidance clinics became a fertile training resource for social workers, psychiatrists, and psychologists. *Child psychiatrists* traditionally assumed the role of principal child therapists and medical administrators, while psychologists functioned mainly as mental testers, diagnostic evaluators, and researchers. But with the rapid development of *clinical psychology* following World War II, the roles and functions of psychologists in child clinics broadened to include psychotherapy; behavior therapy; family, school, and other agency consultation; diagnosis; training; research; and administration. It is now recognized that no discipline is equipped with the necessary skills and experience to deal effectively with all facets of child psychopathology, although many perform similar and overlapping functions.

Psychoanalysis continued to dominate the field as Freud's student Melanie Klein and his daughter Anna Freud introduced modifications in the 1920s that made his theory and treatment method more applicable to children. Klein replaced free association with play techniques (see Chapter 6) on the grounds that play was a natural activity of children and that it revealed the same sources of anxiety and unconscious conflicts as words did for adults. Anna Freud used play, especially drawings, as well as dreams to understand and treat children's problems, and she elaborated on her father's notions of the ego and its defensive functions. In 1950 Erik Erikson's book *Childhood and Society* made an enormous impact on the field. In the book he analyzed both the human life cycle and identity in terms of a psychosocial stage theory, as contrasted to Freud's psychosexual stages of development (see Chapter 3) (Erickson, 1950).

Pediatric medicine became interested in the psychological aspects of child care largely as a result of psychoanalytic theory, the mental testing movement, normative data from child psychology, and Watson's environmental view of learning. Pediatricians who were thrust into the position of giving advice about child-rearing practices now could offer suggestions that were based on the important psychological ingredients of development. In 1945 Benjamin Spock, a pediatrician, published a manual entitled *Baby and Child Care* that rapidly became the bible for millions of parents, as it answered virtually all their questions about child rearing (Spock, 1968).

Unbelievable growth and diversification have characterized the field of psychology over the last three to four decades. With some exceptions, prior to World War II psychology was concerned with its own advancement as a science as well as with seeking data that would be useful for understanding and predicting human behavior. After the war formal doctoral programs in clinical psychology were established combining didactic course work, research requirements, and supervised clinical experience. Within recent years specialty training in child clinical psychology has been offered in many university graduate programs. In addition, the science-practice orientation is very much evident in the field of child psychology, where job opportunities within education, pediatrics, juvenile corrections, and early child-care programs are quite usual.

Research, training, and service programs designed to improve the health and welfare of children were stimulated especially by federal funds during the 1960s. Presidents Kennedy and Johnson and their administrations were involved significantly in the problem of mental retardation and in supporting special programs for the culturally disadvantaged.

Although still in its infancy, the field of childhood psychopathology is currently flourishing. There now exist more exciting ideas, more adequately controlled and systematic research, more graduate and professional training programs, and more service facilities and programs than were thought possible some twenty or thirty years ago. In a relatively brief time, and in spite of meager and stormy beginnings, students of developmental psychopathology have made great strides in understanding and treating abnormal behaviors of children. Nevertheless, there is much more to learn and much more to be done. We hope the remaining chapters will challenge some readers to contribute their own research and to add new insights and directions to the field.

SUMMARY

Interest in the study of child psychopathology is of recent vintage. Prior to the seventeenth century children were thought of as little adults without personalities of their own; and they lacked distinctive clothes, play activities, literature, and schools. Nor were they excluded from any topic of discourse. As childhood came to be considered a period of life separate from adulthood, children became the object of controversy among parents, the Church, and the State, who all vied for their control. In this chapter we looked at this struggle in a historical context, considering children as a labor force, the problem of child abuse, and the child welfare movement.

No fixed beginning can be established for the emergence of the field of child psychopathology, although many divergent forces appearing in the late nineteenth century and early twentieth century were influential in its development. Except for the area of mental retardation, early ideas about adult psychopathology and the field of psychiatry took little notice of childhood disorders. We noted here the impact of past and recent developments as regards mental retardation, intelligence tests and other psychological tests, child psychology, psychoanalysis, the mental hygiene movement, and child guidance clinics. We also noted later developments, especially in the training of educational specialists, social workers, child psychiatrists, clinical psychologists, and clinical child psychologists.

REFERENCES

ABRAMOVITZ, R. Parenthood in America. *Journal of Clinical Child Psychology,* 1976, 5, 43–46.

ANASTASI, A. (ed.). *Individual Differences.* New York: John Wiley, 1965.

ARIES, P. *Centuries of Childhood,* trans. Robert Baldick. New York: Vintage Books (Random House), 1962.

"THE BATTERED CHILDREN." *Newsweek,* October 10, 1977, 112–115.

BEERS, C. W. *A Mind That Found Itself.* New York: Longmans, Green, 1908.

BERLIN, I. N. We Advocate This Bill of Rights. In I. N. Berlin (ed.), *Advocacy for Child Mental Health.* New York: Brunner/Mazel, 1975, pp. 1–10.

BLAIN, D. Twenty-five Years of Hospital and Community Psychiatry: Community Psychiatry: 1945–1970. *Hospital and Community Psychiatry,* 1975, 26, 605–609.

BROWN, F. J. *The Sociology of Childhood.* Englewood Cliffs, N.J.: Prentice-Hall, 1939.

COUGHLIN, B. J. United Nations Declaration of the Rights of the Child. In A. E. Wilkerson (ed.), *The Rights of Children.* Philadelphia: Temple University Press, 1973, pp. 3–23.

DE MAUSE, L. The Evolution of Childhood. In L. de Mause (ed.), *The History of Childhood.* New York: The Psychohistory Press, 1974, pp. 1–73.

DENNIS, W. The Effect of Restricted Practice Upon the Reaching, Sitting, and Standing of Two Infants. *Journal of Genetic Psychology,* 1935, 47, 17–32.

DENNIS, W. Historical Beginnings of Child Psychology. *Psychological Bulletin,* 1949, 46, 224–235.

DEUTSCH, A. *The Mentally Ill in America.* New York: Columbia University Press, 1949.

ERIKSON, E. H. *Childhood and Society.* New York: W. W. Norton and Co., 1950.

FREUD, S. Analysis of a Phobia in a Five-Year-Old Boy. In *Collected Papers,* Vol. III, trans. Alix and James Strachey. New York: Basic Books, 1959.

FREUD, S., and BREUER, J. On the Psychical Mechanisms of Hysterical Phenomena. In *Collected Papers,* Vol. 1, trans. Joan Riviere. New York: Basic Books, 1959.

GESELL, A. *Infancy and Human Growth.* New York: Macmillan, 1928.

GESELL, A., THOMPSON, H., and AMATRUDA, C. S. *The Psychology of Early Growth*. New York: Macmillan, 1938.

GOODENOUGH, F. L. *Mental Testing: Its History, Principles, and Applications*. New York: Holt, Rinehart and Winston, 1949.

GREENLEAF, B. K. *Children Through the Ages*. New York: McGraw-Hill, 1978.

HARMS, E. *Origins of Modern Psychiatry*. Springfield, Ill.: Chas. C Thomas, 1967.

KADUSHIN, A. Child Welfare Services Past and Present. *Journal of Clinical Child Psychology*, 1976, *5*, 51–55.

KANNER, L. *Child Psychiatry*, 4th ed. Springfield, Ill.: Chas. C Thomas, 1972.

KIESLER, S. B. Federal Policies for Research on Children. *American Psychologist*, 1979, *34*, 1009–1016.

LANE, H. *The Wild Boy of Aveyron*. Cambridge, Mass.: Harvard University Press, 1976.

LIEF, A. *The Commonsense Psychiatry of Dr. Adolf Meyer*. New York: McGraw-Hill, 1948.

LOMAX, E. M. R., KAGAN, J., and ROSENKRANTZ, B. G. *Science and Patterns of Child Care*. San Francisco: W. H. Freeman and Co., 1978.

LYMAN, R. B., JR. Barbarism and Religion: Late Roman and Early Medieval Childhood. In L. de Mause (ed.), *The History of Childhood*. New York: The Psychohistory Press, 1974, pp. 101–181.

MCLAUGHLIN, M. M. Survivors and Surrogates: Children and Parents from the Ninth to the Thirteenth Centuries. In L. de Mause (ed.), *The History of Childhood*. New York: The Psychohistory Press, 1974, pp. 101–181.

MORA, G. History of Psychiatry. In A. M. Freedman and H. I. Kaplan (eds.), *Comprehensive Textbook of Psychiatry*. Baltimore, Md.: Williams and Wilkins, 1967, pp. 2–34.

PAVLOV, I. P. *Lectures on Conditioned Reflexes*. New York: Liveright, 1928.

POTTER, H. W. Mental Retardation in Historical Perspective. In S. I. Harrison and J. F. McDermott (eds.), *Childhood Psychopathology: An Anthology of Basic Readings*. New York: International Universities Press, 1972, pp. 733–743.

RIE, H. E. Historical Perspective of Concepts of Child Psychopathology. In H. E. Rie (ed.), *Perspectives in Child Psychopathology*. Chicago: Aldine-Atherton, 1971, pp. 3–50.

ROSEN, M., CLARK, G. R., and KIVITZ M. S. (eds.). *The History of Mental Retardation: Collected Papers*, Vol. 1. Baltimore, Md.: University Park Press, 1976, pp. XIII–XXIV.

SEARS, R. R. Your Ancient Revisited: A History of Child Development. In E. M. Hetherrington (ed.), *Review of Child Development Research*, Vol. 5. Chicago: University of Chicago Press, 1975, pp. 1–73.

SHEPHERD, R. E., JR. The Abused Child and the Law. In A. E. Wilkerson (ed.), *The Rights of Children*. Philadelphia: Temple University Press, 1973, pp. 174–189.

SOBEL, S. B. Psychology and the Juvenile Justice System. *American Psychologist*, 1979, *34*, 1020–1023.

SPINETTA, J. J., and RIGLER, D. The Child-Abusing Parent: A Psychological Review. *Psychological Bulletin*, 1972, *77*, 296–304.

SPOCK, B. *Baby and Child Care*, new rev. ed. New York: Pocket Books, 1968.

STIER, S. Children's Rights and Society's Duties. *Journal of Social Issues*, 1978, *34*, 46–58.

STRICKLAND, C. E. American Attitudes Toward Children. In E. Blishen (ed.), *Encyclopedia of Education*, Vol. II. New York: Macmillan, 1970, pp. 77–92.

TAKANISHI, R. Childhood as a Social Issue: Historical Roots of Contemporary Child Advocacy Movements. *Journal of Social Issues*, 1978, *34*, 8–28.

TUCKER, M. J. The Child as Beginning and End: Fifteenth and Sixteenth Century English Childhood. In L. de Mause (ed.), *The History of Childhood*. New York: The Psychohistory Press, 1974, pp. 229–257.

WALK, A. The Prehistory of Child Psychiatry. *British Journal of Psychiatry*, 1964, *110*, 754–767.

WATSON, J. B. Psychology as the Behaviorist Views It. *Psychological Review*, 1913, *20*, 158–177.

WATSON, J. B. *Behaviorism*. New York: W. W. Norton and Co., 1925.

WATSON, J. B. *Psychological Care of Infant and Child*. New York: W. W. Norton and Co., 1928.

WATSON, J. B., and RAYNER, R. Conditioned Emotional Reaction. *Journal of Experimental Psychology*, 1920, *3*, 1–4.

WATSON, R. I. *Psychology of the Child: Personal, Social and Disturbed Child Development*. New York: John Wiley, 1959.

WHITE, S. H. The Learning Theory Tradition and Child Psychology. In P. H. Mussen (ed.), *Carmichael's Manual of Child Psychology*, Vol. 1, 3rd ed. New York: John Wiley, 1970, pp. 657–701.

WILKERSON, A. E. (ed.). *The Rights of Children*. Philadelphia: Temple University Press, 1973.

ZILBOORG, G., and HENRY, G. W. *History of Medical Psychology*. New York: W. W. Norton and Co., 1941.

2

THE NATURE OF CHILDHOOD PSYCHOPATHOLOGY: Definition, Classification, and Scope

PROLOGUE

Mr. and Mrs. S. called their local mental health clinic to request a psychological evaluation for Scott, their nine-year-old son, who was evidencing difficulties in school and at home. Mrs. S. reported that Scott's academic performance had deteriorated significantly within the last two years and that he tended to be rebellious and hostile much of the time. In addition, Scott had wet his bed at night for the last three years and was unable to get along with his parents, siblings, peers, or teachers. More recently he was involved in several thefts and had evidenced persistent lying.

Mrs. S. indicated that Scott was the youngest of her three sons and that she divorced their father three years earlier, when Scott was about six years old. A year later she remarried a man ten years her senior, who had never been married before. At present Mr. S. owns and operates a small foreign-car repair shop and needs to work long hours to provide "nicely but not lavishly" for his family. He tends to be a perfectionist, demanding of himself and others, and especially critical of his stepsons when they fail to meet his high expectations. Mrs. S. is demanding as well, but she is also high strung, easily upset, and full of self-doubts about her ability to cope with her sons, husband, and homemaking responsibilities.

In contrast to Scott, his older brothers (ages twelve and fifteen) are described as "model children." Mr. and Mrs. S. characterize them as straight A students, outstanding athletes, very popular with peers, and easily managed and well-behaved at home. Apparently, they have been a great source of pride to their parents, while Scott has been disappointing and troublesome.

Scott was a full-term baby who was conceived at a time when Mrs. S. and her first husband initially began to battle over his drinking problem and his infidelity. Scott's birth was uncomplicated, and he seemed to be a healthy and happy baby. He was bottle fed, and from all indications his physical, motor, and language development were within normal limits during the first several years. He was successfully toilet trained by his second birthday, and his mother reported that he slept well at night and was easy to care for during the day. He was rarely sick, except for a mild case of the mumps at age four and occasional colds and sore throats. Scott's academic performance was excellent in the first grade, but his schoolwork fell off dramatically, and he began to wet the bed at about the time his parents were divorced. His mother and brothers became very critical of him, tending to pick on him and to use him as a scapegoat for their own pent-up frustrations and anger. His academic difficulties worsened when his mother remarried, and subsequently he was required to repeat the second grade.

It didn't take very long before his stepfather joined the others and added another critical voice in the household to which Scott retaliated with angry acting-out behaviors. He fought with his brothers, talked back to his mother, and fabricated stories to avoid doing what was asked of him. In school he began to bully and fight with younger boys and to take their belongings and hide them in other places. His teachers noted that he seemed to enjoy tormenting other children, but they could not find any effective way to control his aggressive actions.

Shortly before his referral, Scott stole a neighbor's bicycle and took some money from his mother's purse. He rode around for hours, staying away long past dinner time. His parents became frantic and feared something terrible might have happened to him. On his arrival home Scott returned the bike to the neighbor's garage and then entered the back door of his house as if nothing unusual had happened. He was greeted by a set of relieved, but very angry, parents. A few days later Mr. and Mrs. S. decided that Scott needed professional help.

What prompted Scott's parents to seek the assistance of a psychologist? Was it their concern about his stealing and his staying out late? Was it prompted by his past misbehaviors, together with his recent misbehaviors? Was it a reaction to their own frustrations and anger in failing to manage Scott? Or was it their realization that Scott's behavioral patterns were deviant from those of his brothers and from other children of his age? Whatever the reason (or reasons), their decision to call for psychological help rested on some vague and implicit notion they held about what constitutes abnormal behavior. While all of us have some general idea about aberrant behavior, there is no single definition on which everyone would agree or which would completely satisfy most professional workers. Recognizing this variability, it would be useful to define the domain of abnormal behavior as it will be used here. In addition, we need to grapple with the issues and problems associated with the classification of children's disorders, so that we may better understand what groupings have been proposed, how the various categories are used, and how reliable they are. Finally, we need to consider the scope of the problem, the procedures used to measure the frequency of abnormal conditions, and the sources of error associated with these measures.

WHAT IS PSYCHOPATHOLOGICAL BEHAVIOR?

Scott's case illustrates that psychopathology is probably easier to recognize than to define. Mr. and Mrs. S. had ample opportunity to evaluate Scott's behaviors in light of his previous personality, its appropriateness to his life circumstances, and its effect on him and others. They may have viewed his academic decline and bedwetting at age six as a temporary but understandable response to the stress of his parents' divorce. But the fact that these behaviors persisted and worsened, with the appearance of hostile and antisocial acts, only emphasized to his parents the seriousness of Scott's problem and their inability to deal with it on their own. At the time of the referral, Mr. and Mrs. S. recognized Scott's behavioral patterns as abnormal, but their conclusion probably was based on multiple and vague criteria which were neither sufficiently explicit nor generalizable beyond the single instance of their son. Therefore, it would be useful to delineate an explicit set of comprehensive criteria by which the adequate identification of abnormal behaviors can be made.

Statistical Criterion

Abnormal behavior may be thought of as deviant in the sense that it deviates statistically from the normal, the usual, the most common, or the typical reaction found in the majority of the population. But this criterion is limited, because it implies that normality is restricted to those behaviors that are most common; it regards as deviant many attributes which society considers very favorable, such as the unusual abilities of the extremely bright child or the gifted athlete. Moreover, this criterion includes within the bounds of normality such highly common practices as alcohol abuse as well as other drug abuses found among high school students, even though society views these behaviors as deviant and undesirable. The fact that few children go through life completely free of behavioral and adjustment difficulties implies by statistical standards that behaviors such as temper tantrums, fears, overactivity, bedwetting, lying, and stealing are normal (Werry and Quay, 1971; Johnson et al., 1973). Yet factors other than mere occurrence—such as persistence, age of onset, or the appearance of a combination of some of these behaviors (as evidenced by Scott)—may override statistical considerations in differentiating normal from abnormal behavior.

In addition to these limitations, the statistical criterion is too broad and vague, defining normal behavior only in terms of what the majority does. Thus, the next two sections will deal with more specific statistical criteria, noting cultural values and changes in behavior that occur with development.

Cultural Norms

Historically certain behaviors have been sufficiently distinctive to be labeled abnormal. Some of these behaviors appear to be universal, since they can be found in similar forms all over the world. In fact, studies have shown that such psychopathological behaviors as hallucinations, delusions, phobias, and sexual deviations are evident across different cultures (Copeland, 1968; Al-Issa, 1969; Dohrenwend and Dohrenwend, 1974). At the same time differences among cultures have been reported both in the incidence of abnormal behaviors and in the specific ways they are expressed. Although suicide and alcoholism are well-known universal phenomena, suicide is rare among Muslims, and compulsive drinking is unusual among Jews, Muslims, and Mormons (Coleman et al., 1980).

The specific content of a disordered behavior, such as a delusion, also is influenced by cultural factors. A delusion of persecution in Africa may take the form of a fixed belief that some large, wild, and dangerous animal is out there for the sole purpose of stalking and destroying the deluded person. In this country the delusional content might focus on the false belief that the person is under the electronic surveillance of foreign agents who plan to seize and murder him. Therefore, a distinction must be made between the basic characteristics of abnormal behaviors that are uniform in all cultures and those features that vary because of cultural differences. In general, behaviors which reduce, interfere with, or disrupt the individual's personal and social adjustment are considered abnormal in all societies. However, the specific form these disruptive behaviors take, the explanation given for them, and their frequency of occurrence vary from culture to culture. The processes and functions underlying human behavior (normal and abnormal) are the same in all societies, while the specific behavioral expressions are influenced largely by one's culture. Obviously then, what is regarded as abnormal by one culture may very well be viewed as normal in another.

The first criterion of psychopathology, the *cultural norm*, recognizes that every culture establishes approved standards and expectations for the behavior of its members. Cultural norms change from time to time, but usually there is a "lag" between the introduction of the change and its widespread acceptance by the culture. Typically cultural norms are more specific and restrictive in their prohibitions, in contrast to the greater flexibility allowed for their sanctions. In addition, there is usually more latitude and leeway given to children in terms of what they may and may not do. For example, our culture prohibits adults from performing certain aggressive acts, such as physical assault and stealing, while similar aggressive responses are subtly permitted for children. Without imposing a great penalty, we allow children to fight, attack each other, and take things that don't belong to them. Moreover, cultural norms provide standards of behavior that are situationally defined. For the adolescent, nudity is permissible in the privacy of his or her home, or even in the less-than-private locker room at the school gym; but it is a definite "no-no" when he or she is out in a shopping mall or on the way to school.

Developmental Norms

Knowledge of the developmental process is essential in making decisions about whether a child's behavior is normal or abnormal, although statistical averages (as we have already noted) are limited in defining abnormality. We know that most children are toilet trained before, and are continent after, the age of three. By this standard Scott's bedwetting deviates significantly from developmental norms, since he has been enuretic since the age of six. Of course, if Scott were younger (for example, four years old), the deviation would be less extreme and more difficult to categorize as abnormal. In general, the greater the deviation from developmental norms, the more agreement there will be regarding the abnormality of the behavior.

However, not all developmental deviations reflect abnormality in the sense of impaired or insufficient progress. Some children walk unaided at an earlier age than the norm or have vocabularies and linguistic skills that far exceed the average. Most, but not all, instances of rapid or early development are looked upon as positive indications of exceptional abilities. It is at the slow end of the continuum that developmental deviations have their major significance as indicators of abnormality.

Frequency, Intensity, and Duration

For discussion purposes let us consider the question: Is pulling hair from one's head abnormal? While many might respond affirmatively, others might ask for additional information before answering. If pulling hair occurred only once—or at the most, twice—the answer might change to "no." If, however, pulling hair was a frequent event, the answer would be "yes." Therefore, frequency is an important dimension in defining abnormal behaviors. In this regard we should note that the absence or rarity of a response may be just as significant as high *frequency*. Scott's infrequent expression of warm and positive feelings is as indicative of abnormality as is his excessive lying or his frequent bedwetting.

Another characteristic useful in determining whether a behavior is abnormal is *intensity* or *degree*. If pulling hair merely involved the removal of a single strand of hair rather than large clumps, the behavior would be considered within normal limits. However, when behaviors are evident in extremes of intensity or degree, they generally fall outside the bounds of normality and inside the range of abnormality.

Similarly, we need to include the dimension of *duration* in distinguishing normal from abnormal behavior. Scott's lying and stealing take on greater significance if they are manifest over a long period of time rather than over a brief time span. The greater the persistence of deviant behaviors, the more likely they are to be considered as falling within the domain of abnormality.

AREAS OF IMPAIRED FUNCTIONING

Intellectual and Cognitive

In the management of everyday affairs, we expect that normal people will function well within their intellectual capabilities, even though most people do not operate at maximum efficiency most of the time. A healthy fourteen-year-old of superior intelligence who cannot remember his name, address, or whereabouts would strike most of us as odd and abnormal.

Cognitive malfunctioning is present when a disparity exists between ability and actual performance in areas such as attention, comprehension, judgment, learning, memory, thinking, and perception. The larger the difference between a person's capabilities and his or her actual performance, the greater the likelihood of abnormal behavior. Children of average or higher intelligence who are extremely distractible, unable to carry out simple instructions, or unable to learn the difference between friend and foe—and those who cannot recall important, recent, or past events—illustrate cognitive impairment.

For the most part, normal thought processes tend to be logical, coherent, organized, and appropriate to the situation. Gross disruption and impairment of these patterns, together with peculiar content—known as a thought disorder—usually are good indicators of abnormal behavior. Wouldn't you think there was something radically wrong with an eleven-year-old boy who responded characteristically to simple questions such as "How are you today?" with "My God! The world is coming to an end. The weasel stole all of the bees . . . no more honey . . . no more money. The heck with you, you S.O.B. What do you have against fried flies?"

A particularly important instance of cognitive dysfunction is in the child's perception of reality. During normal development we learn to move about unimpaired in our environment by interpreting external cues. We learn that distant objects look smaller than nearer ones, and we learn to correct our perception when these cues are incorrect, such as when we view things that are submerged in water. With practice and successful experiences our confidence in these perceptions of physical objects and space increases. From time to time we check our impressions with those of others, especially when in doubt. Misperceptions or *hallucinations* occur when a person sees, hears, or smells something that is not present in the external world of reality. Hallucinatory experiences may involve any of the senses, although visual and auditory misperceptions are most frequently noted. Beliefs that are based on false premises are known as *delusions*, which are faulty perceptions or incorrect appraisals of reality or the actual behavior of others.

The ramblings of a five-year-old child about his or her imaginary playmate may be normal, but similar behavior in a teenager would be properly labeled as abnormal. The belief that the moon dangerously pollutes the atmosphere because it is made of blue cheese is distinctly abnormal in a college graduate, although it may be within normal limits for a gullible retardate who was misled by an older sibling. Thus, in order to be useful as a criterion of abnormal behavior, cognitive dysfunction must be considered in light of intellectual potential, developmental norms, frequency, duration, and degree of impairment.

Emotional Expression and Control

Some of the most vivid illustrations of abnormal behavior come from the emotional area of human functioning. Scenes of wild, explosive, and unpredictable emotional expressions are often used to describe the behavior of those considered abnormal. Extreme or sudden fluctuations of moods, infantile or inappropriate emotional expression—or lack of any emotional expression at all, and irrational but persistent fears are some of the emotional signs of personal instability. "A proper emotional development prepares the individual to appreciate the pleasurable aspects of emotion and to cope adaptively with the unpleasant. The well-rounded personality is not flat or wholly intellectual but expressive and emotionally responsive in a disciplined manner" (Nash, 1970, p. 306).

During the course of development children learn to alter the way they express emotions. Infants show fear by crying, while teenagers may respond by avoiding or withdrawing from the feared stimuli. Children also learn to size up the situation in terms of what emotion is appropriate and what manner of expression is acceptable. With maturity, people are expected to increase the degree of control they exercise over their feelings. Thus, over time youngsters may show acquired changes in the expression of anger—from frantic temper tantrums, to direct physical attack, to verbal expression of anger, and so forth.

Deviations in emotional expression and control are varied and numerous. Emotional behavior can be *inappropriate* to the situation—as in the show of elation over the news of the death of a loved one—or *insufficient* or *exaggerated*—as reflected in either indifference or a prolonged grief reaction to a broken engagement. There may be either too little or too much control exercised over emotional responsivity, as seen in impulsive acting-out behavior or in emotional constriction and inhibition. In addition, emotional regression or the use of emotional expressions evident in an earlier period of development may indicate abnormal behavior. Temper tantrums in a twelve-year-old who had since learned to express anger verbally are a sign of emotional regression and emotional immaturity. Here again the greater the deviation from normal developmental patterns, the greater is the likelihood that the behavior would be regarded as abnormal.

Personal Discomfort. Sometimes *personal discomfort* is considered a useful criterion of abnormal behavior, because it is frequently (but not necessarily always) a byproduct of such a state. Worry, anxiety, fears, and despondent feelings often become so pervasive and all-consuming that some—or many—areas of functioning are affected adversely. When personal discomfort in any form is enduring and sufficiently troublesome to interfere with normal functioning, it may be considered abnormal. However, we must keep in mind that not all abnormal emotional behaviors are painful or uncomfortable. Seriously regressed psychotics may show silly emotional responses and a readiness to inflict pain on others or themselves without any apparent sign of personal distress. Those in prolonged states of euphoria (even if inappropriate) appear to be ecstatically happy. Sexual deviants and drug users apparently derive a great deal of pleasure from their abnormal behaviors.

Interpersonal Relations

It is well recognized that humans are not solitary creatures but rather are social animals who require relationships with others for their well-being. To function adequately in society a person must acquire the capacity to interact with others on friendly and cooperative terms and maintain relationships of mutual respect, agreement, and responsibility. Because this is such an important area of human functioning, deviations from the expected patterns, expecially those in which the rights of others are offended or violated, are considered abnormal. Typically disruptions in a person's ability to cope with interpersonal relationships are associated with or lead to impaired functioning in many areas. Behaviors such as social withdrawal and isolation, suspiciousness, fear, hatred of others, and uncooperativeness make almost any facet of life difficult to manage.

Nevertheless, not all deviant interpersonal relations fall within the domain of abnormal behavior. Rudeness, insensitivity, deceit, and infidelity are among the behaviors that are socially deviant but not in and of themselves abnormal. Similarly, criminal acts of murder, rape, and theft—while deviant—cannot be classed as abnormal without further qualifications.

What, then, are the necessary additional considerations? If the behavior is committed by a person who is rational and otherwise shows no signs of cognitive impairment, we think of the act—albeit vulgar, immoral, or criminal—as outside the domain of abnormality. If, however, the behavior is performed by a person whose judgment, thinking, memory, or perception is disturbed, we consider the behavior abnormal. Emotional dysfunction is another factor that helps differentiate abnormal social behaviors from other kinds of deviant interactions. When emotional instability is present along with deviant interpersonal behavior, the social interaction is more likely to be abnormal than criminal. Therefore, in order to use interpersonal deviancy as a criterion of abnormal behavior, it is necessary to apply it in conjunction with the other criteria of cognitive and emotional dysfunction.

In summary, there is no single criterion for defining abnormal behaviors. However, for our purposes we define such behaviors as (1) those that persistently deviate from cultural and developmental norms in frequency and intensity and (2) those that are evidenced by impairment in one or more of the following areas of human functioning: intellectual and cognitive emotional expression and control, personal distress, and interpersonal relationships.

THE CLASSIFICATION OF PSYCHOPATHOLOGY

In the field of behavior disorders, a classification system arranges those individuals exhibiting abnormal behavior into diagnostic groupings according to certain common characteristics. From the very beginning, classification has been influenced greatly by a disease-oriented view of psychopathological behavior. This influence dates back to the contributions of Hippocrates, although the major impetus came in the nineteenth century, when Emil Kraepelin undertook the careful compilation of clinical records and histories of hospitalized patients. On the basis of these data, he constructed a classification system that was essentially descriptive; all his observations and clinical findings were used as diagnostic criteria. The data included symptoms and clusters of symptoms, etiology (when known), physiological changes, and observations about the course and outcome of the behavior.

Several other contributors helped to shape the present-day classification of abnormal behavior. For example, Eugen Bleuler (1857–1939) worked extensively with the disorder known as dementia praecox, or schizophrenia, and brought about significant changes both in the name and the concept of that disorder. Bleuler's lucid description of schizophrenia and its subcategories not only replaced the Kraepelinian view of the disorder, but it also significantly modified its classification. Adolph Meyer (1866–1950) argued against the Kraepelinian bias, which focused on the study of symptomatology and especially protested the inclination to view symptoms as signs of specific brain lesions. He took a broader approach, claiming that abnormal behaviors were faulty life adaptations produced by many factors (psychological, social, physiological, and constitutional) and not exclusively by brain pathology. He introduced the concept of reaction types as a substitute for the narrowly conceived disease entities.

Because no single system of classifying abnormal behavior had been adopted as the official standard in the field, diversity prevailed. Clinicians either modified existing systems or constructed their own to meet their special needs and those of the clinical facilities in which they worked. The result was "a polyglot of diagnostic labels and systems, effectively blocking communication and the collection of medical statistics" (APA, *Diagnostic and Statistical Manual*, 1965, p. v). This state of confusion triggered off several attempts to establish a standard nomenclature that would be nationally accepted and used.

American Psychiatric Association's Classification Systems

DSM–I and DSM–II. In 1927 the New York Academy of Medicine moved to establish a standard nomenclature of disease that would be nationally accepted. The first edition, entitled *Standard Classified Nomenclature of Disease*, was published in 1933 and was followed by two revisions, the last of which appeared in 1942. During World War II, however, psychiatrists found this system to be inadequate, since it dealt effectively with only about 10 percent of the total cases seen. Following the war the American Psychiatric Association undertook a revision of the system. Using material received from the Army and Veterans Administration, ideas from psychiatric training programs, suggestions from their own members, and data from the literature, they drafted a proposed revision. In 1951 they published the *Diagnostic and Statistical Manual* (DSM-I). Curiously, the manual virtually ignored childhood disorders per se, except for the inclusion of a few conditions listed along with adult syndromes in a manner somewhat reminiscent of the way children were viewed before childhood was discovered. In 1968 a second revision was published, known as DSM-II, which consisted of ten major categories. For the first time one of these categories was devoted exclusively to children ("Behavior Disorders of Childhood and Adolescence") and included the following subcategories: behavioral disorders, hyperkinetic reaction, withdrawing reaction, overanxious reaction, runaway reaction, unsocialized aggressive reaction, group delinquent reaction, and other reactions. In addition, another major category, transient situational disturbances, dealt with special symptoms most commonly found in children. These additions, albeit far from adequate, represented a substantial shift on the part of the American Psychiatric Association toward recognizing child psychopathology.

DSM–III. DSM-III is the latest and most radical revision of the classification system, not only in its attempt to be specific and inclusive but also in its rather extensive provisions for childhood disorders (APA, *Diagnostic and Statistical Manual of Mental Disorders: DSM-III*, 1980). Work on DSM-III began in 1974. Beginning in 1975, a task force from the American Psychiatric Association (APA) presented a series of drafts at each annual meeting of the association until the document was finally approved in 1979. In the interim the special task force established liaison committees with other professional organizations, held and sponsored relevant conferences, and conducted field trials of the new system. These involved 12,667 patients, who were evaluated by 550 clinicians working in more than 200 different facilities across the country.

The new classification system consists of sixteen major categories plus two others for recording special and not otherwise classifiable conditions (see Table 2–1). It also provides operational criteria that spell out the specific clinical behaviors required for each diagnostic category, as well as a multiaxial framework which enables the diagnostician to code the patient on additional dimensions. There are five axes: two dealing with the various categories of mental disorders; one for

Table 2-1 Summary of DSM-III Categories

Disorders Usually First Evident in Infancy, Childhood, or Adolescence
- Mental Retardation
- Attention Deficit Disorders
- Conduct Disorder
- Anxiety Disorders of Childhood or Adolescence
- Other Disorders of Infancy, Childhood, or Adolescence
- Eating Disorders
- Stereotyped Movement Disorders
- Other Disorders with Physical Manifestations
- Pervasive Developmental Disorders
- Specific Developmental Disorders

Organic Mental Disorders
Substance Use Disorders
Schizophrenic Disorders
Paranoid Disorders
Psychotic Disorders Not Elsewhere Classified
Affective Disorders
Anxiety Disorders
Somatoform Disorders
Dissociative Disorders (Hysterical Neuroses, Dissociative Type)
Psychosexual Disorders
Factitious Disorders
Disorders of Impulse Control Not Elsewhere Classified
Adjustment Disorders
Psychological Factors Affecting Physical Condition
Personality Disorders
V Codes for Conditions Not Attributable to a Mental Disorder That Are a Focus of Attention or Treatment
Additional Codes

designating nonmental medical disorders; one for rating the severity of psychosocial stressors; and one for characterizing the highest level of adaptive functioning the patient achieved within the last year.

The major category in DSM-III devoted to childhood psychopathology is more extensive and inclusive than the one that appeared in the two previous editions. It is designated as Disorders Usually First Evident in Infancy, Childhood, or Adolescence, and each of its subcategories is summarized in Table 2-2. Psychosexual disorders, particularly gender disturbances occurring during childhood and adolescence, are not included in this section, although they are covered in the adult part. Surprisingly, this major category establishes no age limit to distinguish childhood from adolescence and, in fact, includes subcategories that may be more appropriate for the college years (Identity Disorder) or for older adults, if the present condition dates back to early childhood (Attention Deficit Disorder). Childhood disorders resembling those seen in adults but that may not develop into the adult condition are given separate subcategories in this section. In addition, any other diagnostic category offered elsewhere in DSM-III may be applied to children.

In order to describe fully the current psychiatric and medical conditions of the patient, DSM-III allows for the multiple diagnoses on Axes I, II, and III. The system has more categories for many of the conditions included in DSM-I and II, and it also includes a number of additional categories not noted in the earlier editions. Further, DSM-III actually excludes or changes the classification of some conditions previously regarded as important. For example, it omits Neurotic Disorders as a major category, although separate neurotic disorders are covered in other categories of the system. In addition, psychophysiological or psychosomatic disorders are no longer cate-

Table 2-2 Summary Description of DSM-III's Disorders Usually First Evident in Infancy, Childhood, or Adolescence[a]

The disorders in this section usually arise and are evident in infancy, childhood or adolescence, although no arbitrary age limit is used to define childhood or adolescence. The diagnoses may be applied to adults if they manifest the condition from childhood and no adult category applies. When childhood conditions closely resemble adult disorders in essential features the diagnostic categories correspond to adult disorders and are not included in this section.

1. *Mental Retardation*
   Three essential features must be present: (1) significant subaverage intellectual functioning, (2) concurrent impairment in adaptive behavior, and (3) onset before the age of eighteen. The diagnosis is made regardless of the nature of the etiological factors, although a known biological cause should be coded on Axis III. When mental retardation develops after age eighteen, it is designated as dementia and is coded within the organic mental disorders section. There are four subtypes of mental retardation reflecting the degree of intellectual impairment. These are labeled as mild, moderate, severe, or profound depending on an IQ criterion.

2. *Attention Deficit Disorder*
   This category is characterized by developmentally inappropriate short attention and impulsivity. The active disorder includes two subtypes: Attention Deficit Disorder with Hyperactivity, and Attention Deficit Disorder without Hyperactivity. There is also a residual subtype in which hyperactivity is no longer present, although the other signs of the disorder persist. The operational criteria for *inattention* include any three of the following: (1) frequent failure to complete things started, (2) frequent failure to listen, (3) distracted easily, and (4) difficulty in concentrating on tasks requiring sustained attention. *Impulsivity* includes three or more of the following: (1) acting before thinking frequently, (2) excessive shifting from one activity to another, (3) difficulty in organizing work not due to cognitive impairment, (4) requires a great deal of supervision, (5) calling out in class frequently, and (6) finding it difficult to await turn in games or group situations. With respect to *hyperactivity* two or more of the following must be present: (1) excessive running about or climbing on things, (2) excessive fidgetiness or difficulty in sitting still, (3) excessive difficulty in remaining seated, (4) excessive movement during sleep, and (5) constantly "on the go" or acts as if "driven by a motor."

3. *Conduct Disorder*
   The disorder involves repetitive and persistent patterns of misconduct such as delinquent acts, destructiveness or other violations of the rights of others beyond the ordinary mischief and pranks of children and adolescents. It includes four subtypes: *Undersocialized, Aggressive; Undersocialized, Nonaggressive; Socialized, Aggressive;* and *Socialized, Nonaggressive.* The *Undersocialized* subtypes fail to form a normal degree of affection, social bond, and empathy with others. Meaningful peer relations are generally absent, and these youngsters do not extend themselves to others without obvious and immediate benefit. They are manipulative and callous. They show a general lack of concern for others and fail to evidence appropriate feelings of guilt for their actions. The *socialized* subtypes manifest social attachment to others, although they may be manipulative and evidence little guilt for actions against persons to whom they are not attached. The *aggressive* subtypes display repetitive and persistent patterns of aggressive behavior that violate the rights of others through physical violence against other people or thefts involving confrontation with the victim. The *nonaggressive* subtypes evidence a persistent pattern of actions which conflicts with norms for their age such as violation of a variety of important rules established at home and in school, persistent truancy, substance abuse, persistent lying, running away from home, vandalism and stealing (but without confrontation of a victim). For these youngsters, the aggressive conduct described for the aggressive subtypes are absent.

4. *Anxiety Disorders*
   There are three disorders in this category in which anxiety is the predominant clinical feature. The anxiety is focused on specific situations for two of these disorders: Separation Anxiety Disorder and Avoidant Disorder of Childhood or Adolescence, while the anxiety is generalized to a variety of situations in the third disorder, Overanxious Disorder.

(*continued*)

Table 2-2 (cont.)

A. *Separation Anxiety Disorder*
This disorder is characterized by excessive anxiety of at least two week duration over separation from those to whom the child is attached.

B. *Avoidant Disorder of Childhood or Adolescence*
This disorder involves persistent and excessive shrinking from contact with strangers, a desire for affection, acceptance, and warm relationships with family and other familiar figures, and avoidant behavior severe enough to interfere with social functioning with peers for at least six months duration.

C. *Overanxious Disorder*
This disorder is characterized by non-specific and generalized excessive worry and fearful behavior for at least six months which is not attributable to a recent psychosocial stressor.

5. *Other Disorders of Infancy, Childhood, or Adolescence*

A. *Reactive Attachment Disorder of Infancy*
Poor emotional development involving absence of age-appropriate signs of social responsiveness and apathetic mood together with poor physical development (failure to thrive) occurring before eight months of age are the essential characteristics of this disorder. Infants with this disorder fail to receive the type of care that typically leads to affectional bonding with others.

B. *Schizoid Disorder of Childhood or Adolescence*
This disorder is characterized by an impairment in one's capacity to form social relationships. The operational criteria include: no close friendship with similar aged peers; no evident interest in forming friendships; an absence of pleasure from peer interactions; avoidance of nonfamilial social contacts; an absence of interest in group activities with other children; and the disturbance is present for at least three months.

C. *Elective Mutism*
Continuous refusal to speak in social situations and school in children who are able to comprehend and speak language are the chief characteristics of this disorder.

D. *Oppositional Disorder*
This disorder begins after three years of age and before age 18 and involves a pattern of disobedient, negativistic, and provocative opposition to authority figures, although violation of the basic rights of others (as in Conduct Disorder) is not evident.

E. *Identity Disorder*
This disorder involves severe subjective distress over one's inability to reconcile various parts of the self into a relatively coherent and acceptable sense of self. Uncertainty about various issues relating to identity is evident and the disturbance is of at least three months duration.

6. *Eating Disorders*
This category includes several conditions that involve gross disturbances in eating behavior.

A. *Anorexia Nervosa*
This disorder is characterized by intense fear of becoming obese, disturbance of body image, significant weight loss, refusal to maintain a minimal normal body weight and amenorrhea (in females) which are not attributable to a known physical disorder.

B. *Bulimia*
This disorder involves episodic binge eating with the awareness that this eating pattern is abnormal; fear of being unable to voluntarily stop eating; depressed mood; and self-deprecating thoughts following the eating binges which are not attributable to Anorexia Nervosa or a known physical disorder.

C. *Pica*
Persistent eating of nonnutritive substances for at least one month.

D. *Rumination Disorder of Infancy*
This disorder is characterized by repeated regurgitation without nausea or associated gastrointestinal illness but with a weight loss for at least one month following a period of normal functioning and development.

Table 2-2 (cont.)

7. *Stereotyped Movement Disorders*
This classification includes several disorders characterized by abnormalities of gross motor movement.
   A. *Transient Tic Disorders*
   This disorder involves recurrent, involuntary, repetitive, rapid and purposeless movements (tics) which can be voluntarily suppressed for minutes to hours, vary in intensity, and persist for one month but no longer than 12 months.
   B. *Chronic Motor Tic Disorder*
   This disorder is characterized by recurrent, involuntary, repetitive and purposeless movements involving no more than three muscle groups at one time. The tics are unvarying in intensity, and persist for at least a year.
   C. *Tourette's Disorder*
   Recurrent tics including multiple vocal tics which can be voluntarily suppressed for minutes to hours and occurs between the ages of 2 and 15 years. The movements can vary over weeks or months in intensity, frequency and location of the symptoms.
   D. *Atypical Tic Disorder*
   This category is for the diagnosis of tics that cannot be classified adequately in any of the previous categories.
   E. *Atypical Stereotyped Movement Disorder*
   This disorder involves head banging, rocking, repetitive hand movements consisting of quick, rhythmic, small hand rotations, or repetitive voluntary movements that typically involve the fingers or arms. They are distinguishable from tics in that they consist of voluntary movements and are not spasmodic. Children with these disorders are not distressed by the same symptoms as those with tics.

8. *Other Disorders with Physical Manifestations*
This classification includes categories in which the predominant disturbance is in a physical function involving speech, urination, defection, or sleep.
   A. *Stuttering*
   The operational criteria for this disorder includes frequent repetitions or prolongation of sounds, syllables, or words, or frequent, unusual hesitations and pauses that disrupt the rhythmic flow of speech.
   B. *Functional Enuresis*
   Persistent involuntary voiding of urine by day or night not due to a physical disorder that is considered abnormal for the age of the individual and that occurs at least twice a month for children between the ages of five and six and once a month for older children. The disorder is called *primary* if it has not been preceded by a period of urinary continence for at least one year, and *secondary* if it has been preceded by urinary continence for at least one year.
   C. *Functional Encopresis*
   This disorder involves repeated or involuntary passage of feces of normal or near-normal consistency into places not appropriate for that purpose in the individual's own sociocultural setting and which is not attributable to any physical disorder. At least one such event per month should occur after the age of four.
   D. *Sleepwalking Disorder*
   This disorder involves repeated episodes of a sequence of complex behaviors that often progress, without full consciousness or later memory, to leaving the bed and walking about after the onset of sleep (between 30 and 200 minutes) and lasts from a few minutes to about a half hour. The individual typically sits up and carries out perseverative motor movements, and then, in addition to walking, performs semi-purposeful motor acts. During the episode the individual has a blank, staring face and is relatively unresponsive to the attempts of others to influence the sleep walking or to communicate with him or her. There is amnesia for the route traversed and what happened during the episode, although there is no other impairment of mental activity or behavior upon awakening.
   E. *Sleep Terror Disorder*
   This disorder involves repeated episodes of abrupt awakening from sleep (after 30 to 200

(*continued*)

Table 2-2 (cont.)

minutes of sleep) lasting between one and ten minutes. Typically, the individual sits up in bed with intense anxiety and evidences agitated and perseverative motor movements, a frightened expression, dilated pupils, profuse perspiration, pilo-erection, rapid breathing, and quick pulse. The person is unresponsive to the attempts of others to comfort him or her, is unable to recount a complete dream sequence, and in the morning is amnesic for the entire episode.

9. *Pervasive Developmental Disorders*
Disorders in this classification are characterized by distortions in the development of multiple basic psychological functions involved in the development of social skills and language. Many basic areas of psychological development are affected at the same time and to a severe degree. They differ from specific developmental disorders in two ways: (1) the specifics show a delay in time or rate of specific discrete functions while the pervasives evidence a marked distortion of the timing, rate, and sequence of many psychological functions; and (2) the specifics appear as if they are passing through an earlier normal developmental stage, while the pervasives manifest severe qualitative abnormalities that are not normal for any stage of development.
   A. *Infantile Autism*
   This disorder begins before 30 months of age and involves pervasive lack of responsiveness to other people, gross deficits in language development, and peculiar speech patterns (when speech present) such as immediate and delayed echolalia, metaphorical language and pronoun reversal. Bizarre responses to various aspects of the environment are present but there is an absence of delusions, hallucinations, loosening of associations, and incoherence as noted in Schizophrenia. Two other subclasses of this diagnosis are available: *Infantile Autism, Full Syndrome Present* (for instances which currently meet the criteria for Infantile Autism), and *Infantile Autism, Residual State* (for instances where the criteria for Infantile Autism were once met but the current clinical picture no longer meets the full criteria).
   B. *Childhood Onset Pervasive Developmental Disorder*
   This disorder develops after 30 months and before twelve years of age and involves a profound disturbance in social relations and multiple oddities of behavior. Impaired social relations include: lack of appropriate affective responsivity, inappropriate clinging, asociality, and a lack of peer relationships, while oddities of behavior include: sudden excessive anxiety, constricted or inappropriate affect, resistance to change in the environment or insistence on doing things in the same manner, oddities of motor movement, speech abnormalities, hyper- or hypo-sensitivity to sensory stimuli, and self-mutilation. There is an absence of delusions, hallucinations, incoherence, or marked loosening of associations. Subcategories are provided for the Full Syndrome Present (currently meets the criteria), Residual State (previously met the criteria but current clinical picture no longer meets the full criteria), and Atypical (for those instances that cannot be classified as either Infantile Autism or Childhood Onset Pervasive Developmental Disorder).

10. *Specific Developmental Disorders* (Axis II)
These disorders are coded on Axis II and are diagnosed only when there is a delay in development that is not an essential criterion for another disorder. The coding carries no etiological implications, and all Specific Developmental Disorders should be diagnosed since a given child may have more than one.
   A. *Developmental Reading Disorder*
   The essential feature of this disorder is a significant impairment in the development of reading skills not explicable in terms of mental age or inadequate schooling. In school, the child's performance on tasks requiring reading skills is significantly below his or her intellectual capacity. The diagnosis can only be made by individually administered IQ tests and a variety of academic achievement tests that contain reading subtests.
   B. *Developmental Arithmetic Disorder*
   This disorder involves arithmetic achievement that is significantly below expected level (as measured by performance on stardardized, individually administered tests of arithmetic achievement) given the child's schooling, chronological age and mental age (as measured by an individually administered IQ test). In addition, the child's performance in school on tasks requiring arithmetic skills is significantly below his/her intellectual capacity.

Table 2-2 (cont.)

C. *Developmental Language Disorder*
This category includes three major types of language disorder:
(1) *Expressive Type*—characterized by a failure to develop vocal expression (encoding) of language while understanding or decoding skills remain intact and inner language is evident.
(2) *Receptive Type*—characterized by a failure to develop comprehension (decoding) and vocal expression (encoding) of language.
(3) *Articulation Disorder*—characterized by a failure to develop consistent articulations of the later-acquired speech sounds such as r, sh, th, f, z, l, or ch. When omissions occur or substitutes are made for these sounds, it gives the impression of "baby talk."

D. *Mixed Specific Developmental Disorder*
This category is used when there is more than one Specific Developmental Disorder, but none is predominant.

E. *Atypical Specific Developmental Disorder*
This category is used when there is a Specific Developmental Disorder not covered by any of the above specified categories.

[a] Description of these categories based on material included in DSM-III, 1980.

Reprinted by permission of American Psychiatric Association. From *Diagnostic and Statistical Manual of Medical Disorders*, 3rd ed.

gorized as mental disorders, but rather the physical condition (asthma, colitis, ulcer, hypertension, and so forth) is noted on Axis III. The disorder is diagnosed on Axis I only when psychological factors are associated with either the onset or exacerbation of the physical condition. DSM-III also deals with childhood psychoses differently than before by relabeling this major diagnostic category as Pervasive Developmental Disorders and excluding Childhood Schizophrenia as one of its subcategories. The decision to eliminate this widely used subcategory serves to restrict Schizophrenia (if it occurs in childhood) to the criteria designated for the adult form of the disorder; this tends to minimize the abusive practice of using Childhood Schizophrenia as an all-inclusive category for psychosis in children.

In general, DSM-III does not deal with personality disorders of childhood and adolescence as completely as other systems. It does contain major categories for Conduct Disorders and Other Disorders of Infancy, Childhood, or Adolescence, but in neither of these categories are the Compulsive or Hysterical Personality Disorders included. In fact, the absence of a major category for Personality Disorders for Children and Adolescents, and its recommended use on Axis II (an axis intended for either adult personality disorders or for learning disorders of childhood), suggests that DSM-III places less importance than prior editions on this category for youngsters. However, this deemphasis is discrepant with research findings obtained with the GAP classification system, which indicated that Personality Disorders is one of four major categories (along with Reactive Disorders, Neurotic Disorders, and Psychotic Disorders) that accounted for 83 percent of the diagnoses made by experienced clinicians (Freeman, 1971).

Evaluation of DSM-III. Although DSM-III is a relatively new classification system, it is important that it receive critical appraisal, since it is the official nosology of American psychiatry and is likely to be the primary (if not exclusive) system used by clinicians working in various mental health settings for years to come. In contrast to previous editions, DSM-III is a more complex system which provides for multiaxial coding, a greater number of diagnostic categories, and more explicit operational criteria for each diagnostic subtype. These features, as well as DSM-III's greater emphasis on objectivity, offer the prospect that this new system will prove to be significantly more reliable and valid than prior versions.

However, even at this early date criticisms of DSM-III have appeared in the literature. It has been said that the boundary lines used by the system to define mental disorders are too broad and inclusive and are too closely tied to a traditional disease-model of psychopathology. For these reasons the American Psychological Association officially endorsed the system with reservations, claiming that under its broadened range of categories, such commonplace behaviors as smoking would be included and considered to be a mental disorder (APA Monitor, 1980). More specifically, several writers have leveled criticism at DSM-III's inclusion of Specific Developmental Disorders (such as reading and arithmetic disabilities, and articulation problems) as mental disorders, since there is no tangible evidence to corroborate either the presence of a disease process or disordered physiology underlying these developmental problems (Schacht and Nathan, 1977; Garmezy, 1978; Nathan, 1979). Moreover, Harris (1979) contends that these conditions cannot be considered legitimate mental disorders, even though they may in fact pose serious difficulties for the children who have them. In this context the American Psychological Association expressed concern over DSM-III's practice of classifying almost any childhood problem as a stigmatizing mental disorder rather than labeling it a maladaptive behavior (APA Monitor, 1980). The practice of calling developmental and other childhood problems mental disorders may adversely affect the child's self-concept and the way in which he or she is perceived by others. Further, it may be harmful to assume that treatment of mental disorders (in a disease model) should come under the direction and control of medical practitioners rather than specially trained teachers.

Behaviorally oriented clinicians tend to quarrel with DSM-III and other systems rooted in the medical-disease model because such systems assume that specific mental disorders are characterized by a certain set of symptoms which reflect an underlying pathology (or disease process). Inasmuch as behavioral clinicians prefer to assess specific maladaptive behaviors as well as the environmental conditions that maintain them, they are inclined to argue that the diagnoses of DSM-III have limited implications for treatment choice and outcome (Harris, 1979).

Finally, some observers challenge the inclusion in DSM-III of disorders which deal with specific behaviors—such as repetitive movements (tics), eating, sleeping, as well as bladder and bowel control—as separate mental disorders. They suggest that these deviations are more likely to be symptoms associated with or indicative of other psychopathological conditions than to be actual disorders or syndromes themselves.

Notwithstanding these criticisms and areas of controversy, DSM-III is clearly more comprehensive and explicit in diagnostic criteria and categories than the previous two editions. Further, it gives every indication of being significantly more reliable and valid than any classification system yet developed. In addition, DSM-III should provide reassurance to those concerned with the tendency of classification systems in general to neglect the "whole" individual; DSM-III, with its multiaxial orientation, looks at children and adults from many perspectives.

Child Classification Systems

The GAP System. Although the need for a uniform classification system for children and adolescents had been noted for years (Group for the Advancement of Psychiatry, 1957), it was not until 1966 that the Committee on Child Psychiatry of the Group for the Advancement of Psychiatry (GAP) completed and published their proposed system (Group for the Advancement of Psychiatry, 1966). At the time of publication, there were at least twenty-three other child classification systems in use, illustrating the diversity and diagnostic confusion that has characterized the field.

The GAP system consists of ten major categories ordered (although poorly) along the dimension of prognosis and ranging from healthy responses to the most severe disorders. A summary of these categories and the subcategories noted for each are included in Table 2–3. Embracing the psychosomatic, developmental, and psychosocial views, the system can best be characterized as a clinical descriptive scheme that can be used by clinicians of varying backgrounds. While the category of Healthy Responses has never been used in any system, it is included here to minimize the practice of clinicians to exaggerate minor childhood problems for classification purposes. For example, the new category gives the clinician the opportunity to categorize bedwetting in a two-year-old as a healthy response rather than calling it abnormal. Another new category, Developmental Deviations, deals with deviations in maturational rate or sequence in personality development. While frequently noted in children, they are not adequately classified under other systems.

The WHO System. In 1969 The World Health Organization (WHO) published a multiaxial classification system for childhood disorders (Rutter et al., 1969). This system includes the following four axes: (1) clinical psychiatric syndrome, (2) intellectual level (IQ), (3) associated etiological biological factors, and (4) any associated etiological psychosocial factors. Thus, a psychotic child who (1) is severely retarded and (2) has epilepsy (3) would be coded on three of the four axes. The advantages of classifying children on various relevant dimensions offered by the WHO system is now available in the new multiaxial look of DSM-III.

Factor-Analytic System. A statistical technique known as *factor analysis* has been used empirically to isolate clusters of characteristics observed in children, which clusters then become the major categories of the classification system. The effectiveness of this statistical approach rests on the nature and character of the items on which each child is rated, since the final cluster of symptoms is derived from these initial data. Consequently, factor-analytic classifications differ from one investigator to another, because the original variables under study and the items used to measure them are likely to be divergent. An example of a factor-analytic classification scheme is the one proposed by Achenbach (1966), who found two general clusters which he called *internalizing* and *externalizing,* or *personality problems* and *conduct problems.* In addition to the general clusters, the system also includes specific symptom clusters that are either subsumed by the general clusters or peculiar to certain developmental periods. Some of the internalizing symptoms include phobias, insomnia, stomachaches, and seclusiveness, while externalizing symptoms include destructiveness, stealing, and running away. These data have been replicated with new samples of children and have been used to show that externalizing boys were independently rated as more impulsive and aggressive, while internalizing boys were considered more passive as well as more inclined to stay longer in psychotherapy and to improve with treatment (Achenbach and Lewis, 1971). Several other studies using these two general clusters with children from clinics and schools indicate relationships that support the validity of the categories (Achenbach, 1974).

Other Systems. Other and more specific classification schemes have been used for research purposes, especially where investigators are concerned with studying one or relatively few psychopathological conditions. Usually these miniature systems specify a set of diagnostic criteria that are more behavioral and more amenable to the careful selection of clinical populations than is possible with the more traditional and global systems. For example, the DeMyer-Churchill system (DeMyer et al., 1971) provides a set of criteria to distinguish psychotic children (see Chapter 8) into subgroups that are not included in

Table 2–3 Psychopathological Disorders in Childhood: Proposed Classification

1. *Healthy Responses*

This category assesses the positive strengths of the child and tries to avoid the diagnosis of healthy states by the exclusion of pathology. The criteria for assessment are the intellectual, social, emotional, personal, adaptive, and psychosocial functioning of the child in relation to developmental and situational crises.

Healthy responses:

1. Developmental crisis
2. Situational crisis
3. Other responses

2. *Reactive Disorders*

This category is based on disorders in which behavior and/or symptoms are the result of situational factors. These disturbances must be of a pathological degree so as to distinguish them from the healthy responses to a situational crisis.

3. *Developmental Disorders*

These are disorders in personality development that may be beyond the range of normal variation in that they occur at a time, in a sequence, or in a degree not expected for a given age level or stage in development.

Developmental Deviations:

1. Deviations in maturational patterns
2. Deviations in specific dimensions of development
3. Motor
4. Sensory
5. Speech
6. Cognitive functions
7. Social development
8. Psychosexual
9. Affective
10. Integrative
11. Other developmental deviation

4. *Psychoneurotic Disorders*

These disorders are based on unconscious conflicts over the handling of sexual and aggressive impulses that remain active and unresolved, though removed from awareness by the mechanism of repression. Marked personality disorganization or decompensation, or the gross disturbance of reality testing is not seen. Because of their internalized character, these disorders tend toward chronicity, with a self-perpetuating or repetitive nature. Subcategories are based on specific syndromes.

Psychoneurotic Disorders:

1. Anxiety type
2. Phobic type
3. Conversion type
4. Dissociative type
5. Obsessive-compulsive type
6. Depressive type
7. Other psychoneurotic disorder

5. *Personality Disorders*

These disorders are characterized by chronic or fixed pathological trends, representing traits that have become ingrained in the personality structure. In most but not all such disorders, these trends or traits are not perceived by the child as a source of intrapsychic distress or anxiety. In making this classification, the total personality picture must be considered and not just the presence of a single behavior or symptom.

Personality Disorders

1. Compulsive personality
2. Hysterical
3. Anxious
4. Overly dependent

Table 2-3 (cont.)

5. Oppositional
6. Overly inhibited
7. Overly independent
8. Isolated
9. Mistrustful

Tension-discharge disorders:
1. Impulse-ridden personality
2. Neurotic personality disorder

Sociosyntonic personality disorders:
1. Sexual deviation
2. Other personality disorder

6. *Psychotic Disorder*

These disorders are characterized by marked, pervasive deviations from the behavior that is expected for the child's age. They are revealed in severe and continued impairment of emotional relationships with persons; loss of speech or failure in its development; disturbances in sensory perception; bizarre or stereotyped behavior and motility patterns; marked resistance to change in environment or routine; outbursts of intense and unpredictable panic; absence of a sense of personal identity; and blunted, uneven, or fragmented intellectual development. Major categories are based on the developmental period with subcategories in each period for the listing of a specific syndrome, if known.

Psychotic Disorders:
1. Psychoses of infancy and early childhood
   a. Early infantile autism
   b. Interactional psychotic disorder
   c. Other psychosis of infancy and early childhood
2. Psychoses of later childhood
   a. Schizophreniform psychotic disorder
   b. Other psychosis of later childhood
3. Psychoses of adolescence
   a. Acute confusional state
   b. Schizophrenic disorder, adult type
   c. Other psychosis of adolescence

7. *Psychophysiologic Disorders*

These disorders are characterized by a significant interaction between somatic and psychological components. They may be precipitated and perpetuated by psychological or social stimuli of stressful nature. These disorders ordinarily involve those organ systems innervated by the autonomic nervous system.

Psychophysiologic Disorders:
1. Skin
2. Musculoskeletal
3. Respiratory
4. Cardiovascular
5. Hemic and lymphatic
6. Gastrointestinal
7. Genitourinary
8. Endocrine
9. Of Nervous system
10. Of organs of special sense
11. Other psychophysiologic disorders

8. *Brain Syndromes*

These disorders are characterized by impairment of orientation, judgment, discrimination, learning, memory, and other cognitive functions, as well as by frequent labile affect. They are basically caused by diffuse impairment of brain tissue function. Personality disturbances of a psychotic, neurotic, or behavioral nature also may be present.

(*continued*)

Table 2-3 (cont.)

Brain Syndromes:
1. Acute
2. Chronic

9. *Mental Retardation*

10. *Other Disorders*
This category is for disorders that cannot be classified by the above definitions or for disorders we will describe in the future.

Reprinted by permission from *Psychological Disorders in Childhood: A Proposed Classification*, Group for the Advancement of Psychiatry, 419 Park Avenue South, New York, N.Y. 10016.

DSM-III, GAP, or other systems previously described. Similarly, a checklist prepared by Rimland (1971) to differentiate one group of psychotic children from other groups (discussed in Chapter 8) is still popular with researchers studying childhood psychoses.

RELIABILITY OF CLASSIFICATION

From the time of Kraepelin to the present, the classification of abnormal behavior has had as its principal goals the understanding of etiology, the prediction of the course and outcome of the condition, and the appropriate selection of treatment for the various abnormal behaviors. To a large extent the usefulness of a classification scheme depends on the degree of consistency or agreement achieved in categorizing abnormal behavior. If little agreement is obtained, the system has very limited pragmatic value.

Measures of Reliability

Reliability may be measured in three ways:

1. Observer agreement—a measure of agreement on categorization by two or more observers.
2. Consistency agreement—a measure of agreement on categories over time, such as between the initial and final diagnosis.
3. Frequency agreement—a measure of agreement between two or more random samples of the same population with regard to the frequency of cases falling into each diagnostic category (Zubin, 1967).

Reliability Findings

Most studies of reliability have been concerned with observer agreement and have been based on the adult categories specified in DSM-I. We should also note that data obtained from many of these studies, especially the earlier ones, are difficult to interpret because of their methodological shortcomings. These shortcomings involve (1) very small and unrepresentatitive samples of patients, (2) lack of control for rater differences in training and experience, and (3) dearth of information about patients on which ratings were based (Beck, 1962). More carefully designed studies have consistently shown that agreement is high when the classification is restricted to a few major categories that are grossly distinct from each other. However, reliability estimates sharply decline when a greater number of categories, and more specific diagnostic categories, are included (Hunt, Witson, and Hunt, 1953; Schmidt and Fonda, 1956; Kreitman et al., 1961; Sandifer, Pettus, and Quade, 1964).

In general, consistency of diagnosis over time as a reliability measure yields even lower estimates than that obtained from studies of observer agreement (Zubin, 1967). However, this finding may be more indicative of the dramatic changes that can take place in the symptoms of a patient from one period of time to another than of poor rater reliability. This is particularly true of those patients who after a brief period of hospitalization show a decrease in agitated and anxiety-generated behavior because they are now in a more secure and protected environment. In addition, the increased use of drugs to treat patients and make them more manageable has tended to bring about symptom changes over time.

Frequency agreement is illustrated by a study involving 538 women who were admitted to a large midwestern psychiatric hospital for the first time (Pasamanick, Dinitz, and Lefton, 1959). The patients were assigned to one of three autonomously operated wards on the basis of bed availability. There were no differences among the patients on the three wards with respect to marital status, age, education, urban-rural residence, or type of admission (voluntary or involuntary). Three different psychiatrists were placed in charge of each ward. In this way a situation was constructed that provided each psychiatrist with equal access to patient information from other professional workers as well as with the "same type" of patient to diagnose. The results showed marked discrepancies among the samples with respect to the frequency with which the three major diagnostic categories were used. In this connection Zubin noted that of four studies he reviewed (including Pasamanick and associates), only one showed agreement among samples. He concluded: "In general, the results of comparative studies of random samples with regard to distribution of diagnoses do not yield a consistent picture regarding reliability" (1976, p. 388).

Interest in assessing the reliability of the classification of children's disorders is recent, primarily because there was no single system that could be used uniformly until the appearance of the GAP proposal. Since its publication, the GAP scheme has been the subject of several investigations. One study found that two of the GAP categories accounted for 75 percent of the 200 cases sampled (Personality Disorder and Psychotic Disorder). Six other categories were used sparingly (from about 4 to 8 percent), while the two new categories (Healthy Responses and Developmental Deviation) were hardly used at all (Sabot, Peck, and Raskin, 1969). Another study attempted to determine the effectiveness of the GAP system over a twelve-month period (Bemporad, Pfeiffer, and Bloom, 1970). In contrast, the new categories were found to be useful for this sample of 310 children in that they accounted for almost 24 percent of the cases. Moreover, the distribution of the cases among the GAP categories between these two studies differed markedly in almost all instances. It is difficult to resolve the large discrepancies between these two studies because the second study did not describe the patients with respect to socioeconomic level, race, age, educational level, and family structure. It is entirely possible that some of the differences in the findings were attributable to the substantial differences in the population sampled.

The most extensive reliability study to date involved the diagnosis by twenty experienced child psychiatrists of forty-four cases (case histories and diagnoses) submitted by members of the GAP subcommittee (Freeman, 1971). The results indicated that four categories (Reactive Disorders, Neurotic Disorders, Personality Disorders, and Psychotic Disorders) accounted for 83 percent of the diagnoses, while the remaining categories accounted for only 17 percent. The two new categories (Healthy Responses and Developmental Deviation) were rarely used, once again raising the question of their value in a classification system. The reliability of the four frequently used categories was between 61 and 72 percent. There was no evidence that diagnostic agreement is higher for any specific age group.

Data were also gathered to measure consistency over time, as the twenty clinicians were required to rediagnose a sample of selected cases some three months later. The clinicians placed 86 out of a total of 120 diagnoses in the same category as before, yielding a 72 percent agreement. This figure is even more impressive in light of the fact that three cases accounted for twenty-six of the thirty-four disagreements recorded and that three cases were responsible for low agreement even in the initial ratings. These findings demonstrate fairly high reliability for the four categories used most frequently and show a decrease in reliability when more specific subcategories are employed.

Field trials and tests of interrater reliability between two clinicians evaluating the same patient on each of the five axes were completed using earlier draft versions of DSM-III. A total of 670 adult patients were evaluated by approximately 300 clinicians; the latter showed higher diagnostic agreement for major categories (on Axis I) than previously found with DSM-I or DSM-II (Spitzer, Forman, and Nee, 1979). In contrast, the interrater diagnostic reliability for 124 child and adolescent patients evaluated by approximately 84 clinicians was generally lower than that reported for adult patients, but higher than that reported using the GAP classification system (Beitchman et al., 1978). Given DSM-III's apparent degree of objectivity and its explicit diagnostic criteria, it is disappointing to find preliminary data that indicate no significant increase in diagnostic reliability with children between DSM-III and DSM-II (Mattison et al., 1979). No data are available as yet with which to evaluate the reliability of the other classification systems discussed earlier.

EVALUATION OF CLASSIFICATION

Evidently, the reliability of psychiatric classification is low, except when diagnosis is restricted to a few broad categories. Although much of this evidence comes from studies using an outdated system primarily intended for adults, similar inferences seem to be supported by data involving children and a classification scheme for child psychopathology (GAP). Diagnostic accuracy becomes increasingly more difficult as more categories are used and finer discriminations are required. The validity question—that is, how well diagnosis meets its goals—is extremely difficult to answer, since the goals of classification are so numerous and diverse.

Classification has been seriously criticized on additional grounds. Some have considered it unscientific because it confounds etiology, symptoms, and outcome as the bases for diagnosis. Commenting on this diversity of principles, Draguns and Phillips stated: "This confusion not only makes for conceptual inelegance; it implies an ever continuing process of diagnosis terminated only at the point of patient's death. Ultimately, this orientation makes diagnosis intrinsically uncertain and unknowable" (1971, p. 5). The use of behavioral description as the basic data for classification has been suggested as an alternative (Zigler and Phillips, 1961). Both etiology and prognosis would be treated as correlates of the particular class to which their relationship is known; but they would not be handled as inherent attributes of the various categories.

Another major criticism is that classification implies separate and mutually exclusive entities. Yet there is considerable overlapping in symptomatology among the categories. For example, it has been found that the symptom of depression occurred in 65 percent of patients diagnosed as manic-depressive, in 58 percent of those diagnosed as psychoneurotic, and in 31 percent of those diagnosed as character disordered (Zigler and Phillips, 1961).

It has been estimated that about 5 percent of the disagreement in diagnosis is attributable to the inconsistent behavior of the patient, 32.5 percent to the inconsistent behavior of the diagnostician, and 62.5 percent to the inadequacy of the classification system (Ward et al., 1962). If this appraisal is correct, diagnostic reliability can be increased to some extent by reducing those disagreements introduced by the clinician. Improving clinicians' training in the uniform use of the classification scheme would go a long way toward minimizing this source of error.

The issue of attaching psychiatric labels to children has aroused some controversy. Diagnostic labels, especially those reflecting serious disorders, may stick to the child over the years and possibly influence later evaluations, even when such labels are no longer appropriate. Labeling may stigmatize the child and set him or her apart from peers, and it may encourage others to expect the child to behave in a way commensurate with the label. Unfortunately, diagnostic categories appear real and valid to many observers. However, we now know that they lack the precision and reliability to warrant such confidence. For these reasons, and to protect children from future abuses, many clinicians are reluctant to fix a diagnostic label to children who evidence abnormal behaviors if there is a chance that in the future others might have access to the diagnosis. On the other hand, it can be argued that diagnostic labels need not be abused or misinterpreted if the clinician exercises care in the evaluation as well as good judgment about who has access to it. The diagnosis should serve as the basis for a treatment plan and should be helpful in later evaluations of the child, acting as a model for comparison and as a measure of the child's progress.

For the present, DSM-III and to a lesser extent the GAP proposal enjoy official status and widespread use throughout the country. Within the limitations already noted, classification brings uniformity to the ordering of psychopathology and continues to serve an important communication function among professionals. While we must be aware of its shortcomings, it would be premature to either ignore or completely reject the current system. Meehl supported this position when he remarked: "There is a sufficient amount of etiological and prognostic homogeneity among patients belonging to a given diagnostic group, so that the assignment of a patient to his group has probability implications which it is clinically unsound to ignore" (Meehl, 1959, p. 103). More recently it has been argued that classification is essential for research and fundamental to the clinician in organizing the multifaceted aspects of mental disorders (Shakow, 1968). Over the years classification has increased our knowledge of psychopathology, and further important insights should be forthcoming with increased efforts to improve both the system and the process. We are drawn to the conclusion that the student must be familiar with the diagnostic categories presently used—they represent handles that systematically open the storehouse of available knowledge in the field. In addition, they stress the orderly and careful accumulation of observations so necessary for making diagnostic decisions.

SCOPE OF CHILDHOOD PSYCHOPATHOLOGY

Measures Used

Statistical data about the occurrence of abnormal behavior may be arrived at in three different ways: through *incidence, prevalence,* and *expectancy*. Incidence refers to the total number of new cases of a disorder that occur within a specified population and period of time. Prevalence is a more extensive measure in that it refers to the total number of cases (old and new) present in a given population during a specified time interval.

The major difference between incidence and prevalence measures is that the latter reflect both incidence and duration. For example, if we interpret as incidence data the often-cited statistic that over one-half of all hospital beds are occupied by the mentally ill, we would conclude erroneously that there are more people who evidence abnormal behavior than is actually the case. However, if we understand this finding as prevalence data, we recognize the fact that the internment for mental disorder is much longer than the time required for other hospitalized conditions. Therefore, the statistic should not be taken to mean that one-half of all new hospital admissions each year consists of mentally ill people, but rather that mental patients occupy half of the beds available because their hospital stay is relatively longer (Kramer, 1957; Malzberg, 1963).

The probability that a person will fall into a specific category of abnormal behavior sometime during his or her lifetime is an expectancy measure. Although informative, an expectancy measure is biased, since it does not take into account the individual's age when the question is considered. The longer one lives, the greater the number of years available in which to demonstrate abnormal behavior. Therefore, it is more useful to talk about one's risk of acquiring a behavioral disorder if one lives to a certain age. In this way the risk is expressed as a conditional probability, not as a joint probability of both living to such an age and becoming mentally ill. For example, the probability of living to the age of ninety and being mentally ill is less than the chance of having a behavioral disorder if one does live to the age of ninety.

Sources of Error in Measurement

Unfortunately, all these measures are subject to several sources of error. Typically frequency figures of abnormal behavior come from public and private clinics and hospital census records. These data do not include instances of abnormal behaviors that are tolerated or go unrecognized within some subcultures of our society. For example, school phobias (fear of and refusal to go to school) are more likely to go unnoticed in a low socioeconomic urban area than in an upper-middle-class urban neighborhood, because truancy is implicitly sanctioned in the former subculture. In addition, the measures do not reflect the number of less severe cases that are handled within the confines of the family, or those cases that are masked by physical symptoms such as asthma. There is a strong tendency for some parents to postpone as long as possible the professional attention needed by their disturbed children. For that matter, some professionals tend to shy away from using diagnostic labels connoting severe abnormal conditions to reduce the danger that the diagnosis will adversely affect how others react to the child in the future.

Moreover, official statistics are not adjusted in terms of the availability of services and facilities. Therefore, they do not include those cases that are unadmitted because facilities are either nonexistent or unavailable due to overcrowded conditions. A more serious source of error is the great diversity among professionals and institutions with regard to the definition and classification of abnormal behavior. Therefore, all these measures are affected in an unsystematic way by the variability of the diagnostic labels used to categorize abnormal behaviors.

Scope of the Problem

In spite of these limitations in measuring the extent of childhood psychopathology, we do know from available estimates that abnormal behaviors in children and adolescents represent a sizeable and serious contemporary problem. This is especially relevant in light of the 1970 census figures, which indicate that we are a nation of young people: Approximately 50 million (or 26 percent) of our citizens are classified as minors, and half of this total figure are under the age of ten.

Few studies to determine the frequency of abnormal behaviors in very young children (infancy through preschool years) have been carried out. In fact, there are no adequate criteria of psychopathology for this age period other than some rare psychotic conditions or infrequent, biologically caused forms of mental retardation (see Chapters 8 and 10). At this age level some prevalence data are available on specific forms of maladaptive behaviors involving disruptions in such daily functions as eating, sleep, and elimination (to be discussed in later chapters). However, fewer studies have provided comprehensive overall figures on the frequency and severity of emotional problems in young children. Richman, Stevenson, and Graham (1975) interviewed mothers of a large random sample of three-year-old children who lived outside of London. They found that 7 percent of the children had moderate to severe problems, and 15 percent evidenced mild behavioral problems. A similar estimate of disorders in North American preschool children was reported by Minde and Minde (1977).

Prevalence figures for older children indicate that up to 10 percent of all school-age youngsters require professional attention for abnormal behaviors. They indicate also that children now constitute about 34 percent of the total population served by outpatient mental health centers, as compared to 27 percent in 1967 (Bower, 1969; Garmezy, 1975). Studies carried out on ten- and eleven-year-old children from the Isle of Wight and from England's urban areas found estimates ranging from 6.8 to 19.4 percent of the children who evidenced a significant degree of emotional disturbance (Rutter, Tizard, and Whitmore, 1970; Miller et al., 1974). Rates of disorder in adolescents tend to run at or near 20 percent in various Western countries and in some of the developing countries (Leslie, 1974; Krupinski et al., 1967; Lavik, 1977; Minde, 1976).

Thus, the overall estimates of the scope of the problem range from about 7 percent in very young children to about 20 percent in adolescents, and these data seem to reflect a positive relationship between prevalence and age. This relationship is also evident when admission figures to state and county mental hospitals are examined. It has been shown that 1 percent of hospital admissions was for children under five years of age, 7 percent for children between the ages of five and nine, 30 percent for those between the ages of ten and fifteen, and 63 percent for adolescents between the ages of fifteen and seventeen (Taube and Meyer, 1975). However, according to Redick (1973), the age at which children most frequently are referred for professional attention is between ten and fourteen. While these data are interesting, they do not account for the presumed relationship between prevalence and age. It is likely, however, that factors as a function of age such as increased behavioral repertoire, less opportunity for parents to deny and hide children's problems, and the increasing number of possible areas of disturbed and impaired functioning account to a great extent for this relationship.

It has been known for a long time that boys outnumber girls in practically every diagnostic category of abnormal behavior, although as yet no satisfactory explanation for this finding is available. In some instances the male-female ratio is as high as 5:1 (Gilbert, 1957; Morse, Cutler, and Fink, 1964; Redick, 1973; Behar and Stringfield, 1974). Equally puzzling is the fact that this relationship tends to hold until late adolescence. However, it dissipates in adulthood to the point where females may even exceed males in those abnormal conditions where unequal sex distributions are found. For hospitalized children the boys exceed girls in every age group, but especially between the ages of five and nine (Taube and Meyer, 1975).

Although the problem of aberrant behaviors in children is greater than we would wish, we can look to the future with optimism, knowing that the field now provides formal training for its professional workers. Moreover, the encouraging advances obtained through research make it more reasonable than ever before to expect that abnormal behaviors of children will be identified earlier, treated more effectively, and—to a greater extent—prevented.

SUMMARY

In this chapter we defined abnormal behavior in terms of the following criteria:

1. Cultural norms: the established standards and expectations approved by the culture for the behavior of its members

2. Developmental norms: the expectations based on our knowledge of the developmental process
3. Intellectual and cognitive functioning: an apparent disparity between ability and actual performance in attention, comprehension, judgment, learning, memory, thinking, and perception
4. Emotional expression and control: characterized by insufficient or exaggerated emotional reactions, inappropriate emotional expressions, infantile emotional reactions, moods of despondency, extreme elation, sudden fluctuations, or too little or too much emotional control
5. Coping in interpersonal relations: disruptions in or inability to cope with interpersonal relations; social withdrawal; isolation; suspiciousness; fear and hatred of others; and uncooperativeness. This criterion must be used in conjunction with the other criteria of cognitive and emotional dysfunction.

We also argued that the characteristics of frequency, intensity or degree, and duration are necessary in applying the above criteria in defining the domain of abnormal behavior.

We presented summaries of the new psychiatric classification system (DSM-III) and of the GAP proposal for categorizing children's disorders. In addition, we considered the WHO multiaxial classification for childhood disorders, Achenbach's factor-analytic system, and other miniature schemes for research purposes.

We discussed measures of reliability and research findings. In general, reliability of classification is fairly high when few and broad categories are used; but it declines sharply when a greater number of categories, and more specific categories, are included. We reviewed major criticisms and problems inherent in the classification system, although we concluded that classification brings order and uniformity to psychopathology and serves an important communication function among professionals.

We also considered the problems associated with estimating the frequency of occurrence of abnormal behavior, and we defined incidence, prevalence, and expectancy measures. All these measures are affected by the variability of the diagnostic labels used to categorize abnormal behavior, by the availability of service facilities, by instances that are either tolerated or unrecognized within some subcultures of our society, and by the inclination of families to deny or ignore the problem. We then presented some overall estimates of the scope of the problem.

EPILOGUE

Both the immediate and long-term course for Scott could be described as disappointing and unsuccessful. Scott was seen on and off at a local mental health clinic for a period of three years, during which time he was placed on a trial dose of amphetamine and given separate blocks of sessions in individual and group therapy. The clinic staff was initially impressed with Scott's acting-out behavior, and they viewed him as a hyperkinetic boy who could be controlled and treated effectively with medication. However, his mother and teachers observed no improvement in his behavior, and the medication was discontinued. He was assigned to a therapist and seen weekly in individual sessions for five months, and then on a twice-a-month basis for approximately a year. Finally, he was placed in a group which met weekly, although Scott's attendance was sporadic.

At first Scott and his parents seemed to be of one mind in their quest for professional help, but after the trial of amphetamine and its failure to bring about significant changes, they became resistant. Scott continued to act out in school and at home, fought with his parents about coming to the clinic, and often did not come home directly from school on those afternoons he was scheduled for treatment at the clinic. Soon Mrs S. evidenced her resistance to the clinic's efforts by indicating to the therapist that Scott's appointment time conflicted with her need to fix dinner for her family. She said also that her husband was unwilling to leave work to bring Scott in for his appointment. It was clear that parental motivation waxed and waned as a function of Scott's acting out and the amount of trouble he stirred up. Interestingly enough, Scott's interest in treatment paralleled his parent's motivational patterns and the level of difficulty he was in either in school or at home. For reasons unknown, the clinic tolerated Scott's missed appointments, poor motivation, and dwindling interest without confrontation. Finally, treatment was terminated because the family said that they were pessimistic about Scott's prospects for improvement and the clinic's ability to treat him. Possibly, the absence of a careful diagnostic workup and the failure to arrive at a diagnosis were significant factors in the clinic's ineffectiveness.

REFERENCES

ACHENBACH, T. M. The Classification of Children's Psychiatric Symptoms: A Factor-Analytic Study. *Psychological Monographs*, 1966, *80* (Whole No. 615), 1–37.

ACHENBACH, T. M. *Developmental Psychopathology*. New York: Ronald Press, 1974.

ACHENBACH, T. M., and LEWIS, M. A Proposed Model for Clinical Research and Its Application to Encopresis and Enuresis. *Journal of the American Academy of Child Psychiatry*, 1971, *10*, 535–554.

AL-ISSA, I. Problems in the Cross-Cultural Study of Schizophrenia. *Journal of Psychology*, 1969, *71*, 143–151.

APA, DSM-II: *Diagnostic and Statistical Manual of Mental Disorders*, 2nd ed. Washington, D.C.: American Psychiatric Association, 1980.

APA, DSM-III: *Diagnostic and Statistical Manual of Mental Disorders*, 3rd ed. Washington, D.C.: American Psychiatric Association, 1980.

APA Monitor. Council: Divisions, Dues, and DSM-III. November 1980, Vol. 11, 1, 10, and 11.

BECK, A. T. Reliability of Psychiatric Diagnoses. I. A Critique of Systematic Studies. *American Journal of Psychiatry*, 1962, *119*, 210–216.

BEHAR, L., and STRINGFIELD, S. A Behavior Rating Scale for the Preschool Child. *Developmental Psychology*, 1974, *10*, 601–610

BEITCHMAN, J. H., DIELMAN, T. E., LANDIS, J. R., BENSON, R. M., and KEMP, P. L. Reliability of the Group for Advancement of Psychiatry Diagnostic Categories in Child Psychiatry. *Archives of General Psychiatry*, 1978, *35*, 1461–1468.

BEMPORAD, J., PFEIFFER, C., and BLOOM, W. Twelve Months Experiences with the GAP Classification of Childhood Disorders. *American Journal of Psychiatry*, 1970, *127*, 658–664.

BOWER, E. M. *The Early Identification of Emotionally Handicapped Children In School*, 2nd ed. Springfield, Ill.: Chas. C Thomas, 1969.

COLEMAN, J. C., BUTCHER, J, N., and CARSON, R. C. (eds.). *Abnormal Psychology and Modern Life*, 6th ed. Glenview, Ill.: Scott, Foresman and Co., 1980.

COPELAND, J. Aspects of Mental Illness in West African Students. *Social Psychiatry*, 1968, *3*, 7–13.

Council: Divisions, Dues, and DSM-III. *APA Monitor*, November 1980, *11*, 1, 10, and 11.

DEMYER, M. K., CHURCHILL, D. W., PONTIUS, W., and GILKEY, K. M. A Comparison of Five Diagnostic Systems for Childhood Schizophrenia and Infantile Autism. *Journal of Autism and Childhood Schizophrenia*, 1971, *1*, 175–189.

DOHRENWEND, B. P., and DOHRENWEND, B. S. Social and Cultural Influences on Psychopathology. *Annual Review of Psychology*, 1974, *25*, 417–452.

DRAGUNS, J. G., and PHILLIPS, L. *Psychiatric Classification and Diagnosis: An Overview and Critique*. Morristown, N. J.: General Learning Press, 1971.

FREEMAN, M. A Reliability Study of Psychiatric Diagnosis in Childhood and Adolescence. *Journal of Child Psychology and Psychiatry and Allied Disciplines*, 1971, *12* (1), 43–54.

GARMEZY, N. The Experimental Study of Children Vulnerable to Psychopathology. In A. Davids (ed.), *Child Personality and Psychopathology: Current Trends*, Vol. 2. New York: John Wiley, 1975, pp. 171–216.

GARMEZY, N. DSM III: Never Mind the Psychologist—Is It Good for the Children? *Clinical Psychologist*, 1978, *31* (3–4), 4–6.

GILBERT, G. M. A Survey of Referral Problems in Metropolitan Child Guidance Centers. *Journal of Clinical Psychology*, 1957, *13*, 37–42.

Group for the Advancement of Psychiatry, Committee on Child Psychiatry: The Diagnostic Process in Child Psychiatry. GAP Report No. 38, August 1957.

Group for the Advancement of Psychiatry, Committee on Child Psychiatry: Psychopathological Disorders in Childhood: Theoretical Considerations and a Proposed Classification. GAP report No. 62, June 1966.

HARRIS, S. L. DSM III: Its Implications for Children. *Child Behavior Therapy*, 1979, *1*(1), 37–46.

HUNT, W. A., WITSON, C. L., and HUNT, E. B. A Theoretical and Practical Analysis of the Diagnostic Process. In P. H. Hoch and J. Zubin (eds.), *Current Problems in Psychiatric Diagnosis*. New York: Grune and Stratton, 1953, pp. 53–65.

JOHNSON, S., WAHL, G., MARTIN, W., and JOHANSSON, S. How Deviant Is the Normal Child? A Behavioral Analysis of the Preschool Child and His Family. In R. Rubin, J. Brady, and J. Henderson (eds.), *Advances in Behavior Therapy: Proceedings of the Association for Advancement of Behavior Therapy, 1969–73*, Vol. 4. New York: Academic Press, 1973, pp. 35–54.

KRAMER, M. A. A Discussion of the Concepts of Incidence and Prevalence as Related to Epidemiologic Studies of Mental Disorder. *American Journal of Public Health*, 1957, *47*, 826–840.

KREITMAN, N., SAINSBURY, P., MORRISEY, J., TOWERS, J., and

SCRIVENER, J. The Reliability of Psychiatric Assessment: An Analysis. *Journal of Mental Science,* 1961, *197,* 887–908.

KRUPINSKI, J., BAIKIE, A. G., STOLLER, A., GRAVES, J., O'DAY, D. M., and POLKE, P. A Community Mental Health Survey of Heyfield, Victoria. *Medical Journal of Australia,* 1967, *1,* 1204–1211.

LAVIK, N. Urban-Rural Differences in Rates of Disorder: A Comparative Psychiatric Population Study of Norwegian Adolescents. In P. J. Graham (ed.), *Epidemiological Approaches in Child Psychiatry.* New York: Academic Press, 1977, 223–251.

LESLIE, S. A. Psychiatric Disorder in the Young Adolescents of an Industrial Town. *British Journal of Psychiatry,* 1974, *125,* 113–124.

MALZBERG, B. Mental Disorders in the United States. In A. Deutsch and H. Fishman (eds.), *Encyclopedia of Mental Health,* 6 Vols. New York: Franklin Watts, 1963.

MATTISON, R., CANTWELL, D. P., RUSSELL, A. T., and WILL, L. A Comparison of DSM-II and DSM-III in the Diagnoses of Childhood Psychiatric Disorders. *Archives of General Psychiatry,* 1979, *36,* 1217–1222.

MEEHL, P. E. Some Ruminations on the Validation of Clinical Procedures. *Canadian Journal of Psychology,* 1959, *13,* 102–128.

MEYER, A. *The Commonsense Psychiatry of Doctor Adolph Meyer,* ed. A. Lief. New York: McGraw-Hill, 1948.

MILLER, F. J. W., COURT, S. D. M., KNOX, E. G., and BRANDON, S. *The School Years in Newcastle-upon-Tyne.* London: Oxford University Press, 1974.

MINDE, K. Child Psychiatry in Developing Countries. *Journal of Child Psychology and Psychiatry,* 1976, *17,* 79–83.

MINDE, K., and MINDE, R. Behavioral Screening of Preschool Children: A New Approach to Mental Health. In P. J. Graham (ed.), *Epidemiological Approaches in Child Psychiatry.* New York: Academic Press, 1977, 139–164.

MORSE, W. C., CUTLER, R. L., and FINK, A. H. *Public School Classes for the Emotionally Handicapped: A Research Analysis.* Washington, D.C.: Council for Exceptional Children, 1964.

NASH, J. *Developmental Psychology: A Psychobiological Approach.* Englewood Cliffs, N.J.: Prentice-Hall, 1970, p. 306.

NATHAN, P. E. DSM III and Schizophrenia—Diagnostic Delight or Nosological Nightmare? *Journal of Clinical Psychology,* 1979, 35 (2), 477–479.

PASAMANICK, B., DINITZ, S., and LEFTON, M. Psychiatric Orientation and Its Relation to Diagnosis and Treatment in a Mental Hospital. *American Journal of Psychiatry,* 1959, *116,* 127–132.

REDICK, R. *Utilization of Psychiatric Facilities by Persons Under Eighteen Years of Age. United States, 1971.* Statistical Note 90. Department of Health, Education and Welfare, 1973.

RICHMAN, N., STEVENSON, J. E., and GRAHAM, P. J. Prevalance of Behaviour Problems in 3-Year-Old Children: An Epidemiological Study in a London Borough. *Journal of Child Psychology and Psychiatry,* 1975, *16,* 277–287.

RIMLAND, B. The Differentiation of Childhood Psychoses: An Analysis of Checklists for 2,218 Psychotic Children. *Journal of Autism and Childhood Schizophrenia,* 1971, 2, 161–174.

RUTTER, M., LEBOVICI, S., EISENBERG, L., SNEVNEVSKIJ, A. V., SADOUN, R., BROOKE, E., and LIN, T. Y. A Triaxial Classification of Mental Disorders in Childhood. *Journal of Child Psychology and Psychiatry,* 1969, *10,* 41–61.

RUTTER, M., TIZARD, J., and WHITMORE, K. (eds.). *Education, Health and Behaviour.* London: Longmans, 1970.

SABOT, L. M., PECK, R., and RASKIN, J. The Waiting Room Society. *Archives of General Psychiatry,* 1969, *21,* 25–32.

SANDIFER, M. G., JR., PETTUS, C., and QUADE, D. A Study of Psychiatric Diagnosis. *Journal of Nervous and Mental Disease,* 1964, *139,* 350–356.

SCHACHT, T., and NATHAN, P. E. But Is It Good for the Psychologists? Appraisal and Status of DSM-III. *American Psychologist,* 1977, 32, 1017–1025.

SCHMIDT, H. W., and FONDA, C. P. The Reliability of Psychiatric Diagnosis. *Journal of Abnormal and Social Psychology,* 1956, 52, 262–267.

SHAKOW, D. The Role of Classification in the Development of the Science of Psychopathology with Particular Reference to Research. In M. M. Katz, J. O. Cole, and W. E. Barton (eds.), *The Role and Methodology of Classification in Psychiatry and Psychopathology.* Public Health Service Publication No. 1584. U.S. Department of Health, Education, and Welfare, Public Health Service, 1968, pp. 116–143.

SPITZER, R. L., FORMAN, J. B. W., and NEE, J. DSM-III Field Trials: I. Initial Interrater Diagnostic Reliability. *American Journal of Psychiatry,* 1979, *136,* 815–817.

TAUBE, C. A., and MEYER, N. G. *Children and State Mental Hospitals.* DHEW Statistical Note 115. Publication No. (ADM) 75-158. Rockville, Md.: U.S. Department of Health, Education and Welfare, 1975.

WARD, C. H., BECK, A. T., MENDELSON, M., MOCK, J. E., and ERBAUGH, J. K. The Psychiatric Nomenclature: Reasons for Diagnostic Disagreement. *Archives of General Psychiatry,* 1962, 7, 198–205.

WERRY, J. S., and QUAY, H. C. The Prevalence of Behavior Symptoms in Younger Elementary School Children. *American Journal of Orthopsychiatry,* 1971, *41,* 136–143.

ZIGLER, E., and PHILLIPS, L. Social Competence and Outcome in Psychiatric Disorder. *Journal of Abnormal and Social Psychology,* 1961, 63, 264–271.

ZUBIN, J. Classification of the Behavior Disorders. *Annual Review of Psychology,* 1967, *18,* 373–406.

3

NORMAL AND ABNORMAL PERSONALITY DEVELOPMENT

PROLOGUE

There was a CHILD WENT FORTH EVERY DAY,
And the first object he looked upon and received with wonder or pity or
love or dread, that object he became,
And that object became part of him for the day or a certain part of the
day or for many years or stretching cycles of years.

The early lilacs became part of this child,
And grass, and white and red morning glories, and white and red clover,
and the song of the phoebe-bird,
And the March-born lambs, and the sow's pink-faint litter, and the
mare's foal, and the cow's calf, and the noisy brood of the barnyard,
or by the mire of the pondside . . . and the fish suspending themselves
so curiously below there . . . and the beautiful curious liquid . . . and
the waterplants with their graceful flat heads . . . all became part of him.

. . . .His own parents . . . he that propelled the fatherstuff at night, and
fathered him . . . and she that conceived him in her womb and birthed
him . . . they gave this child more of themselves than that,
They gave him afterward every day . . . they and of them became part of
him.

. . . .These became part of that child who went forth every day, and who
now goes and will always go forth every day.
And these became of him or her that peruses them now.

(*Leaves of Grass* by Walt Whitman,
edited by Malcolm Cowley. Published
by Viking Penguin, Inc., 1959, pp. 138–139)

The cry of new life sets off the exhilarating feelings of parental pride and duty, of unfulfilled dreams and lofty aspirations, of fears of failure, and of uncertainties about the future. Nowhere in the animal kingdom does the newborn go forth with as much attention from so many, and for such a prolonged period of time. Whitman views the child as profoundly influenced and molded by both environmental and hereditary forces; in this regard he can be said to hold an interactionist position of human development, which is widely accepted today. In his beautiful poem Whitman captures the importance of the various conditions that take on maximum significance in the life of the child, although he paints the child as only a passive participant in the growth process.

In our society we strongly prefer the growing child to be above statistical average in physical, mental, emotional, or social development, and we become distraught when the child displays almost any feature that is below average. In fact, the only deviance in children we find acceptable is that of exceptionality; all else brings unhappiness and disappointment. Low birth weight (say of four pounds two ounces) is regarded not only as below average but also as abnormal (premature). On the other hand, a baby of eight pounds two ounces (while above average) may be considered healthy and robust. But there is a point at which above-average characteristics become abnormal, as in obesity, hyperactivity, and the unusually rapid growth of gigantism. Since either extreme may be abnormal, how can we hope to recognize deviance without some basic understanding of normal development?

Almost all parents experience some anxiety about their child's normality (especially their firstborn) with respect to eating or sleeping patterns, motor and physical growth trends, language progress, socialization, and cognitive performance. In the absence of developmental norms, there is no tangible way of either measuring or assessing the progress of children as they grow and mature.[1] It is commonplace for parents to seek this sort of normative data from their pediatricians and from others who either have children or have experience with them. As students interested in abnormal behaviors of children, we too must have a good grasp of (1) what constitutes normal development, (2) factors affecting it, and (3) its methodological and interpretative limitations.

In this chapter we try to provide a framework of normal and abnormal personality development from which developmental psychopathology can be better understood. Obviously, we cannot hope to present in one chapter all the details ordinarily included in a single course or in a text devoted exclusively to this topic. For our purposes, therefore, we shall consider the basic principles of development, some of the major variables influencing its course, and the theoretical positions that are currently prominent.

GENERAL PRINCIPLES OF DEVELOPMENT

Data about child behavior and growth has made it possible to discern certain orderly patterns of human development. The most widely accepted principles deal with the

[1] A detailed presentation of these developmental norms can be found in Gesell, Ilg, Ames, and Rodell, 1974.

direction and progression of physical growth and motor development.

Directions of Development

There are two principles concerned with the directional flow of physical development. These state that growth and motor development generally proceed from the head to the tail (cephalocaudal growth) and from the central axis to the periphery (proximodistal growth) of the human body. Both growth principles are manifest in prenatal and postnatal development. The head of the human fetus develops initially, while the lower portions form later on. Similarly, the central axis of the human fetus develops before the formation of the limb buds from which the hands, fingers, and toes subsequently appear. Postnatally, cephalocaudal growth is illustrated in the disproportionate size of the infant's head in relation to the torso and the even smaller legs. In fact, the newborn's head approximates the size of the adult's, whereas the torso—and especially the legs—are expected to grow a great deal more before they reach adult proportions. In addition, the infant's head is functionally more mature than the torso and extremities in that the mouth, eyes, and ears are functional before grasping appears and prior to the use of the legs and feet. The proximodistal growth and motor development in the infant can be seen in the development of hand use. First the baby uses the hand (reaching) as a whole unit through gross movements of the arm up to the shoulder. Months later the baby gains control of fingers or can make oppositional movements of thumb and finger in picking up things.

Progression of Development

Two principles have been identified to describe the progression of development. The first states that progress occurs in patterns from the general to the specific (sometimes called the principle of differentiation) or from the simple to the complex. Newborns have undifferentiated reactions to painful stimuli, since their behavior is gross and general rather than specific. The pain of being pricked accidentally by a pin will elicit a generalized reaction; babies will cry, kick, and vigorously move their arms, but months later their reaction will be noticeably more specific in the sense that they probably will cry and try to avoid the painful pinprick.

The second principle (asynchronous growth) states that different parts and subsystems of the human organism develop at different rates and times, and that the various parts of a person do not grow equally or all at once. In a way this has been implicit in what has been discussed thus far. The head, in both size and function, develops earlier than the lower and more peripheral regions. Asynchronous growth occurs prenatally and postnatally in spurts that have implications for what can be expected of children during different periods of development. For example, in our culture adolesence is a period in which there is a tremendous growth spurt that levels off in the beginning of adulthood. Development of both primary and secondary sexual characteristics occurs rapidly during this period, although almost no changes in these characteristics take place between late infancy and puberty.

Personal and Social Development

This general principle deals with personality and social development. It describes the child's progress from an undifferentiated and almost totally dependent organism to a distinctive and independent self. In contrast to physical and motor development, personal growth and social growth are much more difficult to measure, and more likely to cause controversy.

At birth babies do not know their names or have any observable awareness of who they are as separate and intact organisms. They learn about their own bodies and the world around them through sensory and motor exploration; and they develop a self-concept gradually through their interactions with the environment. Coincidentally, as their competency to cope without assistance increases, they are both more inclined to and able to think and act on their own. They can be expected to exhibit increased self-control and regulation of their feelings and behavior as they become more familiar with the contingencies of specific situations and the consequences of their responses. In broad perspective the helpless, dependent, emotionally volatile, and undifferentiated self of the infant matures over time into a more independent, emotionally controlled, responsible, and distinctive self as he or she reaches adulthood.

Maturation and Readiness

Maturation refers to physical alterations in size and "qualitative changes in tissues or in anatomical and physiological organization" (Stone and Church, 1973, p. 191). With respect to child development, maturation is extremely important: These physiological transformations make it possible for new behaviors to emerge—that is, they render the child biologically ready to acquire a new behavior without a great deal of practice or preparation. For instance, maturation must occur before a child can walk, although a child's readiness to walk will not in and of itself result in locomotion unless the opportunity is provided. Studies have shown that either severe deprivation of or extensive practice in walking prior to maturational readiness will affect the age at which the child walks, although maturation sets the general limits for when such motor skills occur (Dennis and Najarian, 1957; Zelazo, Zelazo, and Kolb, 1972). Similarly, only when babies reach a particular stage of maturation are they able to bring bladder and bowel sphincters under control. Fastidious or eager parents who begin toilet training before these changes occur are likely to engage in a losing battle with their child and precipitate unnecessary anxiety and conflict for all parties concerned. Knowing about and understanding maturation can go a long way toward minimizing needless parent-child strife and increasing the child's chances of successfully acquiring new behaviors.

FACTORS AFFECTING DEVELOPMENT

Development is an active process that consists of "two essential components: the notion of a system possessing a definite structure and a definite set of pre-existing capacities; and the notion of a sequential set of changes in the system, yielding relatively permanent but novel increments not only in its structure but in its mode of operation as well" (Nagel, 1957, p. 17). Thus, we think of development as involving sequential and orderly changes over time in the organism's structure and function. Research has shown that the factors affecting development are multitudinous, ranging from biological factors—which include heredity, congenital factors, maturation, temperament, prenatal and postnatal care, drugs, and nutrition—to sociopsychological factors— emphasizing race, social class, cultural context, family, school, peer relationships, early neonatal experiences (especially the effect of mother and father), and the learning potential of the newborn. Obviously, the space limitations of this section preclude an exhaustive discussion of these factors. However, for our purposes we will focus on heredity, temperament, parent-child interaction, the school, and peer relations as they influence later personality development.

Heredity and Environment

Psychology has historically debated the relative roles of heredity and environment as determinants of human structure and function. Past inquiry emphasized the relative contributions of either nature or nurture; however, a new interactional approach considers the potential impact of each factor as it varies on a continuum, allowing for greater or lesser interplay of the other factor in determining behavior (Anastasi, 1958; Cohen, 1976). For example, the causal effects of genetic factors may be so extensive as to produce a debilitating and irreversible condition such as Down's Syndrome (a form of mental retardation we will discuss in Chapter 11) and to significantly limit the opportunity of environmental forces to influence the developmental outcome. On the other hand, the potential effect of an inherited allergy (such as hay fever) is less extensive, since there is ample opportunity for environmental conditions (reducing the amount of pollen) to control the outcome.

Similarly, there are two categories of environmental factors—organic accidents and cultural heritage—that represent continua ranging from direct to indirect in their impact on development (Anastasi, 1958). Birth complications such as prolonged delivery, the use of forceps, or breech delivery may seriously impair the baby's oxygen supply (anoxia), leading to the destruction of brain cells and mental retardation. In contrast, less direct influence on intellectual development may occur in children who have acquired sensory defects (visual or auditory) and for whom educational opportunities and enrichment may be restricted by their organic impairment. Similarly, the potential impact of cultural heritage can vary considerably. For example, a variable such as race may either have little effect or else it may so severely restrict both the individual's motivation and social chances as to negate the influence of other genetic attributes.

In this interactional context heredity may be thought of as providing the basic biological organization within which the organism's physical structure and personality can develop. We know that genetic factors can determine such physical characteristics as eye color, skin pigmentation, texture and color of hair, baldness, color blindness, and blood type. We also know that heredity accounts for other human characteristics that are more or less affected by experience—such as height, intelligence, and temperament. Further, it accounts for areas of genetic predisposition that are only manifested in the presence of certain noxious environmental conditions (for example, the mental disorder known as schizophrenia) (Rosenthal, 1970). Therefore, it is important to keep in mind that people differ in both their genetic make-up (except for monozygotic twins) and their environmental experiences, making it unlikely that they will develop in the same way or be capable of responding in the same manner to similar experiences (Cohen, 1976).

Temperament in Normal and Abnormal Development

Parents and others who have had the opportunity to observe babies at birth will attest to their differences in temperament. Indeed, research inquiries into the significance of temperament not only have identified specific infant reaction patterns that have consequences for personality development but also have suggested relationships between temperament and childhood behavioral disorders (Thomas and Chess, 1977).

In years past it was assumed that infants were similar to each other and were uniformly affected by parental behaviors and practices. However, we know now from studies of temperament that babies differ in their disposition to respond and that they vary considerably in their reactivity to parental actions (Thomas and Chess, 1977; Thomas and Chess, 1980; Kagan, Kearsley, and Zelazo, 1978; Kagan, 1982). In fact, this research has emphasized the stimulus value of the child and its contribution to the interaction between the child and his or her family members.

Based on the longitudinal studies undertaken by Thomas, Chess, and Birch (1970) over a twenty-year period, the concept of temperament has come to refer to individual differences in inborn potentials for action, characterized by particular behavioral styles and significantly affected by the interplay of environmental forces. These investigators established the following nine categories on which the infant's behavioral style or temperamental reactivity can be classified:

1. Activity level—the relative proportion of active to inactive periods
2. Rhythmicity—regularity of biological functions of hunger, sleep and wakefulness, and excretion

3. Approach and withdrawal to new situations and people
4. Adaptability to new situations
5. Threshold of responsiveness—the intensity of stimulation needed to evoke a discernible response
6. Intensity of reaction—the energy of the response
7. Quality of mood—the amount of pleasant, friendly, and joyful behavior versus unpleasant, unfriendly, and crying behavior
8. Distractibility—the degree to which extraneous stimuli change behavior
9. Attention span and persistence—time spent on an activity and the effect of distraction on activity

Using these nine reactive patterns, the investigators showed that after the first ten years of life, children were remarkably stable and consistent in temperamental reactivity (Thomas, Chess, and Birch, 1970). For example, a child rated positive on the approach-and-withdrawal category at one year of age approached strangers without fear and slept well in new surroundings; at ten years the same child went to camp happily and loved to ski the first time. In addition, three temperamental constellations were statistically factored out of the basic nine categories, each with its own characteristic style of relating to life situations (Thomas, Chess, and Birch, 1968; Thomas and Chess, 1977). The *difficult child* type included those children who evidenced irregularity in biological function, negative withdrawal responses to new stimuli, frequent and loud crying periods, slow adaptability to change, and frustration resulting in frequent tantrums. In contrast, the *easy child* grouping was characterized by regularity, adaptability, smiling at strangers, accepting some frustration, positive approach responses to new stimuli, and predominantly positive moods of mild to moderate intensity. Somewhere in between these two patterns was the third constellation, the *slow-to-warm-up* group, consisting of youngsters who showed initial negative responses of mild intensity to new stimuli, which responses became positive if given time to warm up; slow adaptability; and some irregularity in biological functioning.

While these groupings are broad and imprecise, it is significant that 70 percent of those children from the original population who later evidenced emotional problems and needed psychiatric attention were classified as difficult, while only 18 percent were identified as easy. Moreover, difficult children represented 10 percent of all the children sampled by these investigators (a figure that corresponds to other estimates of occurrence of abnormal behaviors in children), while 40 percent fell into the easy category (Thomas and Chess, 1977). Similar percentages of difficult and easy infants were reported by Carey (1970), who constructed a temperament questionnaire fashioned after the interview used earlier by Thomas, Chess, and Birch (1968). In general, these findings suggest the possibilities that useful predictions about childhood psychopathology can be made from early temperament measures and that disorders can be prevented through the early identification of high-risk children.

In this context Thomas and Chess (1977) emphasized "the goodness of fit" between the child and the environment. They posited that when there is a significant discrepancy between the child's temperamental dispositions and environmental demands, severe stress and psychopathological development are likely to occur. However, follow-up questionnaire data on the above infants when they were between three and seven years old suggested that temperament constellations do not remain stable after infancy (Carey and McDevitt, 1978). More specifically, only 30 percent of the 187 children sampled (via mother's responses to the Carey Temperament Questionnaire) remained in their original temperament grouping. Sixty-six percent showed a change in temperament by shifting from one category to the next closest category (that is, from the "easy" to the "slow-to-warm-up" category), and 4 percent showed the most extreme change by shifting two categories (from the "easy" to "difficult" category, or vice-versa).

The work of Thomas and Chess has been criticized on the grounds that their sample was not representative of the general population of infants; rather, the subjects came primarily from middle-class, highly educated Jewish families. Moreover, many of the subjects were siblings or pairs of twins, which would tend to introduce a similarity bias in the results (Persson-Blennow, and McNeil, 1979).

Another view of temperament has been proposed by Buss and Plomin (1975), who suggested that individual differences are governed by four temperaments: activity, emotionality, sociability, and impulsivity. These are depicted as dimensions (each ranging from one extreme to the other). The potential to occupy some place on the dimension of each temperament is inherited, although the final form the inherited tendency takes depends on environmental influences. Every person represents some combination of the four temperaments. Buss and Plomin claim that the proposed nine temperaments of Thomas and associates have not been substantiated as truly inherited and that if this criterion were applied, both views would identify similar temperaments.

In 1978 Torgersen and Kringlen carried out a twin study in Norway based on the Thomas and Chess categories of temperament. They interviewed mothers of thirty-four monozygotic twins and sixteen dizygotic twins (same-sex twin pairs) when their children were two months and nine months old. The results showed that identical twins were more similar than fraternal twins at two months of age in regularity, threshold, and intensity. Also, they were more similar than fraternal twins on all nine temperament categories by the time they reached nine months of age. These data tend to support the inheritance of temperament as defined and measured by Thomas and Chess.

Research on temperament has added to the understanding of individual differences, of the interplay between heredity and environment in the stability of reactive patterns over time, and of the early identification of probable psychopathology. But equally important, inquiry on temperament has called attention to the influence of temperamental reactivity on parental responses to the child. For too long theorists have focused on the effect first of the mother and now of both the mother and father as shapers of the child's personality, without fully appreciating the multidirectional components of parent-child interactions. As Buss and Plomin state:

> The child is not merely the passive recipient of environmental shaping. Our theory assumes an interaction between the child and the forces that mold his personality. He is an initiator who in part makes his own environment. He is a reinforcer, selectively rewarding or punishing agents in his environment for the way they behave toward him. And he is a responder, who modifies the impact of the environment on his personality. This is a considerably more complex model of personality development than that of the child as a blank slate on which the environment writes. But we suggest that it is a true picture of what actually happens. (1975, p. 237)

Parent-Child Interaction

Attachment. Bowlby (1958, 1969, 1973, 1980) used the term *attachment* to describe the formation of a reciprocal affective bond between the infant and its mother as a way of reducing chronic infantile anxiety and as a necessary process for later healthy psychological development. Bowlby suggested biological and evolutionary origins for attachment. He posited that human infants inherit species-specific but modifiable behavioral systems such as sucking, crying, smiling, vocalizing, listening, and looking as well as various motor patterns which make it possible for attachment to occur and for the species to survive. Another major figure in the study of attachment, Mary Ainsworth, cited the similarity of attachment patterns found in cross-cultural data to support the etiological view that human attachments are universal and innate (Ainsworth, 1967, 1978). However, the evidence which did the most to bolster this view came from animal studies in an area of inquiry known as *imprinting*.

Critical periods and imprinting. As early as 1873 D. A. Spalding reported that newborn chicks approached and followed the first moving object they saw. Their attachment response was innate and had to occur within a particular and brief period of time (later called critical period) in order for them to establish an enduring attachment to a particular object. More recently the work of Lorenz (1952) and of Hess (1959, 1972) has shown that (1) newborn ducks can be imprinted to such varied objects as the experimenter, decoys, milk bottles, flashing lights, and mechanical toys; (2) the attachment to these objects is relatively permanent; and (3) the attachment bond is stronger when the newborn duckling is engaged in physical exercise during imprinting or when the imprinted stimulus is a relatively big and moving object.

Does imprinting and the idea of critical periods carry over to human infants? No definitive answer is yet available. In general, those who argue against the analogy emphasize that the plasticity and high adaptability of human behavior make the notion of an early and very brief critical period unlikely. The terms *sensitivity* or *increased and heightened receptivity* are preferred for humans, because critical periods place undue importance on either the first few days of life or a very brief time span (Field, 1977; Hunt, 1979).

Infants begin to show affective attachments to specific others about six or seven months after they have developed a preference for humans over inanimate objects and after they have learned to differentiate familiar from unfamiliar persons (Ainsworth, 1973). Babies as young as two weeks of age tend to look longer at their mother's faces than at strangers, giving support to the idea that they can recognize their mothers very early in life (Carpenter, 1975). Moreover, by the time infants reach two months of age, their discrimination of people becomes even sharper; not only can they differentiate their parents from strangers, but they can also discriminate between their mothers and fathers (Yogman et al., 1977). Although Bowlby focused on the mother as the primary object of initial attachment, later research has consistently broadened the view to include attachments with fathers and to a lesser extent with others who do not provide caretaking functions (Ainsworth, 1967). Indeed, multiple rather than exclusive attachments are preferable for development, since children who experienced multiple caretakers (as in kibbutzim in Israel) evidenced less stranger and separation anxiety than those who experienced an almost exclusive relationship (Ainsworth, 1967; Maccoby and Feldman, 1972). This finding holds when the multiple caretakers respond favorably, attentively, and affectionately to the infants. Where only the basic physical needs of the infants are met when they are cared for by multiple but changing caretakers, infants become apathetic, withdrawn, and depressed and are unable to develop an attachment relationship (Spitz and Cobliner, 1966). Babies who have successfully established a secure attachment have the basis from which to establish other areas of competency and from which to actively explore and gain mastery of object play and the social environment (Sroufe, 1978).

The Child as a Stimulus. Richard Bell (1968) first emphasized that the child acts as a stimulus in the parent-child relationship. Bell examined the autonomy-control issue of child rearing and found that active children elicit upper-limit control behavior from parents, presumably as a means of reducing and redirecting the behaviors of the child that exceed parental limits. He noted, in contrast, that parents set lower-limit controls for lethargic children in order to stimulate their behavior up to parental expectations. Thus, Bell showed that the responses of young children can serve to modify the behaviors of adults. Thomas and Chess (1977) similarly observed that to a large extent parental responses are a function of the child's temperamental constellation, which determines the smoothness or turmoil of management routines. Mothers prefer children of the "easy child type," because these youngsters reassure them that they are adequate, healthy, and loving mothers; "difficult" children tend to make mothers feel threatened, resentful, or anxious. The researchers also stress the uniqueness of the child and the potential danger involved in assuming that there is one child-care practice that is favorable for all types of children. They claim that the child who is unable to respond to the currently favored child-rearing practice is under severe stress and is at risk for the development of psychopathology.

Brazleton (1969) also emphasizes the uniqueness of the newborn baby by describing three types of infants (average, quiet, and active) and their development. He suggests that babies manifest unique qualities that are obvious from birth onward and that these qualities set the tone of parental reactions to the child. More specifically, parental reactions are a function of an interaction between parents' preconceived notions of child rearing and the nature of the infant. Brazleton adopts the view that the neonate influences the environment as much as it affects him or her, and he advises new mothers to be aware of the special characteristics of their babies and to find individualized ways to respond to them. When the expectations of the mother are not met with regard to such matters as the appearance of the baby, its level of activity, or the ease or difficulty with which it nurses, the attachment relationship may be delayed or even damaged (Blehar, Lieberman, and Ainsworth, 1977). Fortunately, much of the early damage is reparable if the disappointed mothers can shift and interact with their infants in mutually gratifying and positive ways (Hunt, 1979; Hunt et al., 1976).

Within recent years the effect of the infant on its caretaker has been the subject of increasing systematic study, for which several promising research strategies have been developed (Lewis and Rosenblum, 1974). One strategy, involving the manipulation of certain stimulus characteristics of the infant to determine their effects on the caregiver, has been used to experimentally produce visual defects and drug-induced bodily malformations in infant animals (Lindburg, 1969; Berkson, 1974). The findings indicated that the defective animals were either treated like younger animals or given additional help and attention by their mothers. Another research strategy consists of examining certain biological aspects of infants (sex, physical stature, arousal level) and assessing their impact on the caretaker. For example, Korner (1974) found that the aversive properties of crying behavior in early infancy were a good initiator of maternal attention and that irritable babies received more maternal attention and stimulation than "good" ones. Korner also stressed the importance of maternal factors in establishing the affectional bond between mother and child, especially when dyadic mismatch occurs; that is, when the mother is either unable or unwilling to respond to the infant's cues. For example, one mother who is afraid of spoiling her child may fail to provide the soothing he or she requires, while another mother who needs to cuddle her baby may be disappointed and ungratified if her child fails to respond to cuddling.

Other investigators prefer studying the interactive, dynamic, and changing dyad of mother-child relationships rather than using strategies which focus on a single component of the system. For example, Brazleton and his associates (1974) used detailed film studies to look at behavioral components of mother-child interactions. They discerned five kinds of experiences mothers can provide for their babies. These include (1) the reduction of interfering activity by soothing the child when he or she is irritable or by attending to the baby's discomforts; (2) encouraging the child to be more alert and receptive; (3) creating an atmosphere of expectancy for further interaction; (4) accelerating the child's attention to receive and send messages by smiling and vocalizing in response to the baby's efforts to do these things; and (5) allowing for reciprocity by being sensitive to the child's cues and giving him or her time to respond.

Normal and Abnormal Effects of Mothering. Largely due to the influence of Freudian theory and to western society's assignment of mothering and early child care to women, we have for years viewed the mother as the most important interactive influence in the child's early development. During infancy it is the mother (typically) who becomes a powerful reinforcer, an influential stimulus, and an object of the baby's responses. She satisfies the infant's needs by feeding, comforting, or easing pain; she stimulates the child to respond by her own actions of talking, moving about, and playing; and she permits the child to explore her presence as he or she fingers her face, squeezes her nose, pulls her hair, or tugs at her beads. It is through these interactions that the infant becomes attached to the mother and gains sufficient sensory stimulation and need gratification for the development of a healthy personality.

Although Freud emphasized the importance of early mothering on later personality development, it was Margaret Ribble (among others) who undertook a substantial study of its effects from a psychoanalytic point of view (Ribble, 1944). On the basis of careful observations of 600 infants, Ribble noted that sensory experiences (tactile, kinesthetic, and auditory stimulation) provided by the mother were essential for stable personality development and that the failure to have these sensory experiences result in both biological and psychological damage to the child. In psychology the significant experimental breakthrough came with the creative work of Harry Harlow and his associates, who conducted a series of studies in which infant monkeys were reared with two kinds of inanimate surrogate mothers: a wire-mesh one and one covered with terry-cloth material. Harlow and Zimmerman (1959) separated infant monkeys from their mothers twelve hours or less after birth and reared and fed them by using either wire or cloth surrogate mothers. Regardless of their prior mothering experience, baby monkeys clearly preferred the cloth mother, spending more time clinging to her than to the wire mother. In addition, the experimenters found that monkeys reared with the cloth mother evidenced a sense of security that enabled them to explore a fear-arousing stimulus, whereas the monkeys reared with the wire mother exhibited fear and avoidance in this situation. These findings identified tactile stimulation as a principal ingredient of the mother-child relationship.

However, Harlow soon discovered that tactile stimulation was not the only important variable for normal development. Regardless of which surrogate mother the monkeys had, those raised in isolation from peers later showed abnormal behaviors that included aggressiveness, self-mutilation, withdrawal, social indifference, and inability to imitate heterosexual behavior (Harlow, 1962). Harlow concluded: "Since it is age-mate or peer affection even more than maternal affection that is basic to the success or failure of a monkey's or human's subsequent social and sexual life (Harlow and Harlow, 1962), one can defend the position that the mother's primary personal-social function is to aid and abet the infant in making age-mate adjustment" (Harlow and Harlow, 1971, p. 205).

The infant's need for kinesthetic stimulation usually dispensed by the mother in cuddling, rocking, and holding her baby while walking has only recently become the subject of experimental study. The available evidence indicates that monkeys who experience early maternal deprivation develop distinct stereotyped patterns of body rocking (Berkson and Mason, 1964). In an effort to identify the specific aspects of maternal deprivation that leads to body rocking, Mason (1968) compared two groups of rhesus monkeys raised with either a stationary or a mobile artificial mother. Infant monkeys tested at ten months showed typical body-rocking patterns when reared with a stationary mother, while those raised with mobile surrogates showed no such behavior. These findings support the view that rocking is a sensory need of infant monkeys and perhaps of humans. Additional evidence of the importance of vestibular stimulation (motion) in facilitating behavioral development comes from research with premature human infants. Those premature babies who were exposed systematically to motion achieved greater motor and auditory-visual responses than those who did not receive vestibular stimulation (Neal, 1970).

This line of investigation has helped us identify some of the specific variables associated with early mothering and their effects on later personality development. Another related line of investigation has focused on the effects of maternal deprivation. A study observing institutionalized infants who received different amounts of care and handling dramatically demonstrated the debilitating effects of maternal deprivation. A two-year follow-up indicated that the children who remained in the deprived institutional setting showed both profound intellectual and motor retardation and a higher incidence of disease and mortality (Spitz, 1945). Spitz described a syndrome, called anaclitic depression, that he saw in some of the deprived children during the second half of their first year. "The children would lie or sit with wide open, expressionless eyes, frozen, immobile faces, and a faraway expression as if in a daze, apparently not perceiving what went on in their environment" (Spitz and Wolf, 1946, p. 314). He believed that the debilitating effects (both physiological and psychological) of maternal deprivation could be arrested and reversed if mothering was resumed within three months and if the deprivation didn't continue beyond the first year of the infant's life. The infant's response to maternal deprivation has been described as falling into three stages: protest, despair, and detachment from mother after the infant is reunited with mother (Bowlby, 1960). Later animal studies have confirmed both the protest and despair stages, but they have failed to corroborate the detachment stage (Seay, Hansen, and Harlow, 1962; Seay and Harlow, 1965; Spencer-Booth and Hinde, 1966; Kaufman and Rosenblum, 1967; Spencer-Booth and Hinde, 1971; Schlottman and Seay, 1972).

While the mother-child relationship traditionally has been viewed as unique and of critical importance to later personality development (largely because the mother typically has assumed the role of the primary caregiver), the work of Ribble and later of Harlow and his associates has brought into sharper focus the more essential effects of early sensory experiences (rather than the mother per se) on the child's development. Moreover, the popular idea that the mother is the most important figure in the infant's life because she spends the most time with the infant is unsupported by research data, which show that the time spent in interacting is a poor predictor of the quality of the relationship between infant and parent. In fact, the most important factor is the quality of the relationship, evidenced by the intact relationships found between working mothers and their children (Bossard and Boll, 1966). Additional research, as we shall see, indicates that a number of people (besides the mother) and environmental stimuli play an influential role in the development of the child.

Normal and Abnormal Effects of Fathering. Until recently the role of the father in child development has been obscured by the emphasis placed on the importance of mother-infant relationships and by the assumption that the father merely serves as an aid to the mother in nurturing the child before the age of three. At present we know that fathers hold, touch, talk to, and kiss their babies as much as mothers do, provided they are given ample opportunities to engage in such contact and interactions (Parke and O'Leary, 1976). It has also been shown that infants between seven and thirteen months of age are more attached to their parents than to strangers, and that they show just as much attachment for either parent (fathers or mothers) during this period of their lives (Lamb, 1977). In fact, a recent study indicated that infants react more positively to play with their fathers than with their mothers (Clarke-Stewart, 1978).

In addition, eighteen-month-old infants chose fathers more often than mothers as play partners when given a choice. However, rather than reflecting the child's preference for a specific parent, this may actually be related to the more physical and rough-type play of fathers as contrasted to mothers' greater emphasis on cognitive play activities (Weinraub and Frankel, 1977). Even though fathers spend less time with their infants, it is also apparent that many are responsive to their cues, enjoy interacting with them, and become early and enduring central figures in their social worlds. But as most of us know from our own observations, babies seek out their mothers more frequently than fathers during times of stress (Lamb, 1976).

In a well-controlled and informative study, Santrock (1972) set out to determine the effect of father absence on third and sixth graders' IQ and achievement scores. The subject sample was sufficiently large to permit analysis of onset of father absence at birth to two years, three to five years, six to nine years, ten to eleven years, and twelve to thirteen years of age. The study also explored the type of absence; that is, death, divorce, desertion, separation, or presence of a stepfather. Subjects were Caucasian boys and girls who came from lower-socioeconomic homes. Both IQ and achievement scores were most depressed for boys whose fathers died when the child was between the ages of six and nine. The other forms of father absence had the most detrimental effect on cognitive development during the period from birth to two years for both girls and boys. Boys whose fathers were absent consistently scored lower than either father-absent girls or father-present boys. Moreover, when fathers who were absent because of divorce, separation, or desertion were replaced through remarriage during the first five years of the child's life, the effect on the cognitive development of boys—although not on girls—was positive. In addition, Hoffman (1971) studied the relationship of father absence to moral development in seventh-grade Caucasian boys and girls from low- and middle-socioeconomic-level homes. He found clear evidence that father absence had a detrimental effect on conscience development in boys, although not on girls.

Using measures of parent-child relations, internal-external locus of control, and self-concept, Moerk (1973) compared the test scores of the sons of imprisoned fathers and of divorced fathers with those of juvenile delinquents and normal youngsters. Profiles of sons of imprisoned fathers were more similar to those of juvenile delinquents and less similar to the normal controls than were the profiles of the sons of divorced fathers. Absence of father has also been linked with alcoholism in young men whose fathers were in the home until the boys were fifteen years of age; with hospitalized female alcoholics evidencing serious behavioral problems; and with suicide attempts and drug addiction in both males and females (Jacobs and Teicher, 1967; Oltman and Friedman, 1967; Rosenberg, 1969; Rathod and Thompson, 1971).

The importance of the father for daughters is illustrated in a rather elaborate study involving seventy-two adolescent firstborn daughters (aged thirteen to seventeen) whose parents lived together or were divorced, or whose fathers had died (Hetherington, 1973). Noteworthy among the extensive findings were the indications that girls who had grown up without fathers felt insecure and apprehensive in relating to male peers and adults, although they expressed these feelings in different ways. Girls of divorced parents reported more heterosexual activity, while those whose fathers had died tended to be more sexually inhibited. Higher self-esteem and positive feelings about the father were noted more frequently for daughters whose fathers had died than for those whose parents were divorced.

Although a good deal more data are needed to explicate the impact of the father on the personality development of the child, several trends have been noted (Radin, 1976; Parke and Sawin, 1977). Paternal nurturance seems to be more highly correlated with the cognitive competence of boys than of girls, and father absence before the age of five seems to be particularly damaging to the cognitive functioning of young boys. In addition, father absence in the early years hinders the mathematical skills of girls, and it is associated with a cognitive profile in college men that is more typical of females. For both sexes authoritarian paternal behavior or intense paternal involvement in the problem-solving activities of the child is related to reduced academic competence. Fathers do well at many of the traditional feminine tasks of child care, but unlike mothers, they tend to provide more physical stimulation for their babies than verbal stimulation. Baby boys seem to benefit more than girls from interactions with their fathers, not only cognitively but in social situations as well. In fact, as early as age five months, baby boys show less fear of strangers and less apprehension on being left alone when fathers have taken care of them and played with them. Thus,

> A father influences his children's mental development through many and diverse channels: through his genetic background, his manifest behavior with his offspring, the attitudes he holds about himself and his children, the behavior he models, his position in the family system, the material resources he is able to supply for his children, the influence he is able to exert on his wife's behavior, his ethnic heritage, and the vision he holds for his children. Finally, when he dies or separates from the family, the memories he leaves with his wife and children continue to exert an influence, perhaps equal to the impressions he made on the youngsters when he was physically present. (Radin, 1976, p. 270)

The Total Interacting System—The Family. Thus far we have discussed the three main characters in a one-child family unit primarily as single components of a complex interacting system; however, we have considered each (the child, the mother, and the father) as influencing and being influenced by the behaviors of others. Figure 3-1 schematically depicts the interplay that initially has the greatest impact on the child's personality and social development. As children grow older, the family's almost exclusive control over and impact on them decrease and give way to other major sources of influence, such as the school and peer groups, although their ties to the family are never completely broken or abandoned (Cohen, 1976). Throughout a person's life the family provides a sense of security, role differentiation, and group membership that not only facilitates adaptive and effective functioning within society but also serves to perpetuate itself through marriage and procreation. Unfortunately, our research technology has not yet permitted adequate study of the multidirectional interplay of forces within a family unit, other than to examine the effects of single or dyadic components on the child's development (as illustrated in the foregoing discussion).

One dyadic relationship, that of husband-wife, has been of interest not only because it changes to some extent when a child arrives, but also because the quality and nature of this relationship sets the tone of harmony or disharmony, cooperation or antagonism, consistency or inconsistency, and stability or instability for the family unit. According to Lidz:

Figure 3-1 Schematic illustration of family multidirectional interaction system

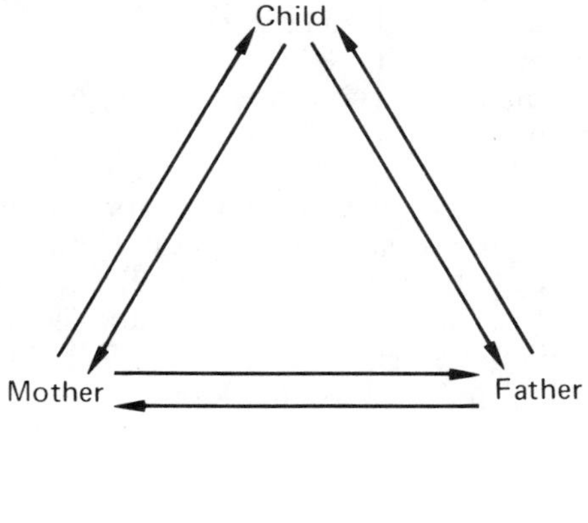

> A coalition between the parents is necessary not only to give unity of direction but also to provide each parent with the support essential for carrying out his or her cardinal functions. The wife, for example, can better delimit her erotic investment to maternal feelings when her wifely sexual needs are being satisfied by her husband. The tendency of small groups to divide up into dyads that create rivalries and jealousies is diminished markedly if the parents form a unity in relation to their children. The child's tendency to possess one or the other parent for himself alone—the essence of the Oedipal situation—is overcome if the parental coalition is firm, frustrating the child's fantasies and redirecting him to the reality that requires repression of such wishes. If the parents form a coalition not only as parents but also as a married couple, the child is provided with adult models who treat one another as alter egos, each striving for the partner's satisfaction as well as for his own. The child then grows up valuing marriage as an institution that provides emotional gratification and security, and thus, gains a long-range goal to pursue. (1970, p. 29)

Indeed, several different kinds of faulty parental coalitions have been found in families that evidence psychotic or other abnormal conditions (Lidz, Fleck, and Cornelison, 1965). For example, chronic disharmony between parents is a coalition that exerts undue pressure on the child to take sides with one of the two warring parents. This seriously impedes identification with either parent, since each is deprecated by the other. A skewed parental coalition is characterized by a severe abnormal disorder in one parent, with the other passively submitting and appeasing the disturbed spouse to keep the marriage intact. Obviously, such a lopsided coalition requires extreme passivity on the part of the accommodating parent (leading one to wonder about his or her emotional stability), and it provides a family environment for children in which abnormal behaviors and unrealistic views of the world are implicitly, if not explicitly, sanctioned. Minuchin and associates (Minuchin, Rosman, and Baker, 1978) studied hospitalized psychosomatic children and their families over a period of ten years and found that a child can become anorectic (refuse to eat) if he or she has learned to relate in highly enmeshed patterns and if the family is predominantly child-oriented, carefully protective and hypervigilant over the child's psychobiological needs, and restrictive of the child's autonomy. In this setting the child learns to become a sensitive observer of intrafamilial happenings, dependent on and receptive to assessment by parents and very loyal to the values of the family. Substantial areas of the child's bodily and psychological functioning persist from earlier times as a subject in which others are interested and over which others retain control. The youngster fails to develop age-appropriate coping skills, and a crisis develops during adolescence because the child is quite conflicted between the wish to join in with peer groups and attachment and orientation toward the family. Characteristically, anorectic families tend to focus on bodily functions manifested in the form of somatic complaints, which are then reinforced in order to detour conflict by family members, especially when disequilibrium threatens their family system.

Where these or other faulty parental coalitions exist, children often are caught in a struggle either to support one or the other parent or to invest a great deal of their energies in keeping the family intact—all at the expense of their own development (Lidz, 1970). Children also may serve as scapegoats for parental strife, and they even may act in ways that will lead to parental disfavor; in this way they can conceal the underlying marital disharmony and keep it from becoming an open battle leading to divorce. The failure of parents to achieve an effective coalition inevitably draws the child into the conflictual situation producing anxiety and insecurity as well as role models that interfere with normal personality development.

The School

Apart from the family, no institution has a greater and more continuous impact on the child's social and personality development than our educational system. When we consider that for many years children spend half of their waking lives in school, it is not surprising that this becomes the center not only for academic instruction but also for the acquisition of social skills and competence. Cohen (1976) likens the school to the family in its form and mode of operating (although not in content), since in both situations the child is placed into a relatively self-contained unit and is expected to be responsive to adult controls. However, entrance into school usually represents the child's first prolonged separation from the familiar and comforting family environment. In this new setting demands are made to do things that are not always rewarding, and greater independence is required.

What the child experiences, how the child perceives school, and whether school will positively or negatively affect the child's motivation to learn, persevere, act independently, cope with frustrations, and acquire a sense of competence and self-worth will depend largely on teacher-pupil relationships. In our society, preschool, kindergarten, and first-grade teachers are likely to be women, who perform functions that are similar to those customarily assumed by the mother (Mussen, Conger, and Kagan, 1974). They compliment and reward the child's desirable behaviors and reprimand undesirable behaviors; they may provide nurturance in the form of cookies and juice; and they help the child get in or out of outer garments during the winter months or on rainy days. Teachers may also provide entertainment, since they play games and read stories to children, much like their mothers are apt to do. Yet some writers have suggested that the early and continued exposure of children, especially boys, to women teachers may foster the attitude that school is more appropriate for girls than for boys. This attitude may in part account for the higher academic achievement of girls in the first several grades.

Perhaps more important than the teacher's sex is his or her personal characteristics and their effect on the child's academic and social progress. In general, children make their greatest social, emotional, and academic progress with teachers who are warm, flexible, and encouraging of creative expression and who are authoritative in providing direction and guidance. In contrast,

> optimal academic and personal growth will not be stimulated in most students by the teacher who is either rigidly authoritarian, hostile, or unresponsive to student needs, or the one who is indecisive and uncertain, poorly trained, narcissistic, or preoccupied with his or her own anxieties and personal problems. (Mussen, Conger, and Kagan, 1974, p. 495)

Of course, not all children perceive and react to the same teacher in the same way. Consequently, it is even more important for the teacher to be aware that the child's motivation to learn and the building of his or her self-worth are facilitated by prior successes and drastically impaired by repeated failure.

Teachers of socioeconomically disadvantaged youngsters should recognize that their potential influence on these students may be even greater than that of teachers of middle-class children; the culturally deprived child is likely to be more vulnerable to the stress of new situations as a result of earlier family experiences that have been deficient in nurturance and support (Yee, 1968). In addition, disadvantaged children often come from environments that prepare them poorly for the demands of the school. Often they lack the attention skills necessary in classroom and laboratory situations (Whiteman and Deutsch, 1968; Knopf and Kirchner, 1974; Knopf and Mabel, 1975). These children also tend to be less motivated and less ambitious in their academic aspirations than their middle-class counterparts. Further, they typically attend schools that are overcrowded, physically deteriorated, and lacking in adequate resources (Mussen, Conger, and Kagan, 1974).

Peer Relations

As the child grows older, peer relations become increasingly important as a source of influence in social and personality development. The opportunity for peer interactions provides children with normative standards by which they can compare and to some extent modify their own feelings, thoughts, and actions. Peer groups begin to form early in middle childhood as the child extends his or her interpersonal ties beyond the immediate family (Mussen, Conger, and Kagan, 1974). Initially these groups consist of informal and tenuous associations that over time evolve into more structured, stable, and cohesive organizations that sometimes involve special rituals and paraphernalia (such as the Scout groups for boys and girls).

The peer group is an alternative social unit to the family.

> [It] is formed through a community of equals, where status and leadership patterns are defined through natural group processes; consequently, the peer group provides an exercise in communal formation where positions are earned (and subject to change) as a result of skill and democratic procedures, rather than imposed or assumed as a function of prior conditions and obligations. (Cohen, 1976, p. 83)

Consequently, membership in a group affords social status and enhances self-esteem, whereas rejection from a group can have serious negative effects. Peer groups also offer companionship in age-appropriate interests and activities and provide opportunities for children to explore new experiences that are group sanctioned. Sometimes peer values conflict with those held by parents, in which case the resolution will likely depend on the relative strength of the child's relationship to the parents and the group (Hartup, 1970). Finally, peer relationships serve to foster a sense of responsibility and commitment to others, which is necessary for adaptive functioning within our society (Hartup, 1977).

THEORIES OF NORMAL DEVELOPMENT

Having considered the basic principles by which development occurs as well as some of the important variables that influence its course, we turn now to a discussion of the three most viable and promising theoretical views of normal development: the psychoanalytic view, the cognitive-developmental view, and the learning view. These approaches have been singled out for presentation because they have had a great impact on researchers, educators, and other child-care workers, and because together they provide a broad but understandable perspective of the developing child.

Psychoanalytic Theory

Sigmund Freud. As noted in Chapter 1, Freud's theoretical contributions not only added legitimacy to the study of children per se but also focused lasting attention on the critical role of the early years of childhood in determining a person's basic character structure. In fact, Freud believed that personality was essentially formed by the end of the child's fifth year of life, and that in the main, later growth involved an elaboration of the already-established basic structure. Since we are interested in normal development, we shall deal with those aspects of Freud's psychoanalytic theory that bear directly on this subject, leaving for later consideration (Chapter 4) his theoretical contributions to psychopathology.

According to psychoanalytic theory, the personality consists of three major systems: the id, the ego, and the superego.[2] Although each component has its own functions, characteristics, and guiding principles, in the normal personality each interacts with the other components, and together they operate in an integrated fashion.

1. *The id.* This is the inherited and original energy system of the personality that is present at birth, and from which the ego and the superego are later energized and differentiated. The id represents the world of subjective reality, and its activities are governed by what Freud called the pleasure prin-

[2] Much of this section is based on Freud, 1922, 1959, 1957, and 1933.

ciple—that is, the seeking of pleasure and the avoidance of pain. It is entirely amoral, unaware of the demands of external or objective reality, and incapable of making judgments. Thus, Freud viewed the newborn infant as a pleasure-bound organism seeking immediate gratification of impulses without regard for or knowledge of objective reality. This is evidenced by the crescendo cry of the baby who won't stop until he is fed and who seems oblivious to the fact that his parents are preparing the food.

In seeking immediate gratification, the id functions largely by a primary process that includes motor actions or mental images of the desired object if it isn't immediately available (imagining and grabbing at the mother's breast when hungry). However, images alone cannot reduce tension states (mental images of food do not satisfy hunger); they must be augmented by a secondary process that permits the developing child to interact appropriately with the objective world of reality to satisfy its needs. In addition, the id's demands for immediate satisfaction are likely to lead the infant into dangerous conflicts with the external environment (such as the baby's getting hurt when reaching for a desired object or touching a hot burner), since the id is cut off from the external world and knows nothing of ensuring the organism's survival. Finally, as the caregiver tries to foster self-control skills in the child by gradually witholding immediate and continuous gratification, the infant is forced to deal with the demands of the environment.

2. *The ego.* It is within this context that the ego develops to facilitate the aims of the id by acquiring skills that enable the child to achieve pleasure in ways that are within the bounds of objective reality. The ego emerges from the id as the component of the personality that is concerned with reason, the preservation of the organism, and the modification of the pleasure principle (but not its nullification). Guided by the reality principle (keeping experiences within external constraints), the ego employs the *secondary process* (thought processes that distinguish the subjective from the objective worlds of reality) to delay tension states until an appropriate object is found that satisfies the need. The ego also protects the child by making use of the sensations of anxiety as warning signals of danger, which in turn prompt safer responses. As the executive of the personality, the ego controls cognitive and intellectual functioning and acts as a mediator between id impulses and the demands of reality, and between the id and the superego.

3. *The superego.* This is the last system of the personality to develop, and it is as unbending and unreasonable as its original source, the id. As the moral component of the personality, the superego represents the cultural past—it incorporates the traditional values of society and the more specific values of parents. It is recognized by its judicial functions (the conscience), rendering judgments about right and wrong and striving for perfection and for the ideal. In trying to control the impulses of the id, the superego seeks to permanently block the id's gratification. This is in contrast to the ego's efforts to postpone gratification. The superego keeps a careful watch over the ego, attempts to direct it, and threatens to punish it for id gratification. When the ego and the superego are in complete agreement, there is little to distinguish them, but when the ego fails to block the impulses of the id, tensions flare up and the superego becomes visible as pangs of conscience.

4. *Psychosexual stages of development.* In addition to describing the essential components of the personality, Freud's major contribution to human development was his view of infant sexuality and its connection to a temporal series of differentiated stages by which personality develops. Surprisingly, Freud formulated this aspect of psychoanalytic theory largely from observations of his adult patients, who repeatedly evidenced childish traits and recalled early childhood experiences that seemed to be determinants of their current behaviors. He posited excessive frustration or indulgence of the child's needs as the two primary causes of disruption in the normal

growth process, and he specified fixation and regression as ways in which growth can either be permanently halted at a particular stage of development or temporarily reverted to earlier forms of behavior.

Freud also believed that all behaviors are determined by (unconscious) drives, known as instincts, that activate internal tensions and prompt actions that remove or lessen the tension. Instincts are the inborn energy states of the id that give rise to tension. They are reducible to the two fundamental drives of sexuality and aggression. Freud conceived of sexuality as broadly corresponding to pleasure-seeking activities and erogenous strivings for bodily satisfaction (not strictly tied to genital satisfaction). He regarded aggression as the need to destroy objects.

According to Freud, the sexual drive, which he characterized as libidinal energy and tension, develops through a time-ordered series of stages that are associated with various erotic areas of the body. These stages constitute the sequential periods of growth that every child must pass through for the formation of normal personality. The child's failure to deal effectively with libidinal tension at each stage of psychosexual development leads to either fixation or regression as well as to adjustment problems later in life.

The first stage, known as the *oral period*, occurs during the initial eighteen to twenty-four months of the infant's life. Stimulation of the erogenous zones of the lips and mouth by objects such as nipples, toys, and fingers provide pleasure and relieve libidinal tension.

During the second period, called the *anal phase*, the anus becomes the site of sexual stimulation and gratification. This stage extends from about eighteen months to approximately three years of age (roughly corresponding to the period of toilet training), during which time the child seems to derive sensual pleasure from the retention and expulsion of fecal matter.

The *phallic stage* occurs between the third and fifth year of the child's life, when the genitals become the primary focus of sexual excitation and pleasure. Soon thereafter the child enters the *oedipal period*, when the libidinal source of gratification becomes an external object; that is, the opposite-sex parent becomes the object of libidinal pleasure instead of the youngster's own genitals and body. The child views the parent of the same sex as an obstacle and as a source of interference with the sexual desire for the other parent. The child's wish to replace and eliminate the same-sex parent arouses guilt and fear of retaliation as well as a sense of inadequacy. This period is conflictual and tumultuous for the child, but it is resolved through a process of identification with the same-sex parent (being like him or her).

The longest psychosexual stage of development, known as the *latency period*, begins at about age six and extends through preadolescence. It is a stage where sexual tensions and activities are dormant, where the child can recover from the turmoil of the oedipal phase, and where further identification with the same-sex parent occurs. The final period, the *genital stage*, takes place during adolescence. This is the time when the sexual drive is heightened and the opposite sex becomes the sexual object for those who have developed normally.

The psychosexual stages of development are significant not only as focuses of sensual pleasure but also as important sources of parent-child interactions in which enduring patterns are established for the gratification of the child's needs. During the early periods the baby is exposed to adults who facilitate his or her pleasure-seeking activities and who gradually impose limits on them. According to Freud, the manner in which libidinal needs are satisfied or frustrated has important implications for the child's social development and for the formation of specific character traits. For example, Freud proposed bipolar personality traits associated with each stage of psychosexual development and believed that manifestations of either extreme of the trait reflected fixation (caused by indulgence or frustration) at that particular developmental level. Thus, an excessively indulged person fixated at the oral level would evidence traits of optimism, gullibility, and admiration, while the orally frustrated fixated person would show pessimism, suspiciousness, and envy (Maddi, 1972). In this way Freud's theory described the means by which specific personality attributes are initially acquired; and he more broadly suggested that the nature of the child's experiences during each stage of development determines the form that personality structure will take.

Erik Erikson. Erikson used a Freudian psychoanalytic orientation to fashion a view of personality development that has come to be more palatable than Freud's to most child-care workers. In contrast to Freud, Erikson placed greater emphasis on the ego than on the id in personality development, stressed the importance of social and cultural influences beyond the mother-father-child triangle, and adopted a more optimistic view of human nature, discerning components conducive to growth in every personal and social crisis (Erikson, 1963; Maier, 1965).

Psychosocial stages of development. Erikson proposed eight stages of development, including the adult years, thus reflecting his belief that the individual constantly redevelops his or her personality in passing from one phase to the next. Moreover, he maintained that development follows a universal course and that each person must face and master a central problem at each stage of development. A person's successful resolution of each conflict contributes to ego strength, while failure results in carrying over problems that impair attempts to resolve the new problems of later phases. Table 3–1 describes the major characteristics of both Freud's and Erikson's stages of development.

During phase 1 (first year of life) the infant is faced with the central problem of acquiring a sense of basic trust while overcoming basic distrust. Trust, the cornerstone of the personality, enables the infant to feel comfortable and to experience a minimum of fear in new situations. Distrust can lead to such serious consequences as the withdrawal reaction of a psychotic child. The quality of the maternal relationship is critical in determining the amount of trust the infant will derive.

Phase 2 coincides with Freud's anal stage. It is concerned with the conflict of autonomy versus self-doubt and shame. During this period children discover that their behavior is self-determined and that they can function with a sense of autonomy, especially as they develop new motor skills. At the same time children experience doubt about giving up the dependency they enjoy and about their ability to be autonomous. Self-doubt is most likely to occur in the absence of parental regulations and controls, while shame results from excessive disapproval from parents and others, as well as from censorship and from the failure to attain high expectations set by

Table 3–1 Freud's and Erikson's Stages of Development

Freud		*Erikson*	
Age	*Stage*	*Age*	*Stage*
Birth–1 year	Oral	Infancy	Trust versus Mistrust
1–3 years	Anal	Early Childhood	Autonomy versus Shame, Doubt
3–5 years	Phallic	Middle Childhood	Initiative versus Guilt
5–12 years	Latency	Late Childhood	Industry versus Inferiority
12–adult	Genital	Adolescence	Identity versus Role confusion
		Young Adulthood	Intimacy versus Isolation
		Middle Adulthood	Creativity versus Stagnation
		Maturity	Integrity versus Despair

others. Erikson maintains that a combination of freedom for the child to do some things unaided and parental regulation of other activities encourages the development of autonomy.

Phase 3 involves the conflict over the acquisition of a sense of initiative versus overcoming a sense of guilt. This period closely coincides with Freud's phallic and oedipal stages and with the preschool period. At this time children make new conquests, master ambulatory skills, and reach out to expand their activities and abilities (Maier, 1965). Initiative is encouraged by parental behaviors that include both approval and regulation. Guilt occurs both because the child develops a superego and because of the oedipal relationship.

Phase 4 (corresponding to Freud's latency period) focuses on the conflict of industry versus inferiority. Children during middle childhood begin to gain recognition for their accomplishments. Usually they start formal schooling with a determination to master new skills. In the process they begin to develop work habits that will be important later on. The danger at this stage is that the child may develop a sense of inadequacy and inferiority that comes from the youngster's previous level of lesser production and competence. During this period children see their involvement with peers of the same sex as essential.

Phase 5, beginning with adolescence, is concerned with the conflict of identity versus role confusion. The occurrence of rapid physiological changes along with the challenge of impending tangible adult tasks create conflicts in adolescents about their role in the world. Teenagers become overly concerned with their inability to settle on an occupational goal, while they readily "overidentify" with peer-group heroes. Some integration of past identification occurs during this phase, but in the main, adolescents search for peer social values to guide their identity.

Erikson's delineation of phases 6, 7, and 8 emphasizes the fact that development continues beyond childhood and youth. Here we have the conflicts of intimacy versus isolation, generativity versus stagnation, and ego integrity versus despair. The crisis in phase 6 arises from the avoidance of intimacy because of fear of failure and of ego loss, which may result in feelings of isolation. The hazardous task of establishing a permanent relationship with a suitable spouse may very well be the battleground of this conflict. In phase 7 adults become primarily concerned with guiding the next generation by developing a strong marital union and by having children, while in the last phase adults must learn to accept and adapt to the successes and failures of daily living and go forward without despair, unafraid of death. Erickson ties ego-integrity to basic trust when he comments: "... healthy children will not fear life, if their parents have integrity enough not to fear death" (Erikson, 1963, p. 269).

Cognitive-Developmental Theory

In contrast to psychoanalytic theory, the cognitive-developmental approach stresses both the higher mental processes and intellectual factors as the basic ingredients and integrative threads of human development (Cohen, 1976). It does not compartmentalize development into discrete areas of experiences—such as social, emotional, or intellectual—nor does it have any need to make assumptions about unconscious processes or major systems of the developing organism.

Jean Piaget. The work of Jean Piaget is voluminous, highly original, and couched in unfamiliar and difficult-to-understand constructs. But unmistakably, it is one of the most influential works in child development. Piaget's theory stresses the universal nature of intellectual development and views development as an evolutionary process that is innate and fixed (Flavell, 1963; Maier, 1965; Tuddenham, 1966). Like Erikson, he holds to the assumption that development progresses through successive stages for all children; however, he believes the rate of progress varies from child to child. Although Piaget studied perception, moral attitudes, and motivation—among other areas—his overriding interest was in learning how knowledge develops and changes (Tuddenham, 1966).

Piaget's cognitive theory begins with the idea that motor action is the source from which mental operations develop; that is, early sensorimotor activities of infants markedly influence later cognitions. Infants begin life with innate reflexes, some of which are modifiable through experience and become the behavioral elements from which more complex and symbolic forms of cognitive behavior develop. Piaget's penchant for ordering a relationship (that is similar in form and structure) between biological and mental structure is illustrated by his assumption that a *schema* exists in the mind that corresponds to each innate reflex and, later, to each behavior sequence. Schema, an important concept in Piaget's theory, refers to the organization of all experiences of a particular kind into a cognitive structure that can change with learning.

Intelligence is the ability to adapt, and adaptation depends on the dual learning processes of *assimilation* and *accommodation.* Assimilation refers to the tendency to incorporate external reality into some meaningful structure (schema), while accommodation is "the process by which a schema *changes* so as to adapt better to the assimilated reality" (Tuddenham, 1966, p. 21).

The stages of cognitive development. Piaget divides cognitive development into the following four stages, which roughly correspond to age periods: *the sensorimotor stage*—birth to approximately two years; *the preoperational stage*—two to seven years; *the stage of concrete operations*—seven to eleven years; and *the stage of formal operations*—eleven to fifteen years and older (Tuddenham, 1966).

Piaget devotes more detailed analysis to the sensorimotor period than to any other, perhaps because of the opportunities he had to observe his own three children during this time. He divides this period into six substages, beginning with the infant's use of reflexes and progressing to the acquired behavioral patterns of voluntary movements and active exploration. The child progresses from a very self-centered existence to one that is object-centered. "During this period the various sensory spaces of vision, touch, and the rest, are coordinated into a single space and objects evolve from their separate sensory properties into *things* with multiple properties, permanence, and spatial relationships to other objects" (Tuddenham, 1966, p. 215). The introduction of the concept of object permanence is important as an explanatory base for the child's memory (mental images) of objects beyond his or her immediate sensory experiences with them.

Language acquisition and development highlight the preoperational stage and enable the child to shift from total reliance on motor activity to an increased use of symbolic activity (cognitive), ranging from problem solving to concerns dealing with the environment. Initially the child is the center of the world, but through *decentering,* a time scale and a spatial world independent of the child begin to emerge. Two-year-old children have egocentric thoughts that are specific to the situation and reflective only of their point of view. Sometime around four years of age, children begin to view the world less subjectively as their perspective gradually widens. The child's reasoning is still distorted during this phase, since the child tends to attend to one essential feature of a problem while neglecting other important aspects. Piaget illustrates this by presenting a child with two identical elongated vases containing the same amount of water. If the water in one vase is poured into a short and broad-based jar, the child will insist that the amount of water in the vase is greater than the amount in the jar. Piaget contends that the child has focused only on the height of the vase without attending to other dimensions.

The stage of concrete operations ushers in the capacity to reason, albeit at a concrete level. For the first time the child can produce mental representation of a series of actions, such as tracing with paper and pencil the route the child travels to and from school. The child also recognizes the notion of conservation and sees volume, weight, length, and number as constant, even when minor changes in their external appearance are introduced (such as shifting water from one vase to a jar). The child learns to reason in relational terms and is able to discern that the concept of shorter or taller, for example, is relative to two or more objects and not absolute characteristics of each. In addition, the child learns to classify, number, and order things in relation to an organized whole, which leads to a notion of certainty about the world. During the last phase of intellectual development, the phase of formal operations, the adolescent is capable of thinking about all the possible solutions to a problem by systematically exploring the possibilities and checking the effectiveness of each. Adolescents can think in hypothetical terms, and they are capable of forming abstractions and dealing with symbols. For Piaget, the capacity to formulate hypotheses and to handle logical relationships brings intellectual growth to its peak (Tuddenham, 1966).

Kohlberg—Moral Development. Another example of a cognitive-developmental theory is the one offered by Kohlberg. This theory deals with moral development and involves the concepts of reason and judgment. Kohlberg's research is largely an outgrowth of the earlier work of Piaget, who viewed morality as a system of rules for conduct that the child forms from the influences of parents and other significant adults, as well as from the child's own experiences (Cohen, 1976).

> According to Piaget, the interaction of individual growth factors and social experiences instrumental in the development of moral judgment may be distinguished by reference to four successive and invariant stages of emergence. These include a period of motor development, followed by an egocentric stage, leading to a period of cooperative effort, and, finally, terminating in the child's recognition of moral principle in the establishment of social order. (Cohen, 1976, pp. 177–178)

Although Piaget's view has been greeted with mildly favorable reactions, the work of Kohlberg is more complete and detailed and currently provides an important extension of the cognitive-developmental approach to the development of moral judgment. A descriptive summary of Kohlberg's three levels of moral judgment and its six stages of development is given in Table 3–2 (Kohlberg, 1967).

Kohlberg's research evaluating moral judgment employs a set of stories, each containing a moral dilemma. The child is asked to make moral judgments concerning the behaviors of the characters in the story (Kohlberg, 1969). Some evidence suggests that Kohlberg's view of moral development involves a component of cognitive growth, since the stages he proposes correlate moderately well with IQ (Hoffman, 1970). Additional data are available that support his claim that all children go through the same successive stages of development (Kohlberg, 1969). However, other observers have raised serious questions about the validity of the developmental stages (Bandura, 1969a; Hoffman, 1970). The latter researchers are learning theorists who prefer to view development as continually changing and as a function of maturational growth and learning—not as a set of discrete and invariant stages. In general, stage theorists such as Freud, Erikson, Piaget, and Kohlberg hold a maturational view of development in which biological factors play a central role in the sequential and orderly unfolding of behavior. In contrast, learning theorists emphasize environmental conditions that give rise to the acquisition of behavior and those that maintain or produce changes in behavior (Cohen, 1976).

Learning Theory

The importance of learning to the developing child is difficult to exaggerate; its influence pervades almost every aspect of his or her functioning. It plays a role in eating, bowel

Table 3-2* Kohlberg's Classification of Moral Judgment into Levels and Stages of Development

Basis of Moral Judgment Levels	*Stages of Development*
I Moral value resides in external, quasi-physical happenings, in bad acts, or in quasi-physical needs rather than in persons and standards.	Stage 1: Obedience and punishment orientation. Egocentric deference to superior power or prestige, or a trouble-avoiding set. Objective responsibility.
	Stage 2: Naively egoistic orientation. Right action is that instrumentally satisfying the self's needs and occasionally others'. Awareness of relativism of value to each actor's needs and perspective. Naive egalitarianism and orientation to exchange and reciprocity.
II Moral value resides in performing good or right roles, in maintaining the conventional order and the expectancies of others.	Stage 3: Good-boy orientation. Orientation to approval and to pleasing and helping others. Conformity to stereotypical images of majority of natural role behavior, and judgment by intentions.
	Stage 4: Authority- and social-order-maintaining orientation. Orientation to "doing duty" and to showing respect for authority and maintaining the given social order for its own sake. Regard for earned expectations of others.
III Moral value resides in conformity by the self to shared or sharable standards, rights, or duties.	Stage 5: Contractual legalistic orientation. Recognition of an arbitrary element or starting point in rules or expectations for the sake of agreement. Duty defined in terms of contract, general avoidance of violation of the will or rights of others, and majority will and welfare.
	Stage 6: Conscience or principle orientation. Orientation not only to actually ordained social rules but to principles of choice involving appeal to logical universality and consistency. Orientation to conscience as a directing agent and to mutual respect and trust.

*From Cohen, 1976, p. 181. Reprinted with permission of Macmillan Publishing Co., Inc.

and bladder control, language development, interpersonal relations, emotional expression, motivation, thinking, remembering, perceiving, motor skills, and in the formation of attitudes and values. Although limited by biological factors, *learning is the process by which environmental forces bring about lasting changes in behavior through practice.* For example, the child who is born deaf will be unable to learn normal speech patterns, and no amount of practice will enable the paraplegic to learn to run or play soccer. Learning results in long-lasting behavioral change, as distinguished from temporary alterations that occur from fatigue, drugs, or adaptation. Practice or experience is essential to differentiate learning from the effects of physical maturation or of biological factors such as brain injury or damage. Changes in behavior that result from learning may be either desirable or undesirable, since the process of acquisition makes no distinction between good and bad behaviors.

There are many learning theories that attempt to account for human behavior. However, before we can discuss even a select sample of learning theories, we must become familiar with the basic concepts and with the different kinds of learning.

Reinforcement. The concept of reinforcement is extremely important in a discussion of the learning process. If the occurrence or removal of an event or condition leads to the strengthening of a stimulus-response (S-R) connection or to the increased probability that a response will be emitted, the event or condition may be referred to as a *positive or negative reinforcer.* Positive reinforcement usually is thought of as a reward that either meets the biological requirements of the organisms (primary)—such as food, water, or rest—or meets the learned needs (secondary) of the individual—such as approval, recognition, or affection. Negative reinforcement involves the removal of an unpleasant or aversive consequence that strengthens avoidance or escape behavior, as illustrated in the student who does an extra term paper to avoid failing the course. In contrast, *punishment* is a condition or event presented after a response occurs that will decrease the probability that the response will be emitted; that is, it will weaken the S-R association. Table 3-3 describes more fully the characteristics of positive and negative reinforcement and punishment. Under optimal conditions punishment is the most effective way of eliminating an unwanted response. However, in real-life situations, punishment is rarely given with either sufficient intensity or suddenness to have more than transient effects. Just how effective punishment can be in eliminating behavior permanently is illustrated by the one trial learning of the child who gets burned by touching a hot burner on a stove, or by the child who is shocked by putting his or her finger into a light socket. In most human situa-

Table 3-3* Characteristics of Reinforcement and Punishment

Positive Reinforcement	*Negative Reinforcement*	*Punishment*
1. Produced by instrumental behavior 2. Increases the probability of a particular instrumental response 3. Increases the intensity of a particular instrumental response 4. Sustains instrumental responses that have been learned 5. Elicits respondent emotional behaviors that induce approach behavior (enthusiasm, zest, encouragement, joy, excitement, pleasure)	1. Consists of the removal of unwanted consequences 2. Strengthens instrumental avoidance behavior 3. Strengthens instrumental escape behavior 4. Increases the behavior that removes it 5. Resembles positive reinforcement when instrumental responses remove certain aversive consequences (shortening a prison sentence by good behavior; receiving reduced work load as reward for good work) 6. Resembles punishment when instrumental responses simply prevent punishment (performing a job to avoid punishment by the boss, cleaning one's room to prevent mother's nagging)	1. Used to weaken behaviors, but frequently ineffective 2. Consists of following instrumental responses by an unpleasant consequence, or removing one that is desired 3. Suppresses behavior, but does not necessarily weaken it 4. May instigate other instrumental responses that accomplish the same goal (being caught stealing during the day instigates stealing at night) 5. May result in conditioned emotional responses (ulcers, chronic headache, resentment, and other psychosomatic processes; anger, hatred, fear, anxiety, distrust) 6. May result in avoidance or escape behaviors (active avoidance; learning what to do to avoid the punishment; passive avoidance; learning what not to do to avoid or escape from the punishment) 7. If mild, may stimulate alternative behaviors

**Note:* Reinforcement strengthens, punishment weakens. Strictly speaking, punishment cannot be avoided: An angry parent who is motivated to punish his child will administer the punishment in spite of the child's cries, protests, and pleadings. If punishment can be avoided or escaped, then we are dealing with negative reinforcement.

tions punishment is not administered at maximum strength initially. Parents typically begin to correct their child's behavior by gentle verbal prods that may escalate into screams, exile, and eventually spanking, without much success in curbing the unwanted behavior. If punishment is to be used, the most extreme form should be employed at the outset, but the ethical and moral problems involved keep most of us from doing what should be done when we choose to use punishment as a way of changing behavior.

In many instances reinforcement is difficult to identify until after learning takes place. In this sense it is not independent of learning but is inferred from it. We know that food, water, or the cessation of pain are reinforcers for hungry, thirsty, or hurting animals, although we often don't know in advance, especially when we deal with complex human behaviors, what specific reward will reinforce learning. For these instances the work of Premack (1965) has been most useful. Premack notes that reinforcing stimuli (rewards) control responses; that is, food controls eating and water controls drinking in the sense that these responses are highly likely to occur in the presence of these stimuli. In contrast, a response to be reinforced, such as social interaction for a withdrawn child, will occur less frequently in the presence of people than eating will in the presence of food. According to Premack's Principle, the opportunity to engage in higher-probability responses will reinforce lower probability responses. By observing a person's behavior, one can determine which behaviors are most likely to be emitted. Once having determined that these behaviors have a high probability of occurrence, the opportunity to perform any of these preferred behaviors can be employed as reinforcers for wanted behaviors. Thus, the experimenter can gain control over low-probability desired behavior by manipulating the subject's opportunity to perform preferred behaviors, such as permitting a child to watch TV only after homework is done. In this way reinforcers can be dependent on learning and identified in advance.

Kinds of Learning. There are numerous experimental paradigms (or arrangements) employed by psychologists to study the learning process, although for our purposes we shall discuss only three major types: classical conditioning; operant conditioning; and imitation learning, or modeling.

1. *Classical conditioning.* First introduced by Ivan P. Pavlov, the Nobel Prize–winning Russian physiologist, this paradigm involves the pairing of a previously neutral stimulus, *the conditioned stimulus* (CS), with a stimulus called *the unconditioned stimulus* (UCS), which consistently elicits a specific response, called *the unconditioned response* (UCR). The basic experimental paradigm is schematically illustrated in Figure 3–2. Pavlov showed that through successive temporal pairing of the CS (the onset of a light or the sound of a buzzer) with the UCS, which serves as the reinforcer (the sight of meat powder), the CS comes to elicit a specific response of salivation, called *the conditioned response* (CR). Through this simple procedure Pavlov showed that a new stimulus-response connection could be established through learning. He also showed that a CR could be diminished and eventually eliminated from the animal's repertory in the absence of the UCS. The progressive weakening of a CR under these conditions is known as *extinction*, although there are special occasions, referred to as *spontaneous recovery*, when an extinguished CR reappears.

Another principle uncovered by Pavlov, *stimulus generalization*, provides an explanation for our ability to respond appropriately to new stimuli as long as they are similar to familiar ones. Generalization occurs when a similar stimulus, but not one identical to the original, elicits the same response. The closer the similarity to the original stimulus, the more completely will the new stimulus substitute for it. Thus, a child who has been scratched by a Persian cat will avoid not only Persian cats but also other kinds of cats, and to a lesser extent other four-legged furry animals. The effect of generalization can be reduced through a process known as *discrimination*, in which

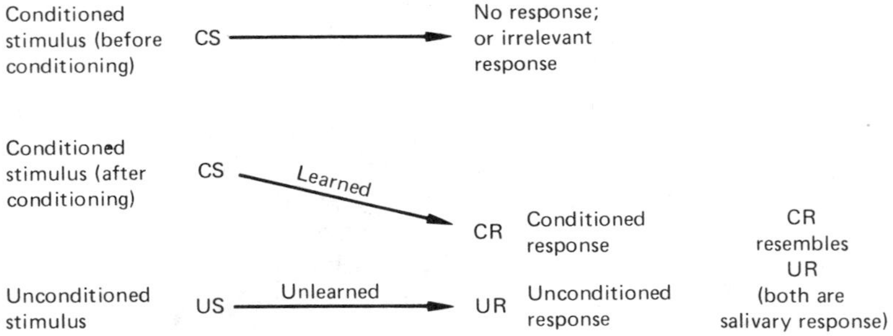

The association between the unconditioned stimulus and the unconditioned response exists at the start of the experiment and does not have to be learned. The association between the conditioned stimulus and the conditioned response is a learned one. It arises through the pairing of the conditioned and unconditioned stimuli followed by the unconditioned response (i.e., reinforcement). The conditioned response resembles the unconditioned one (though they need not be identical).

Figure 3-2 A diagram of classical conditioning. (From *Introduction to Psychology,* 3rd ed., by Ernest R. Hilgard, Copyright © 1962 by Harcourt Brace Jovanovich, Inc. Reprinted with permission.)

the association between a particular CS and a CR is reinforced through conditioning, while the CRs to similar CSs are eliminated through extinction. In this way the organism learns to discriminate stimuli and to respond to the appropriate one.

After a CS acquires the ability to elicit a CR, it may be successfully paired (this time serving as the UCS) with a new CS, which eventually will also elicit the same CR. This *higher-order conditioning* is an important finding; it extends the possibilities of learning through conditioning in our daily lives.

2. *Operant conditioning.* Unlike the sequence of events in classical conditioning, where the reinforcer is paired with the CS and is presented *before* the response is made, operant conditioning employs a sequence where reinforcement is given *after* the organism makes the appropriate response. Because reinforcement is contingent on what the organism does, operant conditioning is sometimes referred to as *instrumental learning* (the response is instrumental in obtaining reinforcement). No such contingency exists in classical conditioning, because the organism is reinforced (the UCS is presented) regardless of what response is given. However, responses that are classically conditioned are considered to be *elicited* and under direct stimulus control in that they are reflexlike and specific to the UCS (such as salivation to food, eyeblink to a puff of air to the eyelid, or leg flexion to an electric shock to the animal's hind limb).

In contrast, operant responses are *emitted* in the sense that they are available in the organism's response repertory, and they appear spontaneously rather than as a response to a specific stimulus. The stimulus situation in this kind of learning is nonspecific, as in an operant chamber (sometimes called a Skinner box, referring to B. F. Skinner, a major contributor to our understanding of operant conditioning) shown in Figure 3–3, where the hungry animal must make a bar-pressing response before it receives food as a reinforcer. In this way the animal's behavior of bar pressing "operates" on the environment to produce the effect of obtaining food.

Operant conditioning can and does occur without the reinforcer following the responses every time (continuous reinforcement). In fact, experimental studies have used different schedules of *intermittent reinforcement,* where reinforcement may occur after a fixed number of nonreinforced responses or at variable time intervals between reinforcements. Many of the principles found with

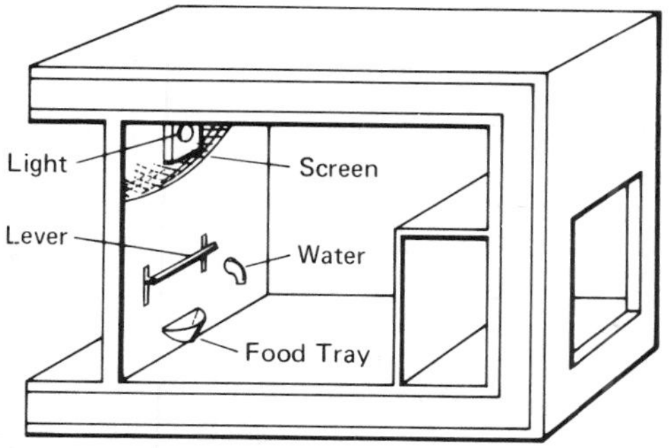

Figure 3–3 The diagram shows the interior arrangement of the box used in operant conditioning of the rat. The space behind the panel at the left contains additional apparatus. This box has been named a "Skinner-box" after its developer. (From Skinner, 1983) (From Hilgard, 1962, p. 259. Reprinted with permission.)

classical conditioning—such as extinction, spontaneous recovery, and generalization—apply equally to operant conditioning. In addition, novel or new responses that are not already available in the organism's repertory can be learned through a procedure known as *shaping*. Initially approximations of the wanted response are reinforced, followed by the reinforcement of responses that are increasingly similar to it, until finally, only the appropriate response is reinforced. (The trainer in a marineland show is likely to use this technique in teaching a porpoise to play basketball or retrieve a ball.)

3. *Imitation learning, or modeling.* Whereas reinforcement plays a central role in the two kinds of learning already discussed, neither reinforcement nor overt practice is necessary in imitation learning. This type of learning takes place by observing another person, or a *model*, make a response or a set of responses. Can you recall putting a piece of white chalk or a candy cigarette up to your lips, taking a deep breath, and then exhaling to imitate the adult cigarette smoker? Especially for the developing child, the opportunities for imitation learning are almost limitless—both in such obvious behaviors as emotional expressions and in more subtle behaviors such as attitudes toward others. The first time a four-year-old vocalizes anger by using a four-letter word, the child probably is imitating someone (probably a family member) who had used the expression earlier and probably often.

The work of Bandura (1969 1969b, 1971) has stimulated interest in modeling. He maintains that exposure to various modeling situations may produce previously unexhibited behavior, inhibit or disinhibit responses, or serve as facilitators for existing responses. The retention and delayed reproduction of modeled behavior requires representational or symbolic mediation (Bandura, Grusec, and Menlove, 1966).

Examples of Learning Theory. The views of Dollard and Miller, Rotter, and Bandura (and their followers) have been selected as illustrations of learning theories that have generated considerable research. Although these approaches deal with the acquisition of both normal and abnormal behaviors, our discussion of them will focus primarily on normal personality development, leaving for Chapter 4 (as we have done with the psychoanalytic view) much of what they and other learning theorists have to say about psychopathology.

1. *Dollard and Miller* (1950). Dollard and Miller introduced one of the earliest learning models of personality, attempting to translate psychoanalytic theory into a system (S-R) largely based on conditioning and drive-reduction postulates. They described four essential components of learning—*cue, response, drive,* and *reinforcement*—in which cues determine the nature of the responses (that is, what response will occur as well as when and where it will take place), and learning consists of the establishment of cue-response connections (S-R). S-R bonds are strengthened when the responses to the cues produce drive-reduction (reinforcement). According to this view, drive is a motivational state that impels or energizes the organism to respond (without specific direction). Any event or response that reduces the strength of a drive is reinforcing, leading to an increased probability that the response will be repeated.

Drives must be present in the organism in order for learning to occur, whether they are primary (innate)—such as hunger, thirst, sex, and pain—or secondary (acquired)—such as fear, anxiety, or the need for money or achievement. Reward or reinforcement is also necessary for the maintenance of an S-R connection. Thus, for learning to take place, the organism must want something (drive), must notice something (cue), and must do something (response) that reduces the strength of the drive (reinforcement).

In this system responses are thought to be arranged in a hierarchy (at first innate) with respect to their probability of occurrence to a particular cue. When a response is reinforced, its probability of recurring increases, and its relative position within the hierarchy changes. Thus, the hierarchy of a child's responses at any given time is a function of previous learning. Responses may be extinguished in the absence of reinforcement, and they may generalize to similar stimuli or to different stimuli through labels or symbols (such as words designating a class of objects). Dollard and Miller also differentiate between instrumental responses and cue-producing responses, suggesting that the former are directly observable responses that accomplish drive reduction, while the latter usually occur within the individual (such as mental thoughts or images) to produce information that may be linked with instrumental responses.

Dollard and Miller's principle of reinforcement replaces Freud's concept of the pleasure principle, while their account of higher mental processes and description of learned drives and skills more clearly amplifies Freud's view of the ego. Conflict plays an important role in their theory, as it did in Freud's, as the underlying basis of neuroses (see Chapter 12). They define conflict as competing or opposing responses that tend to block or inhibit overt behavior (instrumental responses), leaving the drive unsatisfied and creating tensions that continue or increase. Most conflicts involve competition between drives and inhibitory emotional responses such as fear and guilt. Those caught in a conflict are likely to experience the tensions of the unsatisfied drive as well as the distress of the intense fear that prevents the occurrence of instrumental responses that would reduce the drive. Dollard and Miller agree with Freud's emphasis on early childhood experiences, noting that conflicts can and do occur early in life, at a time when the young child is poorly equipped to deal with them. Inhibiting emotions (fear or guilt) often become associated with primary drives, forming the basis of life-long tensions and ensuring the presence of fear or guilt when drives are present and even reduced. For example, the baby who responds to a drive state (such as the discomfort of a soiled diaper) by crying, and who in turn is scolded or verbally reprimanded by a fastidious mother, is not only thwarted in trying to satisfy the tension state but also learns to fear or feel guilty about the gratification of needs. Moreover, Dollard and Miller suggest that conflicts occurring before the child develops language are unconscious (outside the child's awareness and not accessible to the higher mental processes) and much more difficult to treat later on.

2. *Rotter's social learning theory.* (Rotter, Chance, and Phares, 1972). In 1954 Julian Rotter first described his particular approach to social learning, postulating the three basic theoretical concepts of *behavior potential* (B.P.), *expectancy* (E.), and *reinforcement value* (R.V.) to account for human behavior in complex social situations. Rotter arranged these concepts in the seemingly simple equation B.P. = f (E. + R.V.), without making any mathematical assumptions about the relationship between expectancy and reinforcement value (although he favors a multiplicative one). The formula states that the probability of occurrence of a particular behavior in a specific situation (behavior potential) is a function of *both* the subjectively held probability (expectancy) that the behavior in question will be reinforced, and the value of the reinforcer (reinforcement value) to the re-

sponder (Rotter, Chance, and Phares, 1972). A fourth basic concept, the *psychological situation,* implicit in the formula, was used to reflect the stimulus complex to which the organism reacts and to acknowledge the selectivity of reactions to diverse kinds of stimulation.

Rotter thinks of behavior in broad terms as including any response made to a meaningful stimulus that is directly or indirectly measurable. He regards reinforcement (either internal or external) as any event that changes the potential for occurrence of a given behavior, while he thinks of reinforcement value as the relative preference for one of a number of reinforcements to occur if the probability of occurrence for all of them is equal. Rotter defines expectancy as the subjectively held probability that a specific reinforcement or set of reinforcements will occur in a given situation or situations.

The developing child acquires a number of expectancies as he or she tries to satisfy needs. The boy who repeatedly fails to get his father to play with him soon develops a generalized expectancy that he will be rejected by his father. If the boy's need to engage father in play is strong (reinforcement value), he is likely to persist in his efforts, although the expectancy of achieving the goal is low. If, on the other hand, the boy's need for father is reduced (for example, through interactions with another highly valued male figure, such as a teacher or a grandfather), his attempts to gain his father's attention will fall off considerably. However, the boy carries the generalized expectancy into new situations, so that he is likely to expect rejection in a new encounter with an adult male. Only through subsequent interactions with this adult can the generalized expectancy be modified to more closely correspond to the adult's actual behavior, assuming that the reinforcement value of this adult is sufficiently high for the boy to pursue additional encounters.

3. *Bandura's social learning theory.* Combining some innovative principles of imitation learning with the established procedures of operant conditioning, Bandura and Walters introduced a social learning theory that attempted to more adequately account for the acquisition of novel responses in children and adults (Bandura and Walters, 1963). They emphasized the importance of imitation (modeling) in the learning of both deviant and conforming behaviors, and they cited numerous examples where modeling occurs, such as sex-linked roles, vocational roles, child-rearing practices, and learning to perform specific acts such as lacing a shoe. Imitation learning may occur through direct modeling or through symbolic modeling, although the mode of modeling will affect the rate and level of learning. Bandura describes imitation as an active process that is determined by four interrelated subprocesses: attention, retention, motoric reproduction, and incentive and motivation (Bandura, 1969b).

Attention is necessary, since imitation would not be possible if the observer failed to attend to the model or failed to notice the distinctive characteristics of the model's behavior. Retention of the model's behavior or modeling situation is also necessary in order for the child to reproduce it without the continued presence of the external model. The process of motoric reproduction, although complex, must be available in order for the child to actually perform the modeled behavior. Finally, incentive and motivation must be present if overt performance of the modeled sequence is to occur. Here Bandura distinguished between learning and the capacity to reproduce modeled behavior on the one hand, and its activation into overt performance on the other. A youngster may learn a modeled sequence and be capable of reproducing it, yet the child may not perform it either because of negative consequences or because of the absence of incentives. Behavior is maintained through direct reinforcement given to the individual, through vicarious reinforcement given to the model (but not to the observer), or through self-rewards or self-punishments.

Bandura and Walters used data from both

field and laboratory studies to support the influence of modeling and of patterns of reinforcement in the learning of prosocial and deviant aggressive, dependent, and sexual behaviors. For example, they showed that aggressive-punitive parents are likely to produce aggressive children, especially if the parents (models) are highly successful in controlling rewards. Moreover, frustrated children, who under ordinary conditions would respond with aggression, can be taught novel patterns; that is, they would exhibit unaggressive and inhibited behavior after observing the inhibited behavior of a model. Whether the aggressive behavior of the model was rewarded or punished also differentially affected the behavior of the children who were observers. Those who observed aggression being rewarded showed more aggressive behavior than those who observed punishment administered as a result of the model's aggressive behavior.

Research has also shown that positive reinforcement will increase the child's aggressive behavior and that the effects of this reinforcement will transfer to new social situations. As expected, punishment tends to inhibit aggressive responses, although a great deal of punishment-training may lead to aggression directed to objects or persons who are not the punitive agent (displaced aggression). While there is less research evidence available about the effect of reinforcement on dependency and sexual behavior, Bandura and Walters propose that "reinforcement variables modify these classes of responses in much the same manner as they modify aggression" (1963, p. 160).

SUMMARY

This chapter was primarily intended to provide a framework of normal personality development from which developmental psychopathology can be better understood. The basic principles of development, the major variables influencing its course, and the theoretical positions that have generated research were considered.

Human development follows a set of lawful and orderly general principles. Growth and motor development proceed from head to tail (cephalocaudal growth) and from the central axis to the periphery (proximodistal growth) of the human body. Moreover, development progresses from the general to the specific (differentiation) and at different rates at different times (asynchronous growth). All these principles are evident prenatally and postnatally, and they apply to both structure and function. In the area of personality and social development, the child progresses from an undifferentiated and almost totally dependent organism to a distinct and independent self.

Maturation refers both to physical alterations in size and to qualitative changes in tissues or in anatomical and physiological organization. It is extremely important for child development: These physiological transformations make the organism biologically ready to learn new behaviors. Without maturation, no amount of practice or preparation would be sufficient for certain new behaviors to emerge.

Development involves sequential and orderly changes over time in the organism's structure and function. It is affected by many factors. The variables of heredity and temperament, the multidirectional effects of the parent-child interaction, and the influence of the school and of peer relations were considered as they affect later personality development.

The final section of the chapter was devoted to a discussion of the three major theoretical views of personality development: the psychoanalytic approach, the cognitive-developmental approach, and the learning approach. These views were singled out because they have had a great impact on researchers, educators, and other child-care workers, and because collectively they provide a broad but understandable perspective of the developing child. The views of both Freud and Erikson were considered under psychoanalytic theory; those of Piaget and Kohlberg were explored within the cognitive-developmental framework; and those of Dollard and Miller, Rotter, and Bandura were looked at as representative of learning theory. In explicating these views, emphasis was placed on normal development, leaving for later consideration the theoretical underpinnings of abnormal behavior.

REFERENCES

AINSWORTH, M. D. S. *Infancy in Uganda: Infant Care and Growth of Love.* Baltimore, Md.: Johns Hopkins Press, 1967.

AINSWORTH, M. D. S. The Development of Infant-Mother Attachment. In B. M. Caldwell and H. N. Ricciuti (eds.), *Review of Child Development Research,* Vol. 3. Chicago: University of Chicago Press, 1973, pp. 1–94.

AINSWORTH, M. D. S., BELL, S. M., and STRAYTON, D. J. Infant-Mother Attachment and Social Development: Socialization as a Product of Reciprocal Responsiveness to Signals. In M. Richards (ed.), *The Integration of a Child into a Social World.* Cambridge, England: Cambridge University Press, 1974, pp. 99–135.

AINSWORTH, M. D. S., BLEHAR, M. C., WATERS, E., and WALL, S. *Patterns of Attachment: A Psychological Study of the Strange Situation.* Hillsdale, N.J.: Lawrence Erlbaum Associates, 1978.

ANASTASI, A. Heredity, Environment, and the Question of "How?" *Psychological Review,* 1958, *65,* 197–208.

BANDURA, A. Social Learning of Moral Judgments. *Journal of Personality and Social Psychology,* 1969a, *11,* 275–279.

BANDURA, A. *Principles of Behavior Modification.* New York: Holt, Rinehart and Winston, 1969b.

BANDURA, A. *Social Learning Theory.* Morristown, N.J.: General Learning Press, 1971.

BANDURA, A., GRUSEC, J. R., and MENLOVE, F. L. Observational Learning as a Function of Symbolization and Incentive Set. *Child Development,* 1966, *37,* 499–506.

BANDURA, A., and WALTERS, R. H. *Social Learning and Personality Development.* New York: Holt, Rinehart and Winston, 1963.

BELL, R. Q. A Reinterpretation of the Direction of Effects in Studies of Socialization. *Psychological Review,* 1968, *75,* 81–95.

BERKSON, G., and MASON, W. A. Stereotyped Behavior of Chimpanzees: Relation to General Arousal and Alternative Activities. *Perceptual and Motor Skills,* 1964, *19,* 635–652.

BERKSON, G. Social Responses of Animals to Infants with Defects. In M. Lewis and L. A. Rosenblum (eds.), *The Effect of the Infant on Its Caregiver.* New York: John Wiley, 1974, pp. 233–250.

BLEHAR, M. C., LIEBERMAN, A. F., and AINSWORTH, M. D. S., Early Face-to-Face Interaction and Its Relation to Later Infant-Mother Attachment. *Child Development,* 1977, *48,* 182–194.

BOSSARD, J. H., and BOLL, E. S. *The Sociology of Child Development,* 4th ed. New York: Harper and Row, 1966.

BOWLBY, J. Separation Anxiety. *International Journal of Psychoanalysis,* 1960, *41,* 89–113.

BOWLBY, J. *Attachment. Attachment and Loss,* Vol. I. New York: Basic Books, 1969.

Bowlby, J. The Nature of the Child's Tie to His Mother. *International Journal of Psychoanalysis,* 1958, *39,* 350–373.

BOWLBY, J. Separation, Anxiety and Anger. *Attachment and Loss,* Vol. II. New York: Basic Books, 1973.

BOWLBY, J. *Attachment and Loss,* Vol. III. New York: Basic Books, 1980.

BRAZLETON, T. B. *Infants and Mothers: Differences in Development.* New York: Delacorte Press, 1969.

BRAZLETON, T. B., KOSLOWSKI, B., and MAIN, M. The Origins of Reciprocity: The Early Mother-Infant Interaction. In M. Lewis and L. A. Rosenblum (eds.), *The Effect of the Infant on its Caregiver.* New York: John Wiley, 1974, pp. 49–76.

BUSS, A. H., and PLOMIN, R. A *Temperament Theory of Personality Development.* New York: John Wiley, 1975.

CAREY, W. B. A Simplified Method for Measuring Infant Temperament. *Journal of Pediatrics,* 1970, *77,* 188–194.

CAREY, W. B., and MCDEVITT, S. C. Stability and Change in Individual Temperament Diagnoses from Infancy to Early Childhood. *Journal of the American Academy of Child Psychiatry,* 1978, *17,* 331–337.

CARPENTER, G. Mother's Face and the Newborn. In R. Lewin (ed.), *Child Alive.* London: Temple Smith, 1975.

CLARKE-STEWART, K. A. And Daddy Makes Three: The Father's Impact on Mother and Young Child. *Child Development,* 1978, *49,* 466–478.

COHEN, S. *Social and Personality Development in Children.* New York: Macmillan, 1976.

DENNIS, W. *Children of the Creche.* New York: Appleton-Century-Crofts, 1973.

DENNIS, W., and NAJARIAN, P. Infant Development. *Psychological Monographs,* 1957, *71* (436).

DICAPRIO, N. S. *Personality Theories: Guides to Living.* Philadelphia: Saunders, 1974.

DOLLARD, J., and MILLER, N. E. *Personality and Psychotherapy.* New York: McGraw-Hill, 1950.

ERIKSON, E. H. *Childhood and Society,* 2nd ed. New York: W. W. Norton and Co., 1963.

FIELD, T. M. Effects of Early Separation, Interactive Deficits, and Experimental Manipulations on Infant-Mother Face-to-Face Interaction. *Child Development,* 1977, *48,* 763–771.

FLAVELL, H. H. *The Developmental Psychology of Jean Piaget.* Princeton, N.J.: Van Nostrand Reinhold, 1963.

FREUD, S. *Beyond the Pleasure Principle,* trans. C. M. Hubback. London: International Psychoanalytic Press, 1922.

FREUD, S. *The Ego and the Id,* trans. J. Riviere. London: Institute of Psychoanalysis and Hogarth Press, 1957.

FREUD, S. Instincts and Their Vicissitudes, trans. J. Riviere. In *Collected Papers,* 1st ed., Vol. 4. New York: Basic Books, 1959.

FREUD, S. *New Introductory Lectures to Psychoanalysis,* trans. W. J. H. Sprott. New York: W. W. Norton and Co., 1933.

GESELL, A., ILG, F. L., AMES, L. B., and RODELL, J. L. *Infant and Child in the Culture of Today,* rev. ed. New York: Harper and Row, 1974.

HARLOW, H. F. The Heterosexual Affectional System in Monkeys. *American Psychologist,* 1962, *17,* 1–9.

HARLOW, H. F., and HARLOW, M. K. Psychopathology in Monkeys. In H. D. Kimmel (ed.), *Experimental Psychopathology: Recent Research and Theory.* New York: Academic Press, 1971, pp. 203–229.

HARLOW, H., and ZIMMERMAN, R. Affectional Responses in the Infant Monkey. *Science,* 1959, *130,* 421–432.

HARTUP, W. W. Peer Interaction and Social Organization. In P. H. Mussen (ed.), *Carmichael's Manual of Child Psychology,* 3rd ed., Vol. 2. New York: John Wiley, 1970, pp. 361–456.

HARTUP, W. W. Peers, Play, and Pathology: A New Look at the Social Behavior of Children. *Newsletter, Society for Research in Child Development,* Fall 1977, 1–3.

HESS, E. H. Imprinting. *Science,* 1959, *130,* 133–141.

HESS, E. H. "Imprinting" in a Natural Laboratory. *Scientific American,* 1972, *227,* 24–31.

HETHERINGTON, E. M. Girls Without Fathers. *Psychology Today,* 1973, *6*(9), 47–52.

HILGARD, E. R. *Introduction to Psychology,* 3rd ed. New York: Harcourt Brace Jovanovich, 1962.

HOFFMAN, M. Moral Development. In P. Mussen (ed.), *Carmichael's Manual of Child Psychology.* New York: John Wiley, 1970, pp. 261–359.

HOFFMAN, M. L. Father Absence and Conscience Development. *Developmental Psychology,* 1971, *4,* 400–406.

HUNT, J. McV. Psychological Development: Early Experience. *Annual Review of Psychology,* 1979, *30,* 103–143.

HUNT, J. McV., MOHANDESSI, K., GHODSSI, M., and AKIYAMA, M. The Psychological Development of Orphanage-Reared Infants: Interventions with Outcomes (Tehran). *Genetic Psychology Monograph,* 1976, *94,* 177–226.

JACOBS, J., and TEICHER, J. D. Broken Homes and Social Isolation in Attempted Suicides of Adolescents. *International Journal of Social Psychiatry,* 1967, *13,* 139–149.

KAGAN, J. *Psychological Research on the Human Infant: An Evaluative Summary.* New York: William T. Grant Foundation, 1982.

KAGAN, J., KEARSLEY, R. B., and ZELAZO, P. R. *Infancy: Its Place in Human Development.* Cambridge, Mass.: Harvard University Press, 1978.

KAUFMAN, I. C., and ROSENBLUM, L. A. Depression in Infant Monkeys Separated from Their Mothers. *Science,* 1967, *155,* 1030–1031.

KNOPF, I. J., and KIRCHNER, G. L. Differences in the Vigilance Performance of Second-Grade Children as Related to Sex and Achievement. *Child Development,* 1974, *45,* 490–495.

KNOPF, I. J., and MABEL, R. M. Vigilance Performance in Second Graders as a Function of Interstimulus Intervals, Socioeconomic Levels, and Reading. *Merrill-Palmer Quarterly of Behavior and Development,* 1975, *21,* 195–203.

KOHLBERG, L. Stage and Sequence: The Cognitive-Developmental Approach to Socialization. In D. A. Goslin (ed.), *Handbook of Socialization Theory and Research.* Chicago: Rand McNally, 1969, pp. 347–480.

KOHLBERG, L. Moral and Religious Education and the Public Schools: A Developmental View. In T. Sizer (ed.), *Religion and Public Education.* Boston: Houghton Mifflin, 1967, pp. 164–183.

KORNER, A. F. The Effect of the Infant's State, Level of Arousal, Sex, and Ontogenetic Stage on the Caregiver. In M. Lewis and L. A. Rosenblum (eds.), *The Effect of the Infant on its Caregiver.* New York: John Wiley, 1974, pp. 105–120.

LAMB, M. E. (ed.). *The Role of the Father in Child Development.* New York: John Wiley, 1976a.

LAMB, M. E. The Role of the Father: An Overview. In M. E. Lamb (ed.), *The Role of the Father in Child Development.* New York: John Wiley, 1976b, pp. 1–61.

LAMB, M. E. Twelve-Month-Olds and Their Parents: Interaction in a Laboratory Playroom. *Developmental Psychology,* 1976, *12,* 237–244.

LAMB, M. E. Father-Infant and Mother-Infant Interaction in the First Year of Life. *Child Development,* 1977, *48,* 167–181.

LEWIS, M., and ROSENBLUM, L. A. (eds.). *The Effect of the Infant on its Caregiver.* New York: John Wiley, 1974.

LIDZ, T. The Family as the Developmental Setting. In E. J. Anthony and C. Koupernik (eds.), *The Child in His Family,* Vol. 1. New York: Wiley-Interscience, 1970, pp. 19–39.

LIDZ, T., FLECK, S., and CORNELISON, A. *Schizophrenia and the Family.* New York: International Universities Press, 1965.

LINDBURG, D. G. Behavior of Infant Rhesus Monkeys with Thalidomide-Induced Malformations: A Pilot Study. *Psychonomic Science,* 1969, *15,* 55–56.

LORENZ, K. Z. *King Solomon's Ring* (trans. Marjorie Kerr Wilson). New York: Thomas Y. Crowell, 1952.

MACCOBY, E. E., and FELDMAN, S. S. Mother-attachment and Stranger-reactions in the Third Year of Life. *Monographs of the Society for Research in Child Development,* 1972, 37 (1 Serial No. 146).

MADDI, S. R. *Personality Theories: A Comparative Analysis,* rev. ed. Homewood, Ill.: Dorsey Press, 1972.

MAIER, H. *Three Theories of Child Development.* New York: Harper and Row, 1965.

MASON, W. A. *Early Social Deprivation in the Nonhuman Primates.* New York: The Rockefeller University Press and Russell Sage Foundation, 1968.

MINUCHIN, S., ROSMAN, B. L., and BAKER, L. *Psychosomatic Families: Anorexia Nervosa in Context.* Cambridge, Mass.: Harvard University Press, 1978.

MOERK, E. L. Like Father Like Son: Imprisonment of Fathers and the Psychological Adjustment of Sons. *Journal of Youth and Adolescence*, 1973, *2*(4), 303–312.

MUSSEN, P. H., CONGER, J. J., and KAGAN, J. *Child Development and Personality*, 4th ed. New York: Harper and Row, 1974.

NAGEL, E. Determinism and Development. In D. B. Harris (ed.), *The Concept of Development*. Minneapolis: University of Minnesota Press, 1957, pp. 15–24.

NEAL, M. V. The Relationship Between a Regimen of Vestibular Stimulation and the Developmental Behavior of the Premature Infant. Doctoral dissertation, New York University, 1970. *Dissertation Abstracts International*, 1970, *30*(10–A), 4151.

OLTMAN, J. E., and FRIEDMAN, S. Parental Deprivation in Psychiatric Conditions: III. In Personality Disorders and Other Conditions. *Diseases of the Nervous System*, 1967, *28*, 298–303.

PARKE, R. D., and O'LEARY, S. E., Father-Mother-Infant Interaction in the Newborn Period: Some Findings, Some Observations, and Some Unresolved Issues. In K. Riegel and J. Meacham (eds.), *The Developing Individual in a Changing World: Social and Environmental Issues (Vol. 2)*. The Hague: Mouton, 1976, pp. 653–663.

PARKE, R. D., and SAWIN, D. B. Fathering: It's a Major Role. *Psychology Today*, 1977, *11*, 109–113.

PERSSON-BLENNOW, I., and MCNEIL, T. F. A Questionnaire for Measurement of Temperament in Six-Month-Old Infants: Development and Standardization. *Journal of Child Psychology and Psychiatry*, 1979, *20*, 1–13.

PREMACK, D. Reinforcement Theory. In D. Levine (ed.), *Nebraska Symposium on Motivation*. Lincoln, Neb.: University of Nebraska Press, 1965, pp. 123–180.

RADIN, N. The Role of the Father in Cognitive, Academic, and Intellectual Development. In M. E. Lamb (ed.), *The Role of the Father in Child Development*. New York: John Wiley, 1976, pp. 237–276.

RATHOD, N. H., and THOMPSON, I. G. Women Alcoholics. *Quarterly Journal of Studies of Alcohol*, 1971, *32*, 45–52.

RIBBLE, M. Infantile Experience in Relation to Personality Development. In J. McV. Hunt (ed.), *Personality and the Behavior Disorders*. New York: Ronald Press, 1944, pp. 621–651.

RIEGEL, K. F., and MEACHAM, J. A. (eds.). *The Developing Individual in a Changing World: Social and Environmental Issues*, Vol. 2. The Hague: Mouton, 1976.

ROSENBERG, C. M. Determinants of Psychiatric Illness in Young People. *British Journal of Psychiatry*, 1969, *115*, 907–915.

ROSENTHAL, D. *Genetic Theory and Abnormal Behavior*. New York: McGraw-Hill, 1970.

ROTTER, J. B., CHANCE, J. E., and PHARES, E. J. *Applications of a Social Learning Theory of Personality*. New York: Holt, Rinehart and Winston, 1972.

SANTROCK, J. W. Relation of Type and Onset of Father Absence to Cognitive Development. *Child Development*, 1972, *43*, 455–469.

SCHLOTTMAN, R. S., and SEAY, H. Mother-Infant Separation in the Java Monkey (Macaca Irus). *Journal of Comparative and Physiological Psychology*, 1972, *79*(2), 334–340.

SEAY, B., HANSEN, E., and HARLOW, H. Mother-Infant Separation in Monkeys. *Journal of Child Psychology and Psychiatry*, 1962, *3*(3–4), 123–132.

SEAY, B., and HARLOW, H. Maternal Separation in the Rhesus Monkey. *Journal of Nervous and Mental Disease*, 1975, *140*(6), 434–441.

SPENCER-BOOTH, Y., and HINDE, R. A. Effects of Six Days Separation from Mother on 18- to 32-Week Old Rhesus Monkeys. *Animal Behavior*, 1971, *19*(1), 174–191.

SPENCER-BOOTH, Y., and HINDE, R. A. The Effects of Separating Rhesus Monkey Infants from Their Mothers for Six Days. *Journal of Child Psychology and Psychiatry*, 1966, *7*, 179–197.

SPITZ, R. A. Hospitalism: An Inquiry into the Genesis of Psychiatric Conditions in Early Childhood. In O. Fenichel et al. (eds.), *The Psychoanalytic Study of the Child*, Vol. 1. New York: International Universities Press, 1945, pp. 53–64.

SPITZ, R. A., and WOLF, K. M. Anaclitic Depression: An Inquiry into the Genesis of Psychiatric Conditions in Early Childhood. In O. Fenichel et al. (eds.), *The Psychoanalytic Study of the Child*, Vol. II. New York: International Universities Press, 1946, pp. 313–342.

SPITZ, R. A., and COBLINER, W. G. *The First Year of Life*. New York: International Universities Press, 1966.

SROUFE, L. A. Emotional Development in Infancy. In J. D. Osofsky (ed.), *Handbook of Infant Development*. New York: John Wiley, 1978, pp. 462–516.

STONE, L. J., and CHURCH J. *Childhood and Adolescence*, 3rd ed. New York: Random House, 1973.

THOMAS, A., and CHESS, S. *Temperament and Development*. New York: Brunner/Mazel, 1977.

THOMAS, A., CHESS, S., and BIRCH, H. The Origin of Personality. *Scientific American*, 1970, *223*(2), 102–109.

THOMAS, A., CHESS, S., and BIRCH, H. *Temperament and Behavior Disorders in Children*. New York: New York University Press, 1968.

THOMAS, A., and CHESS, S. *The Dynamics of Psychological Development*. New York: Brunner/Mazel, 1980.

TORGERSEN, A. M., and KRINGLEN, E. Genetic Aspects of Temperamental Differences in Infants. *Journal of the American Academy of Child Psychiatry*, 1978, *17*, 433–444.

TUDDENHAM, R. D. Jean Piaget and the World of the Child. *American Psychologist*, 1966, *21*, 207–217.

WEINRAUB, M., and FRANKEL, J. Sex Differences in Parent-Infant Interaction During Free Play, Departure, and Separation. *Child Development*, 1977, *48*, 1240–1249.

WHITEMAN, M., and DEUTSCH, M. Social Disadvantage as Related to Intellective and Language Development. In M. Deutsch, I. Katz, and A. R. Jensen (eds.), *Social Class, Race, and Psychological Development*. New York: Holt, Rinehart and Winston, 1968, pp. 86–114.

WHITMAN, W. *Leaves of Grass*, ed. M. Cowley. New York: Viking, 1959, pp. 138–139.

YEE, A. H. Source and Direction of Causal Influence in Teacher-Pupil Relationships. *Journal of Educational Psychology*, 1968, 59, 275–282.

YOGMAN, M. J., DIXON, J., TRONICK, E., ALS, H., and BRAZELTON, T. B. The Goals and Structure of Face-to-Face Interaction Between Infants and Fathers. Paper presented at the biennial meeting of the Society for Research in Child Development, New Orleans, March 1977.

ZELAZO, P. R., ZELAZO, N. A., and KOLB, S. "Walking" in the Newborn. *Science*, 1972, *176*, 314–315.

4

ETIOLOGICAL MODELS OF PSYCHOPATHOLOGY

PROLOGUE

Eric was a short, obese, somewhat effeminate fourteen-year-old who achieved poorly in school despite his above-average intelligence-test scores. In class he was described as restless, distractible, inattentive, irritating to others, and disinterested. The victim of frequent physical and verbal attacks from his peers, Eric allowed himself to be bullied without ever fighting back. He had no friends and showed no interest in any activity outside of the home. He refused to participate in sports, join clubs, attend parties, or venture out by himself once he returned home from school. Apart from fighting almost endlessly with his seventeen-year-old sister, Eric enjoyed helping his mother cook, clean, or perform any of her routine household chores. He liked to watch TV for hours on end while gorging himself on large quantities of candy, pretzels, potato chips, and soda pop.

Eric's parents were also short and obese. His father owned a small business that required working long hours, which fact he used to justify his reluctance to assume any responsibilities at home. Consequently, he saw his role as financial provider for the family, and his wife's as manager of the home. Eric's mother accepted her position as the key figure in the family with assertiveness, zeal, and an air of self-sacrifice. She was nurturant, indulgent, and overprotective, especially to Eric, whom she treated as "her baby." She protected him from his sister whenever they fought, kept his poor school performance from his father, and denied that Eric was obese or that he had any social or personal problems.

Eric was born prematurely and kept in an incubator for two weeks before he could leave the hospital. He gained weight rapidly, slept well, and seemed to be a healthy and happy infant. He had no serious illnesses or accidents and suffered no brain injury or surgery. His motor and language development were within normal limits. Everything went well until Eric enrolled in school at the age of six. His initial difficulty in separating himself from his mother quickly turned into a full-blown problem. He feigned illness to avoid going to school or created such disturbances in school that his mother had to be called to take him home. After several months of these daily battles, and out of sheer frustration, his mother angrily insisted that he go to school and that he be kept there regardless of his acting-out behaviors. Through the cooperation of the principal and his mother's persistent resolve, Eric's school refusal subsided. However, from that time on his academic performance was consistently below his potential, and his behavior was troublesome to both teachers and peers. After years of denying the problem and hoping for some change, Eric's mother finally sought professional help.

Eric's behavior can be understood in a number of ways, depending on our frame of reference and how we choose to conceptualize the basis of his difficulties. His problem could be attributed to some sort of disease process, to hereditary or environmental forces, or to some combination of both. It might even be blamed on demons, evil spirits, or supernatural influences. Because no single frame of reference can account for the full range of abnormal conditions, and because each conception charts different directions and consequences, we need to examine a sample of currently influential models. Although the models are not completely independent of each other, we have taken the liberty of grouping them into two broad—and somewhat arbitrary—categories (the medical-disease and the environmental models) to facilitate their exposition and understanding.

THE NATURE OF ETIOLOGICAL MODELS

Definition

Etiological models are frames of reference that provide a broad and cohesive way of understanding and explaining abnormal behaviors. While these models make basic etiological assumptions that often have the ring of plausibility, they seldom are completely verified by scientific evidence. Their causal assumptions give rise to different interpretations of the available research data and lead to other assumptions and inferences as the model is elaborated and developed. Usually models generate their own vocabularies and technical terms, reflecting their particular orientation and emphasizing their uniqueness. But as we shall see, the explanations offered by models tend to overlap in varying degrees, sometimes to the extent that they blur the models' boundaries as distinct frames of reference.

Implications and Consequences

While etiological models generate useful research hypotheses, initially they encourage studies designed to either support or challenge the model. However, once a model achieves widespread acceptance, alternative positions become more peripheral and less influential, often regardless of their validity. All too frequently the model may persist because of its plausibility and because its advocates maintain an almost unalterable faith in its premise. This is true with demonology, where proponents continue to believe in supernatural forces despite the absence of scientific support. Contemporary interest in witchcraft, demons, and the occult is reflected in the success of the TV shows *Bewitched* and *Tucker's Witch* as well as in the popularity of books and subsequent movies such as *The Omen*, *The Exorcist*, and *Poltergeist*. It also is evidenced in colloquialisms such as "I don't know what possessed me to do . . . ," or "I'd sell my soul if I could only have . . . ."

The adoption of a model not only increases the resistance to other views but also helps determine who is identified as abnormal, the criteria used, the treatment, the kinds of institutional provisions available, and the public attitude toward those labeled abnormal. An illustration may help demonstrate what an etiological model is and the consequences that follow its adoption.

With recent years frequent reports of unidentified flying objects (UFOs) have strengthened the belief that these objects come from other planets in the solar system, even though no verifiable evidence exists to support this view. In fact, people have always tried to find rational explanations for inexplicable events as a way of understanding themselves and their environment. That many have long believed that other planets are inhabited by some form of life was dramatically illustrated on a Sunday night in 1938 (Halloween), when approximately 1 million people became panic stricken while listening to a radio broadcast of the Mercury Theatre. Orson Wells and a company of players dramatized a version of "The War of the Worlds" by H. G. Wells so realistically that many listeners became terrified and fled from the fictitious invading monsters from Mars (Cantril, 1940).

The popular comic strips "Buck Rogers" and "Flash Gordon," widely syndicated in those days, and more recent TV shows and movies such as *Star Trek, Star Wars, Battlestar Galactica, The Martian Chronicles, E. T. The Extra-terrestrial,* and *Close Encounters of the Third Kind* attest to the public's continued fascination with the idea that other planets are inhabited by some form of life. Science fiction of this sort has gained considerable credibility in the last several decades, having been stimulated and reinforced by almost unbelievable technological advances, especially in space exploration. In addition, international tensions and conflicts have heightened our fears of being attacked by alien forces. Therefore, it is not surprising that many people believe that UFOs are spaceships from other planets.

Let us suppose for a moment that this was the prevalent view in our society. Under these circumstances we could reasonably conjecture certain highly probable consequences. Our country, and perhaps others, would be prompted to construct some sort of identification and warning systems to capture one of the vessels and learn who and what sent it into our world as well as the nature of its scientific technology. Special public funds would be allocated for a detection program and for a rapid increase of our own space exploration efforts. Mobilization of national resources would be associated with a sharp rise in the number of reported sightings of UFOs, along with growing public fears of infiltration. It is even possible to imagine that unexplained deaths, disappearances, epidemics, or mysterious happenings would be attributed to the evil acts of space creatures, particularly if these events were coupled with UFO sightings. If fear turned into panic, military control and even military rule would become more acceptable and, indeed, welcomed by many.

As far-fetched as this UFO fantasy may seem, it does illustrate that once an etiological model achieves widespread acceptance, it determines a number of important events, regardless of the validity of its premise. The model assumed that UFOs were the vehicles of potentially hostile creatures from outer space. The assumption set into motion a number of important actions because of its ring of plausibility and its concurrence with a longstanding popular belief. When augmented by enormous public fear and anxiety, the original premise became increasingly difficult to question and/or test. As acceptance increased, fewer tests of the model occurred, and scientific advances tended to focus on technological improvements within the system. In such cases invariably the development of alternate etiological models is retarded, sometimes for long periods of time.

MEDICAL-DISEASE MODELS

The primary explanatory model of abnormal behavior in our society is medical, complete with its own language, institutions, professional personnel, and types of remediation: Its basic assumption is that some sort of disease is present. Both laypeople and professionals widely use and accept such words as *mental illness, mental health,* and *mental patient* to describe the disorder, the institutional program, and the specific person who manifests abnormal behavior. Moreover, mental patients receive care in mental hospitals or clinics and services from a mental health "team," frequently led by a physician called a psychiatrist. Federal, state, and local governments continue to mount programs to "stamp out mental illness" by allocating funds to build institutions, train personnel, and support research within this medical-disease model. In our society we hospitalize the mentally ill because we consider them "sick" and incapable of caring for themselves, in spite of the fact that no tangible disease has been demonstrated.

The disease model of psychopathology is a broad category incorporating a number of specific causal models. It was adopted from physical medicine, where there is abundant evidence for the etiological link between organic pathology and physical symptoms. The model makes a leap of faith, hoping that similar biophysical causes eventually will be connected to mental and behavioral symptoms. It assumes that the pathological process occurs within the organism and that the cause may be genetic, biochemical, neurophysiological, or intrapsychic in nature.

The Genetic Model

From the time of Darwin and Galton, heredity has been acknowledged as an important determinant of both the biological and the psychological make-up of people. The well-known nature-nurture controversy is as much a part of contemporary psychology as it was of psychology in the days of William James, although we have a better understanding of human genetics today than ever before. With regard to psychopathology, at least two positions have been posited: (1) the view that genetic factors are primary and sometimes exclusive determinants and that they are only minimally and superficially influenced by environmental forces; and (2) the more moderate notion that heredity disposes the person to act in certain ways but that these predispositions can be modified by learning as well as by one's life experiences. However, in order to better understand these models, we need to digress a bit to consider some of the basic elements of genetics and the research methods used to study the role of genetics in psychopathology.

Chromosomes and Genes. Chromosomes are long threadlike bodies that can be seen with the aid of an electron microscope in the nucleus of every human cell. Each cell contains twenty-three pairs, or a total of forty-six chromosomes, that can be studied by special techniques of photographic enlargements. Pictures of pairs of chromosomes are then arranged according to a prescribed order, known as karyotype, by which comparisons can be made with the karyotype of a standardized human cell. In this way chromosomal abnormalities can be identified.

All body cells reproduce by dividing into new cells, with forty-six chromosomes in each. As the cell divides, each chromosome splits lengthwise down the middle, and each half moves to opposite sides of the cell. Later, when the cell divides down the center, each new cell is left with the same forty-six chromosomes that were included in the original cell. This process of body cell division is referred to as *mitosis.* In contrast, germ cells, which produce the sex cells (sperm and ova), undergo a different pattern of division in their final stage, known as *meiosis.* At this point the number of chromosomes in each germ cell is reduced to twenty-three pairs. Thus, one member from each of the twenty-three pairs of chromosomes goes into either the new sperm or egg cell, and each parent contributes an equal number (twenty-three) of chromosomes to the fertilized ovum at the time of conception

Genes are tiny bodies that are presumed to be arranged linearly, by the thousands, in each chromosome. They are thought to be the transmitters of heredity, although for many years little was actually known about them. It was not until 1953 that their biochemical structure and the basis for their action was discovered (Watson and Crick, 1953), and not until 1969 that a single gene was isolated (Shapiro et al., 1969).

It now is known that genes are composed of a complex chemical substance called *deoxyribonucleic acid* (DNA). Each DNA molecule consists of two chains (with five-carbon sugars) twisted around each other in the form of a helix that resembles a spiral ladder. The chains are linked by pairs of chemicals that appear much like rungs of the ladder. In every DNA molecule (see Figure 4-1) there are thousands of these chemical linkages or rungs. DNA has two primary functions: genetic replication from one generation to another and transferring information (genetic code). The coded information in a DNA molecule is transmitted to a single-strand molecule known as *ribonucleic acid* (RNA), which then moves into the cytoplasm of the cell. Acting as a messenger, RNA initiates certain chemical reactions that eventually determine bodily structure and function.

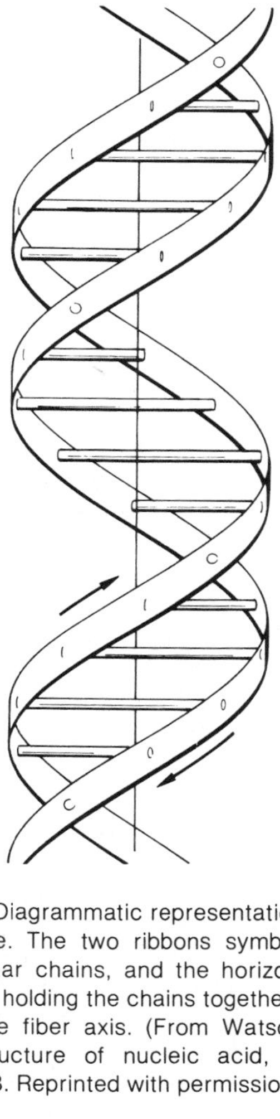

Figure 4-1 Diagrammatic representation of a double DNA molecule. The two ribbons symbolize the two phosphate-sugar chains, and the horizontal rods the pairs of bases holding the chains together. The vertical line marks the fiber axis. (From Watson and Crick, Molecular structure of nucleic acid, *Nature,* 171, 737–738, 1953. Reprinted with permission.)

Mendel's Laws of Genetic Transmission. Almost one hundred years before genes were experimentally confirmed, an Austrian monk named Gregor Mendel hypothesized their existence through long and careful cross-fertilization studies of the garden pea. Working with red-flowering and white-flowering strains of peas, Mendel found that the offspring were the same color in successive generations when plants of the same strain were paired—that is, red with red and white with white. He maintained that this inherited factor (later called a gene) was preserved and passed along unchanged from generation to generation. After he crossbred the two strains (red and white), he noted that the first offspring were red. However, if he mated these offspring, the next generation resulted in an average of three red to one white plant, suggesting that the inherited factor is evident in predictable proportions in crossbreeding.

On the basis of such studies, Mendel

discovered the phenomena of dominance, recessiveness, and intermediate hybrid, and he formulated his now classic principles of genetic transmission. He said that genes were found in pairs, with each gene being either dominant or recessive. A gene is dominant when it determines the characteristic under the control of that pair of genes, whereas it is recessive when the characteristic will only be manifest if both genes of the pair are recessive. An intermediate hybrid refers to a compromise in the characteristic that may result from crossbreeding (a pink offspring from the pairing of red and white).

While much of Mendel's theorizing has been confirmed, geneticists recently have shown that human genetic transmission is more complex and that there are many exceptions to Mendel's principles (Dobzhansky, 1962; Rosenthal, 1970, 1971; Plomin, DeFries, and McClearn, 1980). For many human characteristics genes do not act according to the simple dominant-recessive Mendelian principles. Instead, genes may show *partial dominance* over other genes; *partial penetrance,* in which a dominant gene fails to produce a trait 100 percent of the time as expected; or *polygenic inheritance,* in which complex combinations of gene pairs, rather than just one pair, determine human traits. In spite of the complexity found in human genetics, there are more than one thousand characteristics tentatively identified as single-gene effects in humans (Plomin, DeFries, and McClearn, 1980). For example, a disorder known as Huntington's Chorea, which is characterized by the loss of motor control and progressive deterioration of the central nervous system, is caused by a single dominant gene, whereas Phenylketonuria (PKU), a type of severe mental retardation (see Chapter 11), is caused by a single recessive gene. Interestingly, most mental characteristics which have been identified as inherited through single-gene transmission seem to be deleterious.

Certainly, it would be easier to study the role of inheritance in determining abnormal behavior if human characteristics were as simple in their genetic features as those found by Mendel in his studies of the garden pea. However, heredity does not directly produce psychopathology in the sense that specific genes correspond to specific behavioral abnormalities. Instead, genes should be thought of as providing the basic biologic organization in which psychopathology can develop. Therefore, human genetics must concern itself with observable traits or *phenotypes* (the physical features and behavioral patterns of an individual), and it must be content for the present to make inferences about the genetic trait or *genotype* (the genetic potential of an individual that may produce the trait).

Research Methods

1. *Pedigree method.* Much of the early thinking about the role of heredity in abnormal behavior was stimulated by Darwin's theory of natural selection and by the work of his cousin, Francis Galton, who observed strong hereditary ties between certain distinguished British families and some of the most intellectually outstanding Englishmen of that time. Even more celebrated and influential was Goddard's study of the Kallikak family (Goddard, 1912), which, like Galton's, used the pedigree method to show the role of heredity in determining abnormal behavior. Goddard studied the descendants of Martin Kallikak (a coded name for a soldier in the American Revolutionary War), who fathered children by two women, one mentally retarded and the other intellectually normal. Unwittingly, Kallikak had created a set of circumstances that was of potential scientific merit. The pairing of a normal father with both a normal and a mentally retarded mother made it possible to compare the offspring from both unions with respect to the incidence of mental retardation and other abnormalities. Goddard traced the descendants from each union through successive generations. He found that a large number of descendants of the retarded mother were feebleminded and manifested other forms of abnormal behavior, whereas all the descen-

dants of the normal mother were normal. Goddard used the data to support the conclusion that the observed abnormal behaviors were genetically transmitted by the retarded mother.

More explicitly, the pedigree method consists of tracing the incidence of a trait or phenotype in all family members over several generations in order to make inferences about the genotype and genetic principle involved. It is a naturalistic method, in which data are dependent on selected and infrequent accidents of nature that are too unrepresentative of the general population to warrant firm conclusions. While pedigree studies are of limited value, they have the potential of uncovering tentative relationships that can be further explored by more rigorous and statistically adequate methods.

2. *Family studies.* These studies are intended to determine whether or not a familial resemblance exists for the behaviors in question. The *contingency* or *family-risk method* represents an improvement over pedigree studies, using large samples of relatives of index cases or probands (known carriers of the trait under study) both to assess the degree to which the trait is related to blood ties and to compare the incidence of the trait found in the experimental group with that noted in a sample drawn from the normal population. The greater the relationship between the trait and the closeness of blood ties (parents, siblings, and children as contrasted to uncles, nieces, and cousins), and the higher the incidence of the trait in the family group as compared to normal controls, the more convincing the evidence for genetic transmission. Yet caution must be exercised in drawing causal inferences from family-risk studies; correlation data (the relationship between the incidence of a trait and heredity closeness) merely reflect a relationship between two variables, and not cause and effect. It is quite possible that other unaccounted-for variables, such as the environmental impact of being reared in a psychopathological home, may contribute significantly to the positive correlation obtained. Without proper control for environmental factors, the data from contingency studies cannot be regarded as unequivocal with respect to the influence of heredity on abnormal behavior.

3. *Twin study method.* This method uses the essential ingredients of the contingency method to provide more precise genetic and, potentially, other controls. This approach uses monozygotic (identical) twins who originate from the same fertilized ovum and have the same genotypes of genetic structure, and dizygotic (fraternal) twins who have only half of their genetic structure in common (much like ordinary siblings). A concordance rate is established by computing the percent of cases in which both members of a twin pair manifest the trait in question. When identical twins show a higher concordance rate for the trait than fraternal twins, we have presumptive evidence of a genetic influence. However, this is based on the assumption that identical twins and fraternal twins are exposed to the same environmental conditions, an assumption that has been seriously questioned and weakened with the observation that environmental influences are more similar for identical than for fraternal twins.

Although twin studies have been widely used and offer numerous advantages, the method has been criticized in terms of the reliability of the techniques used to classify zygosity. It has also been questioned with respect to the assumption that the environments of both types of twins are fairly equal (Mittler, 1971). However, recent improvements in technique now allow for the accurate determination of zygosity (Plomin, DeFries, and McClearn, 1980). Moreover, some researchers now note that although monozygotic twins may experience more similar environments than dizygotic twins, the weight of the research evidence indicates that these similarities do not appear to greatly affect behavior. On the basis of an experimental study involving the trait of weight, Fischbein (1978) concluded that twin studies must be carried out longitudinally in order to properly evaluate the heredity-environment interaction. The experiment showed that weight, which is thought to be primarily determined by genetics, appears instead to be the consequence of our heredity-environment interaction, especially for females, when studied longitudinally.

4. Adoption studies. These studies have been used as a control for the effect of environmental factors and have been reviewed favorably as a method of studying genetic influences among humans (Plomin, DeFries, and Loelin, 1977; Plomin, DeFries, and McClearn, 1980). One type of adoption study compares the incidence of a disorder in two groups of children who have been placed in presumably "normal" foster homes but who differ in family genetics with regard to the disorder under study. More specifically, one group of children (the index cases) are the product of one biological parent who evidences the disorder, while the other group (the control cases) come from two biologically "normal" parents. If the incidence of the disorder is more common among the index cases than among the controls, genetic transmission can be inferred. If, however, incidence rates are equal in both groups, the disorder can be attributed to factors other than genetics. While this method recognizes the importance of controlling for environmental influences, it nevertheless provides no certainty that the foster environment is "normal" or that one or more members of the foster family are not affected by some psychological disorder. Related questions raised by adoption studies are: How representative are adoptive parents and adoptees of the population in general? and Is the placement of adoptees with adoptive parents selectively carried out so that the genetic similarity between them is artificially increased (Plomin, DeFries, and Loehlin, 1977; Plomin, DeFries, and McClern, 1980)?

A more sophisticated adoption study method is the *cross-fostering approach.* A group of children from biologically "normal" parents are placed in foster homes in which one or both of the adopted parents are affected by the disorder. They are compared with a group of children placed in "normal" foster homes whose biological parents (at least one) evidence the disorder. The incidence rates of the disorder found in the adoptees for each group are then used to reflect the relative potency of hereditary and environmental factors. This approach greatly reduces the confounding environmental factors found in most other methods.

5. Risk studies. More recently researchers have favored the predictive studies involving the early identification of high-risk children (youngsters who have one biological parent manifesting the disorder but who have not themselves shown signs of the disturbance at the time of initial study) and super high-risk children (those with both biological parents affected by the disorder). This research strategy, which has been especially popular in studying schizophrenia (an adult psychotic condition), includes the longitudinal assessment of the impact of environmental factors on children who are at risk for that disorder (Mednick and McNeill, 1968; Mednick, 1973; Hanson, Gottesman, and Heston, 1976; Erlenmeyer-Kimling, 1976). This approach prospectively examines populations considered to be either high-risk or super high-risk to identify vulnerable persons at an early age in order to determine the characteristics that are associated with the development of the disorder and to establish preventive intervention.

Illustrations of Genetic Models. Having reviewed the basic elements of human genetics and the research strategies that have been used, we can now consider the two primary etiological models: (1) the view that genetic factors are primary and exclusive determinants of abnormal behavior and (2) the position that heredity predisposes the person to act in certain ways, but that these predispositions are modified by learning as well as by one's life experiences.

1. Genetics as primary determinant. Franz Kallmann, a pioneer in and significant contributor to the field of behavioral genetics, argues for the central role of heredity in the development of various forms of abnormal behaviors.

> The importance of genetic elements in the organization of behavior patterns rests on the interdependence of organic structure and psychologic function throughout the life of the individual. There is no behavior without an organism, no organism without a genotype, and no physiologic adaptedness without continuous and integrated gene activity. (1973, p. 25)

While crediting environmental forces as being the coequal of heredity (after conception), Kallmann downplayed its impact by restricting its effect to the limits established by the individual's genetic constitution. Whether it be through genetic transmission, enzymatic control, or mutative effects, it is a person's genetic composition and action that primarily determine whether normal or abnormal behaviors appear.

2. *Heredity-environment interaction.* In contrast to this rather extreme view, there is a middle ground that seems more palatable to most behavioral scientists. One variant suggests that both inheritance and environment play an important explanatory role in accounting for individual differences among people. Morphological differences in the form and structure of the organism's biological systems and in the psychological processes have a substantial hereditary basis.

> Individual infants are endowed with far reaching anatomical distinctiveness; each has a distinctive endocrine system, and a highly distinctive nervous system; a highly distinctive brain. The same distinctiveness carries over into the sensory and biochemical realms, and into their individual psychologies. It is not surprising, therefore, that each individual upon reaching adulthood exhibits a distinctive pattern of likes and dislikes not only with respect to trivialities, but also with respect to what may be regarded as the most important things in life. (Williams, 1973, p. 35)

While Williams calls attention to the importance of genetic factors, he also includes environmental influences. Accordingly, people are born with innate and distinctive biological characteristics that are modified by learning and everyday life experiences in different ways, depending upon their genetic potentialities.

A similar proposition is the view of genetic vulnerability, which holds that psychopathology is manifested when innate biological characteristics interact with noxious environmental variables. Vulnerability is a predisposition that increases the risk of breakdown but doesn't assure its occurrence, unless the person lives in an unpleasant environment that prompts the learning of certain maladaptive behaviors (Mednick, Schulsinger, and Schulsinger, 1975). To a great extent the idea of genetic vulnerability (also psychological and sociological vulnerability) has been bolstered by "risk" research, which encompasses both the predisposing factors that establish the person's adaptation threshold and the stress factors of life experiences that combine with these inherited characteristics to produce abnormal behavioral patterns (Garmezy, 1975).

At this point in time few researchers would deny the importance of the genetic model and its great potential as an explanatory basis of psychopathology. However, the most reasonable position is the one so clearly stated by Zubin:

> We designate a disorder as genetic when we are still ignorant of its environmental parameters and vice versa. In most so-called genetic disorders, the hereditary component is necessary but not sufficient. It is the interaction of both hereditary and environmental factors that is both necessary and sufficient for producing a disorder. (1972, p. 290)

The Biochemical Model

The biochemical and genetic models overlap in the sense that genes supply the blueprint for chemical structure. The overlap is also evident in instances where genes may be responsible for the absence or excess of certain enzymes needed for normal mental functioning; where errors of metabolism are inherited; and where genetic vulnerability provides the basis for biochemical changes underlying abnormal behaviors (Kety, 1973; Zubin, 1969). The biochemical model is substantially derived from and nourished by drug studies.

The search for biochemical agents as the etiological basis of mental illness, especially of schizophrenia, has had a long and elusive history. If virulent germs and toxins can cause physical diseases, it seems only reasonable to suppose that similar factors can cause diseases of the mind. In fact, much of the biochemical research on psychopathology can be characterized as a quest for a psychotoxic agent that is both necessary and sufficient to produce mental illness (Kety, 1969). Moreover, etiological research has tended to follow the various trends in medicine. For example, when bacteria were discovered to be the cause of some diseases, researchers suggested that bacteria in the person's intestinal flora produced a toxin that disrupted the central nervous system (Brill, 1969). When medical attention shifted to viruses, researchers sought a viral cause for mental illness. Similarly, the discovery of hereditary metabolic diseases prompted the search for some deficiency or aberration in biochemical pathways as the cause of abnormal behaviors (Kety, 1969). Recent advances in the fields of biochemistry and neuropharmacology have led to a number of hypotheses concerning possible alterations in the metabolism of certain brain chemicals (neurochemicals). In the last fifteen years considerable attention has focused on a particular group of naturally occurring neurochemical substances that are classified as *monoamines*. The three common substances that have been extensively studied are *serotonin, dopamine,* and *norepinephrine*. In order to understand the possible relationship of these compounds to psychopathological processes, it is necessary to discuss briefly their roles as *neurotransmitters*, or mediators of neural communication, in the central nervous system.

Stages of Neural Transmission. The *neuron* (nerve cell) is the basic functional unit in the central nervous system. Information is transferred in the brain in five stages through the interaction of neurons across *synapses* (spaces between neurons) by chemical substances called *neurotransmitters*—such as dopamine (DA) and norepinephrine (NE) (Julian, 1975). Thus, any increase or decrease in the action of these substances will affect neural communication and, ultimately, behavior. The stages of transmission include (1) synthesis, (2) storage, (3) release, (4) receptor activation, and (5) re-uptake/degradation, which are schematically represented in Figures 4–2 and 4–3. As shown in Figure 4–2, neurotransmitters are manufactured in the *cell body* of the neuron,[1] then transported down through the *axonal processes* and packaged. In the second stage neurotransmitters are stored in the axon *terminal* of the *presynaptic neuron* (the nerve cell which actively releases the neurotransmitter). Third, information is transmitted in a two-step process: (1) the *electrical* stage, in which the information received by the presynaptic neuron (cell 1) is translated into an electrical nerve impulse that is carried down the axon to its terminal; and (2) the *chemical* step, in which the nerve impulse, upon reaching the terminal, causes the release of the neurotransmitter

Figure 4–2 Neuronal communication

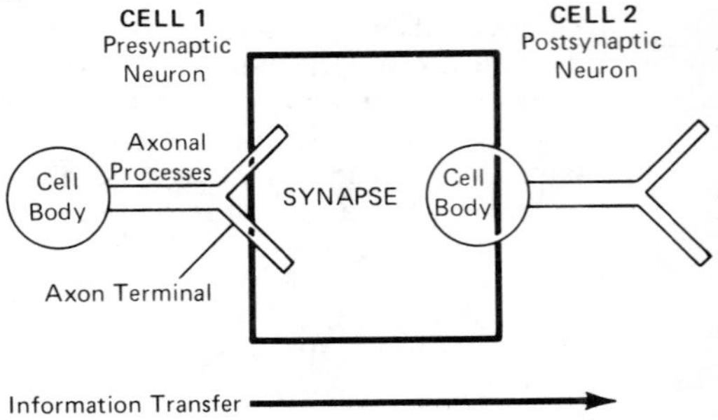

[1] According to Goldfarb and Wilk (1976), much of the synthesis occurs within the presynaptic terminal as well.

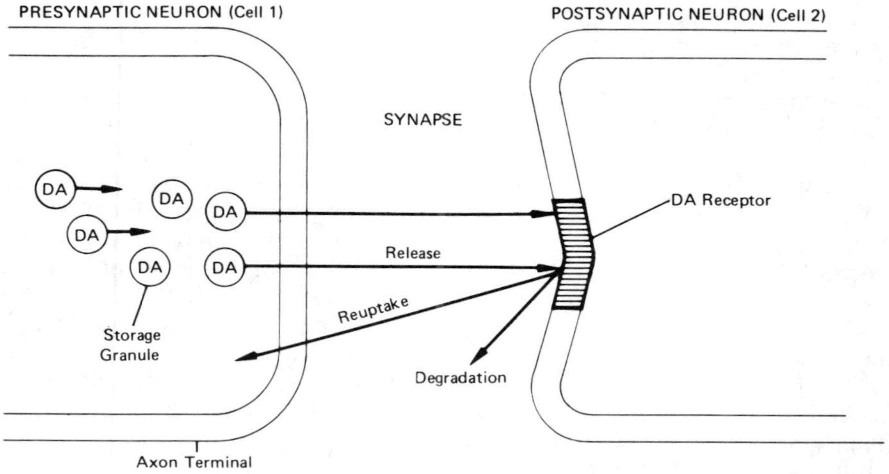

Figure 4-3 Synaptic transmission in the dopaminergic (DA) neuron

into the synaptic cleft and onto an adjacent *postsynaptic* neuron (cell 2, the nerve cell which receives the information in the form of the neurotransmitter) (see Figure 4-3, which is an enlargement of the synaptic area shown in Figure 4-2). In the fourth stage the neurotransmitter activates specific sites called receptors on the postsynaptic neuron, and in the last stage it is released back into the synaptic cleft, where it is either metabolized (degraded) or taken back up into the terminal of the presynaptic cell. This transmission of a biochemical message can activate the second neuron and start the process all over again.

Recent advances in research techniques have made it possible to map pathways of neurons in the brain that are mediated by specific neurotransmitters (DA, NE, and serotonin) and have, therefore, changed our perspective regarding brain and behavior relations (Iversen, 1980). Formerly the focus was on the isolation of particular areas or loci in the brain controlling specific functions (such as eating, sleeping, and aggressive behaviors). The current emphasis is on identifying conduction systems (of neurons) as mediators of behavior.

Illustrations of Biochemical Models. Broadly speaking, the biochemical model posits an imbalance of monoamines in the production of psychopathology. This takes the form of either single-substance hypotheses, where an individual transmitter is said to have elevated or depressed neuronal activity of some sort, or hypotheses positing the interaction of two or more of the monoamines to account for the imbalance (Fredrickson and Richelson, 1979; Iversen, 1980). Biochemical research has progressed primarily along two lines of inquiry: (1) direct measure of neurotransmitter action and metabolism and (2) indirect examination of neurotransmitter action by way of pharmacological evidence. More specifically, direct assessment of neurotransmitter action involves measuring the monoamine or its metabolites in the cerebrospinal fluid, urine, or blood, and counting in post-mortem fluorescent microscopy the neurons and receptors affected by catecholamines (NE and DA). Pharmacological evidence includes the examination of the effects that certain exogenous drugs have on the behavior and neurotransmitter levels of humans with naturally occurring psychopathology, and the investigation of exogenous drug effects on animals and humans with drug-induced psychopathology (Fredrickson and Richelson, 1979; Iverson, 1980). Animals are frequently used in such studies; not only do they present a simplified form of complex human phenomena (Kokkinidis and Anisman, 1980), but the laws governing animal experimentation are far more lenient.

Much of the recent biochemical research has focused on the disorder known as schizophrenia and the so-called "dopamine hypothesis." Essentially, this view suggests that schizophrenia results from an imbalance of DA systems and, specifically, an excess of DA at either the synaptic sites or the receptor sites in the brain. Initially the research noted a clinical resemblance between amphetamine psychosis and paranoid schizophrenia. When used at *high* doses with normal subjects for long periods of time, amphetamine—a central nervous system stimulant drug—produces a behavioral syndrome that mimics schizophrenia. It includes such behaviors as stereotypes, compulsive grooming, scanning, heightened fear and anxiety, suspiciousness, delusions, and hallucinations. In contrast, the administration of amphetamine in *low* doses (too low to produce psychotic symptoms in normals) to schizophrenic subjects exacerbates their symptoms (West 1974; Snyder et al., 1974; Snyder, 1978; Davis, 1974, 1978). It has also been shown that amphetamine acts at the biochemical level by enhancing the release and preventing the reuptake of DA and NE at the central nerve terminals (Groves and Rebec, 1976). These actions serve to increase the amounts of DA and NE in the synapse and thus, ultimately, to raise the activity of these neurotransmitters in the brain. Recent post-mortem studies have confirmed the presence of a neurochemical imbalance in schizophrenic patients and have bolstered the earlier findings from drug studies supporting the DA hypothesis (Bowers, 1980).

Antipsychotic drugs (such as chloropromazine and haloperidol), used either to treat schizophrenics or as antidotes to amphetamine psychosis, act as DA and NE receptor blockers, serving to diminish the effects of these neurotransmitters in the central nervous system (Snyder et al., 1974; Stanley et al., 1980).

Finally, elevated levels of DA or NE metabolites have been found in the urine of schizophrenic patients during periods of severe symptomatology (Arieti and Brody, 1974). Thus, on the basis of the evidence of the biochemical model of amphetamine psychosis, along with pharmacological data strongly suggestive of disordered monoamine metabolism, in the case of schizophrenia there is a strong link between biochemistry and behavior.

Critique of Biochemical Model. While promising, the DA hypothesis has its limitations: It is not yet known in which of the five stages of neural transmission the malfunctioning occurs, or if the feedback or regulatory mechanisms of the DA system may be malfunctioning (Bower, 1980). Langer, Brown, and Docherty, (1981) have suggested that DA receptors are supersensitive in schizophrenics, while Alpert and Friedhoff (1980) argued that there is inadequate support for the DA hypothesis, since the evidence is primarily pharmacologic. Finally, in reviewing biochemical studies of children with autism, childhood schizophrenia, and related developmental disabilities, Ritvo (1977) found no specific biochemical abnormalities consistently identified with these disorders.

The biochemistry of psychopathology is a highly complex and technical area of research, fraught with difficult methodological problems. It often rests on the questionable assumption that descriptive differences in peripheral measures (such as blood levels of monoamines) have etiological implications for underlying central brain mechanisms. Typical studies have attempted to correlate specific symptomatology with biological and/or physiological findings (Boulton, 1971), while ethical considerations have prevented more direct experimental approaches with humans. Research has also been hampered by poor diagnostic agreement about what constitutes a given disorder, and by subject variables that are contaminated by the consequences of mental illness, such as diet, prior treatment, long-term hospitalization, recent stressful experiences, and level of physical activity (Chassen, 1967; Kety, 1960; Klerman, 1971; Selye, 1974; Kety, 1969). In sum, any proposed relationship between biochemical changes in the metabolism of neurotransmitters of the brain and certain observable behaviors or subjective experiences requires, at least at this time, a "leap" from chemistry to behavior without sufficient direct evidence to make the journey valid (Mendels and Frazer, 1974).

Despite these methodological limitations and the promising indication that neurotransmitter aberrations in the central nervous system are associated with some of the more severe forms of abnormal behavior, the search for a causal biochemical factor continues. However, mental disorders are complex psychobiological phenomena that are no more likely to have a single cause than are such traits as weight, personality, and intelligence.

The Neurophysiological Model

This model assumes that the etiology of abnormal behavior resides in brain pathology which is either inherited, congenital, or acquired. It maintains that normal cognitive and behavioral functioning depend on the anatomical and physiological integrity of the brain and that defects, insults, or damage which violates this important organ provides the physical basis for disordered thinking and behavior. To a great extent the model overlaps with both the genetic and the biochemical views, since it acknowledges the crucial role of genetic transmission or aberrations, as well as of metabolic and biochemical changes in affecting brain function. But the neurophysiological model is broader and in some ways more general than the others, including a wider array of etiological agents, such as congenital abnormalities, acquired intrauterine aberrations or diseases, Rh incompatibilities, prenatal effects of X-irradiation and drugs, toxemias of pregnancy, premature births, and traumatic brain insults during or after birth. The relationship between any of these events and the emergence of abnormal behaviors is often correlational and not indicative of cause and effect. Even when a causal link is more evident, knowledge of the specific details bridging the aberrant brain structure or function to behaviors is, as yet, far from complete.

Several research methods have been used to investigate the neurophysiological model. One of the most widely used is the production of *brain lesions* by cooling, radiation, electrolysis, or chemical means and the *ablation* of brain tissue in specific areas to assess its associated behavioral effects. Another investigative device is the *electrical stimulation* of the brain, as illustrated in a study by Smith (1980). In addition, the *electroencephalogram* (EEG), an instrument which records the electrical activity of the brain, has been used by researchers for more than fifty years to try to differentiate mental patients from normals and to obtain information about the reactivity of the central nervous system of disordered persons (Abrams and Taylor, 1979, 1980). Increased technical sophistication also has made it possible to use the EEG to measure cerebral responses evoked (*evoked potential*) by *sensory stimulation* such as flashes of light, electrical shock, or auditory clicks. Unfortunately, the EEG has not proved useful in diagnosing most psychiatric conditions, although it has been effective in identifying epilepsy and organic brain lesions and in diagnosing those hyperactive children who respond well to stimulant medication (Goldstein and Sugarman, 1969; Satterfield, Cantwell, and Satterfield, 1974). Although evoked responses have been found to be associated with various forms of psychopathology, very little specificity in the response characteristics has been evident thus far (Shagass and Straumanis, 1969; Shagass et al., 1980). Another relatively recent technique, known as *contingent negative variation* (CNV) and thought to be associated with attention, has shown differences in children with learning disabilities. It is now being used with psychotic children to reveal the impairment in the central nervous system that underlies mental processes such as attention, expectation, and motivation (Cohen, Offner, and Palmer, 1967; Small, DeMyer, and Milstein, 1971; Beatty, 1975; Bachneff and Engelsmann, 1980). *Peripheral measures* of the autonomic nervous system also have been used to make inferences about mental activity and psychopathology. One such index, skin conductance (GSR), measures the change in skin resistance resulting from alterations in sweat-gland activity, which is thought to indicate arousal or emotionality. Mednick and Schulsinger (1968) investigated skin conductance in children of schizophrenic mothers and found that the GSR is predictive of later schizophrenia, while Zahn (1977) and Venables (1977) reported some early results from an ongoing large-scale longitudinal study of approximately 1,800 three-year-old children living in two representative communities on the island of Mauritius. This differs from earlier high-risk studies, since it includes children of various racial backgrounds. The initial assessment carried out in 1973 included behavioral observations of play and mother-child interactions, and psychophysiological measurements of skin conductance, EEG, and heart rate. Venables found two abnormal GSR groups, hyper- and hypo-responders, and he was able to identify some children who showed the same hyperresponsive pattern of skin conductance as that manifested by high-risk children who later became schizophrenic. Venables concluded that the skin conductance measure reflects the underlying neural impairment of attention found in schizophrenia.

At present, neurophysiological methods used to examine the etiology and course of psychopathology are hindered by problems of diagnostic inaccuracies, confounding effects of institutionalization and medication, and the incomplete understanding of the intricacies of the human brain. Indeed, we probably are less knowledgeable about neurophysiological factors and their implications for abnormal behaviors than we are about the variables associated with either the genetic or biochemical models.

Psychoanalytic Model

Freud's View. Fashioned and modified over forty years by Sigmund Freud, the psychoanalytic model is perhaps the most complete medical model discussed so far. While it has attracted ardent and unshakable supporters as well as severe critics, few would question its profound influence on the fields of personality and psychopathology. In its simplest form Freud's theory rests on two essential assumptions: *psychic determinism* and the *unconscious*.

Freud believed that every human act, whether it is directly observable—such as a smile—or only noted through self-report—such as a fantasy—occurs as a function of prior mental events, and not as a matter of happenstance. Previous events and experiences of the organism (both internal and external) determine all facets of a person's behavior. Therefore, one of Freud's major tasks consisted of trying to find and then eliminate the psychic determinants of abnormal behaviors.

The other cornerstone of psychoanalytic thinking is the unconscious, an inference made early by Freud to explain the thoughts, wishes, memories, information, and experiences of which his neurotic patients were unaware (Hogan, 1976). He proposed that people banish (repress) unpleasant experiences and unacceptable feelings from consciousness because of their threatening nature. In addition, he suggested that the unconscious contains memories of preverbal infantile experience and informally acquired information that are almost impossible to recover. Similar memory difficulties are encountered with repressed (emotionally charged) material, because the person has learned to use a variety of psychological defenses to prevent it from becoming conscious. Freud also proposed another level of accessibility, called the *preconscious*, to account for mental content that was presently unavailable to the person but which could be readily brought into awareness. Recognizing the difficulty in obtaining direct evidence to demonstrate the unconscious (since we can only know about the material after it has been transformed into consciousness), he nevertheless argued for its existence. Freud inferred its presence from behaviors such as slips of the tongue, misplacing of objects, jokes, neurotic symptoms, recurrent patterns that lead to negative consequences, and excessive protestations. He used the technique of free association to uncover unconscious material. He interpreted lateness and missed appointments as signs of unconscious resistance to treatment and focused on the hidden (latent) content of dreams to understand the unconscious.

Anxiety plays a central role in Freud's theoretical view. It may arise from fear of the real dangers in the external world, from fear of punishment for the expression of libidinal drives, and from feelings of guilt about acting in ways that are discrepant with the values of society and the family (Hogan, 1976). Anxiety, therefore, is a tension state determined by external factors that serves both as a danger signal and as a motivator to reduce the tension through such acts as withdrawing from a dangerous situation, inhibiting an unacceptable impulse, or following a moralistic course. The responsibility for coping with anxiety resides with the ego, which utilizes a variety of defense mechanisms for this purpose. All people, both normal and abnormal, use defenses to reduce anxiety, although the abnormal personality relies heavily on a smaller repertoire of defenses than the healthy personality. Table 4–1 presents some of the major defense mechanisms described by Freud.

In his paper, "Neurosis and Psychosis" (Freud, 1959), Freud discussed the relationship between the ego and the id that gives rise to the abnormal behaviors characteristic of neurosis and to the failure of the ego to deal with the environment (the outer world) that results both in the loss of reality and in psychosis. More specifically, he viewed neurosis as arising from the ego's rejection (through repression) of the expression of an instinctual impulse. The repressed impulse persists in seeking expression until it finds an alternate way of gratification (a symptom) which the ego is unable to control. However, this maneuver threatens the integrity of the ego, and the ego fights back against the symptom as it had previously struggled to prevent the expression of the original impulse. This intrapsychic conflict between the ego and the id represents the essential basis of the clinical manifestations of a neurosis. (A more extensive discussion of the psychoanalytic view of neurosis is presented in Chapter 12.)

In contrast, Freud saw psychosis as originating in the ego's inability to cope with the demands of the outside world; instead, the ego creates a world that is less threatening, more gratifying of primitive impulses, but quite removed from reality. In a psychosis reality (the outer world) is replaced by the new world the ego has substituted for it.

Freud's view of human existence is rather pessimistic, full of tension and conflicts that at best can only be temporarily reduced and resolved (Hogan, 1976). Both past and present problems contribute to continued discomfort. Difficulties encountered in handling the various stages of psychosexual development lead to enduring personality traits and to immature and inappropriate sources of libidinal gratification that heighten anxiety and prevent attempts to find more mature ways of obtaining satisfaction. Weak ego development or an excessively strict superego, for example, also increases the likelihood of intrapsychic conflict requiring too much psychic energy to resolve and still deal effectively with reality. Present day-to-day living is hardly possible without tension and intrapsychic conflict. These arise from the tension between the person's demand for instinctual gratification and

Table 4-1 Defense Mechanisms and Their Descriptive Characteristics

Defense	*Description*
Repression:	The process by which the ego bars anxiety-producing memories, ideas, or perceptions from consciousness.
Denial:	Similar to repression, it is the unconscious act of simply denying the existence of painful facts or feelings. Denial enables the individual to avoid anxiety by refusing to admit the truth.
Reaction Formation:	The process by which the ego substitutes actions and feelings directly opposite to those that might be produced by sexual or aggressive impulses. A reaction formation masks threatening feelings.
Displacement:	The transfer of instinctual emotions from one object to another. Displacement permits the release of tensions in a manner that is less anxiety producing; for example, kicking the wall instead of one's mother.
Sublimation:	A way of expressing unacceptable impulses in an acceptable manner. Sublimation channels ego-threatening drives into constructive outlets such as art and science.
Rationalization:	The process of avoiding anxiety by finding justifiable excuses for doing something unacceptable. Rationalization helps the ego maintain self-respect.
Intellectualization:	Similar to rationalization, it is the process of concealing threatening feelings by discussing them in an abstract, intellectual manner.
Projection:	The unconscious act of blaming others or attributing one's faults to others. Projection frees the ego from taking responsibility for faulty actions or traits.
Regression:	The method of dealing with external or internal conflicts by retreating to an immature stage of development. A threatened individual will regress to behaviors that provided comfort in the past.

society's many restrictions and prohibitions against libidinal satisfaction. The struggle between the id (seeking immediate gratification) and the superego (striving for moralistic and ideal behavior) is ever present. Therefore, Freud believed that most people are somewhat neurotic, and that psychological health is not the average state but rather an ideal one.

Critique of the Psychoanalytic Model. Despite the creative and insightful nature of Freud's thinking—and the significant influence his contributions have had, psychoanalytic theory has not enjoyed empirical support. The theory's inclusiveness and generality, along with its substantial number of interacting components, make it impossible to test with the research methods presently available (Sarason, 1966). Apart from the matter of validity, the theory has more recently been criticized on the grounds that Freud was an antifeminist (reflecting the attitude of his time) who viewed women as morally and intellectually inferior to men (Hogan, 1976).

Other Intrapsychic Views. We noted earlier that some of Freud's followers voiced strong opposition to certain aspects of his psychoanalytic theory. Eventually this prompted them to develop positions of their own. Carl Jung, the first to break with Freud, constructed a complicated and somewhat mystical system. In it he rejected Freud's emphasis on sex as the primary source of libidinal energy and instead placed emphasis on the crucial role of the first five years in personality development (Jung, 1964). Jung proposed a distinction between extroverted and introverted personalities and introduced the concept of the collective unconscious which, in addition to the personal unconscious (storehouse of the individual's past experiences—forgotten or repressed), he viewed as a storehouse of innate memories of human beings' shared experiences throughout history. Jung proposed that people everywhere share a common set of instincts as well as universal developmental patterns. He then suggested that this, along with the collective unconscious, accounts for the similarities found among people of different cultures.

Dissatisfied with Freud's attention to sexual instincts and his biological orientation, Alfred Adler stressed environmental and social forces as important determinants of behavior. He conceived of healthy people as social animals who were motivated by the need to meet their communal obligations, to love others, and to fulfill their work objectives. He attributed abnormal behaviors to inferiority feelings (inferiority complexes) that arise from the person's real or imagined failure to achieve self-fulfillment and self-actualization. Harry Stack Sullivan, a more recent dissident, viewed disordered interpersonal relationships as the primary source of internalized anxiety which produced aberrant behaviors. Whatever modifications these or other dissenters introduced, they all assumed (as did Freud) that the etiological origin of abnormal behaviors lies in internal conflicts (intrapsychic) associated with early childhood experiences.

Critique of Medical Models

A major critic of the disease model, especially of the idea that biophysical defects cause mental disorders, has been Thomas Szasz (1960). He argued that a disease of the brain is a defect in the nervous system and should be labeled as such. Moreover, disease should not be used as a causal explanation for problems in living or for the beliefs a person embraces—be they political, religious, or delusional. Szasz noted that the term *mental illness* is widely accepted as referring to deviations from psychosocial, ethical, and legal norms, and that this connotes something quite different from a brain disease. Yet these deviations are claimed (by the model) to be remediable through medical action, an illogical intervention to alleviate problems that are defined by nonmedical criteria. The disease concept of abnormal behaviors, according to Szasz, has outlived its usefulness, and it functions as a myth to obscure the real struggles of human existence and the conflicts in needs, values, and goals that are inherent in day-to-day living.

Other critics of the disease model prefer the concept of *failure of human adaptation* to that of mental illness, since empirical evidence is not readily available to support a disease concept (Draguns and Phillips, 1971). There have been relatively few diseases identified as the basis of abnormal behaviors (general paresis, phenylketonuria, and Tay-Sachs disease are some examples) despite almost a century of searching—and these usually have become part of the field of medicine and are excluded from the domain of psychology. While some of the more extreme and less frequent disorders of childhood may have their etiological origins in biophysical factors, it is doubtful that the disease model will prove fruitful in accounting for or dealing with the vast majority of abnormal behaviors found in children today.

ENVIRONMENTAL MODELS

The basic reason for separately classifying medical-disease models and environmental models rests on the markedly different etiological assumptions made by each. Instead of searching for causal factors within the organism, as the medical views are prone to do, the environmental models focus almost exclusively on *external* variables (sociocultural and psychological) as the primary determinants of abnormal behaviors. However, some environmental models persist in considering aberrant behaviors as diseases in spite of the fact that the analogy of pathogens (between neurophysiological defects and problems in living) is faulty (Szasz, 1960).

Whether they ignore or acknowledge the innate and biological characteristics of the individual, researchers and theorists within the environmental camp believe in the potency of cultural mores, social systems, economic influences, and unique life experiences in shaping (through the learning process) personality patterns. In choosing another etiological orientation, they tend to explore different variables with different investigative tools and designs. They also tend to look for remedial and preventive solutions that are primarily consonant with the causal factors they emphasize. In the section that follows, we shall examine a sample of these views.

Sociocultural Models

These models emphasize the importance of culture and social systems as determinants of abnormal behavior. They study the effect of such global and pervasive variables as the family, race, socioeconomic levels, rural versus urban living, religious affiliation, and cultural attitudes, while often making inferences from correlational data. Sociocultural models tend to oversimplify complicated relationships, since they are prone to deal in broad generalities or in incomplete analysis of specific variables. Yet there are few who would discount their contributions in highlighting the important role played by sociocultural factors in personality development.

The sociological model may approach psychopathology from the perspective of systems theory, where the system is comprised of individuals and various groupings of people. In this scheme of things a system is regarded as an ongoing process which requires equilibrium (a steady state of energy) for its survival. New events that alter and disrupt the equilibrium are stressors which tend to impair the functioning of the system. When this occurs, counteractions—often in the form of new action patterns—result, as a way of restoring equilibrium. These reactions can be adaptive or maladaptive, giving rise to growth or psychopathology (Kaplan, Wilson, and Leighton, 1976). The concept of threshold is important in understanding the role of stress within a system. If changes are either small enough or large and slow enough, the system can adjust easily. However, if changes are sizeable, widespread, simultaneous, or abrupt, the adaptive capacity of the system may be overwhelmed, and the system will function poorly (Kaplan, Wilson, and Leighton, 1976).

One major research paradigm used to study the sociological model is the determination of the incidence and distribution of mental disorders in a population (epidemiological research) to identify high-risk areas and groups as well as the social conditions which are correlated with a high incidence of given disorders. Another paradigm is the cross-cultural approach, in which the relative incidence and specific symptoms of various disorders are compared across cultures. A third research design is the cross-sectional comparison of groups of persons with identifiable disorders or symptoms, both with each other and with normal controls in terms of the existence or frequency of various social factors such as stress, socioeconomic status, and family systems. Finally, a fourth major research approach is the longitudinal analysis of social factors and the occurrence of change in symptoms of psychopathology.

Research areas associated with the sociological model include (1) work on the impact of societal changes (for example, technological change, population increase, demographic movement, war, changes in ideologies and values) on social systems (for example, the total society, the community, or the family); (2) the examination of the differential effects of either social changes or societal demands on specific subgroups (for example, socioeconomic status, race, sex); (3) the analysis of the interaction between the individual and society, with emphasis on the effect of societal demands on the individual's adjustment patterns; and (4) the impact of stressful life events on the person's psychological and physiological functioning.

The majority of studies dealing with the latter area have found modest, but statistically significant, positive relationships between stressful life events and psychopathological symptomatology. For example, self-reported degrees of aggression, paranoid thinking, depression, suicidal thoughts, insomnia, and drinking were reported to be associated with undesirable life events (Vinokur and Selzer, 1975). Later studies have also shown a relationship between undesirable life events and psychological disorder and psychiatric symptoms (Hotaling, Atwell, and Linsky, 1978; Grant et al., 1981).

The most consistently reported relationship is between stressful life events and depression and psychosomatic symptoms. Studies have shown that patients with psychosomatic symptoms have been exposed to a larger number of psychosocial stressors than normal controls (Grant et al., 1981). Paykel (1974) found in a study of 185 depressed patients and matched controls a significant difference between the groups in stressful life events during a six-month period. Depressed patients reported three times as many stressful life events as controls. These included increased arguments with spouse, marital separation, and death of a family member. Cleghorn and Streiner (1979) studied the life experiences of 85 nursing students and found that they verbalized more depressive themes than did controls. Other investigators have also consistently found a significant relationship between depression and stressful life events.

While the sociocultural perspective calls attention to important variables affecting human behavior, it is limited by its almost total emphasis on environmental forces, to the exclusion of the internal characteristics of individuals (biology, motivation, and mental processes) (Hogan, 1976). Also the model explains the mechanisms by which external events result in psychopathology only in theoretical and unempirical terms. One must look to other models (for example, the learning or the neurophysiological models) for explanations of specific behaviors, since this model's data are often correlational and/or accumulated on broad-based variables. For example, while it may be true that some external events result in maladaptive behaviors, the model cannot explain (as can a learning model) how this has occurred (for instance, the external events led to maladaptive behavior because the individual has learned that he or she is "helpless" in the face of certain stressors). It is also true that research based on the sociological model has demonstrated significant relationships between external events and mental health, but in most cases these findings are concerned with symptoms of abnormality and not with symptom clusters characteristic of specific disorders. The major exception to this is depression.

The possibility of new life and increased access to data for the sociocultural models comes from the field of *community mental health*, which bears such diverse and almost indistinguishable labels as community psychiatry, community psychology, social psychiatry, comprehensive mental health, and many others. Its major focus in this country has been on certain socially oriented types of psychiatric and psychological practice. In addition, the techniques and theories of behavioral sciences are now being used to investigate sociocultural variables and to modify the existing body of literature in these areas (Sabshin, 1973).

On the basis of experimental programs developed within several comprehensive mental-health services that markedly reduced their caseload of chronic psychotics, Gruenberg constructed an interesting sociocultural model (Gruenberg, 1973). He used the term *social breakdown syndrome* (S.B.S.) to describe

> the deterioration in social functioning associated with mental disorders which can be prevented both by less harmful responses to those disorders and by changed community attitudes toward the mentally ill and their treatment. (1973, p. 400)

There are seven steps in the development of S.B.S., beginning with the transient experiences everyone encounters—namely, the discrepancy between what one can do and what one is expected to do. Failure to meet these expectations, especially when they persist and the failure is recognized both by self and others, results in self-doubt and increased uncertainty. Actions initiated to meet the demands of the situation are usually unsatisfactory, and the person reacts with feelings of being misunderstood and of anger. These actions and reactions eventually lead to social exclusion or withdrawal, and then to some vague or specific labeling of the person as crazy, mentally ill, or psychotic. The labeling results in admission to the mental hospital, where the environment fosters the further development of S.B.S. Institutionalization brings with it compliance with the hospital's rules, and isolation from family and community. In the end the patient identifies with other patients, and his or her capacity to cope with ordinary social interactions and work tasks deteriorates (from disuse). Gruenberg claims that planned intervention and prevention of S.B.S. can be instituted through knowledge of countermeasures specific to these developing steps.

Learning Models

In contrast to the medical-disease models, the learning approach optimistically views both normal and abnormal behaviors as primarily determined by learning and, in turn, modifiable through the appropriate application of learning principles. Thus, abnormal behaviors are learned maladaptive responses that can be either eliminated or altered in favor of more adaptive ones, without having to make any additional assumption about an underlying disease process. In general, learning models reject both the Freudian notion of the unconscious, with its emphasis on symbolism in psychopathology, and the medical position of disease entities. They prefer the idea that aberrant behavior is either a failure to learn a response or the acquisition of a maladaptive one. Having already described some of the basic principles, paradigms, and theoretical positions of learning (see Chapter 3), we shall in the following discussion illustrate how these principles apply to the formation of abnormal behaviors.

In their effort to translate psychoanalytic theory into learning terms, Dollard and Miller (1950) described a neurosis as originating from an approach-avoidance conflict—that is, a conflict between two or more strong drives that creates internal tension and produces responses that are incompatible. A conflict of this sort is illustrated by a person's strong need for sexual expression with a person of the opposite sex (approach), on the one hand, which is opposed by the person's fear of making overt sexual advances (avoidance), on the other. During development children are required to learn socially acceptable outlets for their drives, especially those that are associated with eating, toilet training, and sexual and aggressive behaviors. As children seek expression of these drives, they are likely, at least on some occasions, to be punished for the responses; for example, aggressive behavior toward parents likely will mean punishment by parents. Dollard and Miller have shown in animal studies that punishment leads to the emergence of fear as a learned drive. Moreover, fear can be conditioned as a response to a previously neutral stimulus, which then takes on the properties of a drive stimulus. In this way it is possible for the same stimulus to elicit both the original drive and the learned fear drive.

In neurosis the individual is unable to reduce the tension of the conflicting drive but continually seeks responses that tend to reduce his or her suffering (subjective state of *misery*). Any response (symptom) that successfully reduces neurotic misery is reinforced, although it is not likely to solve the original conflict. Each successive reinforcement of the symptom increases the probability of its occurrence and strengthens it as a learned habit. For example, Dollard and Miller considered phobias (intense and persistent fears) as learned avoidance responses that are reinforced by the reduction in the strength of the fear drive. Although the original stimulus of the fear is frequently obscured in childhood conflicts over sexual and aggressive impulses (à la Freud), the intense fears transfer to new cues through stimulus generalization, higher-order conditioning, and response-mediated generalization. Phobias persist because those affected usually manage to avoid the phobic situation with behaviors (withdrawal and avoidance) that reduce the fear but do not resolve the basic and underlying conflict (intrapsychic conflict).

While Dollard and Miller's innovative effort brought new respectability to psychoanalytic theory within the camp of empirically minded psychologists, as well as admiration from clinically oriented psychologists for making learning theory relevant to "real" human problems, it also stimulated its share of criticisms. Some observers stated that the theory considered an extremely limited range of animal and human behaviors and that it treated clinical phenomena with no more rigor than did psychoanalysts. In addition, it was charged that the theory's exclusive reliance on drive reduction as a reward mechanism for learning fails to deal effectively with the complexities of most clinical phenomena (Rapaport, 1953). Nevertheless, Dollard and Miller's theoretical model marked the first in a series of subsequent learning formulations attempting to account for and understand human social behavior (including maladaptive behaviors).

According to the social learning view of Julian Rotter, abnormal behaviors are "learned" and "thus maintained because the individual has a relatively high expectancy that such behavior will lead to a reinforcement of value (or avoid or reduce some potential punishment)" (Rotter, Chance, and Phares, 1972, p. 441). Moreover, most abnormal behaviors can be thought of as avoidance behaviors attributable to expectations of punishment or low expectancies of achieving important reinforcements. For example, if a youngster places a high value on athletic success, but expects that he or she will not achieve this end, the youngster is likely to employ avoidance behaviors or symptoms such as withdrawal from peer relations (especially those involving opportunities for athletics). The avoidant behavior eventually leads to the youngster's failure to develop competency, which, in turn, tends to facilitate the development of other deviant behaviors. Withdrawal behavior precludes practice opportunities that could increase the youngster's athletic competence and, instead, may lead to excessive and unrealistic fantasy activities about his or her extraordinary athletic prowess.

Another possible consequence of high need value may result in the person distorting reality or failing to make appropriate discriminations among social situations. If a need is excessive, every occasion becomes an opportunity for its attainment, without regard for the propriety of the situation. Under these circumstances behavior is likely to be inappropriate and to elicit negative reactions from others, which, in the end, will lower the person's expectations about receiving the rewards.

With regard to other aspects of abnormal behavior, Rotter's theory "substitutes either low expectancy for success or high expectancy for failure" (Rotter, Chance, and Phares, 1972, p. 447) for what is clinically considered anxiety. In addition, it rejects the dichotomy between neurosis and psychosis implied in the Kraepelinian classification system, and it attempts to deal specifically with certain forms of abnormal behavior, such as obsessions, compulsions, depressive reactions, and hypochondriacal behavior (frequent somatic complaints).

Bandura's social learning view relies heavily on instrumental conditioning and imitation learning in arguing that abnormal response patterns are learned and maintained by a faulty conditioning history (Bandura, 1968, pp. 293–344). In some instances the faulty prior learning involves a "behavioral deficit" in which there is a failure to acquire adequate responses that would enable the person to cope effectively with the demands of the environment. The failure to learn the requisite skills arises from inadequate modeling and reinforcements and may lead to further adverse effects; insufficient rewards are given for the skills the individual does possess, while at the same time the behavioral deficit is negatively reinforced. Bandura suggests that the low levels of responsiveness of psychotic children and adults are manifestations resulting from behavioral deficits of this sort.

Deviant response patterns also may be attributable to the failure "to respond discriminately to important stimuli" (Bandura, 1968, p. 299) in people who possess "normal" responses in their repertoires. In the course of development, children learn to respond differentially to stimuli in terms of the consequences associated with particular stimuli. For example, they may consistently receive approval (reinforcement) for shedding their clothes at bath or bedtime and consistently receive disapproval (punishment) for undressing at other times. By introducing the discriminable stimuli and the different schedules of reinforcement, the behavior of undressing is brought under stimulus control. Through faulty training or a disruption of previously acquired discriminative responses, behaviors that are inappropriate to the situation may occur. Deviant (abnormal) responses of this sort are evident in psychotic individuals in the form of inappropriate or impoverished affect, delusions, and cognitive dysfunction.

In addition, deviant behaviors may arise when inappropriate stimuli acquire the capacity to produce intense emotional responses. "If a formerly ineffective conditioned stimulus occurs in conjunction with another stimulus which is capable of eliciting unpleasant autonomic responses, the former stimulus itself gradually acquires the power to evoke the same aversive emotional response pattern" (Bandura, 1968, p. 303). These deviant behaviors are manifested as somatic complaints and in psychophysiological disorders (see Chapter 12) such as asthma, ulcers, and hypertension. In addition, conditioned emotional reactions of phobia and other avoidance patterns are acquired in this way.

Bandura also described the faulty prior learning of either defective or inappropriate incentive systems as a condition that results in abnormal behaviors. In this instance, he referred to pleasurable but culturally unacceptable stimuli (sexual, alcohol, drugs), which in themselves function as strong positive reinforcers, and become associated with behaviors considered deviant in our culture, such as homosexuality, transvestism (a male dressing up as a female), or alcoholism. He cites the example of transvestism in a young boy who received the approval of mother, grandmother, and neighbor whenever he dressed up as a girl. In these illustrations, the previous positive reinforcement accounts for the acquisition and maintenance of sexually deviant response patterns.

In addition, Bandura discusses how aversive behaviors such as aggression are acquired, since these behaviors often are thought of as symptomatic of a personality aberration in our society. Experimental studies have shown that aggressive, punitive parents are likely to produce aggressive children, especially if the parents (models) are highly successful in controlling rewards (Bandura and Walters, 1963). Moreover, frustrated children, who under ordinary conditions respond with aggression, can be taught novel patterns in which they exhibit unaggressive and inhibited behavior after they observe the inhibited behavior of a model. Also, whether the aggressive behavior of the model is rewarded or punished can affect the behavior of the observers. Children who observe aggression rewarded are more aggressive than those who observe aggression punished.

Research has also shown that positive reinforcement increases the child's aggressive behavior and that the effects of this reinforcement transfer to new social situations. As expected, punishment tends to inhibit aggressive responses, although a great deal of punishment training may lead to aggression directed toward objects or persons who are not the punitive agent (displaced aggression). While less research evidence is available about the effect of reinforcement on dependency and sexual behavior, Bandura and Walters proposed that "reinforcement variables modify these classes of responses in much the same manner as they modify aggression" (Bandura and Walters, 1963, p. 160).

Humanistic Models

Falling somewhere between the global concepts of sociocultural models and the more specific and mechanistic postulates of learning theories are a group of views known as *humanism* and *existentialism*. They are environmental positions because they stress experience and the individual's reaction both to self and to the external world as essential determinants of behaviors. Instead of expressing concern with either the exploration of the person's unconscious (intrapsychic models) or the recounting and restructuring of past learning experiences (learning models), the humanistic approach tries to understand the whole person in terms of present functioning and capabilities for the future. Both humanism and existentialism are deeply rooted in philosophical ideas which regard human nature in a positive light and which respect the worth of all persons as well as their right to make choices about how they will live their lives.

According to Abraham Maslow, one of the pioneers of the humanistic movement,

> Man demonstrates in his own nature a pressure toward fuller and fuller Being, more and more perfect actualization of his humanness in exactly the same naturalistic, scientific sense that an acorn may be said to be "pressing toward" being an oak tree, or that a tiger can be observed to "push forward" being tigerish, or a horse toward being equine. Man is ultimately not molded or shaped into humanness, or taught to be human. The role of the environment is ultimately to permit him to help him to actualize his own potentialities, not its potentialities. The environment does not give him potentialities and capacities; he has them in inchoate or embryonic form, just exactly as he has embryonic arms and legs. And creativeness, spontaneity, selfhood, authenticity, caring for others, being able to love, yearning for truth are embryonic potentialities belonging to his species-membership just as much as are his arms and legs and brain and eyes. (1968, pp. 160–161)

For Maslow every person has "an essential biological inner nature" which is, within limits, unchangeable, and which is partly unique and partly common to the species. The needs, emotions, and human capacities of this inner nature are either intrinsically neutral or "good," suggesting that people are not innately "evil" but manifest such behaviors as destructiveness, cruelty, and sadism as violent reactions to the frustration of their inner core. Maslow viewed the inner nature as weak and delicate, readily denied and overcome by habit and external forces, although it persists in striving first for survival and then for actualization (self-fulfillment). Thus, Maslow emphasized the presence in all people of inherent tendencies for survival and for actualization, which—if not thwarted or suppressed—lead to both the maintenance and the enhancement of life (Maddi, 1972). Needs associated with the survival tendency include physiological demands, safety, belongingness and love, and esteem, while the actualizing tendency incorporates the need for self-actualization and for cognitive understanding.

According to Maslow, when either of these tendencies is blocked, the person becomes "sick" or evidences maladaptive behaviors (Maslow, 1968). For example, in the course of living, people continually face the conflict between the defensive forces of survival and the forces of growth. People progress and move foward when the anxieties of safety are less than the "delights" of growth, and conversely, they regress or remain static when the anxieties of growth are greater than the "delights" of safety. Healthy people are those who are free to choose growth, while those who are "sick" are thwarted by the fears and anxieties of survival. Thus, the needs associated with the survival tendency (including safety needs) must be gratified before the growth needs can be met and before the person can feel safe enough to take the next step. For example, the young child can only venture forth to explore the surrounding environment when the mother-child relationship is secure. When it is impaired and uncertain, the child will cling to mother and be unable to take the growth step of freely interacting with the environment. Moreover, the maladaptive responses can best be treated when the therapist respects the fears of the "sick" person and provides the security and safety needed for the person to be bold enough to choose growth.

In a similar vein Carl Rogers, one of the earliest and best-known phenomenologists, conceptualized self-actualization as the core tendency of human personality (Maddi, 1972; Rogers, 1959, 1974). By this he meant that every person is born with inherent potentialities and that life experiences are perceived by the individual as either favorable or unfavorable in terms of self-actualization (the realization of these potentialities). The developing child gains a conscious sense of self by learning that it is highly desirable to be favorably regarded by parents, relatives, and others (the need for positive regard). The need for positive regard is internalized in the merging self through approval and disapproval received from others, while the child develops another important need, the need for positive self-regard.

Under unusual circumstances a person may receive unconditional approval from others and thus develop unconditional positive self-regard. This results in an ideal person who experiences no discrepancy between his or her self and potentialities. Less ideal, but more the rule, is the probability that the individual will receive conditional positive regard. The person will then develop conditions of worth that give rise to anxiety about the occurrence of unworthy behaviors. Defenses (much like those noted by Freud) are constructed to deal with the anxiety and to ward off threats to the self. However, when defenses are inadequate, anxiety increases and abnormal behaviors appear.

> So, for Rogers, the way of actualizing your potentialities in the fullest manner is to possess a self-concept that does not include conditions of worth, and therefore precipitates no defenses. It follows from this that you will (1) respect and value all manifestations of yourself, (2) be conscious of virtually all there is to know about yourself, and (3) be flexible and open to new experiences. In this way, the work of becoming what it is in your nature to be can go forward undisturbed. You will be what Rogers calls a *fully functioning* person. (Maddi, 1972, p. 97)

Perhaps even more well known is Rogers's client-centered therapy, in which the therapist provides unconditional positive regard in a warm, reflective, and empathic manner to bolster the client's self-regard. This acceptance presumably decreases the client's need for defenses and facilitates acceptance of previously denied feelings and experiences. With increased freedom to accept their feelings, clients can perceive themselves and others more realistically, and they can form self-perceptions that are more congruent with their potentialities.

The existential view holds that human understanding cannot come from approaches that focus on the specific mechanisms of learning, on the unconscious, or on drive states (May, 1961; Maddi, 1972; Hogan, 1976). To do so is to talk about abstractions that lose sight of the existing human being and to give precedence to mechanisms rather than people. Existentialism is an attitude and an approach to humans instead of a theory or a special ideological school. It stresses the person's "unique pattern of potentialities" and his or her relationship to them as the person struggles to deal with "being" and "nonbeing." Accordingly, the major task that each person must deal with is to become self-aware or to seriously question one's identity and the purpose of one's life. In this process the person discovers that human existence is purposeless, which gives rise to *Angst*, a subjective state of dread or anxiety over the possibility of nonbeing, that also serves as a basic source of motivation. A second motivational force, the *will to power*, permits the person to deal with Angst through knowledge of oneself. However, the anxiety that comes from the potential of nonbeing may, at times, be too high for some people to tolerate and too intense to prompt self-awareness. Therefore, many people choose self-deception; the more they seek self-knowledge, the more they heightened the dread of nonbeing (Hogan, 1976).

To achieve self-awareness and an authentic (honest and true) being, people must accept the discomfort of nonbeing and find the courage to persist by recognizing that they have the power to create their own meaning and existence. This sense of human dignity not only recognizes and accepts the limits set by biological and social forces but also permits the individual to examine the remaining possibilities for freedom of action. People who see no options or alternatives (freedom) in their life circumstances (such as feeling trapped in a bad marriage) confuse the actual limits of the situation with the possible degrees of freedom that may be available. These reactions form the basis of psychopathology in which the individual blames others, since he or she is unwilling to assume the responsibility for, or take the necessary action that would further, his or her authentic being. In this sense psychopathology involves cowardice, self-deception, and a refusal to use one's wits (higher mental processes of symbolization, imagination, and judgment) to construct alternatives in situations where freedom of action was unnecessarily surrendered.

In general, humanistic models, while popular with clinical practitioners, have incurred their share of criticisms on the grounds that they are vague and incomplete (for example, they provide few—if any—specifics with regard to the nature of inherent potentialities). They are also charged with proposing formulations that are unsystematic and unintegrated and with making naive and unverified assumptions. The idea "that man would be a constructive, rational, and socially conscious being, were he free of the malevolent distortions of society" (Millon, 1973, p. 267) is based on unsupported and perhaps romantic assumptions about the nature of man, on which Millon makes the following cryptic comment: "There is something as banal as the proverbialism of a fortune cookie in the suggestion 'be thyself.' Conceiving man's emotional disorders as a failure to 'be thyself' seems equally naive and banal" (Millon, 1973, p. 267).

Critique of Environmental Models

Unlike the medical models—which assume abnormal behaviors are disease entities caused by some sort of biological pathogen—the environmental models make no assumption about an underlying disease process. Instead, these models represent a diverse set of views that primarily emphasize environmental forces (factors external to the organism) as determinants of aberrant response patterns. To the extent that this is true, they can be criticized both for not adequately considering the internal state of the organism and its influence on behavior and for viewing people as passive, without any real impact on the environment. Both the sociological and humanistic models involve variables that are vague and too broad to be either predictive or testable, and neither model sufficiently attends to developmental principles or processes. The learning views tend to be mechanistic, molecular, and too often generalized from data generated from animal studies. Their attention to childhood usually takes the form of retrospective reinforcement histories which cannot be reconstructed with either the accuracy or precision needed to test their formulations. In their focus on behavior (both normal and abnormal), they tend to disregard the internal processes of the organism and to discount (and possibly oversimplify) the psychopathological process itself. Indeed, as we shall see in our discussion of childhood psychosis (Chapter 8), symptoms can be modified or even eliminated without essentially altering the abnormal condition.

Although the environmental models can be additionally criticized for using correlational data to make cause-and-effect interpretations, these models (like the medical models) have not only significantly contributed to our understanding and treatment of childhood disorders but have also kept open alternative and promising avenues for investigating the etiological factors involved in psychopathology. Since it is doubtful that any single approach will provide the data which will enable us to understand this very complex field, there is every reason to encourage the further development of these and other approaches, notwithstanding their methodological limitations.

SUMMARY

Etiological models are frames of reference which provide a broad but cohesive way of understanding and explaining abnormal behaviors. They make causal assumptions which tend to persist in the absence of corroborative evidence. Adoption of a model increases the resistance to alternative views and sets into motion important consequences.

Selected positions within two broad categories of models, *medical-disease* and *environmental,* were discussed. The medical-disease models were described as a group of views which assumed that abnormal behaviors were disease entities and that the pathological process occurred within the organism. Under this rubric genetic, biochemical, neurophysiological, and intrapsychic models were considered.

Although all genetic views acknowledge the importance of heredity as a determinant of both the biological and the psychological make-up of people, they vary in their emphasis on the relative contributions of heredity versus those of environment. One extreme holds that genetic factors are the primary determinants of abnormal behaviors. A more moderate view proposes that heredity disposes the person to act in certain ways, but that these predispositions can be modified by learning as well as by one's life experiences. A variant of this is the view of genetic vulnerability, which posits vulnerability as a predisposition that increases the risk of breakdown.

Stimulated by the varous etiological trends in physical medicine, the biochemical model has focused on the search for a psychotoxic agent causing mental illness. Recent advances in research techniques have made it possible to map pathways in the brain mediated by specific neurotransmitters and to formulate hypotheses concerning the possible alterations in the metabolism of the monoamines in the central nervous system.

The neurophysiological model assumes that the etiology of abnormal behaviors resides in brain pathology which is inherited, congenital, or acquired.

Psychoanalysis and the intrapsychic views of Jung and Adler, who broke with Freud, were also discussed. An overall critique of the medical model was presented, in which the disease concept was faulted as illogical, erroneous, and unsupported by empirical evidence.

The environmental models focus almost exclusively on external variables as primary determinants of abnormal behaviors. Sociocultural models deal with the global variables of social systems and culture as they relate to abnormal behaviors. Such models tend to oversimplify complicated relationships.

The discussion of learning models included Dollard and Miller's translation of psychoanalytic theory into a learning system based on classical conditioning and drive-reduction postulates. Rotter's and Bandura's approaches to social learning and the formation of abnormal behaviors were described. Abnormal behaviors are construed by Rotter as avoidance behaviors attributable to expectations of punishment or to low expectancies of achieving important reinforcements. The avoidance behavior eventually leads to the failure to develop competency, which, in turn, often facilitates the development of other deviant behaviors. Bandura's social learning theory emphasizes operant conditioning and imitation learning in the acquisition of both deviant and conforming behaviors. A number of conditions that give rise to the faulty conditioning history associated with aberrant behaviors were discussed. The theory also used data from both field and laboratory studies to show the influence of modeling and patterns of reinforcement in the learning of aggressive, dependent, and sexual behaviors.

Finally, the humanistic models (self-actualization and existential) were presented. These are environmental positions stressing experience and the individual's reaction both to self and to the external world as essential determinants of behavior. The humanistic approach focuses on the whole person in terms of present and future capabilities. Both humanism and existentialism are approaches to humans rather than theories or ideological schools.

A critique of the environmental models was also included.

EPILOGUE

The evaluation revealed that Eric's adjustment problems were rooted in early but long-standing faulty parent-child relationships, rather than possession, brain pathology, or genetic transmission. His mother's overprotectiveness and her strong inclination to treat Eric as a "baby" had been evident since his birth, possibly because she experienced a mixture of inadequacy, anger, and guilt feelings over his premature birth and/or because she viewed Eric as a substitute for her absent husband. Whatever her reasons, Eric became the beneficiary of her extra maternal care and attention. However, in order to obtain more gratification, she coerced him to behave in ways that would comply with her wishes. She helped to retard his social maturity by encouraging him to share in her household chores, and she literally reduced his chances of success in sports and in relating to his peers by overfeeding him. Eric, in turn, read the contingencies well and behaved accordingly. He preferred being at home where he could be close to his mother and be fed and nurtured by her. Going to school only deprived him of maternal relations and gratification, an event that neither Eric nor his mother really wanted. His father's dedication to his business, and his almost total abdication of parental responsibilities and involvement, presented a distant, disinterested, and ineffective male model for Eric. Like his father, Eric was passive and unassertive because he had learned that he would be indulged by his mother (and perhaps others) if he permitted her to be dominant and overbearing. Eric and his parents (his sister went off to college) became involved in weekly family therapy sessions that were intended to increase everyone's understanding of his or her role as well as of their contributions to Eric's problems. The intention was to create a climate that would facilitate changes. Eric's mother and father had to understand how Eric was both a victim and a participant in their marital conflicts. They needed to resolve their problems with each other and to deal with Eric in ways that would promote his personal growth. At the same time Eric needed to find gratification in activities outside of the home and away from his mother, and to shift his identification toward his father.

After four months of therapy some improvements were noted. The father became more active in family matters and spent more time with his wife and Eric. He drew Eric into the business, which provided Eric with success experiences outside of the home as well as with a male model whom he could emulate. The father's reentry into the family eased the mother's loneliness and decreased her need to hold onto Eric. Eric began to lose weight, to feel better about himself, and to slowly establish relationships with peers. No essential change in this brief period was evident in his academic performance.

REFERENCES

ABRAMS, R., and TAYLOR, M. A. Differential EEG Patterns in Affective Disorder and Schizophrenia. *Archives of General Psychiatry*, 1979, 36, 1355–1358.

ABRAMS, R., and TAYLOR, M. A. Psychopathology and the Electroencephalogram. *Biological Psychiatry*, 1980, *15*, 871–878.

ALPERT, M., and FRIEDHOFF, A. J. An Un-dopamine Hypothesis of Schizophrenia. *Schizophrenia Bulletin*, 1980, 6, 387–390.

ARIETI, S., and BRODY, E. B. *American Handbook of Psychiatry*, Vol. III, 2nd ed. New York: Basic Books, 1974.

BACHNEFF, S. A., and ENGELSMANN, F. Contingent Negative Variation, Postimperative Negative Variation, and Psychopathology. *Biological Psychiatry*, 1980, *15*, 323–328.

BALINSKY, B. I. *An Introduction to Embryology*, 2nd ed. Philadelphia: Saunders, 1965.

BANDURA, A., and WALTERS, R. H. *Social Learning and Personality Development*. New York: Holt, Rinehart and Winston, 1963.

BANDURA, A. A Social Learning Interpretation of Psychological Dysfunctions. In P. London and D. Rosenhan (eds.), *Foundations of Abnormal Psychology*. New York: Holt, Rinehart and Winston, 1968, pp. 293–344.

BEATTY, J. *Introduction to Physiological Psychology*. Monterey, Calif.: Brooks/Cole, 1975.

BOULTON, A. Biochemical Research in Schizophrenia. *Nature*, 1971, *231*, 22–28.

BOWERS, M. B. Biochemical Processes in Schizophrenia: An Update. *Schizophrenia Bulletin*, 1980, 6, 393–403.

BRILL, N. Q. General Biological Studies. In L. Bellak and L. Loeb (eds.), *The Schizophrenic Syndrome*. New York: Grune and Stratton, 1969, pp. 114–154.

CANTRIL, H. *The Invasion from Mars: A Study in the Psychology of Panic*. Princeton: Princeton University Press, 1940.

CHASSEN, J. B. *Research Design in Clinical Psychology and Psychiatry*. New York: Appleton-Century-Crofts, 1967.

CLEGHORN, J. M., and STREINER, B. J. Prediction of Symptoms and Illness Behaviour from Measures of Life Change and Verbalized Depressive Themes. *Journal of Human Stress*, 1979, 5, 16–23.

COHEN, J., OFFNER, F., and PALMER, C. W. Development of the Contingent Negative Variation in Children. *Electroencephalography and Clinical Neurophysiology*, 1967, *23*, 77–98.

COLEMAN, M. Serotonin and Central Nervous System Syndromes of Childhood. A Review. *Journal of Autism and Childhood Schizophrenia*, 1973, 3, 27–35.

DAVIS, J. M. A Two Factor Theory of Schizophrenia. *Journal of Psychiatric Research*, 1974, *11*, 25–29.

DAVIS, J. M. Dopamine Theory of Schizophrenia: A Two-Factor Theory. In L. C. Wynne, R. L. Cromwell, and S. Matthysse (eds.), *The Nature of Schizophrenia: New Approaches to Research and Treatment*. New York: John Wiley, 1978, pp. 105–115.

DELGADO, J. M. R. *Physical Control of the Mind*. New York: Harper and Row, 1969.

DOLLARD, J., and MILLER, N. E. *Personality and Psychotherapy*. New York: McGraw-Hill, 1950.

DOBZHANSKY, T. *Mankind Evolving*. New Haven, Conn: Yale University Press, 1962.

DRAGUNS, J. G., and PHILLIPS, L. *Psychiatric Classification and Diagnosis: An Overview and Critique*. Morristown, N.J.: General Learning Press, 1971.

DURHAM, H. W. Social Structures and Mental Disorder: Competency Hypotheses of Explanation. *Milbank Memorial Fund Quarterly*, 1961, 39, 259–311.

ERLENMEYER-KIMLING, L. Discussion of Genetics and Mental Illness. *Behavior Genetics*, 1976, 6, 285–290.

FISCHBEIN, S. Heredity-Environment Interaction in the Development of Twins. *International Journal of Behavioral Development*, 1978, *1*, 313–322.

FREDRICKSON, P., and RICHELSON, E. Mayo Seminars in Psychiatry: Dopamine and Schizophrenia—A Review. *Journal of Clinical Psychiatry*, 1979, 40, 399–405.

FREUD, S. Neurosis and Psychosis, Trans. Joan Riviere, Vol. II. In E. Jones (ed.), *The Collected Papers of Sigmund Freud*. New York: Basic Books, 1959, pp. 250–254.

GARMEZY, N. The Experimental Study of Children Vulnerable to Psychopathology. In A. Davids (ed.), *Child Personality and Psychopathology: Current Topics*, Vol. 2. New York: John Wiley, 1975, pp. 171–216.

GODDARD, H. H. *The Kallikak Family*. New York: Macmillan, 1912.

GOLDFARB, J., and WILK, S. Neuroanatomy, Neurophysiology, and Neurochemistry. In S. D. Glick and J. Goldfarb (eds.), *Behavioral Pharmacology*. St. Louis, Mo.: Mosby, 1976, pp. 14–57.

GOLDSTEIN, L., and SUGARMAN, A. A. EEG Correlates of Psychopathology. *Proceedings of the American Psychopathological Association*, 1969, 58, 281–309.

GRANT, I., SWEETWOOD, H. L., YAGER, J., and GERST, M. Quality of Life Events in Relation to Psychiatric Symptoms. *Archives of General Psychiatry*, 1981, 38, 335–339.

GROVES, P. M., and REBEC, G. C. Biochemistry and Behavior: Some Central Actions of Amphetamine and Antipsychotic Drugs. *Annual Review of Psychology*, 1976, 27, 91–127.

GRUENBERG, E. M. From Practice to Theory—Community Mental-Health Services and the Nature of Psychoses. In T. Millon (ed.), *Theories of Psychopathology and Personality: Essays and Critiques,* 2nd ed. Philadelphia: Saunders, 1973, pp. 399–403.

Hanson, D. R., Gottesman, I. I., and Heston, L. L. Some Possible Childhood Indicators of Adult Schizophrenia Inferred from Children of Schizophrenics. *British Journal of Psychiatry,* 1976, *129,* 142–154.

Hogan, R. *Personality Theory: The Personological Tradition.* Englewood Cliffs, N.J.: Prentice-Hall, 1976.

Hotaling, G. T., Atwell, S. G., and Linsky, A. S. Adolescent Life Changes and Illness: A Comparison of 3 Models. *Journal of Youth and Adolescence,* 1978, *7*(4), 393–403.

Iversen, S. D. Brain Chemistry and Behaviour. *Psychological Medicine,* 1980, *10,* 427–539.

Julian, R. M. *A Primer of Drug Action.* San Francisco: Freeman, 1975.

Jung, C. G. *Man and His Symbols.* Garden City, N.Y.: Doubleday, 1964.

Kallmann, F. J. The Genetics of Human Behavior. In T. Millon (ed.), *Theories of Psychopathology and Personality: Essays and Critiques,* 2nd ed. Philadelphia: Saunders, 1973, pp. 24–28.

Kaplan, B. H., Wilson, R. N., and Leighton, A. H. *Further Explorations in Social Psychiatry.* New York: Basic Books, 1976.

Kety, S. S. Biochemical Hypotheses and Studies. In L. Bellak and L. Loeb (eds.), *The Schizophrenic Syndrome.* New York: Grune and Stratton, 1969, pp. 155–171.

Kety, S. S. Biochemical Hypotheses of Schizophrenia. In T. Millon (ed.), *Theories of Psychopathology and Personality: Essays and Critiques,* 2nd ed. Philadelphia: Saunders, 1973, pp. 92–103.

Kety, S. S. Recent Biochemical Theories of Schizophrenia. In D. D. Jackson (ed.). *The Etiology of Schizophrenia.* New York: Basic Books, 1960, pp. 120–145.

Klerman G. Clinical Research in Depression. *Archives of General Psychiatry,* 1971, *24,* 305–319.

Kokkinidis, L., and Anisman, H. Amphetamine Models of Paranoid Schizophrenia: An Overview and Elaboration of Animal Experimentation. *Psychological Bulletin,* 1980, *88,* 551–579.

Langer, D. H., Brown, G. L., and Docherty, J. P. Dopamine Receptor Supersensitivity and Schizophrenia: A Review. *Schizophrenia Bulletin,* 1981, *7,* 208–224.

Lehmer, M. Navajos Want Their Own Schools. *San Francisco Examiner and Chronicle,* December 14, 1969, p. D–4.

Maddi, S. R. *Personality Theories: A Comparative Analysis,* rev. ed. Homewood, Ill.: Dorsey Press, 1972.

Maslow, A. H. *Toward a Psychology of Being,* 2nd ed. Princeton: Van Nostrand Reinhold, 1968.

May, R. *Existential Psychology.* New York: Random House, 1961.

Mednick, S. A. Breakdown in High-Risk Subjects: Familial and Early Environmental Factors. *Journal of Abnormal Psychology,* 1973, *83,* 469–475.

Mednick, S. A., and McNeill, T. F. Current Methodology in Research on the Etiology of Schizophrenia: Serious Difficulties Which Suggest the Use of the High-Risk Group Method. *Psychological Bulletin,* 1968, *70,* 681–693.

Mednick, S. A., and Schulsinger, F. Some Premorbid Characteristics Related to Breakdown in Children with Schizophrenic Mothers. In D. Rosenthal and S. S. Kety (eds.), *The Transmission of Schizophrenia.* New York: Pergamon Press, 1968, pp. 267–291.

Mednick, S. A., Schulsinger, H., and Schulsinger, F. Schizophrenia in Children of Schizophrenic Mothers. In A. Davids (ed.), *Child Personality and Psychopathology: Current Topics,* Vol. 2. New York: John Wiley, 1975, pp. 217–252.

Mendels, J., and Frazer, A. Brain Biogenic Amine Depletion and Mood. *Archives of General Psychiatry,* 1974, *30,* 447–451.

Merton, R. Anomie, Anomia and Social Interaction. In M. B. Clinard (ed.), *Anomie and Deviant Behavior.* New York: Free Press, 1964, pp. 213–242.

Millon, T. (ed.). *Theories of Psychopathology and Personality: Essays and Critiques,* 2nd ed. Philadelphia: Saunders, 1973.

Mittler, P. *The Study of Twins,* Middlesex, Eng.: Penguin Books, 1971.

Murphy, E., and Brown, G. W. Life Events, Psychiatric Disturbance and Physical Illness. *British Journal of Psychiatry,* 1980, *136,* 326–338.

Nauta, W. J. H. The Problem of the Frontal Lobe: A Reinterpretation. In J. V. Brady and W. J. H. Nauta (eds.), *Principles, Practices and Positions in Neuropsychiatric Research.* New York: Pergamon Press, 1972, pp. 167–187.

Paykel, E. S. Life Stress and Psychiatric Disorder: Applications of Clinical Approach. In B. S. Dohrenwend and B. P. Dohrenwend (eds.), *Stressful Life Events: Their Nature and Effects.* New York: John Wiley, 1974, pp. 135–149.

Paykel, E. S., Emms, E. M., Fletcher, J., and Rassaby, E. S. Life Events and Social Support in Puerperal Depression. *British Journal of Psychiatry,* 1980, *136,* 339–346.

Plomin, R., DeFries, J. C., and Loehlin, J. C. Genotype-Environment Interaction and Correlation in the Analysis of Human Behavior. *Psychological Bulletin,* 1977, *84,* 309–322.

Plomin, R., DeFries, J. C., and McClearn, G. E. *Behavioral Genetics.* San Francisco: W. H. Freeman and Co., 1980.

Rapaport, D. A Critique of Dollard and Miller's *Personality and Psychotherapy. American Journal of Orthopsychiatry,* 1953, *23,* 204–208.

Ritvo, E. R. Biochemical Research with Hyperactive Children. In D. P. Cantwell (ed.), *The Hyperactive Child: Diagnosis, Management and Current Research.* New York: Spectrum Publ., 1975, pp. 83–91.

Ritvo, E. R. Biochemical Studies of Children with the Syndromes of Autism, Childhood Schizophrenia and Related Developmental Disabilities: A Review. *Journal of Child Psychology and Psychiatry,* 1977, *18,* 373–379.

ROGERS, C. R. A Theory of Therapy, Personality, and Interpersonal Relationships as Developed in the Client Centered Framework. In S. Koch (ed.), *Psychology: A Study of a Science*, Vol. 3. New York: McGraw-Hill, 1959, pp. 184–256.

ROGERS, C. R. In Retrospect: Forty-Six Years. *American Psychologist*, 1974, *29*, 115–123.

ROSENTHAL, D. *Genetics of Psychopathology*. New York: McGraw-Hill, 1971, p. 3.

ROSENTHAL, D. *Genetic Theory and Abnormal Behavior*. New York: McGraw-Hill, 1970, p. 2.

ROTTER, J. B., CHANCE, J. E., and PHARES, E. J. *Applications of a Social Learning Theory of Personality*. New York: Holt, Rinehart and Winston, 1972.

SABSHIN, M. Theoretical Models in Community and Social Psychiatry. In T. Millon (ed.), *Theories of Psychopathology and Personality: Essays and Critiques*, 2nd ed. Philadelphia: Saunders, 1973, pp. 386–394.

SAGER, C. J. Alienation Can Be Said to Epitomize Our Times. *Roche Reports*, 1968, *5*(8), 1–2, 11.

SARASON, I. G. *Personality: An Objective Approach*. New York: John Wiley, 1966.

SATTERFIELD, J. H., CANTWELL, D. P., and SATTERFIELD, B. T. Pathphysiology of the Hyperactive Child Syndrome. *Archives of General Psychiatry*, 1974, *31*, 839–844.

SELYE, H. *Stress Without Distress*. Philadelphia: Lippincott, 1974.

SHAGASS, C., ROEMER, R. A., STRAUMANIS, J. J., and AMADEO, M. Topography of Sensory Evoked Potentials in Depressive Disorders. *Biological Psychiatry*, 1980, *15*, 183–207.

SHAGASS, C., and STRAUMANIS, J. J. Evoked Potentials and Psychopathology. *Proceedings of the American Psychopathological Association*, 1969, *58*, 22–53.

SHAPIRO, J., MACHATTIE, L., ERON, L., IHLER, G., IPPEN, K., and BECKWITH, J. Isolation of Pur Lac Operon DNA. *Nature*, 1969, *224*, 768–774.

SMALL, J. G., DEMYER, M. K., and MILSTEIN, V. CNV Responses of Autistic and Normal Children. *Journal of Autism and Childhood Schizophrenia*, 1971, *1*, 215–231.

SMITH, B. L. Cortical Stimulation and Speech Timing: A Preliminary Observation. *Brain and Language*, 1980, *10*, 89–97.

SNYDER, S. H. Dopamine and Schizophrenia. In L. C. Wynne, R. L. Cromwell, and S. Matthysse (eds.), *The Nature of Schizophrenia. New Approaches to Research and Treatment*. New York: Wiley, 1978, pp. 366–375.

SNYDER, S. H., BANERJEE, S. P., YAMAMURA, H. I., and GREENBERG, D. Drugs, Neurotransmitters, and Schizophrenia. *Science*, 1974, *184*, 1243–1253.

STANLEY, M., LAUTIN, A., ROTROSEN, J., GERSHON, S., and KLEINBERG, D. Metoclopramide: Antipsychotic Efficacy of a Drug Lacking Potency in Receptor Models. *Psychopharmocology*, 1980, *71*, 219–225.

SZASZ, T. S. The Myth of Mental Illness. *American Psychologist*, 1960, *15*, 113–118.

THOMAS, W. I., and ZNANIECKI, F. *The Polish Peasant in Europe and America*, Vols. I and II. New York: Dover, 1958.

VAUGHN, H. G., JR. Some Reflections on Stimulation of the Human Brain. In J. Zubin and C. Shagass (eds.), *Neurobiological Aspects of Psychopathology*. New York: Grune and Stratton, 1969, pp. 66–77.

VENABLES, P. H. The Electrodermal Psychophysiology of Schizophrenia and Children at Risk for Schizophrenia: Controversies and Developments. *Schizophrenia Bulletin*, 1977, *3*, 28–48.

VINOKUR, A., and SELZER, M. L. Desirable versus Undesirable Life Events: Their Relationship to Stress and Mental Distress. *Journal of Personality and Social Psychology*, 1975, *32* (2), 329–337.

WALTER, W. G. The Contingent Negative Variation as an Aid to Psychiatric Diagnosis. In M. L. Kietzman, S. Sutton, and J. Zubin (eds.), *Experimental Approaches to Psychopathology*. New York: Academic Press, 1975, pp. 197–205.

WATSON, J. D., and CRICK, R. H. C. Molecular Structure of Nucleic Acids: A Structure for Deoxyribose Nucleic Acid. *Nature*, 1953, *171*(4356), 737–738.

WEST, A. P. Interaction of Low-Dose Amphetamine Use with Schizophrenia in Outpatients: Three Case Reports. *American Journal of Psychiatry*, 1974, *131*, 321–323.

WILLIAMS, R. J. The Biological Approach to the Study of Personality. In T. Millon (ed.), *Theories of Psychopathology and Personality: Essays and Critiques*, 2nd ed. Philadelphia: Saunders, 1973, pp. 29–38.

WITTKOWER, E. D., and FRIED, J. Some Problems of Transcultural Psychiatry. *International Journal of Social Psychiatry*, 1958, *3*, 242–252.

ZAHN, T. P. Autonomic Nervous System Characteristics Possibly Related to a Genetic Predisposition to Schizophrenia. *Schizophrenia Bulletin*, 1977, *3*, 49–60.

ZUBIN, J. The Biometric Approach to Psychopathology Revisited. In J. Zubin and C. Shagass (eds.), *Neurobiological Aspects of Psychopathology*. New York: Grune and Stratton, 1969, pp. 281–309.

ZUBIN, J. Scientific Models for Psychopathology in the 1970's. *Seminars in Psychiatry*, 1972, *4*(3), 283–296.

Part 2 METHODS OF EVALUATION AND INTERVENTION

5

COMPONENTS OF THE ASSESSMENT PROCESS:

Clinical Observation, the Interview, Psychological Tests, and Behavioral Assessment

PROLOGUE

After months of urging by the school principal, Mrs. B. telephoned the psychologist for an appointment for Freddy, her nine-year-old son. Although Freddy, a third grader, achieved at an academic level far below his intellectual potential, his social immaturity, isolation, and withdrawal worried the school officials even more. Mrs. B. balked at the psychologist's suggestion that she and her husband be interviewed first to obtain a more complete picture of Freddy's present problems and past history. She stated that both she and Mr. B. worked and couldn't get away and that, after all, it was Freddy who needed professional attention. Several appointment times were offered, but Mrs. B. angrily rejected them, saying she couldn't make any arrangements without checking with her husband. Days later, Mrs. B. telephoned again to set a definite time for their first visit. She reluctantly gave the psychologist permission to speak to the principal about Freddy, only after she repeatedly warned that he would be difficult to contact.

Mr. and Mrs. B. arrived separately, but on time for their appointment, seating themselves across from each other in an empty waiting room. The psychologist's greeting interrupted their silence and stark separateness. Mrs. B. quickly stood up and extended a firm hand, while Mr. B. rose slowly and timidly placed his limp hand into the clinician's. Mrs. B. was a tall woman whose big-boned frame and sturdy, matronly appearance made her look older than her stated age of forty-two. She was stylishly dressed with jet black hair which was obviously coiffed by a hairdresser.

Although not a pretty woman, Mrs. B. created an air of attractiveness and poise in the way she put herself together. In sharp contrast, Mr. B. was several inches shorter, overweight, balding, and dressed in a worn and loosely fitting suit, suggesting that he had been even heavier at one time. He looked older than forty-one years, yet his appearance was discrepant with his boyish awkwardness in meeting people and his passive-dependent relationship with his wife.

Mr. and Mrs. B. had married after they had both turned thirty. Neither had been married before, nor had they dated very much prior to their meeting. They wanted children immediately but had to wait several years, because they had difficulty conceiving. The mother had always worked as a bookkeeper, and the father as a salesman. However, Mrs. B. quit her job when Freddy was born and did not return to full-time employment until he was three years old. At that time Mr. B. became seriously ill with ulcerative colitis, which required several hospitalizations and eventually surgery. Mrs. B. went back to work to help support the family, leaving Freddy in a preschool and in the care of a housekeeper. When he entered the first grade, the housekeeper was discharged to cut expenses. However, their concern over Freddy's safety during the few hours between the close of school and the end of his mother's work day prompted them to require that he stay close to home and not wander beyond their fenced yard. Freddy more than complied with their wishes in that he rarely, if ever, went out of doors after he returned from school. He chose to change into his pajamas and watch TV while holding on to his favorite baby blanket until his mother arrived home at about 5:30 P.M. He made no friends, even though a number of boys his age lived in the neighborhood. Since Freddy was left alone so much, his parents never went out in the evenings or on weekends without taking him along.

The mother reported that Freddy was a fussy eater who often refused to eat the meals she prepared. On these occasions his father would interrupt his own dinner to go out and buy Freddy's favorite hamburger and french fries. The parents also had great difficulty in putting Freddy to bed at a regular and reasonable time, although after awhile Mr. B. usually resolved the problem by agreeing to Freddy's request that he sleep with him. Mr. B.'s frequent indulgence of his son met with Mrs. B.'s disapproval, opposition, and intense anger. However, the open battles between the parents over Freddy's management were short-lived, because his mother feared that the conflict would precipitate another hospitalization for her husband.

In this chapter we shift emphasis from the broad and substantive issues of the field to an in-depth look at the assessment process. We will see how the clinician arrives at a diagnosis and a treatment plan for children like Freddy. We shall look at who and what the clinician evaluates, the techniques available for accumulating information, and the information needed, as well as the way in which it is used. Hopefully, this will remove the cloud of mystery that often surrounds the clinical process and further our understanding of the significance of these data for the various clinical conditions we will present in later chapters.

REFERRAL

All clinical interactions begin with a *referral,* which brings the child and the family to the attention of the clinician. Most clients[1] do not seek professional help on their own, and they usually experience some degree of resistance in admitting that "something is wrong."

Frequently the behaviors of troubled children are a plea for help and a means of attrac-

[1] *Client* is used in this chapter to refer to the child and the parents, recognizing that in most instances diagnosing abnormal behavior in children minimally involves this trio.

ting the attention of some responsible adult. Acting-out children who disrupt class, fight with others, and refuse to obey rules attract more than their share of attention. Less noticeable to most adult observers are those aberrant behaviors of children that do not affect the lives of others. Excessive daydreaming, withdrawal from social interactions, disruptive sleep patterns, and unwillingness to try any new activity because of an intense fear of being physically hurt are some examples of adjustment problems that may be as serious as acting-out behaviors. However, these are more likely to go on for longer periods of time before professional services are sought.

The nature of the referral often provides the clinician with early clues which aid in evaluating the referrant's understanding and willingness to do something about the problem. For example, in her first telephone call Mrs. B. communicated her reluctance to accept either the principal's initial referral or any involvement in her son's maladjustment. In addition, she readily constructed barriers to block a meeting with the psychologist, reflecting her resistance to becoming part of the evaluation and to admitting that problems exist.

In general, families who are aware of their problems and who willingly seek professional help are more cooperative and easier to work with than those who show resistance. Those who are either unable or unwilling to face up to their problems not only require the direction of others to secure help but also show poor motivation to alter their behavioral patterns. Mr. and Mrs. B. refused to acknowledge Freddy's deviant behaviors, although both his poor school performance and his lack of social adjustment were obvious to everyone else. It was the principal's unwillingness to tolerate Freddy's deteriorating behavior that pressed Mrs. B. into calling the psychologist. Although both recognition of one's problems and self-motivation are desirable, their absence does not preclude a favorable outcome. It is important that the clinician have an early awareness of the referrant's motivation in order to construct a strategy that will increase cooperation and motivation.

Resistance to outside intervention is not uncommon in parents who, like Mrs. B., wish to believe that this is a "passing phase" which the child will eventually "outgrow." Parental reluctance to seek clinical services is understandable, since the referral may imply that parents are responsible for the child's problems, that they have failed to be "good" parents, or that they conceived a damaged offspring. In addition, parental resistance may reflect a basic unwillingness to change their own behaviors or to give up using the child as a vehicle for expressing their conflicts.

It is also often the case that children are reluctant to receive professional help; it may cause them to feel put-down, unloved, and blamed for the problem. Consequently, they are likely to react with anger and anxiety to being singled out and brought to a specialist for help. Some youngsters may resist because they equate the need for psychological assistance with an open admission of a serious disability. In this instance they may wish to deny or conceal their difficulties because their integrity is threatened. Still others may show reluctance because they are fearful of the unknown and of what the "doctor" might do to them. Whatever the circumstances, the clinician must be aware as early as possible of the presence of fears and resistances and their potential effect on the relationship and the information gathered.

In addition, the referral should provide the clinician with an orientation to the referrant's major problems. A telephone conversation with the referrant can yield information about the primary symptoms, their duration, their onset (gradual or sudden), their effects on the functioning of the referrant and others, and the measures that have been tried to deal with them. It is also important to know the results of recent medical evaluations and the kind and dosage of current medication, since the latter may have possible confounding effects on the assessment of the client. Armed with this information, the assessment process begins to take shape even before the referrant arrives for the initial visit. In those instances where a client is self-referred, some preliminary intake procedure (either informally on the telephone or by some prepared written questionnaire) is often employed.

CLINICAL METHODS

Typically the diagnostic process attempts to classify the abnormal behaviors, arrive at working hypotheses about causal factors and construct a plan to remediate the condition. In later sections we shall discuss the clinical methods by which these goals are met: *clinical observations, the interview, psychological tests,* and *behavioral assessment.* Keep in mind that while each of these methods offers advantages and disadvantages, the clinician does not typically rely on only one approach for gathering diagnostic information. Instead, he or she recognizes that careful assessment involves a combination of methods to yield data that is reliable, complete, and accurate.

Clinical Observations

Observation is the chief method of study for every field of scientific inquiry, although its limitations are more pronounced when it is applied to the clinical setting. Human behavior is so complex and changeable that it overloads the sheer observational capacities of the observer. A child in a play situation may do many things (laugh, talk, run, throw, hit or catch a ball, and become involved in a fight with a playmate) within a timespan of only a few minutes. Obviously, all the behaviors evidenced cannot be accurately recorded. Laughing, for example, is sufficiently complex in itself to make the human observer's task extremely difficult. The observer must make decisions about what constitutes a laugh and what prompts it, as well as note all the facial, bodily, and auditory components of the laugh. However, in the clinical setting not one but many behaviors are observed at the same time, increasing the difficulty of the task and reducing the chances of obtaining high agreement between different observers.

Errors in Clinical Observation. Clinical observations are subject to the biases of the clinician (*observer bias*). For example, a particular behavior might be interpreted to confirm a working clinical hypothesis. In addition, clinicians might overlook or underrate other behaviors that do not coincide with their a priori notions. Because the intrusion of observer bias is ever present, clinicians must not only be aware of this source of error but also must guard against distorting what they see.

The client is another potential contributor to observational error (*subject bias*), especially early in the clinical interaction. Since most clients want to put their best foot forward, we can expect them to temporarily adopt behaviors that will create a favorable impression. Some may be guarded and defensive because they fear being studied or fear the prospect of being viewed as "crazy." Still others may attempt to behave in ways that they believe are expected of them. Any of these conditions will make the client's behaviors difficult to note and even more hazardous to interpret.

Areas of Clinical Observation. In spite of these limitations, observation is an important and useful clinical method in generating diagnostic hypotheses that can be rejected or supported by further study. A sensitive and well-trained clinical observer can gain valuable information from the following five categories of the client's behaviors: (1) general physical appearance and attire, (2) emotional gestures and facial expressions, (3) gross and fine motor acts, (4) the quality of the relationship between the client and others, and (5) the client's verbalizations.

1. *General appearance and attire.* Almost everyone is well practiced in forming initial impressions of strangers through their physical appearance and dress. Although clinicians use similar cues, their assessment is not in-

tended to serve as an early basis of interpersonal attractiveness or as a guide for ensuing social interactions. Rather, it will be used as a source of data on the physical, social, and personality characteristics of the client. In this light, clinicians look for extremes, incongruities, and peculiarities in both physical appearance and attire as early diagnostic clues that may require further evaluation. Is the child well proportioned and formed, or does the child show physical deformities or abnormalities that should be noted for later study with respect to their organic and/or psychological implications for the child's adjustment? Similarly, observations about the client's general health, cleanliness, body surface signs (bruise marks, cuts, sores, scars, hair distributions and other secondary sexual characteristics, and so forth), and the condition and propriety of the client's clothes may provide gross indications of some diagnostic possibilities that can be ruled either in or out by additional data. For example, emaciation in a fifteen-year-old girl is one of the physical manifestations of a disorder known as anorexia nervosa (see Chapter 12), and an extremely large or small head—disproportionate to the rest of the body—in a five-year-old suggests macro- or microcephalous (congenital disorders that usually result in severe mental retardation). Black or blue bruise marks on the face and arms of a child may be the result of a convulsive disorder, accident proneness, or physical assault. Needle marks on the arm of an adolescent may indicate drug abuse, while extremely chafed and irritated hands may be the result of a handwashing compulsion.

Within limits acceptable to society, the child and the parents are expected to be dressed and groomed in ways that are appropriate to their age, socioeconomic status, vocation, and—to some extent—educational level. Any gross disparity is worthy of note, although on closer examination some will not be of diagnostic significance. But the shabby, baggy, and worn condition of Mr. B's clothes gave the unmistaken impression of a downtrodden, dejected, and spiritless man who might be depressed. Moreover, Mr. B.'s attire was in sharp contrast to the smart way in which Mrs. B. was dressed and groomed and to Freddy's freshly cleaned and pressed shirt and trousers. This suggested gross neglect that was discrepant with his family, his middle-class socioeconomic level, and his job as a salesman.

2. *Emotional gestures and facial expressions.* Most of us have learned to note and interpret body movements, gestures, and expressions as clues to the emotional state and reaction of those with whom we interact. The shrug of the shoulder that connotes either disapproval or apathy, the clenched fist and gritting of teeth that communicates anger, the hung head and the slumped bodily attitude that suggests dejection, and the wide open smile accompanied by hand clapping that expresses pleasure and approval illustrate some of these behaviors. We learn early to look for these signs to help us get along with those around us. The disapproving glance of a parent or teacher represents a nonverbal communication often sufficiently potent to control our behavior. For more than fifty years psychologists have demonstrated that subjects can successfully identify emotions represented in either posed or candid photographs of faces (Munn, 1940; Schlosberg, 1952, 1954; Izard, 1971). Two additional studies support the notion that emotional gestures and facial expressions can provide valuable clues in the diagnostic interview (Ekman, 1964, 1965).

At the first meeting, the clinician looks for signs of tension, apprehension, fear, and other emotional states as well as for inappropriate emotional reactions that may be evidenced in the client's facial and body expressions. Additional observations should occur during subsequent meetings so that the clinician can confirm, reject, or elaborate initial impressions. Moreover, patterns of emotional responsivity should emerge over time and in different stimulus contexts. Thus, it is important not only for the clinician to observe signs of the initial emotional reaction but also to continue the observations to discern changes in emotionality, appropriateness, consistency of emotional reactions, and the range of the child's emotional repertoire.

3. *Gross and fine motor acts.* Motor behavior interests the clinician because it is an area of responsivity that is affected by neurological, physiological, pharmacological, and psychological variables. Disturbances in motor behavior vary in degree or kind. The general activity level of the child should be noted, especially at either extreme. *Overactivity* represents heightened motor output in which there are quick and successive motor acts that are rarely completed or goal directed. An example of this is the hyperkinetic child (see Chapter 10), who is characterized by restlessness, fidgeting, flitting from one activity to another, and an inability to sit still for even a moment without getting into something (often destructively).

Underactivity, sometimes known as psychomotor retardation, represents reduced and slowed motor output that may be indicative of endocrine imbalance, drug effects, depression, mental retardation, or psychosis. The extreme of underactivity—paralysis or muscular weakness (asthenia)—may reflect a neurological disorder, psychoneurosis (hysterical paralysis of the conversion reaction), depression, or the effects of heavy sedation.

In addition to the general activity level, certain kinds of unusual motor behaviors are of diagnostic importance. A *tic* is an involuntary spasmodic twitching of the face or body parts that is repeated at frequent intervals. Its origin usually has an emotional component (anger, anxiety, grief, or shame), making it a valuable bit of diagnostic data. The child's unsolicited repetition and imitation of motor acts performed by the examiner or others is called *echopraxia.* This motor disturbance is most often associated with childhood psychosis. Another peculiar kind of motor behavior is known as *perseveration,* in which movements and actions just performed by the child are repeated. The initial action is usually appropriate for the stimulus, but its repetition is inappropriate. Perseveration should be noted because it is often an associated characteristic of brain pathology, mental retardation, and psychosis. *Ritualistic* or *compulsive* motor behaviors such as performing a prior sequential set of acts before performing another activity may be diagnostic clues of an obsessive-compulsive neurotic reaction (discussed in Chapter 12).

4. *Quality of relationships.* Children almost never come to the evaluation sessions unattended, a circumstance that provides the clinician with opportunities to observe the nature of the relationship between both parents and between the child and the parents. For example, the scene of silence, separateness, and emptiness enacted by Mr. and Mrs. B. in the waiting room, along with Mrs. B.'s domination of her husband in the initial interview, communicated a good deal about their relationship. Mrs. B.'s inclination to be aggressive and dominant was extended to her relationship with Freddy, where it was noted that she criticized and directed his activities as they waited for the psychologist. A child and mother who totally ignore each other, sitting at different ends of an uncrowded waiting room and showing no visible sign of interest in each other, convey a picture of coldness and distance in their relationship. The kinds of interactions observed should provide the clinician with sources of rich but tentative interpretative data, which the clinician can reject or later confirm.

5. *Verbalizations of the client.* Verbal language is not only a unique characteristic of people but also represents the principal source of data used by the clinician in diagnosing abnormal behavior. As a trained observer, the clinician must listen carefully to both the *formal structure* of the client's verbalizations and the *content* of what the client says, because each of these areas can reveal important diagnostic information.

The formal structure of language is first learned in the home environment. It consists of such characteristics as grammar, sentence structure, choice of words, speed, flow, and length. It is then modified and developed in school and constantly practiced within a cultural setting. It should tell us something of the client's educational level and the subculture that has been influential. The way language is structured should provide an estimate of the client's intellectual level and current functioning. For example, a middle-class Caucasian child of thirteen who speaks in short monosyllabic phrases with poor grammatical structure is probably intellectually limited. Table 5–1 summarizes some of the major deviations in the formal structure of verbal language indicative of disordered thought beyond the slips of the tongue, digressions from the main topic, or interruptions in the flow of ideas found in the speech of most people.

Observations of language content provide an important source of diagnostic data, since they permit a glimpse of human functioning in areas that tend to be impaired when abnormal conditions exist. In fact, careful listening to the content of verbal language should reveal what people think, what they have learned and remembered, how they see themselves and their environment, and what they feel. Various signs of disordered thinking, especially in extreme forms, are readily apparent in the client's language content. For example, *bizarre ideas* such as "My limbs are made of jelly," or "The ear of corn can't hear if it is cooked too long" characterize the language content found in some psychotic children. Similarly, the expression of fixed beliefs based on false premises, known as *delusions,* characterizes paranoid thinking. Delusions are not ordinarily shared by other members of the client's educational and socioeconomic group, a fact which helps to distinguish them from common superstitions as well as from religious and political beliefs. The two most commonly observed types of delusions are those of grandeur and persecution, although other types are known.

Content of speech may also reveal signs of memory impairment; partial or total inability to recall—a condition known as *amnesia*—may be evident in what the client says. *Anterograde amnesia* refers to loss of memory of those matters that occurred after the event that precipitated the amnesia and tends to become progressively worse. This type of am-

Table 5–1 Deviations in Language Structure Indicative of Disordered Thinking

	Description
Neologisms	The coining of new words, i.e., "jampow" created to refer to the draining of one's strength by excreting feces.
Incoherence	Phrases connected without reason or logical sequence. "I am made of bones and blood much as the wind bends the trees and Napoleon feels his heart."
Verbigeration	Extreme of incoherence consisting of a flow of unrelated words.
Word Salad	Speech that includes neologisms, incoherent, and illogical phrases sequenced so that they lack meaning. "The world is jampow! What's the use (laughs) . . .no matter, the sky is purple. Let my face burn, cut the trees down, and we will shout thy commands."
Tangential or Circumstantial	Long winded, indirect, and round-about speech that includes irrelevant details to the extent that the original objective is forgotten.
Flight of Ideas	Continuous, rapid flow of speech in which the client jumps from one thought to another without any apparent connection.
Clang Associations	The sound of the word touches off a series of punnings and/or rhymings. "Goodbye! . . .sky and eye. . .don't fly, lie, die, die. . ."
Pressure of Speech	Markedly rapid speech that is almost impossible to interrupt.
Mutism	Absence of speech.
Blocking	Low verbal output in which there are numerous instances of sudden breaks (silence) in the stream of speech occurring to interval stimulation.

nesia is characteristic of degenerative brain pathology, whereas *retrograde amnesia,* the loss of memory for things that took place prior to the precipitant event (usually emotional trauma or head injury), may be indicative of either a neurotic reaction or brain damage. Sometimes brain-damaged people fill in the gaps in their memory with imagined experiences they believe have really happened. This type of memory impairment, *confabulation,* is illustrated by the brain-injured adolescent who recounts for the clinician the events of her day by saying she visited her parents in a neighboring city when in fact she never left the hospital. In contrast, *hyperamnesia* refers to the unusual ability to recall minute and sometimes insignificant details learned in the distant past. This exaggeration of memory may be evident in childhood psychosis, paranoid and manic states, and obsessive-compulsive neurotic reactions.

In addition, language content may indicate impairment of perceptual functioning. The ten-year-old child who sees snakes covering his bed is likely to be *hallucinating,* perceiving something that does not actually exist. Hallucinations of this sort may be suggestive of extremely high fever, toxic drug reactions, brain disorders, and psychotic reactions. Any of the senses may be involved in hallucinations, although visual and auditory experiences are most frequently observed.

Finally, the content of verbal language gives the clinician important diagnostic data about the client's range of emotions, the quality of feelings, the appropriateness of the emotional expression to the situation, and the degree of control exercised over impulses and feelings. Mrs. B.'s pervasive anger toward her husband, the school principal, and the examiner were reflected in what she said. Her words did not convey either elation or despondency, or inappropriateness of feelings (disparity between expressed feelings and the context in which the feelings occur), which may have suggested a psychotic reaction. Instead, Mrs. B.'s verbalizations revealed a cold, controlling, aggressive, and domineering woman who encouraged immaturity and dependency in both Freddy and her husband.

The Interview

In today's world almost everyone has had some experience with the interview. We tend to think of it as a formal conversation between two or more people that has been prearranged for a specific purpose—be it admission to school, membership in a club, job placement, market research, or census taking. How the interview is conducted varies widely, depending on the orientation and training of the interviewer. For example, the psychoanalytically oriented clinician would want to know a great deal about the child's past history, especially early experiences, while the behaviorist would emphasize current unwanted behaviors and the conditions that maintain them. In addition, the nature of the interview may be influenced by the setting and the purpose of the interview, as well as by the special characteristics of the interviewee. A study of nine different interview schedules showed that only three kinds of information (identifying data, present problem, and family history) were included in all of them, while many other types of information were common to only a few schedules (Peterson, 1968).

The Initial Interview. This is the first of perhaps several interactions between the client and the clinician, and it is sometimes referred to as the intake interview. Although the intent may be to gather diagnostic data, it is difficult to separate diagnostic sessions from therapeutic ones. Consequently, a primary objective of the initial interview is to establish a positive relationship between clinician and client (known as *rapport*). The clinician must be sensitive to and aware of the client's attitudes and feelings about being evaluated. The clinician should remember that it is the client and not the clinician who feels scrutinized and who may enter into this first meeting with feelings of anxiety and mistrust. For various reasons parents may not adequately prepare their youngsters for the interview, and may thus heighten the child's anxieties and fears. Clinicians can lessen these difficulties by instructing parents to discuss with the child prior to the visit what to expect and why the interview is necessary, and by dealing with these matters early in the session.

In working with young children, special problems of rapport may arise because of their limited verbal abilities, their fear of strangers, and their reluctance to separate from their mother. The clinician can inspire trust and make the situation less formidable by introducing play materials and by either playing or watching the child play. Moreover, giving the child freedom to move about the room realistically acknowledges the fact that the child can't sit still for a long period of time. Freedom of movement loosens up the situation to the extent that it will increase the child's spontaneity and verbalizations.

As a matter of practice, many clinicians (including the author) hold the initial interview with both parents, followed by several separate sessions with the child, for which each parent is asked to bring the child to at least one session. At the end of the evaluation process, a feedback session is held for the parents and—whenever possible—the child, to discuss the findings and recommendations. The initial interview serves the multiple purposes of establishing rapport, eliciting information about the child's problems, seeing how parents relate to each other, and obtaining historical data on the family and the child. In addition, it can give parents some help in learning how to prepare their child for subsequent visits. An account of the present problem is a natural starting point for most parents, since their chief complaints are likely to be uppermost in their minds. Following this discussion the interview can turn to a detailed history in which a systematic study of the antecedent conditions that contributed to the child's personality and present difficulties are highlighted. This procedure is known as a *case history*, and—much like the interview itself—it can vary considerably. A sample case history form is outlined and summarized in Table 5–2.

Sometime before the initial parent interview is over, the clinician describes what will be done with the child during the next two sessions and also tells the parents that they will be asked to take several tests while the clinician works with the child. When the parent and the child appear for the next session, they are told that the parent will be taking some tests in the outer office while the child and the clinician are together. In almost all cases the child is reassured by the knowledge that the parent is nearby and that both mother and father are actively involved in the evaluation process.

Critical Evaluation of the Interview. Although the interview is the most important and frequently used clinical method for diagnosing and understanding clients, it is a procedure that is subject to several sources of error that may significantly reduce its reliability. We know from earlier discussions that interviewers vary greatly with respect to their purpose, the way they gather information, and, more subtly, the way they establish rapport. Therefore, by keeping interview differences to a minimum, interview agreement for diagnosis or prognosis could be increased. This could be accomplished by more routine use of a standardized interview format in which the clinician asks the same set of questions and accumulates the same set of data from every client seen. An example of a *standardized* or *structured interview*, as it is called, is the Psychiatric Evaluation Form: Diagnostic Version (Spitzer et al., 1967–1968), which is partially shown in Table 5–3.

Sometimes the resolution of one problem leads to others. In adding more structure and uniformity to the interview, the clinician gives up the freedom to wander and shift about from area to area in ways that seem to best fit the client and to obtain maximum information. Moreover, the standardized interview imposes a style of inquiry that may be neither comfortable for the interviewer nor

Table 5-2 Summary of a Case History

	Area of Inquiry	*Information*	*Implication*
I.	Prenatal, Birth, and Early Development	Pregnancy planned, legitimate, difficult?	Rejection
		Delivery: breach, section, induced?	Brain injury
		Mother's physical and emotional condition?	Infection, drugs, anxiety, depression.
		Infant's weight, height?	Premature birth
		Feeding: breast, bottle, problems, weaning? Sleep-patterns; restlessness, colic, problems associated with bedtime? Toilet training: when, what problems, enuresis, how handled? Motor patterns: crawl, walk, write, language patterns, talk?	Mother-child interaction and early signs of abnormal development and behavior, in eating, sleeping, toilet training, gross and fine motor coordination, and language acquisition.
II.	Medical History	Patterns of illness and sequela, head injuries or signs of brain dysfunction, surgery.	Parental and client reaction to illness. Brain damage, emotional trauma, fears, anxieties.
III.	Educational History	Amount of education, grades, relations with school authorities and peers, and behavioral problems like truancy, dismissals. . . .	Intellectual and achievement pattern. Relations to both authority and peers. Acting out and delinquency.
IV.	Work History	Sequence of jobs held, how long, reasons for termination, special vocational skills.	Achievement motivation, reliability, sense of responsibility. . . .
V.	Social History	Nature of social adjustment, choice of interpersonal relations, social activities, interests, hobbies, and sexual adjustment and experiences such as masturbation, homosexuality, heterosexuality, sex fantasies, and particular difficulties. Handling of anger, and circumstances that give rise to hostile feelings. Drug or alcohol use.	Ability and kind of relationships, style of relating, range of interest, sex orientation, difficulties, and emotional reactions. Quality of feelings, acting out and delinquency. Drug or alcohol abuse.
VI.	Family History	Parents alive, other members of family . . . living together or when and how did separation occur. Indications of epilepsy, mental illness, or other diseases, and emotional stability.	Kinds of parental models, genetic influences, relations within family structure.

suitable for motivating the client to be productive.

Clinicians are responsible for charting and maintaining the direction of the interview as well as for its contents. Additionally, they are required to serve as recorders, observers, and skilled professionals who know how to pursue pertinent information while avoiding the blind alleys of unimportant material. Under these circumstances it is not surprising that inaccuracies and errors are inadvertently introduced into the process by the interviewer. Untrained interviewers are likely to be so overly attentive to the mechanics of these functions that they often lose sight of their major objective—the client. Interview errors

Table 5-3 Psychiatric Evaluation Form–Diagnostic Version

INTERVIEW GUIDE	SCALES
ORIGINAL COMPLAINT **If a psychiatric patient:** Now I would like to hear about your problems or difficulties and how they led to your coming to the (hospital, clinic).	**The time period for this section is the past month.**
GENERAL CONDITION Tell me how you have been feeling recently. (Anything else been bothering you?)	
PHYSICAL HEALTH How is your physical condition? Does any part of your body give you trouble? Do you worry much about your health?	**PHYSICAL HEALTH** 214 **SOMATIC CONCERNS** Excessive concern with bodily functions; preoccupation with one or more real or imagined physical complaints or disabilities; bizarre or unrealistic feelings or beliefs about his body or parts of body. **Do not include mere dissatisfaction with appearance.** ? 1 2 3 4 5 6
If necessary, inquire for doctor's opinion about symptoms or illnesses. When you are upset do you react physically...like [stomach trouble, diarrhea, headaches, sick feelings, dizziness] ?	215 **CONVERSION REACTION** Has a motor or sensory dysfunction which conforms to the lay notion of neurological illness, for which his doctors can find no organic basis (e.g., paralysis or anesthesia). ? 1 2 3 4 5 6
	216 **PSYCHOPHYSIOLOGICAL REACTIONS** Is bothered by one or more psychophysiological reactions to stress. Examples: backache, headaches, hypertension, dizziness, asthma, spastic bowel. **Note: the reaction may or may not involve structural change.** ? 1 2 3 4 5 6
APPETITE-SLEEP-FATIGUE **Disturbances in these areas are often associated with Depression, Anxiety, or Somatic Concerns.** What about your appetite for food? Do you have any trouble sleeping or getting to sleep? (Why is that?) How easily do you get tired?	
MOOD **This section covers several moods. The interviewer must determine to what extent the symptoms are associated with either one or the other or several of the dimensions.** What kinds of moods have you been in recently?	**MOOD** 217 **ELATED MOOD** Exhibits or speaks of an elevated mood, exaggerated sense of well being or optimism, or feelings of elation. Examples: Says "everything is great," jokes, witticisms, silly remarks, singing, laughing, or trying to get others to laugh or smile. ? 1 2 3 4 5 6
What kinds of things do you worry about? (How much do you worry?) What kinds of fears do you have? (Any situation... activities...things?) How often do you feel anxious or tense? (When you are this way, do you react physically...like sweating, dizziness, cramps?)	218 **ANXIETY** Remarks indicate feelings of apprehension, worry, anxiety, nervousness, tension, fearfulness, or panic. When clearly associated with any of these feelings, consider insomnia, restlessness, physical symptoms (e.g., palpitations, sweating, dizziness, cramps), or difficulty concentrating, etc. ? 1 2 3 4 5 6

(continued)

PEF-D 2

What about feeling restless?

219 **PHOBIA**
Has an irrational fear(s) of a particular object(s) or situation(s) which he tends to avoid. Consider number, interference in life and degree of irrationality.

? 1 2 3 4 5 6

How often do you feel sad, depressed, or blue?

When was the last time you felt like crying?

How do you feel about yourself?
(When you compare yourself with other people, how do you come out?)

Is it hard for you to concentrate on things?

Do you enjoy things now as much as usual?

220 **DEPRESSION**
Remarks indicate feelings of sadness, depression, worthlessness, failure, hopelessness, remorse, guilt, or loss. When clearly associated with any of these feelings, consider crying, insomnia, poor appetite, fatigue, loss of interest or enjoyment, difficulty concentrating, or brooding, etc.

? 1 2 3 4 5 6

221 **GUILT**
Feels he is either unworthy, sinful, evil, or has done something terrible, or feels he is being punished for his misdeeds.

? 1 2 3 4 5 6

OBSESSIONS-COMPULSIONS
Do you get thoughts that don't make sense that you can't get rid of or put out of your mind?

Is there any act which you have to repeat over and over or which you cannot resist repeating...like constantly washing your hands or constantly checking things or anything like that?

222 **OBSESSIONS-COMPULSIONS**
Has thoughts which occur repeatedly against his resistance, the content of which he regards as senseless, or performs some act or routine which he cannot resist repeating excessively (e.g., handwashing).

? 1 2 3 4 5 6

SUICIDE-SELF MUTILATION
When a person gets upset, depressed, or feels hopeless, he may think about dying. Do you?

Have you recently thought about killing yourself?
If yes: Determine degree of preoccupation, and presence of threats, gestures, or attempts.

(What about hurting yourself physically... other than suicide?)

223 **SUICIDE-SELF MUTILATION**
Suicidal thoughts, preoccupation, threats, gestures, or attempts, and thoughts or acts of self mutilation.

? 1 2 3 4 5 6

SOCIAL ISOLATION AND SUSPICION-PERSECUTION
This section covers both Social Isolation and Suspicion-Persecution. The interviewer must determine to what extent the symptoms are associated with either one or the other or both dimensions.

How are you getting along with people?

What kinds of trouble do you have with people?
(What about your family?)

Do you have much to do with [your neighbors, co-workers, students, the other people here] ?

How do you usually feel when you are with people?

How do people generally seem to feel about you?

Whom do you feel you can trust the most?

Do you feel you have to be on guard with people?

SOCIAL ISOLATION AND SUSPICION-PERSECUTION

224 **SOCIAL ISOLATION**
Avoidance of contact or involvement with people; preference for being alone; feelings of isolation, rejection, or discomfort with people.

? 1 2 3 4 5 6

225 **SUSPICION-PERSECUTION**
From mild suspiciousness to belief that he is being persecuted. Examples: distrustfulness; feels mistreated, taken advantage of or tricked; feels that people are staring at him or talking about him when they aren't; believes he is being poisoned, his mind is being read, controlled, or influenced by others, or that there is a plot against him. **Do not include feelings or beliefs which are completely justified by the situation.**

? 1 2 3 4 5 6

* Spitzer, Endicott, Mesnikoff & Cohen, 1967–1968. Reprinted with permission from New York State Psychiatric Institute.

may also be introduced by transient personal events, such as fatigue from too much partying the night before or preoccupation about a sick child at home. Some interviewers bring with them certain biases, whether it be their inclination to overinterpret sexual data or an overemphasis on the inadequacies and deficiencies in clients rather than on their strengths and resources. Daily (1960) identified a "pathology bias" in some clinicians who tend to see symptoms of abnormal behavior in everyone.

Another important source of interview error comes from the interviewee, whose predetermined attitudes, expectations, and feelings about the interview may influence what he or she says, what areas he or she will discuss truthfully, and how much cooperation will take place. In addition, clients are subject to the same sorts of transient effects from personal events as is the interviewer. These may unduly color their usual behavior pattern on a given day, and they may be erroneously interpreted if they are not confirmed by additional observations made over several separate occasions.

Apart from sources of errors that lower the reliability of the interview, questions concerning its predictive validity have also been raised (Sarbin, 1943; Kelly and Fiske, 1951; Meehl, 1954; Matarazzo, 1965). Inherent complexities and sources of error involved in the interview process itself, as well as the poorly defined areas selected for prediction, hinder the ability of the clinician to produce unequivocal answers. To illustrate, we need only look at the problem of predicting school success. How well have we identified the characteristics an individual must possess in order to succeed in school? Even if we could agree that both intelligence and motivation are important factors, we could not agree on the weight that should be assigned to each in arriving at a predictive formula. Obviously, if we were dealing with a graduate program in which candidates for admission were all intellectually bright, we probably would give more attention to factors such as motivation and past demonstrated performance in a known setting.

The problem of prediction is further complicated by the poorly defined criteria of school success. Should we use grade point average as our criterion, and, if so, is a C average adequate as a measure of success, or should it be set higher, say B or A? Should the student's participation in extracurricular activities be included, and how much weight should it be given? What about using eventual job placement as a criterion? But how do you grade or measure the quality of jobs, and how do you account for fluctuations in the job market at the time placement is made? Obviously, the problems involved in making predictions, be they from interviews, test results, grades, or other indicators of past performance, are numerous and complex.

As a method, the interview cannot be indicted for predictive inefficiency any more than most other methods. It is essential in establishing rapport between client and clinician. It is also useful in providing the clinician with firsthand observations and information needed to diagnose and understand the client. Further, it serves as a potential base for improving interpersonal relations between the client and others. Recent advances aimed at decreasing major sources of error, such as the standardized interview and computer interviewing, offer promise for more effective and systematic study of the interview process and its future clinical application.

Psychological Tests

Of all the clinical methods available for diagnosing abnormal behavior, psychological tests[2] are more closely identified with psychologists than with any other group of mental health specialists. Since the close of the nineteenth century, psychology has continued to make substantial contributions to the devel-

[2] Only a sample of the available tests can be included here. For a more detailed and extensive coverage of tests, the most recent volume of Buros's *Mental Measurement Yearbook* is recommended as a valuable reference.

opment of tests which measure a wide range of human behaviors. These efforts have produced a degree of precision and objectivity that is simply not attainable with other assessment approaches. Essentially, the test method provides a standard procedure in which the same stimuli are presented to every client in a prescribed manner. Responses are then categorized in objective and quantitative terms. Many psychological tests have been devised to more reliably measure behaviors that are elicited in the course of clinical observations and during the interview. However, there are other tests that measure behaviors which are not readily discernible in the clinical interaction, for example, fantasies, specific aspects of memory, perception, or academic achievement. Therefore, the use of psychological tests in the diagnostic process serves the dual function of increasing the accuracy and reliability of data already available through other clinical methods, and of providing additional data not accessible otherwise.

Intelligence Tests. No area of psychological testing has enjoyed greater success or more public acceptance than that of intelligence testing. It was the first test area to be widely recognized and the first of many to have been developed as a response to specfic social needs. Today belief in the IQ as an index of intelligence has implications for many aspects of a person's life. In the clinical setting assessing intelligence is almost always important, because it establishes an overall baseline estimate of the child's intellectual capacities. It also provides an evaluation of the child's functioning efficiency in a variety of cognitive areas where impairment may be of diagnostic significance. Intelligence tests are numerous and diverse: They are designed for all ages, for either group or individual administration, and for people who have verbal, motor, and/or educational disadvantages or handicaps.

1. The Binet Scales. These scales appeared at the turn of the twentieth century (as noted in Chapter 1) and represented the first major breakthrough in intelligence testing. The scales were translated into English, revised several times, and improved as a psychometric instrument largely through the efforts of Lewis Terman and his associates at Stanford University (Terman, 1916; Terman and Merrill, 1937, 1960). Although the term *intelligence quotient* (IQ) was first introduced by William Stern, it was Terman who was largely responsible for its current popularity, since he used it in his revision of the scales to express mental development and brightness. The IQ is computed by dividing mental age (MA—that is, the sum of the months of credit a respondent received for items passed—by chronological age (CA)—the actual age of the respondent in months. The obtained ratio is then multiplied by 100. Thus, the IQ score of 100 is set as the average and reflects the child's mental ability to perform at a level equal to his or her actual age. In using the formula MA/CA × 100, the obtained IQ score provides a quantitative expression of the degree to which the child falls above or below the average. The latest revision of the Stanford-Binet (Form L-M) incorporates the best subtests from the 1937 L and M scales. As in previous editions the scale consists of six subtests for age levels from two years to adulthood. At the youngest level the child is required to put each cutout of a circle, square, and triangle into its appropriate hole in a form board, identify parts of a boy depicted on a large picture, build a tower with blocks, and point to the correct picture when a word is presented (such as *airplane, telephone, hat* and so forth). At age five the child is asked to complete an incomplete drawing of a man, to imitate the examiner in folding a piece of paper into a triangle, to define words such as *ball, hat,* and *stove,* to copy a figure of a square, and so forth. Most children find the subtests interesting and pleasurable.

2. The Wechsler Scales. Because he was critical of the Stanford-Binet test on the grounds that it yielded only one score—heavily influenced by verbal skills—David Wechsler set out to construct a test of intelligence that would not only measure the aggregate of abilities involved in intelligence but also would provide separate scores for its important components (Wechsler, 1955). In addition, Wechsler devised a new method of calculating IQ that was not dependent on the erroneous assumption that there is a linear relationship between MA and CA. He showed that intelligence does not proceed by equal amounts throughout its development. Instead, it tends to increase until the very late teens and then level off for a brief period, before it gradually declines with age. Therefore, Wechsler did away with the MA score and defined IQ in terms of deviation units from the average scores obtained by people of a given age (which, incidentally, is the procedure for computing IQ adopted in the 1960 revision of the Stanford-Binet).

The first of Wechsler's tests appeared in 1939, but it was later substantially revised and called the Wechsler Adult Intelligence Scale (WAIS). The enormous popularity of the Wechsler tests with individuals ranging in age from sixteen to sixty-four prompted the construction of two new tests that essentially followed the same format—but were to be used for preschool and school-age children: the Wechsler Intelligence Scale for Children (WISC) and its recent revision (the WISC-R), and the Wechsler Preschool and Primary Scale of Intelligence (WPPSI) (Wechsler, 1974).

WISC-R consists of twelve subtests, six of which are considered verbal in nature and six nonverbal. Separate IQ scores are obtained for each grouping of subtests; that is, both a Verbal Scale IQ and a Performance Scale IQ are computed. When the total weighted score of all of the subtests is computed, a third IQ, known as the Full Scale IQ, is established. The subtests of both the verbal and the performance Scales, along with a sample item and a brief description of the tasks involved, are summarized in Table 5–4. By and large, clinicians have found the Wechsler Scales very useful; they not only provide three separate IQ scores, but they also yield separate subtest scores that can be examined for potential diagnostic clues associated with areas of either impaired or enhanced intellectual functioning.

3. *The McCarthy Scales of Children's Abilities.* Published in 1972, the test is a well-standardized measure of cognitive ability in children ranging in age from two and a half to eight and a half. In consists of eighteen tests grouped into one or more of six scales involving cognitive functioning and motor coordination, and it provides a general intelligence score which is regarded as comparable to the Binet and WPPSI IQ scores (Sattler, 1982). McCarthy intended the test to provide information about diverse behaviors that are of diagnostic significance in the early identification of retarded children and those with uneven developmental patterns. However, the validity of her test and its goals have not been determined as yet (Kaufman and Kaufman, 1977; Hunt, 1978; Sattler, 1982).

4. *Other tests of intelligence.* Several other intelligence tests are particularly suitable for either special circumstances or certain populations. The Binet, Wechsler, and McCarthy scales are expensive, requiring a highly trained examiner, a one-on-one test administration, and a relatively long period of time to complete.

The Peabody Picture Vocabulary Test (PPVT) and the Slosson Intelligence Test (SIT) are examples of two individually administered tests that are less costly than those noted above; they require less time to administer and can be given by relatively untrained examiners. The PPVT consists of a graded set of cards, each containing four line drawings from which the child matches the word presented by the examiner (Dunn, 1959, 1965). The test applies to children from age two and a half to eighteen, and it can be administered in about fifteen minutes. The SIT can be used for children and adults, and it can be given in approximately twenty minutes. It

Table 5-4 Description of Subtests of the WISC-R and Sample Items

Verbal Scale Subtests	
Information	A simply stated set of questions that require memory of previously learned facts. (What must you do to make water boil?)
Similarities	A set of paired items that require verbal abstraction of similarity. (In what way are an apple and a banana alike?)
Arithmetic	A set of computation questions and problems. (At 8¢ each, how much will 3 candy bars cost?)
Vocabulary	A set of words to define. (What does "umbrella" mean?)
Comprehension	A set of questions dealing with judgment and common sense ways of coping with different situations. (What is the thing to do when you cut your finger?)
Digit Span	Immediate memory of a series of orally presented numbers. (I am going to say some numbers. When I am finished, say them right after me . . . 8–4–2–3–9.)
Performance Scale Subtests	
Picture Completion	Twenty simple line drawings, each with an important missing element. (Look at the picture and tell me what important part is missing?)
Picture Arrangement	A series of cards presented in a jumbled sequence. (Put the cards in the right order so they tell a story that makes sense.)
Block Design	Blocks are used to reproduce a series of designs. (Take these blocks and make a design with them that looks like the one on this card.)
Object Assembly	Scrambled pieces must be correctly assembled to make an object. (Put these pieces together correctly.)
Coding	Symbols attached to numbers must be correctly substituted in a series of numbered boxes. (Write in the open box the symbol that goes with the number above it.)
Mazes	A supplementary test requires finding one's way through a set of mazes, with a minimum of wrong turns and in the shortest period of time.

consists of items taken from the Binet Scale and from the Gesell Institute of Child Development Behavior Inventory (Slosson, 1963). Both the PPVT and the SIT are quick measures of intelligence and useful screening instruments, although they should not be regarded as suitable substitutes for either the Binet or WISC (Sattler, 1974, 1982; Himmelstein, 1972).

The Extended Merrill-Palmer Scale (1978) is an individually administered set of tests of cognitive ability applicable to preschool children between the ages of three and five years eleven months. It requires a trained examiner and about one hour to administer. The psychometric qualities of the test are questionable: No information is provided on test-retest reliability, while part-whole reliability is low. Neither standard errors of measurement nor validity data are presented, and the standardization sample is not representative of the United States with respect to minority membership and socioeconomic status (Sattler, 1982). In contrast, many clinicians have found the Progressive Matrices Test (Raven, 1938, 1947a, 1947b; Sattler, 1982) useful as a supplemental measure of intelligence for individuals with severe language, hearing, or physical impairments; it is easily administered and does not require a wholly intact sensorium (Bortner, 1978; Sattler, 1982). It is a nonverbal test of reasoning ability in which the child completes a matrix of figural symbols by choosing the appropriate missing symbol from a group of symbols. Another nonverbal test favored by clinicians is the Porteus Maze Test (Porteus, 1965), which is easy to administer, fun to take, and helpful in identifying both children and adults who fall in the borderline range of intelligence. The latest revision of the Columbia Mental Maturity Scale, published in 1972, is regarded by Egeland (1978) as a substantial improvement over earlier versions and as an extremely useful screening measure of intelligence in subjects who require a nonverbal and a minimal motor response test. Kaufman considers the Columbia as among the best brief tests available for evaluating preschool children.

One of the oldest and most widely used group intelligence tests is the Otis-Lennon Mental Ability Test, which includes six levels appropriate for schoolchildren from kindergarten through twelfth grade (Otis and Lennon, 1967). Like other group tests, the Otis is economical, but it has the disadvantages of precluding examiner observations and of penalizing children who are slow or poor readers and who are relatively unstimulated and unmotivated by an objective paper-and-pencil test.

If for some reason—perhaps for child adoption or due to early suspicion of mental retardation—an infant must be evaluated, the clinician may find an infant scale useful. For example, the Bayley Scales of Infant Development (BSID) is a well-constructed and standardized measure of infant development for children from two to thirty months of age (Bayley, 1969). Bayley wisely cautions that the scales are not intended to predict a child's future abilities; rather, they are useful in identifying impairments in development that may suggest diagnostic inferences with respect to neurological defects, emotional disturbances, or sensory and environmental deficiencies. It should be emphasized that attempts to assess the intelligence of an infant have been uniformly unsuccessful. Infant intelligence tests are highly unreliable, and their validity with respect to future measures of intelligence have been quite low (McCall, Hogarty, and Hurlburt, 1972).

As useful as intelligence tests have been, they are not trouble-free or without limitations. For some time the IQ was assumed to have a constant meaning regardless of the age of the child and regardless of what test was used to obtain it. We know that unless certain constant relationships are maintained between the dispersion of test scores at each age and the averages for successive ages, the IQ cannot remain constant either for individuals or for groups (Stodolsky and Lesser, 1967; Sattler, 1974; Sattler, 1982). Moreover, tests of intelligence differ in their construction, norms, variability, and ways of calculating IQ, so that an IQ obtained from one is not the same as that derived from another (Anastasi, 1976). It is erroneous to think of an IQ as an absolute number referring to the relative amount of brightness a person possesses. Like all test scores, an IQ can vary as much as plus or minus fifteen points from one test administration to another. To avoid misinterpretations, clinicians rarely—if ever—report the obtained IQ score to the parents and child. Instead, they discuss the findings in terms of a descriptive range (retarded, borderline defective, dull normal, average, bright normal, superior, and very superior) of functioning. Also, many intelligence tests have limited applicability, since they have traditionally excluded black and other minority groups from their normative population. Clinicians must exercise care in selecting the test that is most appropriate for each client and in interpreting the results in light of the available norms for that test.

Most psychologists tend to divide personality tests into two types: self-report inventories and projective tests.

Self-report inventories are characterized by structured stimuli (test items) to which a client responds with a fixed number of specific choices. Frequently they are paper-and-pencil tests which can be administered easily to many people at the same time and which can be scored rapidly and objectively. While they are designed to measure discrete personality traits, most have been intended for use with literate adult and adolescent populations.

The *Minnesota Multiphasic Personality Inventory* (MMPI) is unquestionably the best-known and most widely used personality test of the self-report type (Hathaway and McKinley, 1953). Its success and popularity can be attributed largely to the care exercised by the authors in its original construction and to the voluminous research literature that has accumulated over the last thirty years. It was developed as an inexpensive diagnostic instrument which is easily administered to most people (usually adults), and as a psychometric device which eliminates many of the deficiencies of other inventories. It consists of nine clinical scales that describe the major psychiatric disorders. In addition, it has three validity scales that serve as internal checks on the respondent's tendency (1) to attribute socially desirable traits to herself or himself, (2) to be careless or confused and thus give an invalid answer, and (3) to be either too open or too defensive. Early clinical application of the MMPI dampened the original idea that a deviant elevation on a single clinical scale would correspond to the psychiatric diagnosis of the client. However, those who administered the MMPI soon found that the instrument could be effectively used in making diagnostic decisions when combinations of scale scores (profile patterns) were interpreted (Dahlstrom, Welsh, and Dahlstrom, 1972, 1975). Within recent years computer programs have become available for scoring and interpreting the MMPI. The response can be scored, analyzed, and readied for a printout in narrative form in less time than it takes most people to say "Minnesota Multiphasic Personality Inventory" (Fowler, 1969).

In spite of its popularity and demonstrated value in the diagnostic process, the MMPI is not without limitations. It is a test on which many normal persons achieve elevated scores on the clinical scales. In addition, disturbed persons with some superficial knowledge of abnormal behavior can minimize their psychopathology by not admitting to items that are characteristic of their disorder. The test may be too time consuming (taking about one and a half hours), and it may be inappropriate for persons who are either illiterate or have low reading competence. Although it is neither designed for or useful with young children, its demonstrated value in predicting juvenile deliquency has encouraged clinicians to include it in their test batteries for preadolescent and adolescent youngsters (Hathaway and Monachesi, 1953, 1963). In addition, it is sometimes a fruitful test to give to parents while the clinician works with the child, especially for those parents with suspected psychopathology.

Projective tests involve the presentation of unstructured and ambiguous stimuli to which people may respond freely. Test stimuli are standard in the sense that the same set is presented to each examinee in the same order and with the same instructions. However, the purpose for which the test is intended and the variables it is designed to assess are concealed from the respondent. In contrast to self-report inventories, the stimulus meaning of the projective test items are determined more by the responder than by the predetermined design of the test constructor. The open and free style of responding to projective devices allows wide variations in the number, length, and content of responses, as well as in interpretations that reflect the unique aspects of the respondent's personality

Projective tests come in an extensive and diverse assortment of stimuli and task requirements that make categorization difficult (Lindzey, 1959). The stimulus material ranges from ink blots to pictures of people, animals, and scenes, as well as geometric designs, cartoons, words, and incomplete sentences. Most projective tests assume that every response is psychologically determined and that the test stimuli provide ample opportunity for eliciting a sampe of answers that reflect the person's basic personality. It is further assumed that the test's ambiguity and hidden intent will make the respondents both less defensive and freer to reveal their personalities. Accordingly, a great deal may be inferred from these test responses, including the person's fantasies, defense mechanisms, unconscious motives, latent feelings, and sources of anxiety. Interpreters of projective tests typically adopt a holistic frame of reference, stressing the interaction among personality variables and the totality of personality.

The Rorschach (Ink Blots). Introduced in 1921 by the Swiss psychiatrist Hermann Rorschach, the test consists of a standard series of ten ink blots, five achromatic and five chromatic (Rorschach, 1921, 1942). Although a form is available for group administration, typically the test is given in a fixed sequential order to one person at a time. The test administration includes three separate phases known as *free association, inquiry,* and *testing the limits.* During free association the client is simply required to look at each card and to say aloud what it looks like. The examiner records the client's verbal and nonverbal responses as well as the time taken for the first association and for all associations to each card. The most crucial and difficult phase of administration is the inquiry, because it involves conducting a short nondirective interview to obtain answers concerning the location, the stimulus determinants, and the content of each response. This information enables the examiner to score the responses formally sometime later. When testing young children, some clinicians conduct the inquiry after the child has responded to each card rather than wait until the free association is completed on all ten blots; this avoids the possibility of the child forgetting. Testing the limits involves yet another presentation of the ten cards. It is useful in special circumstances, such as when few responses are given, or when the examiner wants to see if the client is capable of perceiving good form or popular responses.

The Rorschach test uses scores to describe the stimulus characteristics of the test responses and to reflect specific psychological processes. Recent norms for children and adolescents have been published by Levitt and Truumaa (1972). Interpreting Rorschach protocols involves understanding the conventional psychological meaning attached to the scoring categories and learning how and when to modify these interpretations, since scores are considered in the context of other scores. The interpretive process is quite complex because it is not only tied to the psychological meaning of a given scoring category and its relationship to other scores, but also to certain considerations such as the frequency of scores and their patterns and distribution. In addition, the formal structure and the content of the verbal response are analyzed and play an important part in such interpretation.

How effective is the Rorschach test as a psychodiagnostic instrument and as a measure of personality? After more than fifty years of clinical use, and a voluminous literature that exceeds four thousand published papers and books, there is still no clear-cut answer to this question. The issue is complicated by the conflict between research findings and the favorable experiences of clinicians who show continued confidence in its usage. As a psychometric instrument or a test, the Rorschach incorporates so many glaring weaknesses and inadequacies that it is clearly found wanting. The diversity of scoring systems and the idiosyncratic practices of clinicians introduce inconsistencies into interpretation that, in turn, lower predictive accuracy (Exner, 1969). Moreover, Rorschach scores do not occur with frequencies that even approximate a normal distribution. Evidence based on 337 Rorschach protocols not only supports this finding but also notes that almost half the scoring categories show average response frequencies of less than one (Knopf, 1956). In short, half the scoring categories are rarely called into use, making them almost useless both for differential diagnosis and as important indicators of psychological attributes.

Recent reviews of the Rorschach uniformly conclude that it is useful not as a psychometric instrument but rather as a rich source of structured information about an individual's personality (McArthur, 1972; Rabin, 1972; Reznikoff, 1972; Dana, 1978). There is a growing view that the Rorschach can be useful in personality theorizing (Peterson, 1978) and as a clinical source of information if it is treated as a standard interview in which formal scoring is abandoned and only the content of the protocol is examined (Zubin, Eron, and Schumer, 1965; Dana, 1978). This position holds that it is the content of the Rorschach record, and not the formal perceptual determinants, that is the important ingredient for the success and clinical usefulness of the test. Nevertheless, in a recent review of literature, Peterson (1978) concluded that the Rorschach continues to lack predictive validity, although this failure does not seem to deter its strong adherents from using it.

The Thematic Apperception Test (TAT). In 1935 Morgan and Murray introduced the TAT as a method of studying fantasy. They observed that literary works often reflect the authors' experiences, even though these are distorted in fiction writings. Moreover, they contended that one could discern from the writings of a particular author certain common underlying patterns, attitudes, needs, and interests that reflect the author's personality.

As originally conceived, the TAT is a storytelling device that consists of thirty ambiguous black and white pictures plus one blank card. Some cards are intended for boys, girls, men, or women; but all thirty-one cards are seldom used with any given individual. Usually the examiner administers ten cards that seem appropriate for the client. The examiner asks the respondent to make up a story that includes what is going on in the picture, what led up to the events depicted, how it turns out, and how people are feeling and thinking. The examiner may record the story along with side comments and nonverbal behaviors, or the respondent may be asked to write it. Although there are formal scoring systems available, these are primarily used for research, seldom for clinical practice. Instead, clinicians usually analyze the stories as a sample of verbal behavior much like that obtained in an interview.

Occasionally the respondent's identification with the hero is so intense that it evokes obvious autobiographical data, as is the case in the following story made up for Figure 5–1 by an adolescent client who was briefly hospitalized because of severe attacks of anxiety.

> This, to me, is the scene of a boy who just learned about his father's death, and he went back to his room to cry where nobody could see him. Where should I go from here? Again the boy is wondering why his father had to die at an early age, and nobody will tell him. Eventually he forgets about this, but he always had doubts in his mind about certain things that happened. Actually, this struck me as very personal. There is a question of religion involved, and the lack of any medical treatment. That's how my father died when he was forty-nine and I was about twelve years old. He probably died of a cerebral hemorrhage. It happened that this was a Christian Science family, and the boy wondered if medical treatment might have saved this tragedy, but he was never allowed to voice his opinion because of strict religious training. The boy's mother believed vigorously, and was very religious, and the boy had the impression that his father was going along with the mother rather than believing himself. It turned out that the boy finally leaves home, goes out on his own, raises his own family, and buries the feeling.

In the almost fifty years since the TAT was first introduced, and with more than 2000 references on it during that time, it is astonishing there is so little information about the test's standardization, reliability, and validity. Nevertheless, recent research has attempted to establish a relationship between real-life behaviors and components of TAT performance; to measure and evaluate certain motives, especially the achievement motive; to study variations of TAT administration; and to examine the content of TAT stories both as it reflects personality tendencies and as an aid

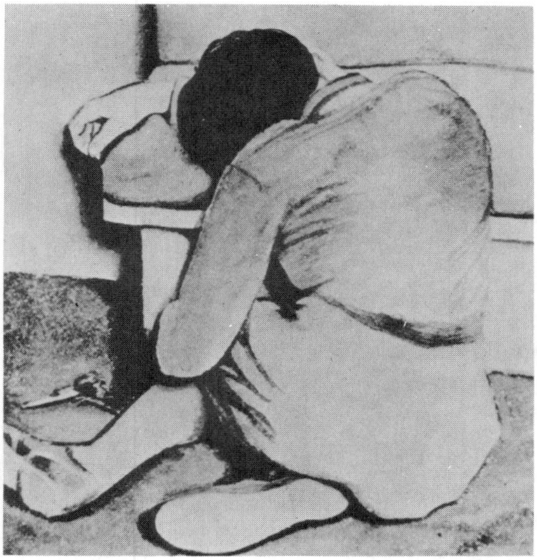

Figure 5-1 (Reprinted by permission of the publishers from Henry A. Murray, *Thematic Apperception Test*, Cambridge, Mass.: Harvard University Press, Copyright © 1943 by the President and Fellows of Harvard College, © 1971 by Henry A. Murray.)

in establishing normative data (Swartz, 1978). Research findings seem to be equivocal with respect to the TAT's effectiveness in differentiating diagnostic categories. However, Swartz concludes his review of the literature with an overall favorable evaluation of this well-established clinical instrument (Swartz, 1978).

Storytelling Techniques for Children. Bellak (1954) designed a TAT-like test called the *Children's Apperception Test* (CAT) for children between the ages of three and ten. The CAT is based on the belief that it is easier for children to identify with animals than with the adult figures of the TAT. The ten pictures show animals in various situations and are intended to elicit responses focusing on the psychosexual development and conflicts initially postulated by Freud as occurring in young children. For example, Card 10 of the CAT was constructed to provide information about the child's toilet training, as shown in Figure 5-2.

Research with the CAT has produced some normative data, but few studies have been directed toward validating the predictive accuracy of interpretations. As a matter of fact, there is evidence that casts doubt on the CAT's clinical usefulness and on Bellak's original assumption that children will more readily identify with animals than with human figures. Several studies have shown that children tell longer stories, manifest more feelings, and evidence greater identification when responding to human pictures than when they respond to the animal pictures of the CAT (Zubin, Eron, and Schumer, 1965).

Constructed for children between the ages of eight and fourteen, the *Michigan Picture Test* (MPT) consists of fifteen pictures (plus one blank card) of various people and scenes —such as a classroom, a family in a variety of activities, and so forth (Andrew et al., 1953). Although the MPT normative data are quite adequate, and some of the responses have been related to outside measures of maladjustment in children, the MPT has not enjoyed widespread clinical use.

Drawing Techniques. In 1926 Florence Goodenough introduced a technique for measuring intellectual levels of children from their drawings of a man (Goodenough, 1926). At the same time she suggested that her test was also capable of reflecting personality factors. Since then other writers have been even more impressed with this observation. Some even contend that drawings yield more and richer data about personality than intelligence. Moreover, it is generally assumed that a human figure drawing is an unconscious projection of oneself and that psychodiagnostic clues are qualitatively reflected in the drawing (Machover, 1949; Hammer, 1958; Klapfer and Faulbes, 1976). There are a number of variants of the draw-a-man test. The best known is described by Machover, who asks the client first to draw a picture of a person on a blank sheet of white paper and then to draw a person of the opposite sex on a sep-

Figure 5-2 (Reprinted by permission of the author, Leopold Bellak, M.D. and the publisher, C.P.S., Inc., P.O. Box 83, Larchmont, New York 10538.)

arate sheet. In addition, she proposed thirty-three questions to ask children, to obtain more specific information about their performance (Machover, 1960, pp. 238–257).

Tests that require drawings of human figures are easy to administer and require little time and cost. As an added bonus, they have been known to offer fanciful but contradictory interpretations; for example, inadequacy feelings are reflected in the drawing of either very small figures or very large ones; and both intellectual strivings and feelings of intellectual inadequacy are given as interpretations of a drawing of a large head (Urban, 1963). Drawing is a technique that has enjoyed a degree of clinical popularity exceeded only by the substantial body of negative findings concerning its validity.

Sentence Completion Techniques (SCT). Growing out of the word association technique, where the client responds to a set of stimulus words with the first word that comes to mind, the SCT consists of a series of sentence stems that the client completes. For example, a client might be asked to complete the following:

I am afraid____________________.
I got mad____________________.
The people I like best____________.
My main trouble is______________.

The SCT is an extremely flexible device for measuring personality in that the stimuli (sentence stems) can readily be manipulated to assess specific areas of personality and to meet the requirements of different populations and situations. Thus, it is not surprising that there are many forms of the SCT that are applicable to children, adults, females, and males in such diverse settings as the classroom, the mental health clinic, and the workplace.

As with other projective techniques, the SCT assumes that the responses reveal information about the client's personality. Interpretation usually involves content analysis that ranges in clinical practice from formal scoring to intuitive inspection. Reliability and validity estimates are higher than those reported with most other projective techniques, making the SCT highly useful in clinical practice and research.

Tests of Neurological Impairment. The possibility that the abnormal behaviors of a child are the result or the byproduct of some central nervous system dysfunction is an option that is almost always under consideration in the psychodiagnostic process. Unfortunately, the area of brain dysfunction, which includes many vague but interchangeable terms such as *brain damage, organic brain disorders, organicity, central nervous system damage,* or *dysfunction,* is quite complex and imprecise. Reference to any of these labels suggests the illogical struggle to fit under one broad rubric a set of very heterogeneous conditions that only belong together because "something" has happened to the brain. There is room in this category for such diverse causal agents as tumors and lesions, infections, toxic agents, brain injuries, and biochemical and hormonal imbalances. These circumstances are further complicated by the fact that there is no one-to-one relationship between brain damage and specific behavioral manifestations, although certain behavioral changes in memory, attention span, and perceptual-motor coordination, among others, have been associated with the performance of individuals with known brain damage. Moreover, since behavior is frequently determined by multiple factors, it is not easy to determine when a given behavioral change is the product of psychological or organic influences, or both.

Therefore, it is not surprising that behavioral tests designed to determine the presence of brain damage, not to mention its location or extent, have encountered serious predictive difficulties. What is surprising is how well some tests actually do work in the clinical setting. We shall discuss several examples of tests intended specifically to assess brain damage, although we should also note that the clinician uses data obtained from many of the other tests (personality and intelligence) already presented in this chapter.

1. The Bender-Gestalt Test. First introduced in 1938 by Lauretta Bender (1938), the test consists of nine figures printed on separate white cards. The figures were taken from designs initially used by Wertheimer to demonstrate principles of perceptual organization. (See Figure 5–3.) They are given in a fixed order to both children and adults with the simple request to copy each design on one unlined sheet of white paper. Research has shown that simple changes in the instructions given to the respondent, and whether or not the individual is permitted to move the stimulus cards, affect differences in test performance (Hutt, 1969).

Bender provides neither normative data nor a formal scoring system. Rather, she prefers to inspect the child's performance intuitively and make interpretations about perceptual organization and maturation, perceptual motor coordination, and neurological impairment. Koppitz (1964) has developed one of several scoring systems based on specific errors (distortions, rotations, integration failures, and others) found in the responses of young children ranging in age from five to ten. Only its ease and economy, as well as the occasional indication from the reproductions of possible brain damage, seem to justify the popularity and widespread use of the Bender-Gestalt Test in clinical practice.

2. Graham-Kendall Memory-for-Designs Test. Inasmuch as memory is an area of functioning that often is affected by brain damage, tests that involve memory are impor-

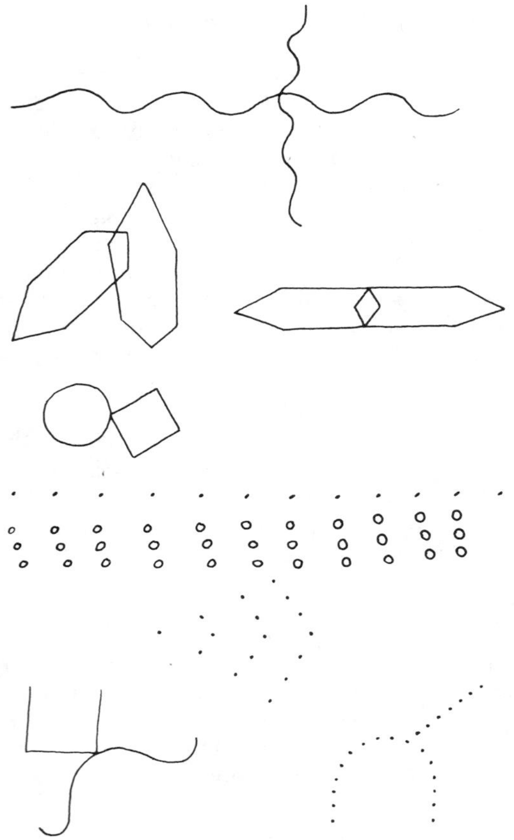

Figure 5-3 (From the Bender Gestalt Test as published by the American Orthopsychiatric Association.)

tant in the clinician's repertoire. The Graham-Kendall Test requires an individual to draw from memory designs that are presented and exposed for five seconds. The test consists of fifteen figures, similar to those of the Bender except that they have been selected for their demonstrated capacity to discriminate between normal and brain-damaged persons between the ages of nine and sixty. A highly reliable scoring system is available that is easy to use, especially by inexperienced examiners.

3. *The Revised Benton Visual Retention Test (Benton, 1963).* This test includes three alternate forms of a set of ten designs which the child is asked to copy and draw from memory. Presumably, the test taps visual memory, visual perception, and visual-motor abilities. Since its earlier publication, a set of detailed norms have been added to the literature (Rice, 1972; Sattler, 1982).

4. *Halstead Neuropsychological Test Battery for Children and the Reitan-Indiana Neuropsychological Test Battery for Children.* Both these tests contain a variety of cognitive and perceptual-motor tests as well as an intelligence test (for the Halstead) which some have regarded as clinically useful in identifying neurological impairment in children. At present the information concerning the reliability and validity of these batteries is limited, and their clinical utility seems to be confined to relatively few individuals who have been trained to use them (Sattler, 1982).

In the course of a psychodiagnostic work-up, there are instances where special tests are used to answer specific questions or to provide data that would fill in existing gaps in the information already available. This is particularly true in evaluating children who are referred because they are experiencing some difficulties in school. It is often not enough to assess their intelligence, because these results do not shed enough light on the child's actual performance or academic achievement.

A wide assortment of achievement tests are available for primary, middle, and high school grades that measure achievement in a variety of academic subjects, such as reading, spelling, arithmetic, social studies, and science. Typically these tests are of the paper-and-pencil variety and can be administered by the teacher to a group of youngsters. Most achievement tests are easily and quickly scored, and they provide the user with national and sometimes regional norms, so that the individuals' scores may be compared with the performance of others. The addition of data on the child's achievement allows the clinician an opportunity not only to make these comparisons but also to relate the child's achievement scores to his or her overall intellectual abilities. The clinician can then more precisely determine whether or not the child's academic performance is discrepant with his or her overall capacity, in which subject areas the child is deficient and/or accelerated, and what performance patterns evidenced by the child may serve as potential clues for differential diagnosis.

5. *Illinois Test of Psycholinguistic Abilities (ITPA) (Kirk, McCarthy, and Kirk, 1968).* This test was designed to assist in the diagnosis of learning disabilities and mental retardation. It can be given to children between two and ten years of age, and it includes ten cognitive subtests which tend to focus on the visual and auditory reception and processing of information. The standardization population consisted of children of average intelligence who came from families with slightly above-the-national-average income and educational levels. Thus, the norms have restricted applicability, since minority and lower-income groups are underrepresented. Research aimed at evaluating the ITPA for diagnosing reading disorders has yielded both positive and negative findings, leaving unanswered as yet the question of its effectiveness in diagnosing learning disabilities (Carroll, 1972). More recent evaluations led Silverstein (1978) to ponder whether the test does more than assess general intelligence, as it purports to do; while Sattler (1982) concludes that its clinical usefulness is limited.

Behavioral Assessment

Behavioral assessment involves procedures that are unlike those used in psychological testing and diagnostic interviewing, since this approach aims neither to uncover personality traits or dynamics of the client nor to arrive at a diagnostic classification of the client's present condition. Instead, behavioral assessment sets out to (1) determine the frequency of unwanted behaviors in specific situations, in order to obtain a reliable estimate of the magnitude of the problem; (2) identify the variables that are currently maintaining the client's abnormal behaviors; and (3) evaluate the responses the client is capable of making, in order to design the most effective treatment plan. Techniques used to accumulate data for these objectives include behavioral interviews, behavioral observations, and inventories and behavioral surveys such as behavior checklists and self-report measures.

Behavioral Interview. Although it differs from the traditional diagnostic interview discussed earlier, the behavioral interview is an important tool in establishing a good working relationship with parents and child. Instead of focusing on historical information to understand or classify the underlying psychopathology, the behavioral interview takes a more contemporary perspective. It seeks information about the child's present problem behaviors and the antecedent and consequent stimuli that may maintain them. The clinician may ask the parents to aid in the assessment process by monitoring and recording the target behaviors and by allowing the clinician to come into the home and/or school to make observations. The behavioral clinician emphasizes objective and specific descriptions of behavior that may require training parents to be more objective, accurate, specific, and reliable in their reporting (Mash and Terdal, 1976; Evans and Nelson, 1977). In addition, the behavioral interview is more flexible and less restricted to a particular place or time than the traditional interview. It may take place in the home, the classroom, or over the phone, and it may involve several interviews with different people. Table 5–5 illustrates a sequential interview guide which one behavioral clinician has found useful in accumulating behavioral data and in training parents.

Behavioral Observation.

1. *Direct observation* of the child's actual behavior in a variety of settings and situations provides the primary assessment data for the behaviorally oriented clinician. Accordingly, the clinician—aided by observations of the child's problem behaviors reported by parents, teachers, pediatrician, and other involved people—begins the assessment by de-

Table 5-5 Summary of an Interview Guide for Parents[a]

Sequential Points To Be Covered

1. Have the parents establish general goals and complaints.
2. Have the parents reduce the general goals and complaints to a list of discrete behaviors which require an increase or decrease in frequency.
3. Have the parents select from the ranked list a single problem behavior on which to concentrate their efforts.
4. Have the parents specify in behavioral terms the precise behavior that is presently occurring and which they desire to change.
5. Have the parents specify in behavioral terms the precise behavior which they desire.
6. Have the parents discuss how they may proceed to the terminal behavior in a step-by-step manner.
7. Have the parents list positive and negative reinforcers which they think will be effective in bringing about behavior changes.
8. Have the parents discuss what deprivations are possible.
9. Have the parents clearly establish what they want to do, either to increase or decrease a behavior or to do both.
10. Have the parents discuss the situation in which the desired behavior should occur.
11. Have the parents discuss the situation in which the undesired behavior should not occur.
12. Have the parents determine a situation which increases the likelihood that some form or portion of the desired behavior occurs.
13. Have the parents discuss how they may increase desired behavior by immediately giving a positive reinforcer following the behavior.
14. Have the parents discuss how they may increase desired behavior by immediately terminating a negative reinforcer following the behavior.
15. Have the parents discuss how they may decrease undesired behavior by withholding the reinforcers which follow it.
16. Have the parents discuss how they may decrease undesired behavior by removing a positive reinforcer.
17. Have the parents discuss how they may decrease undesired behavior by time-out.
18. Discuss with the parents how they may pattern the reinforcers they give to the child.
19. Have the parents discuss how they may vary the reinforcers they give to the child.
20. Have the parents discuss how they may apply two or more procedures simultaneously.
21. Have the parents rehearse verbally the entire program.

[a] From Holland, 1976. Reprinted with permission from the Springer Publishing Co.

lineating the target behaviors to be observed. This is usually followed by a *baseline* observational period in which either the frequency or the duration of the target behavior is systematically recorded on a daily basis or on the days when the child is in the situation where the behavior occurs. In this way the frequency of temper tantrums or the duration of rocking behavior serves as a baseline from which to measure at a later date the effect of behavior therapy.

Baseline observational data can be obtained in the actual setting in which the target behavior occurs (such as in the home and school) or in the clinic. Frequency measures are easy to obtain and can be recorded by the clinician and/or the person appropriate to the setting. This has the added benefit of making everyone concerned much more aware of the problem behavior. By dividing the number of times the target behavior occurs by the time of the specified observational period, the clinician can obtain a *response rate*. In instances where it is desirable to observe several behaviors at the same time, *interval recording* or *time-sampling* is ordinarily favored. This method divides each observation session into small time intervals (about twenty seconds) in which the clinician records the presence (+) or absence (0) of each behavior. Since only one occurrence of each behavior is recorded for each interval, the method fails to yield an exact frequency tally of the behaviors under study. To obtain a measure of the duration of the behavior, or *response duration,* the clinician notes the time interval between the beginning and the termination of the target behavior.

In order to identify the stimuli that maintain the target behavior, the clinician also records changes in environmental stimuli before and after the behavior occurs. Those stimuli that precede the target behavior, called *antecedent stimuli,* may be signals to the child that reinforcement will be given when the behavior is emitted, as illustrated in the attention and assistance a boy receives if he waits until father comes home before doing his homework. The stimuli events that occur after the behavior is emitted are known as *consequences* or *consequent stimuli,* and they may serve as reinforcers that increase the probability that the behavior will occur again. In this instance the boy's refusal to do his homework until the evening is reinforced by his being permitted to play or watch TV. Information about the antecedent and consequent stimuli is necessary for the preparation of a behavioral intervention plan, since these stimuli play an important role in the maintenance of the unwanted behavior. Most often the clinician gathers this information from the initial interview with the parents, from reports of teachers and others who have observed the child's problem behavior, and through direct observation of the child in a variety of settings.

2. *Situational observation* is another widely used behavioral observation technique. Behavior sampling may occur in a clinical setting where the clinician can make observations in a systematic manner and under relatively controlled conditions. As an illustration, a youngster with a phobia for dogs might be asked to participate in a Behavioral Avoidance Test (BAT) in which he enters a room which houses a caged dog. He is asked to approach and, if possible, to pet the dog, while his behavior is observed and monitored by the clinician (Bandura, Grusec, and Menlove, 1967). The BAT is used both to assess the severity of the youngster's phobia and to evaluate the effectiveness of the behavior therapy. Situational observations may also be used to assess mother-child interactions, for example, with regard to understanding the antecedent and consequent stimuli reinforcing the child's passive and compliant behaviors. Under these circumstances the clinician might observe and record the mother's behavior toward the child whenever the child attempts to be assertive, as well as what she does when the child is passive. In this way the clinician can accumulate valuable data about both the child's target behavior and some of the stimuli that maintain it. Situational observations allow the clinician to structure the situation in order that certain behaviors will occur, and they also permit comparisons of the child's behavior within and between situations. Problems associated with this type of behavioral observation include determining which situation is best for eliciting the desired behaviors, and the uncertain extent to which one can generalize from these simulated situations to everyday situations (Evans and Nelson, 1977).

Inventories and Behavioral Surveys. These measures have been used by behavioral clinicians in conjunction with direct and situational observations as a way of providing initial data about problem behaviors. However, this approach is, in general, subjective, and it runs the risk of low reliability. Rating scales of the sort described below vary considerably in number of items and specificity and types of behaviors included; the way items are rated and scored; and the age for which behaviors are appropriate. For the most part such measures are characterized by a series of items on which clients or others rate the client's behavior with respect to the presence or absence, or the degree of intensity, of particular events or behaviors. The following are some scales that fall under this category.

1. *The Behavior Problem Checklist (BPC)* is a three-point scale for rating traits of problem behavior in childhood and adolescence (Quay, 1977). Its three primary subscales (Conduct Problems; Personality Problems; Inadequacy-Immaturity) are derived from a factor analysis of fifty-eight items describing deviant behavior, and a fourth subscale (Socialized-Delinquency) is derived from factor-analytic studies of case histories. The BPC has been used to differentiate dimensions of deviance, select different treatment programs, measure changes in behavior produced by drugs and psychological interventions, and determine systematic differences among children with divergent patterns of deviance (Quay, 1977).

2. *The Conner's Teacher Rating Scale* (Conners, 1969) consists of thirty-nine items which are rated (by teachers) on a four-point scale. A factor analysis of the items produced the following five factors: Defiance or Aggressive Conduct Disorder, Daydreaming or Inattentive Dimension, Anxious-Fearful Dimension, Hyperactivity, and Health Factor. This scale was used to assess the behavioral changes of hyperactive children in a behavior modification program which was successful in lowering their hyperactivity (O'Leary et al., 1976). It was also used successfully in studies which have demonstrated the relationship between hyperactivity and sustained attention in young children (Kirchner, 1975; Hayim, 1980).

3. *The Fear Survey Schedule-II (FSS-II)* consists of fifty-one fears (empirically selected) that adolescents and college students can rate in terms of seven different intensities ranging from "none" to "terror" (Greer, 1976). Ratings on such items as sharp objects, dead bodies, failing a test, arguing with parents and hypodermic needles enable the clinician to assess the various fear stimuli that the client tends to avoid. The FSS-II is often used as a research tool in selecting subjects who differ on specific fears.

Evaluation of Behavioral Assessment. Behavioral assessment is a relatively new but exciting development that provides a detailed and systematic analysis of problem behaviors and the environmental stimuli that maintain them. It is an approach that is intimately tied to treatment; therefore, it has the additional advantage of generating data that are used to evaluate the effectiveness of behavior therapy. If the treatment program fails, the clinician can then reexamine the data, gather more, and reformulate and test another remediation plan. While the traditional psychodynamic approach faults the behavioral orientation principally on the grounds that the latter deals only with symptoms and ignores the underlying basis of the disorder, there is little evidence that the criticism is warranted. Technical advances in behavioral assessment have been abundant during recent years, and more extensive information may be found in the following publications: Gelfand and Hartmann, 1975; McReynolds, 1975; Mash and Terdal, 1976, Ciminero, Calhoun, and Adams, 1977; and Markolin, 1978.

SUMMARY

In this chapter we looked at the clinical process and the methods used by clinicians in diagnosing abnormal behavior. We discussed and evaluated clinical observations, the interview, psychological tests, and behavioral assessment. In addition, a variety of specific behaviors that have potential value as diagnostic clues were identified and described.

The clinical process is initiated through a referral made either directly by the client or through the intervention of others. Those who are self-referred are likely to be more aware of their problems and more motivated to change their behavioral patterns than those who are directed to the clinician by others. Children are rarely, if ever, self-referred, although they may either directly or indirectly "cry out" for help.

The referral also serves to provide the clinician with an initial orientation to the client's major problems. Sometimes it provides additional information about the symptoms and what, if anything, has been done to deal with them. The diagnostic process is intended to gather sufficient data to classify the abnormal behavior, identify the causes or arrive at a working hypothesis about causal factors, and construct a remedial plan.

Observations of behaviors should be systematically made within each of the following areas: (1) general appearance and attire, and bodily surface signs; (2) emotional gestures and facial expressions; (3) gross and fine motor acts; (4) quality of relationship between client and others; and (5) verbalization of the client.

The interview is a formal conversation between two or more people that has been prearranged for a specific purpose. Interviews may be structured or unstructured. How they are conducted varies widely, depending on the orientation and training of the interviewer, the setting and purpose of the interview, and the characteristics of the interviewee.

Rapport between the client and the clinician is the primary objective of the initial interview, along with the gathering of information about the client's current problems and symptoms, when and how they first appeared, the circumstances surrounding their development, and the stimulus events that seem to evoke them. The case history study, which systematically reviews certain important past areas of the client's life, is undertaken by some clinicians.

Problems of reliability and validity associated with the interview process include its complexity and variability, interviewer and interviewee biases, and its questionable efficiency in making predictions. Recent advances such as the standardized interview and computer interviewing provide opportunities for greater systematic study of the interview process.

Psychological tests are useful devices for obtaining important information about people. These instruments enable psychologists to collect data in a standard, prescribed, and quantifiable manner.

Intelligence tests are widely used, as illustrated by the Binet and the Wechsler Scales. These instruments make possible the assessment of baseline cognitive capabilities, as well as the identification of specific intellectual impairments. Although IQ scores are often used in decision-making processes, they are not without their limitations.

Other types of intelligence measures may be used with special populations. Large numbers of people can be quickly assessed through the use of group intelligence tests. The Bayley Scales of Infant Development are employed to identify impairment of a baby's functioning. For nonverbal individuals the Porteus Maze Test is best in assessing intellectual level.

A second well-known type of psychological test is personality measure. Such tests include self-report inventories and projective tests. Self-report inventories, such as the MMPI, are structured devices that permit rapid and objective scoring. Projective tests, on the other hand, enable the free and open assessment of the needs, drives, and attitudes of people.

Several tests of brain damage that claim to identify central nervous system dysfunction were discussed. Generally, these tests require the copying of figures from cards (as in the Bender-Gestalt) or the reproduction of designs from memory (as in the Graham-Kendall Memory-for-Design Test). We also discussed special tests of academic achievement and those used to assess deficits in a wide array of mental functions.

Behavioral assessment sets out to (1) determine the frequency of unwanted behaviors in specific situations so as to obtain a reliable estimate of the magnitude of the problem; (2) identify the variables that are currently maintaining the client's abnormal thoughts, feelings, and behaviors; and (3) evaluate the responses the client is capable of making, in order to plan the most effective treatment plan. It includes the behavioral interview as well as direct and situational observations of the child's actual behavior in a variety of settings and situations in which a baseline measure of the target behavior is obtained. Other sources of behavioral assessment involving inventories and behavioral surveys were also discussed.

EPILOGUE

Unfortunately there is little to say about what happened to Freddy and his family; Mr. and Mrs. B. were unwilling to deal either with the problem or with the results of the psychological evaluation. While they acknowledged that they did not like some of Freddy's behavior at home, they quickly noted that these incidents were minor and only transient (sleeping with his father or refusing to eat what his mother cooks). They completely rejected the possibility that Freddy's infantile patterns were in any way related to what they were doing. They excused Freddy's social withdrawal on the grounds of economic circumstances that required them to hold down full-time jobs. Being unable to accept much responsibility for Freddy's adjustment problems or to go along with treatment recommendations that would involve all of them, Mr. and Mrs. B. focused on the principal and the school as scapegoats. Accordingly, they felt it was the school that failed in helping Freddy to adjust better; and they said that probably the school was to blame for providing an environment where such behaviors could develop. This became both the source of their anger and their justification for withdrawing Freddy from the school. Thus, they saw themselves as the injured parties—the family whose problems were the symptoms of Freddy's mistreatment at school, and the family who spent money it could not afford to have Freddy in a private school that did him in.

At the end of the term, Mr. and Mrs. B. transferred Freddy to a local public grade school, believing that they had taken a positive and major step in resolving his problems. They steadfastly refused additional sessions with the psychologist or any form of therapeutic assistance. They avoided in-depth conversations with the school principal about Freddy, telling the school that they were removing him because of financial difficulties. No further follow-up was possible.

REFERENCES

ANASTASI, A. *Psychological Testing,* 4th ed. New York: Macmillan, 1976.

ANDREW, G., HARTWELL, S. W., HUTT, M. L., and WALTON, R. E. *The Michigan Picture Test.* Chicago: Science Research Associates, 1953.

BALL, R. S., MERRILFIELD, P., and STOTT, L. H. *Extended Merrill-Palmer Scale.* Chicago: Stoelting, 1978.

BANDURA, A., GRUSEC, J. E., and MENLOVE, R. L. Vicarious Extinction of Avoidance Behavior. *Journal of Personality and Social Psychology,* 1967, *5,* 16–23.

BAYLEY, N. *Bayley Scales of Infant Development Manual.* New York: The Psychological Corporation, 1969.

BELLAK, L. *The Thematic Apperception Test and the Children's Apperception Test in Clinical Use.* New York: Grune and Stratton, 1954.

BELLAK, L., and BELLAK, S. S. *Children's Apperception Test* (C.A.T.), 4th ed. P.O. Box 83, Larchmont, N.Y.: C.P.S., Inc., 1961 (now published by Grune and Stratton, 381 Park Avenue South, New York, N.Y.)

BENDER, L. A Visual Motor Gestalt Test and Its Clinical Use. *The American Orthopsychiatric Association Research Monographs,* No. 3, 1938.

BENDER, L. *Instructions for the Use of Visual Motor Gestalt Test.* New York: The American Orthopsychiatric Association, 1946.

BENE, E., and ANTHONY, J. *Manual for the Family Relations Test.* London: National Foundation for Educational Research in England and Wales, 1957.

BENTON, A. L. *Benton Visual Retention Test,* rev. ed. New York: Psychological Corporation, 1963.

BORTNER, M. Review of the Progressive Matrices. In O. K. Buros (ed.), *The Eighth Mental Measurement Yearbook.* Highland Park, N. J.: Gryphon Press, 1978, pp. 764–765.

CARROLL, J. B. Review of the ITPA. In O. K. Buros (ed.), *The Seventh Mental Measurements Yearbook,* Vol. 1. Highland Park, N. J.: Gryphon Press. 1972, pp. 819–823.

CIMINERO, A. R., CALHOUN, K. S., and ADAMS, H. E. (eds.). *Handbook of Behavioral Assessment.* New York: John Wiley, 1977.

CONNERS, C. K. A Teacher Rating Scale for Use in Drug Studies with Children. *American Journal of Psychiatry,* 1969, *126,* 884–888.

DAHLSTROM, W. G., WELSH, G. S., and DAHLSTROM, L. E. *An MMPI Handbook: Vol. 1: Clinical Interpretation. A Revised Edition.* Minneapolis: University of Minnesota Press, 1972.

DAHLSTROM, W. G., WELSH, G. S., and DAHLSTROM, L. E. *An MMPI Handbook, Revised Edition: Vol. 2, Research Applications.* Minneapolis: University of Minnesota Press, 1975.

DAILY, C. A. The Life History as a Criterion of Assessment. *Journal of Counseling Psychology*, 1960, *7*, 20–23.

DANA, R. H. In O. K. Buros (ed.), *The Eighth Mental Measurement Yearbook,* Vol. 1. Highland Park, N. J.: Gryphon Press, 1978, pp. 1040–1047.

DUNN, L. M. *Expanded Manual for the Peabody Picture Vocabulary Test.* Minneapolis: American Guidance Service, 1965.

DUNN, L. M. *Peabody Picture Vocabulary Test Manual,* Nashville, Tenn.: American Guidance Service, 1959.

EGELAND, B. R. Review of the Columbia Mental Maturity Scale. In O. K. Buros (ed.), *The Eighth Mental Measurement Yearbook.* Highland Park, N. J.: Gryphon Press, 1978, pp. 298–299.

EKMAN, P. Body Position, Facial Expression and Verbal Behavior During Interviews. *Journal of Personality and Social Psychology,* 1964, *68*, 295–301.

EKMAN, P. Differential Communication of Affect by Head and Body Cues. *Journal of Personality and Social Psychology,* 1965, *2*, 726–735.

EVANS, I. M., and NELSON, R. O. Assessment of Child Behavior Problems. In A. R. Ciminero, K. S. Calhoun, and H. E. Adams (eds.), *Handbook of Behavioral Assessment.* New York: John Wiley, 1977, pp. 603–681.

EXNER, J. E., JR. *The Rorschach Systems.* New York: Grune and Stratton, 1969.

FOGEL, M. Picture Description and Interpretation in Brain Damaged Patients. *Cortex,* 1967, *3*, 433–448.

FOWLER, R. D., JR. Automated Interpretation of Test Data. In J. N. Butcher (ed.), *MMPI Research Developments and Clinical Applications.* New York: McGraw-Hill, 1969, pp. 105–126.

GELFAND, D. M., and HARTMANN, D. P. *Child Behavior Analysis and Therapy.* Elmsford, N. Y.: Pergamon Press, 1975.

GOODENOUGH, F. L. *Measurement of Intelligence by Drawings.* Yonkers, N. Y.: World Press, 1926.

GREER, J. H. The Development of a Scale to Measure Fear. In E. J. Mash and L. F. Terdal (eds.), *Behavior Therapy Assessment.* New York: Springer, 1976, pp. 155–166.

HAMMER, E. F. (ed.). *The Clinical Application of Projective Drawings.* Springfield, Ill.: Chas. C Thomas, 1958.

HATHAWAY, S. R., and MCKINLEY, J. C. *Manual for the Minnesota Multiphasic Personality Inventory.* Minneapolis: University of Minnesota Press, 1943.

HATHAWAY, S. R., and MONACHESI, E. D. *Adolescent Personality and Behavior: MMPI Patterns of Normal, Delinquent, and Other Outcomes.* Minneapolis: University of Minnesota Press, 1963.

HATHAWAY, S. R., and MONACHESI, E. D. (eds.). *Analyzing and Predicting Juvenile Delinquency with MMPI.* Minneapolis: University of Minnesota Press, 1953.

HAYIM, NANCY S. An Investigation of the Relations among 3 Behavioral Measures of Attention. Unpublished master's thesis, Emory University, 1980.

HIMMELSTEIN, P. Review of the Slosson Intelligence Test. In O. K. Buros (ed.), *The Seventh Mental Measurements Yearbook.* Highland Park, N. J.: Gryphon Press, 1972, pp. 765–766.

HOLLAND, C. J. An Interview Guide for Behavioral Counseling with Parents. In E. J. Mash and L. F. Terdal (eds.), *Behavior Therapy Assessment.* New York: Springer, 1976, pp. 99–108.

HUNT, J. V. McCarthy Scales of Children's Abilities. In O. K. Buros (ed.), *The Eighth Mental Measurement Yearbook.* Highland Park, N. J.: Gryphon Press, 1978, pp. 309–311.

HUTT, M. L. *Hutt Adaptation of the Gestalt Bender Test,* 2nd ed. New York: Grune and Stratton, 1969.

IZARD, C. E. *The Face of Emotion.* New York: Appleton-Century-Crofts, 1971.

KAUFMAN, A. S. Review of the Columbia Mental Maturity Scale. In O. K. Buros (ed.), *The Eighth Mental Measurement Yearbook.* Highland Park, N. J.: Gryphon Press, 1978, pp. 299–301.

KAUFMAN, A. S., and KAUFMAN, N. L. *Clinical Evaluation of Young Children with the McCarthy Scales.* New York: Grune and Stratton, 1977.

KELLY, E. L., and FISKE, D. W. *The Prediction of Performance in Clinical Psychology.* Ann Arbor, Mich: University of Michigan Press, 1951.

KIRK, S. A., MCCARTHY, J. J., and KIRK, W. D. *Illinois Test of Psycholinguistic Abilities,* Rev. ed. Urbana, Ill: University of Illinois Press, 1968.

KLOPFER, W. G., and TAULBEE, E. S. Projective Tests. *Annual Review of Psychology,* 1976, *27*, 543–567.

KIRCHNER, G. L. Differences in the Vigilance Performance of Highly Active and Normal Second-Grade Males under Four Exceptional Conditions. Unpublished Doctoral Dissertation, Emory University, 1975.

KNOPF, I. J. Rorschach Summary Scores in Differential Diagnosis. *Journal of Consulting Psychology,* 1956, *20*, 99–104.

KOPPITZ, E. M. *The Bender Gestalt Test for Young Children.* New York: Grune and Stratton, 1964.

LEVITT, E. E., and TRUUMAA, A. *The Rorschach Technique with Children and Adolescents.* New York: Grune and Stratton, 1972.

LINDZEY, G. On the Classification of Projective Techniques. *Psychological Bulletin,* 1959, *56*, 158–168.

MCARTHUR, C. C., A Review of the Rorschach. In O. K. Buros (ed.), *The Seventh Mental Measurements Yearbook.* Highland Park, N.J.: Gryphon Press, 1972, pp. 440–443.

MCCARTHY, D. A. *Manual for the McCarthy Scales of Children's Abilities.* New York: Psychological Corporation, 1972.

MACHOVER, K. *Personality Projection in the Drawing of the Human Figure.* Springfield, Ill.: Chas. C Thomas, 1949.

MACHOVER, K. Sex Differences in the Developmental Pattern of Children as Seen in Human Figure Drawings. In A. I. Rabin and M. R. Haworth (eds.), *Projective Techniques with Children*. New York: Grune and Stratton, 1960, pp. 238–257.

MARKOLIN, D., II (ed.). *Child Behavior Therapy*. New York: Gardner Press, 1978.

MASH, E. J., and TERDAL, L. F. (eds.). *Behavior Therapy Assessment*. New York: Springer, 1976.

MATARAZZO, J. D. The Interview. In B. B. Wolman (ed.), *Handbook of Clinical Psychology*. New York: McGraw-Hill, 1965, pp. 403–450.

MCARTHUR, C. C. A Review of the Rorschach. In O. K. Buros (ed.), *The Seventh Mental Measurements Yearbook*, Vol. 1. Highland Park, N. J.: Gryphon Press, 1972, pp. 440–443.

MCCALL, R. B., HOGARTY, P. S., and HURLBURT, N. Transitions in Infant Sensorimotor Development and the Prediction of Childhood IQ. *American Psychologist*, 1972, *27*, 728–748.

MCREYNOLDS, P. (ed.). *Advances in Psychological Assessment*, Vol. 3. San Francisco: Jossey-Bass, 1975.

MEEHL, P. E. *Clinical versus Statistical Prediction: A Theoretical Analysis and a Review of the Evidence*. Minneapolis: University of Minnesota Press, 1954.

MUNN, J. L. The Effect of Knowledge of the Situation upon Judgment of Emotion from Facial Expressions. *Journal of Abnormal and Social Psychology*, 1940, *35*, 324–338.

MURRAY, H. A. *Thematic Apperception Test*. Cambridge, Mass.: Harvard University Press, 1943.

O'LEARY, K. D., PELHAM, W. E., ROSENBAUM, A., and PRICE, G. H. Behavioral Treatment of Hyperkinetic Children: An Experimental Evaluation of Its Usefulness. *Clinical Pediatrics*, 1976, *15*, 510–515.

OTIS, A. S., and LENNON, R. T. *Otis-Lennon Mental Ability Test*. New York: Harcourt, Brace, & World, 1967.

PETERSON, R. A., In O. K. Buros (ed.), *The Eighth Mental Measurement Yearbook*. Highland Park, N. J.: Gryphon Press, 1978, pp. 1042–1044.

PETERSON, D. R. *The Clinical Study of Social Behavior*. New York: Appleton-Century-Crofts, 1968.

PORTEUS, S. D. *Porteus Maze Test. Fifty Years Application*. Palo Alto, Calif.: Pacific Books, 1965.

QUAY, H. C. Measuring Dimensions of Deviant Behavior: The Behavior Problem Checklist. *Journal of Abnormal Child Psychology*, 1977, *5*, 277–288.

RABIN, A. I. A Review of the Rorschach. In O. K. Buros (ed.), *The Seventh Mental Measurement Yearbook*, Vol. 1. Highland Park, N. J.: Gryphon Press, 1972, pp. 443–446.

RAVEN, J. C. *Progressive Matrices*. London: Lewis, 1938.

RAVEN, J. C. *Advanced Progressive Matrices*. London: Lewis, 1947a.

RAVEN, J. C. *Coloured Progressive Matrices*. London: Lewis, 1947b.

REZNIKOFF, M. A Review of the Rorschach. In O. K. Buros (ed.), *The Seventh Mental Measurement Yearbook*, Vol. 1. Highland Park, N. J.: Gryphon Press, 1972, pp. 446–449.

RICE, J. A. Benton's Visual Retention Test: New Age, Scale Scores, and Percentile Norms for Children. Paper presented at the meeting of the American Psychological Association, Honolulu, September 1972.

RORSCHACH, H. *Psychodiagnostik*. Methodik und Ergebnisse eines Wahrnehmungs-diagnostischen Experiments (Deutenlassen Bon Zufallsformen). Bern and Leipzig: E. Bircher, 1921.

RORSCHACH, H. *Psychodiagnostics: A Diagnostic Test Based on Perception*. New York: Grune and Stratton, 1942.

SAGON, NANCY HAYIM. An Investigation of the Effects of Rewards and Feedback on Sustained Attention and Activity Levels of First Grade Children. Unpublished doctoral dissertation, Emory University, 1982.

SARBIN, T. R. A. A Contribution to the Study of Actuarial and Individual Methods of Prediction. *American Journal of Sociology*, 1943, *48*, 593–602.

SATTLER, J. M. *Assessment of Children's Intelligence*. Philadelphia: Saunders, 1974.

SATTLER, J. M. *Assessment of Children's Intelligence and Special Abilities*. Boston: Allyn and Bacon, 1982.

SCHLOSBERG, H. The Description of Facial Expressions in Terms of Two Dimensions. *Journal of Experimental Psychology*, 1952, *44*, 229–237.

SCHLOSBERG, H. Three Dimensions of Emotion. *Psychological Review*, 1954, *61*, 81–88.

SILVERSTEIN, A. B. Note on the Construct Validity of the ITPA. *Psychology in the Schools*, 1978, *15*, 371–372.

SLOSSON, R. L. *Slosson Intelligence Test for Children and Adults* (SIT). New York: Slosson Educational Publications, 1963.

SPITZER, R. L., ENDICOTT, J., MESNIKOFF, A., and COHEN, G. *Psychiatric Evaluation Form: Diagnostic Version*. Biometric Research, New York State Psychiatric Institute, 1967–1968.

STODOLSKY, S. S., and LESSER, G. S. Learning Patterns in the Disadvantaged. *Harvard Educational Review*, 1967, *37*, 546–593.

SUINN, R. M., and OSKAMP, S. *The Predictive Validity of Projective Measures*. Springfield, Ill.: Chas. C Thomas, 1969.

SWARTZ, J. D. A Review of the Thematic Apperception Tests. In O. K. Buros (ed.), *The Eighth Mental Measurements Yearbook*. Highland Park, N. J.: Gryphon Press, 1978, pp. 1127–1130.

TERMAN, L. M. *The Measurement of Intelligence*. Boston: Houghton Mifflin, 1916.

TERMAN, L. M., and MERRILL, M. A. *Measuring Intelligence*. Boston: Houghton Mifflin, 1937.

TERMAN, L. M., and MERRILL, M. A. *Stanford-Binet Intelligence Scale: Manual for the 3rd Revision*. Form L.M. Boston: Houghton Mifflin, 1960.

URBAN, W. H. *The Draw-A-Person Manual*. Western Psychological Services, 1963.

WECHSLER, D. *Manual for the Wechsler Intelligence Scale*

for Children-Revised. New York: The Psychological Corporation, 1974.

WECHSLER, D. *Manual for the Wechsler Adult Intelligence Scale.* New York: The Psychological Corp., 1955.

WERNER, M., STABENAU, J. R., and POLLIN, W. Thematic Apperception Test Method for the Differentiation of Families of Schizophrenics, Delinquents and 'Normals.' *Journal of Abnormal Psychology,* 1970, *75,* 139–145.

ZUBIN, J., ERON, L. D., and SCHUMER, F. *An Experimental Approach to Projective Techniques.* New York: John Wiley, 1965.

6

TREATMENT APPROACHES

INTRODUCTION

Knowing what's wrong with children like Freddy is of little practical value unless something can be done to correct their problems and promote their normal development. You will recall that Mr. and Mrs. B. sought professional help not because they recognized a need for it but because they felt pressured by the school principal. They participated reluctantly in the diagnostic process but promptly rejected the findings and the treatment recommendations, since they saw the school's failure to meet Freddy's needs as the real problem. They angrily went through the motions of visiting the psychologist to placate the school and to show that they were not neglectful parents, but they had no expectation that the evaluation would have any meaning or impact. In the process they grew even more convinced that Freddy was the victim of the school's incompetence and unwillingness to work with him, and their hostile feelings toward the school carried over to their relationship with the psychologist.

Although diagnosis and treatment may involve different techniques and goals, the two processes are not unrelated or independent of each other; the success of each is greatly influenced by the nature of the relationship between client and clinician. The relationship (although colored by prior events and feelings) formally begins when the client and practitioner first meet. Ideally, it grows until the child and parents experience positive feelings of confidence, trust, acceptance, and safety. Without this sort of rapport, clients such as Mr. and Mrs. B. tend to be defensive, unproductive, unreceptive, and resistant to working with the clinician. Perhaps Mr. and Mrs. B.'s strong negative feelings about the clinical sessions were unalterable, but hindsight suggests that greater effort by the psychologist to allay their anxieties and deal with their anger may have brought about a more meaningful relationship and a different outcome. The important point is that rapport is a necessary initial step, whether the goal is diagnostic or therapeutic. It forms the basis for all subsequent clinical interactions and influences the extent to which the client will accept and carry out the clinical findings and treatment recommendations.

Freddy's case also illustrates several other general issues associated with treatment approaches. As so often happens, the parents knew little about their psychologist other than that he was recommended by the school as a competent professional. They accepted the school's referral without fully realizing that practitioners differ widely in terms of their training, theoretical orientation, technical skills, experience, and personal style—and these differences introduce considerable variability into the quality and kinds of services they may receive. As we have already seen (Chapter 2), diversity among clinicians contributes to the problems of reliability in the classification of abnormal behaviors, as well as to differences in etiological formulations (Chapter 4) and treatment choices. Clinical practice is still more of an art than a science, and it is an area with little uniformity in the way a given case is evaluated, conceptualized, and treated. The state of the art is such that each clinician has ample leeway to bring something of his or her own to a given clinical interaction, so that even those with similar training, experience, and theoretical bent are likely to vary with respect to specifics.

Such heterogeneity in clinical practice must be recognized as unsystematic variations of the treatment approaches that will be described in this chapter. Moreover, and perhaps of greater significance, heterogeneity represents a serious liability to the scientific study of treatment methods, making replication virtually impossible and restricting the possibility of either combining the data obtained from separate studies using the same treatment method or comparing the relative effectiveness of different methods.

Freddy's parents chose to reject the treatment recommendations of the psychologist, preferring instead to transfer Freddy to another school. Unfortunately, we shall never know how Freddy fared in the new school environment, since Mr. and Mrs. B. refused further contact with the clinician. But even under more favorable and cooperative circumstances, it would be extremely difficult to accumulate data that would adequately assess the effectiveness of their remedy. All too often treatment outcome and follow-up studies (when available) rely on parental reports which may be colored by their own needs and wishes. It would be foolhardy to accept Mr. and Mrs. B's observations as the sole measure of treatment outcome; not only did they choose the particular remedy, but they consistently demonstrated their inclination to lessen and deny their son's problems. Similarly, the therapist's progress reports may be subject to bias arising out of the need to see improvement in the child and to validate the treatment. In either event a more accurate appraisal of treatment outcome could be achieved through behavioral ratings made by independent observers—those who are not involved in the treatment—who have ample opportunity to sample the child's behavior in different settings. In addition, the evaluation could be further enhanced if ratings were obtained on the specific target behaviors purported to change with treatment.

But even these precautionary measures are not sufficient to enable us to arrive at a definitive conclusion about the impact of the treatment. While Mr. and Mrs. B. might be inclined to attribute Freddy's improvement to the change of schools, his progress could have been the result of one or more less apparent factors for which there are no controls. In the absence of (1) data from a larger sample of youngsters who were given the same treatment as Freddy and who were similar to him in age, intelligence, sex, educational level, socioeconomic class, and apparent adjustment problems; (2) an untreated matched control group and a placebo control group; and (3) data indicating specific ways in which the two schools were similar and different, Mr. and Mrs. B.'s conclusion is no more warranted than one interpreting Freddy's progress as the result of chance, developmental factors, changes within the family, or the like.

The placebo effect refers to changes or benefits achieved from a treatment that has no known value other than the client's belief that it will help. The fact that something is being done or taken internally for the problem, even though the measure has no known curative effects, is frequently sufficient to produce significant changes (Shapiro, 1971). Indeed, some writers claim that the expectation of help is as powerful as specific treatments—if not more so—in bringing about behavioral changes (Frank, 1961; Bergin, 1971). Consequently, a placebo control is necessary to determine the effects of the specific treatment beyond that which may be produced by a placebo condition.

Even if these additional research data and controls were available, we would still need long-term follow-up data to rule out transient effects and to assess the extent to which the treatment approach brought about durable changes. In short, the intent of this analysis is to highlight the difficulties one encounters in doing research in this area, to specify some of the complex experimental demands that must be met, and to forewarn the reader that much of the available research literature fails in one or more ways to meet these methodological requirements.

Finally, Freddy's story raises the question, What constitutes treatment? We may tend to think of therapy as an intervention that actively involves the child and family, and that is designed and carried out by a professional. In the strictest sense Freddy was given a home remedy fashioned by his parents, who believed that their son's academic failures and social immaturity were directly attributable to a damaging school situation. On the basis of their etiological formulation, Mr. and Mrs. B. took the logical action of changing Freddy's school environment. Environmental manipulation as a treatment approach has a long history, dating back to Hippocrates, who prescribed removing some of his patients from the family setting (Zilboorg and Henry, 1941). Contemporary medical and psychological practice continues to employ such environmental changes as bed rest, a vacation, removal of a pet from the home, a change of residence to a drier or warmer climate, transfer to a different school, and so forth as viable treatments for a variety of diseases and abnormal behaviors. Should the distinction between treatment and nontreatment be made on the basis of the therapist's qualifications? Should it be restricted to procedures that are based on some theoretical or rational grounds? Does it require the active participation and involvement of the client? As Davison and Neale have stated: "These are difficult questions, and as in other areas of abnormal psychology, there is a lack of total agreement on the various points" (1974, p. 459).

Since there are a number of treatment approaches for abnormal behaviors that have little or inadequate theoretical or rational basis (for example, electric convulsive therapy, psychosurgery, drug therapy), and some that vary considerably in the degree of participation by the client (hypnosis, behavior modification, psychotherapy), we cannot justifiably use either theoretical basis or client participation as criteria for defining treatment. To reflect the diversity of approaches in current practice, we favor the broad definition of treatment that includes any intervention or agent designed to alleviate or alter abnormal behaviors and facilitate normal personality development. The issue of who dispenses the intervention is essentially a social-ethical matter; society gives license to certain trained and qualified individuals as a means of protecting itself from charlatans. In this sense conversations with friends, play, recreational activities, or hot baths may be therapeutic in their effect but cannot be considered treatment per se by societal standards.

The primary intent of this chapter is to describe a representative sample of treatment approaches used to remove or alleviate abnormal behaviors in children. While general in nature, these descriptions will emphasize the assumptions, rationale, and operational requirements of various treatment methods. We will focus to a lesser extent on a critical appraisal of their effectiveness, since subsequent chapters will include more detailed evaluations of specific clinical entities. Although there is no single acceptable way of classifying treatment methods, for pedagogical reasons we have organized them under the categories of *psychological, somatic,* and *milieu* approaches. Thus, we will characterize and distinguish them by their rationale and by what is done with or to the client.

PSYCHOLOGICAL APPROACHES

Individual Psychotherapies

Psychotherapy as a treatment form began with the work of Sigmund Freud and Joseph Breuer who, toward the end of the nineteenth century, explored various procedures by which hysteria (a neurotic reaction also known as *conversion reaction*) could be treated (Urgan and Ford, 1971). While today psychotherapy is conducted in numerous ways and has numerous goals, it can be broadly defined as a psychologically planned and ongoing (at regular intervals) interaction between a trained person—the therapist—and a client who has adjustment problems. As it is practiced today, Freud's method of psychoanalysis involves frequent meetings (as many as three to five each week) between the client and the therapist (known as the psychoanalyst) over a prolonged period that may range from one to ten years. Traditional psychoanalysts seat themselves out of view of their clients, who are asked to lie on a couch so that they can more comfortably and freely report whatever comes into their minds (free association), be it feelings, sensations, memories, or associations. Through the interpretation of free associations and dreams, conflicts that once were unconscious become conscious, and presumably this greater self-awareness enables the client to live a more conflict-free life (Fine, 1973).

Freud thought of his psychoanalytic method primarily as a treatment for adult neurotics, although in 1909 he published the now-celebrated case history of a five-year-old phobic boy, Little Hans, who was analyzed by his father under Freud's supervision (Freud, 1955). Little Hans's case was important to Freud as a means of confirming his theoretical formulation of infant sexuality as the origin of adult neurotic symptomatology. It also demonstrated that insight (understanding of the intrapsychic conflict) could dissolve phobic (neurotic) symptoms. However, it was years later that the psychoanalytic treatment of children was developed and undertaken, primarily through the leadership of Melanie Klein and Freud's daughter Anna (Lesser, 1972). Few children today undergo classical psychoanalysis, although analytic concepts have been incorporated in a number of psychotherapies. In a review in which a variety of therapy approaches (including the psychoanalytic) were examined, Koocher and Pedulla (1977) found that psychoanalytic theory still remains a potent force, although it is more frequently used by psychiatrists than psychologists. However, they concluded that regardless of theoretical orientation, different approaches do not vary significantly in cases involving children. For example, most psychologists and psychiatrists use art as a therapeutic medium, and most employ parents as part of the treatment plan.

Play Therapy. Essentially, Anna Freud and Melanie Klein introduced play as a procedural modification of psychoanalysis.[1] They reasoned that preadolescent children are unable to free associate because of their limited linguistic development and their less mature (than adults) ego organization. Accordingly, play—and not free association—was regarded as the natural communication channel of children, enabling them to freely and safely express their rich fantasy life and reveal their unconscious processes and basic conflicts (Hammer and Kaplan, 1967). It has also been suggested that play facilitates the establishment of rapport by reducing the communication barrier between child and therapist and by making the therapeutic sessions more interesting to the child (Freud, 1946b; Watson, 1951). But playing per se is not to be construed as therapy (although its effects may be therapeutic); rather, it is an activity that enables the therapist to understand the child, and which the therapist uses to promote the child's growth.

1. *Psychoanalytic Play Therapy,* as formulated by Anna Freud in 1926 and in subsequent publications (Freud, 1946a, 1946b, 1965), emphasized the differences between child and adult analysis. She correctly viewed children as relatively unmotivated for treatment, since they usually don't seek help voluntarily, and they tend to see their problems as caused by the environment and not within themselves. In addition, she noted that children are unable to free associate and are unlikely to develop a transference neurosis (the repetition of neurotic conflicts that are focused on the therapist in analysis) equal to that formed by an adult. Freud regarded both play with toys and other activities such as drawing, painting, modeling, and dramatic role play as particularly useful in establishing a positive working relationship between the child and the therapist. It also helps in assessing the child's fantasies and unconscious conflicts.

Free play was used not as a substitute for free association but as a technique that allowed the child to externalize internal (unconscious) material. By structuring the form and content of the play, the child has the opportunity to play out intrapsychic conflicts. The therapist can thereby strengthen the child's ego functioning, helping the child identify and verbalize what he or she is experiencing and feeling. In the course of analysis the analyst interprets these feelings and experiences to increase the child's conscious awareness of unconscious drives, past emotional traumatic experiences, and other sources of anxiety that impede functioning. Freud also emphasized the importance of working with the child's parents, since the course and outcome of the treatment is likely to be greatly influenced by their willingness to support the treatment and accept change in their child.

In contrast, Klein's approach, which is favored in Great Britain, equates the use of play with free association and assumes that children are capable of developing transferences in the course of analysis that can be interpreted and understood in a way similar to adult analysis (Klein, 1949). Klein and her followers advocate the use of free play, especially with preschool children. Unlike Freudians, they interpret the play early in the analysis and in symbolic terms (for example, the shape of an object represents male or female genitalia) that imply a direct relationship between the symbol and the unconscious conflict. They do not offer intermediate levels of interpretation or a progression of interrelated interpretations before they symbolically connect the child's play with its primitive libidinal impulse. Consequently, this ap-

[1] For a more detailed description of play therapy, the reader is referred to Hammer and Kaplan, 1967; and Axline, 1964.

proach has been criticized on the grounds that it reflects an overly simplistic view of the child's psychodynamics as well as of the child's readiness to understand and deal with the original unconscious sources of anxiety (Lesser, 1972).

2. *Nondirective Play Therapy* with children grew out of Carl Rogers's client-centered therapy for adults and his view that all people possess the drive for self-realization and the capacity to solve their own difficulties (Rogers, 1951). Consequently, Rogers designed a treatment approach that encouraged self-realization by providing his clients with unconditional positive regard (unqualified acceptance), clarification of their thoughts and feelings through reflections, and opportunities for directing their own courses of action without interpretation or influence by the therapist. Virginia Axline fashioned her nondirective play therapy for children after Rogers's approach by assuming that play can serve as a substitute for words and can be just as therapeutic, provided that the children are given complete acceptance and freedom of expression (Axline, 1969). Play takes place in a setting where the child's importance, integrity, and self-worth are emphasized and where he or she is free to express feelings without fear of censure or reprisals. The therapist reflects back to the child the feelings and attitudes expressed through play to help the child recognize and clarify his or her feelings and gain a better self-understanding. Throughout therapy it is the child, and not the therapist, who is responsible for growth and self-realization.

Consistent with her positive view of human nature, Axline believes that children can be successfully treated in play therapy without treating the parents. While she notes that parental treatment may facilitate the therapeutic outcome for the child, she stresses the importance of the alliance between the therapist and the child, which must not be endangered by the therapist's involvement in the treatment of the parents.

3. *Filial Therapy* is a variant of play therapy in which parents are trained to conduct nondirective play with their emotionally troubled children (Guerney, 1964). Parents meet with the psychologist in groups on a weekly basis to learn the principles of nondirective play therapy and to air their children's problems for group discussion. Research data indicate that parents improved in ratings obtained on such behaviors as empathy, involvement, reflection of feelings, and permitting the child more self-direction, and they continued to improve after three post-training play sessions (Stover, Guerney, and O'Connell, 1971).

4. *Indications and Contraindications for Play Therapy*. In general, clinicians agree that play is a useful therapeutic technique for preadolescent children, especially for those who have limited verbal facility because of either developmental or psychogenic factors (Hammer and Kaplan, 1967). Children for whom this medium is appropriate would include the preschooler, the mute or linguistically handicapped, the socially shy, the inhibited, the withdrawn, the emotionally constricted, the fearful, the obsessive ruminator, the daydreamer, and the fantasy-ridden youngster. For these children play helps to establish rapport while also providing a natural activity through which they can discharge pent-up feelings, act out conflicts, and externalize psychic energies that were internalized as fantasies or obsessive thoughts. Play does not exclude or discourage verbal interactions between the child and therapist, although typically it is the major vehicle of expression and communication in therapy. Hammer and Kaplan (1967) note that play therapy, especially free play, is contraindicated for adolescents and children who evidence a high degree of emotional arousal or low cortical control of excitation, such as impulsive, acting-out, or hyperkinetic (hyperactivity caused by brain damage) youngsters. These children must learn to exercise more control over their feelings and impulses—a goal which can be better accomplished in situations with relatively low levels of stimulation,

and where structure and constraints are externally imposed on their acting-out tendencies.

A note of caution must be added: These indications and contraindications are based on clinical experience and not on empirical findings. In fact, only a few studies have been done on play therapy processes; and of those dealing with outcomes, most have been based on small numbers of cases and inadequate methodologies. After reviewing the available literature, Ginott (1961) and Lebo (1964) concluded that it is impossible to determine if changes that have occurred in children are attributable to play therapy per se or to a number of other possible factors, such as the placebo effect, spontaneous remission, increased attention or concern from significant others, and the like.

The effectiveness of play therapy in treating personality problems must be experimentally confirmed. Thus far, for example, there is no evidence to indicate the superiority of play therapy over dancing lessons in treatment of shyness, or its superiority over boxing lessons in the treatment of aggressiveness (Ginott, 1961, p. 154).

Verbal One-to-One Therapies. Verbal forms of one-to-one interactions between a therapist and a child differ widely. The following are some examples.

1. *Reality Therapy* is an interesting and relatively recent form of psychotherapy that differs markedly from the traditional psychoanalytic and client-centered approaches. The therapist focuses on the present while actively and deliberately encouraging the child (1) to make a value judgment about his or her behavior, (2) to make a plan that would achieve the desired goal, and (3) to be committed to the plan (Glasser, 1965, 1969; Barr, 1974). Reality therapy assumes that people are accountable for their own actions and that responsible behaviors on their part will result in their happiness. In behaving responsibly, children satisfy their basic needs for involvement and self-worth without hurting others; as a result, they feel good about themselves and others. The therapist finds unacceptable such comments as "I can't help it," "I am unhappy," or "My father never showed me any affection," because the therapist emphasizes the positive—or what the client can do. In addition, the therapist deals with the present, since nothing can be done to change the past.

Interpretations and attempts to provide insight are never part of the therapy in as much as these techniques serve to prompt excuses for irresponsible behaviors and to delay efforts to formulate and commit oneself to a plan of action that will change unwanted behaviors. In adapting reality therapy principles to the classroom, Glasser (1969) suggested three different kinds of meetings between the teacher and groups of students to help solve both behavioral and educational problems. In addition, he noted that his approach was very successful in treating institutionalized delinquent girls—about 80 percent left the institution without returning. However, there are sufficient ambiguities about these data to warrant a much more guarded conclusion (Glasser, 1965).

2. *Transactional Analysis* has recently been adopted by a number of clinicians as a form of psychotherapy for work with children. Essentially, transactional analysis focuses on intrapsychic learning as interpersonal "games" (Berne, 1972). As applied to groups of children, Roth (1977) has found this technique effective in male adolescents in residential treatment programs, and Garber (1976) has employed this approach to alter self-perception in delinquent boys on probation. This therapy is quite new in terms of its application to children, and its potential value has yet to be empirically demonstrated.

Critique of verbal therapies. While it is neither possible nor fruitful to attempt to describe other approaches here, some general comments concerning psychotherapy are in order. Reports based on reviews of the research literature by Bergin (1966), Levitt (1971), and Barrett, Harupe, and Miller (1978) provide us with a summary of the current status of psychotherapy and highlight specific problems inherent in psychotherapy research with children.

Although Bergin's review focused on psychotherapy with adults, his conclusions are still relevant to the practice of psychotherapy with children. He noted the following:

1. The subsequent adjustment of people who receive psychotherapy may be better or worse as compared to those who were not afforded such treatment. The fact that the outcome may be positive or negative speaks more to our need to determine the characteristics of those who get better and those who do not, and under what conditions, than to any decision to abandon the treatment form as ineffective.
2. Spontaneous remission (improvement over time) occurs in control subjects who did not receive psychotherapy. Not only does this finding underscore the importance of adequate control groups in studying the effectiveness of a given treatment form, but it also emphasizes the need to institute research that would tell us more about the variables producing spontaneous remission.
3. Progress in psychotherapy seems to be related to some characteristics of the therapist (such as personal adjustment, interpersonal warmth, empathy, and experience) that should be controlled for in research studies and taken into account in the selection of a therapist.
4. The client-centered approach to psychotherapy is the only one that has shown consistently favorable results, while studies of classical psychoanalysis (over long periods of time) have produced the poorest outcomes. However, Levitt's findings based on outcome studies of child psychotherapy over a period of thirty-five years (up to 1960) are even more pessimistic: The data fail to demonstrate the effectiveness of psychotherapy with children beyond a spontaneous recovery rate of between 60 and 70 percent.
5. Not only are traditional psychotherapies of questionable effectiveness, but also they are of limited pragmatic value, since they are only applicable and available to a small number of those who need treatment for abnormal behaviors. We need to develop alternative treatment methods that are suitable and feasible for the many more people for whom treatment has not as yet been available.
6. The more recent behavior therapies should be studied more extensively, since they have demonstrated considerable promise.

In discussing child psychotherapy research, Levitt (1971) identifies (but offers no solutions) several unique problems. In a more recent review Barrett and associates (1978) cover similar ground and concur with Levitt's approach and conclusions. The fact that children change as a function of developmental processes may account for the spontaneous remission in "normal children" of behaviors usually regarded as manifestations of emotional problems, such as enuresis, disruptions of sleep, persistent fears, and temper tantrums (MacFarlane, Allen, and Honzik, 1954; Lapouse and Monk, 1959). These behaviors tend to disappear without the assistance of therapeutic intervention as the child grows older; but in all likelihood their remission is attributable to the child's development of new or more effective coping skills to handle stress. Levitt argues, with some support from the literature, that overly anxious mothers tend to seek professional help for symptomatic children such as these, and these children may then be counted as therapeutic successes, although a developmental remission probably would have occurred without treatment.

In addition, Levitt notes that symptoms that are indicative of an abnormal condition also may drop out because of developmental changes, only to be replaced by other symptoms. He refers to this empirical finding as *developmental symptom substitution* and suggests that it reflects the probable occurrence of certain symptoms at certain ages (such as school phobia that most frequently occurs during the grade school years, and delinquency during adolescence). Without adequate experimental controls and follow-up data, one might erroneously attribute the disappearance of the first symptoms to the effectiveness of treatment, not knowing that a second set of symptoms has emerged later. Developmental factors may be responsible for the disappearance of the original set of symptoms and the reappearance of other ones, while in fact the child has made no significant improvement in adjustment with or without therapy. Levitt also points out that the common practice of treating both the child and one or more members of the family makes it extremely difficult to study separate treatment effects. If mother and child are treated separately and the child's outcome is favorable, we cannot draw any specific conclusions about the effectiveness of the child's therapy without knowing (1) the relative contribution of the mother's therapy or (2) the accumulative benefit of both therapeutic interventions.

Finally, the recent tendency reflected increasingly in the literature to combine two or more treatments into a single intervention approach makes it extremely difficult to assess the relative effectiveness and contribution of each component to the improvements (if any) noted in the clients. For example, studies have combined implosive therapy and hypnosis in treating obsessive-compulsive children, or they have used multiple behavioral techniques (relaxation, systematic desensitization, positive reinforcement, and gradual extinction) to treat severe separation anxiety, or they have tried a combination of behavioral training, structured group activities, individual psychotherapy, and parental involvement to treat children with encopresis Scrignas, 1981; Phillips and Wolpe, 1981; Artner and Castell, 1979). Although significant improvements have typically been reported in the treated children, most of the studies are not designed to allow for an analysis of the contribution made by each component.

The dim view taken by Levitt, Bergin, and others about psychotherapy has by no means gone unchallenged, since it simply does not conform to the experience of those practicing clinicians who can cite numerous instances of successful treatments. One recent study comparing neurotic patients who were treated with psychotherapy to an untreated group of controls showed that the treated patients significantly improved over the controls at the end of treatment (Andrews and Harvey, 1981). Moreover, the researchers showed a small relapse rate after two years for the successfully treated patients. The reaction of Lawrence Kubie—a well-known psychiatrist, analyst, and teacher—reflects the position of those who defend psychotherapy:

> We will soon be ashamed of the extent to which we may have been turned against the term by the recent flood of ignorant, naive and biased attacks on psychotherapy as a field. While pretending to be scientific, these studies have violated important principles of research design. Certainly a precise investigation of the psychotherapeutic process . . . is urgently needed. But we do not yet have reliable techniques by which to make meaningful evaluation of results. Anyone who pretends today that he is making accurate evaluations or comparisons is merely exhibiting naivete, bias, and ignorance. (1971, p. 23).

Cognitive Therapies. Broadly speaking, these treatment procedures[2] apply learning principles to covert cognitive activities and events. While behavior therapy focuses on overt behaviors, the more recent cognitive approaches include a person's covert experiences as behavioral data and view the person's inner world of thoughts, perceptions, attitudes, and other cognitive activities as central to the development of normal and abnormal behaviors (Kendall and Hollon, 1979). Homme (1965) and Cantela (1967) argued for the legitimacy of covert cognitive events as behavioral data and opened the way for other investigators to develop intervention approaches by which to modify unobserved behaviors. Cognitive therapies deal with both internal and external behaviors as appropriate targets for treatment, and they assume that these behaviors are subject to the same prin-

[2]For in-depth coverage and discussion of cognitive therapies, see Mahoney, 1974, 1977; Meichenbaum, 1974, 1977; and Stuart, 1977.

ciples and laws of learning. Several illustrations of cognitive approaches will be presented below.

1. Influenced in part by the work of Russian psychologists, Luria (1961, 1969), Vygotsky (1962), Meichenbaum and Goodman (1971), and Palkes and associates (1972) combined cognitive modeling and rehearsal of self-instructions to teach grade school children what to do before taking action. The idea was to teach impulsive children greater self-control through self-instructional training, which presumably allows them to stop and think of what to do before overtly responding. While impulsive children improved in their self-control at the end of training, the initial gain failed to hold over time and failed to generalize to the classroom situation. In fact, while reviews of the literature consistently show that the cognitive behavior modification approach is effective in treating children with self-control problems, there is little evidence that the treatment effects generalize across situations or over time (Meichenbaum, 1979).

2. Kendall and Finch (1979a, 1979b) developed a clinical intervention program for the treatment of impulsivity within various childhood disorders. Their subjects were classified as impulsive according to their scores on the Matching Familiar Figures Test (MFF) (presumably reflecting an impulsive cognitive style). Subjects were placed in a cognitive training program which included self-instructional training, relevant search-and-scan behavior, and exposure to the modeling of self-instructions and of efficient task behaviors. In addition, the procedure involved a response-cost where rewards were lost contingent on errors made by the subject during training. Initially the therapist performed the task while talking aloud to himself. Next the child was asked to perform the task while talking aloud. Then the therapist, followed by the child, performed additional tasks while whispering. Finally, the therapist, followed by the child, performed the task while using covert instructions. The results showed that the treated children obtained lower impulsive scores on the MFF after treatment and at follow-up. Moreover, a later study indicated that the treated impulsive children significantly increased their on-task verbalizations, asked more task-related questions, and decreased their off-task verbal behavior. However, the results were disappointing in that the improvements were not evident at follow-up (Kendall and Finch, 1979a, 1979b).

3. Another cognitive therapy, and one of the earliest developed, is rational-emotive therapy (RET) (Ellis, 1959, 1970). RET focuses on the modification of the person's inappropriate and perfectionistic self-demands and unrealistic beliefs; if unaltered, these lead to maladaptive behaviors and the emotional reactions of self-depreciation and depression. The therapy attempts to restructure the person's belief system and increase his or her feelings of self-worth. Techniques used include rational confrontation (disputing the illogical beliefs that give rise to the negative behavioral and emotional consequences); the assigning of practice or homework in between therapy sessions, to introduce new activities and new ways of thinking; and the use of reinforcement (giving self tangible rewards for doing homework and/or encouraging client to make covert statements of praise when appropriate). RET, to a greater degree than other cognitive therapies, stresses verbal persuasion (carried on in the form of a deductive debate) to produce changes in the belief system, while inductive processes are emphasized in other cognitive therapies (Hollon and Beck, 1979). These inductive processes involve collaboration between the therapist and the client in gathering monitored cognitive and behavioral data to test the hypothesis generated during the course of treatment. In contrast, the deduction in RET is reflected in the therapist's attempt to persuade the client that he or she is holding on to an irrational belief.

Several attempts to apply RET to children have been noted in the literature. De Guiseppe (1977) outlined the procedures he used to establish rational self-statements in two children. First the therapist demonstrated the use of rational self-statements; then the child modeled the use of the statements; and finally the child faded the verbal modeling into covert responses. Reinforcement was applied at each stage of this progression. Knaus (1977) developed a rational emotive program for use in the schools in which the emphasis is on experiential learning through the presentation of a planned sequence of emotional lessons. One example cited involved the use of pantomime to help students learn that not all people express their emotions in the same way. Finally, the work of DeVoge (1974) illustrates a behavioral approach to RET where the consistent reinforcement of rational statements (for example, "I don't like school, but I can stand it") increased self-controlled behaviors in children.

The relatively recent development of cognitive therapies, and the popularity they currently enjoy, reflect a promising addition to the treatment approaches available to clinicians. However, the failure of initial improvements in behaviors to persist over time and to generalize to relevant situations are significant indications that further research and continued evaluation of cognitive therapies are needed.

Behavior Therapies. Broadly speaking, behavior therapy—or behavior modification—refers to the treatment of abnormal behaviors by methods and techniques that have been derived from experimental psychology and the principles of learning. Although its beginnings can be traced to the 1920s, the meteoric rise of behavior therapy as a body of literature and as a promising treatment approach has occurred only within the last twenty-five years (O'Leary and Wilson, 1975). Laboratory experiments in this country and in Russia demonstrated the acquisition of a phobic reaction through classical conditioning in a little boy (named Albert) (Watson and Rayner, 1920); the extinction of children's fears by the pairing of the feared object with food (something highly pleasant) (Jones, 1924a); and the treatment of sexual perversions and alcoholism through conditioning procedures (Yates, 1970). Some years later Dunlap (1932) described the acquisition of maladaptive habits and the methods he devised to weaken or eliminate them, while the Mowrers (Mowrer and Mowrer, 1938) showed that enuretic children can be treated successfully by conditioning procedures that involved the sounding of a loud buzzer as soon as the child wet an electrically wired pad placed on the bed.

Unlike other practitioners, behavior modifiers find it unneccessary to diagnose psychopathology or to use traditional assessment techniques to uncover the origins of abnormal behavior. Rather, they need to assess the current conditions that influence either the occurrence of the behavior in question or its failure to occur (Ross, 1972). In addition, the construction of a realistic behavioral plan requires that the therapist learn as much as possible about the child's capabilities; that is, his or her response repertoire and the range of stimuli that can be processed, as well as those stimuli that have reinforcement value for maintaining the behavior. Initially the therapist, together with the parents and the child, identifies the specific behavior (*target behavior*) to be modified, which then makes the treatment goal clear to all parties concerned and establishes a clear-cut behavioral criterion for the evaluation of treatment outcome. Treatment strategy is then devised in terms of whether the desired effect involves (1) a decrease in the emission of a target behavior, (2) an increase in the occurrence of a wanted response or class of responses, or (3) a combination where the rate of wanted behaviors is increased and unwanted ones are eliminated.

1. Decrease of target behavior. Jones (1924a,b) was the first to suggest that the pairing of an incompatible experience (the enjoyment of eating a favored food) with the gradual presentation of a fear-evoking stimulus (the furry rabbit) would lead to the elimination of a learned fear response. Later Wolpe (1958) referred to this principle as *reciprocal inhibition* and proposed a procedure called *systematic desensitization* (sometimes known as *counterconditioning*) for the treatment of learned fear in adults. Desensitization pairs the incompatible response of relaxation (induced by suggestion, hypnosis, or drugs) with a graded series of anxiety stimuli in such a way as to prevent the occurrence of the fear response (avoidance) and allow the anxiety to extinguish. Wolpe's method involves the training in muscle relaxation, the preparation (by the therapist and the client) of a hierarchy of fear-evoking stimuli (arranged in order from the least to the most fearful), and finally, the actual desensitization. In the last stage the client relaxes and is asked to imagine the least fearful stimulus, then the next in the hierarchy, and so on, until the client reports that relaxation has given way to anxiety. At this point relaxation is reestablished; the process is then repeated until the client successfully goes through the entire hierarchy without anxiety.

Wolpe's approach has been modified for children, since training in deep muscle relaxation is difficult to accomplish with youngsters (Lazarus and Abramovitz, 1962; Wolpe and Lazarus, 1966). The modification, known as *emotive therapy,* uses imagery of pleasurable scenes that are incompatible with anxiety and that are, in effect, substitutes for muscle relaxation. While the child enjoys the pleasurable fantasy, the anxiety-arousing stimulus is gradually introduced (much like Jones gradually introduced a rabbit as the child ate his favorite food) via the previously constructed hierarchy of the least to the most fearful stimulus.

Systematic desensitization has been used successfully with a wide range of phobias (Garvey and Hegrenes, 1966; Chapel, 1967; Lazarus and Rachman, 1967; Bandura, 1969; Obler and Terwilliger, 1970) and for anxiety (Levine and O'Brien, 1980), although the paucity of research leaves its claim to effectiveness virtually unsubstantiated (Lazarus and Abramovitz, 1962).

In contrast to desensitization, where therapy is conducted in a way that minimizes anxiety arousal, *flooding* or *implosive therapy* is based on the principle of maximal anxiety arousal. This approach involves the induction of intense anxiety by exposing the client to highly threatening stimuli. The idea is to induce and sustain high levels of anxiety without relief, until the aversive reactions are extinguished (Stampfl and Levis, 1967; Watson and Marks, 1971). Flooding has been used successfully in treating phobic and obsessive-compulsive reactions, although thus far most of the studies have been done with adults (Boulougouris and Bassiakos, 1973; Mathews and Shaw, 1973; Morganstern, 1973; Watson, Mullett, and Pillay, 1973; Emmelkamp, 1974; Keane and Kaloupek, 1982; Testa, 1981; Boudewyns and Shipley, 1982).

Modeling is another behavioral technique that has been effective in reducing avoidance behaviors in children, as evidenced by a carefully controlled study in which children fearful of a dog reduced their avoidance behavior after being exposed to a fearless peer model who comfortably approached the feared animal (Bandura, Grusec, and Menlove, 1967). *Extinction* of a target behavior also can be brought about by discontinuing the reinforcement given the child (usually by parents) for some unwanted behavior. Extinction may be accomplished through the use of punishment or through a technique known as *time out,* in which the child is isolated from positive reinforcing conditions for a period of time. Strong punishment (electric shock and slapping) has been shown to extinguish self-destructive and mutilating behaviors of psychotic children, while a combination of mild punishment and time out was effectively used in the treatment of a five-year-old acting-out and destructive child (Boardman, 1962; Lovaas et al., 1965; Lovaas et al., 1973).

Positive reinforcement can be used indirectly to decrease unwanted target behaviors by giving rewards when low-frequency prosocial behaviors occur. For example, hyperactivity or the social unresponsiveness of schizophrenic children (the target behavior) can be effectively reduced by positively reinforcing attentive and more sedentary behaviors, such as listening to the teacher or sitting quietly (Patterson et al., 1965; Doubros and Daniels, 1966; Lovaas et al., 1973).

2. *Increase of prosocial behaviors.* This can be accomplished most effectively by behavioral strategems that use either positive reinforcement or modeling. By making the reinforcement or the reward contingent on the performance of some wanted response, children can be taught a variety of social behaviors. They can also be taught to improve their academic habits and performance and to emit new responses (Stolz, Wienckowski, and Brown, 1975). There have been numerous successful applications of positive reinforcement for the purpose of increasing prosocial behaviors. They have been evidenced in such diverse behaviors as the smiling of an infant at an adult, toilet training, cooperation between schizophrenic children, social interaction between severely retarded youngsters, and increased creativity in young children's block building (Brackbill, 1958; Hingtgen, Saunders, and DeMyer, 1965; Madsen et al., 1969; Whitman, Mercurio, and Caponigri, 1970; Goetz and Baer, 1973). Moreover, the use of tokens as reinforcers (sometimes referred to as token economy systems), which can be accumulated and cashed in at some later time for privileges or for some tangible item, has tended to offset the problem of a child becoming satiated with a particular reinforcer, and it has given teachers and the personnel of institutions greater opportunities for the control and management of relatively large groups of children (Ayllon and Azrin, 1968; O'Leary and Drabman, 1971; Kazdin, 1977).

Another application of positive reinforcement is known as *contingency contracting,* in which the therapist and the client agree together on the behavioral goals and the reinforcement to be received when the goals are reached. For example, a contract between a child and parents might deal with such matters as the child agreeing to do homework on a daily basis, to go to bed at a specified hour, or to perform certain household chores in exchange for something he or she wants from the parents. Therefore, both parties involved in the contract agree to meet their commitments so that when one party changes behavior, the other provides reinforcement for that behavioral change. Behavioral contracting has been effectively used within families of delinquents to reduce such behaviors as sexual promiscuity, drug abuse, and truancy (Stuart, 1971; Stuart, Jayaratne, and Tripoldi, 1976) and in a family of an adolescent to eliminate disturbed sleep behaviors (Framer and Sanders, 1980).

New behaviors also can be acquired through modeling when the model (actual, depicted, or imagined) demonstrates the desired behavior (Rachman, 1972). Recent work in assertiveness training illustrates the application of modeling for persons who have difficulty in asserting themselves. Successful results have been reported when the client is taught to imagine people who are engaged in assertive behavior, or when clients are exposed to a model who role plays and demonstrates assertiveness (Hersen et al., 1973; Kazdin, 1974; Stolz, Wienckowski, and Brown, 1975).

3. *Combining procedures.* The *decrease* of maladaptive behaviors and *increase* of adaptative ones is a favored strategy of behavioral therapists, since it both deals with the child's problem behavior and provides him or her with alternative and socially acceptable ways of responding. The approach has been applied to a wide range of problems, including school phobia, social behaviors of psychotic and mentally retarded children, and the antisocial behaviors of delinquents. For example, when a school-phobic child was given positive reinforcement for going to school, coupled with the discontinuance of positive consequences of staying at home, and the mother experienced aversive consequences when the child failed to attend school, school refusal was effectively extinguished and the child achieved regular school attendance (Ayllon, Smith, and Rogers, 1970). By using a favored food as a positive reinforcer, a psychotic boy was taught to wear his eye glasses. Further, his disruptive table manners were modified by removing his plate or removing

him from the dining room when he ate with his fingers, ate from the plate of others, or threw food (Wolf, Risley, and Meers, 1964). Similarly, a combination of punishment and positive reinforcement was used to reduce undesirable mealtime behavior of mental retardates and to increase their desirable eating responses (Henriksen and Doughty, 1967). Behavioral intervention that included token reinforcement, a contract system, and time out from reinforcement significantly reduced aggressive and nonconforming responses and markedly improved family relations and functioning in a group of acting-out boys (Patterson and Reid, 1973).

4. Evaluation of behavior therapies. In the aggregate, behavior therapy has demonstrated considerable promise as a treatment approach for a wide range of abnormal behaviors and for a substantial age range in children and adolescents. Because assessment of target behaviors is typically an integral part of the treatment process, evaluation of outcome in behavioral terms is readily accomplished. However, much of the research data in this area are based on single cases or on very small samples in a research design in which the subject is his or her own control (*ABAB* design). Studying too few subjects makes the kind of interpretation and conclusions drawn from the results rather tentative, while the *ABAB* design makes it impossible to compare the effectiveness of behavior therapy with other treatment methods in a single study (Ross, 1972). In addition, follow-up data over long periods of time are generally not available either to assess the durability of the behaviors modified with behavior therapy or to unequivocally answer the nagging question of symptom-substitution. While the research data support the overall effectiveness of behavior therapy, the sobering thoughts of Ross (1972) place its evaluation in a more appropriate perspective.

> It is unlikely that behavior therapy, as presently conceived and practiced, is the treatment of choice for every conceivable form of psychological disorder and it is to be hoped that, in addition to the conditioning and social learning paradigms now applied in treatment, other aspects of psychology, such as the study of cognitive processes, modeling procedures, developmental phenomena, physiological correlates, and group dynamics, will eventually be brought to bear on clinical problems. (p. 309)

Group and Family Therapies

In this section we shall describe some of the widely used psychotherapies that involve multiple clients who are brought together at regular intervals to engage in psychologically planned verbal and nonverbal interactions with each other and with one or more therapists. Group therapy may be distinguished from family therapy on the basis of the blood-tie relationships of the participants and on theoretical grounds. In practice, however, the therapist is faced in both situations with the similar problem of working with several clients at the same time. In group therapy several emotionally disturbed children (usually unknown to each other) meet together with a therapist to share and express their conflicts and feelings, to promote the development of social behaviors, and to support each other as they attempt to solve their problems. In contrast, in family therapy the family is the single interacting social system in which the behaviors of each member are the product of the pressures existing within that system. Abnormal behaviors of a child represent expressions of family transactions and pathology that can best be resolved through the participation and treatment of the family as a unit, and not through isolated attempts to bring about changes in the child (Bell, 1975).

Group Therapies. In current practice group therapy may take a variety of forms, depending on such factors as the age of the child, the type of psychopathology, and the theoretical preference of the therapist. However, all types of group therapy provide a social and economic advantage over individual psychotherapy, since a group therapist can offer treatment services to a larger number of clients and at a reduced cost per client for each therapy session. In addition, group therapy recognizes that humans are social animals whose growth and development are greatly influenced by the attitudes and values held by the group.

1. *Activity group therapy.* Introduced by Slavson, this method was designed for prepubescent youngsters of the same age and sex who have been rejected (directly through dislike or neglect or indirectly through overprotectiveness) by parents, siblings, school, and peers (Slavson, 1970; Slavson and Schiffer, 1975). These children are described as overtly hostile toward the world, refusing to interact with it, and demonstrating either antisocial or nonsocial behaviors. Activity groups provide a sanctuary for these children where the stress of their disharmony with the environment is removed and replaced by a social setting characterized by acceptance and "unconditional love." Tendencies toward open expressions of aggression or withdrawal are tolerated and permitted to run their course (emotional release) without censure or interpretation from the therapist, although the other members of the group may exert control over these actions.

The emphasis in such groups is placed on activities that are functionally related to the clinical needs of the children, and age- and sex-appropriate play materials are used either separately or as a group project. However, verbal interactions can and do occur in the therapy sessions. The therapist assumes a neutral and impartial role but also serves as a model of restraint and of other socially desired behaviors, and as a reinforcer of desirable behaviors as they appear. Permissiveness and praise from both the therapist and other members of the group increase the child's feelings of self-worth and gratify his or her need for status and success.

Typically Slavson works with children between the ages of seven and fourteen in groups containing from three to eight children. Hammer and Kaplan (1967) differ somewhat from Slavson in defining the abnormal conditions that can be treated effectively by activity group therapy. They suggest that the treatment is most appropriate for youngsters with behavioral disorders who are not extreme in their overt aggressive tendencies, as well as for mildly neurotic children without intense or pervasive anxiety. In addition, children who are overly inhibited, emotionally constricted, or fearful of close interpersonal relations are said to be suitable for this treatment form. Nevertheless, we still lack adequate empirical research on which children are helped by such therapy and which are not.

2. *Group play therapy.* Like individual play therapy, this treatment form may follow psychoanalytic or nondirective theoretical lines, or some variant of both. It is usually intended for young children between the ages of five and nine for whom play is a natural mode of expressing conflicts, feelings, and fantasies that have impeded personality development and social adjustment. A playgroup should consist of no more than six children who are homogeneous with respect to age and sex (Schiffer, 1969). Psychoanalytically oriented therapists have suggested that the presence of several children makes the therapy less threatening and facilitates the early establishment of rapport (Ginott, 1961; Schiffer, 1969). They also have claimed that group play provides opportunities for catharsis (emotional release), the subsequent reduction of guilt and anxiety, enhancement of self-worth through support and reinforcement given by the therapist and the group members, and the development of social skills and activities in which sublimation (acceptable outlets for id impulses) can occur. Nondirective playgroups closely follow the approach used by Axline in her individual play therapy, in which play is the primary vehicle through which children express and clarify their feelings, and where growth and self-realization are promoted by a therapeutic attitude of unconditional acceptance.

3. *Verbal group therapy.* This is viewed by its proponents as particularly suitable for adolescents who may regard play as too childlike and for whom peer relations and group af-

filiation are important (Berkovitz and Sugar, 1975). As contrasted to individual psychotherapy, group therapy comforts adolescents with the reassurance that others are "in the same boat." It also provides them with safety in numbers, to help diffuse the fear and distrust frequently associated with adult therapists. Although adolescents may enter group therapy as a result of parental or other external pressures, the group does not become viable unless and until its members experience a sense of belonging and accept the responsibility of participation (MacLennan and Felsenfield, 1968).

Group therapy has been described as appropriate for a variety of settings (outpatient, hospital, school, and residential) as well as for different patient populations. Also, there are divergent ideas concerning the group composition (in terms of such variables as age, sex, and types of psychopathology) (Hammer and Kaplan, 1967; Reckless, 1968; Franklin and Nottage, 1969; Yalom, 1970; Berkovitz, 1972; Sugar, 1975). For example, Sugar (1975) suggested that young adolescents between twelve and fourteen years of age should be placed in groups that are homogeneous in age (not greater than a three-year age span) and sex to increase peer harmony and interests and to avoid the additional stress of relating to the opposite sex before a better self-understanding is achieved. Grouping for middle to late adolescents tends to become increasingly heterosexual, since these youngsters now are faced with the real problem of relating to the opposite sex. Sugar also acknowledged that clinicians have varying opinions about the composition of the group with respect to the homogeneity or diversity of psychopathology. Anderson (Anderson and Marrone, 1977) described a method of group therapy for emotionally disturbed children where regular sessions were held in the school, and teachers acted as cotherapists. Anderson reported that their method was more effective than group or individual treatment given outside the school, although neither the outcome variables nor adequately controlled treatment comparisons were provided. It is noteworthy that most of the variations and applications of group therapy described in the literature reflect clinical experience, preference, and bias, and not differences that are firmly rooted in empirical data.

Family Therapies. From a historical perspective family therapy is a relatively recent innovation. It took on significance for clinical practice in the mid-1950s and early 1960s, with the appearance of a body of literature describing the procedure and its theoretical basis (Brown, 1972). Family therapy has been influenced primarily by two views: psychoanalysis and systems theory (Offer and VanderStoep, 1975). Psychoanalytically oriented family therapists find family interviews useful not only in diagnosing the psychopathology of the child and the family but also in forming a basis on which to build a suitable treatment strategy. If, for example, the evaluation revealed that the child's problem was intrapsychic, individual psychotherapy would be indicated. On the other hand, family therapy would be the preferred treatment for children whose problems were primarily interpersonal (Kramer, 1970). In addition, analytically oriented therapists view the child as the outlet for the expression of unresolved parental conflicts, as well as the conduit through which parental anxieties are reexperienced in day-to-day family transactions. The child, then, becomes the victim and—to some extent—a participant in unresolved parental battles which are enacted in daily family interactions (such as that described between Mr. and Mrs. B. in their management of Freddy).

In contrast, systems theorists (usually behaviorally oriented nonmedical practitioners) regard the diagnostic process and the concern over psychopathology as potential sources of interference with an open and flexible interaction between the therapist and the family. These therapists perceive the family as a unit—a biosocial system—in which there is reciprocal interaction among the members, and where the child's disturbance fulfills a psychologically meaningful function for that system. Consequently, changes in the child's behavior without concomitant changes in the family system may result in the appearance of new symptoms in family members or the destruction of the family as a unit. Within this perspective Mr. and Mrs. B.'s reluctance to seek professional help and their refusal to accept treatment might be interpreted as their resistance to changing the family interactive patterns (albeit maladaptive) that have successfully kept their family system intact.

In practice family therapy varies widely, as evidenced by a survey of 300 therapists who described differences in procedures. These ranged from the use of family therapy as an extension of or supplement to individual therapy, to discrepant views about which family members should be included in the treatment and what kinds of emotional disturbances are effectively treated by this approach (Group for the Advancement of Psychiatry, 1975). For example, John Bell (1975), a pioneer in family therapy, begins with a joint interview of both parents (1) to obtain their version of the child's problems, (2) to gain historical data about the child's development, and (3) to inform them about his approach to family therapy. He tells the parents that while he will act as a referee to assure that every member of the family has an opportunity to participate in the sessions, he will be especially supportive of the child (or children) both to gain his or her confidence and to provide a safe setting for the open expression of feelings. Usually the parents and all the children over eight years of age then convene, while Bell gives a similar summary of his role to the children, telling them that the parents are willing to change and that everyone can work together to decide on the plans for the family.

Following these initial sessions Bell describes his approach to family therapy in three sequential phases. In the *child-centered phase* the child is encouraged to express his or her thoughts and feelings about what makes the family unhappy. According to Bell, children typically use this opportunity to voice their irritation over some aspect of the rules and routine of their family lives, such as bedtime hours, having to keep their room clean, or the issue of who gets to watch which T.V. show and when. Bell works with these complaints, asking the child for solutions that perhaps parents can accept. Solutions are to be for a trial period and are subject to future discussions. The *parent-centered phase* starts when "everything is going good" for the child, although considerable hostility has accumulated on the part of the parents during the first phase of therapy. Bell permits the expression of these feelings; however, he tries to safeguard the rapport he has with the child by telling the parents that the child must also have a say in the matter. Further, he notes that the child's behavior corresponds to developmental norms (when this is so) and helps the child explain the reasons for his or her actions. This phase of therapy usually involves the catharsis of negative feelings and the greater understanding of both the emotional ties between family members and the nature of parental problems. The final stage of therapy, the *family-centered phase*, occurs when many of the referral problems have disappeared. The sessions during this stage are punctuated with laughter and reports of the family enjoying shared activities and working together to solve problems.

Unlike Bell, Haley (1963, 1981) approaches family therapy with the idea that family members engage in a power struggle with the therapist and that the therapist must construct various strategies to maintain authoritative control. Family members consistently try to wrestle control in whatever way they can, and they strive to render the therapist ineffective, perceiving the latter as a threat to the equilibrium of the family. Haley responds to these defensive ploys by forcing the family to look at itself and by pressing for more open and direct communication with him and among family members. He downplays psychodynamics, interpretation, and insight as useful ingredients for therapy, and he emphasizes the importance of relationships within the family system and the need to establish different interpersonal operations within the family for therapy to be effective.

Block (1976) advocates a procedure in which all family members are initially included in a series of open-ended contracts concerning family problems. These contracts are dealt with in separate sessions that include only those members of the family necessary for that phase of the work. Presumably, this method is intended to reduce the scapegoating of a particular child, to eliminate symptomatic behavior, and to establish the family system as the unit of the malfunction. Other variations of family therapy include multiple families meeting together in group therapy, a combination of family and group therapy, social networks in which families and their support systems are brought together for regularly scheduled therapy sessions, Adlerian family therapy, brief family therapy, and behaviorally oriented family therapy (Mendell, 1975; Attneave, 1976; Strelnick, 1977; Baideme, Kern, and Taffel-Cohen, 1979; Ostensen, 1981; Hafner et al., 1981).

Family therapists also tend to categorize families as a way of describing different family structures and patterns, and as a diagnostic indication for therapy and therapy outcome. However, as Brown so aptly noted:

> A satisfying classification seems not yet at hand. Descriptive characterizations of families are everyday language among family therapists. These include such terms as *sick* families, *chaotic* families, *multiple-problem* families, *psychosomatic* families, *obsessional-compulsive* families, *regressive* families, *hostile* families, *hypomanic* families, *sensitive* families, *violent* families, families with a sense of destiny, families with purpose, stable families, stable-unstable families, likeable families and difficult families. (1972, p. 986, emphasis added)

Outcome Research with Group and Family Therapies. Although the literature on group and family therapy is extensive, relatively few adequately controlled studies on the effectiveness of these treatment methods are available. A recent review of group psychotherapy included only studies that met the following criteria: (1) They provided quantitative pre- and posttherapy measures of behavioral and psychosocial adjustment and (2) they did not combine group therapy with any other treatment intervention (Abramowitz, 1976). These studies tended to focus on immaturity, social isolation, poor self-concept, and academic achievement as the four major problem areas of the identified children. The survey showed that about one-third of the studies yielded positive outcome results, about one-third reported mixed outcomes (some positive, some negative, and some with no change), while the remaining one-third yielded findings of no improvement. There were no apparent differences among types of group therapy, although behavioral approaches were overrepresented in both the positive and mixed results. These outcome data are far from impressive in demonstrating the effectiveness of group therapy.

Unfortunately, the empirical support for family therapy is no greater than it is for group therapy, in spite of the enthusiasm of its proponents. The results of a recent study are fairly typical in that they shed more light on the many methodological problems involved in outcome research than on the question of whether or not family therapy is effective. Sigal, Barrs, and Doubilet (1976) compared treated and untreated families with respect to the following criteria of effectiveness: (1) status of presenting symptoms at least a year after termination, (2) appearance of new symptoms, and (3) parental reports of satisfaction. They found that on follow-up the treated families were no better or worse than the untreated families. However, their measures of effectiveness were not objective, the assignments of families to either the experimental or control groups were not random, and the untreated group, in fact, saw a therapist for one or two sessions before terminating themselves. Indeed, it is difficult to do meaningful (well-controlled) outcome studies because, as Ross points out:

> ...relevant control groups are hard to find, therapies and therapists are difficult to equate, a sufficient number of subjects with the same problem behavior is rarely available, and objective criterion measures are often unacceptable or irrelevant to therapists of a different theoretical orientation. (1972, p. 307)

SOMATIC APPROACHES

Somatic therapies, including *shock therapy* (chemical or electrical), *psychosurgery,* and *psychoactive drugs,* are radical forms of treatment that must be administered under medical supervision. With the exception of drug therapy, these therapies are used infrequently with children, since they are poorly understood and produce unfavorable neurophysiological effects (Shaw, 1966).

Shock Therapy

Lauretta Bender (1953), a chief proponent of shock treatment, used both Metrazol (a convulsion-producing drug) and electric shock with schizophrenic children (see Chapter 8) as a means of stimulating the maturation and patterning of what she regarded as an inadequately developed nervous system in these youngsters. She claimed that 25 percent of the shock-treated children on long-term follow-up had higher adjustment ratings than members of the nonshock group (4 percent). However, Eisenberg (1957) argued convincingly against Bender's claim by showing that a very high percentage of the shock-treated group (89 percent) continued to be schizophrenic at the time of follow-up and that approximately 25 percent of psychotic children could be expected to recover spontaneously, without any treatment. Bender's use of shock treatment has been regarded by others as indiscriminate, distasteful, and ineffective (Wing, 1966; Werry, 1981). In the end she abandoned it in favor of LSD and other psychotomimetic drugs (Bender, Goldschmidt, and Sankar, 1962).

Psychosurgery

This procedure was introduced in 1936 by Moniz and again in 1942 by Freeman and Watts (1950) for chronic and difficult-to-manage adult mental patients and for individuals suffering from intractable pain. Crude surgical procedures were used in severing or removing portions of the prefrontal lobe of the brain to disconnect the nerve fibers that normally connect the frontal lobe and the dorsomedial nucleus of the thalamus (believed to be the center of emotions). In 1951 two Japanese neurosurgeons, Narabayashi and Uchimura, introduced human stereotaxic surgery, in which the amygdala (part of the temporal lobe and the limbic system) was destroyed. This surgery was designed to treat behavioral problems in children and adults who evidenced hyperexcitability, destructiveness, and violent behaviors (Narabayashi, 1972). The procedure was extended to feeble-minded epileptic patients who also were violent and uncontrollable. Narabayashi reported that there were no fatalities in well over a hundred surgical cases, and that 67 percent showed improvement consisting of calm, obedient, and cooperative behaviors. The calming effect was even stronger in children, who showed better improvement than adults. Other investigators in different parts of the world (India, the United States, Japan, and South America) have since reported favorable findings in which hostile, aggressive, destructive, and uncontrollable children and adults have been made more manageable and docile by the surgical destruction of the amygdala or the posterior hypothalamus (Heimburger, Whitlock, and Kalsbeck, 1966; Balasubramaniam, Kanaka, and Ramamurthi, 1970; Sano et al., 1970; Guttierez et al., 1976; Reixach, Torres, and Reis, 1977).

Psychosurgery has been sharply criticized on both socioethical and methodological grounds. Some argue against using such a radical and potentially dangerous procedure with human subjects when the surgical effects (either good or bad) are inadequately documented, and where controls (when used) are subjected to "sham" operations in which a superficial incision is made in the cerebral cortex and a small portion of the skull is removed (Breggin, 1972). In addition, the vast majority of studies thus far reported have used unclear criteria for patient selection, and there have been few, if any, objective measures (other than the biased observations of the surgeon) to assess either short or long-term outcome. Many other serious methodological flaws (too few subjects, no control groups, and so forth) prevent these studies from yielding definitive results (Mark and Ervin, 1970; Valenstein, 1973; Shevitz, 1976). Indeed, the justification for the continuance of psychosurgery with patient populations can come only after it has survived the most careful empirical scrutiny possible and after unequivocal confirmation of its benefits are firmly established.

Psychoactive Drug Therapy

This is clearly the major somatic approach in clinical practice today, especially with children, having gained its popularity from demonstrations of its effectiveness and in some cases from its superiority over other treatment methods with adult mental patients (Group for the Advancement of Psychiatry, 1975). Unfortunately, the application of drug therapy to children and adolescents has occurred in spite of the fact that there is a dearth of adequately controlled studies demonstrating its benefits or comparing its effectiveness with other therapies for this age groups (Christensen and Sprague, 1973; Gittelman-Klein, 1975). The effect of drug treatment in children with disorders other than hyperkinesis or minimal brain dysfunction (see Chapter 10) has been studied infrequently, unsystematically, and with a lack of concern for determining long-term adverse consequences.

The paucity of studies may be attributable largely to the difficulties a researcher may encounter in trying to assess the efficacy of drugs in light of the many, almost insurmountable methodological problems involved. There is no single diagnostic classification system for children and adolescents that is uniformly used by clinicians; nor is there evidence of high reliability among practitioners who diagnose from the same classification schema. Outcome criteria are often difficult to specify and even more difficult to evaluate, since too few objective measuring devices (behavioral rating scales, psychological tests) of demonstrated reliability and validity are available. Moreover, drug effects may be confounded or obscured by developmental changes in the child, obvious and subtle changes in the child's environment (loss of a parent, change of school, change in parental attitudes and child-rearing practices), or inadequate supervision of the child's drug intake (Lucas, 1970). Lucas also noted that physicians often are reluctant to prescribe high doses of drugs to children they see on an outpatient basis, whereas they would feel safe enough to give such high doses in the more controlled inpatient setting. Under these conditions many drug-treated outpatients are not likely to receive the therapeutic dose of the drug that is necessary to produce a beneficial effect (Sprague and Sleaton, 1975). Finally, the problem of suggestion, or the placebo effect (discussed earlier in this chapter), is especially important in drug therapy—not only because it requires an appropriate control group, but also because it requires withholding treatment from some children who need remediation.

For our purposes we will consider three major categories of psychoactive drugs and their effects: stimulants, tranquilizers, and antidepresants. Table 6–1 lists the generic and trade names for some of the more widely used drugs under each major category.

1. *Stimulant drugs* were first used for the treatment of acting-out behavioral disorders in children in 1937 by Bradley, who reported that children showed marked improvement in school performance—especially in arithmetic—a decrease in mood swings, and a calmer, more comfortable adjustment (Bradley, 1937). After more than ten years of experience with

Table 6-1 Generic and Trade Names of Psychoactive Drugs within Each Major Category

	Generic Name	*Trade Name*
1. Stimulants		
	Amphetamine	Benzedrine
	Dextroamphetamine	Dexedrine
	Methylphenidate	Ritalin
	Magnesium Pemoline	Cyclert
2. Tranquilizers		
Phenothiazines	Chlorpromazine	Thorazine
	Triflupromazine	Vesprin
	Thioridazine	Mellaril
	Fluphenazine	Permitil
	Trifluoperazine	Stelazine
Thioxanthenes	* Thiothixene	Navane
	Chlorprothixene	Taractan
Butyrophenones	* Haloperidol	Haldol
Dihydroindolones	Molindone	Moban
3. Antidepressants		
	Imipramine	Tofranil, Presamine, Pramine, Imavate
	* Amitriptyline	Elavil
	* Nortriptyline	Aventyl
	* Phenelzine	Nardil
	* Nialamide	Niamid
	* Tranylcypromine	Parnate

*Not recommended for children under twelve years of age.

Benzedrine and Dexedrine, Bradley (1950) found improvement on such variables as academic performance, drive for achievement, attention span, school adjustment, and control of behavior in 60 to 75 percent of the treated children. Fifteen to 25 percent were unchanged, and 10 to 15 percent were worse.

Since the appearance of Bradley's early work, many other studies have been reported in which stimulant drugs were used to treat certain conditions (psychoneuroses, psychopathic personality, schizophrenia, delinquency, and hyperkinesis) and an array of disruptive behaviors (temper outbursts, fighting, hyperactivity, restlessness, disobedience, lying, and defiance) (Office of Child Development, 1971; Conners, 1972b). However, the most systematic research with stimulant drugs has involved minimal brain dysfunction (MBD). Here a paradoxical effect is noted: The drug has a calming, rather than a stimulating, effect on these hyperactive children (Conners, 1972a). The weight of the evidence thus far accumulated indicates that stimulant drugs (amphetamine, dextroamphetamine, methylphenidate, magnesium pemoline) have a positive effect on the disruptive, impulsive, and acting-out symptoms of children evidencing MBD (Werry et al., 1970; Weiss et al., 1971; Dykman, McGrew, and Ackerman, 1974; Page et al., 1974; Lambert et al., 1976). Moreover, Walden and Thompson (1981) claim that drugs do not eliminate the causes of hyperactivity but instead make the child more manageable in the classroom. More specifically, Ritalin and Dexadrine are reported to be the two most effective compounds for managing children with attention deficit disorder with hyperactivity (Klein et al., 1980).

In addition, a number of studies have examined more specific effects of stimulant drugs on various spheres of functioning in MBD children. With respect to activity level and motor performance, these drugs seem to lower aimless and non-goal-directed activity and to improve motor steadiness, accuracy, and reaction times, suggesting faster but more controlled and effective motor performance (Knights and Hinton, 1969; Sprague, Barnes, and Werry, 1970). This salutary effect on motor performance apparently extends to other areas, as reflected in studies that indicate higher intelligence-test scores (IQs) in children treated with stimulant drugs. In fact, the elevation occurred primarily in performance IQs (based on motor and nonverbal responses) or on tests involving perceptual-motor coordination, spatial relations, human figure drawings, and the tracing of one's way through a maze with a pencil (Connors and Rothschild, 1968; Millichap et al., 1968; Knights and Hinton, 1969). However, two recent studies showed that Ritalin does not enhance learning in underachieving children; it may, in fact, conceal learning problems from teachers who may erroneously equate behavioral changes in the classroom with positive changes in achievement (Rie, Rie, and Stewart, 1976a, 1976b).

The results of studies dealing with the effect of stimulants on mood and personality have been sketchy, inconsistent, and unsystematic. While there are data that indicate that these drugs produce happier, more cooperative, more energetic, and more task- and achievement-oriented youngsters, a committee of experts apparently was unimpressed with the evidence, since it concluded that stimulants do not produce mood improvement effects (Connors, 1972b). In a recent review of research on stimulant drugs, Whalen and Henker (1976) proposed that in evaluating the effectiveness of these medications it is important to consider their potency in causing attributional change and to determine where the responsibility of the disorder lies (in external conditions versus internal dysfunctions).

The known side effects of stimulant drugs include loss of appetite and weight, insomnia, headaches, abdominal pain, irritability, aggressiveness, and tearfulness (Aman and Werry, 1974; Campbell and Small, 1978). Moreover, recent data suggest that the long-term administration of stimulants adversely affects growth in terms of height and weight (Safer, Allen, and Barr, 1972; Quinn and Rappoport, 1975; Safer and Allen, 1975).

2. *Tranquilizers* (see Table 6–1) have been credited with radically changing the practice of adult psychiatry, particularly in reducing the length of hospitalization for many seriously disturbed mental patients and in keeping so many of them functioning within the community. However, their usefulness with emotionally troubled children is limited to the control of certain symptoms, such as severe hypermotility, excitability, insomnia, and stereotyped behaviors, and to effects that are usually quite small (Brummit, 1968; Fish, 1968; Campbell, 1976). In fact, the risks with major tranquilizers seem to be greater than the gains—tranquilizers are known to impair cognitive functioning and learning as well as to produce serious extrapyramidal symptoms (tremors and excessive salivation), dyskinetic symptoms (abnormal movements of the face, neck, jaw, and tongue, as well as difficulties in swallowing), and convulsive seizures (Campbell and Small, 1978).

Many sedeatives and minor tranquilizers are now employed with anxious and neurotic children, because their unfavorable effects are minimal (Yaffe and Danish, 1977). Those most commonly used in clinical practices include the minor tranquilizers (such as Valium and Librium) and the antihistamine sedative (such as Benadryl).

However, Patterson and Pruitt (1977) conclude that "there is no absolute documentation of benefit for the use of sedatives and minor tranquilizers in children.... Drugs are not a substitute for the care and caring that should be given by the health professional to the affected child and the parents" (p. 176).

3. *Antidepressant drugs* have been neither studied nor used extensively with children,

although tricyclic amines have shown some effectiveness in treating enuresis and school phobias in children between the ages of six and fourteen and with adolescents who manifest moderate to severe depression (Gittelman-Klein and Klein, 1971, 1973; Bakwin and Bakwin, 1972; Campbell and Small, 1978; Klein et al., 1980). Conners (1972) also noted some interesting but tentative findings worthy of further exploration. These suggest that antidepressant drugs (imipramine) may have a positive effect on behavioral disorders and MBD, similar to their effect on depression.

4. *The socioethical aspects of drug therapy with children* have begun to receive attention. Recently public concern was aroused by newspaper accounts claiming that as many as 20 percent of our school-aged children showed learning and behavioral characteristics of MBD and that large numbers of these youngsters (between 300,000 and 2,000,000) were being drugged to control and manage their classroom behavior (Brown and Bing, 1976). The fact that MBD is an ambiguous and little-understood condition and that stimulants and tranquilizers were increasingly used without data on their long-term effects and for a disorder about which the experts cannot agree brought a storm of public protests (Ladd, 1973). Local physicians defended their practice, and they were supported by a panel of experts brought together by the Office of Child Development and the Department of Health, Education and Welfare, who were favorable about the effects of these drugs in treating MBD children (Office of Child Development, 1971). Apparently, parents of the treated children and the school officials involved also were unperturbed by the situation, although one well-known educator, Edward T. Ladd, sharply criticized the practice and raised some important issues (Ladd, 1973). Ladd noted five serious risks involved in the use of these drugs: (1) the possibility of the drugs producing undesirable physiological effects, even addiction; (2) the possibility of faulty diagnoses, since the diagnostic judgment is frequently based on teachers' observations of the child's behavior; (3) the possibility that this practice will further encourage a positive attitude toward taking "pills" in a culture already inclined to think of chemical substances as a "cure-all"; (4) the likelihood that the use of drugs deprives children of opportunities for controlling and regulating their own behavior and for developing independence; and (5) the belief that drug use infringes on the legal rights and civil liberties of children, since it is doubtful that the schools have a legal right to attempt to control their students' hyperactive behaviors.

Eisenberg (1971) dealt with the issue of drug therapy from another perspective. He described the medical reluctance and the ethical concerns of experimental drug research with normal children, and he held this largely responsible for the paucity of laboratory data on the effectiveness and the safety of the various drugs used today. He also highlighted the need to know the long-term effects of chronic drug use on the growth and development of children, because adverse and permanent consequences are real possibilities. Eisenberg then discussed the principles of drug therapy he believed should be followed when administering drugs to children as part of a larger therapeutic program.

MILIEU APPROACHES

Milieu approaches. These treatment methods are ongoing experiences in which the daily environment is ordered, arranged, and planned as either a partial or a complete therapeutic program. While there are numerous possibilities for such programs, the prototype is ordinarily thought of as a residential treatment facility where the treatment philosophy is expressed in almost every aspect of the environment—including the attitudes and activities of the staff, the design of living, the way the child is managed, and the specific therapeutic programs the child is offered (Shaw, 1966). Obviously, not all inpatient units meet these standards, since some provide only custodial care while others offer no more than hospital maintenance, regular visits with a therapist, and a structured and controlled setting. Residential treatment centers are typically quite expensive, but they are very valuable when either the child or the family is too disturbed to be managed and treated on an outpatient basis. Under these conditions the residential program may be the best solution; it provides the child with a total therapeutic environment as well as with the external controls necessary to prevent the child from becoming involved in self-destructive behaviors and/or conflicts with society. However, whenever possible, most therapists prefer to keep the child in the home and functioning in the community by using alternative milieu approaches, such as special education programs and summer camps. In describing these approaches, it is important to recognize that at this time few—if any—controlled studies exist evaluating the effectiveness of one treatment relative to another, determining which aspects of the milieu approach contribute most significantly to improvement, or highlighting the specific ways in which children benefit, if at all.

Residential Treatment Centers

These vary widely in size, philosophy, goals, and methods, but as a milieu approach they all provide children with greater tolerance and consistency as well as with firmer control. They also provide more frequent contacts with adults who are warmer and more understanding of their problems than those adults encountered on the outside. While not all aspects of a residential facility are of equal therapeutic value, Redl (1972) compiled a list of important ingredients that might make a difference in the treatment of disturbed children when organized in accord with the therapeutic goals. Redl stresses that the social structure of a residential facility more closely resembles a harem society or a sleep-away camp than a family unit and that the roles, responsibilities, pecking order, and communication network of the staff must be articulated clearly to avoid confusion and mixed messages. Routines, rituals, and regulations of daily living should be managed within the context of therapeutic goals, since they have a strong impact on the child's behavior, such as whether he or she is encouraged to control impulses or act them out. Since other youngsters and their personality characteristics (and psychopathology) have significant but possibly different stimulus values and effects on different children, it is important to order the interpersonal living arrangements in ways that best meet the psychological needs of each child. Redl also stresses the importance of staff attitudes and feelings, the daily assessment of each child's behaviors in terms of their implications, the planning of activities, and the proper use of space, equipment, and time.

Residential centers offer multifaceted programs, and they employ a multidiscipline professional staff to carry them out. Professionals include psychiatrists, clinical psychologists, psychiatric social workers, psychiatric nurses, special education teachers, language therapists, occupational and recreational therapists, and child-care workers. In performing their respective roles, staff members should each have an understanding of the individual child and his or her psychopathology, as well as maintain continuous communication with other staff members so that efforts are coordinated within the total treatment plan. The child's therapist usually directs the therapeutic program, which involves decisions about living arrangements, visitors, the activities in which the child will participate, and the short- and long-term goals the staff and child should accomplish. When indicated, the therapist also meets with the child in regularly scheduled sessions of individual or group psychotherapy. Milieu residential centers rely heavily on their special school as an integral part of the treatment plan, not only to provide continuing education but also to function as a prime force in promoting the child's social, physical, and emotional development. Language specialists (to remediate reading and speech problems), occupational therapists (to help the children learn to manipulate craft materials in an organized and constructive way), and recreational therapists (to plan and supervise athletic and play activities) are almost always available as supportive components of this milieu approach. In addition, a cadre of nurses usually function as ward or cottage supervisors, as administrators of medications and arrangers of daily activities, and as supervisors of child-care workers who are responsible for managing the children in the morning, at mealtimes, during free-activity periods, and at bedtime.

Project Re-Ed, launched by federal funds and consisting of residential schools under the state mental health departments of Tennessee and South Carolina, is an example of a residential milieu that emphasizes an educational approach in helping emotionally disturbed children adapt to living at home and within the community (Hobbs, 1966). Unlike residential treatment centers where psychotic and severely disturbed children are "treated" for their psychopathology, project Re-Ed is designed to service children who are less disturbed and for whom institutionalization is not required. The children range from six to twelve years of age, possess average or higher intelligence, but are often academically deficient. They are enrolled in the residential schools in groups of eight, with teams of teacher-counselors, teacher-counselor trainees, teacher aides, and resource specialists (art, music, and physical education) assigned to work with each group. Volunteer workers and professional consultants from the fields of psychiatry, psychology, social work, and education are also available. Children live in the schools during the week and spend weekends with their families at home. The thrust of the program is two-fold: (1) reeducating the children to live effectively in the outside world by enhancing self-competence and teaching them to cognitively control their behavior, and (2) training a new type of mental health worker, the teacher-counselor.

The evaluative results of one study suggest that Re-Ed has promise as a milieu approach (Weinstein, 1969). Ratings made by parents, teachers, and referring agencies showed that 75 percent of the children were regarded as moderately to greatly improved after six months with respect to their symptomatology, although no academic improvement was noted. Moreover, the project demonstrated a significant reduction in per child cost (about one-third less) over the expenditures necessary in the psychotherapeutically oriented residential centers).

Special Education Programs

Various estimates have been cited indicating the numbers of school-age children who are emotionally disturbed or who require special help for emotional difficulties or academic problems, or both. One investigator suggested that three children in the average classroom evidence a classifiable abnormal condition, while another reported a figure of nine when mild and moderate problems were included (Glidewel and Swallow, 1968; Bower, 1969). When the number of children in kindergarten through third grade who have received special help from a professional worker or who have had to repeat a grade is considered, the estimate reaches the staggering figure of 41 percent (Rubin and Balow, 1971). The fact that the bulk of the mentally retarded and sensory handicapped children are not included in these estimates makes the sheer demand and need for special education programs more apparent, especially in light of recent legislation that guarantees the right of every child to publicly supported education.

Special education programs are now available for mentally retarded, sensory handicapped, emotionally disturbed, and learning disabled children in either full-day schools, self-contained classes, or resource rooms. The social stigma, the isolation from normal peers, and the self-limiting availability of resources associated with full-day schools and self-contained programs are among the disadvantages noted by educators who argue against this form of special education. The concept of the resource room was developed to overcome some of the criticisms of the isolated special class. Students are provided with a classroom as well as with a special education teacher with whom they work during several periods of the day; for the remainder of the school day, they attend regular classes.

Summer Camps

Full-day and sleep-away camps for emotionally disturbed and mentally retarded children provide recreational programs as well as opportunities for the development of social, personal, and physical skills. Children may develop peer relations and group affiliation, a sense of independence and personal competence, and new skills in crafts and outdoor athletic activities. Special academic instructional programs are sometimes available in reading as well as in other areas where the child needs help. Group therapy and activities planned to meet therapeutic goals for each child (similar to a residential treatment center) reflect the program emphasis of a few of the camps—usually those that are quite expensive and limited in the number of children they can handle. Groves (1981) argues for the importance of camping as an experience that aids the child's ability to cope with and adjust to the social environment.

SUMMARY

In this chapter we initially discussed the issues associated with treatment approaches, such as rapport and the heterogenity of clinical practice, as well as the methodological problems involved in evaluating treatment outcome, the relative merits of different therapies, and the durability of behavioral changes. We also considered the question of what constitutes treatment, and we arrived at a broad definition that would satisfy our purposes and reflect the diversity of approaches in current practice. Therefore, treatment is here regarded as any intervention or agent designed to alleviate or alter abnormal behaviors and facilitate normal personality development. The remainder of the chapter was devoted to descriptions, and to a lesser extent critical appraisals, of various *psychological, somatic,* and *milieu* treatment approaches. Tables 6–2, 6–3, and 6–4 summarize the treatment methods described under each of these categories.

Table 6–2 Psychological Treatment Approaches

METHOD	
I. Individual Psychotherapies	Psychologically planned interaction between therapist and client.
A. Play Therapy	Suitable for prepubertal children where play rather than words is natural mode of expression.
1. Psychoanalytic	Procedural modification of psychoanalysis in which play is used as media of expressing and understanding unconscious processes and conflicts.
2. Nondirective	Adapted from client-centered therapy in which the feelings and attitudes of child are reflected and clarified by therapists.
3. Filial Therapy	Variant of nondirective play in which parents are trained to conduct therapy.
B. Verbal One-to-One Therapies	Planned verbal interaction between therapist and client.
1. Reality Therapy	Individual talk therapy which stresses the present and encourages the child to make a value judgment of his/her behavior, to develop a plan to achieve the desired goal, and to be committed to that plan.

(*continued*)

Table 6-2 (cont.)

METHOD	
2. Transactional Analysis	Psychotherapy which focuses on intrapsychic learning and interpersonal games.
C. Cognitive Therapies	Intervention procedures which apply learning principles to covert cognitive activities and events. Illustrations include a combination of cognitive modeling and self-instruction rehearsal to increase self-control of impulsive children; self-instructional training, relevant search-and-scan behavior, and exposure to the modeling of self-instructions and of efficient task behaviors to increase self-control; and rational-emotive therapy, in which the therapist disputes the client's irrational expectations and beliefs to increase his/her self-worth.
II. Group and Family Therapy	Involve multiple clients and are distinguishable on the basis of blood-tie relations of participants and on theoretical grounds.
A. Group Therapy	Multiple clients meeting together in planned group experience intended to foster personal and social development.
1. Activity Group	Designed for prepubertal children; play activities for each child or the group are used to enhance self-worth and imitation of socially desired behaviors.
2. Group Play	
a. Psychoanalytic	Offers children emotional release, reduction of guilt and anxiety, and more acceptable outlets for id impulses.
b. Nondirective	Offers opportunities for self-realization under conditions of unconditional acceptance.
3. Verbal Group	Suitable for adolescents who are reassured and comforted by presence of others and for whom peer relations and group affiliation are important.
B. Family Therapies	Members of the family are brought together for treatment.
1. Psychoanalytic	Diagnoses psychopathology of child and family, and views the child as the victim and participant of unresolved parental conflicts.
2. Systems Theory	Views diagnosis as interference with open interaction between therapist and family, and perceives the family as a biosocial system in which there is a reciprocal interaction among family members.
III. Behavior Therapies	Treatment of abnormal behaviors by methods derived from experimental psychology and the principles of learning.
A. Decreasing Target Behaviors	
1. Reciprocal Inhibition: Systematic Desensitization and Emotive Imagery	Pairing of incompatible responses of relaxation or imaging pleasurable scenes with a graded series of anxiety stimuli to prevent fear response and extinguish anxiety.
2. Flooding or Implosive Therapy	Induces the arousal of maximal anxiety without relief until the aversive reactions are extinguished.
3. Modeling	Learning to reduce avoidance behaviors through vicarious imitation of a model.
4. Extinction	Target behavior eliminated through the discontinuance of reinforcement, by punishment or time out.
B. Increasing Prosocial Behaviors	
1. Positive Reinforcement	Making reinforcement (reward) contingent on the performance of some wanted response.

(*continued*)

Table 6-2 (cont.)

METHOD	
a. Token Economy	Use of tokens as reinforcers which can be accumulated and later cashed in for desired privilege or tangible item.
b. Contingency Contract	Therapist and client agree on behavioral goals and the reinforcement to be received when goals are reached.
2. Modeling	New behaviors are acquired by means of a model (actual, depicted, or imagined) who demonstrates the desired behavior.
C. Combined Procedures	Strategies that involve the decrease of maladaptive behaviors and the increase of adaptive ones.
1. Positive Reinforcement, Discontinuance of Positive Consequences, and Aversive Consequences	Reward for wanted behavior, remove rewards from target behavior, and punish parents when child fails to emit wanted response.
2. Positive Reinforcement and Punishment	Use of reward for wanted behavior and aversive controls for unwanted ones.

Table 6-3 Somatic Treatment Approaches

Method	
I. Shock Treatment (Chemical or Electrical)	Electric current passed through two electrodes attached to the skull, or chemical substances used to produce convulsions. Has been tried with psychotic children by Bender primarily, but with no demonstrated benefits.
II. Psychosurgery	Sterotaxic destruction of the amygdala or posterior hypothalamus in children who evidenced hyperexcitability as well as violent, uncontrollable behaviors. No fatalities reported, with claims of positive calming effects. The approach has been criticized on both socioethical and scientific grounds.
III. Psychoactive Drug Therapy	The use of certain chemical substances to alter mood and behavior, although there is a dearth of adequately controlled studies.
A. Stimulants	Used for acting-out behaviors, hyperactivity, and minimal brain dysfunction in which a paradoxical effect is noted wherein the drugs have a calming rather than a stimulating effect. The evidence suggests a positive effect on symptoms of MBD children, improvement in goal-directed activity, motor steadiness, and reaction time. Treated MBD children also show higher performance IQs, but no consistent changes in mood and personality.
B. Tranquilizers	Usefulness limited to the control of certain symptoms and to effects that are usually quite small. Risks of side effects seem to be greater than benefits.
C. Antidepressants	Neither studied nor used extensively with children, although tricyclic amines show promise with enuretics, school phobics, and adolescent depressions.

Table 6-4 Milieu Treatment Approaches

METHOD	
I. Residential Treatment Centers	Multifaceted programs with multidiscipline staff providing live-in environment that is ordered, arranged, and planned as a total therapeutic program. Children receive greater tolerance and consistency, firmer control, and more frequent contacts with understanding adults than they would get on the outside. Centers are usually psychodynamically oriented and quite expensive, but useful for psychotic or very severely disturbed children and/or families.
A. Project Re-Ed	Residential milieu approach that emphasizes an educational approach to emotionally disturbed children. It also was designed to train a new type of mental health worker, the teacher-counselor. Results of one study thus far showed that the project has promise in decreasing symptoms and in reducing cost of residential treatment.
II. Special Education Programs	Specially designed instructional programs given by trained teachers for the retarded, sensory handicapped, emotionally disturbed, and learning disabled children either in full-day schools, self-contained classes, or in resource rooms.
A. Day Schools or Self-contained Classes	Criticized because of their social stigma, the isolation of children from normal peers, and their limited access to material resources.
B. Resource Rooms	Developed to overcome some of the criticisms of full-day or self-contained classes. Provides students with special education teacher with whom to work for several periods of the day, but rest of the day students attend regular classes.
III. Summer Camps	Either full-day or sleep-away summer camps are available for emotionally disturbed and retarded children. Recreational, social, and academic programs are offered.

REFERENCES

ABRAMOWITZ, C. V. The Effectiveness of Group Psychotherapy with Children. *Archives of General Psychiatry*, 1976, 33, 320–326.

AMAN, M. G., and WERRY, J. S. Methylphenidate in Children: Effects on Cardiorespiratory Function in Exertion. In C. K. Conners (ed.), *Clinical Use of Stimulant Drugs in Children*. Amsterdam: Excerpta Medica, 1974, pp. 119–131.

ANDERSON, N., and MARRONE, R. T. Group Therapy for Emotionally Disturbed Children: A Key to Affective Education. *American Journal of Orthopsychiatry*, 1977, 47, 97–103.

ANDREWS, G., and HARVEY, R. Does Psychotherapy Benefit Neurotic Patients? A Reanalysis of the Smith, Glass and Miller Data. *Archives of General Psychiatry*, 1981, 38, 1203–1208.

ARTNER, K., and CASTELL, R. Therapy of Encopretic Children on a Ward for Psychosomatic Diseases. *Praxis Der Kinderpsychologie und Kinderpsychiatrie*, 1979, 28, 119–132.

ATTNEAVE, C. L. Social Networks as a Unit of Intervention. In P. J. Guerin, Jr. (ed.), *Family Therapy: Theory and Practice*. New York: Gardner Press, 1976, pp. 220–231.

AYLLON, T., and AZRIN, N. H. *The Token Economy: A Motivational System for Therapy and Rehabilitation*. New York: Appleton-Century-Crofts, 1968.

AYLLON, T., SMITH, D., and ROGERS, M. Behavioral Management of School Phobia. *Journal of Behavior Therapy and Experimental Psychiatry*, 1970, 1, 125–128.

AXLINE, V. M. *Dibs in Search of Self*. Boston: Houghton Mifflin, 1964.

AXLINE, V. M. *Play Therapy*, rev. ed. New York: Ballantine Books, 1969.

BAIDEME, S. M., KERN, R. M., and TAFFEL-COHEN, S. The Use of Adlerian Family Therapy in a Case of School Phobia. *Journal of Individual Psychology*, 1979, 35, 58–69.

BAKWIN, H., and BAKWIN, R. M. M. *Behavior Disorders in Children*, 4th ed. Philadelphia: Saunders, 1972.

BALASUBRAMANIAM, V., KANAKA, T. S., and RAMAMURTHI, B. Surgical Treatment of Hyperkinetic and Behavior Disorders. *International Surgery*, 1970, *54*, 18–23.

BANDURA. A. *Principles of Behavior Modification*. New York: Holt, Rinehart and Winston, 1969.

BANDURA, A., GRUSEC, J. E., and MENLOVE, F. L. Vicarious Extinction of Avoidance Behavior. *Journal of Personality and Social Psychology*, 1967, *5*, 16–23.

BARR, N. The Responsible World of Reality Therapy. *Psychology Today*, 1974, *7*(9), 64–68.

BARRETT, C. L., HARUPE, I. E., and MILLER, L. Research on Psychotherapy with Children. In S. L. Garfield and A. E. Bergin (eds.), *Handbook of Psychotherapy and Behavior Change*, 2nd ed. New York: John Wiley, 1978, pp. 411–435.

BELL, J. E. *Family Therapy*. New York: Jason Aronson, 1975.

BENDER, L. Childhood Schizophrenia. *Psychiatric Quarterly*, 1953, *27*, 633–681.

BENDER, L., GOLDSCHMIDT, L., and SANKAR, D. Treatment of Autistic Schizophrenic Children with LSD-25 and UML 491. *Recent Advances in Biological Psychiatry*, 1962, *4*, 170–177.

BERGIN, A. E. Some Implications of Psychotherapy Research for Therapeutic Practice. *Journal of Abnormal Psychology*, 1966, *71*, 235–246.

BERGIN, A. E. The Evaluation of Therapeutic Outcomes. In A. E. Bergin and S. L. Garfield (eds.), *Handbook of Psychotherapy and Behavior Change: An Empirical Analysis*. New York: John Wiley, 1971, pp. 217–270.

BERKOVITZ, I. H. On Growing a Group: Some Thoughts on Structure, Process and Settings. In I. H. Berkovitz (ed.), *Adolescents Grow in Groups: Experiences in Adolescent Group Psychotherapy*. New York: Brunner/Mazel, 1972, pp. 6–28.

BERKOVITZ, I. H., and SUGAR, M. Indications and Contraindications for Adolescent Group Psychotherapy. In M. Sugar (ed.), *The Adolescent in Group and Family Therapy*. New York: Brunner/Mazel, 1975, pp. 3–26.

BERNE, E. *What Do You Say after You Say Hello?* New York: Bantam Books, 1972.

BLOCK, D. A. Including the Children in Family Therapy. In P. J. Guerin, (ed.), *Family Therapy: Theory and Practice*. New York: Gardner Press, 1976, pp. 168–181.

BOARDMAN, W. K. Rusty: A Brief Behavior Disorder. *Journal of Consulting Psychology*, 1962, *26*, 293–297.

BOUDEWYNS, P. A., and SHIPLEY, R. H. Confusing Negative Practice with Flooding: A Cautionary Note. *Bahavior Therapist*, 1982, *5*, 47–48.

BOULOUGOURIS, J. C., and BASSIAKOS, L. Prolonged Flooding in Cases with Obsessive-Compulsive Neurosis. *Behavior Research and Therapy*, 1973, *11*, 227–231.

BOWER, E. M. Mental Health. In R. Ebel (ed.), *Encyclopedia of Educational Research*, 4th ed. New York: Macmillan, 1969, pp. 811–828.

BRACKBILL, Y. Extinction of the Smiling Response in Infants as a Function of Reinforcement Schedule. *Child Development*, 1958, *29*, 115–124.

BRADLEY, C. The Behavior of Children Receiving Benzedrine. *American Journal of Psychiatry*, 1937, *94*, 577–585.

BRADLEY, C. Benzedrine and Dexedrine in the Treatment of Children's Behavior Disorders. *Pediatrics*, 1950, *5*, 24–36.

BREGGIN, P. R. The Return of Lobotomy and Psychosurgery. *Congressional Record*, February 1972, *118*(26) E1602–E1612.

BROWN, J. L., and BING, S. R. Drugging Children: Child Abuse by Professionals. In G. P. Roocher (ed.), *Children's Rights and the Mental Health Profession*. New York: John Wiley, 1976, pp. 219–228.

BROWN, S. L. Family Group Therapy. In B. B. Wolman (ed.), *Manual of Child Psychopathology*. New York: McGraw-Hill, 1972, pp. 969–1009.

BRUMMIT, H. The Use of Long Acting Tranquilizers with Hyperactive Children. *Psychosomatics*, 1968, *9*, 157–159.

CAMPBELL, M. Biological Interventions in Psychoses of Childhood. In E. Schopler and R. J. Reichler (eds.), *Psychopathology and Child Development: Research and Treatment*. New York: Plenum, 1976, pp. 243–270.

CAMPBELL, M., and SMALL, A. M. Chemotherapy. In B. B. Wolman, A. O. Ross, and J. Egan (eds.), *Handbook of Treatment of Mental Disorders in Childhood and Adolescence*. Englewood Cliffs, N.J.: Prentice-Hall, 1978, pp. 9–27.

CANTELA, J. R. Covert Sensitization. *Psychological Reports*, 1967, *20*, 459–468.

CHAPEL. J. L. Treatment of a Case of School Phobia by Reciprocal Inhibition. *Canadian Psychiatric Association Journal*, 1967, *12*, 25–28.

CHRISTENSEN, D. E., and SPRAGUE, R. L. Reduction of Hyperactive Behavior by Conditioning Procedures Alone and Combined with Methylphenidate (Ritalin). *Behavior Research and Therapy*, 1973, *11*, 331–334.

CONNERS, C. K. Psychological Effects of Stimulant Drugs in Children with Minimal Brain Dysfunction. *Pediatrics*, 1972a, *49*, 702–715.

CONNERS, C. K. Pharmacotherapy of Psychopathology in Children. In H. C. Quay and J. S. Werry (eds.), *Psychopathological Disorders of Childhood*. New York: Wiley-Interscience, 1972b, pp. 316–347.

CONNERS, C. K., and ROTHSCHILD, G. H. Drugs and Learning in Children. In J. Hellmuth (ed.), *Learning Disorders, Volume III*. Seattle, Wash.: Special Child Publications, 1968, pp. 191–224.

DAVISON, G. C., and NEALE, J. M. *Abnormal Psychology: An Experimental Clinical Approach*. New York: John Wiley, 1974, p. 459.

DE GIUSEPPE, R. A. The Use of Behavior Modification to Establish Rational Self-statements in Children. In A. Ellis and R. Grieger (eds.), *Handbook of Rational Emotive Therapy*. New York: Springer Publishing Co., 1977, pp. 376–378.

DeVoge, C. A Behavioral Approach to RET with Children. *Rational Living,* 1974, *9,* 23–26.

Doubros, S. G., and Daniels, G. J. An Experimental Approach to the Reduction of Overactive Behavior. *Behavior Research and Therapy,* 1966, *4,* 251–258.

Dunlap, K., *Habits: Their Making and Unmaking.* New York: Liveright, 1932.

Dykman, R. A., McGrew, J., and Ackerman, P. T. A Double Blind Clinical Study of Pemoline in MBD Children: Comments on the Psychological Test Results. In C. K. Conners (ed.), *Clinical Use of Stimulant Drugs in Children.* Amsterdam: Excerpta Medica, 1974, pp. 125–129.

Eisenberg, L. The Course of Childhood Schizophrenia. *Archives of Neurology and Psychiatry,* 1957, *78,* 69–83.

Eisenberg, L. Principles of Drug Therapy in Child Psychiatry with Special Reference to Stimulant Drugs. *American Journal of Orthopsychiatry,* 1971, *41,* 371–379.

Ellis, A. Rational Psychotherapy. *Journal of General Psychology,* 1958, *59,* 35–49.

Ellis, A. *Reason and Emotion in Psychotherapy.* New York: Lyle Stuart, 1962.

Emmelkamp, P. M. G. Self-observation versus Flooding in the Treatment of Agoraphobia. *Behavior Research and Therapy,* 1974, *12,* 229–237.

Fine, R. Psychoanalysis. In R. Corsini (ed.), *Current Psychotherapies.* Ithaca, Ill.: Peacock, 1973, pp. 1–33.

Fish, B. Drug Use in Psychiatric Disorders of Children. *American Journal of Psychiatry,* 1968, *124,* 31–36.

Framer, E. M., and Sanders, S. H. The Effects of Family Contingency Contracting on Disturbed Sleep Behaviors in a Male Adolescent. *Journal of Behavior Therapy and Experimental Psychiatry,* 1980, *11,* 235–237.

Frank, J. D. *Persuasion and Healing: A Comparative Study of Psychotherapy.* New York: Schocken Books, 1961.

Franklin, G., and Nottage, W. Psychoanalytic Treatment of Severely Disturbed Juvenile Delinquents in a Therapy Group. *International Journal of Psychotherapy,* 1969, *19,* 165–175.

Freeman, A. M., and Watts, J. W. *Psychosurgery in the Treatment of Mental Disorders and Intractable Pain,* 2nd ed. Springfield, Ill.: Chas. C Thomas, 1950.

Freud, A. *The Ego and the Mechanisms of Defense* (1936). *New York: International Universities Press,* 1946a.

Freud. A. *The Psychoanalytical Treatment of Children: Lectures and Essays.* London: Imago, 1946b.

Freud, A. *Normality and Pathology in Childhood.* New York: International Universities Press, 1965.

Freud, S. *Analysis of a Phobia in a Five-Year-Old Boy* (1909), Vol. 10, standard ed. London: Hogarth, 1955.

Garber, J. A Psychoeducational Therapy Program for Delinquent Boys: An Evaluation Report. *Journal of Drug Education,* 1976, *6,* 331–342.

Garvey, W. P., and Hegrenes, J. R. Desensitization Techniques in the Treatment of School Phobia. *American Journal of Orthopsychiatry,* 1966, *36,* 147–152.

Gittelman-Klein, R. (ed.). *Recent Advances in Child Psychopharmacology.* New York: International Arts and Science Press, 1975.

Gittelman-Klein, R., and Klein, D. F. Controlled Imipramine Treatment of School Phobia. *Archives of General Psychiatry,* 1971, *25,* 204–222.

Gittelman-Klein, R., and Klein, D. F. School Phobia: Diagnostic Considerations in the Light of Imipramine Effects. *Journal of Nervous and Mental Disease,* 1973, *156,* 199–215.

Ginott, H. G. *Group Psychotherapy with Children: The Theory and Practice of Play-Therapy.* New York: McGraw-Hill, 1961.

Glasser, W. *Reality Therapy: A New Approach to Psychiatry.* New York: Harper and Row, 1965.

Glasser, W. *Schools Without Failure.* New York: Harper and Row, 1969.

Glidewell, J., and Swallow, C. *The Prevalence of Maladjustment in Elementary Schools.* Chicago, Ill.: University of Chicago Press, 1968.

Goetz, E. M., and Baer, D. M. Social Control of Form Diversity and the Emergence of New Forms in Children's Blockbuilding. *Journal of Applied Behavior Analysis,* 1973, *6*(2), 209–217.

Group for the Advancement of Psychiatry (GAP). *Pharmacotherapy and Psychotherapy: Paradoxes, Problems and Progress,* 1975, Vol. IX, Report No. 93.

Groves, P. Camping—Its Past and Future Contribution to Adolescent Development. *Adolescence,* 1981, *62,* 331–334.

Guerney, B., Jr. Filial Therapy: Description and Rationale. *Journal of Consulting Psychology,* 1964, *28,* 304–310.

Guttierez, L. F., Vallejo, C., Chacon, C., and Vargas, L. Surgical Treatment of Mental Disorders by Functional or Stereotaxic Neurosurgery. *Revista Columbiana de Psiquiatria,* 1976, *5,* 402–409.

Hafner, R. J., Gilchrist, P., Bowling, J., and Kalucy, R. The Treatment of Obsessional Neurosis in a Family Setting. *Australian and New Zealand Journal of Psychiatry,* 1981, *15,* 145–151.

Haley, J. *Reflections on Therapy and Other Essays.* Chevy Chase, Md.: Family Therapy Institute of Washington, D.C., 1981.

Haley, J. Strategies of Psychotherapy. New York: Grune and Stratton, 1963.

Hammer, M., and Kaplan, A. M. *The Practice of Psychotherapy with Children.* Homewood, Ill.: Dorsey Press, 1967.

Heimburger, R. F., Whitlock, C. C., and Kalsbeck, J. E., Stereotaxic Amygdalectomy for Epilepsy with Aggressive Behavior. *Journal of the American Medical Association,* 1966, *198,* 741–745.

Henriksen, K., and Doughty, R. Decelerating Undesirable Mealtime Behavior in a Group of Profoundly Retarded Boys. *American Journal of Mental Deficiency,* 1967, *72,* 40–44.

Hersen, M., Eisler, R. M., Miller, P. M., Johnson, M. B.,

and PINKSTON, S. G. Effects of Practice, Instructions and Modeling on Components of Assertive Behavior. *Behaviour Research and Therapy*, 1973, *11*, 443–451.

HINGTGEN, J. N., SAUNDERS, B. J., and DEMYER M. K. Shaping Cooperative Responses in Early Childhood Schizophrenics." In L. P. Ullmann, and L. Krasner (eds.), *Case Studies in Behavior Modification*. New York: Holt, Rinehart and Winston, 1965, pp. 130–138.

HOBBS, N. Helping Disturbed Children: Psychological and Ecological Strategies. *American Psychologist*, 1966, *21*, 1105–1115.

HOLLON, S. D., and BECK, A. T. Cognitive Therapy of Depression. In P. C. Kendall and S. D. Hollon (eds.), *Cognitive-Behavioral Interventions: Theory, Research, and Procedures*. New York: Academic Press, 1979, pp. 153–203.

HOMME, L. E. Perspectives in Psychology: XXIV Control of Coverants, the Operants of the Mind, Vol. 24. *Psychological Record*, 1965, *15*, 501–511.

JONES, M. C. The Elimination of Children's Fears. *Journal of Experimental Psychology*, 1924 (a), *7*, 382–390.

JONES, M. C. A Laboratory Study of Fear. The Case of Peter. *Journal of Genetic Psychology*, 1924 (b), *31*, 308–315.

KAZDIN, A. E. Effects of Covert Modeling and Model Reinforcement on Assertive Behavior. *Journal of Abnormal Psychology*, 1974, *83*, 240–252.

KAZDIN, A. E. *The Token Economy*. New York: Plenum, 1977.

KEANE, T. M., and KALOUPEK, D. G. Imaginal Flooding in the Treatment of a Posttraumatic Stress Disorder. *Journal of Consulting and Clinical Psychology*, 1982, *50*, 138–140.

KENDALL, P. C., and FINCH, A. J. Analyses of Changes in Verbal Behavior Following a Cognitive Behavioral Treatment for Impulsivity. *Journal of Abnormal Child Psychology*, 1979a, 7(4), 455–463.

KENDALL, P. C., and FINCH, A. J. Developing Nonimpulsive Behavior in Children. Cognitive-Behavioral Strategies for Self-control. In P. C. Kendall and S. D. Hollon (eds.), *Cognitive-Behavioral Interventions: Theory, Research, and Procedures*. New York: Academic Press, 1979b, pp. 37–79.

KENDALL, P. C., and HOLLON, S. D. Cognitive Behavioral Interventions: Overview and Current Status. In P. C. Kendall and S. D. Hollon (eds.), *Cognitive-Behavioral Interventions: Theory, Research, and Procedures*. New York: Academic Press, 1979, pp. 1–9.

KLEIN, D., GITTELMAN, R., QUITKIN, F., and RIFKIN, A. Diagnosis and Drug Treatment of Childhood Disorders. In D. Klein, R. Gittelman, F. Quitkin, and A. Rifkin (eds.), *Diagnosis and Drug Treatment of Psychotic Disorders: Adults and Children*. Baltimore, Md.: Williams and Wilkins, 1980, pp. 590–756.

KLEIN, M. *The Psycho-analysis of Children* (1932). London: Hogarth, 1949.

KNAUS, W. J. Rational Emotive Education. In A. Ellis and R. Grieger (eds.), *Handbook of Rational Emotive Therapy*. New York: Springer Publishing Co., 1977, pp. 398–408.

KNIGHTS, R. M., and HINTON, G. G. The Effects of Methylphenidate (Ritalin) on the Motor Skills and Behavior of Children with Learning Problems. *The Journal of Nervous and Mental Disease*, 1969, *148*, 643–653.

KOOCHER, G. P., and PEDULLA, B. M. Current Practices in Child Psychotherapy. *Professional Psychology*, 1977, *8*, 275–287.

KRAMER, C. H. Psychoanalytically Oriented Family Therapy: Ten Year Evolution of a Private Child Psychiatry Practice. *Family Institute of Chicago Publications*, 1970, No. 1., 1–42.

KUBIE, L. S. A Doctorate in Psychotherapy: The Reasons for a New Profession. In R. R. Holt (ed.), *New Horizon for Psychotherapy: Autonomy as a Profession*. New York: International Universities Press, 1971, pp. 11–36.

LADD, E. T. Pills for Classroom Peace? In A. Davis (ed.), *Issues in Abnormal Child Psychology*. Monterey, Calif.: Brooks, Cole, 1973, pp. 289–296.

LAMBERT, N. M., WINDMILLER, M., SANDOVAL, J., and MOORE, B. Hyperactive Children and the Efficacy of Psychoactive Drugs as a Treatment Intervention. *American Journal of Orthopsychiatry*, 1976, *46*, 335–352.

LAPOUSE, R., and MONK, M. A. Fears and Worries in a Representative Sample of Children. *American Journal of Orthopsychiatry*, 1959, *29*, 803–818.

LAZARUS. A. A., and ABRAMOVITZ, A. The Use of "Emotive Imagery" in the Treatment of Children's Phobias. *Journal of Mental Science*, 1962, *108*, 191–195.

LAZARUS, A. A., and RACHMAN, S. The Use of Systematic Desensitization in Psychotherapy. *South African Medical Journal*, 1967, *31*, 934–937.

LEBO, D. The Present Status of Research on Nondirective Play Therapy. In M. R. Haworth (ed.), *Child Psychotherapy: Practice and Theory*. New York: Basic Books, 1964, pp. 421–430.

LESSER, S. R. Psychoanalysis with Children. In B. B. Wolman (ed.), *Manual of Child Psychopathology*. New York: McGraw-Hill, 1972, pp. 847–864.

LEVINE, R. A., and O'BRIEN, R. M. Treatment of Anxiety about College Tests with Negative Practice and Systematic Desensitization: Some Negative Findings. *Psychological Reports*, 1980, *46*, 823–829.

LEVITT, E. E. Research on Psychotherapy with Children. In A. E. Bergin and S. L. Garfield (eds.), *Handbook of Psychotherapy and Behavior Change: An Empirical Analysis*. New York: John Wiley, 1971, pp. 474–494.

LOVAAS, O. I., FREITAG, G., GOLD, V. J., and KASSORLA, I. C. Experimental Studies in Childhood Schizophrenia: Analysis of Self-Destructive Behavior. *Journal of Experimental Child Psychology*, 1965, *2*, 67–84.

LOVAAS, O. I., KOEGEL, R., SIMMONS. J. Q., and LONG, J. S. Some Generalizations and Follow-Up Measures on Autistic Children in Behavior Therapy. *Journal of Applied Behavioral Analysis*, 1973, *6*, 131–166.

LUCAS, A. R. Psychopharmacologic Treatment. In C. R. Shaw (ed.), *The Psychiatric Disorders of Childhood,* 2nd ed. New York: Appleton-Century-Crofts, 1970, pp. 436–456.

LURIA, A. R. Speech and Formation of Mental Processes. In M. Cole and I. Maltzman (eds.), *A Handbook of Contemporary Soviet Psychology.* New York: Basic Books, 1969, pp. 121–162.

LURIA, A. R. *The Role of Speech in the Regulation of Normal and Abnormal Behaviors.* New York: Liveright, 1961.

MACFARLANE, J. W., ALLEN, L., and HONZIK, M. *A Developmental Study of the Behavior Problems of Normal Children Between 21 Months and 14 Years.* Berkeley, Calif.: University of California Press, 1954.

MACLENNAN, B. W., and FELSENFIELD, N. *Group Counseling and Psychotherapy with Adolescents.* New York: Columbia University Press, 1968.

MADSEN, C. H., HOFFMAN, M., THOMAS, D. R., KOROPSAK, E., and MADSEN, C. K. Comparisons of Toilet Training Techniques. In D. M. Gelfand (ed.), *Social Learning in Childhood.* Belmont, Calif.: Brooks Cole, 1969, pp. 124–132.

MAHONEY, M. J. *Cognitive Behavior Modification.* Cambridge, Mass.: Ballinger, 1974.

MAHONEY, M. J. Reflections on the Cognitive-Learning Trend in Psychotherapy. *American Psychologist,* 1977, 32, 5–13.

MARK, V. H., and ERVIN, F. R. *Violence and the Brain.* New York: Harper and Row, 1970.

MATHEWS, A., and SHAW, P. Emotional Arousal and Persuasion Effects in Flooding. *Behavior Research and Therapy,* 1973, *11,* 587–598.

MEICHENBAUM, D. H. *Cognitive-Behavior Modification.* Morristown, N.J.: General Learning Press, 1974.

MEICHENBAUM, D. H. *Cognitive-Behavior Modification: An Integrative Approach.* New York: Plenum, 1977.

MEICHENBAUM, D. H. (ed.). Cognitive Behavior Modification with Children. *Cognitive Behavior Modification Newsletter,* 1979, 4, 1–10.

MEICHENBAUM, D. H., and ASARNOW, J. Cognitive-Behavioral Modification and Metacognitive Development: Implications for the Classroom. In P. C. Kendall and S. D. Hollon (eds.), *Cognitive-Behavioral Interventions: Theory, Research, and Procedures.* New York: Academic Press, 1979, pp. 11–35.

MEICHENBAUM, D. H., and GOODMAN, J. Training Impulsive Children to Talk to Themselves: A Means of Developing Self-control. *Journal of Abnormal Psychology,* 1971, 77, 115–126.

Mendell, D. Combined Family and Group Therapy for Problems of Adolescents: A Synergistic Approach. In M. Sugar (ed.), *The Adolescent in Group and Family Therapy.* New York: Brunner/Mazel, 1975, pp. 231–247.

MILLICHAP, J. G., AYMAT, F., STURGIS, L. H., LARSEN, K. W., and EGAN, R. A. Hyperkinetic Behavior and Learning Disorders III: Battery of Neuropsychological Tests in Controlled Trial of Methylphenidate. *American Journal of Diseases of Children,* 1968, *116,* 235–244.

MORGANSTERN, K. P. Implosive Therapy and Flooding Procedures: A Critical Review. *Psychological Bulletin,* 1973, 79, 318–334.

MOWRER, O. H., and Mowrer, W. M. Enueresis: A Method for Its Study and Treatment. *American Journal of Orthopsychiatry,* 1938, 8, 436–459.

NARABAYASHI, H. Stereotaxic Amygdelectomy. In B. E. Eleftheriou (ed.), *The Neurobiology of the Amygdala.* New York: Plenum, 1972, pp. 459–483.

OBLER, M., and TERWILLIGER, R. F. Pilot Study on the Effectiveness of Systematic Desensitization with Neurologically Impaired Children with Phobic Disorders. *Journal of Consulting and Clinical Psychology,* 1970, 34, 314–318.

OFFER, D., and VANDERSTOEP, E. Indications and Contraindications for Family Therapy. In M. Sugar (ed.), *The Adolescent in Group and Family Therapy.* New York: Brunner/Mazel, 1975, pp. 144–160.

OFFICE OF CHILD DEVELOPMENT, DEPARTMENT OF HEALTH, EDUCATION AND WELFARE. *Report of the Conference on the Use of Stimulant Drugs in the Treatment of Behaviorally Disturbed Young School Children.* Washington, D.C., 1971.

O'LEARY, K. D., and DRABMAN, R. Token Reinforcement Programs in the Classroom: A Review. *Psychological Bulletin,* 1971, 75, 379–398.

O'LEARY, K. D., and WILSON, G. T. *Behavior Therapy: Application and Outcome.* Englewood Cliffs, N.J.: Prentice-Hall, 1975.

OSTENSEN, K. W. The Runaway Crisis: Is Family Therapy the Answer? *American Journal of Family Therapy,* 1981, 9, 3–12.

PAGE, J. G., BERNSTEIN, J. E., JANICKI, R. S., and MICHELLI, F. A. A Multiclinic Trial of Pemoline in Childhood Hyperkinesis. In C. K. Conners (ed.), *Clinical Use of Stimulant Drugs in Children.* Amsterdam: Excerpta Medica, 1974, pp. 98–124.

PALKES, H., STEWART, M., and FREEDMAN, J. Improvement in Maze Performance on Hyperactive Boys as a Function of Verbal Training Procedures. *Journal of Special Education,* 1971, 5, 337–342.

PATTERSON, G. R., and REID, J. B. Intervention for Families of Aggressive Boys: A Replication Study. *Behavior Research and Therapy,* 1973, *11,* 383–394.

PATTERSON, G. R., JONES, R., WHITTIER, J., and WRIGHT, M. A. A Behavior Modification Technique for the Hyperactive Child. *Behavior Research and Therapy,* 1965, 2, 217–226.

PATTERSON, J. H., and PRUITT, A. W. Treatment of Mild Symptomatic Anxiety States. In J. M. Weiner (ed.), *Psychopharmacology in Childhood and Adolescence.* New York: Basic Books, 1977, pp. 169–178.

PHILLIPS, D., and WOLPE, S. Multiple Behavioral Techniques in Severe Separation Anxiety of a Twelve-Year-Old. *Journal of Behavior Therapy and Experimental Psychiatry,* 1981, *12,* 329–332.

QUINN, P. O., and RAPPOPORT, J. L. One Year Follow-Up of Hyperactive Boys Treated with Imipramine or Methylphenidate. *American Journal of Psychiatry*, 1975, *132*(3), 241–245.

RACHMAN, S. Clinical Applications of Observational Learning, Imitation, and Modeling. *Behavior Therapy*, 1972, 2, 379–397.

RECKLESS, J. B. Pseudosociopathic Neurotic Behavioral Disturbances in Adolescent Girls. *North Carolina Medical Journal*, 1968, *29*, 1–12.

REDL, F. The Concept of "Therapeutic Milieu." In J. K. Whittaker and A. E. Trieschman (eds.), *Children Away from Home: A Sourcebook of Residential Treatment*. Chicago, Ill.: Aldine, Atherton, 1972, pp. 55–70.

REIXACH, G. R., TORRES, D., and REIS, A. Psychosurgery in Mental Diseases and Behavior Disturbances. *Arquivus de Neuro-Psiquitria*, 1977, *35*, 210–217.

RIE, H. E., RIE, E. D., and STEWART, S. Effects of Methylphenidate on Underachieving Children. *Journal of Consulting and Clinical Psychology*, 1976a, *44*, 250–260.

RIE, H. E., RIE, E. D., STEWART, S., and AMBUEL, J. P. Effects of Ritalin on Underachieving Children: A Replication. *American Journal of Orthopsychiatry*, 1976b, *46*, 313–322.

ROGERS, C. R. *Client-Centered Therapy: Its Current Practice, Implications, and Theory*. Boston: Houghton Mifflin, 1951.

ROSS, A. O. Behavior Therapy. In H. C. Quay and J. S. Werry (eds.), *Psychopathological Disorders of Childhood*. New York: John Wiley, 1972, pp. 273–315.

ROTH, R. A Transactional Analysis Group in Residential Treatment of Adolescents. *Child Welfare*, 1977, *56*, 776–786.

RUBIN, R., and BALOW, B. Learning and Behavior Disorders: A Longitudinal Study. *Exceptional Children*, 1971, *38*, 293–299.

SAFER, D. J., and ALLEN, R. P. Side Effects from Long-Term Use of Stimulants in Children. In R. Gittelman-Klein (ed.), *Recent Advances in Child Psychopharmacology*. New York: International Arts and Sciences Press, 1975, pp. 109–122.

SAFER, D. J., ALLEN, R., and BARR, E. Depression of Growth in Hyperactive Children on Stumulant Drugs. *New England Journal of Medicine*, 1972, *287*(5), 217–232.

SANO, K., MAYANAGI, Y., SEKINO, H., OGASHIWA, M., and ISHIJIMA, B. Results of Stimulation and Destruction of the Posterior Hypothalamus in Man. *Journal of Neurosurgery*, 1970, *33*, 689–707.

SCHIFFER, M. *The Therapeutic Play Group*. New York: Grune & Stratton, 1969.

SCRIGNAR, C. B. Rapid Treatment of Contamination Phobia with Hand-Washing Compulsion by Flooding with Hypnosis. *American Journal of Clinical Hypnosis*, 1981, *23*, 252–257.

SHAPIRO, A. K. Placebo Effects in Medicine, Psychotherapy, and Psychoanalysis. In A. E. Bergin, and S. L. Garfield (eds.), *Handbook of Psychotherapy and Behavior Change: An Empirical Analysis*. New York: John Wiley, 1971, pp. 439–473.

SHAW, C. R. *The Psychiatric Disorders of Childhood*. New York: Appleton-Century-Crofts, 1966.

SHEVITZ, S. A. Psychosurgery: Some Current Observations. *American Journal of Psychiatry*, 1976, *133*(3), 266–270.

SIGAL, J. J., BARRS, C. B., and DOUBILET, A. L. Problems in Measuring the Success of Family Therapy in a Common Clinical Setting: Impasse and Solutions. *Family Process*, 1976, *15*(2), 225–232.

SLAVSON, S. R. An Introduction to Group Therapy. New York: International Universities Press, 1970, p. 1.

SLAVSON, S. R., and SCHIFFER, M. *Group Psychotherapies for Children: A Textbook*. New York: International Universities Press, 1975.

SPRAGUE, R., BARNES, K., and WERRY, J. Methylphenidate and Thioridazine: Learning Activity and Behavior in Emotionally Disturbed Boys. *American Journal of Orthopsychiatry*, 1970, *40*, 615–628.

SPRAGUE, R. L., and SLEATON, E. K. What Is the Proper Dose of Stimulant Drugs in Children? In R. Gittelman-Klein, (ed.), *Recent Advances in Child Psychopharmacology*. New York: International Arts and Sciences Press, 1975, pp. 79–108.

STAMPFL, T. G., and LEVIS, D. J. Essentials of Implosive Therapy: A Learning-Theory-Based Psychodynamic Behavioral Therapy. *Journal of Abnormal Psychology*, 1967, *72*, 496–503.

STOLZ, S. B., WIENCKOWSKI, L. A., and BROWN, B. S. Behavior Modification: A Perspective on Critical Issues. *American Psychologist*, 1975, *30*, 1027–1048.

STOVER, L., GUERNEY, B. G., JR., and O'CONNELL, M. Measurements of Acceptance Allowing Self-Direction, Involvement and Empathy in Adult-Child Interaction." *Journal of Psychology*, 1971, *77*, 261–269.

STRELNICK, A. H. Multiple Family Group Therapy: A Review of the Literature. *Family Process*, 1977, *16*(3), 307–325.

STUART, R. B. Behavioral Contracting within Families of Delinquents. *Journal of Behavior Therapy and Experimental Psychiatry*, 1971, *2*, 1–11.

STUART, R. B. *Behavioral Self-Management: Strategies, Techniques, and Outcome*. New York: Brunner/Mazel, 1977.

STUART, R. B., JAYARATNE, S., and TRIPOLDI, T. Changing Adolescent Deviant Behavior through Reprogramming the Behavior of Parents and Teachers: An Experimental Evaluation." *Canadian Journal of Behavioural Science*, 1976, *8*, 132–44.

SUGAR, M. The Structure and Setting of Adolescent Therapy Groups. In M. Sugar (ed.), *The Adolescent in Group and Family Therapy*. New York: Brunner/Mazel, 1975, 42–48.

TESTA, J. A. Group Systematic Desensitization and Implosive Therapy for Death Anxiety. *Psychological Reports*, 1981, *48*, 376–378.

Urgan, H. B., and Ford, D. H. Some Historical and Conceptual Perspectives on Psychotherapy and Behavior Change. In A. E. Bergin and S. L. Garfield (eds.), *Handbook of Psychotherapy and Behavior Change: An Empirical Analysis*. New York: John Wiley, 1971, pp. 3–35.

Valenstein, E. S. *Brain Control: A Critical Examination of Stimulation and Psychosurgery*. New York: John Wiley, 1973.

Vygotsky, L. *Thought and Language* (trans. Eugenia Hanfmann and Gertrude Vakar). Cambridge, Mass.: M.I.T. Press, 1962.

Walden, E. L., and Thompson, S. A. A Review of Some Alternative Approaches to Drug Management of Hyperactivity in Children. *Journal of Learning Disabilities*, 1981, *14*, 213–217.

Watson, J. P., Mullett, G. E., and Pillay, H. The Effects of Prolonged Exposure to Phobic Situations upon Agoraphobic Patients Treated in Groups. *Behavior Research and Therapy*, 1973, *11*, 531–545.

Watson, J. P., and Marks, I. M. Relevant and Irrelevant Fear of Flooding: A Crossover Study of Phobic Patients. *Behavior Therapy*, 1971, *2*, 275–293.

Watson, J. B., and Rayner, R. Conditioned Emotional Reactions. *Journal of Experimental Psychology*, 1920, *3*, 1–14.

Watson, R. I. *The Clinical Method in Psychology*. New York: Harper and Row, 1951.

Weinstein, L. The Project Re-ED Schools for Emotionally Disturbed Children: Effectiveness as Viewed by Referring Agencies, Parents and Teachers. *Exceptional Children*, 1969, *35*, 703–711.

Weiss, G., Minde, K., Douglas, V., Werry, J., and Sykes, D. Comparison of the Effects of Chlorpromazine, Dextroamphetamine and Methylphenidate on the Behavior and Intellectual Function of Hyperactive Children. *Canadian Medical Association Journal*, 1971, *104*, 20–25.

Werry, J. S. The Childhood Psychoses. In G. D. Burrows and J. S. Werry (eds.), *Advances in Human Psychopharmacology*, Vol. 2. Greenwich, Conn.: Jai Press, Inc., 1981, pp. 245–263.

Werry, J. S., Sprague, R. L., Weiss, G., and Minde, K. Some Clinical and Laboratory Studies of Psychotropic Drugs in Children: An Overview. In W. L. Smith (ed.), *Drugs and Cerebral Function*. Springfield, Ill.: Chas. C Thomas, 1970, pp. 134–144.

Whalen, C. K., and Henker, B. Psychostimulants and Children: A Review and Analysis. *Psychological Bulletin*, 1976, *83*, 1113–1130.

Whitman, T. L., Mercurio, J. R., and Caponigri, V. Development of Social Responses in Two Severely Retarded Children. *Journal of Applied Behavior Analysis*, 1970, *3*, 133–138.

Wing, J. Diagnosis, Epidemiology and Etiology. In J. Wing (ed.), *Early Childhood Autism: Clinical, Educational, and Social Aspects*. Oxford: Pergamon Press, 1966, pp. 3–50.

Wolf, M. M., Risley, T. R., and Meers, H. L. Application of Operant Conditioning Procedures to the Behavior Problems of an Autistic Child. *Behavior Research and Therapy*, 1964, *1*, 305–312.

Wolpe, J. *Psychotherapy by Reciprocal Inhibition*. Stanford University Press, 1958.

Wolpe, J., and Lazarus, A. A. *Behavior Therapy Techniques: A Guide to the Treatment of Neuroses*. Oxford: Pergamon Press, 1966.

Yalom, I. D. *The Theory and Practice of Group Psychotherapy*. New York: Basic Books, 1970.

Yaffe, S. J., and Danish, M. The Classification and Pharmacology of Psychoactive Drugs in Childhood and Adolescence. In J. M. Weiner (ed.), *Psychopharmacology in Childhood and Adolescence*. New York: Basic Books, 1977, pp. 41–47.

Yates, A. J. *Behavior Therapy*. New York: John Wiley, 1970.

Zilboorg, G., and Henry, G. W. *A History of Medical Psychology*. New York: W. W. Norton and Co. 1941.

Part 3 CLINICAL SYNDROMES OF INFANCY AND EARLY CHILDHOOD

7

ABNORMALITIES OF INFANCY AND EARLY CHILDHOOD: Eating, Sleeping, and Elimination

PROLOGUE

Sandy was a four-year-old girl who was referred by her pediatrician because she refused to feed herself and to eat table food. Instead, she ate only strained foods and, at that, restricted her diet to oatmeal, cottage cheese, and occasionally some types of fruit. Several months before the referral, Sandy underwent successful surgery for a congenital heart defect, and she now was in fine health. Actually, her feeding problem was longstanding, having begun when she almost choked on a piece of string bean at nine months of age. Frightened by this event, her mother cautiously refrained from giving Sandy any table foods for several weeks. Later, when she tried to introduce solid foods, Sandy balked, and this was the beginning of many battles over food. Sandy managed to win most of the battles; she was fragile and her parents did not want to risk aggravating her already-weakened health.

Sandy was feeding herself by the age of twenty months, although her refusal began around this time, following another battle over food. The pediatrician advised that Sandy would learn to eat solid foods if she were forced to do so by not having other foods available as alternatives. The mother instituted this strategy, and Sandy responded by crying for thirty-six hours as she persisted in her refusal to eat table foods. It was when she began to have dry heaves that her mother became afraid to continue the struggle. Not only did Sandy receive strained foods again, but she also capped her victory when her mother shortly thereafter succumbed to her demands to be fed. (Reprinted with permission from *Journal of Behavioral Therapy, 3.* Bernal, M. E. Behavioral treatment of a child's eating problem. Copyright 1972, Pergamon Press, Ltd.)

Sandy's story illustrates how a basic function such as eating can be a potential seedbed for the development and maintenance of abnormal behaviors. Infants do little else but eat, sleep, and eliminate waste; in turn, parental energies are almost totally consumed by these functions. These are the basic rhythmic patterns of infancy that come in for early habit training and regulation and that greatly influence the nature of the later relationships between mother and child. Before Sandy was a year old she had already exercised control over her mother's (parent's) behavior. This was especially true when they quarreled about eating, because this battleground heightened her mother's anxiety about Sandy's health.

Nurturing parents quickly become powerful reinforcers as they satisfy the child's essential needs of hunger, thirst, comfort (avoidance of pain), and sleep. At the same time the child serves to gratify the mother's[1] need to love and be needed. As both mother and child strive to bring these basic functions under increased control, the interplay provides frequent opportunities for irritability, impatience, conflict, and tension. For example, the inconsistent mother who may be either stringent or lax about the child's bedtime reinforces irregular sleep patterns that are likely to be a source of continued conflict. Similarly, the failure of the young child to respond positively to toilet training efforts made before he or she is physiologically ready may evoke feelings of disappointment and anger in the mother who interprets the child's behavior as obstinate and uncooperative.

In this chapter we shall consider abnormal behaviors associated with eating, sleeping, and elimination, because these functions predominate early mother-child interactions, establishing patterns that may persist and lead to later adjustment problems. In addition, these functions are so paramount during infancy that any or all of them are likely to evidence impairment when the young child's physical, social, or personal equilibrium is seriously disturbed.

[1] Mother here and henceforth refers to the mothering parent who could be either mother or father or both.

PROBLEMS OF EATING

Undoubtedly, eating is the foremost activity of awakened babies, especially during their first year of life. The infant's biological need and total dependence on adults for food and emotional security become linked with the patterns of eating and hunger in ways that have profound implications for later physical and personality development. The weight of this responsibility falls on the mothering parent, who eagerly but anxiously follows the pediatrician's feeding instructions. Minor deviations from the expected eating pattern produce sufficient concern in the inexperienced mother to prompt her to call the doctor for advice and reassurance. Pediatricians usually attempt to deal with the more serious eating problems, but they seldom refer the baby for psychiatric or psychological assistance unless other abnormal behaviors also are manifested. There are some disturbances of eating that are serious only because they are potential sources of stress between mother and child, and others that additionally may result in physiological damage to the child. The following problems—listed in DSM-III as eating disorders—will be discussed in this section: Rumination Disorder of Infancy, Pica, and Anorexia. In addition, we shall discuss Colic and Obesity, although these problems are not included in the new classification system. A discussion of Bulimia and Anorexia Nervosa will be postponed until Chapter 11, since these two eating disorders typically occur at age twelve and later.

Colic

Because of its early onset and symptom picture, colic—strictly speaking—is not a disturbance of eating, although it is included here because it is often associated with hunger and feeding. It is a condition characterized by loud and persistent crying, which occurs within the first few weeks of the infant's life and lasts for about three to five months. The infant appears to be suffering from intestinal cramps or pain that is inferred from the sound and character of the cry as well as from the physical signs of abdominal distention and flexion of the legs. Initially worried parents look for its cause in factors related to eating, such as the type or temperature of the baby's formula, or the possibility that the baby swallowed too much air as he or she ingested food.

Colic is found more frequently among first-born infants, and there are those who report that it is rarely observed while the baby is in the hospital (Kessler, 1966). For these reasons it has been conjectured that psychological factors, principally anxiety, tension, and ambivalence in the mother, play a significant causal role in producing colic. However, Illingworth (1954) found that 66 percent of the babies he studied showed symptoms of colic before leaving the hospital, and 85 percent manifested symptoms within their first fifteen days of life. Furthermore, neither overfeeding nor underfeeding, the diet of nursing mothers, the techniques of feeding, swallowing air, spoiling the baby, or allergy were implicated as causative factors. Supporting a psychogenic view is the study by Lakin (1957), who reported that mothers of colicky infants were more tense and anxious during pregnancy, less sure of themselves, less adjusted to

Sidelight 7-1

Because Americans live in relative abundance and are well fed, we may find it difficult to believe that as many as one-half of the world's children suffer some degree of malnutrition. Severe malnutrition may be either a protein deficiency (*kwashiorkor*) or an overall deficit of food or calories (*marasmus*). Kwashiorkor often occurs at or after weaning when the infant who was fed on milk, known to be high in protein, is given as a replacement starchy foods that are low in protein. The condition produces stunted growth, swelling, skin sores, and dislocation of dark hair color to red or blond. Infantile marasmus frequently results from early cessation of breast feeding, overdilution of the bottle-fed formula, or gastrointestinal infection that occurs early in infancy. There is extreme retardation of development and wasting away of tissues in babies affected by marasmus.

Severe malnutrition of this sort is extremely rare in the United States, and only evident in one to two percent of children in the world. Moderate malnutrition or chronic undernutrition is much more common, affecting about half of the world's children, and between twenty to thirty percent of children under six years of age in this country, especially those from low-income families. Few preschool children have insufficient protein intake, whereas the preponderance of malnutrition comes from insufficient intake of calories. A surprising finding is that there is an iron deficiency in more than fifty percent of American children between one and five years of age, and that this inadequacy is not restricted to lower socioeconomic levels.

Animal research has shown that malnutrition between the third trimester of pregnancy and through the first year of life can produce irreversible brain deficits both in reduction in the size of the brain and in the number of brain cells. In addition, severe malnutrition that occurs prenatally or during infancy leads to permanent abnormal behaviors in animals, including apathy, reduced exploratory behavior and problem-solving ability. More direct evidence of the effect of malnutrition in humans indicates that malnourished babies have short attention spans, poor concentration, poor fine motor coordination, and impaired ability to learn. It is also known that undernourished children are more susceptible to infection than well-fed youngsters, because their body defenses against disease are impaired. Irreversible effects on human behavior are probably rare, since they occur only when severe malnutrition has been of long duration during infancy and continued through childhood with undernutrition. Iron deficiency (the most frequent form of undernutrition) may lead to anemia, decrease in attentiveness and persistence, and an increase in irritability (sidelight based on Read and Felson, 1976).

their maternal role, and less satisfied with their marriage than were mothers of noncolicky babies. In contrast, the well-known pediatrician Benjamin Spock suggested that many colicky infants are easily startled and unusually tense, active, and restless, which he was inclined to view as innate characteristics (Spock, 1963).

Although the etiology of colic has not been established, almost all observers agree that the condition is temporary and presents no substantial physical danger to the infant. The major consideration and deleterious effect lies in the potential damage colic can produce in the mother-child relationship. Consider, if you will, the prolonged distress of the infant who is in pain that cannot be readily alleviated and the anxiety, guilt, fatigue, and frustration of the parent who day after day is faced with the almost futile task of trying to bring some relief to the suffering baby. Surely, this situation is charged with emotion and tension for both mother and child, which can seriously mar their future relationship.

There is no known specific treatment for colic, although the distressed baby seems to gain temporary relief from being picked up, held, and walked. Parents are best advised about the temporary nature of the condition and about the fact that their baby is not in any physical danger. At the same time they need to know that they are not responsible for the discomfort, so that their guilt and/or feelings of inadequacy are allayed. With patience, tender care and concern, and sharing between parents of the baby's needs, both parents and child can weather this stormy period without ill effects.

Rumination Disorder of Infancy

This is a very rare disorder that usually begins between three and twelve months of age and that is equally common in both boys and girls. It involves the repeated ejection from the mouth of partially digested food, which is then chewed and reswallowed without any apparent signs of nausea, retching, or gastrointestinal disorder. The disorder typically develops following a period of normal functioning and results in weight loss and failure to gain weight. Consequently, the disorder can be serious and may result in a mortality rate of 25 percent from malnutrition (DSM-III, 1980). Progressive malnutrition occurs, especially in severe cases, because vomiting and rumination take place immediately after each feeding, and eventually developmental delays occur in all areas of functioning. Babies with this condition are noted to assume a particular posture: They strain and arch their backs while their heads are held back, and sucking movements of the tongue are evident. While the babies appear to find the symptoms pleasurable, caretakers are understandably discouraged and often disgusted by them. Their failure to feed, the noxious odor of their vomit, and the mess their rumination creates may lead to aversion and underestimation of these babies by the feeding parents. Little, if any, information is available about the causes, familiar patterns, and treatment alternatives for this disorder, although spontaneous remissions are common (DSM-III, 1980).

Obesity

Obesity is a condition that is all too well known in our society, affecting more than 50 *million* overweight Americans and some 10 to 15 percent of our adolescent population. Gross obesity occurring either during childhood or at puberty is both a physical and a psychological disability that may have serious consequences for later life. There is some evidence to indicate that excessive weight gains in infancy are associated with a high incidence of obesity at ages six, seven, and eight (Eid, 1970). It is also likely that fat children will become obese adults, because overfed babies have a permanent increase in the total number of fat cells in the body (Brook, Lloyd, and Wolf, 1972). In addition, the degree of obesity in childhood is related to excesses in weight in the adult years. Abraham and Nordsieck (1960) found that 80 percent of those children who were considered extremely obese were also fat as adults, as contrasted to 42 percent of the boys and 18 percent of the girls judged to be average in weight who later became obese adults. Thus, the long-range outlook for obese youngsters is pessimistic, notwithstanding temporary losses in weight during adolescence or at other periods of their lives.

Obesity is clinically diagnosed either by a body weight that is greater than 20 percent of the norm for height and weight, or by skinfold measurements (pinching the skin in the triceps area) to obtain an estimate of subcutaneous fat. The obvious symptom of obesity is a marked excess of body fat. Obese children do not differ from nonobese youngsters in food habits, food choices, or the proportion of calories derived from various foods. However, when obese and nonobese children in the third to fifth grades were studied, it was found that the obese youngsters ate snacks faster and ate more food from their plates than the nonobese controls (Geller et al., 1981). These investigators contend that obese children have different eating styles than nonobese youngsters and that their peculiar pattern is related to a social context which encourages and rewards such behavior. Stager (1981) tested the hypothesis that external responsiveness and environmental characteristics jointly determine excessive weight gain and the maintenance of obesity. Children between the ages of eight and eleven were studied with respect to both their visual and auditory responsivity to external cues and their socioeconomic status. Stager found that the greatest percentage of obese subjects were in the lower socioeconomic–external responding group, followed by the lower socioeconomic–internal responding group, and the middle socioeconomic–external group. The lowest percentage was evident in the middle socioeconomic–internal responding subjects. Moreover, obese children evidence a higher frequency of *abnormal inactivity* (expend far less energy) than nonobese controls. This finding is particularly important in light of the fact that the reduction of activity is not accompanied by a corresponding decrease in food intake (Bullen, et al., 1963; Mayer, 1966). The clinical behavior of these youngsters has been described as immature, excessively dependent on the mother, shy, fearful, timid, clumsy, slow, and apathetic (Bruch, 1941, 1957). In addition, most obese people are tall as children but are below average in height as adults (Lloyd, Wolfe, and Whelen, 1961; Illingwoth, 1971). This growth pattern is attributable to an early, but temporary, spurt in skeletal maturation. Also, the characteristic of tallness rules out rare endocrine disorders as the cause of obesity, because hormonally produced obesity is typically found in children who are short in stature.

It is quite clear that there is no single cause of obesity; instead, the condition can arise from numerous factors. Hereditary tendencies toward obesity are strongly inferred from studies that have consistently reported a significant relationship between obesity in the child and the same condition in one or both parents. It has been estimated that from 69 to 80 percent of fat children have one or two obese parents (Carrera, 1973). While suggestive, the evidence is not persuasive or conclusive: Obesity can be explained equally well on environmental grounds. However, the significance of environmental factors is undermined by the observations of Bakwin and Bakwin (1972), who noted that the customary relationship that exists between obese children and their parents does not exist—to any significant extent—between the weights of adopted children and their foster parents. Most observers now agree that even if genetic factors are involved in obesity, heredity does not in any precise way set the body weight of the child; it merely establishes the boundaries within which the child's weight will vary, depending on caloric intake and psychological factors.

Contrary to the widespread belief that obesity in childhood is the result of endocrine disorders, it is now recognized that most fat children do not have any demonstrable hormonal disturbance.

Far more attention has been given to psychogenic considerations, where mother-child relationships have been viewed as critical. For example, after extensive work on obesity, Bruch (1961) suggested that the frequent feeding of the child by the mother on occasions when the child is not hungry produces a deficit in the ability to correctly identify the bodily sensations of hunger and satiation. Accordingly, the child fails to learn the specific behaviors relevant to these sensations. Children reared under these circumstances do not know when they are hungry and when they are satiated. Another learning interpretation emphasizes the family occurrence data, suggesting that obese children imitate the eating behaviors of their obese parents, who serve as their models. A more Freudian view of obesity regards eating and excessive oral gratification as a manifestation of deep-seated, but thwarted, needs for love and affection from a mother who is rejecting, but who attempts to conceal her feelings by overzealous demonstrations of nurturance. The child seeks comfort and escape from anxiety and stress by self-indulgence through eating, which reinforces ties to and dependency on the mother.

While there is no overwhelming evidence favoring one psychogenic view over another, there is ample data indicating that psychological factors are significantly related to obesity. The research literature reports that there are emotional disorders and psychological disturbances in anywhere from 40 to 81 percent of the obese children and adolescents studied (Tolstrup, 1953; Ostergaard, 1954; Bruch, 1955; Monello and Mayer, 1963). There is also evidence indicating that chronically obese children who have been brought for medical treatment have more undifferentiated and immature body images than their nonobese peers (Nathan, 1973).

Whether obesity is caused by psychological variables, or vice versa, is as yet uncertain; although it may be more important to underscore the damaging effects of obesity on the personal and social adjustment of many of these children. Fat youngsters are often embarrassed, ridiculed, and rejected by their peers, and they are unable to successfully compete in athletic and other play activities. They often become social isolates with strong inclinations both to withdraw from potential sources of failure and conflict and to reduce their anxiety by eating (Mobbs, 1970). In addition to the psychological dangers of obesity, there are physical problems associated with this condition. Many of these youngsters walk late and have orthopedic problems of the legs and feet. Obese infants have a higher incidence of lower respiratory infections than nonobese babies, and these ailments are especially dangerous and serious in very obese children (Hutchinson-Smith, 1971). Furthermore, individuals who have been obese since childhood are likely to have a shortened life span, because they are prone to such potentially fatal conditions as hypertension and cardiovascular disease.

Obesity in children is particularly difficult to treat: Most youngsters manifest neither sustained motivation for long-term self-control of food intake or activity level nor independence from parents, who hold the major responsibility for providing them with a proper diet. Bruch (1957) found that individual psychotherapy was ineffective when obesity was the only complaint, because these children failed to cooperate. She suggested that treatment focus on increasing the child's awareness of his or her impulses, feelings, and needs, to develop a sense of competence and self-esteem. Group psychotherapy appears to be a more promising treatment procedure, because peer approval is quite important to most of these youngsters (Craddock, 1973). Several studies undertaken recently in the United States and Great Britain have shown significant weight loss in group treatment of obese youngsters who ranged in age from ten to sixteen. However, the group programs varied considerably—from biweekly sessions on diet, nutrition, and exercises during a three-week summer camp program, to sessions over a period of eighteen months. Follow-up data in which the long-term effects are assessed are not yet available.

Diet restrictions, along with increased

physical exercise, are the most obvious and effective means of reducing excess weight, although this approach depends on the cooperation of both parents and child. Typically a favorable initial response is obtained with this approach, but often the enthusiasm of mother and child wanes, and the child regains weight. In order to increase the incentive to participate, and to reinforce the desired changes in the child's eating behavior, behavior modification techniques could be employed. Rotatori, Fox, and Mauser (1982) recently designed a school-based diet program to aid learning disabled children lose weight and improve their appearance and self-esteem. The program included self-monitoring of eating and body weight, stimulus control of eating behavior, and self-reinforcement of new behaviors incompatible with prior eating habits. Overweight girls between the ages of five and ten evidenced a significant weight loss in a behavior modification program involving parental training and contingency contracting (Aragone, Cassady, and Drabman, 1975). However, the treatment effects here and in other behavior therapy studies were not maintained after six months and beyond (Keeley, Shemberg, and Carbonell, 1975). The use of behavior modification in the management of obesity in adults is well established (see reviews by Abramson, 1973; Hall and Hall, 1974; Stunkard and Mahoney, 1976). Social reinforcement from the therapist, from group members, and from important figures in the environment; tangible reinforcers such as tokens, personal valuables, and money; and techniques such as self-monitoring and behavioral contracting are among the many approaches that have been employed successfully (Jeffrey, 1976).

Pica

Pica, which occurs in children over the age of one and disappears in the fourth and fifth year of life, involves the consumption of substances not ordinarily considered edible, such as dirt, clay, plaster, paint, hair, paper, and coal. Children with pica prefer these unnatural sustances and purposefully seek them out, as opposed to normal youngsters of this age, who indiscriminately mouth almost everything they touch. In general, this depraved appetite is not troublesome, although in some special instances it may lead to serious health hazards. The ingestion of lead-based paint from peeling walls or baby furniture, so often characteristic of the economically impoverished, may result in lead poisoning, which can produce brain damage, mental retardation, behavioral disorders, and possibly death. Frequent and repeated eating of hair may result in hairball tumors that can cause intestinal obstruction (Bakwin and Bakwin, 1972). While pica is not restricted to any specific intelligence level, it is more commonly found in mentally retarded children. Not only do such children persist in mouthing objects longer than normal children, but also they are unable to discriminate between food and nonfood substances.

Millican and Lourie (1970, pp. 333–348) found that pica was more frequent among low socioeconomic southeastern black families, whose subculture sanctions the eating of laundry starch and earth containing clay. Furthermore, mothers of children with pica showed a significantly higher incidence of having had pica themselves than mothers of children without pica. For these families learning, either through direct instruction or by way of parental modeling, is substantially implicated as the primary determinant of pica. The authors also noted that children with pica manifested an excessive amount of oral activity—such as thumb sucking, nail biting, and the mouthing of inedible objects—as well as oral disturbances such as feeding problems and retarded speech, or no speech at all. In addition, these children showed a variety of other symptoms, including rocking, head banging, hair pulling, enuresis, nightmares, temper tantrums, fire setting, stuttering, phobias, and compulsive masturbation. Interestingly, mothers who had pica also exhibited signs of oral disturbances in the form of obesity, alcoholism, and drug addiction.

It has often been suggested that pica is caused by a nutritional deficiency, especially of iron, but clinical and laboratory tests as well as double-blind studies in which iron was given intramuscularly failed to support this hypothesis (Millican and Lourie, 1970). Aside from constitutional factors that result in brain damage and mental retardation, with which pica may be associated, there is more evidence supporting an environmental basis for this condition than there is substantiating a biological view. Family disorganization, broken homes, parental neglect, poor physical environment, and poverty conditions all seem to play a causative role (Gutelius et al., 1962; Millican and Lourie, 1970). Eastwell (1979) noticed an increase in pica in adult women from Aboriginal coastal towns of northern Australia. This was later traced to the loss of a worthwhile social role (they were past child-bearing age) for these women. Most observers consider persistent pica beyond the age of six rare but serious: It is frequently a sign of severe psychopathology requiring professional attention and intervention.

There is little known or written about the treatment of pica, principally because it tends to disappear in most children of normal intelligence by age five with proper diet and careful supervision of meals. Since persistent pica is considered a symptom of some serious abnormal disorder, the choice of treatment is usually tied to the eventual diagnosis, and not to the specific eating problem. Millican and Lourie (1970) proposed a program of educational sessions with mothers both to inform them of the potential health hazards of pica and to persuade them to spend more time with their children and to discourage excesses in oral gratification. In addition, these authors suggested psychotherapy for those older children who manifested persistent pica and other abnormal behaviors. Madden and associates (1980) successfully treated pica in three 2-year-old black girls with behavior therapy. Their approach included discrimination training in what substances were not edible, positive reinforcement for not eating pica substances, and overcorrection when pica occurred.

Refusal to Eat (Anorexia)

This is a condition that varies in severity from ordinary fussy appetites to rare life-endangering self-starvation. Mild and moderate forms of refusal to eat appear most frequently in youngsters between the ages of one and five. Generally, these are children with poor appetites who are finicky about foods and resist trying new ones. They chew poorly and insist on the repetition of special rituals associated with eating, such as drinking from a particular cup or being fed by the same person, who is expected to make a game of eating. Although these youngsters usually enjoy good health, they successfully manipulate their parents by the threat of failing health and the prospect of impaired growth and development.

During this age period the child's physical growth is relatively slow as compared to growth during infancy, and weight gains are slight and irregular from month to month. Under these circumstances the child's need for food is less, although many uninformed parents have difficulty accepting this as a normal pattern. Instead, they tend to be so anxious about their child's poor appetite and slow growth rate that they may place undue emphasis on eating and continually battle with the child to alter the feeding pattern. In the course of these events, refusal to eat is reinforced by the additional attention the mother gives to her problem child (something like what Sandy's mother did) and through the satisfaction the child derives from resisting the mother and annoying her. The problem is likely to continue, and perhaps worsen, as long as parents encourage it.

Treating the young child who refuses to eat is not a formidable problem. Simple and direct information about normal physical development and appetite changes as a function of growth patterns can be extremely helpful in reducing parental anxiety and in avoiding parent-child battles over food. Parents need to know that children differ in terms of food preferences and that it is all right for a child to have likes and dislikes. Feeding should be at regular times and intervals, with a minimum of distractions and with regard for the child's needs. Portions should be small to avoid the inevitable problem of forcing the child to finish everything on the plate. Self-feeding should be initiated as early as possible, although parents must understand that the child's table manners will be far from impeccable.

PROBLEMS OF SLEEP

Another essential need of the human organism is sleep, which is periodic and rhythmic in nature. Disruptions or difficulties in sleep can arise in early childhood. While no thoroughly adequate explanation is available to account for the need to sleep, it appears that sleep permits the body to regulate itself and to preserve its energy for later activity. It has also been argued that sleep developed in later species to increase those species' chances of survival. For humans, sleep during the night decreased the number of deaths from predatory animals, from falling off cliffs, and from exhaustion (Webb, 1975). Children vary considerably with respect to their sleep requirements, although most parents have some preconceived notion of how much sleep their children need for normal and healthy development. When the child's sleep pattern fails to correspond to this expectation, parents are likely to enter into an early and prolonged battle with the child over the regulation of sleep—a state of affairs that is fraught with the real possibility of damaging personality development. Sleep disturbances may have their origin in this sort of struggle over training and regulation, or they may be important manifestations of other difficulties the child is experiencing. In either event sleep problems may be considered as falling into two broad categories: those involving failure to go to sleep and those disrupting the continuity of sleep.

Difficulties in Falling Asleep

In infancy babies are unable to sleep when they are experiencing some bodily discomfort arising from hunger, thirst, irritation and pain of wet or soiled diapers, intestinal cramps, indigestion and gas, or extreme temperature conditions. Infants quickly and loudly communicate their distress by crying until they are restored to a more comfortable state, or until they are overcome by their stronger need to sleep. All children have occasional insomnia brought on by physical illnesses such as head colds, earaches, sore throats, itchy skin rashes, and stomach upsets. Emotional or environmental conditions that produce intense feelings or overstimulation at or near bedtime may also interfere with falling asleep. Most parents are understanding and accepting of the infrequent bouts of insomnia, but they are frustrated, angered, and concerned by the child's persistent failure to go to sleep.

By and large, children are not eager to go to bed, and they prefer to postpone bedtime as long as they can. The American household is quite familiar with bedtime rituals that run the gamut from demands for a story, a drink of water, a trip to the bathroom, a round of goodnight kisses for everyone, a bedtime prayer, and finally, being tucked into bed. The parent tiptoes away in eager anticipation of a well-earned period of relaxation, only to hear the child call out for another drink of water or for something else. The ritual surely will continue and become even more embellished if parents participate in and encourage it. In this way the child gains additional parental attention, which may be needed to allay the fears of being left alone, to win a favored position over siblings, or (in Freudian terms) to reduce the child's unconscious fears of losing control over aggressive and sexual impulses while asleep. Some children dread going to sleep because they fear that they will not awaken again or that someone close to them will die.

There are others who are reluctant to retire because they simply have been put to bed earlier than their sleep needs require.

The possible causes of insomnia or of the child's unwillingness to fall asleep are too numerous to detail here. If, however, the problem persists and becomes troublesome, treatment can be appropriately and effectively designed. In order to arrive at an appropriate remedial strategy, it is necessary to assess both the child and the family. The clinician can best determine the factors involved in the child's unwillingness to fall asleep by identifying conflicts between parents, attitudes toward the child, sibling rivalries, child-rearing practices, and the specific aspects surrounding the sleep pattern. The problem may stem from improper training, as evidenced by parental inconsistency, failure to set limits, and reinforcement of behaviors that tend to postpone going to sleep. Under these circumstances treatment can be directed toward the modification of parental practices and the unwanted behaviors associated with sleep. However, if the insomnia originates in the child's intrapsychic conflicts about self-adequacy, guilt feelings about behaviors that are unacceptable, or fears of separation, then more extensive therapeutic intervention may be necessary for both child and parents. Perhaps the simplest form of insomnia to remedy occurs when the child's sleep requirements are less than the preconceived expectations of parents. If the child is happy and active and is in good health, parents can be reassured that the problem will dissipate as they adjust the bedtime hour to conform more closely to the child's needs. Although the rationale is not clear, zinc supplements have been found to be helpful in promoting sleep in infants and children who do not sleep through the night (Hart, 1981).

Disruptions in the Continuity of Sleep

Nightmares and Night Terrors. Most normal children occasionally experience fright reactions during sleep. Only when these reactions are frequent do they require professional consideration and attention. Although both nightmares and night terrors are fear responses that disrupt sleep, they are sufficiently different to be regarded as distinct phenomena. Sleep research has shown that nightmares are relatively common, and they occur during the last third of the night in a stage of sleep known as stage 1 - REM (rapid eye movement), where most dreams take place. In contrast, night terrors are rare, and they occur within the first two hours of the night in stage 4-NREM (non-REM) dreamless sleep, which is also recognized as the period of deepest sleep. Night terrors are also accompanied by severe autonomic discharges marked by steep increases in respiratory rate and amplitude and a profound acceleration in heart rate (Broughton, 1968; Fisher, et al., 1973). They are found more often in boys than girls, and they occur most frequently between the ages of five and seven, decreasing through early adolescence (Jacobson, Kales, and Kales, 1969).

In addition to the differences found in the physiological monitoring of sleep, a number of important differences have been observed in the clinical manifestations of these fright reactions. Table 7–1 summarizes the distinctive clinical features of both nightmares and night terrors.

The causes of nightmares and night terrors are, as yet, little understood. The literature in sleep research consistently indicates that nightmares occur during REM sleep and are properly regarded as a dream phenomena. In contrast, evidence suggests that night terrors are not associated with dream states. Instead, they are more closely akin to an arousal response much like that observed in "sleep drunkenness," where the child is awakened out of stage 4 sleep by a parent, spontaneously walks to the toilet, urinates, and returns to bed without any recollection of what has transpired (Gastaut and Broughton, 1965). On the basis of their extensive physiological study of nightmares and night terrors, Fisher and associates (1973) noted that:

Table 7-1* Differences in the Clinical Picture Between Nightmares and Night Terrors

Nightmares	*Night Terrors*
1. Fearful sleep experience after which the child wakes. The fear may persist for a while, giving way to good orientation and clear realization.	1. Fearful experience taking place in sleep or in a somnolent twilight state, not followed by waking.
2. Slight defense movements or moaning immediately before waking are the only noticeable activities.	2. Facial features are distorted and express terror. The eyes stare, wide open. The child sits up in bed or even jumps to the floor in great agitation, runs helplessly about, clutches at persons or objects, cries out that someone is after him or her, implores an imaginary dog or burglar to leave him or her alone, shouts for help, or screams inarticulately.
3. The child is already awake when the parents notice his or her distress and, after he or she has been calmed, is able to give a coherent account of what has happened.	3. The child, sleeping through the episode, is unable to give any account of his or her distress, which the child is living out in all details while the parents look on and infer from his or her shouts and actions what might go on within the child. The attack cannot be cut short by any amount of calming and reassurance.
4. The child, after waking knows all the persons and objects of his or her surroundings.	4. The persons and objects of the environment are often not recognized and may be mistaken for others and woven into the dream content.
5. No hallucinations ever occur.	5. The child hallucinates the frightening dream objects into the room.
6. There is usually no perspiration.	6. The attack is usually accompanied by perspiration.
7. A long period of waking and conscious going over of the dream situation may follow.	7. Peaceful sleep instantly follows the termination of the reaction.
8. The entire episode rarely lasts longer than one or two minutes.	8. The terror may last for some time, up to fifteen or twenty minutes.
9. The contents are remembered more or less clearly. The incident itself is always recalled.	9. There is complete amnesia for the contents as well as for the occurrence of the episode.

*Reproduced from Kanner, 1972, pp. 478–479, with permission from the Charles C Thomas Publishing Co.

> . . . the night terror is not a dream at all in the ordinary sense, but a symptom, a pathological formation emerging from NREM sleep, brought about by a rift in the ego's capacity to control anxiety. Although the REM nightmare shows evidence of attempts at mastery of the traumatic experience, the night terror seems to be a manifestation of the failure of mastery, which may explain why it may endure unchanged and unabated for periods of a quarter of a century. It is evident that some night terrors have a post-traumatic origin. However, severity of trauma and degree of pre-existing psychopathology do not appear to be sufficiently differentiating factors. (p. 96)

Although it has been demonstrated that night terrors can be produced by the sounding of a buzzer during stages 3 and 4 of NREM sleep, the trigger mechanism of night terrors is still unknown (Broughton, 1968; Fisher et al., 1973). It is conjectured, however, by these investigators that night terrors may be set off by recurrent, ongoing mental activity, or by previous psychological factors, or both.

Most writers follow Freud's view regarding the basis of nightmares. Freud believed that dreams were the product of unconscious impulses and conflicts, particularly those that are aggressive and sexual in nature. It is also possible that previously frightening experiences, and upsetting events of the day—such as peer rejection or failing an important test in school—can precipitate nightmares (Ellis and Mitchell, 1973).

Little has been written on the remedial approaches to nightmares and night terrors. This is probably attributable to the fact that only a relatively small number of children with these fright reactions are brought for professional attention. Further, these conditions ordinarily subside without intervention. Either extensive individual psychotherapy or family therapy is likely to be used in instances where these sleep disruptions persist and become management problems. Several studies have found that the drug Valium reduces the incidence of night terrors by 80 to 90 percent (Kahn et al., 1970; Fisher, et al., 1973; Edwards, and Davis, 1972).

Sleepwalking (Somnambulism). Sleepwalking is a disruption of sleep that is manifest in approximately 6 percent of children (Bakwin and Bakwin, 1972) and which is often triggered by an upsetting emotional experience or event. Night terrors and somnambulism frequently coexist. Further, they share common features; for example, both occur during the first two hours of the night in NREM sleep. In both cases there is a clouding of consciousness, amnesia for the period, and difficulty in waking the victims (Jacobson, Kales, and Kales, 1969). In contrast to those who experience night terrors, sleepwalkers bear no observable sign of fright; instead, they locomote without any emotional display. Walking is carried out with eyes open, with rigid movements that are somewhat unsteady, and with the appearance of having a definite goal. In most instances obstacles are avoided, although occasionally the child will trip over some object in his or her path. Except for their ability to locomote, somnambulists' senses are blunted, and there is potential danger in their activities. They may fall down stairs, climb out of a window, walk out of the house, or run into an object that may inflict injury, but these occasions are rare. However, necessary precautions must be taken by parents to prevent injuries to sleepwalking children.

Sleepwalking may have a genetic basis: The condition is found in two or more members of the immediate family in approximately 40 percent of the cases (Bakwin and Bakwin, 1972). In addition, the concordance rate for monozygotic twins is significantly higher than it is for dizygotic twins. Kales and his co-workers (1980) recently reported results of pedigree studies of twenty-five sleepwalkers and twenty-seven subjects with night terrors. They found that in 80 percent of the sleepwalkers' families and 96 percent of the night terror families, one or more members of the families were affected by either sleepwalking, night terrors, or both. These findings support the hypothesis that night terrors and sleepwalking share a common genetic disposition. Research has linked sleepwalking to disorders of arousal (as in night terror), but the precise nature of the trigger mechanism is unknown. Anxiety, prior fearful experiences, emotional conflict, loud noises, and stomach distress are psychogenic factors that may precipitate somnambulism. It also is possible to induce sleepwalking by standing the sleeping child up, an action that does not have the same effect on the nonsomnambulistic child. Virtually nothing is known about the treatment for this condition; however, most observers agree that drug therapy is usually ineffective. Somnambulism that is frequent and that is associated with night terrors and other problems is ordinarily approached by psychotherapeutic intervention involving the child, the parents, or both.

PROBLEMS OF ELIMINATION

In this section we shall consider *enuresis* and *encopresis,* the two major problems of the rhythmic biological functions of elimination that are associated with, or have their origin in, early childhood. Even more than the problems of eating and sleep, failures in toilet training are likely to be troublesome to parents, prompting them to seek professional attention and intervention. Our culture places a high premium on cleanliness and personal hygiene, reflected in the aversion—and even repugnance—for the "dirty" job of handling soiled or wet diapers. Under these circumstances it is reasonable to expect that the early achievement of bladder and bowel control is desirable. At the same time disturbances in toilet training greatly increase the probability of parent-child conflicts, damage to the child's self-esteem, and problems of social adjustment in school and at home.

Enuresis

Enuresis, like so many other abnormal conditions, is difficult to define because of (1) variability in the age at which it is maturationally possible to establish bladder control (age criteria), (2) differences that occur in the timing and training procedures used for bladder control (training criteria), and (3) disagreement about how often involuntary wetting must occur to be considered as properly falling within this category (frequency criteria). Nevertheless, most observers tend to apply the term arbitrarily to the involuntary passage of urine, primarily during nighttime (nocturnal) sleep, in children past the age of three or four, where the cause is not linked to any demonstrable organic pathology. Most children develop the physiological and social maturity necessary to control the bladder by the age of fifteen to eighteen months, although parental practices differ widely as to when training is initiated and how the control is taught. The question of how often wetting must occur to be regarded as abnormal is not easily answered and is an area of some controversy. Some writers accept the frequency of once a month, while others consider weekly or more frequent wetting as satisfying the criteria for enuresis. While daytime (diurnal) wetting does occur and properly fits the definition of enuresis, nocturnal wetting during sleep is by far more frequent and common. Diurnal wetting rarely occurs in the absence of nocturnal enuresis. It happens at times when the child is so engrossed in play that time out is not taken to go to the toilet, or when the child is under nervous tension that tends to exaggerate the urgency to urinate.

Because of the problems involved in the definition of enuresis, incidence estimates are quite variable and are difficult to compare from study to study. Kanner (1972) reported an incidence of enuresis in 26 percent of the children referred to his clinic for psychiatric consultation. The enuretic children ranged in age from three to fourteen, with the highest frequency occurring between the ages of eight and eleven, and in more boys than girls (62 percent boys, 38 percent girls). Schaeffer (1979) arrived at a similar estimate from a different vantage point by suggesting that approximately 75 to 80 percent of four- and five-year-old children are able to develop nighttime bladder control. It has also been estimated that there are more than 3 million enuretic children in the United States, if the population considered includes youngsters between the ages of three and a half and seventeen (Baller, 1975). Bakwin and Bakwin (1972) estimate that approximately 15 percent of children are enuretic.

Enuresis usually persists from early childhood until the time of referral—almost as a lifelong pattern—in some 78 to 90 percent of the cases (Kessler, 1966; Kanner, 1972). It is more prevalent among children of manual workers and less frequent in children of professional and high-salaried families (Blomfield and Douglas, 1956). The relationship between enuresis and socioeconomic status of the family is even more marked as the age of the children increases. This may be attributable to such factors as differences in attitudes toward cleanliness, accessibility to toilet facilities, consistency in training practices, and possible differences in the temperature of the home, since being cold will increase the tendency to urinate. Enuresis is found at all levels of intelligence, but it rarely occurs as an isolated symptom. Instead, clinical observations indicate that it is highly associated with general immaturity (manifest in such behaviors as whining, moodiness, irritability, restlessness, overactivity, excitability, stubbornness, disobedience, and oversensitivity). It is also related to a wide array of acting-out behaviors (including temper tantrums, nail biting, fear reactions, encopresis, masturbation, tics, health concerns, thumb sucking, stuttering, stealing, and truancy) (Kanner, 1972).

Like night terrors and sleepwalking, enuresis occurs in the first few hours of sleep (NREM), and it is not temporally associated with dream sleep (REM) (Pierce, 1963). This finding was substantiated by Broughton (1968), who also showed more frequent and intense bladder contractions prior to micturition in enuretic children as compared to nonenuretics, and significantly higher heart rates in enuretics before sleep, in stage 4 sleep, during arousal, and after micturition. Broughton hypothesized that it is these autonomic changes that occur throughout the night (independent of bedwetting) which predispose the child to micturition.

Enuresis has been categorized by some as either primary or secondary, depending on whether or not bladder control was ever developed by the child (Lovibond and Coote, 1970; DSM-III, 1980). More specifically, *primary* enuresis refers to those instances of wetting where control of urination has never been established, while *secondary* enuresis refers to wetting that has developed following some period of continence. While this distinction affords some degree of specificity in studying enuretic children, thus far it has not provided evidence of new relationships.

Causes. Since 1550 B.C., when enuresis was first reported, it has been attributed to a variety of unverified causes, such as intestinal parasites, laziness, dreams, deep sleep, weak bladder, acid urine, excessive secretion of urine, weakened musculature, and even allergy (Glicklich, 1951; "Causes of Enuresis," 1969). However, most contemporary writers now believe that the condition is determined by several factors. Although relatively rare (5 to 10 percent of known cases), cases exist in which organic factors produce urinary incontinence. For this reason diseases of the genitourinary tract and the kidneys, congenital malformations of the bladder, lesions of the spinal cord, diabetes, and nocturnal epileptic seizures initially must be explored and ruled out (Ellis and Mitchell, 1973).

The theory that hereditary factors are involved is largely based on the long-established observation that parents and siblings of enuretic children have histories of wetting and that the concordance rate for enuretic monozygotic twins is significantly higher than that for dizygotic enuretic twins (Frary, 1935; Hallgren, 1957; Bakwin, 1971). However, the fact that enuresis seems to run in families cannot be used to support a genetic view, because, as we have noted before, this relationship has been obtained without proper control for environmental factors. It might be just as reasonable to suppose that parents who suffered the problems of enuresis during their childhood would be more accepting of it and more likely to provide faulty toilet training for their youngsters. The confounding of genetic and environmental variables in studies of this sort makes it difficult to evaluate either set of conditions in identifying the etiology of enuresis. Nevertheless, it is entirely possible that some cases of enuresis are determined by a genetic predisposition that is modifiable by environmental factors.

Most instances of enuresis are thought to

be the product of psychological and environmental conditions, primarily of faulty habit training in which the regulation is started too early, too late, or with training practices that are inconsistent and emotionally charged. Training that begins before the child is maturationally ready sets the stage for parental disappointment, anger, and (possibly) rejection of the child. At the same time the child not only senses these parental attitudes and feelings but also reacts to them with anxiety, insecurity, lowered self-esteem, and hostility. Disharmony and strain between parent and child originating from these early failures will make later attempts at training tense and difficult. Training that is initiated too early may reflect parental aversion for the dirty job of handling eliminative wastes, or the premature encouragement of self-sufficiency in the child. In contrast, lack of training, or regulation that begins late, may suggest maternal overprotectiveness and mother's wish to continue the child's dependency as long as possible. Under these circumstances the child may be reinforced for the infantile behavior of wetting. These parents may put the child to sleep with diapers, forget to awaken the child to void during the early portion of the night, or make it difficult for the child to go to the toilet by keeping the household dark and cold.

In this connection MacKeith (1968) proposed a "critical period"—between the ages of one and a half and four and a half—for learning bladder control. Training beyond the upper limit of this age period would be difficult to institute successfully, and wetting is likely to continue for years before it is finally brought under control. In addition, MacKeith emphasized anxiety from situational events such as the birth of a sibling, hospitalization, illness, injury, or moving as important sources of intrusion in the achievement and maintenance of bladder control. To bolster the argument supporting the role of anxiety, MacKeith cited the following data: (1) More than 80 percent of 320 enuretic children had experienced anxiety-provoking conditions in their first three years of life; (2) illness was most common in the third year of life for enuretic children; (3) the prevalence of enuresis is significantly higher at age five among children from severely disturbed families; (4) the incidence of enuresis is much lower than that found in the general population when an anxiety-free training procedure is used; and (5) the physical and mental stress occurring in enuretic children between the ages of two and three is related to the persistence of bedwetting beyond the age of four. More recent data support the implication of anxiety and disturbances in the family as etiological factors in enuresis. They further suggest that the anxiety of the mother is significantly related to the rate of progress the child makes in treatment (Young and Morgan, 1973a).

Even within the psychogenic view of enuresis, there are those who have recognized that it is erroneous to consider one etiology common to all cases. The early work of Gerard highlights this point and illustrates that enuresis can arise from a variety of emotional conflict situations (Gerard, 1939). For example, she notes instances of enuresis that appeared to be regressive, arising out of situational stressors such as the arrival of a new sibling. In addition, she cites cases of revenge, in which the wetting represented retaliation toward a punitive mother and cases that seemed neurotic in nature because the bedwetting was based on unresolved psychosexual conflicts and unconscious fears of castration.

Whatever the primary cause or causes, it is generally agreed that not only is enuresis burdensome to all concerned, but also it is a problem that may contribute to serious adjustment difficulties in the affected child. Parents try rewards for successive nights of dryness, then shaming, and then even more punitive tactics of scolding—without success. They may then adopt a "get-tough" policy by refusing to change pajamas or bed linens, and then resort to spankings. Sometime before parents turn to professional help, they may try a more rational approach, including special remedial activities such as reducing fluid intake in the evening and waking the child several times during the night to take him or her to the toilet. The child becomes the focus of negative attention, with the clear message that he or she has failed to achieve what others have accomplished, and that there is something wrong with him or her. Shame, guilt, feelings of inadequacy, rejection, despondency, and hostility both toward self and others inevitably arise out of this situation for most enuretic children. Problems of alienation and withdrawal from peer relationships must also occur for these children. Therefore, it is advisable to institute remedial measures as early as possible both to maximize the chances of resolving the problem and to minimize the psychological damage associated with it.

Enuresis and Psychopathology. How serious is enuresis, and is it an indication of a larger psychiatric disturbance? These questions have not yet been answered. While general population surveys conducted in Great Britain have shown a relationship between enuresis and psychiatric disorders (especially common neurotic and conduct problems), the overwhelming majority of the children who wet are clearly well adjusted and free from psychiatric disorders (Rutter, Yule, and Graham, 1973; Essen and Peckham, 1976). When nocturnal wetting is accompanied by diurnal wetting, the likelihood of a positive relationship between enuresis and psychopathology increases, as is the case when encopresis (fecal incontinence) is also evident (Bug, 1981).

Treatment Approaches. In days of old the remedies suggested for enuresis included such exotic and repugnant preparations as powdered goat claws or cock trachea, hare's brain in wine, hare's testicles, roast mouse, gastric mucose of a hen, or the roasted bladder of a pig sprinkled on the bed—as well as such painful techniques as pouring collodian on the prepuce, placing an inflated rubber bag in the vagina, clamping the penis, or applying irritants to the glans, or silver nitrate to the urethral passage, to make micturition painful ("Causes of Enuresis," 1969). Fortunately, we can report that treatment advances have progressed considerably since that time, and there are several approaches that seem to work quite well.

The most effective and promising drug therapy is a single dose of imipramine given daily at bedtime. Dinello and Champelli (1968) reviewed some forty papers in which imipramine was used for the treatment of enuresis. These authors found that only seventeen studies used adequate controls, and of these, eleven reported positive results with the drug. In all six studies in which negative findings were obtained, the reviewers noted that the drug dosages were too small. They concluded that imipramine works best with enuretic children (as contrasted to adults) who are frequent bedwetters, when treatment is on an outpatient basis, and when the drug is given in single doses of 50 mg or higher. Bakwin and Bakwin (1972) suggested that the drug be given for an eight-week period at high dosage and then gradually diminished. While imipramine may produce irritability and awakening during the night, these side effects are transient and temporary. In a more recent study the efficacy of placebo, imipramine, and classical conditioning treatment approaches were compared in groups of enuretic schoolchildren between eight and ten years of age. Those treated with either imipramine or conditioning showed more improvement than those in the placebo group after two months (when treatment ended) and after a four-month follow-up. Imipramine-treated youngsters showed an almost immediate improvement after treatment was begun, but the improvement declined considerably after treatment was terminated. In contrast, the conditioning group was slower to show improvement, although the gains were better maintained after the treatment was stopped (Kolvin et al., 1972). These and other findings suggest that relapses are likely to occur when imipramine is used and then stopped (Shaffer, 1977).

Psychological approaches to the treatment of enuresis, primarily those that incorporate the essential paradigm of classical conditioning, are well known, since the Mowrers first introduced the method in 1938 (Mowrer and Mowrer, 1938). The basic procedure consists of the temporal pairing of the interoceptive cues of bladder distension present during bedwetting with the sound of a buzzer or bell that is activated when urine falls on an electrically sensitive pad. The bell serves to awaken the child and is a signal for the child to cease micturition. At the same time it summons the parent to take the child to the toilet to void and to reset the pad and return the child to bed. The object of this conditioning procedure is to replace the buzzer with interoceptive cues in consistently waking the child and in establishing the sphincter responses necessary for continence. Obviously, the effectiveness of the method depends largely on the child's ability to hear the buzzer, and on the cooperation of the parents. Treatment continued in the Mowrers' study until the child achieved seven consecutive dry nights. Then, under conditions of increased fluid intake prior to bedtime, the experimenters administered another series until the child achieved another seven consecutive dry nights. Early objections to this and similar studies centered on three major issues: (1) the absence of control groups, (2) the belief that other symptoms of the presumed underlying emotional disturbance would surface as a substitute for wetting, and (3) the lack of evidence indicating that successes achieved through this method would indeed be maintained over a long period of time.

Studies that have used control groups have appeared in the literature since the 1960s, and they have shown that conditioning was more effective than either no treatment or psychotherapy in producing bladder control (DeLeon and Mandell, 1966; Baker, 1969). Moreover, the Baker study found no evidence of symptom substitution; rather, parents rated their children as happier and more independent than before treatment, and the children themselves scored higher on a measure of self-image and less neurotic on a neurotic inventory. At this point in time there is little doubt that an initial arrest of wetting can be brought about by conditioning in about 90 percent of unselected enuretic cases (Lovibond and Coote, 1970).

The early concern about relapse under a conditioning procedure is still legitimate and very real. When relapse was defined as renewed wetting occurring more than once a week, the relapse rate reached as high as 30 to 40 percent over a two-year period following treatment (Lovibond, 1964; Bug, 1981). Lovibond also found that age, sex adjustment, personality factors, and wetting patterns were unrelated to failure to maintain continence. After examining the relationship of some forty factors to relapse, Young and Morgan (1973b) concluded that relapse is not a function of patient and background variables but rather a product of deficiencies in the treatment. Two additional studies by these authors provide evidence that a procedure of overlearning, in which the child is required to regain bladder control through conditioning trials until achieving fourteen consecutive dry nights (under conditions of increased fluid intake), significantly decreases the relapse rate (Young and Morgan 1972a, 1972b).

Numerous variations on the conditioning treatment approach have been reported in the literature. For example, conditioning on an intermittent basis (with the alarm system operating on some nights and not on others) was tried, on the grounds that it should make the stay-dry response more resistant to extinction. Also, teaching the child sphincter control during the waking state, which will then generalize to the night, has also been tried with success (cited in Ross, 1981). The Dry-Bed Training (DBT) for bedwetting now has growing support in the literature (Azrin, Sneed, and Foxx, 1974; Bollard and Nettelbeck, 1981; Bollard, Nettlebeck, and Roxbee, 1982). DBT involves the use of the standard alarm device along with the introduction of several training features such as waking the child during the night and requiring him or her to urinate, increasing the child's functional bladder control, and punishing the child (for example, dipping him or her into tub of cold water) for having an accident (aversive consequence). These training features without the alarm decrease the frequency of bedwetting, but they are not powerful enough to arrest the enuretic problem (Bollard and Nettelbeck, 1981; Bollard, Nettelbeck, and Roxbee, 1982). The most favorable results are obtained with these three features of DBT and the use of the urine-alarm (Bollard and Nettelback, 1982). Finally, Azrin and Foxx (1974) developed a successful operant program to achieve toilet training in one day. The training involves getting the child familiar and comfortable with the commode, having the child drink large amounts of liquid to assure a great many learning trials, teaching the child through verbal instructions and a model doll the various components of the toileting procedure, and giving positive reinforcement for each appropriate response of the toileting sequence. Verbal disapproval is given for the child's accidents, while dryness (checked every five minutes) is rewarded.

The popularity of psychotherapy as a treatment approach for enuresis was particularly evident during the first half of the twentieth century, when psychoanalytic theory was most influential, and before the usefulness of drug and conditioning therapy was demonstrated. There was strong support for the view that enuresis was a symptom of some underlying emotional conflict and disturbance. In accordance with this assumption, treatment (usually psychodynamically oriented psychotherapy) was aimed at resolving the basic emotional problems rather than at eliminating the symptom. Unless the cause could be treated, symptom removal would not only be temporary but also would result in symptom substitution (the appearance of other symptoms). At present conditioning and drug therapy have proved more effective than psychotherapy, although psychotherapy is still used and recommended for those cases of enuresis in which deep-seated psychological problems are evident.

Encopresis

DSM-III (1980) characterizes functional encopresis as "repeated voluntary or involuntary passage of feces of normal or near-normal consistency into places not appropriate for that purpose in the individual's own sociocultural setting, not due to any physical disorder" (p. 81). Like enuresis, encopresis is considered *primary* if it occurs in a child of four or older who has not had a prior period of fecal continence (for at least one year), while it is referred to as *secondary* if the child has had a period of fecal continence (for a year). Children with encopresis are further distinguished into two types: *retentive* and *nonretentive*. The retentive type tends to withhold feces for long periods of time and to leak fecal-stained fluid from the rectum. Such children are constipated and are likely to have their colons distended by hard feces. The nonretentive type produces fully formed normal stools and defecates in inappropriate places. Retentive encopresis seems to occur equally as often in both sexes, in contrast to the high ratio of males to females reported in the literature for encopresis. Shirley (1938), in one of the earliest studies, found a male to female ratio of 5:1, while Anthony (1958) showed a sex ratio of 6:1 favoring boys. Incidence or prevalence estimates are infrequently cited in the literature, and the data that are available vary considerably, depending on such factors as the size of the sample, the age of the children, the frequency of soiling, and the criterion used with regard to withholding. Shirley (1938) estimated that 3 percent of children evidence encopresis, while Bellman (1966) noted that the prevalence of encopresis decreases sharply to 1½ percent when children over seven years of age are sampled, and it is practically nonexistent by age sixteen.

As objectionable and aversive as soiling may be to parents, it is far less hazardous physiologically to the child than constipation. Persistent withholding results in impacted feces, enlarged colon (megacolon), and loss of tone and sensitivity of the colon that eventually leads to its improper functioning (Ellis and Mitchell, 1973).

As difficult as it may be to interpret these data, it is apparent that encopresis is rare, that it is extremely infrequent beyond age seven, and that it is predominantly found in boys. In Shirley's sample of cases approximately 37 percent obtained IQ scores below seventy (mental retardation), suggesting that limited intelligence may account for these failures in bowel training and control. More recent data indicate that both encopretic and enuretic children are of average intelligence, although the encopretics studied were more socially disadvantaged than those children with enuresis (Krisch and Jahn, 1981). Nevertheless, there are a sizeable number of encopretic children in whom psychogenic factors appear primary. Encopresis was noted as a problem in children who were evacuated from London during the period of heavy German air-raid bombings in World War II (Burns, 1941). Further support for its psychogenic origin comes from the finding that encopretic children who have experienced the emotional stress of separation, arrival of a new sibling, or the illness of a mother also evidence regressive behavior, feeding problems, and temper tantrums (Kanner, 1972). Conflicts between parent and child over bowel control are both more probable and more severe than conflicts arising from bladder regulation because of our greater aversion to one over the other. In addition, defecation becomes the battleground for the child's struggle for assertion and independence, because it is an event that often meets with parental resistance (Anthony, 1957; Erikson, 1963). When the child's efforts are blocked or thwarted, the child may become defiant by soiling or withholding. Reactions of disgust to incontinence may encourage the child to withhold or to conceal the evidence of soiled clothes in order to avoid parental punishment and rejection. The encopretic child also faces social alienation and ridicule from others, which impairs the child's peer relationships, self-concept, and social adjustment. As we shall see in our discussion of childhood psychoses (Chapter 8), encopresis may be an accompanying symptom of this severe form of abnormal behavior.

Treatment Approaches. Before treatment is instituted, incontinence resulting from some organic pathology such as Hirschsprung's disease (neurogenic megacolon that results from an absence of anglionic cells of the rectum or large intestine), or megacolon caused by obstructive lesions, should be ruled out medically. Beyond this, encopretic mental retardates, psychotic children, and encopretic children with less serious associated abnormal behavior have been successfully treated by operant conditioning procedures that used positive reinforcement when appropriate bowel movements were achieved (Neal, 1963; Gelber and Meyer, 1965; Hundziak, Mauer, and Watson, 1965; Balson, 1973). The work of Neal with four hospitalized encopretic children illustrates in a general way the procedures used in operant conditioning. The children were accompanied to the toilet four times daily (after each meal and at bedtime) by a nurse who was known to the child and who tried to reduce the anxiety associated with defecation by permitting the child to close the toilet door if the child wished, or to eat candy and read a comic book. Each child sat on the toilet until either a bowel movement occurred or five minutes had elapsed. Bowel movements were lavishly praised, and the child was given candy or some other appropriate reward. No punishment or critical comments were made when bowel movements were not obtained, and clean pants were given to the child to replace soiled ones whenever soiling occurred. Once the child was free from soiling and was accustomed to sitting on the toilet, the four-times-a-day routine was abandoned and replaced with voluntary trips to the toilet whenever the child felt the sensation of rectal fullness. The child was rewarded for each successful bowel movement. Rapid success—that is, within three months—was achieved in two cases, and in one child after a full year. The fourth case represented a therapeutic failure.

Wright (1973) reported dramatic success (one failure in approximately thirty-six cases) in eliminating encopresis by using a conditioning procedure that involved two positive and one negative reinforcer, morning trips to the toilet, and the use of cathartics. Children unable to defecate were given suppositories and were then permitted to have breakfast. In the event that the suppository did not work, the child was given an enema—a set of conditions that were designed to result in defecation at a specific and regular time (early in the morning). Positive reinforcers were given when defecation occurred, while negative reinforcers were used whenever soiling was noted. Once daily bowel movements were established and soiling was extinguished for two weeks, the use of cathartics was gradually reduced. Their use was completely discontinued when the child had no soiling for eight consecutive weeks.

Encopresis is a dirty problem that frequently comes to the attention of the professional because parents and others find it so objectionable. The prognostic outlook is related to the age of the child, the duration of the condition, and the severity of the underlying or associated psychopathology.

SUMMARY

During early childhood the bodily functions of eating, sleeping, and elimination are of primary interest, as they undergo dramatic modification through maturation and habit training. Behavioral problems may either become evident through or originate in the regulation of these functions. Failures in training may be related to early or continued difficulties in the mother-child relationship, the presence of some serious organic or psychological disorder, and secondary effects that result in subsequent personal and social maladjustment. On the following pages the major problems associated with each of these rhythmic patterns are presented in tabular form.

Table 7-2

A. PROBLEMS OF EATING

Colic

Symptoms	*Related Factors*	*Causal Factors*	*Treatment*
Intestinal pain, abdominal distention, flexion of legs. Incessant and persistent crying.	Begins in first few weeks of life, and lasts three–five months. Found frequently in firstborn. Stressful and disruptive of mother-child relationship.	No known cause. First inclination to look at diet or factors related to eating. Tension and anxiety of mother. Innate tendency.	No known effective treatment. Temporary relief of symptoms by holding, rocking, and walking with baby.

Table 7-2 (*Continued*)

A. PROBLEMS OF EATING			
	Rumination Disorder of Infancy		
Symptoms	*Related Factors*	*Causal Factors*	*Treatment*
Repeated ejection of partially digested food and reswallowing without stomach problems. A pleasurable activity.	Very rare, begins between 3 and 12 months after normal functioning. Weight loss, mortality in 25% of the cases.	No known causes.	No known specific treatment.
	Obesity		
Symptoms	*Related Factors*	*Causal Factors*	*Treatment*
Body weight greater than 20 percent of norm. Excessive body fat. Abnormal inactivity. Immature, dependent on mother, shy, fearful timid, clumsy, slow, and apathetic. Most obese children are tall for their age—a factor that distinguishes obesity from endocrine disease.	Fat infants tend to be obese later in childhood and as adults. Pessimistic outlook. Secondary effects of obesity are in damaging self-esteem, peer relations, and social adjustment; as well as in health hazards. Tall for age rules out hormonal basis of obesity. Below average in height as adults.	No single cause. Hereditary tendencies that may set weight boundaries. Small percentage caused by endocrine disorders. Psychogenic. Rejecting mother tends to overfeed, which leads to child's failure to distinguish correct bodily sensations of hunger and satiation. Modeling of obese parents.	Difficult to treat. Diet restrictions, increased physical exercise, and behavior modification (although no modification program available as yet for children). Individual psychotherapy not effective. Group therapy and special group programs show promise, but no follow-up data available yet.
	Pica		
Symptoms	*Related Factors*	*Causal Factors*	*Treatment*
Purposeful eating of inedible substances beyond age one. Usually disappears during fourth or fifth year of life. Excessive oral activities and feeding and speech problems. Also head banging, rocking, hair pulling, enuresis, nightmares, temper tantrums, etc.	Ingestion of toxic materials such as lead can result in brain damage, mental retardation, and death. Not limited to any specific level of intelligence, although often found in mental retardates. More frequent in low socioeconomic black families of the Southeast.	Not caused by nutritional deficiency. Family disorganization. Modeling of parents.	Little known about treatment. Education of parents. Psychotherapy for older and more persistent cases.

(*continued*)

Table 7-2 *(Continued)*

A. PROBLEMS OF EATING

	Mothers often show pica, obesity, alcoholism, and drug addiction. Pica beyond age of six is rare and considered sign of serious abnormal condition.		

Refusal to Eat

Symptoms	*Related Factors*	*Causal Factors*	*Treatment*
Refusal to eat. Weight loss. Fussy and Variable appetite.		Parental anxiety. Maternal attention reinforces the refusal to eat.	Education and reassurance of parent. Acceptance of child's food preference and regularity of feeding. Small portions and self-feeding. Behavior modification.

B. PROBLEMS OF SLEEP

Falling Asleep

Symptoms	*Related Factors*	*Causal Factors*	*Treatment*
Wakefulness, restlessness, and insomnia. Refusal or reluctance to go to bed. Crying and distress.	Children differ in their sleep needs. Parents often have their own expectations.	Physical discomfort and distress. Emotional and environmental conditions that produce intense feelings and overstimulation. Reinforcement of bedtime rituals. Inconsistent and faulty training.	Modification of parental training practices. Adjust sleep schedule to fit child's needs. Psychotherapy for those cases arising out of intrapsychic conflicts and fears.

Disruptions of Sleep

Symptoms	*Related Factors*	*Causal Factors*	*Treatment*
Nightmares, night terrors, sleepwalking.	Nightmares are frequent and occur during REM sleep, when most	REM nightmares may be attempts at mastery of traumatic experi-	Nightmares are not often brought to attention of professional.

Table 7-2 (*Continued*)

B. PROBLEMS OF SLEEP

See Table 6-1 for differences in clinical picture between nightmares and night terrors.	dreaming occurs. Night terrors are rare, occur in NREM sleep, and are accompanied by severe autonomic discharges. Night terrors are more frequent in boys. Sleepwalking is found in about 6 percent of children, and it occurs in NREM sleep. There is a potential danger of child hurting self while walking. Terrors and sleepwalking frequently coexist.	ences, while terrors may represent failure to master. Terrors are independent of mental activity. Nightmares may be products of unconscious impulses and conflicts. Sleepwalking is often triggered off by upsetting emotional experiences. Sleepwalking is found to run in families and has a higher concordance rate for monozygotic twins than dizygotic twins.	Little is known about their treatment. Severe fright reactions that are frequent and persistent are treated with individual psychotherapy, but no hard data is available to evaluate its effectiveness. Valium has been recommended. Special care needs to be taken so that accidents are prevented for sleepwalkers. Psychotherapy is used for those cases that show sleepwalking, night terrors, and other problems.

C. PROBLEMS OF ELIMINATION

Enuresis

Symptoms	*Related Factors*	*Causal Factors*	*Treatment*
Involuntary passage of urine mostly during the night, but diurnal wetting may also occur. Wetting must be in children beyond age of three or four, occur at least once a month, and not be linked to organic pathology. General immaturity with such behaviors as whining, moodiness, irritability, restlessness, overactivy, excitability, stubbornness, disobedience, oversensitivity, as well as problems of eating, temper, nail biting, fear	Occurs most often between eight and eleven years of age, and in more boys than girls. It usually persists from early childhood. More prevalent in children of manual workers and less frequent in children of professional and high salaried families. Found in all levels of intelligence. Rarely occurs as an isolated symptom. Occurs in NREM sleep.	Only 5 to 10 percent of cases caused by organic pathology. Runs in families, with higher concordance rate for monozygotic twins. Studies, however, confound genetic and environmental factors. Primarily thought of as psychogenic in nature, faulty training, maternal overprotectiveness, situational anxiety, disturbances in the family. No single cause (even psychogenic) that can	Most effective drug is imipramine in daily dose of 50 mg or more for eight weeks and then gradually diminished. High relapse rate after four months. Classical and operant conditioning are best psychological approaches. Relapse rate can be significantly reduced with overlearning. Psychotherapy has been shown to be less effective than conditioning. However it is still used when enuresis is regarded as

(*continued*)

Table 7-2 (*Continued*)

C. PROBLEMS OF ELIMINATION			
reactions, encopresis, tics, health concerns, masturbation, and stealing.	Leads to serious difficulties in personal and social adjustment.	account for all instances of enuresis.	symptom of more serious underlying problem. Conditioning removes symptom without evidence of symptom substitution.
		Encopresis	
Symptoms	*Related Factors*	*Causal Factors*	*Treatment*
Two types: Retentive—Involuntary fecal soiling in child beyond age two or three, not directly related to organic disease. Non-rententive—Involves long periods of constipation and fecal staining that may be serious health hazard. It may lead to psychogenic megacolon and improper functioning of the colon.	Primarily a diurnal condition. It is rare, with an incidence of about 3 percent; male to female ratio of about 5:1 or 6:1. Incidence sharply decreases to $1\frac{1}{2}$ percent beyond age seven. Highly associated with mental retardation, although it occurs in all levels of intelligence. Outlook is related to age of child, duration of the condition, and severity of underlying or associated psychopathology.	Primarily viewed as psychogenic in origin. Situational anxiety. Regressive behavior. Conflict between mother and child. Child seeks independence and self-assertion. He reacts to controlling parent with defiance, hostility, and witholding of feces. In rare instances organic diseases produce incontinence, and these must be ruled out medically.	Traditional individual psychotherapy has been used for chronic and persistent cases or for those where deep-seated psychological problems are apparent. No hard data to evaluate its effectiveness, however. Operant conditioning has been used more recently with promising results.

EPILOGUE

Interested readers will be happy to learn that Sandy's problems of refusal to self-feed and to eat solid foods were successfully treated (Bernal, 1972). Her parents were trained to gradually exert increasing control over her eating habits through restricting normal food intake and through providing her with the opportunity to earn social and food rewards for eating solid foods. Similarly, her parents rewarded Sandy for feeding herself. At the end of thirty-two weeks, Sandy's diet successfully included all table foods, and new foods were introduced. Sandy now fed herself, and her eating behavior improved so noticeably that her parents were no longer concerned.

While this behavioral approach eliminated Sandy's unwanted behaviors, we must not allow this positive outcome to blur our ability to view this treatment method critically. Essentially, we have evidence of symptom (or behavior) removal, but we would need long-term follow-up data to tell us that the symptoms have not reappeared or that new ones have not replaced them. Perhaps more important is the absence of data dealing with the nature of the mother-child battle that gave rise to the symptoms in the first place. In what ways have the relationships between mother and daughter changed? What brought about the change? Is the change the result of the treatment used? What is Sandy's adjustment like with respect to her mother, other members of the family, her nursery school, and so forth? Since there was no untreated child like Sandy to serve as a control subject, we have no way of knowing whether Sandy's eating behaviors would have changed over time without treatment. In fact, we could conjecture that Sandy's successful heart surgery and her clean bill of health were sufficient to allay her parents' fear of doing battle with her. Under these conditions they might be less inclined to cater to Sandy's wishes, and more apt to hold the line in combating her eating problems.

REFERENCES

Abraham, S., and Nordsieck, M. Relationship of Excess Weight in Children and Adults. *Public Health Reports,* 1960, *75,* 263–273.

Abramson, E. E. A Review of Behavioral Approaches to Weight Control. *Behaviour Research and Therapy,* 1973, *11,* 547–556.

American Psychiatric Association. DSM-III: *Diagnostic and Statistical Manual of Mental Disorders,* 3rd ed. Washington, D.C.: American Psychiatric Association, 1980.

Anthony, E. J. An Experimental Approach to the Psychopathology of Childhood Encopresis. *British Journal of Medical Psychology,* 1957, *30,* 146–175.

Aragono, J., Cassady, J., and Drabman, R. S. Teaching Overweight Children Through Parental Training and Contingency Contracting. *Journal of Applied Behaviorial Analysis,* 1975, *8,* 269–278.

Azrin, N. H., Sneed, T. J., and Foxx, R. M. Dry-Bed Training: Rapid Elimination of Childhood Enuresis. *Behaviour Research and Therapy,* 1974, *12,* 147–156.

Azrin, N. H., and Foxx, R. M. *Toilet Training in Less Than a Day.* New York: Simon and Schuster, 1974.

Baker, B. L. Symptom Treatment and Symptom Substitution in Enuresis. *Journal of Abnormal Psychology,* 1969, *74,* 42–49.

Bakwin, H. Enuresis in Twins. *American Journal of Children,* 1971, *121,* 222–225.

Bakwin, H., and Bakwin, R. M. *Behavior Disorders in Children,* 4th ed. Philadelphia: Saunders, 1972.

Baller, W. R. *Bedwetting: Origins and treatment.* New York: Pergamon Press, 1975.

Balson, P. M. Case Study: Encopresis: A Case with Symptom Substitution? *Behavior Therapy,* 1973, *4,* 134–136.

Bellman, M. Studies on Encopresis. *Acta Paediatrica Scandinavia,* 1966, Supplement 170.

Bernal, M. E. Behavioral Treatment of a Child's Eating Problem. *Journal of Behavior Therapy and Experimental Psychiatry,* 1972, *3,* 43–50.

Blomfield, J. M., and Douglas, J. W. B. Bedwetting, Prevalence among Children Aged 4–7 Years. *The Lancet,* 1956, *1,* 850–852.

Bollard, J., and Nettelbeck, T. A comparison of Dry-Bed Training and Standard Urine-Alarm Conditioning Treatment of Childhood Bedwetting. *Behaviour Research and Therapy,* 1981, *19,* 215–226.

Bollard, J., and Nettelbeck, T., and Roxbee, L. Dry-Bed Training for Childhood Bedwetting: A Comparison of Group With Individually Administered Parent Instruction. *Behaviour Research and Therapy,* 1982, *20,* 209–219.

Bollard, J., and Nettelbeck, T. A Component Analysis of Dry-Bed Training for Treatment for Bedwetting. *Behaviour Research and Therapy,* 1982, *20,* 383–390.

Brook, C. G. D., Lloyd, J. K., and Wolf, O. H. Relation Between Age of Onset of Obesity and Size and Number of Adipose Cells. *British Medical Journal,* 1972, *2,* 25–27.

Broughton, R. J. Sleep Disorders: Disorders of Arousal? *Science,* 1968, *159,* 1070–1078.

Bruch, H. Obesity in Childhood and Personality Development. *American Journal of Orthopsychiatry,* 1941, *11,* 467–474.

Bruch, H. Fat Children Grown Up. *American Journal of Diseases of Children,* 1955, *90,* 501.

Bruch, H. *The Importance of Overweight.* New York: W. W. Norton and Co., 1957.

Bruch, H. Transformation of Oral Impulses in Eating Disorders: A Conceptual Approach. *Psychiatric Quarterly,* 1961, *35,* 458–481.

Bruch, H. Developmental Considerations of Anorexia Nervosa and Obesity. *Canadian Journal of Psychiatry,* 1981, *26,* 212–217.

Berg, I. Child Psychiatry and Enuresis. *British Journal of Psychiatry,* 1981, *139,* 247–248.

Bullen, B. A., Monello, L. F., Cohen, H., and Mayer, J. Attitudes Towards Physical Activity, Food and Family in Obese and Nonobese Adolescent Girls. *American Journal of Clinical Nutrition*, 1963, *12*, (1), 1–11.

Burns, C. Encopresis (Incontinence of Faeces) in Children. *British Medical Journal*, 1941, *2*, 767–769.

Carrera, F., III. Obesity in Adolescence. In N. Kiell (ed.), *The Psychology of Obesity, Dynamics and Treatment*. Springfield, Ill.: Chas. C Thomas, 1973, pp. 113–124.

"Causes of Enuresis" (Editorial). *British Medical Journal*, 1969, *2*, 63–64.

Craddock, D. *Obesity and Its Management*, 2nd ed. Edinburgh: Churchill Livingston, 1973.

DeLeon, G., and Mandell, W. A Comparison of Conditioning and Psychotherapy in the Treatment of Functional Enuresis. *Journal of Clinical Psychology*, 1966, *22*, 326–330.

Dinello, F. A., and Champelli, J. The Use of Imipramine in the Treatment of Enuresis (Review). *Canadian Psychiatric Association Journal*, 1968, *13*, 237–241.

Eastwell, H. D. A Pica Epidemic: A Price for Sedentarism among Australian Ex-Hunter-Gatherers. *Psychiatry*, 1979, *42*, 264–273.

Eid, E. E. Follow-up Study of Physical Growth of Chilren Who Had Excessive Weight Gain in First Six Months of Life. *British Medical Journal*, 1970, *2*, 74–76.

Ellis, R. W. B., and Mitchell, R. G. *Disease in Infancy and Childhood*, 7th ed. Baltimore, Md.: William and Wilkins, 1973.

Erikson, E. *Childhood and Society*, 2nd ed. New York: W. W. Norton and Co., 1963.

Essen, J., and Peckham, C. Nocturnal Enuresis in Childhood. *Developmental Medicine and Child Neurology*, 1976, *18*, 577–589.

Fisher, C., Kahn, E., Edwards, A., and Davis, D. Effects of Valium on NREM Night Terrors. *Psychophysiology*, 1972, *9*, 91.

Fisher, C., Kahn, E., Edwards, A., and Davis, D. M. A Psychophysiological Study of Nightmares and Night Terrors. *Journal of Nervous and Mental Disease*, 1973, *157*, 75–98.

Frary, L. G. Enuresis: A Genetic Study. *American Journal of Diseases of Children*, 1935, *49*, 557–578.

Gastaut, H., and Broughton, R. A Clinical and Polygraphic Study of Episodic Phenomena During Sleep. In J. Wortis (ed.), *Recent Advances in Biological Psychiatry*, Vol. VII. New York: Plenum, 1965, pp. 197–221.

Gelber, H., and Meyer, V. Behavior Therapy and Encopresis: The Complexities Involved in Treatment. *Behaviour Research and Therapy*, 1965, *2*, 227–231.

Geller, S. E., Keane, T. M., and Scheirer, C. J. Delay of Gratification, Locus of Control, and Eating Patterns in Obese and Non-Obese Children. *Addictive Behaviors*, 1981, *6*, 9–14.

Gerard, M. W. Enuresis: A Study in Etiology. *American Journal of Orthopsychiatry*, 1939, *9*, 48–58.

Gilbert, G. M. A Survey of "Referral Problems" in Metropolitan Child Guidance Centers. *Journal of Clinical Psychology*, 1957, *13*, 37–42.

Glicklich, L. B. An Historical Account of Enuresis. *Pediatrics*, 1951, *8*, 859–876.

Gutelius, M. F., Millican, F. K., Layman, E. M., Cohen, G. J., and Dublin, C. C. Nutritional Studies of Children with Pica. *Pediatrics*, 1962, *29*, 1012–1023.

Hall, S. M., and Hall, R. G. Outcome and Methodological Considerations in Behavioral Treatment of Obesity. *Behavior Therapy*, 1974, *5*, 352–364.

Hallgren, B. *Enuresis: A Clinical and Genetic Study*. Copenhagen: Munksgaard, 1957.

Hart, J. T. A New Approach to Sidereal Sleeplessness. *Journal of Orthomolecular Psychiatry*, 1981, *10*, 212–214.

Hundziak, M., Mauer, R. A., and Watson, L. S., Jr. Operant Conditioning in Toilet Training of Severely Mentally Retarded Boys. *American Journal of Mental Deficiency*, 1965, *70*, 120–124.

Hutchinson-Smith, B. H. Obesity and Respiratory Infection of Children. *British Medical Journal*, 1971, *1*, 460–461.

Illingworth, R. S. Three Months' Colic. *Archives of Disease in Childhood*, 1954, *29*, 165–174.

Illingworth, R. S. *Common Symptoms of Disease in Children*, 3rd ed. Oxford: Blackwell Scientific Publications, 1971.

Jacobson, A., Kales, J. D., and Kales, A. Clinical and Electrophysiological Correlates of Sleep Disorders in Children. In A. Kales (ed.), *Sleep: Physiology and Pathology, A Symposium*. Philadelphia: Lippincott, 1969, pp. 109–118.

Jeffrey, D. B. Behavioral Management of Obesity. In W. E. Craighead, A. E. Kazdin, and M. J. Mahoney (eds.), *Behavior Modification: Principles, Issues, and Applications*. Boston: Houghton Mifflin, 1976, pp. 394–413.

Kahn, E., Fisher, C., Byrne, J., Edwards, A., and Frosch, A. The Influence of Valium, Thorazine, and Dilantin on Stage 4 Nightmares. *Psychophysiology*, 1970, *7*, 350.

Kales, A., Soldatos, C. R., Bixler, E. O., Ladda, R. L., Charney, D. S., Weber, G., and Schweitzer, P. K. Hereditary Factors in Sleepwalking and Night Terrors. *British Journal of Psychiatry*, 1980, *137*, 111–118.

Kanner, L. *Child Psychiatry*, 4th ed. Springfield, Ill. Chas. C Thomas, 1972.

Keeley, S. M., Shemberg, K. M., and Carbonell, J. Operant Clinical Intervention: Behavior Management or Beyond? Where Are the Data? *Behavior Therapy*, 1976, *7*, 292–305.

Kessler, J. W. *Psychopathology of Childhood*. Englewood Cliffs, N.J.: Prentice-Hall, 1966.

Kolvin, I., Taunch, J., Currah, J., Garside, R. F., Nolan, J., and Shaw, W. B. Enuresis: A Descriptive Analysis and a Controlled Trial. *Developmental Medicine and Child Neurology*, 1972, *14*, 715–726.

Krisch, K., and Jahn, J. Anamnestic Data and Examination Results on 36 Encopretic Children. *Zeitschrift fur Kinderund Jugendpsychiatrie*, 1981, *9*, 16–27.

Lakin, M. Personality Factors in Mothers of Excessively Crying (Colicky) Infants. *Monographs of the Society for*

Research in Child Development, 1957, *22,* Serial No. 64, No. 1.

LAPOUSE, R., and MONK, M. A. Fears and Worries in a Representative Sample of Children. *American Journal of Orthopsychiatry,* 1959, *29,* 803–818.

LLOYD, J. K., WOLFE, O. H., and WHELEN, W. S. Childhood Obesity: A Long-Term Study of Height and Weight. *British Medical Journal,* 1961, *5245,* 145–148.

LOVIBOND, S. H. *Conditioning and Enuresis.* Oxford: Pergammon Press, 1964.

LOVIBOND, S. H., and COOTE, M. A. Enuresis. In C. G. Costello (ed.), *Symptoms of Psychopathology: A Handbook.* New York: John Wiley, 1970, pp. 373–396.

MACKEITH, R. A Frequent Factor in the Origins of Primary Nocturnal Enuresis: Anxiety in the Third Year of Life. *Developmental Medicine and Child Neurology,* 1968, *10,* 465–470.

MADDEN, N. A., RUSSO, D. C., and CATALDO, M. F. Behavioral Treatment of Pica in Children with Lead Poisoning. *Child Behavior Therapy,* 1980, *2,* 67–81.

MAYER, J. Some Aspects of the Problem of Regulation of Food Intake and Obesity. *New England Journal of Medicine,* 1966, *274.*

MILLICAN, F. K., and LOURIE, R. S. The Child with Pica and His Family. In E. J. Anthony and C. Koupernik (eds.), *The Child in His Family,* Vol. 1. *The International Yearbook for Child Psychiatry and Allied Disciplines.* New York: John Wiley, 1970, pp. 333–348.

MOBBS, J. Childhood Obesity. *International Journal of Nursing Studies,* 1970, *7,* 3–18.

MONELLO, L. F., and MAYER, J. Obese Adolescent Girls: Unrecognized "Minority" Group? *American Journal of Clinical Nutrition,* 1963, *13,* 35–39.

MOWRER, O. H., and MOWRER, W. A. Enuresis: A Method for Its Study and Treatment. *American Journal of Orthopsychiatry,* 1938, *8,* 436–459.

NATHAN, S. Body Image in Chronically Obese Children as Reflected in Figure Drawings. *Journal of Personality Assessment,* 1973, *37,* 456–463.

NEAL, D. H. Behavior Therapy and Encopresis in Children. *Behaviour Research and Therapy,* 1963, *1,* 139–150.

OSTERGAARD, L. On Psychogenic Obesity in Childhood. V. *Acta Paediatrica,* 1954, *43,* 507–521.

PIERCE, C. M. Dream Studies in Enuresis Research. *Canadian Psychiatric Association Journal,* 1963, *8,* 415–419.

READ, M. S., and FELSON, D. *Malnutrition, Learning, and Behavior.* National Institute of Child Health and Human Development Center for Research for Mothers and Children, DHEW Publication No. (NIH) 76–1036, April 1976.

ROSS, A. O. Behavior Therapy with Children. In S. L. Garfield and A. E. Bergin (eds.), *Handbook of Psychotherapy and Behavior Change,* 2nd ed. New York: John Wiley, 1978, pp. 591–620.

ROSS, A. O. *Child Behavior Therapy: Principles, Procedures and Empirical Basis.* New York: John Wiley, 1981.

ROTATORI, A. J., FOX, R., and MAUSER, A. Slim Chance: A Weight Control Program for the Learning Disabled. *Academic Therapy,* 1982, *17,* 447–456.

RUTTER, M., YULE, W., and GRAHAM, P. Enuresis and Behaviour Deviance: Some Epidemiological Considerations. In I. Kolvin, R. C. MacKeith, and S. R. Meadow (eds.) *Bladder Control and Enuresis.* London: William Heinemann, pp. 137–147.

SCHAEFFER, C. E. *Childhood Encopresis and Enuresis: Causes and Therapy.* New York: Van Nostrand Reinhold, 1979.

SHAFFER, D. Enuresis. In M. Rutter and L. Hersov (eds.), *Child Psychiatry: Modern Approaches.* Oxford: Blackwell Scientific, 1977, pp. 581–612.

SHIRLEY, H. F. Encopresis in Children. *Journal of Pediatrics,* 1938, *12,* 367–380.

SPOCK, B. *Baby and Child Care* (Revised Cardinal Giant Edition). New York: Pocket Books, 1963.

STAGER, S. F. Externality, Environment and Obesity in Children. *Journal of General Psychology,* 1981, *105,* 141–147.

STUNKARD, A. J., and MAHONEY, M. J. Behavioral Treatment of the Eating Disorders. In H. Leitenberg (ed.), *Handbook of Behavior Modification.* Englewood Cliffs, N.J: Prentice-Hall, 1976, pp. 45–73.

TOLSTRUP, K. On Psychogenic Obesity in Children. IV. *Acta Paediatrica,* 1953, *42,* 289–304.

WEBB, W. B. *Sleep, the Gentle Tyrant.* Englewood Cliffs, N.J.: Prentice-Hall, 1975.

WRIGHT, L. Handling the Encopretic Child. *Professional Psychology,* 1973, Vol. IV, 137–144.

YOUNG, G. C., and MORGAN, R. T. T. Overlearning in the Conditioning Treatment of Enuresis. *Behavior Research and Therapy,* 1972 (a), *10,* 147–151.

YOUNG, G. C., and MORGAN, R. T. T. Overlearning in the Conditioning Treatment of Enuresis: A Long-Term Follow-up Study. *Behavior Research and Therapy,* 1972 (b), *10,* 419–420.

YOUNG, G. C., and MORGAN, R. T. T. Analysis of Factors Associated with the Extinction of a Conditioned Response. *Behavior Research and Therapy,* 1973 (a), *11,* 219–22.

YOUNG, G. C., and MORGAN, R. T. T. Rapidity of Response to the Treatment of Enuresis. *Developmental Medicine and Child Neurology,* 1973 (b), *15,* 488–496.

8

CHILDHOOD PSYCHOSES

Infantile Autism, Childhood Schizophrenia, and Other Childhood Psychoses

PROLOGUE

I don't know where to begin, doctor, except that our pediatrician sent us to you because we are very worried about Henry, our oldest child. Oh, he's a healthy and fine-looking boy . . . and he was such a good baby. He rarely cried or demanded much attention. He seemed content and so self-sufficient that I was able to leave him alone and get other things done around the house. I remember feeling pleased with how easily I managed everything, but also a little resentful that Henry did not appear to need me more. After a while I couldn't help but recognize that he was not interested in anyone, not even toys.

There were times when his eyes were bright and he looked alert. But he would often stare off into space and be so far away. Really, I tried everything to get his attention, but I just couldn't get through to him. We thought that he might be . . . deaf, but his hearing was checked and it was normal. We worried because he didn't walk by himself until months after his second birthday, but we were relieved that he repeated a few words before he was a year old. However, he never really put words together on his own, and he never has really entered into anything resembling a conversation. We struggled for several years to toilet train him but without success. He's five years old now, and he still wets and soils himself.

Henry won't feed himself and he's an absolute disaster at the dinner table. He throws food, bangs on the table, and shoves dishes within his reach until something spills or breaks. He likes to rock back and forth for hours on end, and sometimes he bangs his head as part of his rocking pattern. He doesn't play with other children, and at unexpected times he becomes angry and unmanageable for no apparent reason. My husband and I thought Henry would outgrow whatever stage he was going through, and that things would get better. Believe me doctor, we have tried so hard to be patient with him. It's almost time for him to start school, but we're afraid that he won't be ready . . . (mother breaks into tears), maybe he'll never by ready! Oh doctor . . . help us . . . help us find out what's wrong with Henry.

Henry's mother settled down temporarily after the psychologist reassured her that everything possible would be done to uncover her son's difficulties. However, her basic anxiety came from the nagging fear that Henry was an abnormal child who was suffering from an irreparable disorder. Unfortunately, the psychologist could not dispel her fear, because he viewed Henry's longstanding symptoms—social isolation and inaccessibility, severe impairment of motor and language development, and immature eating and toilet habits—as falling within the broad category of childhood psychosis. But determining exactly what's wrong with Henry is an elusive and complex task that is much like one's first encounter with a mirage—now you see it . . . now you don't.

In spite of long-term interest and lively inquiry by researchers, confusion and controversy continue to characterize the study of childhood psychoses. We still cannot say what label should be used to designate this major category or each specific condition within it; which, if any, of the specific disorders are distinguishable as separate entities; and whether any of these conditions are the same for both children and adults. For example, a cursory review of DSM–II (APA, 1968) will reveal that it lists Childhood Schizophrenia as the only type of psychosis for children, while the GAP classification system (1966) includes a number of other childhood psychotic disorders, dividing psychoses into three age groups and listing within each the conditions appropriate to that particular developmental level. In contrast, the latest classification found in DSM–III (APA, 1980) departs radically from past practice by rejecting the term *psychosis* for children. Instead, DSM–III uses the label *Pervasive Developmental Disorders,* because of the belief that these are disorders that are dissimilar to the psychoses of adults. DSM–III further contends that the new label best describes the many areas of psychological functioning that are affected and disrupted concurrently. DSM–III describes Infantile Autism, Childhood Onset Pervasive Developmental Disorder, and Atypical Pervasive Developmental Disorder as the primary forms of psychoses in children; and it eliminates the diagnosis of Childhood Schizophrenia, which was so popular and widely used in the past. The adult category of schizophrenia can be used in this system for children who evidence the symptoms and meet the behavioral criteria set out in the adult form of the disorder. In clinical practice frequent inconsistencies in diagnostic labeling are fostered by the substantial differences in classification systems and by the tendency to use the various labels interchangeably. The literature reflects disparity in the description of the symptom picture within each category, and even greater disagreement over the diagnostic signs used to discriminate among them. In addition, the difficulty encountered in differentiating childhood psychoses from mental retardation and organic brain syndromes only serves to increase diagnostic confusion. For these reasons data on the incidence, family characteristics, etiological factors, and treatment effects for the separate diagnostic categories are of questionable accuracy—as such, they must be interpreted with caution.

Nevertheless, in this chapter we shall strive to bring some measure of clarity and orderliness to this little-understood but fascinating area of study. While we shall attempt to relate our discussion of psychotic disorders to the categories described in DSM–III, we cannot both faithfully report the literature and adhere strictly to this classification system. For pedagogical reasons, therefore, we have organized this chapter around the presentation of the clinical disorders of Infantile Autism, Childhood Schizophrenia, and Other Psychotic Conditions of Childhood to reflect the past and present emphases and trends in the literature. We shall examine the symptom picture of these disorders, discuss the various criteria used to differentiate between them and other abnormal conditions, consider etiological views, and describe those treatment methods that seem to be most promising.

INFANTILE AUTISM

Clinical Description

Normal babies communicate their desire to be picked up, held, and played with on almost any occasion. They react with animation and enthusiasm to the mere appearance of a familiar person, and they show displeasure when left alone. They enjoy human contact and place unquestioning trust in others. Psychotic children, on the other hand, may as early as four months of age fail to show the normal anticipatory postural movements before being picked up. They remain somewhat stiff and rigid and do not conform to the body of the person holding them. These are the earliest indications of what Kanner (1943) referred to as "extreme autistic aloneness," a primary symptom of infantile autism, in which the child is unable to relate to people and insists on being left alone. Autistic babies show no interest in people or their conversation. An adult who reaches out to such a child is likely to receive an angry or irritated response. These children rarely, if ever, make direct eye contact with others. They may sit motionless, staring into space for hours, as if mentally preoccupied. They may smile to themselves momentarily, but other people are usually unable to attract their attention.

On the basis of case histories and clinical observations, Kanner (1943, 1949) concluded that many youngsters who had been labeled as either deaf or mentally retarded were instead experiencing symptoms associated with infantile autism. He maintained that these children were of good intellectual potential and showed no evidence of auditory impairment. Kanner gave the new syndrome its name both to convey its early onset and to reflect the autistic personality characteristics of inaccessibility, aloofness, and isolation. Although much has been written about autism since, the descriptive standard most widely accepted for the syndrome comes from data compiled by Kanner on the first hundred cases seen at Johns Hopkins Hospital Clinic (Kanner, 1954; Kanner and Lesser, 1958).

Pregnancies of mothers of autistic children were described as normal and uncomplicated, although the rate of premature births in the sample was higher than normal (twelve out of the first hundred cases were born prematurely). Kanner further noted that during the first few months of life, the infant manifested few, if any, apparent abnormal behaviors. Some youngsters appeared apathetic and unresponsive, while others tended to cry excessively. Feeding was a problem sometimes during the second half of the first year or later. The infant either ate very little and showed disinterest in food or else ate a great deal and had an enormous appetite. Parents also noticed peculiar eating habits and food preferences. For example, several studies described autistic children who refused all foods and drank only milk, or who only drank liquids from a transparent container, or who ate chocolate if it was cut in squares, but refused it if it was offered in round pieces (Rimland, 1964).

While autistic children reject human interactions, they have a very active interest in and fondness for inanimate objects, in which they can be absorbed for prolonged periods. Mechanical objects such as light switches, plumbing faucets, and household appliances seem to be especially attractive to these children.

They usually have good motor coordination together with a high level of spatial ability. Numerous reports record the accomplishment of remarkable feats of agility and dexterity for these children at an early age, such as balancing a dime on its edge at age three, or catching and throwing a ball with either hand at age fourteen months (Rimland, 1964).

Insistence on the maintenance of sameness in the environment along with autistic aloneness represent the two principal diagnostic signs of infantile autism. Unless the child introduces the changes, any alteration of furniture, toys, or clothes, or any interruptions of routines (such as bedtime rituals), results in violent temper tantrums and eventual despair. In this regard autistic children demonstrate remarkable memory, since they can notice small changes in their immediate environments, even in places they have not seen in several days.

Approximately 50 percent of autistic youngsters acquire speech. Even when speech is present, there is virtually no conversational interaction, because language is not used as a means of communication. Generally, it is parrotlike, repetitious, monotonous, and noncommunicative. Since these children invest their emotional and intellectual energies in things rather than people, they tend to ignore verbal suggestions and signs of praise or punishment. Often they will repeat TV commercials verbatim or parrot statements made to them by a parent. They may reverse pronouns so that "you" is used in place of "I." The language of autistic children is very literal —the meaning of words does not generalize from one situation to another. For example, "yes" may be used in the specific context, let's say, of wanting a certain toy, but it may not be used as an affirmative response to other things. Part-whole confusion may also be present, so that the expression "hurt my head" may mean "I want comforting," regardless of what part the child may or may not have hurt (Rimland, 1964).

The following case history describes a child who presents the clinical picture of infantile autism:

> The patient, a five-year-old boy, was brought for professional attention because of a history of withdrawn and socially isolated behavior. He was uncommunicative and showed intense insistence on the sameness of the environment, hyperactivity, and repetitive and destructive activity. Both the pregnancy and delivery were normal. He smiled in the early weeks of life, but not necessarily in response to anyone. By the end of the first year his smiling decreased considerably, and it was difficult to get him to smile. He showed little anticipation at being picked up, and he appeared to draw back when held. He did not follow his mother with his eyes, and he was neither alert to nor interested in the environment. Rocking, especially to music, appeared toward the end of the first year. His sleep was poor, and he was selective of and insistent on certain special foods before age one. In spite of this, he showed a rapid weight gain. He sat at six months, stood at seven months, walked at ten and a half months. His brother was born when he was approximately one year old.
>
> During the second year of life, he was hyperactive and destructive. Severe tantrums and unresponsiveness to others were evident in that he neither permitted nor sought physical contact. He became adept at spinning objects and tearing paper, but showed no interest in toys. He spoke a few words at age two, but only for a brief period, and even then, words or vocalized sounds were not used for communication. Instead, he made his demands known by pushing and pulling. Intelligence testing at age three and a half showed a pattern of atypical retardation with successes on a few tasks at his age level.
>
> The patient's mother, age thirty-eight, had been a successful business woman and an active, aggressive person who openly rejected the patient whom she could not control. She reported that since childhood she has been repelled by "little boys," but thought it would be "good for her" to have a boy. The patient's father is a passive and good-natured man who has suffered business reverses in the last several years. Both parents had difficulty in accepting the child's abnormal condition. Neither the patient's sister nor brother show signs of abnormal behavior similar to the patient's.

Clinical examination revealed a hyperactive boy who was out of contact with reality. He spun objects in a highly organized ritualistic manner. Speech was absent as was affective contact. (Adapted from Despert, 1968, pp. 181–182).

Over the years classifying and diagnosing infantile autism has been highly inconsistent; clinicians have been influenced by their own diverse notions of the etiology of the disorder. They have also differed in the way they view mental retardation and organic brain dysfunction as either apart from or part of their formulation of autism (DeMyer, Hingtgen, and Jackson, 1981). Some practitioners have followed Kanner's original observations that autistic children are of normal intelligence, and show no neurological impairment. Accordingly, they have tended to discard from the diagnosis of infantile autism those children who show either mental retardation or neurological signs, or both. We now know that these conditions are not mutually exclusive, and that autistic children who function at the mentally retarded level as preschoolers or earlier continue to be retarded in later childhood. Further, about 18 percent of autistic children develop convulsive disorders by adolescence (Knobloch and Pasamanick, 1975; Rutter and Lockyer, 1967). The fact that DSM-III both allows for the possible inclusion of more than one disorder in arriving at a diagnosis and separates causal factors from the behavioral criteria established for a given disorder should serve to increase the reliability of this new classification system.

Specific Diagnostic Signs of Infantile Autism. Of all the symptoms and characteristics described by Kanner as associated with autism, two were identified as cardinal: *autistic aloneness,* that is, extreme isolation and retrenchment from social interactions evidenced early, and not later than the first year of life; and the *insistence on the maintenance of sameness* in the environment (Eisenberg and Kanner, 1956). Because Kanner emphasized an early age for the onset of the disorder, he considered the failure of the child to speak and abnormalities of speech as secondary symptoms rather than primary ones.

Rimland (1964, 1971) constructed a checklist to be filled out by the child's parents as a quantitative way of identifying autism and

Sidelight 8–1

Discussions about psychotic children typically focus on a description of their symptoms, etiologies, and treatments, with little attention paid to the impact these children may have on their families. In 1972 a book appeared in which Josh Greenfeld gave us a poignant and sometimes painful account of his thoughts, feelings, and reactions to the problems he, his wife (Foumi), and oldest son (Karl) faced in recognizing and coping with his psychotic son, Noah. We hope the following excerpts from this highly recommended book will give us some insight into the family reactions.

4–16–67

"We've decided to stop worrying about Noah. He isn't retarded, he's just pushing the clock hands about at his own slow speed. Yet . . ."

8–16–67

"We took Noah to a pediatrician in the next town, who specializes in neurology. He said that since Noah is talking now there was little cause to worry; that Noah seemed "hypertonic," a floppy baby, a slow developer, but that time would be the maturing agent. We came away relieved. But I also have to admit that lately I haven't worried that much."

9–16–67

I've been reading child-care books. It seems I've been doing everything wrong."

3–11–68

"Noah kept us up half the night, giggling to himself and bouncing in his crib. I became annoyed with him and finally slapped him. He laughed back at me."

7–1–68

"Noah is two. He still doesn't talk, but I do think he's trying to teach himself how to stand up. We're still concerned. And I guess we'll remain concerned until he stands up and walks like a boy."

6–6–69

"Our fears about Noah continue to undergo dramatic ups and downs. Because of his increased opacity, the fact that he doesn't respond when we call his name and fails to relate completely to his immediate environment—a pattern of retardation or autism—we took him to a nearby hospital . . . I guess we both fear that what we dread is so, that Noah is not a normal child, that he is a freak, and his condition is getting worse."

7–14–69

"Somehow the rhythm of our lives, the good fortune of our marriage, seems to have dissipated."

8–1–69

"Meanwhile, last night, as I tried to fall asleep I heard Foumi crying. Why? She was crying for Karl, for the difficulties he would have with other children because he had an abnormal brother. I tried to comfort her, but I know she's right."

9–13–69

"I'm a lousy father. I anger too easily. I get hot with Karl and take on a four-year-old kid. I shout at Noah and further upset an already disturbed one. Perhaps I'm responsible for Noah's problems."

2–19–70

"Foumi keeps complaining about how it's impossible to keep Noah from being destructive about the house. Anything on a table, in a cabinet, on a floor is fodder for him to break. Poor Foumi, she can't afford to take her eyes off him for a second. Poor Noah."

8–70

"I also must note how very few people can actually understand our situation as a family, how they assume we are aloof when we tend not to accept or extend the usual social invitations. Nor have I mentioned the extra expenses a child like Noah entails—those entries I keep in another book."

8–70

"Even more heartbreaking has been the three-year period it has taken us to pierce the organized-medicine, institutionalized-mental-health gauze curtain. Most doctors, if they were unable to prescribe any form of curative aid, did their best to deter us from seeking it. Freudian-oriented psychiatrists and psychologists, if ill-equipped to deal with the problems of those not verbal, tried to inflict great feelings of guilt upon us as all-too-vulnerable parents. Neurologists and pediatricians, if not having the foggiest notions about the effects of diet and nutrition, vitamins and enzymes and their biochemical workings would always suggest such forms of therapy as practiced only by quacks. And county mental-health boards, we discovered, who have charge of the moneys that might be spent helping children like Noah, usually tossed their skimpy fundings away through existing channels that do not offer proper treatment for children like Noah."

8–71

"I still don't know exactly what's wrong with Noah. I only know something is profoundly wrong with him. I still don't know what to do—I only know I must do whatever I possibly can. Although Noah is too young for an institution now, I know I must still accept the very real possibility of his eventual institutionalization. I also know I must try not to feel more sorry for myself than Noah, but some days I forget . . ."

differentiating this disorder from other conditions. He included items that were based on the characteristics Kanner noted for the disorder as well as other items that described features unlike autism. He arrived at a final score based on the subtraction of items dissimilar to autism from those items descriptive of the disorder. Rimland established the score of twenty or greater as the criterion for autism. He showed that while many children with a variety of abnormal conditions were diagnosed as autistic, only 9.7 percent (215 out of 2,218 children) scored twenty or more on his checklist and met his criterion for infantile autism.

Prior and others (1975) analyzed data from 142 cases involving autistic and severely disturbed children with other conditions to find the characteristics that best discriminate autistic children. They found that the following features were most significant: the onset of the disorder before two years of age, the insistence on sameness, the existence of special abilities, and the fine finger coordination that enables unusual dexterity in the manipulation of small objects.

Rutter (1978) and Ritvo and Freeman (1978) in separate papers set forth their criteria for defining the disorder. Common features in both definitions include (1) impaired social development in relating to people, events, and objects, (2) disturbance of language and cognitive skills, and (3) early onset before thirty months of age. In addition, Rutter regards insistence on sameness as an important symptom of autism, while Ritvo and Freeman stress the presence of sensory peculiarities as essential symptoms of the disorder.

According to DSM-III, the diagnostic criteria for infantile autism are as follows:

A. Onset before 30 months of age.
B. Pervasive lack of responsiveness to other people (autism).
C. Gross deficits in language development.
D. If speech is present, peculiar speech patterns such as immediate and delayed echolalia, metaphorical language, pronominal reversal.
E. Bizarre responses to various aspects of the environment, e.g., resistance to change, peculiar interest in or attachments to animate or inanimate objects.
F. Absence of delusions, hallucinations, loosening of associations, and incoherence as in Schizophrenia. (1980, p. 89 and 90)

While the various sets of discriminators noted above illustrate some overlap and agreement with regard to a number of features of infantile autism, they also display a good deal of diversity. Considerable confusion and imprecision would be eliminated if both clinicians and researchers adhered stringently to any one of these sets of discriminators (reporting the criteria used) in the diagnostic process.

Associated Characteristics of Infantile Autism.

1. Family features. In Kanner's first hundred cases he noted a number of characteristics of parents of autistic children, which he regarded as unusual and signficant. These included a high level of educational achievement; a high degree of vocational accomplishment, especially for fathers; high intelligence; and middle to upper-middle class socioeconomic status. Table 8-1 shows the educational level of these parents, demonstrating their significantly higher amount of schooling than is to be expected in the general population, particularly for women in 1954. The fathers included thirty-one businessmen and eight tradesmen; almost all the remaining fathers (sixty-one) were professionals in such fields as engineering, medicine, law, chemistry, writing, dentistry, education, theology,

Table 8-1 Kanner's 100 Cases—Educational Level

	High School Graduate	*Entered College*	*Graduated College*	*Post Graduate Work*
Fathers	96	87	74	38
Mothers	92	70	49	11

Kanner, 1954, pp. 378–385.

psychology, photography, forestry, publishing, and the military. Kanner described the parents as obsessive, preoccupied with abstractions, emotionally cold, and socially distant, with little or no interest in people. He noted further that they were polite, formal, bookish, humorless, and serious individuals who preferred solitary activities. They were undemonstrative but respectful and loyal to their spouses, and they rarely were divorced or separated. Kanner also found that severe mental disorders were extremely rare in these families.

Bender (1959) argued that inferences about high intelligence in the parents of autistic children cannot be made, because Kanner's sample was biased—a special group of people (highly informed, bright, and affluent enough to travel to Baltimore for an appraisal) sought Kanner's services. However, later studies have corroborated the observatrion that parents of autistic children are higher in educational level than parents of other severely disturbed youngsters, although not to the extent originally reported by Kanner (Lotter, 1966; Rimland, 1968; Treffert, 1970). Lotter (1967) demonstrated that parents of autistic children were superior on a vocabulary and nonverbal test to parents of nonautistic but disturbed children and that this superiority tended to hold up within socioeconomic groups. In contrast, Allen and others (1971) found only higher verbal IQs for fathers of autistic children, as compared to fathers of brain-damaged children, when not matched for socioeconomic level. No differences were found between fathers of autistic children and normal children when matched for socioeconomic level. Moreover, no differences were found between mothers of autistic children and mothers of other disturbed children. It has also been shown that there were fewer mental disorders (psychoses and neuroses) in close relatives of autistic children than in parents of other severely disturbed children, as originally noted by Kanner (Cox et al., 1975).

Kanner's observation concerning the personalities and child-rearing practices of the parents of autistic children has stirred yet another controversy in the literature. As we shall see, there are those who view the highly intellectual, obsessive, aloof, and ice-box personality of these parents as the principal causative agent of the disorder. Others, however, favor a biological interpretation.

2. *The course and prognosis of the disorder.* In the early phase of the disorder (within the first three to five years), autistic aloneness, repetitive motor behavior, and absorption in idiosyncratic and self-stimulating behavior (along with speech abnormalities) are quite evident and persistent. Although social adaptation and the appropriateness of behavior continue as problems into adulthood, at about age five or six these youngsters become more socially responsive and less detached from interpersonal interactions than they were before. In middle childhood they compulsively organize and routinize their daily activities, and they may become preoccupied with many sets of facts and/or figures, such as bus or rapid transit schedules, connections, and routes (Rutter, 1978; Wing, 1976). Language problems for those who learn to talk continue into adolescence. Echolalia, concrete use of language, flat monotone speech which is often stiff and formal, and problems with rules that direct conversation in a socially interactive situation are among the speech and language difficulties evident for autistic adolescents (Baltaxe, 1977; Shapiro and Huebner, 1976). In addition, by adolescence up to one-third of these children evidence neurological involvement such as convulsions (Knobloch and Pasamanick, 1975; Deykin and MacMahon, 1979). Infantile autism is a chronic disorder; for many of these children some of the disruptive and incapacitating features persist into adulthood (APA, 1980).

The prognosis is likely to be better in youngsters who have acquired speech as compared to those who are mute. Follow-up studies of sixty-three autistic children in adolescence showed that thirty-two had developed communicative speech by age five, while thirty-one had not. Moreover, one-half of the speaking youngsters achieved a rating of "fair" or "good" on social adjustment, as compared to only one such success in the nonspeaking group of children (Eisenberg, 1956; Kanner and Lesser, 1958). Similarly, Lotter (1974) found that "the ability to use speech communicatively was the best predictor of outcome in late adolescence" (p. 271). This evidence was from an eight-year follow-up of thirty-two autistic children. IQ was found to be a good predictor of outcome. DeMyer and associates (1973) and DeMyer, Hingtgen, and Jackson (1981) report some pessimistic figures both from the literature and from their own study: One to 2 percent recover to achieve independent status, 5 to 19 percent attain "borderline" functioning, while 60 to 75 percent remain in semicomplete or complete dependency on relatives and/or on long-term institutional care.

3. *Prevalence.* Due to diagnostic unreliability, it is difficult to arrive at an accurate assessment of how frequently infantile autism occurs. Nevertheless, all the available data indicate that autism is an extremely rare disorder that occurs in about 2 to 5 per 10,000 cases in children under fifteen years of age (DeMyer, Hingtgen, and Jackson, 1981; APA, 1980). In addition, the data indicate consistently that more boys than girls are affected by this disorder, with a ratio of about 4 males to 1 female (DeMyer et al., 1981; Tsai and Stewart, 1982). For unknown reasons the disorder occurs more frequently in youngsters from upper socioeconomic levels than from lower socioeconomic groups (APA, 1980).

Etiological Views

Psychogenic Considerations. Kanner's early description of and emphasis on the special characteristics of the parents of autistic children—including high intelligence; high educational and occupational levels; marital stability; low incidence of mental illness; and cold, intellectual, and aloof personalities—led to the belief that faulty parental patterns were primary causal factors in the development of the disorder. However, past and current research findings fail to corroborate this position. For example, in the area of child-rearing practices, DeMyer and others (1972) conducted four semistructured interviews with parents of autistic, brain-damaged, and normal children between four and five years of age. The children were matched for age, sex, ordinal position in the family, number and sex of siblings, race, socioeconomic level, and religion of parents. The autistic group consisted of thirty-three youngsters, seven of whom were diagnosed as schizophrenic. The characterization of parents of autistic children as cold, overintellectualized, and nonstimulating was not confirmed. In fact, it was found that parents of brain-damaged children, and not parents of autistics, were the least stimulating, the least warm, and the most restrictive in the physical freedom they permitted their children.

A study using projective techniques (Rorschach and TAT) to compare personality characteristics of parents of psychotic and neurotic children and adult schizophrenics has been used to support Kanner's observation and causal assumption (Singer and Wynne, 1963). The findings indicated that the parents of psychotic children—unlike the other two groups—were cynical, dissatisfied, and superficial. Further, they maintained passive, distant, intellectual, and obsessive interpersonal relationships. Caution must be exercised in interpreting these results, however, since they do not provide evidence warranting a cause-and-effect conclusion. It is not possible to determine whether these parental traits were present prior to the birth of the autistic child, or if they developed later in response to a disturbed child. Moreover, we should also note that no diagnostic distinctions were made in the study concerning the specific types of psychosis, but instead, all psychotic children and their parents were lumped together in one broad diagnostic group. This was done despite the fact that the personality characteristics of parents of autistic children are regarded as quite different than those of parents of schizophrenic children.

Although many etiological factors have been implicated in the search for the definitive cause of autism, a recent review of the literature indicates that the parents of autistic youngsters are similar in personal characteristics to parents of children with brain impairment and other mental disorders. Further, it appears that these parents manifest no psychopathology which could be considered the causal basis for the disorder (DeMyer et al., 1981). In contrast, the recent literature strongly favors the view that attributes the disorder to some as yet unspecified neurological or biological factor or factors. In this connection the National Society for Autistic Children has initiated efforts to facilitate autopsy studies of the few autistic and schizophrenic children who die annually (Schopler, 1976).

Genetic Considerations. In his initial paper on autism, Kanner assumed

> . . . that these children have come into the world with innate inability to form the usual biologically-provided contact with people, just as other children come into the world with innate physical or intellectual handicaps. If this assumption is correct, a further study of our children may help furnish concrete criteria regarding the still diffuse notions about the constitutional components of emotional reactivity. For here we seem to have pure-culture examples of *inborn autistic disturbances of affective contact.* (1943, p. 250)

Albeit vague, Kanner made reference to an inherited and biological etiology for infantile autism, a view that parallels the thesis of genetic vulnerability. More than twenty years later, Rimland (1964) proposed a more specific view of genetic predisposition. He suggested that autistic children (because they come from parents who are intellectually bright) inherit a high capacity for blood circulation in the brain. He further conjectured that this makes them highly susceptible to "oxygen-produced" vascular destruction and damage, especially to the part of the brain stem known as the *reticular formation.* An excess of oxygen damages the connection between incoming sensory information and previously learned material normally stored in the brain. The result is a cognitive dysfunction.

Little data are as yet available with regard to chromosomal or twin studies primarily because autism is so rare, and because the incidence of psychiatric abnormalities is so low in the families of these children. Nevertheless, there are some indications of a high but not perfect concordance for autism in monozygotic twins, and an absence of chromosomal abnormalities in a small sample of autistic children (Judd and Mandell, 1968). More recently Folstein and Rutter (1978) studied the concordance in same-sex monozygotic and dizygotic twins who had autistic and cognitive disorders (which included children diagnosed as autistic). They found a higher concordance for monozygotic twins (36 percent) than for dizygotic twins (0 percent) when at least one twin was diagnosed as autistic, while the concordance for monozygotic versus dizygotic twins with cognitive disorders was even larger (82 percent versus 10 percent respectively). Folstein and Rutter interpreted these findings to indicate a genetic component in the etiology of infantile autism.

Biological Considerations.

1. *Biochemical considerations.* In the past fifteen years or so, a good deal of research has been designed to discover a biochemical "marker" of infantile autism. While no such discriminator has as yet been found, the search continues through diverse lines of inquiry, ranging from studies on hormones to research on neurotransmitters. For example, an isolated study failed to show a thyroid dysfunction in autistic children (Abassi, Linscheid, and Coleman, 1978), while considerable research has explored the role of the monoamines in the development of adult schizophrenia (see Chapter 4) and the child-

hood psychoses. Researchers have measured monoamine levels in the whole blood (Coleman, 1973; Ritvo et al., 1978; Belmaker, Hattab, and Ebstein, 1978; Young et al., 1980), in platelets (Bouillin et al., 1971; Rotman, Caplan, and Szekely, 1980), and in urine (Landgrebe and Landgrebe, 1976; Young et al., 1978) in children diagnosed as autistic. Although differences in monoamine levels are often found when autistics are compared to normal children, they do not appear to be specific for autism, since the same differences are observed in other pathological conditions.

The report of inadequate secretion of hydoroxyindoleacetic acid in autistic children has not been replicated in other studies. Moreover, the finding of higher platelet serotonin levels has been also attributed to the factors of age and activity level, since these variables can significantly elevate serotonin levels as well (DeMyer et al., 1981; Brooker and Mareth, 1982). While still regarded as promising, biochemical studies have thus far failed to yield consistent findings with respect to autistic and severely disturbed children, largely because of major methodological problems such as (1) poor diagnostic agreement; (2) very small samples of subjects; and (3) the many factors (sex, age, activity level, intelligence, presence of a medical disease, treatment method used, diet, and so forth) apart from psychopathology that can bring about alterations in the biochemistry of the body.

2. *Neurobiological considerations.* Neurological Conditions. For more than two decades the literature has implicated neurobiological factors and neurological dysfunction in the etiology of autism and other childhood psychoses. Several studies have shown that almost 50 percent or more of autistic children, as contrasted to less than 20 percent of children in other diagnostic categories, manifest some brain dysfunction or brain disease (Kolvin, Ounsted, and Roth, 1971; Gubbay et al., 1970; Harper and Williams, 1976). Coleman (1979) studied 149 children with infantile autism who also had known neurological conditions and found that about one-third had phenylketonuria (PKU-see Chapter 11) and about one-fifth had rubella (German measles). Chess (1977) followed 243 children between the ages of two and a half and five years who had congenital rubella. She found a high rate of autism but also a high rate of recovery from the autistic symptoms in a large proportion of the cases. She suggested that viral infection of the brain (rubella virus), while not the cause of all instances of autism, is probably the cause in some cases. She also suggested that autism is the final behavioral consequence of a number of different causes. Ornitz (1978) has hypothesized a vestibular dysfunction in autistic children, since they tend to respond abnormally to stimulation of vestibular mechanisms. For example, autistic children are preoccupied with spinning objects, and they spontaneously show peculiar vestibular responses such as whirling, as well as persistent head and body rocking without dizziness or loss of balance.

Biodevelopmental Complications. Evidence appears to be mounting which implicates pre-, peri-, and postnatal complications and risk factors in the etiology of autism. Gillberg (1980) suggests that mothers of autistic children may be at greater risk for autism, since they tend to be significantly older than mothers of nonautistic children. This finding is consistent with studies that indicate a higher rate of unsuccessful pregnancies, more frequent bleeding during pregnancies, more problems during labor, and a greater number of forceps deliveries at birth for mothers of autistic children as compared to controls (DeMyer, 1979; Campbell, Hardesty, and Burdock, 1978; O'Moore, 1972). The fact that several studies indicate that autistic children are delayed in almost all aspects of development as compared to normal controls is consistent with what one would expect based on the findings noted above (Ornitz, Guthrie, and Farley, 1977; DeMyer, 1979). After reviewing the literature, Ornitz and Ritvo (1977) concluded that autism is a behaviorally manifested disease with symptoms that suggest a neuropathophysiological origin which retards the child's development.

EEG and Central Nervous System Activity. The electroencephalogram (EEG) is a popular and widely used measure of central nervous system functioning. However, it has yielded equivocal results with respect to discriminating autistic from nonautistic children. In a study intended to explore the hypothesis that autism may be attributable to anatomical defects of the left temporal lobe, DeLong (1978) and Hauser and colleagues (1975) found sufficient evidence of EEG and pneumoencephalographic (a special procedure in which spinal fluid is replaced with air in order to better view subcortical areas of the brain) abnormalities to support the hypothesis. However, more recent findings give no indication of an EEG pattern that is either unique to autism or indicative of left-sided involvement. In fact, in those autistic children with abnormal EEGs, the findings support bilateral brain abnormalities (Tsai and Stewart, 1982). This variability of findings from study to study is reflected in a review of the literature, which indicates that results have ranged from 13 to 83 percent in the incidence of EEG abnormalities in very young psychotic children (James and Barry, 1980). It may be that autistic children have more EEG abnormalities than normal youngsters; but they do not appear to have more abnormalities than children with other psychiatric conditions. EEG recordings have also been used to help determine whether autistic children are physiologically over- or underaroused. The best evidence at this time indicates that autistic children in a variety of familiar and unfamiliar situations show EEG patterns of high arousal, as well as an increase in stereotyped behavior patterns, in more complex environmental settings (Hutt and Hutt, 1970).

Cerebral Asymmetry. Recently studies suggesting cerebral asymmetry have primarily indicated right-hemisphere processing and left-side dysfunction for autistic children (Blackstock, 1978; Hauser, DeLong, and Rosman, 1975; Hier, LeMay, and Rosenberger, 1978; Hier, LeMay, and Rosenberger, 1979). Blackstock, after having autistic children listen to verbal and musical material, found that autistics favored music and preferred to listen to it with their left ear. Normal controls showed no preference for either type of material, and they were more variable in terms of which ear they listened with. These results were interpreted to suggest that autistic children are primarily right-side processors, a finding which Prior and Bradshaw (1979) also reported. Using computerized brain tomography (CT scan) to search for left-right morphologic asymmetries of the parieto-occipital region of the brain, Hier and others found in two studies that the right side of the brain was larger than the left in autistic children as compared to mentally retarded and nonautistic but neurologically damaged children. These results again point to left-hemisphere dysfunction, which may be a factor in the language difficulties often found in autistic children. Prior (1979) argues also that autistic children have a dysfunction in the left cerebral hemisphere and that the cognitive functions mediated by the left side are more deficient in these children (as compared to nonautistic controls) than those mediated by the right side (for example, verbal, sequential processing, and analytic skills; visual spatial skills; and recognition without analysis).

Unspecified Neurological Deficit. Although unspecific with regard to the nature and location of the damage, some investigators have suggested a neurologically determined deficit. Abnormal behaviors of autistic children are the result of a central disorder of cognition involving deficits both in the use and comprehension of language and in conceptual abilities (Rutter, 1968). Similarly, Ricks and Wing (1975) believe that the difficulty in handling symbols is the central problem in infantile autism, and that this deficit disrupts verbal and nonverbal communication and other aspects of the child's cognitive and social functioning. Experiments have shown that the memory of autistic children is good, but that such children obtain low scores on tests involving concepts, abstractions, or symbolization (Hermelin and O'Connor, 1970).

These findings have led some to favor a neurological view of infantile autism, which claims that the deficit is in the encoding and expressive function of the nervous system rather than in the reception of sensory stimuli from the environment. The behavior of autistic children has been likened to that of brain-damaged youngsters, who are unable to process incoming sensory patterns (auditory and visual) into meaningful experiences because of some neurological deficit (Kugelmass, 1970).

Questionnaire data obtained from parents of autistic, retarded, aphasic, and sensory impaired children revealed behavioral characteristics in autistic children that were similar to those evident in other multiply handicapped youngsters. Autistic children have speech and body orientation problems also found in aphasics. In addition, they have visual abnormalities, abnormal body movements, and a preference for proximal senses similar to the characteristics of partially deaf and blind children (Wing, 1969). These similarities between autistic children and youngsters with perceptual and communication disorders have been interpreted as demonstrating a neurological cause of autism. In support of the biological view, several investigators have found that about one-third of the children with infantile autism strongly evidence neurological damage. Further, seizures have been noted in adolescence in a small, but significant, number of these children (Rutter and Lockyer, 1967; Lotter, 1974).

While the specific nature and location of the impairment remains speculative, there is mounting evidence that strongly implicates neurological factors as the underlying etiology of autism. Nevertheless, psychogenic considerations cannot be ignored, because the quality of the continued interaction of child and family will have important consequences for the child's subsequent adjustment.

CHILDHOOD SCHIZOPHRENIA

Modern-day interest in childhood psychosis began with a paper published by Potter (1933), who outlined a set of diagnostic criteria for childhood schizophrenia, drawn from a sample of six children. Through the years childhood schizophrenia has remained the primary category for classifying psychosis in children, although the diversity of symptoms included within this category has tended to make it increasingly a "catch-all" classification. Moreover, the category has been involved in more than its share of controversy, particularly as regards its distinctiveness from other forms of childhood psychosis, its continuity with or distinctiveness from adult schizophrenia, and the clinical consensus regarding the specific symptoms for its diagnosis. In light of the fact that childhood schizophrenia has been a subject of continuing interest in the clinical and research literature, it was surprising to find that in 1980 the diagnosis was deleted from DSM-III (APA, 1980). Even if one agrees with the DSM-III suggestion that schizophrenia is the same disorder for both children and adults, a problem still arises: DSM-III fails to account for developmental differences that may occur in a disorder in terms of severity, and/or in the way it is clinically expressed, when the disorder begins at substantially different times (that is, early in childhood or during adolescence). In fact, Cantor and her associates (1982) showed that although all their subjects (thirty children and adolescents) were diagnosed as psychotic and met the DSM-III criteria for schizophrenia (except the one which requires evidence of deterioration from a previous level), they could not—strictly speaking—be diagnosed as schizophrenic. In addition, seven subjects evidenced signs of psychosis before they were thirty months old; but because they also manifested a thought disorder (not a criterion of autism), the diagnosis of infantile autism could not be made. Unfortunately, cases of this sort are not accounted for in DSM-III.

Nevertheless, DSM-III provides another

diagnostic category, referred to as Childhood Onset Pervasive Developmental Disorder, which is intended to reflect the criteria frequently used by clinicians to classify childhood schizophrenia. The following are the criteria for the disorder as set forth in DSM-III.

A. Gross and sustained impairment in social relationships, e.g., lack of appropriate affective responsivity, inappropriate clinging, asociality, lack of empathy.

B. At least three of the following:
1. sudden excessive anxiety manifested by such symptoms as free-floating anxiety, catastrophic reactions to everyday occurrences, inability to be consoled when upset, unexplained panic attacks.
2. constricted or inappropriate affect, including lack of appropriate fear reactions, unexplained rage reactions, and extreme mood lability.
3. resistance to change in the environment (e.g., upset if dinner time is changed), or insistence on doing things in the same manner every time (e.g., putting on clothes always in the same order).
4. oddities of motor movement, such as peculiar posturing, peculiar hand or finger movements, or walking on tiptoe.
5. abnormalities of speech, such as questionlike melody, monotonous voice.
6. hyper- or hypo-sensitivity to sensory stimuli, e.g., hyperacusis
7. self-mutilation, e.g., biting or hitting self, head banging

C. Onset of the full syndrome after 30 months of age and before 12 years of age.

D. Absence of delusions, hallucinations, incoherence, or marked loosening of associations. (p. 91)

It will be apparent as the reader progresses that the above criteria are discrepant with the clinical description of childhood schizophrenia found in the literature.

Clinical Description

For reasons already apparent there is no simple, single description of this disorder; instead, many definitions have been proposed by various clinicians. Nevertheless, as noted by Goldfarb and his colleagues:

> Whatever the descriptive label, the criteria for the diagnosis of childhood schizophrenia refer to extreme impairments in human relationships, to inadequate perceptual and conceptual responses, to abnormalities of psychomotor behavior and communication, and to unusual preoccupations. These criteria are broad in scope, and the children classified as schizophrenic are highly diversified in the kind and quantity of their defects. Varied as they may be, however, all schizophrenic children show massive gaps in the framework of their personalities and constitute an enormous burden to themselves, their families, and the community at large. (Goldfarb, Mintz, and Strook, 1969, p. 1)

Childhood schizophrenia usually occurs gradually between the second and eleventh year of life. Most clinicians characterize the disorder as an impairment in *interpersonal relations* and in *motor behavior*. Moreover, they specify that it includes disturbances in *intellectual* and *cognitive functioning, affective responses,* and *language*. Table 8–2 summarizes the diagnostic criteria proposed by various investigators that are most widely used in clinical practice today.

The symptom picture varies with the child's developmental level, age of onset, nature of early experiences, and type of defense mechanisms. Yet in almost all instances there is a profound decrease of interest in the external world of people, events, and activities, together with an absorption in oneself and loss of contact with reality. Like Henry, schizophrenic children don't play with toys, and they refuse to look directly at familiar people. In the presence of people some of these children may only glance upwards or sideways, while others may go as far as covering their ears in response to speech (Norman, 1954, 1955). Paradoxically, their usual avoidance of human contact can be suddenly interrupted by physical clinging, as if extreme fearfulness prompted their behavior (Creak, 1961; Goldfarb, 1963; Despert, 1968).

Table 8-2 Diagnostic Criteria of Childhood Schizophrenia

	Potter (1933)	*Bradley and Bowen (1941)*	*Kaufman, Rosenblum, Heims, and Willer (1957)*	*Bender (1947)*	*Creak (1961)*
I. Social and Interpersonal	Retraction of interest from environment.	Seclusiveness, irritability if disturbed. Decrease in number of personal interests; regressed nature of personal interests. Daydreaming.	Special interest and information (object or area) related to child's pathology; denial of human quality of people.	Inability to relate to people or to play materials. Withdrawal (only for early onset).	Gross and sustained impaired emotional relations with others; unawareness of own identity. Pathological preoccupation with objects.
II. Intellectual and Cognitive	Autistic thinking and acting show poor ties with reality.	Daydreaming.	Distorted time and space orientation.	Perceptual problems.	Abnormal perceptual experiences.
III. Language	Decrease of speech—sometimes mutism.		Disturbances in speech structure and content; mutism; asynchrony of verbal content and tone.	Language disturbances.	Language disturbances.
IV. Affect	Defect in emotional rapport; decrease, rigidity and distortion of affect.	Sensitivity to comment and criticism.	Inappropriate affect.	Lack of concern about bodily secretions.	Acute anxiety.
V. Motor	Hyperactivity, immobility, or bizarre, stereotyped, and perseverative behavior.	Bizarre behavior. Physical inactivity.	Bizarre body movements. Repetitive and stereotyped motions; distorted use of body.	Motor awkwardness; continuation of early reflex patterns; postural reflex responses; bodily dependence.	Distortion in mobility.
VI. Physical Development				Disturbances of normal rhythmic patterns. Unevenness in somatic growth. Dysrythmia in EEG. Disturbance in vasovegetative functioning.	

Schizophrenic children have the blank and unexpressive facial stare suggestive of remoteness and inaccessibility. Parents often comment that they cannot "get close" or "make contact." They may show flatness and inappropriateness of affect along with unpredictable mood changes. At times the child may be extremely withdrawn, while at other times he or she may show sudden, uncontrolled anger and assaultiveness toward self or toward those around him or her.

Intellectual and cognitive deficits also have been reported as part of the symptom picture of schizophrenic children. The literature between 1937 and 1965 indicates that at least one-third of these youngsters scored an IQ of below 80 (Pollack, 1967). A more recent study involving 120 schizophrenic boys indicated that as many as half had IQs below 80 (Walker and Birch, 1974). When compared with nonschizophrenic controls, all the studies surveyed reported that the schizophrenic children were significantly inferior in their intellectual performance. Most observers emphasize disturbances in the thought processes of these youngsters, as evidenced by autistic (highly personalized) thinking, incoherence, neologisms, perplexity, perseveration, and somatic delusions. In addition, obsessions, compulsions, and preoccupation with matters of an abstract character and with sexual material are commonly found in schizophrenic children.

Another prominent characteristic of the disorder is a language disturbance, which is sometimes symptomatic of impaired thought processes. Some schizophrenic children are mute, only rarely uttering single words. Those who do possess speech do not use it to communicate. Instead, they repeat words in parrotlike fashion, use words in bizarre sequences, and give them new and highly personalized meanings. The resultant verbalizations have a wooden quality that fails to convey either the child's feelings or his or her thoughts (Goldfarb, Goldfarb, and Scholl, 1966).

Usually schizophrenic children show some disturbances in bladder and/or bowel control as well as in bodily movements and activity level. They may have alternate periods of *hypoactivity* and *hyperactivity*, which are ordinarily purposeless, repetitious, stereotyped, and rhythmic. Bizarre body movements, such as whirling, body rocking, head banging, rigid posturing, choreiform (spasmodic twitching) hand movements, facial grimacing, and excessive masturbation may be present. An interesting example of this is cited by Despert, who described a four-year-old boy having an acute schizophrenic episode.

> ...[he] stated it very clearly when he complained: "I can't be myself, I'm scared I'm not myself." Identified at intervals with a rhinoceros, a dog, a woodpecker, etc., he exhibited neuromuscular patterns of considerable interest, in that they demonstrated the profound personality disorganization. On many occasions this boy, as a rhinoceros, spontaneously performed movements of the mouth muscles (a sort of a snarl) which, anatomically, are impossible in man, and were so unlike the human face that each time they threw the mother into a panic. Everything happened as if, at such times, even the neuromuscular and vegetative systems had regressed to a lower phylogenic level of functioning. The same was true when, as a dog, he uncovered his upper teeth in a pattern that no human feat of mimicry would make possible. Two years later, when his contact with reality was considerably more normal, he recalled the identifications and, at the physician's suggestion, attempted to reproduce the facial expression, but never succeeded. (1968, pp. 133–134)

Several investigators believe that the general clinical picture of childhood schizophrenia is too broad to fit into one diagnostic category, and they have tried instead to identify several specific subgroups. The best known of these are the three subtypes proposed by Bender (1955).

1. The *pseudodefective syndrome* is characteristic of schizophrenic youngsters who appear retarded from birth, or who, during the first three years of life, regress after reaching a higher level of functioning. These children tend to show

high susceptibility to somatic illnesses, inadequate muscle tone (either hyper- or hyposensitive to stimulation), and immature areas of motor behaviors (clinging, whirling, and rocking).

2. The *pseudoneurotic syndrome* occurs during early or middle childhood and is marked by symptoms such as severe anxiety, phobias, obsessions, stereotyped movements, and compulsive activities. Psychosomatic complaints, or concerns about body boundary, body image, and orientation in time and space, are often present. These children may be highly verbal and intellectually bright.
3. The *pseudopsychopathic syndrome* is seen in children of ten years or older who tend to act out antisocially, and who show paranoid ideation, compulsions, aggressive and potentially dangerous behavior, and little evidence of insight, guilt, and anxiety.

Etiological Views

The etiology or etiologies of childhood schizophrenia and the other childhood psychoses are, at present, little understood and highly speculative. In discussing the genetic, biological, and psychogenic positions, it is important to recognize that they are neither mutually exclusive nor as contradictory as some of their ardent supporters would have us believe. In addition, much of what has already been reported for autistic children applies here, since schizophrenic youngsters were included in those studies.

Genetic Considerations. The bulk of human genetic research has focused on schizophrenia in adults. The extent to which these data are applicable to schizophrenia in children hinges on the unanswered question of whether schizophrenia is the same condition for both age groups. The major study of preadolescent schizophrenics found concordance rates of 71 percent for monozygotic twins and 17 percent for dizygotic twins (Kallmann and Roth, 1956). These data compare favorably to those obtained with adult schizophrenics and suggest that genetic factors (as with adults) are implicated in the development of childhood schizophrenia.

Lauretta Bender, an important contributor to the literature on childhood schizophrenia, stresses the interrelatedness of genetic and biological factors. She believes that the disorder is caused by an inherited vulnerability that is activated by physiological crises, such as damage or trauma occurring prenatally, at birth, or in infancy. She considers childhood schizophrenia a neurological disorder with diffuse pathology involving a maturational lag that begins sometime during the embryonic period. The condition is revealed at all levels and areas of integration within the central nervous systems (Bender, 1961).

In a series of studies spanning almost twenty years, Fish (1971) noted irregularities in the rates of development in various areas in infants who were later diagnosed as schizophrenic. She claims that the neurological impairment is not fixed, but that it is evident in the variability of the child's development, leading to the contradictory impression of retardation and precocity. These infants have arousal and attention problems, and often they are abnormally quiet and lethargic when compared to normals who are quite active. They tend to show gastrointestinal disturbances that include spastic constipation, absence of hunger, difficulty in swallowing solid foods, and an inability to suck. The more severe the lag and disruption in development, the greater the impairment of intellectual and social functioning, and the greater the resistance to modification. Fish sees the poorly integrated biological and psychological functions that are under the control of the central nervous system as the underlying disturbance responsible for the disparate behaviors of childhood schizophrenia.

The problem with this sort of genetic hypothesis is that its specific nature is unelaborated. It is a vague and untestable formulation that posits some predisposing inherited factor that is present in a wide variety of children. Moreover, it presumes that vulnerable youngsters will manifest the disorder only if they are exposed to certain damaging experiences. Until the inherited susceptibility is identified by some physical and/or behavioral evidence, this etiological explanation must remain in the realm of supposition. It is interesting to note that attempts to identify genetic vulnerability in adult schizophrenia by studying biochemical substances excreted in the urine have been promising but inconclusive (Pollin, 1971; Wyatt et al., 1973).

Biological Considerations. Ornitz and Ritvo (1968; 1976), among others, believe that a perceptual disturbance is fundamental to schizophrenia and other psychotic disorders in children. They also believe that the basis for perceptual inconsistency in psychotic children involves central nervous system pathology of a specific, but unknown, type. Perceptual difficulties are evident both in the failure of these children to distinguish between themselves and their environment and in their inability to imitate and to modulate sensory input. The problems they have in maintaining body image can be illustrated in the following clinical observations:

> When asked to locate on a picture the finger that had been touched by the examiner, this child, whom I shall call Ann, had to grasp the involved finger with the other hand while looking for its equivalent in the picture. In a similar fashion, many of the schizophrenic children literally had to hold on to and to keep their eyes on the touched finger in order to identify it on the picture: Or . . . After teasing by another child with the taunt "your mother's ass!" she ran to the counselor, pushed her buttocks toward the latter, and cried "take away ass. I don't like ass!" She seemed confused about whether the buttocks belonged to her or her mother. (Goldfarb, 1963, p. 49)

While schizophrenic children do not differ from normal children in sensory acuities on tests of either visual, auditory, or touch thresholds, they do show receptor aberrations in all modalities. For example: "Cathy was observed today cutting paper with scissors. At one point she continued to cut directly into her skin so as to cause bleeding, without expression of pain" (Goldfarb, 1963, p. 50). It is inferred from these findings that the problem is not caused by impairment of peripheral sensory receptors but is reflective of some deficit in the integration of sensory stimuli within the central nervous system. Ornitz and Ritvo (1968, 1976) stress that no specific cause has been found as yet—and perhaps never will be—because the etiology may be heterogeneous, with one common central nervous system pathway.

The work of Goldfarb and his associates at the Henry Ittleson Center in New York suggests that childhood schizophrenia is caused by multiple factors, which range from organic defects in the child to psychosocial inadequacies within the family. Either variable, or some combination of the two, leads to weakened ego boundaries that leave the child without predictable expectancies and environmental referents. Primary anxiety and panic are clinically evident as the child makes a variety of compensatory attempts (often in vain) to find sameness and constancy in the environment (Goldfarb, 1961).

Fairly extensive research over a decade has shown the following:

1. Schizophrenic children fall into two major groups: organic and nonorganic.
2. Families of organic children are more "normal" than are families of nonorganics.
3. The symptoms of the organic child arise from family-child interactions in which the parents stimulate the child too much, too little, or in a confusing way.

A maternal attitude inventory was administered to mothers of psychotic, mongoloid, and normal children who were matched for age, socioeconomic level, and family size. Mothers were told to answer the inventory in terms of children in general, and not with reference to their own offspring. It was found that mothers of mongoloid children are stricter and more regimented than mothers of psychotic or normal children. However, mothers of psychotic youngsters are more indulgent and more uncertain about their behavior than mothers of the other two groups (Pitfield and Oppenheim, 1964). More recent data show that parents of psychotic children are neither emotionally disturbed nor impaired in their thinking (Schopler and Loftin, 1969). Further, a study by Florsheim and Peterfreund (1974) found that parents of psychotic children fall within the normal range of intelligence.

In an effort to obtain specific information about parental practices, parents of neurotic, schizophrenic, asthmatic, and chronically ill children were given the Rorschach, TAT, and MMPI tests. The groups were similar to each other with respect to age of children, age of parents, size of family, socioeconomic status, and educational level. The results were equivocal in that mothers of schizophrenic children, although more isolated, were quite similar to the mothers of neurotic youngsters. Further analysis of the data showed that there is no difference among the groups of mothers in terms of previously identified characteristics often ascribed to mothers of asthmatic and schizophrenic children (Block, 1969).

One of the earliest studies in this area found that the child-rearing attitudes of mothers of brain-damaged, retarded youngsters are more pathological than the attitudes of mothers of either schizophrenic or normal children. While mothers of schizophenics were found to be more pathological than mothers of normals, the data were interpreted to show maternal attitudes that are the *result* of dealing with impaired children instead of the *cause* of their disturbance (Klebanoff, 1959).

More recent research dealing with family communication and behavioral patterns suggests that parents of schizophrenic children communicate with their children as clearly as those of normal youngsters; differences in family discussions are more likely to be a response to the severity of the child's symptoms—not the basis for the schizophrenic reaction itself (Haley, 1968; Zevin, 1973; Bender, 1974).

At present there appears to be an absence of strong evidence showing that parents of schizophrenic children display distinctive child-rearing attitudes, personality traits, or behavioral patterns that cause their children's condition.

Differentiating Infantile Autism from Childhood Schizophenia

The process of systematically distinguishing one condition from another is complex and difficult, primarily because diagnostic categories (especially those of childhood psychoses) overlap considerably. However, differential diagnosis is important in terms of etiological, therapeutic, and prognostic considerations. How can etiological factors be studied and isolated without differentiating among diagnostic groups? How can the uses and limitations of a therapeutic drug such as penicillin be determined if the clinician cannot differentiate among colds, pneumonia, and lung cancer? Without differential diagnosis the early identification of problems and the specific planning for future treatment and management cannot take place.

Current literature does not shed much light on the differences between autism and childhood schizophrenia. Some view schizophrenia broadly and see no meaningful distinction between the two conditions. Others regard autism as a distinguishable subtype of schizophrenia. Rimland is perhaps the strongest American advocate for considering autism as a separate disorder, claiming "that there is sufficient information at hand to demonstrate clearly that early infantile autism is not the same disease or cluster of diseases which has come to be called childhood schizophrenia, and that autism can and should be distinguished from it at all levels of discourse" (1964, p. 68). Recently, Noll and Benedict (1981), after an extensive review of the literature, concluded that autism and childhood schizophrenia are two distinct and separate disorders.

A summary of the various differences noted by Rimland is shown in Table 8–3. Rimland also constructed two checklists to be completed by the child's parents in an effort

Table 8–3 Summary of Characteristics that Differentiate Infantile Autism from Childhood Schizophrenia

Characteristic	*Early Infantile Autism*	*Childhood Schizophrenia*
Onset	Almost from beginning of life.	Between the second and eleventh year of life.
Course	Continue to show early retardation and detachment as adults.	Gradually develop the delusions and hallucinations typical of adult form of schizophrenia.
Physical Appearance and Health	Handsome, well formed, usually of dark complexion, and almost always in good health.	Light complexion with pale and translucent skin. Poor health from birth and neurologically immature.
EEG	Normal.	Abnormal.
Anticipatory Postural Movements	Absent, and when picked up they are stiff and unresponsive.	Present, and inclined to mold and conform to the body or the holder.
Autistic Aloneness	Considered a principal sign.	Not usually evident.
Perseveration of Sameness	Considered a principal sign.	Uncommon.
Hallucinations	Virtually absent.	Both visual and auditory hallucinations are present.
Motor Performance	Both gross movements and finger dexterity are excellent. Twirling and spinning of small objects is evident.	Poor coordination, motor awkwardness, and clumsiness are typical. Twirling and spinning of small objects is evident.
Language Patterns	Indicating affirmation by repetition, absence of words "yes" and "I," delayed echolalia, part-whole confusion, and metaphoric language are typical.	None of these specific language patterns are ordinarily noted.
Special and Unusual Abilities	Extraordinary feats of memory and/or of music or mechanical performance are typically reported.	No reports of special or unusual abilities.
Personal Orientation	Unoriented, detached, aloof, and oblivious to the environment.	Disoriented, confused, and anxious about their relationship and the environment. More accessible than autistic children.
Conditionability	Classical conditioning is difficult to establish.	Classical conditioning occurs easily and rapidly.
Twins	Unusually high number of twins (especially monozygotic) are found.	No high frequency of occurrence in twins has been observed.
Family Backgrounds	Parents are highly educated, significantly above average in intelligence, and have a low divorce rate. There is also a very low incidence of mental illness found in parents and grandparents.	Unstable home backgrounds are frequently noted with a high incidence of mental illness found in these families.

Adapted from Rimland, 1964, pp. 67–76.

to increase the accuracy of differentiation. Recent results involving more than 2,000 psychotic children showed that the diagnoses given by various professionals varied extensively, with as many as ten different diagnoses given per child (Rimland, 1971). In addition, five diagnostic systems used to differentiate autism from schizophrenia (including Rimland's checklist) were compared (DeMyer et al., 1971). Even though the diagnostic criteria used for autism differed from both Kanner's and Rimland's, the results showed that the Rimland checklist achieved the highest correlation. Continued support of the checklist comes from Davids (1975), who found that Rimland's checklist is most effective in discriminating autism from other disorders.

After an extensive review of the literature, Ward (1970) described two distinguishable types of autism: (1) those involving children who lack object relations, insist on sameness, have been disturbed from birth, but are physically healthy; and (2) those involving children with a history of pre- and perinatal difficulties, developmental and perceptual problems, normal families, and regression after a period of normality. Ward suggested that the lack of object relations from birth, the absence of useful speech, and neurological and developmental dysfunction, along with maintenance of sameness, differentiate autism from other disorders.

In contrast, Rutter (1972), and later DSM-III, argued that the term *childhood schizophrenia* should be abandoned and used only for those who evidence the classical symptoms of adult schizophrenia (regardless of age). Rutter suggested that autism is a separate entity: It occurs earlier than and is clearly distinguishable from other psychotic disorders on seven points (which are similar to those noted in Table 8–3).

At this point there should be little doubt that differentiating between autism and childhood schizophrenia depends on (1) the clinician's position concerning the distinctiveness of the two conditions; (2) the criteria employed for diagnostic decisions; (3) the extent to which symptomatology overlaps; and (4) the reliability of the diagnosis, even when the same criteria are applied. To date there is little agreement and uniformity with respect to any of these variables. Until agreement is reached, significant advances in our knowledge cannot occur.

OTHER PSYCHOTIC CONDITIONS OF CHILDHOOD

Apart from Infantile Autism and Childhood Onset Pervasive Developmental Disorder, which have already been described, DSM-III includes a third category, Atypical Pervasive Developmental Disorder. This classification is to be used for children who evidence distortions in the development of psychological functions necessary for the growth of social skills, and who do not meet the criteria for either autism or childhood onset disorder (APA, 1980). This atypical category presumably allows the clinician to diagnose childhood psychosis in forms other than the two major categories without being more specific and without having to identify other distinct psychotic conditions. Yet descriptions of very rare conditions that are regarded as separate entities have appeared in the literature.

Symbiotic Infantile Psychosis

Clinical Description.

> Rachel, a four-year-old, clung desperately to her mother in a manner that forced mother to attend to her needs exclusively. There seemed to be no pleasure that either Rachel or her mother achieved from this closeness because Rachel was rigid and panic-stricken. She reacted to the slightest frustration with piercing screams that kept mother from leading any independent existence. For example, she could not tolerate mother talking to anyone, either in person or on the telephone. (Adapted from Bergman, 1971, pp. 328–331)

Children like Rachel were first described as not evidencing infantile autism but rather as suffering from symbiotic infantile psychosis

(Mahler, 1952). This very rare syndrome is chiefly characterized by symptoms of intense anxiety and panic over mother-child separation. It occurs between the ages of two and a half and five and is usually preceded by a history of normal development. In sharp contrast to the autistic child, who insists on aloneness, the symbiotic child is virtually unable to tolerate even the briefest separation from the mother. At a time when the normal child becomes increasingly aware of his or her own capacities and individuality, the symbiotic child literally clings to the mother with a strong physical attachment to avoid any prospect of separation. The panic reaction of symbiosis may be triggered off by potential threats of separation, such as the birth of a sibling, enrollment in a nursery school, or developmental periods that require increasing independence.

Symbiotic children are incapable of delineating self-boundaries and of seeing themselves as separate and adequate entities. Therefore, they cannot establish relationships with others, apart from their marked interdependent ties to the mother. Their frustration tolerance is so low that minor deviations in routine or mild thwartings throw them into a state of panic. They may have extreme reactions to small failures, as illustrated by the symbiotic child who gave up walking for months because he had tripped and fallen while moving about in his room. When threatened, symbiotic children exhibit panic-stricken agitation and severe temper tantrums that often are followed by bizarre ideas and behavior. These children rarely display curiosity, exploratory behavior, initiative, or normal aggressiveness. In contrast, they tend to present a rather bland and colorless picture of selflessness. Mahler and Furer (1972) have identified a "symbiotic phase" as part of normal development. They point out that the psychotic child has attained a grossly distorted version of this stage and has not reacted to "inherent maturational pressures toward separation from the mother" (1972, p. 216).

As the psychosis persists, other symptoms emerge. The children become withdrawn, seclusive, and disinterested in their surroundings. Their contact with reality gradually weakens. They stay close to the mother and live a very restricted life, mostly confined to the home. Disturbances in their thinking—such as neologisms, incoherence, and bizarre ideas—become evident, and previously acquired toilet, sleep, and eating habits become disrupted. Eventually these secondary symptoms, together with the tendency to insist on sameness in the immediate environment, overlap with the clinical picture of infantile autism. In fact, the two disorders become almost indistinguishable except for the history of an early intimate relationship between mother and infant (Mahler, 1968).

Rachel's history illustrates the typical picture of symbiotic infantile psychosis:

> Mother maintained that Rachel was an easy baby to care for. She sat up at eight months, crawled by ten, and walked at fifteen months. She toilet trained herself by the age of two-and-a-half years. Her difficulties started in the second year of life when she became intensely negativistic and fearful. It was during this time that mother had to be hospitalized and out of the home for several days. When mother returned, Rachel was even more unresponsive than she had been earlier. In addition, Rachel's parents (who had not been getting along) decided to separate for good when she was two-and-a-half years of age.
>
> At the time of the evaluation, mother and daughter lived together apart from father. Mother had given up all normal social relationships, partly because of Rachel's clinging and partly because of mother's tendency to be overly critical of herself and others. By this time Rachel showed a mixture of symbiotic and autistic behaviors. She did not use language for direct communication or put together words in a spontaneous way. Instead, Rachel quoted from books, records, songs, and television commercials. Although she spoke clearly, her voice was lifeless and unmodulated as were her facial expressions and body movements. Even her frequent shrieks seemed to lack emotional participation.

Motor activities were severely restricted in that she walked cautiously with small steps. She didn't run and was unable to climb, swing, throw a ball, or use her hands in any kind of manipulative activity. Most of her movements were confined to either bouncing from foot to foot or jumping and waving her arms.

Rachel showed no interest in toys, except as objects to chew on and hold in her mouth. She spent hours during the day listening to records or looking at some particular book that caught her fancy. She worked strenuously at shutting out the outside world. When unsuccessful, she reacted with anger and fear. For example, if anyone tried to interest her in a new toy, she would ignore it. However, if she were not permitted to ignore the toy, she would knock it down, drop it, or break into loud shrieks. A trip to the shoe store was an ordeal for mother, who could not quiet Rachel's screams. Rachel was afraid of strangers, especially children, of going in cars, and of all sorts of ordinary household appliances. (Adapted from Bergman, 1971, pp. 328–331)

Etiological Views. Virtually no data exist that bear directly on the influence of genetic factors, probably because the disorder is so rare and because it is frequently diagnosed as autism or schizophrenia. Mahler, except for suggesting constitutional vulnerability, makes no specific references to a biological formulation of this disorder. However, it is entirely possible that due to diagnostic confusion, the biological factors described as significant for infantile autism may be applicable here.

Although the evidence is sparse, Mahler and her students have posited that psychogenic factors may be implicated in the etiology of symbiosis. They suggest that the child, in the normal course of development, is initially totally dependent on the mother (or mothering adult) for survival. Soon this phase is followed by a growing realization by the child that he or she is separate from the mother and that he or she has a body of his or her own—a separate self. In symbiotic psychosis this normal process is said to be disturbed either by constitutional vulnerability or by a mother who fosters the totally dependent relationship and discourages any development of independence on the part of the child. The mother may be overprotective and too attentive to the child, or she may be anxiously possessive and intensely jealous of normal contacts between the child and the outer world, or she may unconsciously view the infant as a representation of her "self" (Mahler, 1968).

The key to the psychogenic view of symbiotic psychosis is a pathological mother, who, for a variety of conjectured reasons, prevents the child from breaking previously established mother-infant ties. Other than clinical reports, no research data directly test this thesis. Even if this position were confirmed, it could neither exclude the genetic and/or biological view nor provide evidence to clarify the question of which came first—the neurologically damaged child or the pathological mother.

Blueberry Syndrome

Recently Levinson (1980) described a disorder which he called the Blueberry Syndrome. Similar in some respects to autism, childhood psychosis, and mental retardation, in other respects the syndrome differs from these conditions. The disorder appears after a normal pre- and perinatal period and in the absence of evidence pointing to brain damage or emotional disturbance. The chief symptoms are an inability to speak, a violent reaction to threatening obstacles and frustration, and an aggressive reaction to any invasion of personal space. Mental retardation is present, but it is viewed as secondary to the language problems. These children do not show social retrenchment, excessive anxiety, or insistence on sameness of the environment, and they are said to come from families of low socioeconomic status. Levinson speculates that the syndrome is caused by a genetic mutation affecting speech—as if it were a regression in the evolutionary process to the time when the human had no speech.

Developmental Psychosis

Another proposed disorder, referred to as a Developmental Psychosis, was described by Noll and Benedict (1981) after they reviewed the literature on childhood psychoses. They presented a detailed case history to illustrate the disorder and to amplify the chief symptoms, which include (1) onset before the age of thirty months; (2) a beginning, autisticlike phase manifested by social withdrawal, impaired communication, and bizarre reactions to the environment; (3) the appearance of some expressive language prior to three years of age; (4) a thought disorder emerging between three and five years of age; (5) cognitive functioning that is low average or better; and (6) frequent occurrence of psychopathology in the families of these children. Noll and Benedict believe that differentiating this disorder from autism and childhood schizophrenia would enhance research by allowing more homogeneous groupings of subjects within a diagnostic category.

DIFFERENTIATING CHILDHOOD PSYCHOSIS FROM MENTAL RETARDATION AND ORGANIC BRAIN SYNDROME

In considering the diagnostic possibilities for any of the childhood psychoses, the suspicion of mental retardation is almost always evident. As you may recall, Kanner's initial cases of autism were thought to involve either feebleminded or deaf children. However, he ruled out mental retardation; autistic children usually demonstrate normal to excellent motor development, alertness, a remarkable memory for details in their environment, and special or unusual musical and mechanical talents. Information from case histories and clinical observations are necessary in this regard.

The most obvious sources of information for differentiating psychosis from retardation are tests of intelligence, even though children affected by either condition may obtain equally low IQs. In this event the clinician examines the child's intratest performance as well as the qualitative aspects of the child's responses, looking for clues that would aid in differential diagnosis. For example, most individually administered intelligence scales have their items arranged in ascending order of difficulty. Usually mental retardates correctly complete successive items until they reach their upper limit. Thereafter their answers are incorrect. Thus, they show little variability in performance until such time as repeated failures occur. In contrast, psychotic children are generally more variable in their performance. They may show a pattern of failing some "easy" items along with succeeding on some "very difficult" ones. While the total number of correct items may be the same for both groups, the important difference is in the variability of successes and failures. To the clinician this unevenness in performance is reflective of higher intellectual potential than the total score would indicate. It suggests impairment of current intellectual functioning by factors other than mental retardation.

In addition, the clinician may examine the responses given to each test item in search of qualitative clues that reveal poor contact with reality and disturbances in thinking. These are characteristics ordinarily associated with psychosis, but not with mental retardation. In this regard some clinicians prefer to use projective techniques to further explore the presence or absence of a thought disorder.

Another condition that may closely resemble psychosis in children is neurological impairment. This is especially true in those instances where language is disturbed and where difficulties are evident in gross and fine motor coordination. In addition, stereotyped ritualistic behavior and severe anxiety reaction to changes in the environment are symptoms that are likely to occur in both psychotic and brain-damaged children. Complicating the diagnostic picture is the fact that psychotic children with IQs of less than 80 have patterns resembling brain-damaged children (Walker and Birch, 1974).

In order to make this difficult differential diagnosis, the clinician may use data from psychological tests purporting to measure behaviors that may be impaired as a function of brain damage. However, many of these sensitive areas of functioning, such as perceptual-motor coordination, visual memory, abstract thinking, organizing part-whole relationships, and attention span, are also affected by the restricted abilities of the mental retardate. Since the overall performance may be equally poor for both abnormal conditions, the clinician may look for additional distinguishing clues in the type of errors committed and in the qualitative aspects of the child's responses (see Figure 8–1 and Figure 5–3 on p. 136).

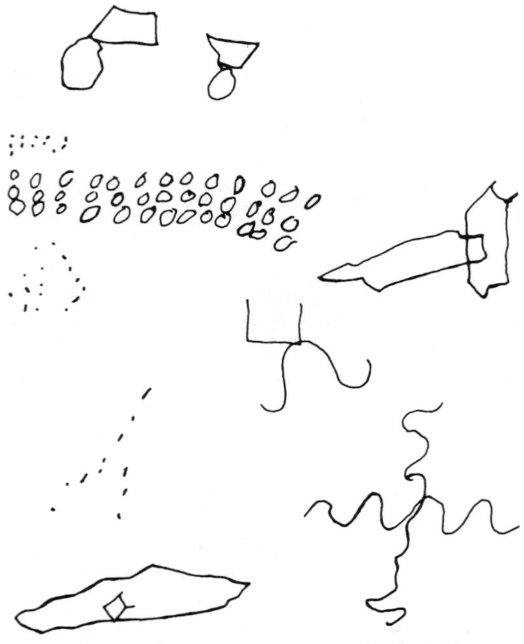
Eight-year-old boy who has a full-scale WISC I.Q. of 112.

FIGURE 8–1 Bender-Gestalt performance of an eight-year-old brain-damaged boy who obtained a full-scale WISC IQ of 112

Additional clues concerning neurological impairment can be obtained from case history materials that may reflect prenatal and birth complications, as well as brain damage from childhood illnesses or accidental injuries. Medical and neurological examinations, including an EEG, can provide further corroborative data. Finally, clinical observations concerning the child's ability and willingness to relate socially is most important in arriving at a differential diagnosis. In most instances psychotic children will show a marked disturbance in their relationship to people, while brain-damaged youngsters ordinarily show normal emotional warmth and social capacity.

INCIDENCE OF CHILDHOOD PSYCHOSES

Considering the general problems of gathering incidence data and the diagnostic confusion associated with childhood psychoses, it should not be surprising that accurate estimates of the frequency of psychosis in children are difficult to come by. A recent report suggests that the incidence of childhood psychoses does not exceed the rate of 6 per 10,000 children (Werry, 1972). However, an accurate breakdown of incidence data for the specific psychotic disorders cannot be reliably obtained at present. Two studies in England found a 4.5 per 10,000 rate of infantile autism in children between the ages of eight and ten (Lotter, 1966; Wing, O'Connor, and Lotter, 1967). However, when the diagnosis was restricted to those children who exhibited only Kanner's two cardinal signs, the incidence rate declined to 2.1 per 10,000 children. On the basis of cases seen over a nineteen-year period, Kanner estimated the incidence of autism as 0.7 per 10,000—a figure that has since been corroborated (Kanner, 1958; Treffert, 1970). After eliminating duplicated cases, these data showed a combined incidence of 3.1 per 10,000 for childhood schizophrenia and autism.

It seems clear from the available estimates

that childhood psychoses occur infrequently, and that the specific psychotic disorders are even rarer. Interestingly, there is consistent evidence of a higher frequency of occurrence of childhood psychosis in boys as compared to girls. Estimates of boy-girl ratios have ranged from approximately 2:1 to slightly higher than 9:1 (Werry, 1972). Although this disproportionate sex distribution is sometimes used to bolster a genetic or biological view of childhood psychosis, there is no substantiated explanation at present for this empirical finding. As a matter of fact, as we shall see repeatedly, for unknown reasons boys typically exceed girls in the frequency of occurrence of most other forms of abnormal behavior.

TREATMENT APPROACHES

Treatment approaches with psychotic children have been numerous and greatly dependent on the etiological position of the therapist. While it is not possible to review all these variations, we shall consider and evaluate a sample of the most widely used or promising procedures under the following broad headings: psychological, education/behavioral milieu, and somatic therapies.

Psychological Therapies

Individual Psychotherapy. Individual psychotherapy is a general term referring to an ongoing interaction between the therapist and the client. However, the nature of the interaction, the techniques used, the goals, the frequency of sessions, and the duration of therapy varies tremendously. Because of this diversity and the difficulty in establishing uniform criteria for improvement, psychotherapy is a formidable treatment method to assess.

Almost all variations of individual psychotherapy have been tried with psychotic children, although the early literature reflected a preference for a psychoanalytic approach. In this context the psychotic child is said to have a severely impaired ego that is either the result of, or further fragmented by, a pathological mother-child relationship. For example, one psychoanalytically oriented therapist suggested that the psychotic child is the victim of gross emotional deprivation from a mother who is very immature, narcissistic, and incapable of emotional relationships (Rank, 1949). This psychodynamic formulation influences both the goal of therapy and the strategy necessary to achieve it. The therapist acts as a mother substitute who, in a totally accepting and loving manner, tries to provide the child with the ego support and emotional gratification that the real mother was unable to give. When the therapist establishes a relationship with the child (a condition that may take several years to accomplish), the therapist turns to the uncovering of traumatic experiences and unconscious conflicts and their resolution. In addition, many clinicians maintain that individual therapy is also necessary for the mother in order to deal with her problems and to help her eventually take over and meet the needs of the child.

Except for anecdotal accounts and clinical case reports, there have been few empirical efforts to evaluate the effectiveness of this approach. In two separate studies no differences were found on any treatment variable between psychotic children who were considered to have either the best or the worst outcome in therapy. Moreover, no differences were found on any treatment variable between psychotic children who were treated with individual psychotherapy for six months and psychotic youngsters who were untreated (Brown, 1960, 1963). In light of these negative results and the great expense involved (both in memory and time), one cannot but wonder whether the gains are sufficient to merit continued clinical confidence in this approach.

Behavior Modification Approaches. At a time when clinicians were discouraged by the failure of individual psychotherapy to dramatically change the behavior of psychotic children, a relatively new and promising approach was introduced. Rooted in basic behavioral research, this approach includes many variations and is known by such diverse labels as behavior modification, behavior therapy, operant conditioning, aversive conditioning, desensitization, and the token economy system.

Although behavior modification had been successfully employed earlier with psychotic adults, Ferster and DeMyer (1962) were among the first to systematically shape the behavior of psychotic children by an operant conditioning procedure in which food was used as reinforcement. Since then reinforcement procedures have been used with psychotic children to increase social responsiveness, eye contact, speech, and imitation in order to facilitate their learning of play, writing, and self-help skills (Hingtgen and Trost, 1966; Blake and Moss, 1967; Lovaas, 1967; Lovaas et al., 1967; Howlin, 1981).

Punishment in the form of electric shock, isolation, and slapping have been used to eliminate unwanted behaviors. Mild electric shock was introduced to decrease a schizophrenic girl's bizarre inattentiveness that was interfering with her academic training (Lovaas et al., 1965). It has also been found to be very effective in controlling the self-mutilative behavior of severely disturbed psychotic children (Lovaas, Schaeffer, and Simmons, 1965). An alternative to the use of punishment for self-mutilators has been reported, in which air splints have been applied to the child's limbs. By controlling the air pressure in the splint, the limbs can be either partially or totally restrained, thus permitting the use of positive reinforcement in shaping new adaptive behaviors (Paul and Romanczyk, 1973).

Tokens acquire reinforcing value through pairings with food. They have been used to train autistic children in school behaviors such as sitting quietly at a desk, identifying objects, answering questions, and matching pictures. More impressive is the finding that children trained this way later were able to transfer these behaviors to a group classroom situation (Martin et al., 1968; Koegel and Rincover, 1974). The success with which parents, teachers, and other caretakers have been trained to carry out operant conditioning procedures has offered hope of providing the child with continued treatment at home or in school (Zimmerman and Zimmerman, 1962; Wolf, Risley, and Mees, 1964; Merbaum, 1973). Using significant laypeople in the therapy of psychotic children provides a continuity and consistency of treatment that increase the likelihood that desirable behaviors learned in therapy will be maintained outside of the treatment setting.

Improvements in the behavior of psychotic children with the behavior modification approach have been impressive, especially in light of the extreme inaccessibility of these children. Without a doubt, this method has brought about dramatic behavioral changes, making these children more manageable in both the home and school environment. It has modified such severely disruptive behaviors as self-mutilation, extreme inattention, lack of eye contact, and refusal to eat with utensils, and it has produced spoken words in children who appeared to be permanently mute.

However, we must inject a critical note. Behavior modification is not the treatment panacea for psychotic children: Treatment effects may be situation specific and reversible, unable to significantly transform the psychotic child into a normal one, or even to change some of the child's impaired functioning to normal levels (Lovaas, Koegel, and Schreibman, 1979; DeMyer et al., 1981). For example, despite the enormous and painstaking efforts involved in increasing the number of words a psychotic child can say, there is no assurance that the gains will lead to the child's using language for communication purposes. In fact, the evidence indicates that with or without operant procedures, improvement in language development rarely brings with it a change from the mechanical and concrete mode of speaking to the spontaneous and communicative one (Rutter, 1968). Within recent years promising reports have described nonverbal language training as a means of improving expressive language in speech-deficient psychotic children (Miller and Miller, 1973; Devilliers and Naughton, 1974; McLean and McLean, 1974).

In 1969 Margaret Creedon began teaching sign language to autistic children with surprising success. The idea has caught on, and now there are scores of programs that use sign language to teach communicative skills to autistic, and even retarded, children (Offir, 1976; Bonvillian, Nelson, and Rhyne, 1981).

Even though the results have been promising, there is no agreement as to why the approach works. Many theorists and researchers of autism have pointed out that a language deficit is at the heart of the disorder. Also, language has been shown repeatedly to be the best predictor of prognosis. There are basically two views: One states that autistic children need all the language cues they can get, and the opposite view claims that these children can only attend to one mode of communication at a time—preferably the visual.

Sign language provides autistic children with a means of interacting with the world. They can request things, ask questions, and even express their feelings. Fulwiler and Fouts (1976) reported on their work with a five-year-old autistic boy. After twenty sessions, not only did he use several signs appropriately, but he also increased his vocal language. These results were observed outside of the training sessions, and he became more attentive and manageable as well.

Although this is only one case (among several), it is an area that is quickly expanding. It is hoped that increased use will prove the effectiveness of sign language in bringing autistic children into contact with the human world.

Enthusiasm for behavior modification is further dampened when we recognize that its therapeutic benefits are lost if they are not constantly reinforced, that the child rarely—if ever—initiates additional changes of his or her own (Pawlicki, 1970). The approach is also limited in that in most cases psychotic children seem to have great difficulties in generalizing what they learned in one situation to new situations. Finally, we must temper our enthusiasm for the use of parents and paraprofessionals as behavioral therapists until such time as their potential and limitations are fully studied.

Special Education/ Behavioral Programs

Great strides in special education/behavioral programs have taken place during the last decade because of the substantial progress made by behavior modifiers and because of the enactment of public law 94–142, which requires public schools to provide appropriate educational programs for all handicapped school-aged children. In fact, this treatment approach at the present time holds the greatest promise for psychotic children and their families. Research has shown that these children can be worked with effectively in small groups rather than, as first thought, only on a one-to-one basis (Rincover and Koegel, 1977). Rincover and Koegel were able to demonstrate that one teacher could gradually shift from teaching one autistic child at a time to handling four children at once. It was also shown in a series of studies that psychotic children made the most progress when the instructional method included structured training which emphasized specific perceptual, motor, and cognitive skills, as compared to either a general regressive therapy approach with no emphasis on development of skills or a permissive classroom setting (Bartak and Rutter, 1973; Rutter and Bartak, 1973). A number of investigators have also shown that teachers can be taught behavioral methods and that the autistic child's school progress is related to the level of training acquired by the teacher (Kozloff, 1973; Marcus et al., 1978; Koegel, Russo, and Rincover, 1977). In the excellent review of the literature by DeMyer and associates (1981), the authors indicated that time out used routinely as a training device has limited value, that generalization is difficult to bring about in autistic children, and that in the last ten years behavioral approaches have produced noticeable improvement in a wide range of behaviors of the psychotic children exposed to these programs.

An illustration of a community-based program of services for autistic children and their parents is the TEACCH program (Treatment and Education of Autistic and Related Communications Handicapped Children) developed by Eric Schopler and Robert Reichler of the University of North Carolina (Reichler and Schopler, 1976; Sloan and Schopler, 1977). The TEACCH program tries to keep the autistic child with his or her parents and within the community, rather than placing the child in an institution. It assumes that autistic children can be educated best in special classes in the public school. The child is evaluated rather extensively, and the findings are discussed with the parents. A contract is made if the child is acceptable to the program and parents agree to place the child in it. Therapists who work with autistic children and their parents typically have no specialized professional training, but they all must have sensitivity and interest in working with this population. Parents also serve as cotherapists in both observing therapy demonstrations and carrying out a home-treatment plan. The treatment program is tailored to the child's needs (for example, eliminating a behavior that is disruptive to learning in the educational program). In addition, the child is placed in self-contained special education classes which include between five and eight children and provide them with individualized developmental programs. While TEACCH offers promise, we must remember that the program is of recent vintage and that its long-range effectiveness has not yet been evaluated (Morgan, 1981).

Milieu Therapy

Perhaps the best-known milieu treatment program for severely disturbed children is the one developed by Bruno Bettelheim at the Orthogenic School in Chicago. Essentially, Bettelheim holds to a psychogenic view of childhood psychosis. According to this view, the hostile rage of the mother severely threatens the child to the point where he or she is afraid to enter into human interactions. Therefore, the child withdraws from the surrounding world. Bettleheim argues that it is necessary to remove the child from the destructive mother-child relationship and place the child in a residential environment designed to satisfy his or her emotional needs. Bettelheim's milieu program includes psychoanalytic therapy (other residential settings may provide somatic and/or behavior therapy), physical and occupational therapy, and a daily life situation that is structured but permissive. Formal school is provided, although the initial emphasis is on nonacademic activities such as caring for animals, drawing, painting, and other simple crafts. In addition to a therapist, the child has a counselor, who is responsible for a small number of children. The counselor, who usually eats with the children, is expected to give support and understanding, to interpret the child's words and actions, and to encourage the child's advances toward ego integration (Bettelheim, 1950).

Bettelheim reported unusually high success with autistic children; of the thirty-nine children he considered, fifteen (48 percent) "rehabilitated," eleven (35 percent) "much improved," and three "somewhat improved." Two showed "no lasting improvement" (Bettelheim, 1966, p. 15). However, his claims are difficult to interpret inasmuch as they were based on "impressions" at the time the children left the Orthogenic School, and inasmuch as the clinical symptoms of these youngsters did not fit Kanner's diagnostic criteria, or even those of researchers who use more inclusive criteria for diagnosing infantile autism.

In evaluating the effectiveness of the Itleson Center's residential program, Goldfarb, Goldfarb, and Pollak (1966) compared thirteen matched pairs of schizophrenic youngsters who were treated either in a day care program or a residential program. While neither treatment program was found to be more effective for organic schizophrenic children, the residential program yielded greater improvement than the day care program for the nonorganics. Milieu therapy provides a full, varied, and extensive treatment plan for these children; and at present it holds the most promise for improving the chances for psychotic children to make future satisfactory adjustments in society. Its greatest limitation is its unavailability in many states as either a public or private facility, and its prohibitive cost when available.

Somatic Therapies

1. Electroconvulsive Shock Treatment (ECT). In 1947 Bender recommended the use of ECT to stimulate the maturation of psychotic children and to reduce their anxiety, making them more amenable to psychotherapeutic intervention (Bender, 1947). She later suggested that ECT promotes some type of reorganization, which results in a more integrated body image (Bender and Keeler, 1952). Follow-up studies of a large number of psychotic children treated with shock claimed that shock produces no intellectual impairment or other adverse effects, and that more than half of the youngsters tested improved socially—especially if they were treated before age seven (Bender, 1960).

A survey of hospital ECT practices found that four of nineteen institutions employed ECT with schizophrenic children (Szurek, Berlin, and Boatman, 1971). Those institutions with the longest and most extensive experience with this treatment used a series of twenty grand mal convulsions, one treatment per day for six days a week.

ECT is a radical treatment that is difficult to evaluate, particularly with regard to its long-term effects. In spite of the favorable results reported by a few clinicians, there is insufficient evidence from well-controlled studies to warrant its unconditional use.

2. Drug Therapies. Drugs are used rather extensively to treat psychotic children or—as some have suggested—to improve the psychotic child's accessibility to stimulation and influence (Eisenberg, 1964; Campbell, Cohen, and Anderson, 1981). It has been stressed recently that drugs in themselves do not eliminate previously learned maladaptive responses, and they do not create new social or personal patterns (Goldfarb, 1970). The use of drugs is rarely sufficient to induce normal behavior, although they may help to reduce symptoms that interfere with the psychotic child's interaction with his or her environment.

Nevertheless, some researchers persist in reporting drug effects in terms of improvement ratings, as if the source of the psychotic disturbance has been ameliorated. Moreover, many studies are inadequately designed or have failed to employ sufficient experimental controls, thus rendering their results difficult to interpret conclusively.

Tranquilizers, antidepressants, megavitamins, and hallucinogenic drugs (LSD) have been used in the treatment of psychotic children. Campbell and her associates (1981) reviewed the literature on pharmacotherapy for autistic children and found that dopamine-blocking psychoactive drugs (for example, the neuroleptics) decrease the symptoms of autism, while dopamine-releasing drugs (stimulants—amphetamines) worsen their condition. Moreover, they report that the less-sedative type of neuroleptics (for example, haloperidol as contrasted to chlorpromazine, the sedative type) are more effective than chlorpromazine in improving the behavior of autistic children. Clinicians have also tried a combination of haloperidol and behavior modification (response-contingent reinforcement) and have found that the combination is better than either treatment alone in improving word imitation in autistic children.

Megavitamin therapy has been proposed as a treatment for psychotic children, but in the main, the results have been negative. Niacinamide and vitamin B_6 have been studied separately. However, the studies showed either no positive gains or invalid results because of seriously flawed designs (DeMyer et al., 1981).

Bender (1966) began giving LSD and UML-491 (a derivative of LSD) to autistic children in 1961 and reported that these children did not show the expected psychotomimetic effects; but they did show heightened mood and responsivity, increased awareness, and a lessening of stereotypic behavior. After six weeks of treatment with either LSD or UML, all the autistic children improved in IQ, schoolwork, motivation, and affect, and they manifested fewer signs of a thought disorder. A review and comparison of seven studies in which psychedelic agents were used with autistic children noted that the studies had not been controlled for the psychedelic agent used, dosage level, frequency, demographic variables, specific disorder, duration, or severity of symptoms (Mogar and Aldrich, 1969). However, in all these studies and in a recent one, similar results were obtained that showed improvement in speech, more interaction with people, and less ritualistic behavior (Simmons, Benor, and Daniel, 1972). Mogar and Aldrich concluded that the effects of LSD are only transient, and that psychotherapy must accompany the use of LSD to effect long-term changes. They also emphasized the fact that follow-up studies must be done to further evaluate the effectiveness of the drug.

As so concisely summarized by DeMyer and colleagues (1981):

> . . . of the drugs studied, nonsedating antipsychotics seemed to offer the most promise, whereas stimulants were usually found to cause great disorganization. Mixed results have been obtained with vitamins, thyroid hormone, and psychedelics. Biogenic amine precursors have not been found to be therapeutic. Antidepressants and lithium may be useful in treatment of specific symptoms; when any of the agents are used, the benefits must be carefully weighed against potential side effects, especially in the pediatric population with its potential for prolonged exposure. (p. 420)

Furthermore, Werry (1981) makes the assessment that pharmacotherapy is not an effective treatment for any of the childhood psychoses, although some antipsychotic (less sedative) drugs have helped in the management of autistic children.

3. Sensory Deprivation. Interesting but scant findings are available at present concerning the use of isolation or sensory deprivation in the treatment of autistic children. Three male autistic children were isolated in a room containing only a mattress and sheet and illuminated by a twenty-five-watt bulb (Schechter et al., 1969). The room temperature was controlled and constant, and meals were brought in. The therapist visited the child two times a day for ten to fifteen minutes, and observations were made every two hours through a window. The authors found that all the boys became increasingly alert to noise, although they were earlier thought to be deaf; further, they engaged in eye contact with the therapist, ate well, seemed happy, and did not try to leave the room when the door was open. At the end of the isolation period (forty, sixty-eight, and seventy-four days) all the boys ran to their parents, sat in their laps, and held them. Follow-up studies of these children (twelve to twenty-four months later) found them to be attending nursery school and living at home as tolerable members of the family.

Isolation therapy is based on the rationale that the autistic child requires sensory reduction because he or she is impaired neurologically in such a way that the child is overwhelmed by incoming stimuli. Considerably more careful research is necessary before the effectiveness and the usefulness of this approach can be determined.

4. Jogging. America's lively interest in jogging and physical fitness finally made its way to autistic children. As if the virtues of jogging need extolling, Kern and colleagues (1982) demonstrated that jogging was effective in reducing self-stimulating behaviors and in increasing appropriate play and academic responses in seven autistic children.

SUMMARY

The area of childhood psychoses that subsumes infantile autism, childhood schizophrenia, and other psychoses is characterized by confusion and controversy. There are divergent views as to whether these are separable conditions and as to the symptomatology included within each category. There is even greater disagreement among clinicians with respect to the diagnostic criteria used to differentiate one disorder from another. In practice these categories are often used interchangeably and inconsistently, so that data with regard to incidence, family characteristics, etiological factors, and treatment effects are imprecise and difficult to interpret.

In general, childhood psychoses occur infrequently (from 2 to 5 per 10,000, under fifteen years of age), and the specific psychotic disorders in children are even more rare (approximately 1 per 10,000 for infantile autism if Kanner's primary diagnostic criteria are used). There is consistent evidence of a higher incidence of childhood psychoses in boys as compared to girls, in a ratio of about 3:1 to 4:1. The clinical description, along with specific diagnostic signs emphasized by various writers; the associated characteristics of the disorder; and the etiological views were presented. Psychogenic factors, once viewed as influential and potent, do not seem to account for the disorder, while biological ones—albeit nonspecific at present—tend to be regarded as the most likely cause.

DSM-III has deleted Childhood Schizophrenia as a diagnostic category, preferring to include Childhood Onset Pervasive Developmental Disorder, which reflects the criteria frequently used by clinicians to classify childhood schizophrenia. DSM-III also suggests that schizophrenia is the same disorder for children and adults, and that, therefore, this category should be used when appropriate for all ages. Nevertheless, we discussed childhood schizophrenia so that past and current trends in the literature could be examined. Through the years childhood schizophrenia has been the central focus of study and the principal classification category of psychoses in children. Other psychotic conditions of childhood (Atypical Pervasive Developmental Disorders, Symbiotic Infantile Psychosis), and new disorders (the Blueberry Syndrome and Developmental Psychosis) were described and discussed. Table 8–4 summarizes the primary characteristics of the clinical picture for infantile autism, childhood schizophrenia, and symbiotic infantile psychosis.

Infantile autism is differentiated from childhood schizophrenia on the basis of age of onset and with reference to Kanner's two primary signs—autistic aloneness and the insistence on sameness in the environment. In addition, autistic children manifest special and unusual abilities, good memory, good motor coordination, and normal EEG patterns, whereas schizophrenic children do not show these characteristics. Features differentiating psychotic disorders from mental retardation and organic brain syndrome were also discussed. Symbiotic psychosis is differentiated from other psychotic conditions by an early and primary panic reaction to the threat of separation from the mother. Secondary symptoms of symbiosis appear as the psychosis progresses, and these are almost indistinguishable from autism. Mentally retarded youngsters typically show no intratest variability on tests of intelligence, but they are apt to be warm and responsive to human interactions, in contrast to psychotic children. Performance on tests purporting to measure behaviors that are often impaired as a function of brain damage, along with medical and neurological data, may be helpful in differentiating brain-damaged children from psychotic and mentally retarded youngsters.

Genetic, biological, and psychogenic views concerning the etiology of childhood schizo-

Table 8-4 Summary of the Clinical Picture of the Three Childhood Psychoses

Clinical Picture	*Infantile Autism*	*Childhood Schizophrenia*	*Symbiotic Infantile Psychosis*
Onset	Gradual from birth.	Gradual between the ages of two and eleven, after period of normal developopment.	Between two-and-a-half to five years after normal devel-development.
Social and Interpersonal	Failure to show anticipatory postural movements; extreme aloneness; insistence on sameness.	Decreased interest in external world, withdrawal, loss of contact, impaired relations with others.	Unable to tolerate briefest separation from mother; clinging and incapable of delineating self.
Intellectual and Cognitive	High spatial ability; good memory; low IQ but good intellectual potential.	Thought disturbance; perceptual problems; distorted time and space orientation; below average IQ.	Bizarre ideation; loss of contact; thought disturbance.
Language	Disturbances in speech; mutism, and if speech is present, it is not used for communication. Very literal; delayed echolalia; pronoun reversal, "I" and "Yes" are absent until age six.	Disturbances in speech; mutism, and if speech is present, it is not used for communication.	
Affect	Inaccessible and emotionally unresponsive to humans.	Defect in emotional responsiveness and rapport; decreased, distorted, and/or inappropriate affect.	Severe anxiety and panic over separation from mother; low frustration tolerance; withdrawn and seclusive as psychosis persists.
Motor	Head banging and body rocking; remarkable agility and dexterity; preoccupied with mechanical objects.	Bizarre body movements; repetitive and stereotyped motions; motor awkwardness; distortion in mobility.	
Physical and Developmental Patterns	Peculiar eating habits and food preferences; normal EEG.	Unevenness of somatic growth; disturbances of normal rhythmic patterns; abnormal EEG.	Disturbed normal rhythmic patterns.
Family	Aloof, obsessive, and emotionally cold; high intelligence and high educational and occupational levels; low divorce rate and low incidence of mental illness.	High incidence of mental illness.	Pathological mother who fosters the symbiosis.

phrenia and the other psychoses of childhood were also discussed, although there is undoubtedly some overlap with the etiology of infantile autism, since there is considerable diagnostic confusion and imprecision. While the data for any particular etiological position are incomplete and inconclusive, mounting evidence and support implicate neurological factors in the development of psychoses in children.

Almost every form of treatment has been tried with psychotic children, including individual psychotherapy, behavior therapy, milieu therapy, electroconvulsive shock treatment, drug therapy, and sensory deprivation; but no treatment approach has been successful in bringing about major improvements in any significant number of psychotic children. Behavior modification approaches have been extremely promising and useful in altering or controlling behaviors, thus making psychotic youngsters much more manageable at home and in school. However, they have generally not been successful in transforming the psychotic child into a normal one. In general, the prognosis for psychotic youngsters is poor, although the evidence suggests that those who have language and show some improvement before age five have a more favorable outlook than those who are mute and who show no signs of early improvement.

EPILOGUE

The diagnosis of childhood schizophrenia, confirmed by separate additional evaluations by a psychiatrist and a neurologist, was poorly received by the family, especially by the father. Primarily because of the father's reluctance and the fact that he had ample financial resources, Henry was taken for a lengthy series of examinations to centers out of the state. The results were usually the same, but the father persisted for more than eighteen months in the hope that he would hear better news and that he would locate someone who would miraculously restore his son to normality. Finally, the father accepted more readily the recommendations made by the local professionals.

Behavior modification helped in toilet training and in increasing Henry's vocabulary, although it did not improve significantly his use of language for communication. He was enrolled in a special day-school program that not only gave his family a much-needed respite during the day but also provided him with continued language, motor, and social training. Socialization gradually occurred in the sense that he was more readily managed, he began to acknowledge the presence of others, and he learned more acceptable eating and personal hygiene habits. While Henry changed in the course of two years, his parents steadfastly refused therapy for themselves to help them deal with their feelings. At this point Henry is easier to manage in school and at home, and he is more pleasant to be around. He likes painting as well as cutting out and pasting pictures in an album; also, he is beginning to learn how to write his name.

REFERENCES

Abassi, V., Linscheid, T., and Coleman, M. Triiodothyronine (T_3) Concentration and Therapy in Autistic Children. *Journal of Autism and Childhood Schizophrenia*, 1978, *8*, 383–387.

Allen, J., DeMyer, M. K., Norton, J. A., Pontius, W., and Yang, E. Intellectuality in Parents of Psychotic, Subnormal, and Normal Children. *Journal of Autism and Childhood Schizophrenia*, 1971, *1*, 311–326.

American Psychiatric Association. *DSM-II: Diagnostic and Statistical Manual of Mental Disorders*, 2nd ed. Washington, D.C.: The American Psychiatric Association, 1968.

American Psychiatric Association. *DSM-III: Diagnostic and Statistical Manual of Mental Disorders*, 3rd ed. Washington, D.C.: The American Psychiatric Association, 1980.

Baltaxe, C. A. Pragmatic Deficits in the Language of Autistic Adolescents. *Journal of Pediatric Psychology*, 1977, *2*, 176–180.

Bartak, L., and Rutter, M. Special Educational Treatment of Autistic Children: A Comparative Study—I. Design of Study and Characteristics of Units. *Journal of Child Psychology and Psychiatry*, 1973, *14*, 161–179.

Belmaker, R. H., Hattab, J., and Ebstein, R. P. Plasma Dopamine-Beta-Hydroxylase in Childhood Psychosis. *Journal of Autism and Childhood Schizophrenia*, 1978, *8*, 293–298.

Bender, L. *Instructions for the Use of Visual Motor Gestalt Test*. New York: The American Orthopsychiatric Association, 1946.

Bender, L. One Hundred Cases of Childhood Schizophrenia Treated with Electric Shock. *Transaction of the American Neurological Association,* 1947, 72, 165–169.

BENDER, L. Twenty Years of Clinical Research on Schizophrenic Children with Special Reference to Those Under Six Years of Age. In G. Caplan (ed.), *Emotional Problems of Early Childhood.* New York: Basic Books, 1955, pp. 503–515.

BENDER, L. Autism in Children with Mental Deficiency. *American Journal of Mental Deficiency,* 1959, 64, 81–86.

BENDER, L. Treatment in Early Schizophrenia. *Progress in Psychotherapy,* 1960, 5, 177–184.

BENDER, L. The Brain and Child Behavior. *Archives of General Psychiatry,* 1961, 4, 531–547.

BENDER, L. D-Lysergic Acid in the Treatment of the Biological Features of Childhood Schizophrenia. *Diseases of the Nervous System,* 1966 (Suppl. 7), 27, 43–46.

BENDER, L. The Family Patterns of 100 Schizophrenic Children Observed at Bellevue, 1935–1952. *Journal of Autism and Childhood Schizophrenia,* 1974, 4, 279–292.

BENDER, L., and FARETRA, G. The Relationship Between Childhood Schizophrenia and Adult Schizophrenia. In A. R. Kaplan (ed.), *Genetic Factors in "Schizophrenia,"* Springfield, Ill.: Chas. C Thomas, 1972, pp. 28–64.

BENDER, L., FREEDMAN, A. M., GRUGETT, A. E., JR., and HELME, W. M. Schizophrenia in Childhood: A Confirmation of the Diagnosis. *Transaction of the American Neurological Association,* 1952, 77, 67–73.

BENDER, L., and KEELER, W. R. The Body Image of Schizophrenic Children Following Electroshock Therapy. *American Journal of Orthopsychiatry,* 1952, 22, 335–355.

BENNETT, S., and KLEIN, H. R. Childhood Schizophrenia: Thirty Years Later. *American Journal of Psychiatry,* 1966, 122, 1121–1124.

BERGMAN, A. I and You: The Separation-Individuation Process in the Treatment of a Symbiotic-Psychotic Child. In J. B. McDevitt and C. F. Settlage (eds.), *Separation-Individuation: Essays in Honor of Margaret S. Mahler.* New York; International Universities Press, 1971, pp. 328–331.

BERGMAN, P., and ESCALONA, S. K. Unusual Sensitivities in Very Young Children. In *Psychoanalytic Study of the Child,* Vols. III–IV. New York: International Universities Press, 1949, pp. 333–352.

BETTELHEIM, B. *Love Is Not Enough.* New York: Free Press, 1950.

BETTELHEIM, B. *The Empty Fortress.* New York: Macmillan, 1966.

BLACKSTOCK, E. G. Cerebral Asymmetry and the Development of Early Infantile Autism. *Journal of Autism and Childhood Schizophrenia,* 1978, 8, 339–353.

BLAKE, P., and MOSS, T. The Development of Socialization Skills in an Electively Mute Child. *Behavior Research and Therapy,* 1967, 5, 349–356.

BLOCK, J. Parents of Schizophrenic, Neurotic, Asthmatic, and Congenitally Ill Children. *Archieves of General Psychiatry,* 1969, 20, 659–674.

BONVILLIAN, J. D., NELSON, K. E., and RHYNE, J. M. Sign Language and Autism. *Journal of Autism and Developmental Disorders,* 1981, 11, 125–137.

BOUILLIN, D. J., BHAGAVAN, H. N., O'BRIEN, R. A., and YOUDIM, M. B. H. Platelet Monoamine Oxidase in Children with Infantile Autism. In M. Coleman, (ed.), *The Autistic Syndromes.* Amsterdam, Holland: North-Holland Publishing Company, 1976, pp. 51–63.

BOUILLIN, D. J., COLEMAN, M., O'BRIEN, R. A., and RIMLAND, B. Laboratory Predictions of Infantile Autism Based on 5-Hydroxytryptamine Efflux from Blood Platelets and Their Correlations with the Rimland E-2 Score. *Journal of Autism and Childhood Schizophrenia,* 1971, 1, 63–71.

BRADLEY, C., and BOWEN, M. Behavior Characteristics of Schizophrenic Children. *Psychiatric Quarterly,* 1941, 15, 296–315.

BROOKER, A. E., and MARETH, T. R. Infantile Autism: Clinical Features, Diagnosis, Etiology, and Prognosis —A Research Review. *Psychological Reports,* 1982, 50, 587–592.

BROWN, J. L. Prognosis from Presenting Symptoms of Preschool Children with Atypical Development. *American Journal of Orthopsychiatry,* 1960, 30, 382–390.

BROWN, J. L. Follow-up of Children with Atypical Development (Infantile Psychosis). *American Journal of Orthopsychiatry,* 1963, 33, 855–861.

CAMPBELL, M., COHEN, I. L., and ANDERSON, L. T. Pharmacotherapy for Autistic Children: A Summary of Research. *Canadian Journal of Psychiatry,* 1981, 26, 265–273.

CAMPBELL, M., HARDESTY, A. S., and BURDOCK, E. I. Demographic and Perinatal Profile of 105 Autistic Children: A Preliminary Report. *Psychopharmacology Bulletin,* 1978, 14, 36–39.

CANTOR, S., EVANS, J., PEARCE, J., and PEZZOT-PEARCE, T. Childhood Schizophrenia: Present But Not Accounted For. *American Journal of Psychiatry,* 1982, 139, 758–762.

CHESS, S. Follow-up Report on Autism in Congenital Rubella. *Journal of Autism and Childhood Schizophrenia,* 1977, 7, 69–81.

COLEMAN, M. Serotonin and Central Nervous Syndromes of Childhood: A Review. *Journal of Autism and Childhood Schizophrenia,* 1973, 3, 27–35.

COLEMAN, M. Studies of the Autistic Syndromes. In R. Katzman (ed.), *Congenital and Acquired Cognitive Disorders.* Research publication of the Association for Research in Nervous and Mental Disease, 1979, Vol. 57, pp. 265–275.

COX, A., RUTTER, M., NEWMAN, S., and BARTAK, L. A Comparative Study of Infantile Autism and Specific Developmental Receptive Language Disorder: II. Parental Characteristics. *British Journal of Psychiatry,* 1975, 126, 146–159.

CREAK, M. Schizophrenia Syndrome in Childhood. Progress Report of a Working Party. *British Medical Journal,* 1961, 2, 889–890.

DAVIDS, A. Childhood Psychosis: The Problem of Differential Diagnosis. *Journal of Autism and Childhood Schizophrenia,* 1975, 5, 129–138.

DeLong, G. R. A Neuropsychologic Interpretation of Infantile Autism. In M. Rutter and E. Schopler (eds.), *Autism: A Reappraisal of Concepts and Treatment.* New York, Plenum Press, 1978, pp. 207–228.

DeMyer, M. K. *Parents and Children in Autism.* Washington, D.C.: Victor H. Winston & Sons, 1979.

DeMyer, M. K., Barton, S., DeMyer, W. E., Norton, J. A., Allen, J., and Steele, R. Prognosis in Autism: A Follow-up Study. *Journal of Autism and Childhood Schizophrenia,* 1973, *3,* 199–246.

DeMyer, M. K., Churchill, D. W., Pontius, W., and Gilkey, K. M. A Comparison of Five Diagnostic Systems for Childhood Schizophrenia and Infantile Autism. *Journal of Autism and Childhood Schizophrenia,* 1971, *1,* 175–189.

DeMyer, M. K., Hingtgen, J. N., and Jackson, R. K. Infantile Autism Reviewed: A Decade of Research. *Schizophrenia Bulletin,* 1981, *7,* 388–451.

DeMyer, M. K., Pontius, W., Norton, J., Baron, S., Allen, J., and Steele, R. Parental Practices and Innate Activity in Normal, Autistic, and Brain Damaged Infants. *Journal of Autism and Childhood Schizophrenia,* 1972, *2,* 49–66.

DesLauriers, A. N., and Carlson, C. F. *Your Child Is Asleep.* Homewood, Ill.: Dorsey Press, 1969.

Despert, J. L. Schizophrenia in Children. *Psychiatric Quarterly,* 1938, *12,* 365–371.

Despert, J. L. *Schizophrenia in Children:* Collected Papers, 1st ed. New York: Brunner/Mazel, 1968.

DeVilliers, J. G., and Naughton, J. M. Teaching a Symbol Language to Autistic Children. *Journal of Consulting and Clinical Psychology,* 1974, *42,* 111–117.

Deykin, E. Y., and MacMahon, B. The Incidence of Seizures among Children with Autistic Symptoms. *American Journal of Psychiatry,* 1979, *136,* 1310–1312.

Eisenberg, L., and Kanner, L. Early Infantile Autism, 1943–1955. *American Journal of Orthopsychiatry,* 1956, *26,* 556–566.

Eisenberg, L. The Autistic Child in Adolescence. *American Journal of Psychiatry,* 1956, *112,* 607–612.

Eisenberg, L. Role of Drugs in Treating Disturbed Children. *Children,* 1964, *11,* 167–173.

Eisenberg, L. Psychiatric Disorders of Childhood, 42.1. Psychotic Disorder. I: Clinical Features. In A. M. Freedman, and H. I. Kaplan (eds.), *Comprehensive Textbook of Psychiatry.* Baltimore, Md.: Williams and Wilkins, 1967, pp. 1433–1438.

Ferster, C. B., and DeMyer, M. K. A Method for the Experimental Analysis of the Behavior of Autistic Children. *American Journal of Orthopsychiatry,* 1962, *32,* 89–98.

Fish, B. Contributions of Developmental Research to a Theory of Schizophrenia. In J. Hellmuth (ed.), *Exceptional Infants: Studies in Abnormalities,* Vol. 2. New York: Brunner/Mazel, 1971, pp. 473–482.

Florsheim, J., and Peterfreund, O., The Intelligence of Parents of Psychotic Children. *Journal of Autism and Childhood Schizophrenia,* 1974, *4,* 61–70.

Folstein, S., and Rutter, M. Genetic Influences and Infantile Autism. In S. Chess and A. Thomas (eds.), *Annual Progress in Child Psychiatry and Child Development.* New York: Brunner/Mazel, 1978, pp. 437–441.

Fulwiler, R. L., and Fouts, R. S. Acquisition of American Sign Language by a Non-communicating Autistic Child. *Journal of Autism and Childhood Schizophrenia,* 1976, *6,* 43–51.

Gillberg, C. Maternal Age and Infantile Autism. *Journal of Autism and Developmental Disorders,* 1980, *10,* 293–297.

Goldfarb, W. *Childhood Schizophrenia.* Cambridge, Mass.: Harvard University Press, 1961.

Goldfarb, W. Self-awareness in Schizophrenia Children. *Archives of General Psychiatry,* 1963, *8,* 47–60.

Goldfarb, W. Childhood Psychoses. In P. H. Mussen (ed.), *Carmichael's Manual of Child Psychology,* Vol. 2. New York: John Wiley, 1970, pp. 765–830.

Goldfarb, W. The Causes and Treatment of Childhood Schizophrenia. From *Program Reports of NIMH: The Mental Health of the Child,* 1971, pp. 293–301.

Goldfarb, W., Goldfarb, N., and Scholl, H. The Speech of Mothers of Schizophrenic Children. *American Journal of Psychiatry,* 1966, *122,* 1220–1227.

Goldfarb, W., Goldfarb, N., and Pollak, R. A. Treatment of Childhood Schizophrenia: A Three Year Comparison of Day and Residential Treatment. *Archives of General Psychiatry,* 1966, *14,* 119–128.

Goldfarb, W., Mintz, I., and Strook, K. *A Time to Heal.* New York: International Universities Press, 1969.

Greenfeld, J. *A Child Called Noah.* New York: Holt, Rinehart and Winston, 1972.

Group for the Advancement of Psychiatry, Committee on Child Psychiatry. *Psychopathological Disorders in Childhood: Theoretical Considerations and a Proposed Classification.* GAP report No. 62, June, 1966.

Gubbay, S. S., Lobascher, M., and Kingerlee, P. A Neurological Appraisal of Autistic Children: Results of a Western Australian Survey. *Developmental Medicine and Child Neurology,* 1970, *12,* 422–429.

Haley, J. Testing Parental Instructions to Schizophrenic and Normal Children: A Pilot Study. *Journal of Abnormal Psychology,* 1968, *73,* 559–565.

Harper, J., and Williams, S. Infantile autism: The incidence of national groups in a New South Wales survey. *The Medical Journal of Australia,* 1976, *1,* 299–301.

Hauser, S. L., DeLong, G. R., and Rosman, N. P. Pneumographic Findings in the Infantile Autism Syndrome. A correlation with Temporal Lobe Disease. *Brain,* 1975, *98,* 667–688.

Hermelin, B., and O'Connor, N. *Psychological Experiments with Autistic Children.* New York: Pergamon Press, 1970.

Hier, D. E., LeMay, M., and Rosenberger, P. B. Autism and Unfavorable Left-Right Asymmetries of the Brain. *Journal of Autism and Childhood Schizophrenia,* 1979, *9,* 153–159.

Hier, D. B., LeMay, M., and Rosenberger, P. B. Autism: Association with Reversed Cerebral Asymmetry. *Neurology,* 1978, *28,* 348–349.

Hingtgen, J. N., and Trost, F. C., Jr. Shaping Cooperative Responses in Early Childhood Schizophrenics: II.

Reinforcement of Mutual Contact and Vocal Responses. In R. Ulrich, T. Statchnick, and J. Mabry (eds.), *Control of Human Behavior* (vol. 1). Glenview, Ill.: Scott, Foresman, 1966, pp. 110–113.

HOWLIN, P. A. The Effectiveness of Operant Language Training with Autistic Children. *Journal of Autism and Developmental Disorders*, 1981, *11*, 89–105.

HUTT, S. J., and HUTT C. (eds.). *Behavior Studies in Psychiatry*. New York: Pergamon Press, 1970.

JAMES, A. L., and BARRY, R. J. A Review of Psychophysiology in Early Onset Psychosis. *Schizophrenia Bulletin*, 1980, *6*, 506–525.

JUDD, L., and MANDELL, A., Chromosome Studies in Early Infantile Autism. *Archives of General Psychiatry*, 1968, *18*, 450–457.

KALLMANN, F. J., and ROTH, B. Genetic Aspects of Preadolescent Schizophrenia. *American Journal of Psychiatry*, 1956, *112*, 599–606.

KANNER, L. Autistic Disturbances of Affective Contact. *Nervous Child*, 1943, *2*, 217–250.

KANNER, L. Problems of Nosology and Psychodynamics of Early Infantile Autism. *American Journal of Orthopsychiatry*, 1949, *19*, 416–426.

KANNER, L. To What Extent Is Early Infantile Autism Determined by Constitutional Inadequacies? *Association for Research on Nervous and Mental Diseases*, Proceedings, 1954, *33*, 378–385.

KANNER, L. The Specificity of Early Infantile Autism. *Zeitschrift fur Kinderpsychiatrie*, 1958, *25*, 108–113.

KANNER, L. *Child Psychiatry*, 4th ed. Springfield, Ill.: Chas. C Thomas, 1972.

KANNER, L., and LESSER, L. I. Early Infantile Autism. *Pediatric Clinics of North America*, 1958, *5*, 711–730.

KAUFMAN, I., ROSENBLUM, E., HEIMS, L., and WILLER, L. Childhood Psychosis: I. Childhood Schizophrenia: Treatment of Children and Parents. *American Journal of Orthopsychiatry*, 1957, *27*, 683–690.

KERN, L., KOEGEL, R. L., DYER, K., BLEW, P., and FENTON, L. The Effect of Physical Exercise on Self-Stimulation and Appropriate Responding in Autistic Children. *Journal of Autism and Developmental Disorders*, 1982, *12*, 399–419.

KLEBANOFF, L. B. Parental Attitudes of Mothers of Schizophrenic, Brain Injured and Retarded and Normal Children. *American Journal of Orthopsychiatry*, 1959, *29*, 445–454.

KNOBLOCH, H., and PASAMANICK, B. Some Etiologic and Prognostic Factors in Early Infantile Autism and Psychosis. *Pediatrics*, 1975, *55*, 182–191.

KOEGEL, R. L., and RINCOVER, A. Treatment of Psychotic Children in a Classroom Environment: I. Learning in a Large Group. *Journal of Applied Behavior Analysis*, 1974, *7*, 45–59.

KOEGEL, R. L., RUSSO, D. C., and RINCOVER, A. Assessing and Training Teachers in the Generalized Use of Behavior Modification with Autistic Children. *Journal of Applied Behavioral Analysis*, 1977, *10*, 197–205.

KOLVIN, I., OUNSTED, C., and ROTH, M. Studies in the Childhood Psychoses: V. Cerebral Dysfunction and Childhood Psychoses. *British Journal of Psychiatry*, 1971, *118*, 407–414.

KOZLOFF, M. A. *Reaching The Autistic Child: A Parent Training Program*. Champaign, Ill.: Research Press, 1973.

KUGELMASS, I. N. *The Autistic Child*, Springfield, Ill.: Chas. C Thomas, 1970.

LANDGREBE, A. R., and LANDGREBE, M. A., Urinary Catecholamine Screening in Autistic Children. In M. Coleman (ed.), *The Autistic Syndromes*, Amsterdam, Holland; North-Holland Publishing Co., 1976, pp. 65–72.

LEVINSON, B. M. The Blueberry Syndrome. *Psychological Reports*, 1980, *46*, 47–52.

LOTTER, V. Epidemiology of Autistic Conditions in Young Children. *Social Psychiatry*, 1966, *1*, 124–137.

LOTTER, V. Epidemiology of Autistic Conditions in Young Children. II. Some Characteristics of the Parents and Children. *Social Psychology*, 1967, *1*, 163–173.

LOTTER, V. Factors Related to Outcome in Autistic Children. *Journal of Autism and Childhood Schizophrenia*, 1974, *4*, 263–277.

LOVAAS, O. I. A Behavior Therapy Approach to the Treatment of Childhood Schizophrenia. In J. P. Hill (ed.), *Minnesota Symposium on Child Psychology*, Vol. I. Minneapolis: University of Minnesota Free Press, 1967, pp. 108–159.

LOVAAS, O. I., FREITAG, G., GOLD, V. I., and KASSORLA, I. C., Experimental Studies in Childhood Schizophrenia: Analysis of Self-Destructive Behavior. *Journal of Experimental Child Psychology*, 1965, *2*, 67–84.

LOVAAS, O. I., FREITAS, L., NELSON. K., and WHALEN, C. The Establishment of Imitation and Its Use for the Development of Complex Behavior in Schizophrenic Children. *Behavior Research and Therapy*, 1967, *5*, 171–181.

LOVAAS, O. I., KOEGEL, R. L., and SCHREIBMAN, L. Stimulus Overselectivity in Autism: A Review of Research. *Psychological Bulletin*, 1979, *86*, 1236–1254.

LOVAAS, O. I., SCHAEFFER, B., and SIMMONS, J. Q. Building Social Behavior in Autistic Children by Use of Electric Shock. *Journal of Experimental Research in Personality*, 1965, *1*, 99–109.

LOWE, L. H. Families of Children with Early Childhood Schizophrenia. *Archives of General Psychiatry*, 1966, *14*, 26–30.

MAHLER, M. S. On Child Psychosis and Schizophrenia: Autistic and Symbiotic Infantile Psychosis. *Psychoanalytic Study of the Child*, 1952, *7*, 286–305.

MAHLER, M. S. *On Human Symbiosis and the Vicissitudes of Individuation, Vol. I: Infantile Psychosis*. New York: International Universities Press, 1968.

MAHLER, M., and FURER, M. Child Psychosis: A Theoretical Statement and Its Implications. *Journal of Autism and Childhood Schizophrenia*, 1972, *2*, 213–218.

MARCUS, L. M., LANSING, M., ANDREWS, C. E., and SCHOPLER, E. Improvement of Teaching Effectiveness in

Parents of Autistic Children. *Journal of the American Academy of Child Psychiatry*, 1978, *17*, 625–639.

MARTIN, G. L., ENGLAND, G., KAPROWY, E., KILGOUR, K., and Pilek, V. Operant Conditioning of Kindergarten Class Behavior in Autistic Children. *Behavior Research and Therapy*, 1968, *6*, 281–294.

MCDERMOTT, J. F., HARRISON, S. I., SCHRAGER, J., LINDY, J., and KILLENS, E. K. Social Class and Mental Illness in Children: The Question of Childhood Psychosis. *American Journal of Orthopsychiatry*, 1967, *37*, 548–557.

MCLEAN, L. P., and MCLEAN, J. E., A Language Training Program for Nonverbal Autistic Children. *Journal of Speech and Hearing Disorders*, 1974, *39*, 186–193.

MERBAUM, M. The Modification of Self-destructive Behavior by a Mother-Therapist Using Aversive Stimulation." *Behavior Therapy*, 1973, *4*, 442–447.

MEYERS, D. I., and GOLDFARB, W. Studies of Perplexity in Mothers of Schizophrenic Children. *American Journal of Orthopsychiatry*, 1961, *31*, 551–564.

MILLER, A., and MILLER, E. E., Cognitive Developmental Training with Elevated Boards and Sign Language. *Journal of Autism and Childhood Schizophrenia*, 1973, *3*, 65–85.

MOGAR, R. E., and ALDRICH, R. W. The Use of Psychedelic Agents with Autistic-Schizophrenic Children. *Behavioral Neuropsychiatry*, 1969, *1*, 44–50.

MORGAN, S. B. *The Unreachable Child.* Memphis, Tenn.: Memphis State University Press, 1981.

NOLL, R. B., and BENEDICT, H. Differentiations Within the Classification of Childhood Psychoses: A Continuing Dilemma. *Merrill-Palmer Quarterly*, 1981, *27*, 175–195.

NORMAN, E. Reality Relationships of Schizophrenic Children. *British Journal of Medical Psychology*, 1954, *27*, 126–141.

NORMAN, E. Affect and Withdrawal of Schizophrenic Children. *British Journal of Medical Psychology*, 1955, *28*, 1–18.

OFFIR, C. W. Visual Speech—Their Fingers Do the Talking. *Psychology Today*, 1976, *10*, 72–78.

O'MOORE, M. A Study of the Aetiology of Autism from a Study of Birth and Family Characteristics. *Journal of the Irish Medical Association*, 1972, *65*, 114–120.

ORNITZ, E. M. Neurophysiologic Studies. In W. Rutter and E. Schopler (eds.), *Autism: A Reappraisal of Concepts and Treatment.* New York: Plenum, 1978, 117–139.

ORNITZ, E. M., GUTHRIE, D., and FARLEY, A. H. The Early Development of Autistic Children. *Journal of Autism and Childhood Schizophrenia*, 1977, *7*, 207–229.

ORNITZ, E. M., and RITVO, E. R. Perceptual Inconstancy in Early Infantile Autism: The Syndrome of Early Infantile Autism and Its Variants, Including Certain Cases of Childhood Schizophrenia. *Archives of General Psychiatry*, 1968, *18*, 76–98.

ORNITZ, E. M., and RITVO, E. The Syndrome of Autism: A Critical Review. *American Journal of Psychiatry*, 1976, *133*, 609–621.

ORNITZ, E. M., and RITVO, E. The Syndrome of Autism: A Critical Review. In S. Chess and A. Thomas (eds.), *Annual Progress in Child Psychiatry and Child Development.* New York: Brunner/Mazel, 1977, pp. 501–530.

PAUL, H. A., and ROMANCZYK, R. G. Use of Air Splints in the Treatment of Self-injurious Behavior. *Behavior Therapy*, 1973, *4*, 320–321.

PAWLICKI, R. Behaviour-Therapy Research with Children: A Critical Review. *Canadian Journal of Behavioural Science*, 1970, *2*, 163–173.

PITFIELD, M., and OPPENHEIM, A. N. Child-Rearing Attitudes of Mothers of Psychotic Children. *Journal of Child Psychology and Psychiatry*, 1964, *5*, 51–57.

POLLACK, M. Mental Subnormality and "Childhood Schizophrenia." In J. Zubin, and G. A. Jervis (eds.), *Psychopathology of Mental Development.* New York: Grune and Stratton, 1967, pp. 460–471.

POLLIN, W. A Possible Genetic Factor Related to Psychosis. *American Journal of Psychiatry*, 1971, *128*, 311–317.

POTTER, H. W. Schizophrenia in Children. *American Journal of Psychiatry*, 1933, *12*, 1253–1270.

PRIOR, M. R., and BRADSHAW, J. L. Hemisphere Functioning in Autistic Children. *Cortex*, 1979, *15*, 73–81.

PRIOR, M. R. Cognitive Abilities and Disabilities in Infantile Autism: A Review. *Journal of Abnormal Child Psychology*, 1979, *7*, 357–380.

PRIOR, M., PERRY, D., and GAJZAGO, C. Kanner's Syndrome or Early-Onset Psychosis: A Taxonomic Analysis of 142 Cases. *Journal of Autism and Childhood Schizophrenia*, 1975, *5*, 71–80.

RANK, B. Adaptation of the Psychoanalytic Technique in the Treatment of Young Children with Atypical Development. *American Journal of Orthopsychiatry*, 1949, *19*, 130–139.

REICHLER, R. J., and SCHOPLER, E. Developmental Therapy: A Program Model for Providing Individualized Services in the Community. In E. Schopler and R. J. Reichler (eds.), *Psychopathology and Child Development.* New York: Plenum, 1976, pp. 347–372.

RICKS, D. M., and WING, L. Language, Communication, and the Use of Symbols in Normal and Autistic Children. *Journal of Autism and Childhood Schizophrenia*, 1975, *5*, 191–221.

RIMLAND, B. *Infantile Autism.* New York: Appleton-Century-Crofts, 1964.

RIMLAND, B. On the Objective Diagnosis of Infantile Autism. *Acta Paedopsychiatrica*, 1968, *35*, 146–161.

RIMLAND, B. The Differentiation of Childhood Psychoses: An Analysis of Checklists for 2218 Psychotic Children. *Journal of Autism and Childhood Schizophrenia*, 1971, *1*, 161–174.

RINCOVER, A., and KOEGEL, R. L. Classroom Treatment of Autistic Children: II. Individualized Instruction in a Group. *Journal of Abnormal Child Psychology*, 1977, *5*, 113–126.

RITVO, E., and FREEMAN, B. J. National Society for Autistic Children Definition of the Syndrome of Autism. *Journal of Autism and Childhood Schizophrenia*, 1978, *8*, 162–169.

RITVO, E. R., RABIN, K., YUWILER, A., FREEMAN, B. J., and GELLER, E. Biochemical and Hematologic Studies: A Critical Review. In M. Rutter and E. Schopler (eds.), *Autism: A Reappraisal of Concepts and Treatments.* New York: Plenum Press, 1978, pp. 163–183.

ROTMAN, A., CAPLAN, R., and SZEKELY, G. A. Platelet Uptake of Serotonin in Psychotic Children. *Psychopharmacology,* 1980, *67,* 245–248.

ROUTTENBERG, A. The Two Arousal Hypothesis: Reticular Formation and Limbic System. *Psychological Review,* 1968, *75,* 51–80.

RUTTER, M. Concepts of Autism: A Review of Research. *Journal of Child Psychology and Psychiatry,* 1968, *9,* 1–25.

RUTTER, M. Childhood Schizophrenia Reconsidered. *Journal of Autism and Childhood Schizophrenia,* 1972, *2,* 315–337.

RUTTER, M. Diagnosis and Definition of Childhood Autism. *Journal of Autism and Childhood Schizophrenia,* 1978, *8,* 139–161.

RUTTER, M. Language Disorder and Infantile Autism. In M. Rutter and E. Schopler (eds.), *Autism: A Reappraisal of Concepts and Treatment.* New York: Plenum, 1978, pp. 85–104.

RUTTER, M., and BARTAK, L. Special Educational Treatment of Autistic Children: A Comparative Study. II. Follow-up Findings and Implications for Services. *Journal of Child Psychology and Psychiatry,* 1973, *14,* 241–270.

RUTTER, M., and LOCKYER, L. A Five to Fifteen Year Follow-up Study of Infantile Psychosis—I. Description of Sample. *British Journal of Psychiatry,* 1967, *113,* 1169–1182.

SCHECHTER, M. D., SHURLEY, J. T., TOUSSIENG, P. W., and MAIER, W. J. Sensory Isolation Therapy of Autistic Children: A Preliminary Report. *Journal of Pediatrics,* 1969, *74,* 564–569.

SCHOPLER, E. Early Infantile Autism and Receptor Processes. *Archives of General Psychiatry,* 1965, *13,* 327–335.

SCHOPLER, E. Childhood Psychosis—Etiology and Autopsy. *Schizophrenia Bulletin,* 1976, *2,* 194–195.

SCHOPLER, E., and LOFTIN, J. Thought Disorders in Parents of Psychotic Children: A Function of Test Anxiety. *Archives of General Psychiatry,* 1969, *20,* 174–181.

SHAPIRO, T., and HUEBNER, H. F. Speech Patterns of Five Psychotic Children Now in Adolescence. *Journal of the American Academy of Child Psychiatry,* 1976, *15,* 278–293.

SIMMONS, J. Q., BENOR, D., and DANIEL, D. The Variable Effects of LSD-25 on the Behavior of a Heterogeneous Group of Childhood Schizophrenics. *Behavioral Neuropsychiatry,* 1972, *4,* 10–16.

SINGER, M., and WYNNE, L. C. Differentiating Characteristics of Parents of Childhood Schizophrenics, Childhood Neurotics, and Young Adult Schizophrenics. *American Journal of Psychiatry,* 1963, *120,* 234–243.

SLOAN, J. L., and SCHOPLER, E. Some Thoughts about Developing Programs for Autistic Adolescents. *Journal of Pediatric Psychology,* 1977, *2,* 187–190.

SZUREK, S. A., BERLIN, I. N., and BOATMAN, M. J. *Inpatient Care of the Psychotic Child.* Palo Alto, Calif.: Science and Behavior Books, 1971.

TREFFERT, D. A. Epidemiology of Infantile Autism. *Archives of General Psychiatry,* 1970, *22,* 431–438.

TSAI, L. Y., and STEWART, M. A. Handedness and EEG Correlation in Autistic Children. *Biological Psychiatry,* 1982, *17,* 595–598.

WALKER, H., and BIRCH, H. G. Intellectual Patterning in Schizophrenic Children. *Journal of Autism and Childhood Schizophrenia,* 1974, *4,* 143–161.

WARD, A. Early Infantile Autism: Diagnosis, Etiology, and Treatment. *Psychological Bulletin,* 1970, *73,* 350–362.

WERRY, J. S. Childhood Psychosis. In H. D. Quay, and J. S. Werry (eds.), *Psychopathological Disorders of Childhood.* New York: John Wiley, 1972, pp. 83–121.

WERRY, J. S. The Childhood Psychoses. In G. D. Burrows and J. S. Werry (eds.), *Advances in Human Psychopharmacology,* Vol. 2. Greenwich, Conn.: Jai Press, 1981, pp. 245–263.

WING, L. Epidemiology and Theories of Aetiology. In L. Wing (ed.), *Early Childhood Autism,* 2nd ed. New York: Pergamon Press, 1976, pp. 65–92.

WING, J. K., O'CONNOR, N., and LOTTER, V. Autistic Conditions in Childhood: A Survey in Middlesex. *British Medical Journal,* 1967, *3,* 389–392.

WING, L. The Handicaps of Autistic Children: A Comparative Study. *Journal of Child Psychology and Psychiatry,* 1969, *10,* 1–40.

WOLF, M. M., RISLEY, T. R., and MEES, H. L. Application of Operant Conditioning Procedures to the Behavior Problems of an Autistic Child. *Behavior Research and Therapy,* 1964, *1,* 304–312.

WYATT, R. J., MURPHY, D. L., BELLMAKER, R., COHEN, S., DONNELLY, C. H., and POLLIN, W. Reduced Monoamine Oxidase Activity in Platelets: A Possible Genetic Marker for Vulnerability to Schizophrenia. *Science,* 1973, *170,* 916–918.

YOUNG, J. G., COHEN, D. J., BROWN, S. L., and CAPARULO, B. K. Decreased Urinary Free Catecholamines in Childhood Autism. *Journal of the American Academy of Child Psychiatry,* 1978, *17,* 671–678.

YOUNG, J. G., KYPRIE, R. M., ROSS, N. T., and COHEN, D. J. Serum Dopamine-Beta-Hydroxylase Activity: Clinical Applications in Child Psychiatry. *Journal of Autism and Developmental Disorders,* 1980, *10,* 1–14.

ZEVIN, B. Family Communication with Schizophrenic and Nonschizophrenic Siblings. *Proceedings of the 81st Annual Convention of the American Psychology Association, Montreal, Canada,* 1973, *8,* 471–772.

ZIMMERMAN, E., and ZIMMERMAN, J. The Alteration of Behavior in a Special Classroom Situation. *Journal of Experimental Analysis of Behavior,* 1962, *5,* 59–60.

Part 4 CLINICAL SYNDROMES OF MIDDLE CHILDHOOD

9

ABNORMALITIES OF MIDDLE CHILDHOOD

Brain Damage, the Epilepsies, and Language Disorders

PROLOGUE

Terry is a tall, muscular, well-built, and handsome eight-year-old boy who was admitted to the psychiatric unit of a general hospital in the Southeast because of an unusual, annoying sensation of pressure in his ears and head. He also seemed unable to concentrate in school or at home, often losing sight of what he was doing. He would repeat irrelevant movements and tasks such as picking at his ear or rapping a pencil on a table. He felt foggy, as if he had cobwebs in his head, and his memory seemed to be impaired. Terry's parents noted that he slept a great deal, and at other times he was listless, drowsy, and lacking in the energy that characterized his previously hectic pace. His orientation toward time was also impaired; he confused recent events with those that happened in the distant past, and vice versa. Moreover, his parents thought they noticed a change in his personality: The once easygoing, happy, patient, and alert boy was now easily irritated, frustrated, impatient, despondent, and very lethargic.

All these symptoms were noticed for approximately five days following an accident in which he fell off a bicycle and hit his head on the asphalt pavement as he landed. At that time he was taken to the emergency room of the hospital, given a neurological examination, X-rays of the head, and an EEG, all of which were negative. He was kept there for several hours and then sent home. His only symptoms were superficial scalp abrasions and a headache. He was told to rest the next day and to gradually resume his normal activities if he felt all right.

Terry is two years older than his brother. His father is a CPA who is tense, irritable, demanding, and punitive to his wife and sons when he drinks, which occurs every weekend. His mother is self-sacrificing, hovering, and overly protective of the boys, but angry, complaining, and quite distant from her husband. They have been married ten years, after a courtship of about one year. They both report that they enjoyed a happy and good marriage for the first two years. Then the father began to drink more and more; it is not uncommon for him to be drunk and stay drunk for at least two days each weekend. He is, however, a good provider. He has high achievement needs and expectations for his sons, his wife, and himself, which often are difficult—if not impossible—to attain.

In the hospital Terry admitted that he hates his father because he mistreats everyone in the family when he drinks. He reported violent fantasies of killing his father, and he alluded to thoughts of protecting his mother from his father's abuses. At the same time, he claimed strong emotional ties to his father, who apparently enjoys some sort of a positive relationship with his sons when sober. Terry confessed to the psychologist, with tears and much apprehension, that on the afternoon of his recent accident, he had gone to visit his bachelor uncle (father's older brother), who persuaded Terry to remove his trousers and underpants. He then fondled Terry's genitals and sodomized the boy. Terry said that he did not know why he permitted the uncle these sexual favors, that it never had happened before, and that it had since troubled him a great deal. In fact, he said that he was so preoccupied with and guilty about this incident that he couldn't think straight, that he was afraid of what his parents might do to him, and that he slept a great deal to keep from thinking about it.

During this hospitalization Terry was given another neurological examination and an EEG. This time the EEG was abnormal, indicating that he must have suffered from a concussion and a posttraumatic organic state.

Terry's story illustrates quite dramatically that symptoms of abnormal behaviors can arise from dissimilar causes, and that the contributions of biological and psychological factors, or some combination of the two, must be carefully considered and assessed in all cases. The facts about Terry may appear obvious and simple, but determining the impact of one set of causal factors on personality change and psychopathology is quite complex and difficult. More specifically, does the positive neurological finding in his case nullify the potential impact of his psychological trauma in producing his symptoms? If we hadn't looked for or had not known about both his bicycle accident and his traumatic experience with his uncle, wouldn't either set of causes have made equally effective explanations for his odd behaviors?

The period of childhood, ranging from age five through preadolescence, is truly a time of remarkable growth—especially in the child's emotional, cognitive, and social functioning. It is also a time of transition for both parents and child, when the world is expanded from the secure and familiar confines of the home to new situations and relationships. Parents transfer some of their child-rearing responsibilities to the school, and to a lesser extent, to other community agencies. At the same time children are called upon regularly to acquire new skills and behaviors in order to meet the demands of a more complex environment.

The role of the school in the child's cognitive and social development cannot be overemphasized. For example, the enthusiasm of the normal child who eagerly looks forward to school may be quickly dampened and transformed to aversion by a hostile and rejecting teacher, or by a humiliating event that results in prolonged peer criticism and alienation, or by some out-of-school event such as Terry experienced. It may also be too confining for those youngsters who are unaccustomed to the sedentary and highly structured demands of the usual classroom setting. Without a sensitive teacher and a flexible school program, many children may experience a disproportionate share of both negative attention and academic failures. These, in turn, almost always lead to self-doubt and feelings of inadequacy. The school's emphasis on academic achievement and competition is communicated early to students, who recognize it and easily decipher the all-too-familiar code names given to groups of fast, intermediate, and slow learners (redbirds, bluebirds, and yellowbirds). At best these conditions can serve to increase motivation and reward for those who are capable of succeeding, while they can heighten anxiety and failure for those who are not. Repeated failures to achieve often result in poor motivation, avoidance of academics, withdrawal and daydreaming, and/or acting-out behaviors which are designed to replace the ego gratification and positive support that are denied these youngsters. In addition, events that occur outside of the school, such as illness or death of a parent, marital discord, disruptions in family and/or peer relations, and social disappointments, may be sufficiently stressful to impede academic progress and personal adjustment. Obviously, the attitudes, values, and stimulation within the home, along with neighborhood peer relationships and participation in a variety of other outside activities, also affect the development of the child.

As in Terry's case, the extent to which children successfully adapt during the school years depends not only on the impact of environmental factors but also on the influence of many biological conditions—and on the interaction of these two major forces. For a considerable period of time the field downplayed the importance of biological variables—particularly brain functions—while it focused on the processes of development and learning and on the impact of environmental factors in molding the child (Ross, 1976). However, it is now recognized that behavior is mediated through the brain and that almost any form of abnormal behavior can stem from brain dysfunction (Harth, 1983). It is clear at this time that there is no single brain disorder—neurological factors are implicated as likely etiological explanations for many forms of childhood psychopathology.

In this chapter we shall discuss a number of disorders whose etiology has been tied—either directly or indirectly—to some sort of neuropathology, and whose symptoms tend to surface most often during the middle years. We shall present past and contemporary theories of brain function, consider the term *brain damage* as well as the causes of this condition, and then cover *the epilepsies and language disorders*. Our discussion of *minimal brain dysfunction, learning disabilities,* and the *hyperkinetic syndrome* will follow in Chapter 10.

THEORIES OF BRAIN FUNCTION[1]

As noted in Chapter 1, Hippocrates and other early Greeks believed that the fluid in the ventricles of the brain governed thought and intellect and that variations in the fluids accounted for differences in and aberrations of personality. Somewhat later the Romans stressed the role of the tissue structures (the solid portions) of the brain. However, their ideas were largely ignored because they did not coincide with the more popular and widely held Greek position. In the 1800s Gall proposed a view of the brain which was the

[1]Much of this section is based on a chapter by C. J. Golden, and G. N. Wilkening, Neuropsychological Basis of Exceptionality. In R. Brown and C. Reynolds (eds.), *Psychological Perspectives on Childhood Exceptionality*. New York: John Wiley, in press.

precursor to the doctrine of localization of specific function. He suggested that the brain was comprised of many individual organs (regarded now as specific cortical areas) which have specific psychological functions (such as reading, talking, friendliness, and so forth), and for which organ size reflected the degree of skill one had in a given area. The idea that every area of the brain has a specific function which is independent from skills represented in other areas of the brain met with resistance and opposition from the scientific community in general, and from one investigator (by the name of Flourens) in particular (Luria, 1980). Flourens carried out a series of experiments in which he removed selective parts of the brains of chickens and pigeons to test Gall's claims. He failed to find evidence to support Gall's localization view, but he did find that the amount of tissue excised was positively related to the extent of impairment. On the basis of this work, Florens proposed an alternative view, which was the forerunner of the equipotential theory of brain function. He suggested that all areas of the brain are equal with regard to its functions and that it is not where (the location) an injury occurs but how much tissue is damaged (the size) that determines the effects of brain injury. Lashley (1929), whose equipotential explanation of brain functioning is well-known, elaborated this view. In fact, both this notion and the opposing one of localization of specific function have dominated the thinking of American psychologists with regard to brain-behavior relationships for many years.

Nevertheless, the failure of both these theoretical positions to adequately explain the clinical and research findings has led to the search for a more viable approach. One well-articulated and highly respected view was offered by Luria, a leading Russian neuropsychologist (Luria, 1973; Golden, 1981). Luria introduced the concept of *functional system* to brain function—(an analogy to other systems of the human body, such as the digestive system)—to suggest that voluntary human behavior is not exclusively governed by a particular area of the brain; rather, in order to produce such a behavior, each area of the brain must function in a systematic way with other areas of the brain. Thus, a functional system of the brain (rather than specific areas) is responsible for a given behavior. Luria also posited *alternative functional systems* to allow for the production of the given behavior by more than one functional system and to describe the organism's ways of enhancing recovery either by substituting the use of lower skills for higher skills, or vice versa, or by changing the nature of the task in an effort to change where in the brain the information is processed. On the basis of physiological and psychological data, Luria allocated specific functions to each brain area. He further suggested that each area shares in the responsibility of one or more functional systems. In his provocative book, Golden (1981) argues that Luria's theory accounts for the current data; and he offers an exciting and illuminating approach to the understanding and the remediation of abnormal behaviors caused by neuropathology. For a more detailed and extensive description of the theory and of its clinical implications for childhood psychopathology, the reader is referred to Luria (1973, 1980).

BRAIN DAMAGE

The term *brain damage* is used frequently in both the clinical and the research literatures as if it referred to a single homogeneous condition. However, it may refer to a variety of disorders, such as cerebral palsy, epilepsy, encephalitis, hydrocephalus, and so forth. It may also refer to different areas and amounts of brain tissue affected and—especially in the case of children—to differences in the age at which the damage occurs (Diller and Birch, 1964; McFie, 1975; Black, 1981). We also know that the symptoms and behavioral characteristics frequently attributed to brain-damaged children—such as attention problems, hyperactivity, intense anxiety perseveration, and emotional lability—over-lap with other forms of psychopathology which have no demonstrable neurological impairment (Berko, Berko, and Thompson, 1970). Consequently, one must be aware that the clinical and/or research groupings of children under the label "brain damage" imply considerable heterogeneity and render the findings low in reliability and poor in validity.

Etiological Factors

Throughout one's lifetime—and even from conception—the possibilities of brain damage are numerous. Nevertheless, the greatest danger seems to occur from conception through the first five years of life.

Prenatal Risks. Much of what happens to the growing fetus during the nine-month gestation period is highly related to variables associated with the mother, on whom the fetus is totally dependent. Animal and human research have shown that maternal malnutrition can decrease the size and number of brain cells in the newborn rat and the rate of myelinization of its nerve fibers, as well as the weight and general health of newborn babies (Winick, 1969; Winick and Rosso, 1975; Benton et al., 1966; Suskind, 1977). However, it should be noted that research on the brain development of newborn babies has shown little evidence for the sort of specific effects noted in animals. Perhaps this is because the malnutrition experienced by mothers in our society is not as great as that experimentally introduced to rodents.

Inherited blood incompatability between mother and fetus, such as Rh positive blood in the fetus (inherited from father) carried by a mother who is negative for the Rh factor, can result in the destruction of red blood cells. The toxic materials produced from this destruction can damage the brain of the fetus. Drugs taken by the mother during pregnancy are likely to cross the placenta and, at times, affect the fetus more than the mother. For example, in the early 1960s a drug known as thalidomide (a sedative) produced severe birth defects and malformations of the offspring when taken by women during the course of their pregnancies. Addictive drugs such as morphine, heroin, and alcohol used excessively by pregnant women can lead to birth defects, premature births, withdrawal symptoms, and drug dependence for the newborn (Abel, 1980). Exposure of expectant women to irradiation, as in X-rays or in the extreme case of nuclear exposure (years ago at Hiroshima), can result in fetal malformation and mental retardation. In addition, infectious diseases transmitted from the mother to the fetus, such as rubella (German measles), mumps, and syphilis can produce malformations and mental retardation in the newborn. There is even some indication that maternal stress is associated with complications of delivery and an increased incidence of children born with congenital abnormalities. This is because heightened emotions tend to increase the secretion of certain hormones in the mother's blood which are transmitted to the fetus through the placenta. Finally, there is an increased risk of infant deaths, defects, and complications during pregnancy and at delivery for babies born to mothers who are either below the age of twenty or older than thirty-five (Walters, 1975; Zarfas and Wolf, 1979). Table 9–1 summarizes these and other prenatal factors and their effects on the newborn.

Perinatal Risks. The greatest risk to the infant during the birth process is deprivation of oxygen, or anoxia, which usually severely affects the lower centers of the brain and the motor functioning controlled by these centers (Towbin, 1981). Cerebral palsy is a major syndrome that results from such damage to the lower centers of the brain. It is an umbrella term used to categorize several types of impaired motor functioning caused by early brain damage of this sort. But, inasmuch as the damage does not involve the thinking portion or system of the brain, intelligence is not usually reduced or impaired in children with this disorder. Anoxia can occur during the

Table 9-1 Prenatal Risk Factors and Their Effects on the Newborn[a]

Prenatal Factors	*Effects*
Inadequate maternal diet	Reduction in growth of brain, below average birth weight, decrease in birth length, rickets
Endocrine disorders	Cretinism, microcephaly
Irradiation	Physical deformities and mental retardation
Rubella	Blindness, deafness, heart abnormalities, stillbirth
Syphilis	Mental retardation, physical deformities, miscarriage
Addictive Drugs	Low birth weight, addiction of infant, possible death after birth from withdrawal
Smoking (tobacco)	Prematurity, low birth weight and length
Alcohol	Mental retardation, below average birth weight
Tetracycline	Discoloration of teeth
Quinine	Deafness
Barbituates	Congenital malformations
DES (diethystilbestrol)	Increased incidence of vaginal cancer in adolescent girls whose mothers were given DES during pregnancy to prevent miscarriage; impaired reproductive performance for these girls
Age of mother—less than 18	Prematurity and stillbirth, increased incidence of Down's syndrome
Age of mother—more than 35	Increased incidence of Down's syndrome

[a]Adapted from J. A. Schickedanz, D. I. Schickedanz, and P. D. Forsyth, *Toward Understanding Children.* Boston: Little, Brown, 1982, p. 95.

birth process because of forced and difficult passage of the fetus through the birth canal, breech delivery, forceps delivery, or the toxic and unfavorable effects of anesthesia used in delivery. The severity of anoxic damage to the brain in the newborn is governed by the intensity and duration of the perinatal complications causing the anoxia (Towbin, 1981). In addition to the anoxic effects on the lower centers of the brain (deep cerebral damage), cortical damage may occur in the mature fetus and newborn as a result of circulatory failure. This type of damage often produces mental retardation, epilepsy, and behavioral disorders or less severe problems such as reading disabilities and tics. Towbin (1981) states that the recovery process is affected by the size and severity of the injury (that is, mild and diffuse injuries are more favorable than severe and focal ones); by the reaction and recoverability of the tissue surrounding the injury; by the structural changes that occur (for example, the sprouting of axons into areas which are deprived of normal synaptic input); and by the reorganization and replacement of function by other areas of the brain following the injury. According to McFie (1975), perinatal lesions in an infant (up to one year old) may show no specific damage inasmuch as transfer of function between the hemispheres of the brain may still occur. If the lesion is unilateral and there is clinical evidence of the damage, it is likely to be located in an area where the same effect would be evidenced in an adult.

Postnatal Risks. Unfortunately, the postnatal period also carries risks of brain damage. Head injuries, most frequently caused by automobile accidents and child abuse, can result in brain damage. The ingestion of toxic materials such as lead-based paints, certain cleaning liquids and their fumes, insecticides and other chemicals, as well as drugs that are kept in most households may well result in brain pathology (Robinson and Robinson, 1976). Diseases such as encephalitis and meningitis, tumors that directly involve the brain, and/or illnesses that are associated with high fever may set off convulsive seizures and result in brain damage as well.

Carter and Gold (1974) described the most important symptoms and signs in diagnosing a neurological disease in infancy and childhood: (1) problems of feeding, vomiting, or complaints of acute abdominal pain; (2) delay of developmental milestones involving speech, motor abilities, and social-adaptive behaviors; (3) an abnormally large head; (4) disturbances of motor functioning, including muscle weakness, unsteady and slow movements, abnormal involuntary movements, slow movements, and sustained muscle spasms of the extremities, trunk, and neck; (5) sensory disturbances; (6) impaired and peculiar visual patterns; and (7) disorders of eye movement, such as nystagmus, strabismus, and diplopia. Other signs include hearing loss, speech problems, changes in personality that are usually sudden and inexplicable, academic problems in youngsters of high ability, convulsions, dizzy spells, vertigo, fainting spells and coma, asymmetry of the face, and a noticeable head tilt.

Both the short- and long-term effects of brain injury are influenced greatly by the age of the child when the injury occurs (Rutter, Graham, and Yule, 1970). In fact, the newborn is more vulnerable to brain damage than older children, although this is offset to a degree by the greater plasticity found in the infant's brain, which allows the transfer of functions from one hemisphere to the other in the event of unilateral damage or in special instances of localized bilateral damage. However, it has also been found that size of the lesion adversely affects this plasticity of the young brain. In general, the larger the lesion (or damage), the greater the impairment and the poorer the prognosis.

THE EPILEPSIES

Epilepsy is a generic term that has long been used to denote a heterogeneous group of organic disorders that evidence disturbances of consciousness which are characterized by seizures or convulsions. It is also well recognized that children are more susceptible to convulsive seizures than adults, probably because of the immaturity of their nervous systems. The epilepsies have been totally ignored in DSM-III, and this omission has aroused criticism, which we endorse (Tu, 1980). This disorder is important in childhood psychopathology: Abnormal mental symptoms and behaviors may accompany or follow epileptic seizures, and the seizures must be distinguished from other disturbances of consciousness which may be psychogenic in origin.

Prevalence and Incidence

Epilepsy is said to be one of the most common neurological disorders, although its frequency of occurrence is difficult to estimate. Prevalence and incidence studies have varied with respect to the number of seizures the subjects have experienced, the frequency of their continuing seizures, the degree to which their seizures were controlled by anticonvulsant medication, and the extent to which the disorder is recorded in medical records. Consequently, estimates have ranged from as low as 0.3 percent to as high as approximately 6 percent of the total population, when the calculation was based on the expectation that one or more seizures occurred at some stage of life (de Ajuriaguerra, 1980; Hopkins, 1981). Incidence figures for the United States more consistently fall between 0.4 percent and approximately 1 percent (Solomon and Plum, 1976; Strub and Black, 1981; Lishman, 1978). Epilepsy occurs more frequently (1.29 percent) in children who are less than one year old than in adults between the ages of twenty and thirty (0.34 percent). The incidence of new cases of epilepsy is highest during two peak periods in infancy and in old age (de Ajuriaguerra, 1980; Hopkins, 1981). Approximately 90 percent of all epileptics develop their first symptoms of the disorder before twenty years of age, while the overall onset of the disorder most frequently occurs between the ages of five and seven (Livingston, 1972).

Classification

The problem of classifying the epilepsies has produced heterogeneous solutions with limited value for diagnosing and treating the disorder (Merlis, 1972; Porter, 1980). Classification systems have been organized around the content of the attacks, the age of onset, the etiology, the EEG patterns, and the location within the brain of the abnormal activity; but none has been completely satisfactory. Recently a useful proposal for an international classification of the epilepsies was put forward (Merlis, 1970; Gastaut, 1970). A simplified and less detailed derivation of this sytem was offered by Lishman (1978) and is presented in Table 9-2. In order to better understand the system and to become familiar with the terminology used to describe the different types of seizures, we shall briefly describe the clinical features of the four major types of seizures: *grand mal, petit mal, Jacksonian*, and *psychomotor*.

Table 9-2 Modified Version of the International Classification of Epileptic Seizures

Varieties of Epilepsy
1. Generalized epilepsies
a. Primary generalized epilepsy (petit mal, grand mal)
b. Secondary generalized epilepsy
2. Focal epilepsies (partial or local epilepsies)
a. With elementary symptomatology (e.g., motor Jacksonian epilepsy)
b. With complex symptomatology (mostly temporal lobe in origin, e.g., with cognitive or affective symptomatology, psychomotor attacks, psychosensory attacks)
3. Unclassifiable and mixed forms

Adapted from Lishman, 1978, p. 296.

Grand Mal Seizures. This type of seizure is dramatic and upsetting; it is the kind of convulsive episode most commonly associated with epilepsy by the general public. Often, but not always, a grand mal seizure begins with an *aura*—a type of warning such as a peculiar odor or a brief tingling in one hand, which ushers in the first phase of the seizure, the *tonic* phase. During this stage there is widespread contraction of muscles, and the body becomes rigid and stiff, often causing the child to fall to the ground. At the same time the contraction of respiratory muscles forces the air in the chest out through the larynx, which may produce a loud noise such as a grunt or cry early in the attack. In addition, jaw and other facial muscles associated with the control of the tongue contract and become rigid, so that the tongue of the child may be bitten or, less frequently, swallowed. Normal breathing is difficult, and the child may become cyanotic (turn a blue color) because his or her oxygen supply is depleted. Saliva may dribble out of the side of the mouth because normal movements of the mouth are disrupted by the muscle contractions. Incontinence of urine may also occur. The tonic phase lasts between one and two minutes, whereupon the seizure enters into the second or *clonic* phase, in which there are vigorous rhythmic (convulsive) movements of the extremities and trunk muscles for a few minutes. The convulsive movements gradually cease, and the child passively falls into a deep sleep. There is no memory for the attack, although the child may suffer from a headache and from stiff and sore muscles.

Petit Mal Seizures. Hopkins (1981) has suggested that this type of seizure is almost exclusively a disorder of childhood, although it may be difficult for parents and others to detect it—the attack is brief and the behavioral manifestations are quite subtle. Petit mal lasts only a few seconds, comes on suddenly and without warning, and essentially represents a brief interruption of consciousness. The child stops what he or she is doing, stares ahead and flutters the eyelids, and then—as the attack subsides—resumes the prior activity. Soon after waking, the child may have contractions of the muscles (myoclonic jerks) for a brief period of time. Petit mal seizures may be as frequent as ten to fifty or even a hundred in a given day.

Jacksonian Seizures. This type of seizure was named for the English neurologist Hughlings Jackson, whose wife suffered from these attacks. Unlike either grand mal or petit mal, the afflicted child is conscious and aware of what is going on and of the symptoms. The seizure typically affects the muscles involved in regulating fine finger and manual dexterity and facial expression. It is evidenced initially in muscle twitching at one corner of the mouth, spreading to the muscles around the eyes, and then to the hands and foot muscles. This spreading from small to larger areas spirals during the attack, often resulting in fatigue and weakness in the muscles for as much as several days afterward.

Psychomotor Seizures. These seizures usually arise in the temporal lobe and involve the automatic and sometimes repeated performance of complex behaviors, without memory of what was done. The attack may be accompanied by emotional experiences such as overwhelming fear, physical sensations such as stomach discomfort, and other sensory experiences such as dizziness. The person may seem confused and may perform irrelevant acts such as picking imaginary lint from clothes, clicking the tongue, or making facial grimaces; less often the person may act out antisocially. This type of seizure is uncommon in children. It is difficult to verify; therefore, it is sometimes employed as a legal defense by defendants in criminal cases to account for actions that are considered discrepant with their premorbid personalities.

Treatment

The treatment goals for children with epilepsy involve the medical control and cessation of all future seizures, and the psychological management of the social, vocational, educational, and other adjustment problems that such children may encounter. Too frequently the emphasis is placed on the first goal because of the medical urgency that a seizure may generate. However, the successful treatment of children with epilepsy must include the management of both the medical and psychological components. The medical approach would include avoidance of known precipitants of seizures—such as certain drugs or stress and anxiety—modification of diet, surgical intervention, implantation of electrodes to stimulate the cerebellum, biofeedback, and the use of anticonvulsant drugs (Hopkins, 1981). Drug therapy, especially the use of carbamazepine for grand mal seizures and sodium valproate for petit mal seizures, has been quite effective in controlling convulsive attacks, although the untoward effects of drugs, the regulation and monitoring of dosages, and the subjects' drug compliance are problems that are related to, and complicate, this sort of treatment (Hopkins, 1981; Strub and Black, 1981; Eeg-Olofsson, 1980).

Psychological management of the epileptic child involves educating both the parents and the child about the nature of the disorder and its medical management. The family must learn the side effects of the anticonvulsant drugs, the importance of drug compliance, the psychosocial variables that may precipitate seizures, and the interaction of anticonvulsant drugs with other drugs, such as the contraceptive pill (Eeg-Olofsson, 1980; Lishman, 1978). Dreisbach and her associates (1982) reviewed the educational problems which are related to epilepsy and indicated that the problems go beyond those directly caused by seizures or anticonvulsant drugs. These authors suggested that the problems include attentional deficits, hyperactivity, delayed reading, coordination/balance deficits, and problems with spatial relationships—which require special training for the teachers and school staff who work with these youngsters. Moreover, either the physician and/or the psychologist must help the parents and child explore their feelings about the disorder and themselves so that misconceptions can be readily corrected, guilt can be allayed, and their self-image can be enhanced. Behavior modification has been tried to reduce seizures, to eliminate the fear of seizures, and to control the precipitant stressors, although much more work needs to be done in this area (Strub and Black, 1981; Balaschak and Mostofsky, 1981; McRae and Cuvo, 1980).

Psychopathology and Epilepsy

For many years there has been a search for—and a strong belief in—the existence of a special "epileptic personality." Tizard (1962) dispelled this idea with an extensive review of the literature, finding that the data were insufficient to support a specific epileptic personality pattern. However, Tizard, and subsequently others, did find a higher incidence of personality disturbances in epileptic populations than expected, especially in temporal lobe epileptics. They also found that difference types of personality disorders may be related to different types of epilepsy (Schmidt and Wilder, 1968; Livingston, 1972; Pincus and Tucker, 1978; and Kogeorgos, Fonagy, and Scott, 1982). While direct comparisons of studies are difficult to make, the data seem to point consistently to a higher-than-expected incidence of intellectual, emotional, and social problems within the epileptic populations. Moreover, when epileptics were assessed recently with respect to their psychiatric state, a significant relationship was found between current affective disorder and a past history of neurotic disorders, although this relationship did not hold for those with temporal lobe epilepsy (Roy, 1979). Another study reported that seizure type was not related to psychosis when temporal lobe and generalized epileptics were compared (Hermann et al., 1981).

Livingston (1972) found a higher incidence of behavioral and personality abnormalities in children who have major motor (grand mal) epilepsy than in those who have other types of epilepsy. He also noted a set of behavioral symptoms or signs occurring in the postconvulsive stage of grand mal seizures which was characterized by disorientation, periods of excitment with hallucinations and delusions, marked restlessness, cognitive confusion, heightened irritability, and unprovoked belligerence and hostility. In addition, Livingston observed that anxiety and depressive states, belligerence and feelings of being "different," feelings of inadequacy and insecurity, and fears are more common and severe in epileptic children than in those who are chronically ill with more socially acceptable disorders. Falconer and Taylor (1970) found explosive and immature aggressiveness in one-third of temporal lobe epileptics, while Herrington (1969) found impulsiveness, antisocial behavior, suspiciousness, moodiness, anxiety, paranoid ideas, depression, and hysterical traits associated with temporal lobe epileptics. However, Lishman (1978) argued that these conclusions lack scientific merit, since they are based on methodologically flawed studies. Nevertheless, the effects of temporal lobectomy (surgical removal of portions of the temporal lobe) on personality characteristics—such as the reduction of aggressiveness and an increase in social and interpersonal warmth—indirectly (if not directly) suggest that the premorbid disturbance in the temporal lobe did, in fact, impair the personality functioning in a certain way (Lishman, 1978). Finally, Lishman's review of the literature (1978), along with other research findings (Lewis et al., 1982; Long and Moore, 1979), showed the following: (1) Epileptics are no more inclined to commit crimes of violence or other punishable crimes than matched controls, although in an adolescent delinquent male epileptic population, there was evidence suggesting a positive relationship between seizures and violence. (2) It is difficult to determine if there is a greater prevalence of neurosis in epileptics than in the general population. (3) Paranoid-hallucinatory psychoses resembling schizophrenia do occur more often than would be expected by chance in epileptics. (4) Epileptics tend to have a higher-than-expected rate of successful suicides and attempts at suicide. (5) Parents of epileptics are more restrictive and have lower expectations for the future achievements of their children than parents of nonepileptic children, suggesting a link between low parental expectations and the epileptic's lowered self-esteem and impaired school achievement.

LANGUAGE DISORDERS

Language acquisition and the ability to speak in words and sentences distinguish human beings from all other living creatures. Normal speech emerges during the second year of life, following a period of spontaneous vocalizations of sounds known as babbling. Once the child begins to talk, language dramatically multiplies from a few spoken words at eighteen months to more than two thousand words at age five (Smith, 1926). At this point the child is verbally fluent and capable of combining words into sentences in ways that reflect a mastery of the complex structure of language. Yet "language development is far from complete when the child reaches his fifth birthday" (Palermo and Molfese, 1972, p. 425).

In light of this rapid progress and because speech is so necessary for the multiple demands of daily living, it is not surprising to find that children with speech problems come to the attention of professionals at an earlier age (between four and five) than children with most other forms of abnormal behavior (usually referred between the ages of eight and nine) (Chess and Rosenberg, 1974). There is also a higher frequency of speech disorders in boys (sex ratio of 3:1) as compared to nonlanguage problems, where boys exceed girls by a 2:1 ratio. Incidence estimates of speech problems in school populations, and referrals to child guidance centers, have been reported in the neighborhood of 5 to 6 percent, while the estimate jumped to 24 percent when referrals to a private practitioner from an upper-middle-class sample were tallied (Gilbert, 1957; Mysak, 1972; Chess and Rosenberg, 1974).

Speech is a complex function that is dependent on the integrity of the brain, on the auditory apparatus, and on the anatomy of the many structures involved in the formation and production of speech—such as lips, tongue, palate, vocal chords, and so forth. Hearing is intimately related to speech: A child who cannot hear will either be unable to speak or will show profound voice and articulation problems, depending on the severity of the hearing loss and the age at which it occurs. For example, partial or complete deafness before age five will result in severe speech problems, even when the child is given extensive training. However, deafness that occurs after nine years of age will have less severe effects, although abnormalities of the voice are likely to be present (Bakwin and Bakwin, 1972). Anatomical defects such as *harelip* and *cleft palate* illustrate structural causes of speech disorders, preventing proper closure of the mouth in the formation of consonants and vowels.

Injuries and diseases of the brain also may result in language disorders, although as we have seen, the term *brain damage* is too broad and heterogeneous to imply specific behavioral effects. Even in those instances where brain damage leads to language problems, the consequences will differ as to what aspect of language is disabled. The mentally retarded may show delayed and slow language development because of cognitive damage, while the cerebral-palsied child may have articulation problems because of damage to the muscular structure involved in the formation of words.

It is important to distinguish speech problems from language problems in assessing a child's difficulties. We must determine whether or not the child has "access to the symbols of the language but is unable to reproduce these symbols, or is he lacking these symbols?" (Rapin, 1977, p. 232). The three primary types of speech problems evidenced in children may be classified as follows: (1) those where children are unable to encode speech adequately—these children grossly distort speech, have defective syntax, and may be mute, although they understand language; (2) those where children cannot adequately produce certain speech sounds, or where they substitute other speech sounds—these children often have the speech of younger children, and the disorder may be no more than a maturational lag; and (3) those where children have a widespread motor disability which also involves speech—these children may have cerebral palsy, with difficulty controlling facial, tongue, and mouth muscles, which are needed to execute the movements for adequate speech (Rapin, 1977).

Aphasia

Aphasia (from the Greek word meaning "without speech") is one of the many possible outcomes of brain damage, although the neurological deficit may be quite difficult to substantiate in children. It is a term used to designate an impairment of symbolic language not only of speech but also of the other language modalities (gestures and writing) and of comprehension of language. Some writers insist that in order for the term *aphasia* to be meaningful with children, there must be evidence that brain damage has occurred and that a loss in previously acquired language has taken place (Swisher, Wooten, and Thompson, 1977). However, others concede that the great number of children who are labeled aphasic do not evidence "hard" neurological signs or demonstrable neurological damage (Stark, 1980). Pick (1973) viewed the aphasias as indications of language breakdown in the normal stages of its production. He said that language is developmental in nature, progressing through a constructive process from cognition to articulate speech. To Pick, disorders of language represent damage to this process at different stages of its progression. Usually the brain damage which produces the aphasia is in the left hemisphere of the brain, although for left-handed people, right-hemisphere damage can also result in aphasia (Strub and Black, 1981). However, Kinsbourne (1975) noted that most children who are aphasic because of right-sided lesions have in all likelihood sustained bilateral damage. In general, the child's ability to recover from injury to the speech area of the brain is amazing, especially as compared to that of the adult. The younger the child, the better the prognosis, with the chances of recovery continuing to be favorable until the early teens. Permanent impairment is likely to occur after this age (Lenneberg, 1964, 1969). Apparently, the recovery for aphasic children is not complete, since it has been found that these children are poorer students after their illness, apparently demonstrating great difficulty in learning new, complex concepts (Alajouanine and Lhermitte, 1965).

Rapin (1977) has stated unequivocally that infants who sustain unilateral brain lesions do not become asphasic, because there is a plasticity in the early developing brain with respect to where language will be organized. According to Rapin, while the early brain is equipotential for language, this plasticity declines with age to the point where brain lesions acquired at or near puberty can result in permanent impairment of language. Although persistent aphasia is not observed following the occurrence of unilateral lesions in early childhood, long-lasting language defects can be evident—but these are likely to be caused by bilateral lesions. It is also known that aphasia in children that is associated with a convulsive disorder (first appearing between four and six years of age) is characterized by impairment in both comprehension and expression of language, but without impairment of nonverbal IQ (Worster-Drought, 1971; Swisher, Wooten, and Thompson, 1977). It has been found that recovery from this type of aphasia is slow, frequently requiring years of remedial training.

Aphasic children often manifest multiple problems, including perceptual, learning, behavioral, and emotional difficulties (Wood, 1964). It has been shown that aphasic children do not have qualitatively different language than children who develop normally; rather they are likely to evidence developmental lag in language. Moreover, aphasic children are not as creative in their language as their normal counterparts (Morehead and Ingram, 1973; Stark, 1980). There is more than ample evidence indicating auditory-perceptual problems in aphasic children; findings show that these children have deficiencies in auditory discrimination, memory, sequencing, closure, and figure-ground relationships (Stark, 1980).

At the present time childhood aphasia is the subject of considerable disagreement and confusion involving the need to corroborate its neurological basis and clarify the imprecise terminology used to describe the specific impairments of the central language process (Perkins, 1977).

The literature dealing with the relationship between speech disorders and intelligence consistently indicates "that the lower the intelligence level, the greater incidence of defective speech" (Eisenson, 1965, p. 769). Schoolchildren with speech problems are characteristically lower in intelligence than controls, and speech defects are more frequently found among mental retardates than among youngsters of normal intelligence. While the relationship between low intelligence and speech disorders is well established, it should not be taken to mean that speech problems are found only in retarded children. On the contrary, they can and do occur in children of all levels of intelligence.

If speech acquisition involves imitation and modeling, then problems of articulation and delayed speech surely can arise from faulty parental reinforcement patterns. Perhaps as a way of prolonging the period of infancy and maintaining dependency, some mothers reward their babies' use of nonverbal communication. Under these conditions the children are rewarded for not speaking, since their needs are met promptly, without the necessity for verbal language. It is also true that some mothers reinforce baby talk, which increases the probability that the child will repeat lisps and other articulation errors. Irwin's (1969) finding that the vocabulary of one-year-old children can be significantly increased by reading to them suggests that some instances of delayed speech may arise in households where there is insufficient verbal stimulation.

In addition, emotional trauma, illness and hospitalization, birth of a sibling, parental rejection, and negativism are among the psychogenic factors implicated in speech disorders.

Of the many types of speech disorders (apart from aphasia), three others will be discussed, primarily because *delayed speech, articulation problems,* and *stuttering* collectively represent more than 80 percent of all the serious speech difficulties found in school-age children ("Need for Speech Pathologists," 1959). In fact, Cantwell and Baker (1980) have shown that children with language delay and other speech problems represent a risk population for the development of psychopathology. These children not only require speech evaluation and therapy but also need psychological assessment and intervention.

Delayed Speech

For most parents the emergence of developmental milestones—the first smile, the first step, the first tooth, or the first spoken word—are eagerly greeted as reassuring signs that their babies are healthy and progressing normally. We tend to regard acceleration in these growth patterns as reflecting superiority, and slowness as some measure of mental or biological inferiority. Inasmuch as there is considerable variability within the normal developmental limits of speech acquisition, simple two-word utterances may not appear before the child is thirty months old. However, failure to talk beyond this age or by the time the child is three is sufficient indication of an abnormal delay in speech (Worster-Drought, 1968). Delayed speech may also refer to speech that appears within the normal age range, but in which there is very slow progress in new word acquisition and in the formation of sentences. Either delayed onset or retarded progress requires prompt and careful evaluation to determine the basis of the problem and what can be done about it.

Causal Factors. Intellectual evaluation of children with delayed speech is of primary importance, since over half the cases are caused by or associated with mental retardation (Bakwin and Bakwin, 1972; de Ajuriaguerra, 1980). Hearing also should be tested early in the evaluation process, because we know that children who suffer a significant hearing loss will have either or both delayed onset of speech and slow language development. It is evident that a severe hearing loss following the normal onset of speech results in the gradual deterioration of the child's speech not only in acquisition but also in articulation, quality of tone, and loudness (Davis and Silverman, 1970).

The suggestion that auditory memory is related to or accounts for some instances of delayed speech has been seriously entertained by some writers, although the results of controlled investigations have been equivocal (Eisenson, 1965). Operationally, auditory memory is studied by the oral presentation of a series (of varying length) of numbers, words, sentences, or nonsense syllables that the subject is asked to recall immediately or at some later time. Eisenson (1965) posited that many children with delayed speech, particularly those who are brain damaged, are impaired in their ability to handle the complex process of analyzing auditory sequences and reproducing them from memory to the listener in an intelligible form. More recently Tallal (1980) reviewed the experimental findings of studies which investigated the nonverbal perceptual abilities of children who had delayed speech. She found perceptual deficits, as evidenced by the difficulty the children had in correctly reacting to stimuli that were presented rapidly. Tallal noted that "language-delayed children have most difficulty both perceiving and producing those speech sounds and syllables that incorporate rapidly changing acoustic spectra" (p. 138). In addition neurological deficits (as noted earlier) can result in delayed speech and language retardation; brain damage, for example, can seriously affect hearing or impair intellectual functioning.

If environmental factors play an influential role in speech disorders, they are probably most significant in delayed speech and articulation problems. According to Emerick and Hatton (1974): "The quantity and quality of language stimulation, motivation to speak, number of siblings, and order of birth, have long been cited as critical to the development of language in the child. . . . A child apparently is capable of learning the basic systems of his language under, or perhaps, in spite of, the most adverse learning conditions. However, he will probably show the effects of his experience in his vocabulary, grammar, and articulation" (p. 107). Perhaps this view will permit us to interpret in another light the well-established findings that children from the ghetto as well as socioeconomically deprived children have impoverished speech, poor language comprehension, and limited vocabularies. They are also reported to use immature and incorrect grammar (Gerber and Hertel, 1969; Perkins, 1977). These language deficiencies are real if we apply middle-class Caucasian standards as the basic yardstick. However, as Baratz (1968, 1969) noted, the speech of lower-class black children is not deficient but instead is reflective of their subculture. These children are not impaired or impoverished in their ability to acquire language; to the contrary, they demonstrate that they can and do learn a complicated language and structure that permits them to communicate effectively within their own subculture. Ghetto children are taught a new linguistic system, that of middle-class society, when they begin their formal schooling—which, in effect, requires them to be bilingual. Lahey (1973) discusses these issues in greater detail and surveys some recent studies that use positive reinforcement and modeling to alter various aspects of the speaking behavior of minority children, while de Ajuriaguerra (1980) describes the problems of bilingualism.

Treatment. Behavior modification procedures have been employed with severely and moderately retarded children, some of whom were brain damaged, to teach them grammatical rules (Guess et al., 1968; Baer and Guess, 1971). By means of imitation and differential reinforcement, it was demonstrated that retardates learned the correct grammatical usage of the training examples, and they generalized appropriately from this limited experience to new instances that were not part of the original practice material. Although only moderately successful, behavior modification has been used to increase the language development of severely psychotic children (see Chapter 8). In addition, verbal stimulation, instructions to parents in encouraging verbalizations from the child, and family and child psychotherapy have been suggested as remedial approaches to children with delayed speech.

Problems of Articulation

Imprecise production of speech sounds frequently is a major characteristic of many types of speech disorders. For this reason alone articulatory problems are the most prevalent of all speech aberrations, representing more than 80 percent of the cases treated by speech therapists in the public schools (Bingham et al., 1961). Defective articulation and the degree of imprecision in producing speech sounds is determined by listening to phonetic behavior. The smallest unit of distinguishable speech sounds is a *phoneme*, which serves as a standard against which articulatory errors can be compared and corrected. According to Perkins (1977), there are four types of faulty articulation in which phonemes are either omitted, substituted, distorted, or added.

With the exception of the high incidence of faulty articulation found in mental retardates, intelligence at higher levels bears no significant relationship to articulatory proficiency (Winitz, 1969). However, after carefully reviewing the literature, Winitz noted a positive relationship between defective articulation and academic achievement, grades, and reading and spelling performance. Additionally, evidence suggests that children with articulatory difficulties show slower development of vocabulary and verbal output, and they tend to be restricted and underdeveloped in the way they arrange words to form phrases or sentences ("Human Communication and Its Disorders: An Overview," 1969; Shriner, Holloway, and Daniloff, 1969; Templin, 1973; de Ajuriaguerra, 1980). The evidence is such that at this time it is not possible to determine whether inadeqaute articulation impairs the development of vocabulary, syntax, and educational performance, or if these are simply part of a more pervasive symptom picture associated with some language or learning disorder. The fact that studies consistently report a higher incidence of articulatory deficits in low-socioeconomic-level children is not surprising, since subculture speech sounds are likely to differ from the standard phonemes used to determine misarticulations (Adler, 1973). Winitz (1969) has suggested that this finding is explicable on the basis of the differences in language stimulation and reinforcement between socioeconomic levels.

Causal Factors. Problems of articulation are attributable to a number of possible factors, the most obvious of which are those physiological, neurological, and sensory conditions that hamper proficiency in the formation of speech sounds. Children who have physiological abnormalities, such as hare lip, cleft palate, dental obstructions, and tongue malformations, are structurally impaired in ways that make normal movement of the speech apparatus difficult. Central nervous system injury or damage that affects hearing, neuromuscular control of the speech mechanism, or respiratory regulation (resulting in either insufficient air supply for speaking or inefficient control of speech sounds) are well-established determinants of articulatory errors (Hardy, 1968; Darley, Aronson, and Brown, 1969; Lishman, 1978). Anyone who has received an injection of Novocaine to reduce the discomfort of dental drilling or extraction can recall the loss of sensation in the tongue, the lips, and part of the face that temporarily reduced their proficiency in articulation. Moreover, auditory acuity and discrimination among pitches of tones, vowels, and consonants, and complex patterns at some level are necessary for accurate articulation. Unfortunately, at present the research evidence is too inconclusive and incomplete to provide specific data as to the precise level of acuity and discrimination needed to enable proper articulation.

At the same time there are many articulatory problems for which no organic cause can be found. These instances are considered to result from faulty learning in which poor speech models, low levels of stimulation and motivation, or some underlying personality disorders are viewed as prime contributors (de Ajuriaguerra, 1980).

Treatment. Most articulatory problems are appropriately treated by a trained speech therapist, since these speech difficulties do not ordinarily give rise to serious emotional or personality consequences. A review of the literature revealed no consistent evidence that either parents of children with cleft palates or the children themselves manifest emotional disturbances to any substantial degree (Goodstein, 1969). Whenever social and personal adjustment problems are associated with misarticulations, speech therapy and psychological intervention may be an effective remedial combination. While it is beyond the scope of our discussion to consider the specific treatment approaches used by speech therapists, it is important to note that learning principles have been increasingly applied to the construction of techniques employed to modify articulatory problems.

Those readers interested in more detailed information are referred to two books that review and describe behavior modification approaches to articulatory and other language disorders (Lahey, 1973; Wolfe and Goulding, 1973).

Stuttering

Although stuttering, or stammering, is easily recognized by most laypeople, it is a condition that specialists in speech pathology find difficult to define; the boundary between stuttering and dysfluence in normal speech (irregularities in the flow of speech) is ambiguous. In fact, the task of making auditory judgments about stuttering is highly unreliable, since listeners (judges) disagree among themselves more than half the time (Perkins, 1977). Nevertheless, we shall, for our purposes, use the term *stuttering* to refer to a particular breakdown in speech fluency characterized by *blocking* (inability to articulate), *repetition*, and *prolongation of speech sounds*.

Blocking is said to be stressful to the stutterer (Jones, 1970, pp. 336–358), as well as a possible consequence of strong anxiety for even normal speakers (Herbert, 1974). It occurs most often in the first words, phrases, or sentences of speech, as is the case with repetitions. The fact that repetitions typically are found in the normal speech of young children makes it all the more understandable that the early diagnosis of stuttering on this basis is difficult. In contrast, the infrequent occurrence of prolongation of vowels in normal speakers of any age may, if present in young children, be of diagnostic significance.

Stuttering begins between the ages of two and five, and almost always before the age of eight. It occurs more frequently in boys, with estimated sex ratios ranging from 3:1 to as high as 8:1 (Jones, 1970; Bakwin and Bakwin, 1972), and it is extremely rare in adult females, (Froschels, 1980). Socioeconomic factors and intelligence are unrelated to stuttering, although vast differences among cultures seem to be evident (Stewart, 1971). Yet stuttering is not universal, since it is unknown in undeveloped areas of the world and among the American Indians. Persistent stuttering is found in only 1 to 2 percent of the population, while transient stuttering appears in 4 or 5 percent (Jones, 1970; Bakwin and Bakwin, 1972). Fortunately, most cases of stuttering are temporary—more than 50 percent recover by puberty without treatment, and 80 percent have normal speech by the time they reach their late teens (Glasner and Rosenthal, 1957; Sheehan and Martyn, 1966, 1967). No satisfactory explanation exists for these findings, although the gradual nature of recovery tends to support a maturational view. Happily, this seems to be the case for four out of every five stutterers.

Causal Factors. While the literature on stuttering is neither sparse nor wanting for causal hypotheses, as yet it has provided no single acceptable explanation. The search for biological or constitutional (including genetic) factors has focused on the exploration of differences between stutterers and nonstutterers in cerebral dominance (neither of the two cortical hemispheres are alleged to be dominant in stutterers, resulting in poor synchrony and control of the central mechanisms of speech), in metabolic organization, in sensory feedback, in EEG recordings, and in air and bone conduction of the auditory mechanism ("Human Communication and Its Disorders: An Overview," 1969; Travis 1971; Perkins, 1977). De Ajuriaguerra (1980) described several studies in which about one-third of the cases were linked to hereditary factors. The data thus far accumulated, although inconsistent, have failed in any substantial way to provide confirmation for a biological view of stuttering.

Psychogenic interpretations of stuttering also have been plentiful in the literature. One large segment of these studies supposes that stuttering is a symptom of a basic neurotic disorder. This view assumes a psychodynamic orientation in which stuttering is a primary expression of anxiety that results from unconscious conflicts. In addition, such studies assume that feelings of embarrassment, failure, and lowered self-esteem associated with stuttering further enhance the development of neurotic reactions and defenses (Barbara, 1959). However, neither aspect of this position is supported by the research evidence. There are neither special personality patterns that can reliably identify stuttering children, nor indications that neurosis occurs more frequently among stutterers than nonstutterers (Goodstein, 1962; Sheehan, 1962).

This is apparently true, in spite of the fact that Johnson (1961), one of the most distinguished researchers in this area, believed that parents of stutterers are more anxious about their children's speech and about other aspects of their children's behavior and tend to be more unrealistic in their demands. The inclination of these parents to be overprotective, critical, perfectionistic, and covertly rejecting has been reported by others, but there is no support for the view that parents of stutterers are grossly maladjusted or emotionally disturbed (Perkins, 1977).

At present the most viable viewpoint seems to be that stuttering is learned, although different theorists have not always emphasized similar environmental conditions and learning paradigms. Johnson and his colleagues (Johnson, 1956; Johnson, et al., 1956) posited that dysfluencies occur in the normal speech of children, which are reacted to by parents of stutterers with negativism and an unrealistic expectation of fluency. Through this type of interaction stuttering becomes a learned avoidance reaction in which the child struggles to avoid all instances of dysfluencies and subsequent negative reactions from parents. Failure to achieve fluent speech is inevitable, and this in turn heightens anxiety and the likelihood of more interruptions in the flow of speech.

Sheehan (1953, 1968) argues that stuttering, cast in a somewhat different light, represents an approach-avoidance conflict in which the child vacillates between the opposing needs to speak and to avoid speaking. The avoidance stems from the embarrassment and other unpleasant feelings the child associates with previous failures in speech fluency. Probably the most sophisticated learning view of stuttering is the *two-process theory* of Brutten and Shoemaker (1967, 1969, p. 51). This view holds that the primary speech disorganization is acquired through classically conditioned anxiety, while the secondary aspects of stuttering (eye blinks, wrinkling the nose) are instrumentally conditioned. Therefore, in order to modify stuttering, both classes of responses must be extinguished.

Treatment. Treatment plans and procedures for stutterers are numerous and diverse, so much so that an extensive review is beyond our scope. Consequently, we shall consider only a sample of the major approaches. Van Riper (1963) proposed a program that combines psychotherapy and speech practice under conditions of progressive stress (similar to desensitization). In fact, this approach effectively reduced or eliminated stuttering in 50 percent of the cases that were followed up five years after therapy. A wide variety of delayed auditory feedback techniques in which very brief delays in hearing one's own voice are used to improve or eliminate (during practice) speech dysfluencies have been employed both to study organic components of the disorder and to treat the condition (Jones, 1970). In general, the results with this approach have been disappointing, although a few stutterers have shown dramatic improvement.

Beginning with the work of Flanagan and his associates (Flanagan, Goldiamond, and Azrin, 1958), principles derived from operant conditioning have been shown to modify stuttering behavior. Early studies demonstrated that the frequency of stuttering can be operantly manipulated. However, as Martin and Ingham (1973) concluded following their critical review of the literature:

> The reports of response contingent stuttering therapy programs of techniques reviewed above are far from satisfactory. There is evidence that the procedures may affect changes within some therapy programs, but the data are difficult to evaluate. Most reports are premature and do not include carefully obtained carryover or follow-up data (p. 126).

For the long-term chronic stutterer, regarded by Jones (1970) as primarily neurotic, psychotherapy along with some technique to interrupt the persistence of stuttering are recommended. Essentially, these individuals need to deal with the anxiety and fear of failure associated with their long history of stuttering; and they need the opportunity to resolve conflicts that have diminished their self-confidence and impaired their social adjustment.

SUMMARY

In this first of several chapters focusing on the period of childhood ranging from age five through preadolescence, we discussed past and contemporary theories of brain function, considered the term *brain damage* and the causes of this condition, and covered two disorders whose etiology has been tied to some sort of neuropathology and whose symptoms emerge most often during this developmental period.

Three theories of brain function were presented briefly: (1) the doctrine of localization of specific function, in which the brain is assumed to have many different areas with specific psychological functions that are independent from skills represented in other areas of the brain; (2) the equipotential theory of brain function, in which all areas of the brain are held to be equal in terms of functions, with each having the potential to take on the function of damaged areas; and (3) the concept of functional system, in which behavior is considered to be not exclusively governed by a particular area of the brain but rather controlled by a functional system of the brain.

The term *brain damage* was discussed as a heterogeneous entity that may refer to many disparate disorders, to different areas and amounts of brain tissue affected, and to differences in the age at which the damage occurs. The symptoms and behavioral characteristics often attributed to brain damage, as well as the etiological factors associated with this condition, also overlap with other forms of psychopathology for which no demonstrable neuropathology exists. The etiological factors of brain damage, and their effects, were presented, organized around prenatal, perinatal, and postnatal risks.

The epilepsies were described as a heterogeneous group of organic disorders which have in common disturbances of consciousness which are characterized by seizures or convulsions. Children are more susceptible to convulsive seizures than adults. Epilepsy is one of the most common neurological disorders, with incidence figures for the United States falling between 0.4 and 1 percent. Approximately 90 percent of all epileptics develop their first symptoms before twenty years of age, although the overall onset most often occurs between the ages of five and seven. Many classifications of the epilepsies have been offered, although in the early 1970s a proposed International Classification of Epileptic Seizures proved to be a useful device. Grand mal, petit mal, Jacksonian, and psychomotor seizures were described, and a discussion of the medical and psychological treatments for the epilepsies was presented. The relationship between epilepsy and psychopathology and personality patterns was also covered.

Language disorders—including aphasia, delayed speech, articulation problems, and stuttering—were described and discussed in terms of their causal factors and treatment approaches.

EPILOGUE

It was apparent from the neurological findings and the psychological assessment that Terry had suffered from a concussion and from some posttraumatic organic state as well as from a psychological trauma caused by his uncle's sexual advances. In this case it is difficult—if not impossible—to give differential or specific weight to each or either of these causes, although the evaluation team believed that organic factors were primary and were intensified by the psychological trauma. Fortunately, Terry's condition improved rapidly, and after sixteen days of hospitalization he was able to return home with a normal EEG and relatively free of his symptoms. While in the hospital, he was treated with sedatives to reduce his anxiety, given bed rest for the concussion, and seen daily by a psychologist in brief psychotherapy to work through and resolve his anxiety and conflicts concerning his sexual feelings and his feelings toward his uncle.

REFERENCES

ABEL, E. L. Fetal Alcohol Syndrome: Behavioral Teratology. *Psychological Bulletin*, 1980, 87, 29–50.

ADLER, S. Articulatory Deviances and Social Class Membership. *Journal of Learning Disabilities*, 1973, 6, 650–654.

ALAJOUANINE, T., AND LHERMITTE, F. Acquired Aphasia in Children. *Brain*, 1965, 88, 653–662.

BAER, D. M., AND GUESS, D. Receptive Training of Adjectival Inflections in Mental Retardates. *Journal of Applied Behavior Analysis*, 1971, 4, 129–139.

Bakwin, H., and Bakwin, R. M. *Behavior Disorders in Children*, 4th ed. Philadelphia: Saunders, 1972.

Balaschak, B. A., and Mostofsky, D. I. Seizure Dis-Disorders. In E. J. Marsh and L. G. Terday (eds.), Behavioral Assessment of Childhood Disorders. New York: Guilford Press, 1981, pp. 601–637.

Baratz, J. Language in the Economically Disadvantaged Child: A Perspective. *American Speech and Hearing Association*, 1968, *10*, 143–145.

Baratz, J. Language and Cognitive Assessment of Negro Children: Assumptions and Research Needs. *American Speech and Hearing Association*, 1969, *11*, 87–91.

Barbara, D. A. Stuttering. In S. Arieti (ed.), *American Handbook of Psychiatry*, Vol. 1. New York: Basic Books 1959, pp. 950–963.

Benton, J. W., Moser, H. W., Dodge, P. R., and Carr, S. Modification of the Schedule of Myelination in the Rat by Early Nutritional Deprivation. *Pediatrics*, 1966, *38*, 801–807.

Berko, F. G., Berko, M. J., and Thompson, S. C. *Management of Brain Damaged Children: A parents' and teachers' guide*. Springfield, Ill.: Chas. C Thomas, 1970.

Bingham, D. S., Van Hattum, R., Faulk, M. E., and Taussing, E. Program Organization and Management. *Journal of Speech and Hearing Disorders*. Monograph Supplement, 1961, *8*, 33–49.

Black, P. Introduction: Changing Concepts of "Brain Damage" and "Brain Dysfunction." In P. Black (ed.), Brain Dysfunction in Children: Etiology, Diagnosis, and Management. New York: Raven Press, 1981, pp. 1–4.

Brutten, E. J., and Shoemaker, D. J. *The Modification of Stuttering*. Englewood Cliffs, N. J.: Prentice-Hall, 1967.

Brutten, E. J., and Shoemaker, D. J. Stuttering: The Disintegration of Speech Due to Conditioned Negative Emotion. In B. Gray., and G. England (eds.), Stuttering and the Conditioning Therapies. Monterey, Calif.: Monterey Institute for Speech and Hearing, 1969, p. 51.

Cantwell, D. P., and Baker, L. Psychiatric and Behavioral Characteristics of Children with Communication Disorders. *Journal of Pediatric Psychology*, 1980, *5*, 161–178.

Carter, S., and Gold, A. Diagnosis of Neurologic Disease. In S. Carter and A. Gold (eds.), *Neurology of Infancy and Childhood*. New York: Appleton-Century-Crofts, 1974, pp. 1–9.

Chess, S., and Rosenberg, M. Clinical Differentiation among Children with Initial Language Complaints. *Journal of Autism and Childhood Schizophrenia*, 1974, *4*, 99–109.

Darley, F. L., Aronson, A. E., and Brown, J. R., Clusters of Deviant Speech Dimensions in th Dysarthrias. *Journal of Speech and Hearing Research*, 1969, *12*, 462–496.

Davis, H., and Silverman, S. R. *Hearing and Deafness*, 3rd ed. New York: Holt, Rinehart and Winston, 1970.

de Ajuriaguerra, J. *Handbook of Child Psychiatry and Psychology*, trans. and ed. R. P. Lorion. New York: Masson Publishing USA, 1980.

Diller, L., and Birch, H. B. Psychological Evaluation of Children with Cerebral Damage. In H. G. Birch (ed.), Brain Damage in Children: The Biological and Social Aspects. Baltimore, Md: Williams and Wilkins, 1964, pp. 27–45.

Dreisbach, M., Ballard, M., Russo, D. C., and Schain, R. J. Educational Intervention for Children with Epilepsy: A Challenge for Collaborative Service Delivery. *Journal of Special Education*, 1982, *16*, 111–121.

Duckett, S. Neuropathological Aspects: I. Congenital Malformations. In P. Black (ed.), *Brain Dysfunction in Children: Etiology Diagnosis, and Management*. New York: Raven Press, 1981, pp. 17–46.

Eeg-Olofsson. O. Treatment of Epileptic Disorders of Children. In P. Robb (ed.), *Epilepsy Up-dated: Causes and Treatment*. Miami, Florida: Symposia Specialists, 1980, pp. 199–211.

Eisenson, J. Speech Disorders. In B. B. Wolman (ed.), Handbook of Clinical Psychology. New York: McGraw Hill, 1965, pp. 765–784.

Emerick, L. L., and Hatton, J. T., *Diagnosis and Evaluation in Speech Pathology*. Englewood Cliffs, N. J.: Prentice-Hall, 1974.

Falconer, M. A., and Taylor, D. C. Temporal Lobe Epilepsy: Clinical Features, Pathology, Diagnosis, and Treatment. In J. H. Price (ed.), *Modern Trends in Psychological Medicine*, Vol. 2. London: Butterworths, 1970, pp. 346–373.

Flanagan, B., Goldiamond, I., and Azrin, N. H. Operant Stuttering: The Control of Stuttering Behavior Through Response Contingent Consequences. *Journal of the Experimental Analysis of Behavior*, 1958, *1*, 173–177.

Froschels, E. Stuttering in Children and in Aphasics. In R. W. Rieber (ed.), *Language Development and Aphasia in Children: New Essays and Translation of Kindersprache und Aphasie by Emil Froschels*. New York: Academic Press, 1980, pp. 211–218.

Gastaut, H. Clinical and Electroencephalographical Classification of Epileptic Seizures. *Epilepsia*, 1970, *11*, 102–113.

Gerber, S. E., and Hertel, C. G. Language Deficiency of Disadvantaged Children. *Journal of Speech and Hearing Research*, 1969, *12*, 270–280.

Gilbert, G. M. A Survey of "Referral Problems" in Metropolitan Child Guidance Centers. *Journal of Clinical Psychology*, 1957, *13*, 37–42.

Glasner, P. J., and Rosenthal, D. Parental Diagnosis of Stuttering in Young Children. *Journal of Speech and Hearing Disorders*, 1957, *22*, 288–295.

Golden, C. J. *Diagnosis and Rehabilitation in Clinical Neuropsychology*, 2nd ed. Springfield, Ill: Chas. C Thomas, 1981.

Goodstein, L. D. Functional Speech Disorders and Personality: A Survey of the Literature. In P. Trapp and P. Himelstein (eds.), *Readings on the Exceptional Child*. New York: Appleton-Century-Crofts, 1962, pp. 399–419.

GOODSTEIN, L. D. Psychosocial Aspects of Cleft Palate. In D. C. Spriesterbach, and D. Sherman (eds.), *Cleft Palate and Communication*. New York: Academic Press, 1969, pp. 201-224.

GUESS, D., SAILOR, W., RUTHERFORD, G., and BAER, D. M. An Experimental Analysis of Linguistic Development: The Productive Use of the Plural Morpheme. *Journal of Applied Behavior Analysis*, 1968, *1*, 297-306.

HARDY, J. Respiratory Physiology: Implications of Current Research. *American Speech and Hearing Association*, 1968, *10*, 204-205.

HARTH, E. *Windows on the Mind: Reflections on the physical basis of consciousness*. New York: Morrow, 1982.

HERBERT, M. *Emotional Problems of Development in Children*. New York: Academic Press, 1974.

HERMANN, B. P., SCHWARTZ, M. S., WHITMAN, S., and KARNES, W. E. Psychosis and Epilepsy: Seizure-Type Comparisons and High-Risk Variables. *Journal of Clinical Psychology*, 1981, *37*, 714-721.

HERRINGTON, R. N. The Personality in Temporal Lobe Epilepsy. In R. N. HERRINGTON (ed.), *Current Problems in Neuropsychiatry*. British Journal of Psychiatry Special Publication. Ashfor, Kent: Headley Brothers, 1969, pp. 70-76.

HOPKINS, A. *Epilepsy: The Facts*. Oxford: Oxford University Press, 1981.

Human Communication and Its Disorders: An Overview. A Report of the Subcommittee on Human Communication and Its Disorders. *National Advisory Neurological Diseases and Stroke Council*, Monograph No. 10 U.S. Department of Health, Education and Welfare, National Institute of Neurological Diseases and Stroke, 1969.

IRWIN, O. C. Infant Speech: Effect of Systematic Reading of Stories. *Journal of Speech and Hearing Research*, 1969, *3*, 187-190.

JOHNSON, W. (ed.), *Stuttering in Children and Adults; Thirty Years of Research at the University of Iowa*. Minneapolis: University of Minnesota Press, 1956.

JOHNSON, W. *Stuttering and What You Can Do About It*. Minneapolis: University of Minnesota Press, 1961.

JOHNSON, W., BROWN, S., CURTIS, J., EDNEY, C., and KEASTER, J. *Speech Handicapped School Children*. New York: Harper and Row, 1956.

JONES, H. G. Stuttering. In C. G. Costello (ed.), *Symptoms of Psychopathology: A Handbook*. New York: John Wiley, 1970, pp. 336-358.

KINSBOURNE, M. *Development and Evolution of the Neural Basis of Language*. Forty-fifth Annual James Arthur Lecture, The American Museum of Natural History. New York: American Museum of Natural History Press, 1975.

KOGEORGOS, J., FONAGY, P., and SCOTT, D. F. Psychiatric Symptom Patterns of Chronic Epileptics Attending a Neurological Clinic: A Controlled Investigation. *British Journal of Psychiatry*, 1982, *140*, 236-243.

LAHEY, B. B. Minority Group Languages. In B. B. Lahey, (ed.), *The Modification of Language Behavior*. Springfield, Ill.: Chas. C Thomas, 1973, pp. 270-315.

LASHLEY, K. S. *Brain Mechanisms and Intelligence:* A Quantitative Study of Injuries to the Brain. Chicago, Ill.: University of Chicago Press, 1929.

LENNEBERG, E. H. (ed.). Language Disorders in Childhood *Harvard Educational Review*, 1964, *34*, 152-177.

LENNEBERG, E. H. On Explaining Language. *Science*, 1969, *164*, 635-643.

LEWIS, D. O., PINCUS, J. H., SHANOK, S. S., and GLASER, G. H. Psychomotor Epilepsy and Violence in a Group of Incarcerated Adolescent Boys. *American Journal of Psychiatry*, 1982, *139*, 882-887.

LISHMAN, W. A. *Organic Psychiatry: The Psychological Consequences of Cerebral Disorder*. Oxford: Blackwell Scientific Publications, 1978.

LIVINGSTON, S. *Comprehensive Management of Epilepsy in Infancy, Childhood and Adolescence*. Springfield, Ill.: Chas. C Thomas, 1972.

LONG, C. G., and MOORE, J. R. Parental Expectations for Their Epileptic Children. *Journal of Child Psychology and Psychiatry and Allied Disciplines*, 1979, *20*, 299-312.

LURIA, A. R. *The Working Brain:* An Introduction to Neuropsychology. New York: Basic Books, 1973.

LURIA, A. R. *Higher Cortical Functions in Man*, 2nd ed. New York: Basic Books, 1980.

MARTIN, R., and INGRAM, R. *Stuttering*. In B. B. Lahey (ed.), *The Modification of Language Behavior*. Springfield, Ill.: Chas. C Thomas, Publisher, 1973, pp. 91-129.

MCFIE, J. *Assessment of Organic Intellectual Impairment*. London: Academic Press, 1975.

MCRAE, S., and CUVO, A. J. Operant Control of Seizure Behavior: Review and Evaluation of Research. *Behavior Research of Severe Developmental Disabilities*, 1980, *1*, 215-248.

MERLIS, J. K. Proposal for an International Classification of the Epilepsies. *Epilepsia*, 1970, *11*, 114-119.

MERLIS, J. K. Treatment in Relation to Classification of the Epilepsies. *Acta Neurologica Latin America*, 1972, *18*, 42-51.

MOREHEAD, D. M., and INGRAM, D. The Development of Base Syntax in Normal and Linguistically Deviant Children. *Journal of Speech and Hearing Research*, 1973, *16*, 330-352.

MYSAK, E. D., and GILBERT, G. M. Child Speech Pathology. In B. B. Wolman, (ed.), *Manual of Child Psychopathology*. New York: McGraw-Hill, 1972, pp. 624-652.

Need for Speech Pathologists. American Speech and Hearing Association, Committee on Legislation. *Journal of the American Speech and Hearing Association*, 1959, *1*, 138-139.

PALERMO, D. S., and MOLFESE, D. L. Language Acquisition from Age Five Onward. *Psychological Bulletin*, 1972, *78*, 409-428.

PERKINS, W. H. *Speech Pathology: An Applied Behavioral Science*, 2nd ed. St. Louis, Mo.: Mosby, 1977.

Pick, A. *Aphasia*. Trans. and ed. J. W. Brown. Springfield, Ill.: Chas. C Thomas, 1973.

Pincus, J. H., and Tucker, G. L. *Behavioral Neurology*. New York: Oxford University Press, 1978.

Porter, R. J. Etiology and Classification of Epileptic Seizures. In P. Robb (ed.), *Epilepsy Updated: Causes and Treatment*. Miami, Fla.: Symposia Specialists, 1980, pp. 1–10.

Rapin, I. Language Disability in Children, In M. E. Blaw, I. Rapin, and M. Kinsbourne (eds.), *Topics in Child Neurology*. New York: Spectrum Publications, 1977, pp. 227–242.

Robinson, N. M., and Robinson, H. B. *The Mentally Retarded Child: A Psychological Approach*, 2nd ed. New York: McGraw-Hill, 1976.

Ross, A. O. *Psychological Aspects of Learning Disabilities and Reading Disorders*. New York: McGraw-Hill, 1976.

Roy, A. Some Determinants of Affective Symptoms in Epileptics. *Canadian Journal of Psychiatry*, 1979, 24, 554–556.

Rutter, M., Graham, P., and Yule, W. A Neuropsychiatric Study in Childhood. *Clinics in Developmental Medicine*, Nos. 35/36. London: Heinemann Medical Books Ltd., 1970.

Schmidt, R. P., and Wilder, B. J. *Epilepsy*. Philadelphia: F. A. Davis Co., 1968.

Sheehan, J. G. Theory and Treatment of Stuttering as an Approach Avoidance Conflict. *Journal of Psychology*, 1953, 36, 27–49.

Sheehan, J. G. Stuttering as a Self-role Conflict. In H. H. Gregory, (ed.), *Learning Theory and Stuttering Therapy*. Evanston, Ill.: Northwestern University Press, 1968, pp. 72–83.

Sheehan, J. G., and Martyn, M. M. Spontaneous Recovery from Stuttering. *Journal of Speech and Hearing Research*, 1966, 9, 121–135.

Sheehan, J. G., and Martyn, M. M. Methodology in Studies of Recovery from Stuttering. *Journal of Speech and Hearing Research*, 1967, *10*, 396–400.

Sheehan, J. G. Projective Studies of Stuttering. In E. P. Trapp, and P. Himmelstein (eds.), *Readings on the Exceptional Child*, New York: Appleton-Century-Crofts, 1962, pp. 419–429.

Shriner, T. H., Holloway, M. S., and Daniloff, R. G. The Relationship Between Articulatory Deficits and Syntax in Speech Defective Children. *Journal of Speech and Hearing Research*, 1969, *12*, 319–325.

Smith, M. E. *An Investigation of the Development of the Sentence and the Extent of Vocabulary in Young Children*. Iowa City, Iowa: University of Iowa Studies in Child Welfare, 1926.

Solomon, G. E., and Plum, F. *Clinical Management of Seizures: A Guide for the Physician*. Philadelphia: Saunders, 1976.

Stark, J. Aphasia in Children. In R. W. Reiber (ed.), *Language Development and Aphasia in Children: New Essays and a Translation of Kindersprache und Aphasie by Emil Froschels*. New York: Academic Press, 1980, pp. 33–44.

Stewart, J. L. Cross-cultural Studies and Linguistic Aspects of Stuttering. *Journal of the All India Institute of Speech and Hearing*, 1971, 2, 1–6.

Strub, R. L., and Black, F. W. *Organic Brain Syndromes: An Introduction to Neurobehavioral Disorders*, Philadelphia: F. A. Davis Co., 1981.

Suskind, R. M. Characteristics and Causation of Protein-Calorie Malnutrition in the Infant and Preschool Child. In L. S. Greene (ed.), *Malnutrition, Behavior and Social Organization*. New York: Academic Press, 1977, pp. 1–17.

Swisher, L., Wooten, N., and Thompson, E. D. Biological Predictors of Language Development. In M. E. Blaw, I, Rapin, and M. Kinsbourne (eds.), *Topics in Child Neurology*. New York: Spectrum Publ., 1977, pp. 213–225.

Tallal, P. Language Disabilities in Children: A Perceptual or Linguistic Deficit? *Journal of Pediatric Psychology*, 1980, 5, 127–140.

Templin, M. C. Developmental Aspects of Articulation. In W. D. Wolfe, and D. J. Goulding (eds.), *Articulation and Learning: New Dimensions in Research, Diagnostics, and Therapy*. Springfield, Ill.: Chas. C Thomas, 1973, pp. 51–83.

Tizard, B. The Personality of Epileptics: A Discussion of the Evidence. *Psychological Bulletin*, 1962, 59, 196–210.

Towbin, A. Neuropathological Aspects: II. Perinatal Brain Damage and Its Sequels. In P. Black (ed.), *Brain Dysfunction in Children: Etiology, Diagnosis, and Management*. New York: Raven Press, 1981, pp. 47–77.

Travis, L. *The Handbook of Speech Pathology and Audiology*. New York: Appleton-Century-Crofts, 1971.

Tu, Jun-bi. Epilepsy, Psychiatry and DSM-III. *Biological Psychiatry*, 1980, *15*, 515–516.

VanRiper, C. G. *Speech Correction: Principles and Methods*, 4th ed. Englewood Cliffs, N. J.: Prentice-Hall, 1963.

Walters, J. Birth Defects and Adolescent Pregnancies. *Journal of Home Economics*, 1975, 67, 23–27.

Winick, M. Food, Time, and Cellular Growth of the Brain. *New York State Journal of Medicine*, 1969, 69, 302–304.

Winick, M., and Rosso, P. Malnutrition and Central Nervous System Development. In J. W. Prescott, M. S. Read, and D. B. Coursin (eds.), *Brain Function and Malnutrition: Neuropsychological Methods of Assessment*. New York: John Wiley, 1975, pp. 41–51.

Winitz, H. *Articulatory Acquisition and Behavior*. New York: Appleton-Century-Crofts, 1969.

Wolfe, W. D., and D. J. Goulding (eds.). *Articulation and Learning: New Dimensions in Research, Diagnostics, and Therapy*. Springfield, Ill.: Chas. C Thomas, Publisher, 1973.

WOOD, N. E. *Delayed Speech and Language Development.* Englewood Cliffs, N. J.: Prentice-Hall, 1964.

WORSTER-DROUGHT, C. Speech Disorders in Children. *Developmental Medicine and Child Neurology,* 1968, *10,* 427–440.

WORSTER-DROUGHT, C. An Unusual Form of Acquired Aphasia in Children. *Developmental Medicine and Child Neurology,* 1971, *13,* 563–571.

ZARFAS, D. E., and WOLF, L. C. Maternal Age Patterns and the Incidence of Down's Syndrome. *American Journal of Mental Deficiency,* 1979, *83,* 353–359.

10

MINIMAL BRAIN DYSFUNCTION, LEARNING DISABILITIES, AND THE HYPERKINETIC SYNDROME

PROLOGUE

Herman is a nine-year-old boy of average intelligence who is of great concern to his third-grade teacher because of poor academic achievement and the recent appearance of behavioral problems. He is unable to read beyond the first-grade level, and his writing is poor and rather uncoordinated. Although his reading difficulties had been noted earlier, he now evidences a reluctance to read aloud in class or to work either in school or at home to improve his reading proficiency. Instead, he is a disruptive influence in school—talking incessantly, poking his classmates, and refusing to remain in his seat for any prolonged period of time. Herman is easily distracted by the sights and sounds around him, and he seems to have attentional and concentrational difficulties. Except for arithmetic, where he clearly achieves at a higher level than most of his peers, his teacher finds little in his school performance that she can reward. Because Herman is clumsy and awkward, he is often excluded from playground and athletic games that require good motor coordination. Numerous school conferences with Herman's parents since the second grade, and the likelihood that he will be required to repeat the third grade, finally convinced his parents to seek professional help.

Herman is the middle son of a family of five, with a sister two years older and another two years younger. He was a planned child, and his mother's pregnancy was uneventful, although he was a breech delivery. He weighed seven pounds eleven ounces, and his motor, language, and social development seemed to be normal for the first eighteen months. When his mother was expecting her third child, she hired a housekeeper to help out with Herman and his older sister. Because the housekeeper was overly fastidious and wanted to impress Herman's mother with the excellent care she was providing the two children, Herman was started on toilet training. He was not readily trained, and after weeks of battling, the training was abandoned. However, his mother attributes his later enuresis to this early failure experience. The housekeeper stressed cleanliness, orderliness, and neatness in dress to the point where Herman soon wanted his clothes changed several times a day so that he could admire himself in the mirror. He also began talking with a lisp (a sort of feminine baby talk); and he showed no interest in activities, games, toys, or even books that were associated with masculine interests or roles. He continued to show feminine interests and preferences similar to those of his older sister, which was reinforced by both mother and the housekeeper, who thought it was "cute." His father is a quiet, passive, and somewhat mousy man who rarely says much at home and almost never asserts himself. He owns and operates a small restaurant and worked long hours to make ends meet. His mother, in contrast, is aggressive, vocal, self-centered, and quite superficial. She is primarily interested in shopping, buying clothes, going to the hairdresser, and making herself look good. She, like the housekeeper, is fastidious and treats the children as manikins to be dressed up and displayed. She is irritated when they dirty themselves, and she does not tolerate play that is in any way messy, rough, or physical. Herman also has a history of running high fevers, even with minor illnesses such as a cold or a sore throat. On several of these occasions he complained of dizzy spells and severe headaches; once he passed out for a brief time. Apart from having his tonsils removed when he was six years old and having frequent colds, his medical history was uneventful.

Practically every elementary classroom teacher and practicing child-clinician recognizes Herman—he represents a sizeable number of school-age youngsters who experience academic difficulties and failure, while evidencing behavioral problems. Within the last two decades there has been considerable confusion and controversy over the specific diagnostic label that one should properly use to categorize Herman's symptoms and problems, the etiological factors underlying his condition, and the best and most effective approach for treating his disorder. Before the mid-1950s Herman's school problems, in all likelihood, would have been regarded as typical of underachievement, although today he probably would be regarded as learning disabled. In days past his academic difficulties would have been called the product of either psychogenic factors (emotional problems and motivation) or demonstrable brain pathology (based on so called "hard" neurological evidence); for many contemporary writers Herman's learning disorder would be attributed to minimal brain dysfunction (based on so-called "soft" neurological signs). There would also be divergent views among practitioners concerning the choice of treatment method, especially as between the somatic and psychological approaches. In fact, the reader can gain some idea about the extent of the confusion surrounding this area by noting that there are more than forty terms currently used in the literature to refer to essentially the same condition as presented by Herman. Yet one is hard pressed to comprehend how such diverse labels as learning disorders, learning dysfunction, minimal brain damage, minimal cerebral dysfunction, or perceptual problem can have the same connotation for classification, etiology, or remediation (McDonald, 1968).

In this chapter we shall consider those disorders believed to be tied in some way to minimal brain pathology and "soft" neurological signs and which occur most often during the period of middle childhood. We shall begin by examining *minimal brain dysfunc-*

tion, its neurological and behavioral features, and its validity and usefulness as a construct. We shall then cover *learning disabilities* and the *hyperkinetic syndrome*.

MINIMAL BRAIN DYSFUNCTION (MBD)

The concept of MBD had its origin in the work of Strauss and his associates (Strauss and Lehtinen, 1947; Strauss and Kephart, 1955), who were interested in identifying those features that best differentiated between retarded youngsters with and without brain damage. Several characteristics emerged from their studies that reliably discriminated between the two groups and were related to brain damage: hyperactivity, impulsivity, distractibility, and aggressiveness. However, it is important to note that they interpreted their findings to mean that these characteristics—especially hyperactivity—are in fact *indicative* of brain damage. This huge and erroneous leap in thinking (taking correlational associations and interpreting them as cause and effect) became the basis for implicating some sort of neuropathology in the etiology of learning disabilities and the hyperkinetic syndrome. The term *MBD* was used to suggest that the damage is barely perceptible; it is verified not by conventional neurological signs or findings but rather by "soft" signs that are of questionable validity. The broader theory posits a continuum of brain impairment, ranging from severe to mild. Mild deficits are not detected by the conventional "hard" neurological signs but are manifest in the disruption of complex psychological functions and behaviors (Strother, 1973). As plausible as this argument may seem, it is difficult to understand how and why the concept of MBD and of its neurological basis has been so extensively accepted and perpetuated by many American writers in the absence of definitive corroborative evidence. In contrast, the idea of MBD is generally rejected by leading English writers as unsound and unsubstantiated (Rutter, Graham, and Yule, 1970; Schaffer, 1973; McFie, 1975).

Attempts to corroborate the concept of MBD empirically have used several different statistical approaches, such as cluster analysis and factor analysis, without much success (Langhorne et al., 1976). For example, on the basis of a cluster analysis of 3,000 children's clinical records, Jenkins (1964) could only statistically identify one dimension which he called brain injury, although the items making up this dimension did not reflect the hyperkinetic syndrome (except in girls) or provide either medical or historical evidence of brain damage. Moreover, the validity of the disorder has been called into question; studies have failed to yield significant intercorrelations between and among those psychological and behavioral features that are essential to the definition of MBD. Further, there is lack of agreement among clinicians and researchers as to what these essential characteristics are (Loney, 1980; Langhorne et al., 1976; Denckla, 1977).

Considerable confusion, controversy, and uncertainty also exist with regard to "soft" neurological signs. How reliable and valid are they, and do they discriminate brain damaged children from other psychiatric populations? Some writers use the term *"soft" signs* to refer to subtle and equivocal indications on conventional neurological tests. Others intend these signs to reflect deficits in neuropsychological functions (involving motor and cognitive behaviors that are often associated with and characteristic of brain-damaged persons). Still others think of "soft" signs as developmental delays or lags in normal development (but not necessarily indicative of permanent damage) (Schain, 1972; Benton, 1973; Strother, 1973; Denckla, 1977). In a recent experiment the relative frequency of primitive reflexes and abnormal postural adjustments were measured (as the "soft" signs reflecting developmental delay) in normal, neurologically handicapped, and emotionally disturbed children ranging in age from 39 to 121 months (Friedlander et al., 1982). However, while the two developmentally abnormal groups of children differed from normals on these measures, they did not differ from each other. The results showed that developmental delays of this sort are related to childhood psychopathology, but they do not differentiate neurologically damaged children from emotionally (but non–brain-damaged) disturbed children.

MBD is one of many terms used to categorize a vague and nonspecific group of children who are considered average or higher in intelligence and who evidence certain learning disabilities and behavioral difficulties (mostly hyperactivity) which are thought to be the result of some sort of neuropathology (Clements, 1966; Wender, 1971). There is considerable disagreement about the symptoms and behavioral characteristics that comprise MBD and little, if any, consensus concerning the "soft" neurological signs that are presumed to differentiate the disorder. Further, there is a paucity of evidence indicating either that the presumed "soft" signs occur as a result of brain pathology or that MBD is caused by neurological impairment. Having arrived at these conclusions on the basis of the available literature, it is difficult to understand the interest and enthusiasm manifest by the field in MBD, or to consider it as either a viable or useful concept and/or syndrome.

LEARNING DISABILITIES

Before the 1960s relatively little interest was shown in learning disabilities. However, some research was done on childhood aphasia and other language disturbances, and some remedial reading programs were established in strong public school systems around the country. Since that time specialists in speech, education, medicine, and psychology have made major contributions to the area. To some extent these professionals were prompted by the interest of an aroused and concerned segment of the citizenry (especially parents of children with learning difficulties). Today we have public funds supporting the training of specialists and enabling public schools to establish special educational programs for children with learning disabilities. The Children with Specific Learning Disabilities Act of 1969, PL 91–230, identified learning disabled children as those who evidence a disorder in either understanding or using language (written or spoken)—in other words, a disorder referred to as handicaps of perception, brain injury, minimal brain dysfunction, dyslexia, developmental aphasia, and so forth. The definition excluded learning difficulties that were due primarily to visual, auditory, or motor handicaps, mental retardation, emotional disturbance, or environmental disadvantages. In 1977 the definition was expanded by the Office of Education to include seven areas of functioning in which learning disabilities can occur, but which can be further reduced to the following categories: receptive and expressive language, reading and writing, and mathematics. Although there are many definitions of learning disabilities, and there are various state and local school provisions for establishing a child's eligibility and for constructing special education programs, there is widespread agreement as to the following: Learning disabled children must show a disparity between their expected and actual academic achievement, but not be mentally retarded, emotionally disturbed, visually or hearing handicapped, or environmentally deprived.

The mentally retarded have been excluded from the category of learning disorders probably because of practical considerations more than ideological ones. Since the definition of learning disabilities requires a discrepancy between expected achievement (based on the child's assets) and actual achievement in one or more specific areas of learning, it follows logically that the retarded child could, by this definition, have a learning disability in which such a disparity might be present. Admittedly, it is much more difficult to establish evidence for specific discrepancies in retarded children. This is due to the pervasive and generalized effect of mental retardation on many areas of functioning, and the fact that the discrepancy is likely to be small (perhaps imperceptible) as the expected capacity decreases in measurable units.

It is also customary to exclude children who are primarily emotionally disturbed from the rubric of learning disability, although the distinction between primary and secondary emotional problems is sometimes difficult to make—and most observers believe that learning disabilities are almost always accompanied by some emotional difficulties (Giffin, 1968; Harris, 1970). Efforts to set learning disabilities apart from psychotic and severely neurotic conditions are based on both practical and substantive considerations. There is marked dissimilarity between these groups in that children with severe emotional disorders are impaired and disturbed in many areas of functioning, whereas those with learning disorders are essentially intact except for a deficit in one or more of the basic learning processes (McCarthy, 1971).

DSM-III (APA, 1980) refers to learning disabilities as *specific developmental disorders* and codes them on a separate axis (II). This is a way of recognizing that no other signs of psychopathology are apparent in many children with this condition and of acknowledging that it is quite controversial to classify these conditions as "mental disorders." Indeed, both the label and concept of learning disabilities have little internal consistency, as evidenced by the large number of divergent terms used interchangeably to describe children with these difficulties (Cruickshank, 1972; Vaughan and Hodges, 1973; Divoky, 1974). In addition, the label is applied differently in various states and school systems, and it is altered by many clinicians and teachers to fit the economic, social, or other unique aspects of a situation at a particular time. It is not applied consistently across situations as if it had integrity and substance of its own (Divoky, 1974; Rist and Harrell, 1982).

Incidence and Prevalence

Accurate incidence and/or prevalence figures are difficult to obtain because of the heterogeneous criteria used to diagnose the condition and because of the controversies that continue over which term, which array of symptoms, and which children fit the category. Nevertheless, available estimates range from 5 to 28 percent of grade school children who show multiple or single signs of learning disability (Wender, 1971; Denckla, 1977; Bryant and McLoughlin, 1972). Most observers agree that learning disabilities represent a large, if not the largest, referral problem in school-aged children.

Reading Disorder

Achievement in reading that is below the child's level of accomplishment in other academic areas or below the child's potential for learning in general is undoubtedly the most frequent specific learning disability. This reason alone would justify its consideration here. But at a different level of discourse, reading disabilities also may serve as a model for the entire field of learning disabilities. Disparities in incidence estimates, definition of terms, etiological views, and remedial approaches are found in both learning disorders in general and reading difficulties in particular.

Authoritative sources estimate that more than 10 percent of the school population in the United States experiences reading problems, and at least one source believes that it may be as high as 20 to 40 percent ("Reading Disorders in the United States," 1969; Goldberg and Schiffman, 1972; de Ajuriaguerra, 1980). Like so many other disorders of childhood, reading problems are found more frequently in boys than in girls, with estimates ranging from 3:1 to 5:1 (Goldenson, 1957; Myklebust and Johnson, 1962; Denckla, 1977;

de Ajuriaguerra, 1980). Interesting, but somewhat puzzling, is the finding that reading problems are ten times more prevalent in western countries than in Japan (Makita, 1968).

While these incidence figures tell us little about the criteria used to establish the disability, or the differential effectiveness of school reading programs across the country, they are impressive in reflecting the enormity and seriousness of the problem. Early acquisition of reading proficiency is a necessary skill for satisfactory progress in most other areas of study; it is also an important determinant of later vocational, economic, and social prospects. Poor readers make poor students and face limited vocational choices and restricted income potential. While cause and effect is not clear, the fact remains that juvenile delinquency and other forms of antisocial behaviors are highly associated with reading difficulties (Margolin, Roman, and Harari, 1955). The repeated experience of failure in reading generalizes to other academic areas and contributes to increasing feelings of inadequacy, alienation, and frustration. Acting-out behaviors and conduct problems in the classroom may provide emotional outlets and gratification of attentional needs. Should this behavioral pattern be reinforced in the absence of other successes, it is possible for it to become dominant. There is evidence that reading failures become chronic and difficult to modify (15 percent success) if the disability is not identified and treated before the fifth grade. In contrast, more than 80 percent of the children diagnosed and remediated as reading problems in the second grade were able within two years to read at their normal grade level (Schiffman and Clemmens, 1966).

Since Kussmaul (1877) used the term *word blindness* to refer to an inability to read in the absence of any demonstrable impairment of vision, speech, or intelligence, many labels have appeared in the literature to designate the same, or a similar phenomenon. In 1937 Orton introduced the term *dyslexia* to describe significant underachieving specific to reading (much below the level of accomplishments in other academic areas) in which there is a persistent tendency to reverse letters and words and a general confusion among words. Other terms, such as *primary reading disability, specific developmental dyslexia, congenital word blindness, developmental lag,* and *specific reading disability* have been used interchangeably and synonymously with *dyslexia.* Generally speaking, the term *dyslexia* is now employed to designate those children of average or slightly-below-average intelligence with specific retardation in reading, who have not been deprived of educational opportunities or who do not show any gross evidence of either sensory or neurological impairment.

Typically dyslexic children have difficulty comprehending written language and competently managing other language functions, such as spelling, writing, and speech. They may be left-handed or ambidextrous, and they tend to be poorly coordinated, awkward, and clumsy. Before beginning school, many are considered intellectually bright—an observation that is periodically supported by their good verbal responses in classroom discussion. Their initial grades in arithmetic are high, but they are likely to decline as reading proficiency becomes more essential in solving written problems and in taking examinations. They frequently show emotional disturbances as a reaction to repeated failures and a lowering of self-esteem.

Tremblay (1982) notes that there are two general types of reading diagnosis: (1) the traditional diagnosis—which determines the grade level for word comprehension and recognition and which tries to determine what reading skills are lacking; and (2) the process diagnosis—which assesses reading problems and ascribes difficulties to various areas presumed to be associated with reading, such as visual and auditory memory, coordination, visual perception, auditory modalities, and so forth. Trembley finds the process type of diagnosis especially faulty, since it tends to identify the deficient area or areas for a given youngster, without concern that the implied causal relationship is unconfirmed and unsubstantiated by research.

Two primary types of difficulties have been suggested, each involving reading impairment in either the auditory or visual modality (Johnson and Myklebust, 1967; Clark, 1973). Dyslexic children with auditory defects have trouble learning to read because they are unable to develop phonetic skills. Auditory perceptions are made, but some defect in the neurological pathway prevents the information from being integrated in the language area of the brain. Thus, these children are said to have poor auditory association with what they see. As a group they are more difficult to remediate than those youngsters with visual defects, especially when auditory spatial perceptions are disturbed. In contrast, youngsters with visual defects typically have phonetic skills, but they are apt to have problems in spelling; in reading maps, graphs, and floor plans; and in dealing with spatial symbols necessary for proficiency in mathematics. They often omit letters in reading a word, thus changing its meaning—such as *mit* for *might.* Recent research has demonstrated significant differences between dyslexic and normal children in visual information and in the perception and organization of broken-up words embedded in ambiguous stimuli (Stanley and Hall, 1973; Feild and Feild, 1974).

Causal Factors. It is apparent that reading problems (much like the broader category of learning disabilities) represent heterogenous conditions for which there is no single cause (Denckla, 1977). Proponents of a genetic view find support in data from twin and family studies that indicate a high prevalence of reading problems in monozygotic twins and in close relatives (parents and siblings) of dyslexic children (Hallgren, 1950; Frisk et al., 1967; Symmes and Rapoport, 1972; Matheny and Dolan, 1974; de Ajuriaguerra, 1980). But as we have noted in previous discussions of genetics, data of this sort can be interpreted to support either a genetic or a social transmission view.

Although evidence of gross neurological involvement or impairment is not usually discernible; there is a persistent assumption by a large segment of contemporary writers that brain dysfunction is the etiological basis of reading disorders and other learning disabilities. This view excludes easily detectable brain damage, which may be responsible for such conditions as cerebral palsy, epilepsy, mental retardation, and sensory disorders. Instead, it refers to instances where no obvious signs of brain pathology are evident, and where inferences are made from certain behaviors that presumably reflect minimal neurological impairment or brain dysfunction. Gross motor functioning such as sitting, crawling, and walking develop normally, while problems in fine motor coordination are likely to be evident. Handedness is often established late, and riding a bicycle is extremely difficult—as is fastening buttons, cutting with scissors, or tying shoelaces. In forming fine motor acts, these children are awkward and clumsy to the extent that they require and usually receive parental assistance. Sharp and sudden mood swings ranging from timidity to violent emotional outbursts—along with hyperactivity, distractibility, and short attention span—are additional characteristics of these youngsters. They have few, if any, friends, either because they have frightened them off through their display of emotional instability and hyperactivity or because other children are forbidden to play with them (Goldberg and Schiffman, 1972).

Evidence supporting a neurological view is indirect and inconclusive. Prematurity and complications of birth and birth weight are among the early and potential signs of neurological impairment that have been shown to be related to later academic problems in more of these children than among normal controls (Wender, 1971). However, it is not at all clear why the vast majority of these high-risk infants never become learning disabled. As noted by Grossman (1966):

> Actually, there is no syndrome, no aggregate of neurological signs, that can be correlated with any specific learning and/or behavior disorder. Indeed, many youngsters with profound aberrations of motor functioning do well in school, in their studies and in their interpersonal relationships. (p. 63)

There are those who regard minimal brain dysfunction as an unproven and strictly inferred diagnosis that has little meaning and application for educational remediation. The extensive study by Paine and his associates (Paine, Werry, and Quay, 1971) showed that minimal cerebral dysfunction is not a homogeneous diagnostic condition but essentially a descriptive label for a diverse set of neurological, behavioral, and cognitive dysfunctions.

Satz (Satz, Rardin, and Ross, 1971) and his associates favor the view that dyslexia is a maturational lag in brain development that differentially impedes progress in those skills that are in primary ascendancy at different times in the child's life. For example, the skills that normally develop early will be delayed in young children with maturational lags, while the skills that show a slower rate of development will be delayed in older youngsters who have this maturational immaturity. Since reading proficiency is dependent on the prior development of perceptual discrimination and analysis, a lag in the maturation of the brain, according to this view, should be evident early in poor perceptual functioning. Moreover, measures of these behaviors should be predictive of subsequent reading disabilities. In a report of a two-year follow-up study of almost 500 kindergarten boys who were initially given an extensive developmental and neuropsychological test battery, Satz and Friel (1974) obtained data that supported their theory.

Another view implicates the long-term effects of nutritional and environmental deprivation as sufficiently potent to produce neurological dysfunction (Hallahan and Cruickshank, 1973). Inasmuch as nutrition is a basic determinant of growth and development, it should also affect the maturation of higher brain functions. For the human infant the first six months of life are probably the most critical as a nutritional period; it is during this time that maximal postnatal brain-cell division occurs. Of equal significance is the maternal, sensory, and environmental deprivation that, according to some writers, can produce neurological deficits or a nondeveloping nervous system capable of producing learning disabilities (Grotberg, 1970).

More recently Money (1982) and Frisch and Rhoads (1982) suggested a link between child abuse and neglect and learning disabilities. Money, especially, notes that there is ample evidence that child abuse and neglect can be a primary cause of IQ impairment and learning disability of a permanent nature, although this explanation has largely been rejected in favor of genetic, neurological, or other quasi-biological causes. Frisch and Rhoads studied 430 children from Hawaii who were referred for evaluation of learning problems. They found an extremely high rate (three and a half times higher than expected in the normal population) of children in their sample who were independently referred for child abuse. Their findings (and those of other researchers) indicate a significant relationship between child abuse, neglect, and maltreatment and subsequent cognitive impairment and deficit.

The psychodynamic influence of Freud highlighted intrapsychic conflicts and motivational variables as important determinants of reading disorders and other learning disabilities. Inhibition of curiosity, repression of scoptophilic impulses (wishes for forbidden and anxiety-laden events), fantasies of aggression, and family tendencies to deny and distort the external reality, among other fanciful notions, have been suggested as causes of learning problems (Kessler, 1966; Heinicke, 1972). More empirically oriented work has shown that academic underachievers, as compared to controls, have poor self-concepts and are more hostile toward their environment (Shaw, 1968). One study also found that boys with learning difficulties experience more specific emotional traumas, but these findings were so general that they would be difficult to replicate (Brodie and Winterbottom, 1967). Families of underachievers tend not to place a high value on formal learning for their children, and they tend to show less mutual acceptance among family members, less sharing and communication, less awareness of each other, and less satisfaction in their family relationships (Morrow, 1970). Mothers of first-born learning disabled children evidenced over-protectiveness toward their disabled youngsters and less concern over the opinions others held about them, while families with learning disabled children who were second born did not behave in this way (Epstein, Berg-Cross, and Berg-Cross, 1980).

In general, the evidence for a psychogenic view of learning disabilities is inconclusive, imprecise, and no more convincing than the support for a biological position. While clinicians believe that emotional factors play an important role in many instances of disturbed learning, the role of these factors as etiological variables still must be demonstrated empirically.

Treatment Approaches. The heterogeneity of terminology and of etiological possibilities in the area of learning disabilities is only exceeded by the diversity of remedial approaches suggested in the literature. Clinical reports and testimonials can be found lauding the effectiveness of almost every treatment method, from psychodynamically oriented psychotherapy, to special training in the development of perceptual motor skills, to behavior modification, to educational remedies, to chemotherapy. In 1972 Heinicke reviewed both a number of his own studies using psychoanalytic psychotherapy and other investigations employing remedial education with children who had reading disabilities. He found that both types of treatment tended to improve reading, although the gains were not sustained after treatment was terminated.

A variety of special training programs designed to facilitate perceptual skills and the neurological organization necessary for learning in general—and reading in particular—have received widespread recognition. The notable contributions of Kephart, Getman, Barsch, and Frostig, along with the controversial work of Doman and Delacato, share (with slight variations) the assumption that early motor development is necessary for normal perceptual development and for later emergence of conceptual abilities in children (Hallahan and Cruickshank, 1973). Doman and Delacato asserted that brain damage or "poor neurological organization" was responsible for most learning disabilities (Doman et al., 1960). Their view as well as their training procedures, which have been negatively evaluated, relied heavily on outdated concepts of localization of function within the brain, and hemispheric dominance (Robbins and Glass, 1969). Training consisted of practice in specific motor patterns to (1) stimulate various areas of the brain, (2) impose hemispheric dominance, and (3) give carbon dioxide to increase blood circulation in the brain.

The use of drugs in the treatment of learning disabilities is a complex and perplexing matter because of the heterogeneity inherent in the disorder. Further, we must consider the variable and sometimes unknown effects drugs have on children. According to Goldberg and Schiffman (1972), a drug such as dilantin is best used with children who have minimal neurological signs and abnormal EEG tracings, while ritalin is recommended for those who are both learning disabled and hyperactive. For emotionally disturbed children thorazine may help to reduce anxiety and increase learning. Stimulant drugs such as the amphetamines may be useful with children who have both behavioral and learning difficulties, but these should not be prescribed beyond the age of twelve. Barbiturates and phenothiazines should not be used, because they are likely to depress learning and contribute to a decline in intellectual functioning. Moreover, the following caution should be sounded whenever drugs are used:

> Laymen and professional people alike will do well, in their involvement in the learning problems of children, to be more aware of the potential dangers in administering drugs to children. The indiscriminate and unsupervised administration of tranquilizers in the home or classroom to children who manifest behavioral and/or learning problems is a form of Russian roulette. (Goldberg and Schiffman, 1972, p. 154)

A technique of repeated reading or some variation of this approach has been described in the literature as increasing the reading fluency of some slow readers (Chomsky, 1978; Moyer, 1979, 1982; Neill, 1980). The approach involves the selection of reading material that the subject can read without difficulty and with a great deal of accuracy. The selection is read and then repeated three or four times, each time at a faster rate than before. When fluency is achieved, a new and more difficult selection is tried. This approach provides for a great deal of practice in reading at the same level of difficulty, and sometimes it is combined with listening activities. The findings, thus far, consistently show increased fluency and speed, along with a decrease in the number of reading errors, both with children of average intelligence and with those who are mentally retarded, and with various age groups (Samuels, 1979; Carver and Hoffman, 1981; Moyer, 1982). While repeated reading shows a great deal of promise much more needs to be learned about this approach. For example, we don't know which slow readers profit from this approach and which do not, and why. We also need to learn more about the task variables and how these affect reading rate and accuracy. Variables such as the level of difficulty of the reading selection, the number of repetitions, the speed of repeated readings, and so forth have yet to be systematically studied.

Usually tangible reinforcement is used to effect positive changes in children who have difficulties in academic achievement. In fact, it has been shown that the combined use of praise and a token facilitates reading acquisition and improves the child's retention of the learned material (Lahey and Drabman, 1974). Ross (1981) noted that reading can be successfully taught by discrimination learning. It has also been demonstrated that behavior modification programs designed to remediate reading problems can be carried out successfully by lay trainers such as high school seniors, parents, and college students (Staats et al., 1967; Ryback and Staats, 1970; Schwartz, 1977). The data, at present, suggest that this is a promising approach that can be effectively used by laypersons to improve reading skills in children. However, it is important to note that decisions about the schedule of reinforcement, the kind of tokens, and the back-up reinforcers used need to be individualized for the subjects by a person who is highly trained and experienced in the technical aspects of operant principles. Although behavior modification has been widely employed to improve the teaching and management of children in the classroom, there are comparatively few studies available that have involved either a substantial number of subjects with specific learning disabilities or follow-up data.

THE HYPERKINETIC SYNDROME

> Beth was five-and-a-half years old at the time her parents arranged for her evaluation at a guidance clinic. The parents noted that they had considerable difficulty in disciplining her and that similar problems were reported by her kindergarten teacher. The teacher also observed that Beth was easily distracted, inattentive, hyperactive, and impaired in visual-motor coordination, raising the possibility of a perceptual problem.
>
> Beth was the oldest of three, and she came from a lower-middle-class background. Mother's pregnancy with Beth went quite well, but the labor

and delivery were difficult in that labor lasted about twenty hours and forceps were necessary to deliver the child. She was born with the umbilical cord wrapped around her neck and she was slightly blue at birth (indicating anoxia). She was in intensive care for the first 48 hours of her life. Her development proceeded at a slower than average rate; she was unable to sit unaided until she was nine months. She crawled at thirteen months and walked at nineteen months. While she spoke (single words) by twenty months, she did not speak in sentences until she was thirty-three months. Toilet training was difficult and completed at three years. However, mother reported that she (Beth) continues to wet the bed on infrequent occasions. When she was two years old, there were four separate times that she fell on her head, but she never lost consciousness or evidenced any symptoms following the accidents.

Mother reported that Beth would not follow her instructions, and that she was frequently given to temper tantrums primarily when Beth was required to do something that she did not want to do. Threats, shouting, and spankings apparently did nothing to change Beth's behavior. The child was extremely active and never played in one place for any length of time. She tired quickly of whatever activity she was involved in, and as she moved from one thing to another she left a litter of toys and objects which she refused to pick up. Beth's constant penchant for getting into trouble through overactivity, short attention span, frequent temper tantrums, and refusals to respond to parental directions tended to place a heavy strain on her interactions with members of her family.

In school, Beth was overactive, highly distractible, and unable to persist in an activity for any length of time. Her teacher noted that she tended to run into or over objects that were in her way, and that her performance on perceptual motor tasks was well below the average (cutting and pasting, drawing, building objects with blocks, and copying letters or numbers).

A neurological examination revealed a normal EEG, and no evidence of either generalized or localized abnormalities in brain functioning. Reflex development and motor coordination were below age level, but not considered grossly abnormal. On the basis of her difficulty in fine motor coordination and in perceptual tasks, the neurologist concurred with the diagnosis of minimal brain damage. (excerpts from Leon, 1974, pp. 35–42)

Children like Beth stand out in a crowd because their activity level and their disruptive behaviors demand attention and usually elicit negative responses from others. They are management problems wherever they are, be it at home or in school, and they require constant supervision because they never seem to respond favorably to corrective measures. Although Beth is clearly hyperactive, the nature of her problem, and what to do about it, are complex issues that have been the subject of considerable clinical and research interest and controversy.

The term *hyperactivity* has been used to connote either a *symptom*—describing heightened activity level—or, more often, a *syndrome*—collectively reflecting a specific disease (Ross and Ross, 1976). It falls short as a purely quantitative measure of behavior, since norms for children's activity level are virtually nonexistent, and because children vary considerably in activity output within themselves across different situations and among themselves in specific situations (Rapoport and Benoit, 1975; Schleifer et al., 1975). To date there are only a few studies that report data on activity level and restlessness in hyperkinetic children who are otherwise physically and intellectually normal (Pope, 1970; Sykes, 1971; Hayim-Sagon, 1982). Pope measured activity level by means of a device (accelerometer) worn on the wrist and ankle that reliably recorded leg and arm movement. She found that greater locomotor and total motor activity, along with shorter attention span, characterized hyperkinetic children. Moreover, her results suggested that excessive activity in the hyperactive child is specific to a situation (found only on difficult tasks) rather than general to all situations. Sykes's (1971) study used a stabilimetric cushion (a device to measure motor activity while the subject is stationary) to measure restlessness and to show that hyperkinetic children were significantly more restless than the controls. More recently Hayim-Sagon (1982) used a specially designed and constructed motion-sensitive chair to measure and record the movements of highly active and normally active first- and second-grade children. She also used teacher ratings to measure the general activity level of the subjects, which she found to be more sensitive and discriminating than the chair. Not only did these studies indicate differences in motor activity between hyperactive and normal children, but they also empirically suggested that the type and amount of activity is influenced greatly by the specific situation.

Even more unsatisfactory is the use of the term *hyperactivity* for a clinical syndrome, since it is questionable that the symptoms from a unitary dimension reflect a common etiology (Werry, 1968). In fact, Werry and associates (1972) have shown that hyperactivity, learning difficulties, and mild or minor neurological dysfunction (three major symptoms often alleged by clinicians to occur together) do not reliably occur together in the same child. Instead, they are more likely to represent three different and distinct clinical disorders. At one time children who are persistently overactive, distractible, impulsive, and emotionally excitable were thought to be neurologically impaired or brain damaged (Strauss and Lehtinen, 1947). However, more recent research has shown that this hyperkinetic behavior pattern is neither an inevitable nor even a likely consequence of brain pathology. Further, the syndrome is often seen in children who show no history or clinical evidence of brain injury (Chess, 1960; Ernhart et al., 1963; Schulman, Kasper, and Thorne, 1965; Stewart et al., 1966; Paine, Werry, and Quay, 1968; Sroufe, 1975). Moreover, Ross and Ross (1976) make the excellent observation that

> . . . there are many statements in the literature accompanied by extensive research evidence that support the view that hyperactivity is a nonspecific symptom occurring in a variety of medical and behavioral disorders and associated with a heterogeneous group of etiological factors. Yet, *for the most part*, research on pharmocologic, behavioral, and educational intervention has treated hyperactive children as a homogeneous group of subjects. As the label *hyperactive child syndrome* is commonly used it implies that there is *one* kind of hyperactive child, a belief that has been detrimental to progress in research on and treatment of hyperactivity. (p. 11)

As a syndrome, hyperactivity has also been known by various interchangeable labels, such as hyperkinesis, minimal brain dysfunction, minimal brain damage, and even learning disability. None of these terms should be taken to imply a specific etiology; instead, the behavioral pattern should be attributed to a variety of causative factors. Because hyperactivity, short attention span, and restlessness often accompany learning problems, some writers have tended to include the syndrome under the general rubric of learning disabilities (Keogh, 1971; Wender, 1971; Minde, 1977). Unfortunately, as we have already seen, the category of learning disabilities is ambiguous and heterogeneous, and it may include a number of specific learning disabilities that either do or do not evidence any behavioral traits of a hyperactive nature. In order to minimize the confounding of these conditions and to identify a more homogeneous syndrome, in this section we shall focus on those children who manifest the behavioral patterns of hyperactivity but who are otherwise physiologically and intellectually normal.

Hyperactivity in children is bothersome, frustrating, exasperating, and extremely troublesome to others, especially to parents and teachers who must deal with it on a daily basis. It is one of the most frequent reasons for referral to child guidance clinics, and it represents about 10 percent of referrals to private practitioners (Chess, 1960; Patterson et al., 1965; Safer, 1971). Other data estimate its occurrence in from 3 to 10 percent of children (Burks, 1960; Stewart et al., 1966;

Comly, 1971; Miller, Palkes, and Stewart, 1973). A more recent review sets the upper limit of occurrence as high as 20 percent (Whalen and Henker, 1976). Hyperkinesis is found more frequently in boys than in girls, with sex ratios ranging anywhere from 5:1 to 9:1 (Eisenberg, 1966; Stevens, Sachdev, and Milstein, 1968; "Report of the Conference on the Use of Stimulant Drugs in the Treatment of Behaviorally Disturbed Young School Children," 1971; Silver, 1971; Trites et al., 1979).

A review of the research literature indicates a fairly consistent behavioral picture associated with the hyperkinetic syndrome (Kleemeier, 1974). One study surveyed five professional groups (pediatricians, teachers, psychologists, psychiatrists, and social workers) with respect to the criteria each used in diagnosing hyperkinesis (Schrager et al., 1966). The professionals were given a fifty-five-item behavioral checklist and were instructed to choose those six behaviors they regarded as most significant in identifying the hyperkinetic syndrome. The six behaviors rated by each group as frequently as 75 percent or more as indicative of hyperkinesis were fidgety, inattentive, hard-to-manage, easily distracted, can't sit still, and low frustration tolerance. In another study, data obtained from an extensive standardized interview of mothers of hyperactive and normal elementary school children were compared (Stewart et al., 1966). Marked differences were found between the groups in such behaviors as overactiveness, can't sit still, can't accept correction, temper tantrums, irritability, destructiveness, unresponsiveness to discipline, defiance, doesn't complete project, doesn't listen to whole story, doesn't follow directions, recklessness, and unpopularity with peers. Table 10-1 shows the behavioral profile of the hyperactive child.

Table 10-1

I. At home
  1. Cannot remain still
  2. Cannot conform to limits or prohibitions
  3. Makes excessive demands
  4. Has sleeping problems
  5. Shows unwarranted aggression
  6. Is general "pest"

II. At school
  1. Is talkative
  2. Fidgets continuously
  3. Cannot concentrate
  4. Has short attention span
  5. Cannot conform to limits or prohibitions
  6. Shows poor school achievement

III. Relationships with other children
  1. Cannot make friends
  2. Fights without provocation
  3. Has poor manners
  4. Is extremely bossy
  5. Disregards rights of others
  6. Is constantly rejected

Ross and Ross, © 1976, p. 276. Reprinted with permission from John Wiley & Sons, Inc.

In addition, some clinicians agree on the typical descriptive patterns of these children, without implicating a specific or single etiology (Stewart and Olds, 1973; Laufer, 1967, pp. 1442–1452). Onset is ordinarily noted early in life (usually before six years of age), and the disorder is especially common in firstborn males. The newborn may be extremely sensitive to external stimuli, tending to respond to them in a massive and undifferentiated manner. The child is very active in the crib and playpen, often wearing the mother out with repeated escapes whenever she turns her back. Successful escapes may lead to a path of destruction as the child touches everything in sight or spills, breaks, empties, and disturbs almost all the contents of the room as he or she moves purposelessly about. The child sleeps little and is reluctant to go to bed, but is often up before someone in the household can prevent him or her from either disturbing the family or getting into some sort of trouble. The child is restless and fidgety at mealtimes and actively disruptive in school, where he or she is apt to be up and out of his or her seat much of the time. Short attention span is to be expected, although occasionally the child may be able to sit for lengthy periods of time watching television or reading a book. Any pressure to complete a task triggers activity and increases the likelihood of failure and interpersonal squabbles. Blurting out an answer in class before being called on, hitting a friend, playing hooky, losing things, or in some other way getting into trouble is characteristic of the hyperkinetic child, probably because the child is impulsive and disinclined to think before acting. The child is also excitable, emotionally labile, and easily frustrated; at one moment the child can be happy, while in the next he or she can be irritable, hostile, or tearful.

Information about the developmental course of hyperkinesis is sparse, especially as regards infancy and the adult years (Campbell, 1976). Nevertheless, Campbell notes that retrospective reports of mothers of hyperactive children suggest that these youngsters slept more, had more eating and colic problems, and tended to be more irritable (during the first six months) than nonhyperactive babies. Moreover, about half the mothers reported a difficult neonatal course. Activity level remained consistent over time during the preschool years and seemed to be predictive of the level of activity observed in the elementary school years. Hyperactivity tends to become most noticeable and troublesome during the elementary school years, when the affected youngsters evidence impulsivity and poor attention, academic achievement, and social functioning. Although it has long been clinically accepted that hyperactivity dissipates with age, particularly during adolescence, the results of recent follow-up studies indicate that children of this sort continue to manifest academic failures, emotional immaturity, impairment in attention and concentration, and even behavioral (antisocial and rebellious) problems (Minde et al., 1971; Weiss et al., 1971; Hoy et al., 1978). While little is known about the course of hyperactivity in adults, preliminary research findings suggest that the adjustment of these individuals improves in the adult years (Campbell, 1976).

Although hyperactivity has been considered a major and prominent feature of the hyperkinetic syndrome, research has demonstrated that impaired attention may be an even more important characteristic than activity level (Kirchner, 1975; Hayim-Sagon, 1982; Douglas, 1972; Goldberg and Konstantareas, 1981). In fact, DSM-III (APA, 1980) reflects this shift in symptom priority, making attention deficits the most important feature—because it is prominent and persistent in almost all cases—and hyperactivity a secondary one—because, if present, it tends to diminish in adolescence. Consequently, DSM-III provides the following categories: Attention Deficit Disorder with Hyperactivity, Attention Deficit Disorder without Hyperactivity, and Attention Deficit Disorder, Residual Type. Tables 10-2, 10-3, and 10-4 give the specific diagnostic criteria noted in DSM-III (APA, 1980, pp. 43 and 44, 44, and 44 and 45, respectively).

Causal Factors

While hyperactivity following some type of brain damage is possible, most hyperkinetic children show no evidence or history that would suggest injury to the central nervous system. Yet many writers in the field still cling to a biological view, including the disorder under the general category of minimal brain dysfunction. This term, like the label learning disabilities, is used to refer to a number of disparate conditions. Consequently, it is imprecise, and perhaps more important, it is misleading. Surely, if brain dysfunction is involved, the damage must be more than minimal to produce such serious and disruptive behavioral patterns. In addition, the vague etiological assumption of this diagnosis tends to confuse and frighten parents, who take it to mean that the child's brain is damaged in some unknown, but irreparable, way. The assumption of minimal brain dysfunction—or the view that neurological, biochemical, or some other biological abnormality causes this disorder—is not supported by the literature at this time (Dubey, 1976; Ross and Ross, 1976).

Two recent reviews of the research on the

Table 10-2 Diagnostic Criteria for Attention Deficit Disorder with Hyperactivity

The child displays, for his or her mental and chronological age, signs of developmentally inappropriate inattention, impulsivity, and hyperactivity. The signs must be reported by adults in the child's environment, such as parents and teachers. Because the symptoms are typically variable, they may not be observed directly by the clinician. When the reports of teachers and parents conflict, primary consideration should be given to the teacher reports because of greater familiarity with age-appropriate norms. Symptoms typically worsen in situations that require self-application, as in the classroom. Signs of the disorder may be absent when the child is in a new or a one-to-one situation.

The number of symptoms specified is for children between the ages of eight and ten, the peak age range for referral. In younger children, more severe forms of the symptoms and a greater number of symptoms are usually present. The opposite is true of older children.

A. **Inattention.** At least three of the following:
   (1) often fails to finish things he or she starts
   (2) often doesn't seem to listen
   (3) easily distracted
   (4) has difficulty concentrating on schoolwork or other tasks requiring sustained attention
   (5) has difficulty sticking to a play activity

B. **Impulsivity.** At least three of the following:
   (1) often acts before thinking
   (2) shifts excessively from one activity to another
   (3) has difficulty organizing work (this not being due to cognitive impairment)
   (4) needs a lot of supervision
   (5) frequently calls out in class
   (6) has difficulty awaiting turn in games or group situations

C. **Hyperactivity.** At least two of the following:
   (1) runs about or climbs on things excessively
   (2) has difficulty sitting still or fidgets excessively
   (3) has difficulty staying seated
   (4) moves about excessively during sleep
   (5) is always "on the go" or acts as if "driven by a motor"

D. Onset before the age of seven.

E. Duration of at least six months.

F. Not due to Schizophrenia, Affective Disorder, or Severe or Profound Mental Retardation.

DSM-III, pp. 43–44.

Table 10-3 Diagnostic Criteria for Attention Deficit Disorder without Hyperactivity

The criteria for this disorder are the same as those for Attention Deficit Disorder with Hyperactivity except that the individual never had signs of hyperactivity (criterion C).

DSM-III, p. 44.

Table 10-4 Diagnostic Criteria for Attention Deficit Disorder, Residual Type

A. The individual once met the criteria for Attention Deficit Disorder with Hyperactivity. This information may come from the individual or from others, such as family members.

B. Signs of hyperactivity are no longer present, but other signs of the illness have persisted to the present without periods of remission, as evidenced by signs of both attentional deficits and impulsivity (e.g., difficulty organizing work and completing tasks, difficulty concentrating, being easily distracted, making sudden decisions without thought of the consequences.

C. The symptoms of inattention and impulsivity result in some impairment in social or occupational functioning.

D. Not due to Schizophrenia, Affective Disorder, Severe or Profound Mental Retardation, or Schizotypal or Borderline Personality Disorders.

DSM-III, pp. 44, 45.

genetics of the hyperactive child syndrome indicate that there is evidence—but not proof—supporting family transmission (1) in the higher prevalence rates of the syndrome in first- and second-degree relatives of probands than in normal controls, (2) in the higher incidence of the syndrome in biological relatives when nonbiological parents of adopted hyperactive children are compared with biological parents of nonadopted hyperactives, and (3) in twin studies that find a higher concordance for monozygotic pairs (Cantwell, 1975; Ross and Ross, 1976). However, the evidence is based on relatively few studies, which were

Sidelight 10-1

The following is a transcript of a doctor's inadequate discussion of the diagnosis and treatment of minimal brain dysfunction with a young mother. This interaction occurred in a university clinic where pediatricians from the community regularly gave volunteer hours; all interactions with the patients were routinely recorded for teaching purposes, and a red indicator light informed the doctor that his conversation was being taped:

Doctor: It seems as though this young man (taps chart) has brain damage, well, uh, not brain *damage,* MBD, that is, minimal brain *dysfunction.*

Mother: (clearly shocked) You mean it's his *brain?* All the school said was that he was hyperkinetic and very distractible.

Doctor: Oh, sure, well, MBD and hyperkinetic are really the same thing. MBD just means that his brain isn't working properly right now so things get a bit out of control especially in school. But he'll probably grow out of it, a lot of these MBD kids are fine by the time they get to adolescence. It's not his intelligence, there isn't anything wrong with *that,* he's a bright boy.

Mother: (sounds very troubled) I never thought of him having anything wrong with his *brain.* How does this brain dysfunction happen, like what caused it? Is it something we did?

Doctor: Well, now, we don't really know what caused it. A lot of this kind of thing happens before birth or at birth. It's pretty difficult to pinpoint the cause. We aren't really sure most of the time how it happened.

Mother: You mean he might have had it all his life?

Doctor: That's right.

Mother: How could he have had it all this time and never had any trouble until he's seven years old and in the second grade?

Doctor: Oh, well, that's when MBD shows up. In school. These MBD children often don't have any trouble until they get in school. But don't worry, we can fix him up with some medication. He'll be fine in school once he's on medication.

Mother: What will the medication do? It's not drugs, it it? What kind of medication is it?

Doctor: It'll quiet him down and he'll get on a lot better in school . . . the teacher'll love him now. The medication we're going to try first is a stimulant called—

Mother: (interrupting) *A stimulant!* That's the last thing he needs. Is that some kind of drug?

Doctor: (coldly) Mrs. A., with these brain-damaged children stimulants have a quieting effect. You'll be *amazed* at the difference. We'll try one kind for a week or two and see how it goes; you just have to play it by ear at the beginning because we never know which kind will work best for a child, and if it doesn't do the trick we'll try another kind. Now you just take this prescription (hands it to the mother and starts to move toward the door) and be sure you don't forget to give them to him morning and afternoon. If these pills work and you forget to give him one you'll really know it, he'll go right back to being a nuisance in class. Now we'll check with you in a week, we have to watch out for side effects . . . they *can* be a problem . . . so we'll check with you in a week. O.K.?

Mother: (reluctantly) O.K., but you didn't tell me if this was drugs. I don't want him getting started on drugs.

Doctor: (showing patient out) Now, now, don't you worry about that, after all, you give him aspirin, don't you? Now you phone me. (Doctor terminates interview) (From *Hyperactivity: Research, Theory and Action,* Ross and Ross, Copyright © 1976. John Wiley & Sons, Inc. Reprinted by permission of John Wiley & Sons, Inc.)

The interview was obviously flawed by the doctor's confusion and by his failure to deal with the mother's anxiety about her son's problem and her role in it. Nevertheless, it reflects the potential danger involved in the etiological assumption inherent in the diagnosis and in the indiscriminate use of drugs in the treatment of the disorder.

frequently marred by methodological inadequacies.

A neurochemical hypothesis of minimal brain dysfunction that involves the catecholamines (dopamine and norepinephrine) has been proposed by a number of investigators (Brase and Loh, 1975). One study generates an interesting model for the minimal brain dysfunction syndrome from data obtained from selective depletion of brain dopamine in developing rats (Shaywitz, Yager, and Klopper, 1976). Neonatal rats depleted of brain dopamine showed increased levels of activity as compared to controls, but their hyperactivity declined as they reached maturity. At the same time the treated rats continued to evidence learning deficits in adulthood. The study suggests that early dopamine depletion produces hyperactivity that declines around the time of puberty; while the cognitive, perceptual, and emotional problems persist. In support of a biological view, Rapoport, Quinn, and Lamprecht (1974) described a group of severely hyperkinetic boys who had a high frequency of minor physical anomalies (large head circumference, low-set ears, curved fingers, large gap between first and second toe, and so forth). These children evidenced a high frequency of either hyperactivity in the father or obstetrical difficulties at birth. In addition, the plasma levels of dopamine-beta-hydoxylase (an enzyme involved in the synthesis of norepinephrine) were correlated positively with the physical anomalies in their sample of youngsters. Those who favor a biological view also tend to cite studies that have found a higher incidence of abnormal EEGs in hyperkinetic children as compared to controls. However, many would argue that the abnormality in EEG tracings alone is insufficient evidence of any specific etiological factor (Stevens, Sachdev, and Milstein, 1968).

Both cortical overarousal and underarousal have been posited as the basic cause of the hyperkinetic syndrome. In 1957 Laufer and Denhoff suggested that hyperactivity is the result of an oversensitivity of the central nervous system to external and internal stimuli. These authors implicated the posterior portion of the forebrain, known as the *diencephalon,* as the site of the dysfunction which, according to the theory, rendered the cortex susceptible to an unusually large amount of stimulation. Burks (1960) similarly concluded that hyperkinesis is the result of overstimulation of the cortex, although he suggested that the dysfunction is located in the reticular formation (a system of nerve paths and connections within the brainstem), which failed to inhibit incoming impulses. Similar theoretical viewpoints emphasizing cortical overarousal have been proposed by Eisenberg (1966), Keogh (1971), and Solomons (1971). However, empirical tests of these theories are essentially unavailable, except for supportive inferences that come from the experimental work of Laufer and his associates (Laufer and Denhoff, 1957; Laufer, Denhoff, and Solomons, 1957).

Quite unexpectedly, Satterfield and Dawson (1971), who had initially set out to test the excessive physiological arousal view of hyperkinesis, found results that were contradictory to this hypothesis but congruent with an underarousal interpretation. They had predicted that hyperkinetic children would have significantly higher basal skin conductance (SCL) than normals, that the frequency of magnitude of the nonspecific skin response (GSR) would be significantly greater, that specific GSRs for the onset of a tone would also be greater, and that the stimulant drugs dextroamphetamine sulfate and methylphenidate would reduce these SCL and GSR levels in hyperkinetic children (making them more like normals). In contrast to their expectations, hyperkinetic children showed lower SCL values, smaller frequencies of nonspecific GSRs, and smaller specific GSRs. All measures changed in the direction of normalcy when the hyperkinetic children received stimulant drugs.

On the basis of these results, it was posited that hyperkinetic children have lower reticular excitation and that their motor hyperactivity is actually an attempt to facilitate and increase sensory input to a more optimal level. Moreover, the apparent paradoxical effect of amphetamines (stimulants acting as depressants) is not paradoxical at all; in fact, the amphetamines act as a stimulant to bring these youngsters up to an appropriate level of arousal. A second study was undertaken in order to replicate these findings (Satterfield et al., 1972). The results indicated that the best responders to drug treatment were those who showed the lowest initial physiological arousal level, and the worst drug responders were those who were considered overaroused. In support of this view, Kleemeier (1974) reexamined the studies that found higher incidence of abnormal EEGs in hyperkinetic children, and she showed that there is a significant relationship between hyperactivity and slow wave activity (or slow cortical activity). The possibility that hyperkinetic children are underaroused continues to gain experimental and conceptual support (Grunewald-Züberbier, Grunewald, and Rasche, 1975; Zahn et al., 1975; Hastings and Barkley, 1978). It promises a rational explanation for the effectiveness of stimulant drugs, and it could open up new vistas in the treatment and educational management of hyperkinetic youngsters.

The notion of diet and allergic reactions to certain foods and additives as causes of hyperactivity has been in the literature for more than fifty years, although it has enjoyed greater popularity in the last decade (Feingold, 1975; Mayron, 1979; Crook, 1980). On the basis of his clinical observations and of mothers' responses to a questionnaire, Crook (1980) found the following foods and additives (in descending order of frequency) to be causes of hyperactivity: sugar, color and flavor additives, milk, corn, chocolate, egg, wheat, potato, soy, citrus, and pork. However, studies investigating the relationship between food, food colors and dyes, and hyperactivity have been unable to substantiate such a link (Harley, Matthews, and Eichman, 1978; Connors et al., 1976; Wender, 1977).

While few would argue against the view that experiential factors are associated with hyperkinesis, the question of whether environmental conditions play a primary causal role in producing the disorder is still very controversial. We know that high degrees of anxiety can be manifested behaviorally in restlessness, impaired learning, distractibility, and emotional excitability (symptoms that at least resemble hyperkinesis). In fact, Chess (1960) found hyperactivity in a variety of disturbed behaviors—in psychotic, neurotic, brain-damaged, and mentally retarded children, and in a group of youngsters she called "physiologic" (not associated with any other pathology). At present we do not have the evidence to resolve this controversy, although we need to be mindful of the emotional components in both parents and child that are often part and parcel of the disorder. It is the rare parent who is not eventually harassed, fatigued, worried, guilt ridden, and angered by the hyperactive child. This child is difficult to manage, frustrating to be with, and quite disappointing to those who hold expectations for the child's academic and social achievement. It is little wonder that the child is rejected, avoided, and disliked by almost everyone with whom he or she comes into contact. The child's self-esteem is typically quite low, and the child is aware that he or she is alienated from others and that there is something radically wrong with him or her.

Conflicts are inevitable between the child and the parents, siblings, teachers, and peers. Tension in the home often increases, and unfortunately, the situation deteriorates before it gets better. The child's behavior worsens, and the child is apt to be blamed for any sort of trouble—whether or not he or she actually has been involved. Environments that are characterized by disorganization, conflicts, destruction, impulsiveness, emotional lability, and restlessness provide modeling opportunities for hyperactivity. Under these living conditions a child either with or without minimal brain dysfunction may evidence a clear symptom picture of hyperkinesis. Regardless of the primary etiology, by the time the family brings the child to a professional, the problem will most likely involve many serious emotional facets that must be dealt with.

Treatment Approaches

Our society's penchant for taking medicines is perhaps most clearly reflected in the preferred treatment approach for hyperactive children. Chemotherapy using two types of drugs, amphetamines and methylphenidate (*stimulants*), and phenothiazines (*tranquilizers*) is so commonplace that teachers and other nonmedically trained professionals, as well as physicians, rely heavily on medication as a first line of defense. The widespread use of drugs, unfortunately, is not supported by a large number of carefully controlled studies or by investigations on long-term drug effects. Ross and Ross (1976) regard much of this drug research as unsystematic and inadequate, with findings that are essentially worthless because of serious methodological flaws and limitations. Central nervous system stimulants, specifically amphetamines, were first used for hyperactive children by Bradley (1937), who described a *paradoxical calming effect* on the children which was positive and effective but was inconsistent with the expected effect of a stimulant drug. Although the early clinical findings were favorable, this form of drug therapy was not used extensively until the late 1950s and through the 1960s, when it became the treatment of choice for many practitioners. Still, other clinicians and researchers were gravely concerned about its widespread popularity and use without there being adequate or sufficient empirical findings to support its effectiveness. The matter became a public controversy when a report appeared in the *Washington Post* (Maynard, 1970) erroneously estimating (later figures were lower) that between 5 and 10 percent of schoolchildren in Omaha, Nebraska, were given stimulant drugs to manage and improve their behavior in the classroom. The report set off investigations and the formation of study panels by the federal government and professional organizations. Nevertheless, it is taking a long time to acquire the much-needed information and data about the drug and its short- and long-term effects.

Millichap and Fowler (1967) reviewed drug studies with hyperactive children who had learning disabilities, and on the basis of that review they compiled the following index of optimum therapies (see Table 10–5). More recent survey data indicate that ritalin is consistently preferred over dexedrine by clinicians as the treatment of choice for hyperactive children, although it was suggested that this preference may have been unduly influenced by Millichap and Fowler's imprecise interpretation of their findings that ritalin showed higher rates of improvement than dexedrine (Sprague and Sleator, 1973; Krager and Safer, 1974; Ross and Ross, 1976). Millichap and Fowler's index suggests that stimulants, especially ritalin, effect greater improvement and less frequent side effects than tranquilizers, although recent reviews of the literature note that with respect to the use of tranquilizers with hyperactive children, the findings are conflicting and inconclusive (Werry and Sprague, 1970; Ross and Ross, 1976).

A number of studies have been done to find the variables that would predict which hyperactive children would benefit from drug therapy and to determine what the most effective dosage would be for a particular child (Sroufe, 1975). Investigators have tried to

Table 10–5 Index of Optimum Therapies

Stimulants	*Dose, Mg per Day*	*Percent Improved*	*Percent Side Effects*
Ritalin	5–60	83	14
Dexedrine	5–30	69	12
Tranquilizers			
Thorazine	10–20	55	25
Deaner	50–150	47	7
Serpasil	0.25–0.5	34	>19

Adapted from Millichap and Fowler, 1967, p. 775.

identify social factors as well as neurobiochemical, neurological, and neurophysiological indices with some modicum of success, although Sroufe (1975), after a careful and extensive review of the literature, concludes that there is as yet no index with proven predictive utility.

Imipramine, a long-acting antidepressant, has been tried with hyperactive youngsters; it is thought to produce less undesirable side effects than central nervous system stimulants such as amphetamines and methylphenidate. One study reported improvement in hyperactive children treated with imipramine during an eight-week period, as compared to deterioration in behavior in those youngsters when they were given a placebo over a period of four weeks (Waizer et al., 1974). However, Rapoport and colleagues (Rapoport et al., 1974) demonstrated that stimulants were more effective than imipramine on all measures of improvement.

Those few studies that have attempted to determine the effect of stimulants and tranquilizers on school achievement generally showed no substantial change when either drug was given in normal clinical doses. If anything, stimulants facilitated performance slightly, while tranquilizers tended to minimally depress some areas (Werry and Sprague, 1970). But too little is known about the effect of these drugs on learning and memory in hyperactive children who have been medicated over a period of several years. Perhaps the greatest problem in evaluating the specific efficacy of this treatment approach is the practice of using drug therapy in some combination with other remedial techniques, such as psychotherapy, special educational programs, and environmental manipulations.

A recent study offers promise that a token reinforcement program can be used as an effective alternative to drug control (Ayllon, Layman, and Kandel, 1975). Ritalin was discontinued in three hyperactive school-aged children after base-line rates of their activity levels and mathematics and reading performance were obtained. Without medication their activity level increased markedly, while the introduction of the reinforcement program (tokens for correct responses in math and reading) controlled their hyperactivity at a level comparable to the base-line data (while subjects were on ritalin). In addition, their math and reading performance increased from a base-line rate of about 12 percent correct to over 85 percent correct on the no-drug reinforcement program. Other behavioral studies have shown improvement in academic performance and classroom behavior for hyperactive youngsters through such techniques as modeling and cognitive behavior modification (Ridberg, Parke, and Hetherington, 1971; Meichenbaum and Goodman, 1971). Interesting as these findings are, we need to accumulate data on many more subjects and over much longer periods of time before we can be confident about using this type of treatment program.

Psychotherapy as an approach for changing the hyperactive child's behavior through the resolution of conflicts and the strengthening of self-esteem has been favored by many clinicians, although little proof of its usefulness is empirically available. Differences among therapists in orientation, techniques, goals, and amount of psychotherapy given are so vast that systematic research is difficult to undertake. When some of these variables are controlled for research purposes, there is the risk that the ensuing evaluation of the effectiveness of psychotherapy will be highly specific to the experimental conditions and not to the usefulness of psychotherapy in general (as clinically practiced or as defined in other empirical studies). For example, the results of the study by Eisenberg and his associates (Eisenberg et al., 1961), which indicated that short-term psychotherapy is not effective in changing the behavior of hyperactive children, cannot be taken as a broad indictment of psychotherapy. The findings must be interpreted within the special conditions of the study, and in light of the criteria used to measure its effects. It seems unreasonable to expect that any form of brief treatment, including psychotherapy, would significantly alter the well-established behavioral patterns of hyperactive children.

Working on the assumption that overactivity in brain-damaged children is attributable to an inability to inhibit and delay incoming and background stimuli, Strauss and Lehtinen (1947) were the first to advocate a maximal reduction of distracting stimuli in the immediate environment as an important aspect of treating these youngsters. Some years later Cruickshank and associates (Cruickshank et al., 1961) used the principles of reduced environmental stimulation and a structured educational program with brain-damaged and hyperactive children in a demonstration pilot project in a public school setting. Their results, although difficult to interpret because of methodological limitations, provided some support for the restricted environment view of Strauss and Lehtinen. Recently data were reported indicating better performance under conditions of reduced environmental stimulation, although familial and brain-damaged mental retardates were used as subjects (Gorton, 1972).

However, contrary to what the hypothesis would predict, data from studies in our laboratory showed that certain extraneous auditory and visual stimuli enhance sustained attentional performance in learning disabled youngsters (Brackup, 1979; Rosenberg, 1980). On the basis of these findings, it is evident that under certain conditions and in certain tasks, irrelevant stimulation does not impair learning and performance as originally proposed by Strauss and Lehtinen. It is also apparent that additional research is needed to test this hypothesis and to determine the conditions under which learning in school and at home is facilitated and maximized for hyperactive and learning disabled youngsters.

SUMMARY

In this chapter we considered those disorders that are viewed as linked in some way to minimal brain pathology and "soft" neurological signs and which occur most often during the period of middle childhood. We discussed minimal brain dysfunction (MBD), its neurological and behavioral features, and its validity and usefulness as a construct. We then covered the hyperkinetic syndrome and learning disabilities.

The concept of MBD originated out of interest in identifying the features that best differentiate between retarded youngsters with and without brain damage. The characteristics of hyperactivity, impulsivity, distractibility, and aggressiveness reliably discriminated between the two groups and were related to brain damage. This led to the erroneous conclusion that these characteristics, especially hyperactivity, were *indicative* of brain damage; and this finding became the basis for implicating some neuropathology in the etiology of the learning disabled and hyperkinetic child. The notion of MBD is used to suggest that the damage is barely perceptible and that it is not demonstrable by conventional neurological signs. Instead, it is evidenced by "soft" signs that are of questionable validity. The empirical basis for MBD was examined, as was the term *"soft" neurological signs.*

The term *learning disability* is one of many labels used interchangeably and imprecisely as a broad category referring to a discrepancy between anticipated and perceived academic achievement in children who otherwise are not handicapped in intelligence, sensory processes, emotional stability, or opportunities to learn. DSM-III uses the term *specific developmental disorders* to categorize learning disabilities; it codes them on a separate axis (II) to acknowledge both that no other signs of psychopathology are apparent with this condition and that it is controversial to classify them as "mental disorders." Learning problems are estimated to occur in between 5 and 28 percent of school-aged youngsters. The specific learning disability of reading was considered because it is found in more than 10 percent of the school population, and because it is illustrative of the issues and areas of controversy characteristic of the entire field of learning disabilities.

Hyperkinesis in children has become a syndrome of increasing interest to clinicians and researchers. The term does not imply a specific etiology, and it is often included under the general rubric of learning disabilities. We considered the hyperkinetic syndrome as a separate condition in order to lessen the confounding of these categories that exists in the literature. DSM-III and recent research emphasize the primacy and persistence of attention deficits in these children, with hyperactivity considered as secondary. The new classification system refers to this disorder as Attention Deficit Disorder either with or without hyperactivity.

The clinical picture, etiological considerations, and therapeutic approaches for the disorders covered in this chapter are summarized in the following tables.

Table 10-6 Learning Disabilities

1. Reading Failures

Clinical Picture	*Etiology*	*Treatment*
Found in more boys than girls (sex ratio ranging from 3:1 to 5:1).	It represents heterogeneous conditions for which there is no single cause.	Heterogeneity of terms and etiological views is only exceeded by diversity of remedial approaches.
Poor readers make poor students who face limited vocational choices and restricted income potential. There is a high association with antisocial behaviors.	High prevalence of reading problems in close relatives of dyslexic children is often used to support a genetic view, but these data can be used equally well to support a social transmission view.	Dynamically oriented psychotherapy has been used and reported, but improvements were not sustained after treatment was terminated.
Reading failure becomes chronic and difficult to modify if not identified before fifth grade.	While evidence of CNS involvement is not usually apparent, many hold some sort of brain dysfunction as the primary cause. Hence, the term *minimal brain dysfunction* is used.	Various special educational programs to improve perceptual skills and neurological organization have been popular, but evidence to date is inconclusive.
Dyslexia is used to designate children of average or slightly below-average intelligence with specific retardation in reading, who have not been deprived of educational opportunities or show any gross evidence of either sensory or neurological impairment.	Some regard minimal brain dysfunction as an unproven and inferred diagnosis that has little meaning and application for educational remediation, while others believe that it will enable further understanding of the neurophysiological basis of learning.	Chemotherapy has been used —with Dilantin best for those with minimal neurological signs, Ritalin for those who are both hyperactive and disabled in learning, and Thorazine for emotionally disturbed children with learning problems. Barbiturates and phenothiazines should not be used.
They have difficulty in comprehending written language and in managing other language functions of writing and speech. They may be left-handed or ambidextrous, and they are poorly coordinated	Maturational lag in brain development is another view which has some empirical support. This arose from a study which	A technique of repeated reading has shown promise in improving the rate and fluency of slow readers.

(*continued*)

Table 10-6 (cont.)

1. Reading Failures

Clinical Picture	*Etiology*	*Treatment*
and awkward. Considered bright intellectually before school and get good grades in arithmetic at first. Emotional disturbances and low self-esteem are noted. Two primary types: impaired in either auditory or visual modality. Auditory defects are more difficult to remediate than visual ones. Significant differences noted in visual information processing, in memory for visual information, and in the perception and organization of broken-up words embedded in ambiguous stimuli.	permitted correct classification of both high-and low-risk children in better than 90 percent of the cases. Psychogenic view involving poor self-image or more fanciful, psychoanalytically derived interpretations tend to be imprecise and difficult to substantiate. However, most clinicians are convinced that emotional factors play an important role in many cases of disturbed learning. Nutritional and environmental deprivation have been recently implicated as potential determinants of neurological dysfunction.	Behavior modification, especially tangible reinforcement, in the management of children in the classroom has been used, but data are too sparse to evaluate. Also, it has been shown that laypersons can be successfully trained to carry out behavioral programs to remediate reading problems.

Table 10-7 Hyperkinetic Syndrome

Clinical Picture	*Etiology*	*Treatment*
Persistent overactivity, distractibility, impulsivity, emotional excitability, low frustration tolerance, short attention span, and in some cases antisocial behavior. Onset is usually early in life, and the behaviors become troublesome to parents and teachers especially when child enters school. It is more frequent in boys (estimates range from 5:1 to 9:1),	Biological view is prevalent although there is usually no evidence or history of brain injury. Both cortical overarousal and underarousal have been suggested as the basic cause. Underarousal is a more viable and promising position, but more data are necessary. Some—but not sufficiently convincing—data exist to support genetic transmission, biochemical factors, and diet and	Chemotherapy is the most favored approach. Two types of drugs are used: stimulants and tranquilizers. Evaluation of drug effectiveness is difficult because there are few controlled studies. However, stimulants seem to be more effective than tranquilizers. Studies assessing the long-term effects of drugs on learning and memory are not available.

Table 10-7 (cont.)

Clinical Picture	*Etiology*	*Treatment*
and it is found in between 3 and 10 percent of elementary school children. Specific learning disabilities may be present. These children are otherwise physiologically and intellectually normal. While hyperactivity declines in adolescence, recent data indicate persistence of academic and social problems throughout the teenage years.	allergic reactions as causal factors. Psychogenic factors such as conflicts and environments that are disorganized, destructive, impulsive, emotional, and restless provide modeling opportunities for hyperactivity. Whether emotional factors are primary or secondary cannot be determined from data available.	Psychotherapy to resolve unconscious conflicts and strengthen self-esteem has been used, but evaluation is difficult at present. A token reinforcement program has been shown to be an effective alternative to drug control. Restriction of environmental stimulation has been tried, with contradictory findings.

REFERENCES

Adler, S. Articulatory Deviances and Social Class Membership. *Journal of Learning Disabilities*, 1973, *6*, 650–654.

American Psychiatric Association. DSM-III: *Diagnostic and Statistical Manual of Mental Disorders*, 3rd ed. Washington, D.C.: American Psychiatric Association, 1980.

Ayllon, T., Layman, D., and Kandel, H. J. A Behavioral Educational Alternative to Drug Control of Hyperactive Children. *Journal of Applied Behavioral Analysis*, 1975, *8*, 137–146.

Baer, D. M., and Guess, D. Receptive Training of Adjectival Inflections in Mental Retardates. *Journal of Applied Behavior Analysis*, 1971, *4*, 129–139.

Bakwin, H., and Bakwin, R. M. *Behavior Disorders in Children*, 4th ed. Philadelphia: Saunders, 1972.

Baratz, J. Language in the Economically Disadvantaged Child: A Perspective. *American Speech and Hearing Association*, 1968, *10*, 143–145.

Baratz, J. Language and Cognitive Assessment of Negro Children: Assumptions and Research Needs. *American Speech and Hearing Association*, 1969, *11*, 87–91.

Barbara, D. A. Stuttering. In S. Arieti (ed.), *American Handbook of Psychiatry*, Vol. 1. New York: Basic Books, 1959, pp. 950–963.

Benton, A. L. Minimal Brain Dysfunction from a Neuropsychological Point of View. *Annals of the New York Academy of Sciences*, 1973, *205*, 29–37.

Bingham, D. S., Van Hattum, R., Faulk, M. E., and Taussing, E. Program Organization and Management. *Journal of Speech and Hearing Disorders*. Monograph Supplement, 1961, *8*, 33–49.

Brackup, E. S. Vigilance in the Learning Disabled: The Effects of Extraneous Speech and a Rest Pause. Unpublished doctoral dissertation, Emory University, 1979.

Bradley, C. The Behavior of Children Receiving Benzedrine. *American Journal of Psychiatry*, 1937, *94*, 577–585.

Brase, D. A., and Loh, H. H. Possible Role of 5-hydroxytryptamine in Minimal Brain Dysfunction. *Life Sciences*, 1975, *16*, 1005–1015.

Brodie, R. D., and Winterbottom, M. R. Failure in Elementary School Boys as a Function of Traumata, Secrecy, and Derogation. *Child Development*, 1967, *38*, 701–711.

Brutten, E. J., and Shoemaker, D. J., *The Modification of Stuttering*. Englewood Cliffs, N. J.: Prentice-Hall, 1967.

Brutten, E. J., and Shoemaker, D. J. Stuttering: The Disintegration of Speech Due to Conditioned Negative Emotion. In B. Gray, and G. England (eds.), *Stuttering and the Conditioning Therapies*. Monterey, Calif.: Monterey Institute for Speech and Hearing, 1969, p. 51.

Bryant, N. D., and McLoughlin, J. A. Subject Variables: Definition, Incidence, Characteristics, and Correlates. In N. D. Bryant and C. E. Kass (eds.), *Leadership Training Institute in Learning Disabilities - Final Report*. Tucson, Ariz.: University of Arizona, 1972, *1*, pp. 5–158.

Burks, H. The Hyperkinetic Child. *Exceptional Children*, 1960, *27*, 18–26.

Campbell, S. B. Hyperactivity: Course and Treatment. In A. Davids (ed.), *Child Personality and Psychopathology: Current Topics,* Vol. 3. New York: John Wiley, 1976, pp. 201–236.

Cantwell, D. P. Genetics of Hyperactivity. *Journal of Child Psychology and Psychiatry, and Allied Disciplines,* 1975, *16,* 261–264.

Carver, R. P., and Hoffman, J. V. The Effects of Practice Through Repeated Reading on Gain in Reading Ability Using a Computer-based Instructional System. *Reading Research Quarterly,* 1981, *16,* 374–390.

Chess, S. Diagnosis and Treatment of the Hyperactive Child. *New York State Journal of Medicine,* 1960, *60,* 2379–2385.

Chess, S., and Rosenberg, M. Clinical Differentiation among Children with Initial Language Complaints. *Journal of Autism and Childhood Schizophrenia,* 1974, *4,* 99–109.

Chomsky, C. When You Still Can't Read in Third Grade: After Decoding, What? In S. J. Samuels (ed.), *What Research Has to Say about Reading Instruction.* Newark, Del.: International Reading Association, 1978, pp. 13–20.

Clarizio, H. F., and McCoy, G. F. *Behavior Disorders in School-Aged Children.* Scranton, Penn.: Chandler Publishing Co., 1970.

Clarke, J. L. Verbal and Nonverbal Learning Disabilities. In M. R. Burkowsky (ed.), *Orientation to Language and Learning Disorders.* St. Louis, Mo.: Warren H. Green, 1973, pp. 54–100.

Clements, S. *Minimal Brain Dysfunction in Children.* NINDB Monograph No. 3. Washington, D. C.: U. S. Public Health Service, 1966.

Comly, H. Cerebral Stimulants for Children with Learning Disorders. *Journal of Learning Disabilities,* 1971, *4,* 484–490.

Connors, C. K., Goyette, C. H., Southwick, D. A., Lees, J. M., and Andrulonis, P. A. Food Additives and Hyperkinesis: A Controlled Double-Blind Experiment. *Pediatrics,* 1976, *58,* 154–166.

Crook, W. G. Can What a Child Eats Make Him Dull, Stupid, or Hyperactive? *Journal of Learning Disabilities,* 1980, *13,* 281–286.

Cruickshank, W. M. Some Issues Facing the Field of Learning Disability. *Journal of Learning Disabilities,* 1972, *5,* 380–388.

Cruickshank, W. M., Bentzen, F. A., Ratzeburg, F. H., and Tannjausser, M. T. *A Teaching Method for Brain Injured and Hyperactive Children: A Demonstration-Pilot Study.* Syracuse, N. Y.: Syracuse University Press, 1961.

Darley, F. L., Aronson, A. E., and Brown, J. R. Clusters of Deviant Speech Dimensions in the Dysarthrias. *Journal of Speech and Hearing Research,* 196, *12,* 462–496.

Davis, H., and Silverman, S. R. *Hearing and Deafness,* 3rd ed. New York: Holt, Rinehart and Winston, 1970.

de Ajuriaguerra, J. *Handbook of Child Psychiatry and Psychology.* Translated and edited by R. P. Lorion. New York: Masson Publishing USA, Inc., 1980.

Denckla, M. B. Minimal Brain Dysfunction and Dyslexia: Beyond Diagnosis by Exclusion. in M. E. Blaw, I. Rapin, and M. Kinsbourne (eds.), *Topics in Child Neurology.* New York: Spectrum Publ., 1977, pp. 243–261.

Divoky, D. Education's Latest Victim, the "LD" Kid. *Learning,* 1974, *3,* 20–25.

Doman, R. J., Spitz, E. B., Zucman, E., Delacato, C. H., and Doman, G. Children with Severe Brain Injuries: Neurological Organization in Terms of Mobility. *Journal of the American Medical Association,* 1960, *174,* 257–262.

Douglas, V. Stop, Look and Listen: The Problem of Sustained Attention and Impulse Control in Hyperactive and Normal Children. *Canadian Journal of Behavioral Science,* 1972, *4,* 259–281.

Dubey, D. R. Organic Factors in Hyperkinesis: A Critical Evaluation. *American Journal of Orthopsychiatry,* 1976, *46,* 353–366.

Eisenberg, L. The Management of the Hyperkinetic Child. *Developmental Medicine and Child Neurology,* 1966, *8,* 593–598.

Eisenberg, L., Gilbert, A., Cytryn, L., and Molling, P. A. The Effectiveness of Psychotherapy Alone and in Conjunction with Perphenazine or Placebo in the Treatment of Neurotic and Hyperkinetic Children. *American Journal of Psychiatry,* 1961, *117,* 1088–1093.

Eisenson, J. Speech Disorders. In B. B. Wolman (ed.), *Handbook of Clinical Psychology.* New York: McGraw-Hill, 1965, pp. 765–784.

Emerick, L. L., and Hatten, J. T. *Diagnosis and Evaluation in Speech Pathology.* Englewood Cliffs, N. J.: Prentice-Hall, 1974.

Epstein, J., Berg-Cross, C., and Berg-Cross, L. Maternal Expectations and Birth Order in Families with Learning Disabled and Normal Children. *Journal of Learning Disabilities,* 1980, *13,* 273–280.

Ernhart, C. B., Graham, F. K., Eichman, P. L., Marshall, J. M., and Thurston, D. Brain Injury in the Preschool Child: Some Developmental Considerations. II. Comparisons of Brain Injured and Normal Children. *Psychological Monographs: General and Applied,* 1963, *77* (No. 574), 17–33.

Feild, C. T., and Feild, H. S. Performance of Subjects with Reading Disabilities on a Series of Perceptual Closure Tasks. *Perceptual and Motor Skills,* 1974, *38,* 812–814.

Feingold, B. F. *Why Your Child is Hyperactive.* New York: Random House, 1975.

Flanagan, B., Goldiamond, I., and Azrin, N. H. Operant Stuttering: The Control of Stuttering Behavior Through Response Contingent Consequences. *Journal of the Experimental Analysis of Behavior,* 1958 *1,* 173–177.

Friedlander, S., Pothier, P., Morrison, D., and Herman, L. The Role of Neurological-Developmental Delay in

Childhood Psychopathology. *American Journal of Orthopsychiatry,* 1982, *52,* 102–108.

Frisch, L. E., and Rhoads, F. A. Child Abuse and Neglect in Children Referred for Learning Evaluation. *Journal of Learning Disabilities,* 1982, *15,* 583–586.

Frisk, M., Wegelius, E. B., Tenhunen, T., Widholm, O., and Hortling, H. The Problem of Dyslexia in Teenage. *Acta Paediatrica Scandinavia,* 1967, *56,* 333–343.

Gerber, S. E., and Hertel, C. G. Language Deficiency of Disadvantaged Children. *Journal of Speech and Hearing Research,* 1969, *12,* 270–280.

Giffin, M. The Role of Child Psychiatry in Learning Disabilities. In H. R. Mykleburst (ed.), *Progress in Learning Disabilities,* Vol. 1. New York: Grune and Stratton, 1968, pp. 75–97.

Gilbert, G. M. A Survey of "Referral Problems" in Metropolitan Child Guidance Centers. *Journal of Clinical Psychology,* 1957, *13,* 37–42.

Glasner, P. J., and Rosenthal, D. Parental Diagnosis of Stuttering in Young Children. *Journal of Speech and Hearing Disorders,* 1957, *22,* 288–295.

Goldberg, H. K., and Schiffman, G. R. *Dyslexia: Problems of Reading Disabilities.* New York: Grune and Stratton, 1972.

Goldberg, J. O., and Konstantareas, M. M. Vigilance in Hyperactive and Normal Children on a Self-paced Operant Task. *Journal of Child Psychology and Psychiatry and Allied Disciplines,* 1981, *22,* 55–63.

Goldenson, R. M. *Helping Your Child to Read Better.* New York: Thomas Y. Crowell, 1957.

Goodstein, L. D. Functional Speech Disorders and Personality: A Survey of the Literature. In P. Trapp and P. Himelstein (eds.), *Readings on the Exceptional Child.* New York: Appleton-Century-Crofts, 1962, pp. 399–419.

Goodstein, L. D. Psychosocial Aspects of Cleft Palate. In D. C. Spriesterbach, and D. Sherman (eds.), *Cleft Palate and Communication.* New York: Academic Press, 1969, pp. 201–224.

Gorton, C. E. The Effects of Various Classroom Environments on Performance of a Mental Task by Mentally Retarded and Normal Children. *Education and Training of the Mentally Retarded,* 1972, *7,* 28–38.

Grossman, H. J. The Child, the Teachers, and the Physician. In W. M. Cruickshank (ed.), *The Teacher of Brain Injured Children: A Discussion of the Bases for Competency.* Syracuse, N. Y.: Syracuse University Press, 1966, pp. 57–67.

Grotberg, E. H. Neurological Aspects of Learning Disabilities: A Case for the Disadvantaged. *Journal of Learning Disabilities,* 1970, *3,* 321–327.

Grunewald-Zuberbier, E., Grunewald, G., and Rasche, A. Hyperactive Behavior and EEG Arousal Reactions in Children's Electroencephalograms. *Clinical Neurophysiology,* 1975, *38,* 149–159.

Guess, D., Sailor, W., Rutherford, G., and Baer, D. M. An Experimental Analysis of Linguistic Development: The Productive Use of the Plural Morpheme. *Journal of Applied Behavior Analysis,* 1968, *1,* 297–306.

Hallahan, D. P., and Cruickshank, W. M. *Psychoeducational Foundations of Learning Disabilities.* Englewood Cliffs, N. J.: Prentice-Hall, 1973.

Hallgren, B. Specific Dyslexia (Congenital and Word Blindness). *Acta Psychiatrica et Neurologica,* Supplementum 65, 1950.

Hardy, J. Respiratory Physiology: Implications of Current Research. *American Speech and Hearing Association,* 1968, *10,* 204–205.

Harley, J. P., Matthews, C. G., and Eichman, P. Synthetic Food Colors and Hyperactivity in Children: A Double-Blind Challenge Experiment. *Pediatrics,* 1978 *62,* 975–983.

Harris, A. J. *How to Increase Reading Ability: A Guide to Development and Remedial Methods,* 5th ed. New York: D. McKay, 1970.

Hastings, J. E., and Barkley, R. A. A Review of Psychophysiological Research with Hyperkinetic Children. *Journal of Abnormal Child Psychology,* 1978, *6,* 413–447.

Hayim-Sagon, N. An Investigation of the Effects of Rewards and Feedback on Sustained Attention and Activity Levels of first-grade Children. Unpublished doctoral dissertation, Emory University, 1982.

Heinicke, C. M. Learning Disturbance in Childhood. In B. B. Wolman (ed.), *Manual of Child Psychopathology.* New York: McGraw-Hill, 1972.

Herbert, M. *Emotional Problems of Development in Children.* New York: Academic Press, 1974.

Hewitt, F. M., Taylor, F. D., and Artuso, A. A. The Santa Monica Project: Evaluation of an Engineered Classroom Design with Emotionally Disturbed Children. *Exceptional Children,* 1969, *35,* 523–529.

Human Communication and Its Disorders: An Overview. A Report of the Subcommittee on Human Communication and Its Disorders. *National Advisory Neurological Diseases and Stroke Council,* Monograph No. 10. U.S. Department of Health, Education and Welfare, National Institute of Neurological Diseases and Stroke, 1969.

Hoy, E., Weiss, G., Minde, K., and Cohen, N. The Hyperactive Child at Adolescence: Cognitive, Emotional, and Social Functioning. *Journal of Abnormal Child Psychology,* 1978, 6, 311–324.

Irwin, O. C. Infant Speech: Effect of Systematic Reading of Stories. *Journal of Speech and Hearing Research.* 1969, 3, 187–190.

Jenkins, R. Diagnosis, Dynamics and Treatment in Child Psychiatry. In R. Jenkins and J. Cole (eds.), *Research Report No. 18.* Washington, D.C.: American Psychiatric Association, 1964.

Johnson, D. J., and Myklebust, H. R. *Learning Disabilities, Educational Principles and Practices.* New York: Grune and Stratton, 1967.

Johnson, W. (ed.). *Stuttering in Children and Adults;*

Thirty Years of Research at the University of Iowa. Minneapolis: University of Minnesota Press, 1956.

Johnson, W. *Stuttering and What You Can Do about It*. Minneapolis: University of Minnesota Press, 1961.

Johnson, W., Brown, S., Curtis, J., Edney, C., and Keaster, J. *Speech Handicapped School Children*. New York: Harper and Row, 1956.

Jones, H. G. Stuttering. In C. G. Costello (ed.), *Symptoms of Psychopathology: A Handbook*. New York: John Wiley, 1970, pp. 336–358.

Keogh, B. Hyperactivity and Learning Disorders: Review and Speculation. *Exceptional Children*, 1971, *38*, 101–109.

Kessler, J. *Psychopathology of Childhood*. Englewood Cliffs, N.J.: Prentice-Hall, 1966.

Kirchner, G. L. Differences in the Vigilance Performance of Highly Active and Normal Second-Grade Males under Four Experimental Conditions. Unpublished doctoral dissertation, Emory University, 1975.

Kleemeier, C. P. A Comparative Evaluation of the Theoretical Relationship Between Arousal and Learning as Demonstrated by the Hyperkinetic Syndrome. Unpublished comprehensive examination paper, Department of Psychology, Emory University, April, 1974.

Krager, J. M., and Safer, D. J. Type and Prevalence of Medication Used in the Treatment of Hyperactive Children. *New England Journal of Medicine*, 1974, *291*, 1118–1120.

Kussmaul, A. Disturbances of Speech. In *Encyclopedia of Practical Medicine*, 1877, *14*, 581–875.

Lahey, B. B. Minority Group Languages. In B. B. Lahey (ed.), *The Modification of Language Behavior*. Springfield, Ill.: Chas. C Thomas, 1973, pp. 270–315.

Lahey, B. B., and Drabman, R. S. Facilitation of the Acquisition and Retention of Sight-Word Vocabulary Through Token Reinforcement. *Journal of Applied Behavioral Analysis*, 1974, *7*, 307–312.

Langhorne, J. E., Loney, J., Paternite, C. E., and Bechtoldt, H. P. Childhood Hyperkinesis: A Return to the Source. *Journal of Abnormal Psyhology*, 1976, *85*, 201–209.

Laufer, M. W. Brain Disorders. In A. M. Freedman, and H. I. Kaplan (eds.), *Comprehensive Textbook of Psychiatry*. Baltimore, Md.: Williams and Wilkins, 1967, pp. 1442–1452.

Laufer, M. W., and Denhoff, E. Hyperkinetic Behavior Syndrome in Children. *Journal of Pediatrics*, 1957, *50*, 463–474.

Laufer, M. W., Denhoff, E., and Solomons, G. Hyperkinetic Impulse Disorder in Children's Behavior Problems. *Psychosomatic Medicine*, 1957, *19*, 38–49.

Lenneberg, E. H. (ed.). Language Disorders in Childhood. *Harvard Educational Review*, 1964, *34*, 152–177.

Lenneberg, E. H. On Explaining Language. *Science*, 1969, *164*, 635–643.

Leon, G. R. *Case Histories of Deviant Behavior: A Social Learning Analysis*. Boston: Holbrook Press, 1974, pp. 35–42.

Loney, J. Hyperkinesis Comes of Age: What Do We Know and Where Should We Go? *American Journal of Orthopsychiatry*, 1980, *50*, 28–42.

McCarthy, J. M. Learning Disabilities: Where Have We Been? Where Are We Going? In D. D. Hammill, and N. R. Bartel (eds.), *Educational Perspectives in Learning Disabilities*. New York: John Wiley, 1971, pp. 10–19.

McDonald, C. W. Problems Concerning the Classification and Education of Children with Learning Disabilities. In J. Hellmuth, (ed.), *Learning Disorders*, Vol. 3. Seattle, Wash.: Special Child Publications, 1968, pp. 371–389.

McFie, J. *Assessment of Organic Intellectual Impairment*. London: Academic Press, 1975.

Makita, K. The Rarity of Reading Disability in Japanese Children. *American Journal of Orthopsychiatry*, 1968, *38*, 599–614.

Margolin, J. B., Roman, M., and Harari, C., Reading Disability in the Delinquent Child: A Microcosm of Psychosocial Pathology. *American Journal of Orthopsychiatry*, 1955, *25*, 25–35.

Martin, R. and Ingham, R. Stuttering. In B. B. Lahey (ed.), *The Modification of Language Behavior*. Springfield, Ill.: Chas. C Thomas, 1973, pp. 91–129.

Matheny, A. P., Jr., and Dolan, A. B. A Twin Study of Genetic Influences in Reading Achievement. *Journal of Learning Disabilities*, 1974, *7*, 99–102.

Maynard, R. Omaha Pupils Given "Behavior" Drugs. *Washington Post*, June 29, 1970.

Mayron, L. W. Allergy, Learning, and Behavior Problems. *Journal of Learning Disabilities*, 1979, *12*, 32–42.

Meichenbaum, D. H., and Goodman, J. Training Impulsive Children to Talk to Themselves: A Means of Developing Self-control. *Journal of Abnormal Psychology* 1971, *77*, 115–126.

Miller, R. G., Jr., Palkes, H. S., and Stewart, M. A. Hyperactive Children in Suburban Elementary Schools. *Child Psychiatry and Human Development*, 1973, *4*, 121–127.

Millichap, J. G., and Fowler, G. W. Treatment of "Minimal Brain Dysfunction" Syndromes. *The Pediatric Clinics of North America*, 1967, *14*, 767–777.

Minde, K. Hyperactivity: Where Do We Stand? In M. E. Blau, I. Rapin, and M. Kinsbourne (eds.), *Topics in Child Neurology*. New York: Spectrum Publications, Inc., 1977, pp. 279–287.

Minde, K., Lewin, D., Weiss, G., Lairgueur, H., Douglas, V., and Sykes, R. The Hyperactive Child in Elementary School: A Five Year Old Controlled Follow Up. *Exceptional Children*, 1971, 38, 215–221.

Money, J. Child Abuse: Growth Failure, IQ Deficit, and Learning Disability. *Journal of Learning Disabilities*, 1982, *15*, 579–582.

Morrow, W. R. Academic Underachievement. In C. G. Costello, (ed.), *Symptoms of Psychopathology: A Handbook*. New York: John Wiley, 1970, pp. 535–559.

Moyer, S. B. Rehabilitation of Alexia: A Case Study. *Cortex*, 1979, *15*, 139–144.

MOYER, S. B. Repeated Reading. *Journal of Learning Disabilities*, 1982, *15*, 619–623.

MYKLEBUST, H. R., and JOHNSON, D. Dyslexia in Children. *Exceptional Children*. 1962, *29*, 14–25.

MYSAK, E. D., and GILBERT, G. M. Child Speech Pathology. In B. B. Wolman (ed.), *Manual of Child Psychopathology*. New York: McGraw-Hill, 1972, pp. 624–652.

Need for Speech Pathologists. American Speech and Hearing Association, Committee on Legislation. *Journal of the American Speech and Hearing Association*, 1959, *1*, 138–139.

NEILL, K. Turn Kids On with Repeated Readings. *Teaching Exceptional Children*, 1980, *12*, 63–64.

ORTON, S. T. *Reading, Writing and Speech Problems in Children*. New York: W. W. Norton & Co., 1937.

PAINE, R. S., WERRY, J. S., and QUAY, H. C. A Study of Minimal Cerebral Dysfunction. *Developmental Medicine and Child Neurology*, 1968, *10*, 505–520.

PAINE, R. S., WERRY, J. S., and QUAY, H. C. A Study of Minimal Cerebral Dysfunction. In D. D. Hammill and N. R. Bartel (eds.), *Educational Perspectives in Learning Disabilities*. New York: John Wiley, 1971, pp. 59–79.

PALERMO, D. S., and MOLFESE, D. L. Language Acquisition from Age Five Onward. *Psychological Bulletin*, 1972, *78*, 409–428.

PATTERSON, G. R., JONES, R., WHITTIER, J., and WRIGHT, M. A. A Behavior Modification Technique for the Hyperactive Child. *Behavior Research and Therapy*, 1965, *2*, 217–226.

PERKINS, W. H. *Speech Pathology: An Applied Behavioral Science*, 2nd ed. St. Louis, Mo.: Mosby, 1977.

POPE, L. Motor Activity in Brain-Injured Children. *American Journal of Orthopsychiatry*, 1970, *40*, 783–794.

RAPOPORT, J. L., and BENOIT, M. The Relation of Direct Home Observations to the Clinic Evaluation of Hyperactive School Age Boys. *Journal of Child Psychology and Psychiatry and Allied Disciplines*, 1975, *16*, 141–147.

RAPOPORT, J. L., QUINN, P. O., BRADBARD, G., RIDDLE, K. D., and BROOKS, E. Imipramine and Methylphenidate Treatments of Hyperactive Boys. *Archives of General Psychiatry*, 1974, *30*, 789–793.

RAPOPORT, J. L., QUINN, P. O., and LAMPRECHT, F. Minor Physical Anomalies and Plasma Dopamine-Beta-Hydroxylase Activity in Hyperactive Boys. *American Journal of Psychiatry*, 1974, *131*, 386–390.

Reading Disorders in the United States. National Advisory Committee on the Dyslexia and Related Reading Disorders. Washington, D.C.: U.S. Department of Health, Education and Welfare, August 1969.

Report of the Conference on the Use of Stimulant Drugs in the Treatment of Behaviorally Disturbed Young School Children. *Journal of Learning Disabilities*, 1971, *4*, 523–530.

RIDBERG, E. H., PARKE, R. D., and HETHERINGTON, E. M. Modification of Impulsive and Reflective Cognitive Styles Through Observation of Film-mediated Models. *Developmental Psychology*, 1971, *5*, 369–377.

RIST, R. C., and HARRELL, J. E. Labeling the Learning Disabled Child: The Social Ecology of Educational Practice. *American Journal of Orthopsychiatry*, 1982, *52*, 146–160.

ROBBINS, M., and GLASS, G. V. The Doman-Delacato Rationale: A Critical Analysis. In J. Hellmuth, (ed.), *Educational Therapy*, Vol. II. Seattle, Wash.: Special Child Publications, 1969, pp. 321–377.

ROSENBERG, R. J. The Effects of Irrelevant Visual Stimuli on Visual Attention in Learning Disabled Boys. Unpublished doctoral dissertation, Emory University, 1980.

ROSS, A. O. *Child Behavior Therapy: Principles, Procedures and Empirical Basis*. New York: John Wiley, 1981.

ROSS, D. M., and ROSS, S. A. *Hyperactivity: Research, Theory, and Action*. New York: John Wiley, 1976.

RUTTER, M., GRAHAM, P., and YULE, W. A Neuropsychiatric Study in Childhood. *Clinics in Developmental Medicine*, Nos. 35/36. London: Heinemann Medical Books, Ltd., 1970, p. 10.

RYBACK, D., and STAATS, A. W. Parents as Behavior Therapy—Technicians in Treating Reading Deficits (Dyslexia). *Journal of Behavior Therapy and Experimental Psychiatry*, 1970, *1*, 109–119.

SAFER, D. J. Drugs for Problem School Children. *Journal of School Health*, 1971, *41*, 491–495.

SAMUELS, S. J. The Method of Repeated Readings. *The Reading Teacher*, 1979, 32, 403–408.

SATTERFIELD, J. H., CANTWELL, D. P., LESSER, L. I., and PODOSIN, R. L. Physiological Studies of the Hyperkinetic Child: I. *American Journal of Psychiatry*, 1972, *128*, 1418–1424.

SATTERFIELD, J. H., and DAWSON, M. E. Electrodermal Correlates of Hyperactivity in Children. *Psychophysiology*, 1971, *8*, 191–197.

SATZ, P., and FRIEL, J. Some Predictive Antecedents of Specific Disability: A Preliminary Two-Year Follow-Up. *Journal of Learning Disabilities*, 1974, *7*, 437–444.

SATZ, P., RARDIN, D., and ROSS, J. An Evaluation of a Theory of Specific Developmental Dyslexia. *Child Development*, 1971, *42*, 2009–2021.

SHAFFER, D. Psychiatric Aspects of Brain Injury in Childhood. A Review. *Developmental Medicine and Child Neurology*, 1973, *15*, 211–220.

SCHAIN, R. J. *Neurology of Childhood Learning Disorders*. Baltimore, Md: Williams and Wilkins, 1972.

SCHIFFMAN, G., and CLEMMENS, R. L. Observations on Children with Severe Reading Problems. In J. Hellmuth (ed.), *Learning Disorders*, Vol. 2. Seattle, Wash: Special Child Publications, 1966, pp. 297–310.

SCHLEIFER, M., WEISS, G., COHEN, N., ELMAN, M., CVEJIC, H., and KRUGER, E. Hyperactivity in Preschoolers and the Effect of Methlphenidate. *American Journal of Orthopsychiatry*, 1975, *45*, 38–50.

SCHRAGER, J., LINDY, J., HARRISON, S., MCDERMOTT, J., and KILLINS, E. The Hyperkinetic Child: Some Consensually Validated Behavior Correlates. *Exceptional Children*, 1966, *32*, 635–637.

SCHULMAN, J. L., KASPER, J. C., and THRONE, F. M. *Brain Damage and Behavior*. Springfield, Ill.: Chas. C Thomas, 1965.

SCHWARTZ, G. J. College Students as Contingency Managers for Adolescents in a Program to Develop Reading Skills. *Journal of Applied Behavior Analysis*, 1977, *10*, 645–655.

SHAW, M. C. Underachievement: Useful Construct or Misleading Illusion. *Psychology in the Schools*, 1968, *5*, 41–46.

SHAYWITZ, B. A., YAGER, R. D., and KLOPPER, J. H. Selective Brain Dopamine Depletion in Developing Rats: An Experimental Model of Minimal Brain Dysfunction. *Science*, 1976, *191*, 305–308.

SHEEHAN, J. G. Theory and Treatment of Stuttering as an Approach Avoidance Conflict. *Journal of Psychology*, 1953, *36*, 27–49.

SHEENAN, J. G. Stuttering as a Self-role Conflict. In H. H. Gregory (ed.), *Learning Theory and Stuttering Therapy*. Evanston, Ill.: Northwestern University Press, 1968, pp. 72–83.

SHEEHAN, J. G., and MARTYN, M. M. Spontaneous Recovery from Stuttering. *Journal of Speech and Hearing Research*, 1966, *9*, 121–135.

SHEEHAN, J. G., and MARTYN, M. M. Methodology in Studies of Recovery from Stuttering. *Journal of Speech and Hearing Research*, 1967, *10*, 396–400.

SHEEHAN, J. G. Projective Studies of Stuttering. In E. P. Trapp and P. Himmelstein (eds.), *Readings on the Exceptional Child*. New York: Appleton-Century-Crofts, 1962, pp. 419–429.

SHRINER, T. H., HOLLOWAY, M. S., and DANILOFF, R. G. The Relationship Between Articulatory Deficits and Syntax in Speech Defective Children. *Journal of Speech and Hearing Research*, 1969, *12*, 319–325.

SILVER, L. A. A Proposed View on the Etiology of the Neurological Learning Disability Syndrome. *Journal of Learning Disabilities*, 1971, *4*, 123–133.

SMITH, M. E. *An Investigation of the Development of the Sentence and the Extent of Vocabulary in Young Children*. Iowa City, Iowa: University of Iowa Studies in Child Welfare, 1926.

SOLOMONS, G. Guidelines on the Use and Medical Effects of Psychostimulant Drugs in Therapy. *Journal of Learning Disabilities*, 1971, *4*, 470–475.

SPRAGUE, R. L., and SLEATOR, E. K. Effects of Psychopharmacologic Agents on Learning Disorders. *Pediatric Clinics of North America*, 1973, *20*, 719–735.

SROUFE, L. A. Drug Treatment of Children with Behavior Problems. In F. Horowitz (ed.), *Review of Child Development Research*, Vol. 4. Chicago: University of Chicago Press, 1975, pp. 347–407.

STAATS, A. W., MINKE, K. A., GOODWIN, W., and LANDEEN, J. Cognitive Behavior Modification: "Motivated Learning" Reading Treatment with Subprofessional Therapy-Technicians. *Behavior Research and Therapy*, 1967, *5*, 283–299.

STANLEY, G., and HALL, R. Short-Term Visual Information Processing in Dyslexics. *Child Development*, 1973, *44*, 841–844.

STEVENS, J. R., SACHDEV, K., and MILSTEIN, V. Behavior Disorders of Childhood and the Electroencephalogram. *Archives of Neurology*, 1968, *18*, 160–177.

STEWART, J. L. Cross-cultural Studies and Linguistic Aspects of Stuttering. *Journal of the All India Institute of Speech and Hearing*, 1971, *2*, 1–6.

STEWART, M. A., and OLDS, S. W. *Raising a Hyperactive Child*. New York: Harper and Row, 1973.

STEWART, M. A., PITTS, F. N., CRAIG, A. G., and DIERUF, W. The Hyperactive Child Syndrome. *American Journal of Orthopsychiatry*, 1966, *36*, 861–867.

STRAUSS, A. A., and KEPHART, N. C. *Psychopathology and Education of the Brain-Injured Child. Vol. 2. Progress in Theory and Clinic*. New York: Grune and Stratton, 1955.

STRAUSS, A. A., and LEHTINEN, L. E. *Psychopathology and Education of the Brain Injured Child*. New York: Grune and Stratton, 1947.

STROTHER, C. R. Minimal Cerebral Dysfunction: A Historical Overview. *Annals of the New York Academy of Sciences*, 1973, *205*, 6–17.

SYKES, D. H., DOUGLAS, V. I., WEISS, G., and MINDE, K. K. Attention in Hyperactive Children and the Effect of Methylphenidate (Ritalin). *Journal of Child Psychology and Psychiatry and Allied Disciplines*, 1971, *12*, 129–139.

SYMMES, J. S., and RAPOPORT, J. L. Unexpected Reading Failure. *American Journal of Orthopsychiatry*, 1972, *42*, 82–91.

TEMPLIN, M. C. Developmental Aspects of Articulation. In W. D. Wolfe and D. J. Goulding (eds.), *Articulation and Learning: New Dimensions in Research, Diagnostics, and Therapy*. Springfield, Ill.: Chas. C Thomas, 1973, pp. 51–83.

TRAVIS, L. *The Handbook of Speech Pathology and Audiology*. New York: Appleton-Century-Crofts, 1971.

TREMBLAY, P. W. Vertical Word Processing: A New Approach for Teaching Written Language to the Learning Disabled Adolescent. *Journal of Learning Disabilities*, 1982, *15*, 587–593.

TRITES, R. L., DUGAS, E., LYNCH, G., and FERGUSON, H. B. Prevalence of Hyperactivity. *Journal of Pediatric Psychology*, 1979, *4*, 179–188.

VANRIPER, C. G. *Speech Correction: Principles and Methods*, 4th ed. Englewood Cliffs, N. J.: Prentice-Hall, 1963.

VAUGHAN, R. W., and HODGES, L. A Statistical Survey into a Definition of Learning Disabilities: A Search for Acceptance. *Journal of Learning Disabilities*, 1973, *6*, 658–664.

WAIZER, J., HOFFMAN, S. P., POLIZOS, P., and ENGELHARDT, D. M. Outpatient Treatment of Hyperactive School Children with Imipramine. *American Journal of Psychiatry*, 1974, *131*, 587–591.

WEISS, G., MINDE, K., WERRY, J. S., DOUGLAS, V., and NEMETH, E. Studies on the Hyperactive Child: VIII.

Five Year Follow-up. *Archives of General Psychiatry*, 1971, *24*, 409–414.

WENDER, P. H. *Minimal Brain Dysfunction in Children*. New York: Wiley-Interscience, 1971.

WENDER, P. H. Food Additives and Hyperkinesis. *American Journal of Diseases of Children*, 1977, *131*, 1204.

WERRY, J. S. Studies on the Hyperactive Child: IV. An Empirical Analysis of the Minimal Brain Dysfunction Syndrome. *Archives of General Psychiatry*, 1968, *19*, 9–16.

WERRY, J. S., and SPRAGUE, R. L. Hyperactivity. In C. G. Costello (ed.), *Symptoms of Psychopathology: A Handbook*. New York: John Wiley, 1970, pp. 397–417.

WERRY, J. S., MINDE, K., GUZMAN, A., WEISS, G., DOGAN, K., and HOY, E. Studies on the Hyperactive Child: VII. Neurological Status Compared with Neurotic and Normal Children. *American Journal of Orthopsychiatry*, 1972, *42*, 441–451.

WHALEN, C. K., and HENKER, B. Psychostimulants and Children: A Review and Analysis. *Psychological Bulletin*, 1976, *83*, 1113–1130.

WINITZ, H. *Articulatory Acquisition and Behavior*. New York: Appleton-Century-Crofts, 1969.

WOLFE, W. D., and GOULDING, D. J. (eds.). *Articulation and Learning: New Dimensions in Research, Diagnostics, and Therapy*. Springfield, Ill.: Chas. C Thomas, 1973.

WOOD, N. E. *Delayed Speech and Language Development*. Englewood Cliffs, N. J.: Prentice-Hall, 1964.

WORSTER-DROUGHT, C. Speech Disorders in Children. *Developmental Medicine and Child Neurology*, 1968, *10*, 427–440.

ZAHN, T. P., ABATE, F., LITTLE, B. C., and WENDER, P. H. Minimal Brain Dysfunction, Stimulant Drugs, and Autonomic Nervous System Activity. *Archives of General Psychiatry*, 1975, *32*, 318–387.

11

MENTAL RETARDATION

PROLOGUE

Regina was a seven-year-old first grader who was a source of great concern to her parents, although they did not openly discuss their fear of what might be wrong with her. References to Regina's apparent "slowness" were met with defensiveness, denial, or attempts to conceal the obvious facts. It was only after several parent-teacher conferences, and the school's insistence that she be placed in a special class for slow children, that her parents agreed to have her evaluated by a clinical psychologist. In the process it was established that Regina was unable to read, write, recognize alphabet letters or numbers, or in any way meet the minimal learning requirements of the first grade. Her history revealed consistent evidence of delay in motor, speech, self-help, and social development, although she was physically normal and emotionally stable. On the basis of all the findings, including her IQ score of 61, she was given the diagnosis of mental retardation—mild.

Regina's story is all too familiar, because it describes youngsters we have known, and it reflects our pessimistic attitudes about the future prospects of those who are diagnosed as mentally retarded. Yet we must not subscribe to the popular notion that Regina is representative of a homogeneous group who share similar behavioral characteristics, comparable educational handicaps, and predictable social and vocational outcomes. In fact, the term *mental retardation,* or synonymous labels such as mental deficiency, feeblemindedness, amentia, or mental handicap, refers to a heterogeneous condition involving many different patterns of assets and limitations, and a diversity of etiologies. Moreover, mental retardation (as we have noted previously) may be associated with or actually mimic the symptoms of a variety of abnormal behaviors to the point where discrimination between the two conditions is difficult. The coexistence of mental retardation and personality disorder is not uncommon, although the underlying nature of the relationship may differ in one of the following ways:

1. The relationship may be coincidental in that the two conditions may be present in the same individual.
2. Both forms of abnormal behavior may be the expression of a single pathological process of the brain.
3. The personality disorder may be the result of a primary deficit in intelligence, reflecting the retardate's limited capacity to cope with stressful situations.
4. The subnormal intelligence may be the product of a primary personality disorder, reflecting behaviors that are characteristically impaired in the particular aberrant personality (Benton, 1964; 1970; Bialer, 1970).

In this chapter we shall consider the major clinical and research issues concerning mental retardation, including the definition, the incidence, the descriptive levels of retardation, the divergent etiological factors, and the institutional and remedial provisions.

DEFINITION

The most current and accepted definition of mental retardation is the one offered by the American Association on Mental Deficiency (AAMD), which states:

> Mental retardation refers to significantly subaverage general intellectual functioning existing concurrently with deficits in adaptive behavior, and manifested during the developmental period. (Grossman, 1973, p. 11)

While this definition emphasizes intelligence, it also acknowledges that intelligence is neither a sufficient nor an exclusive criterion of mental retardation. The additional criterion of deficits in adaptive behavior restricts reliance on measured intelligence and requires evidence of a broader and more consistent nature. For example, it guards against the possibility of misdiagnosing youngsters who for reasons of educational deprivation or sensory handicap (the blind and deaf) cannot be assessed accurately by traditional tests of intelligence. Some writers question the test constructors' assumption that intelligence is normally distributed on a bell-shaped Gaussian curve, on the grounds that the experiential components of intelligence (social and educational) are not equally available to everyone (Wortis, 1970). Wortis points out that current IQ scores show a higher incidence of mental retardation in lower socioeconomic groups, a finding that unduly penalizes this population, which has been deprived of social and educational opportunities afforded others.

The inclusion in the AAMD manual of an adaptive behavior scale by which various aspects of development, social behavior, and independent functioning can be rated is an important step in assessing adaptive behaviors. Unless this scale is refined empirically or new ones are devised, the undue emphasis given to intelligence scores is likely to continue (Robinson and Robinson, 1970). But adaptive capacity is difficult to measure; it rests with social change and is dependent on the individual's life situation. In a society such as ours, in which technological advances and urbanization are commonplace, and where human existence is complex and difficult, we would expect to find many individuals who are unable in some way to adapt to these demands. What sort of adaptive failures indicate mental retardation? Does the increase in impaired adaptive behavior associated with social change mean that mental retardation is on the rise? The problem encountered here can be illustrated in the relationship found between age and the incidence of mental retardation; that is, during infancy and preschool years the incidence is relatively low, but it rises sharply in the school years until the age of fourteen or fifteen, while the number of people first diagnosed as mentally retarded declines in the adult years (Lemkau and Imre, 1969). It is reasonable to conjecture that changes in the level of adaptive behavior account for this relationship: Children who are intellectually sub-average (at least those moderately impaired) can cope successfully with the minimal social demands made during infancy and preschool; while at a later age the demands become more complex, making adaptation more difficult. The fact that there is a decline in the incidence of detection of mental retardation during adulthood suggests that these cases have already been identified, and it is in accord with the finding that many forms of mental retardation are associated with a short life expectancy. If adulthood has been reached without prior evidence of mental retardation, clinicians are inclined to look upon impaired adaptive behaviors as manifestations of an abnormal condition other than mental deficiency.

Because the AAMD definition is purely behavioral in nature and makes no attempt to account for etiological factors, it may be less than satisfactory to those who are primarily concerned with the issues of causation and prevention. Zigler (1967) has argued that a greater degree of order could be brought to the field if distinctions were made between physiological and cultural-familial etiologies. He maintains that the difference between the cultural-familial retardate and the nonretardate is attributable to differing motivational systems and not to mental retardation per se.

It is significant that no implication concerning outcome is included in the current definition. The popular expectation that the mentally retarded are doomed to a life behind institutional walls because they are unable to work or engage in any social relations is intentionally avoided, because it simply isn't true. As we shall see, there are many retardates (especially those falling into the borderline level and even some in the mild category) who are capable of holding employment, of getting married, and of having and raising children.

INCIDENCE AND PREVALENCE

As with so many of the other abnormal conditions we have considered, the incidence of mental retardation is virtually impossible to estimate accurately—it varies with the definition, the diagnostic criteria (especially the IQ cut-off point), and the age and socioeconomic level on which prevalence figures are based. In the absence of a national survey of all instances of mental retardation, incidence estimates tend to come from small sample surveys, extrapolated guesses, and the experience of workers in the field.

Within these limitations mental retardation is recognized as a major problem with an incidence rate exceeded only by mental illness, cardiac disease, arthritis, and cancer (*The First Report to the President on the Nation's Progress and Remaining Great Needs to the Campaign to Combat Mental Retardation,* 1962). Accepting as our standard the IQ score of 70 or below, there is a consensus that more than 6.5 million Americans, or 3 percent of the population, are retarded (Macmillan, 1977; Hallahan and Kauffman, 1978). As substantial as this figure is, there are those who regard it as low, because it fails to include those borderline retarded (IQ scores that fall one standard deviation from the mean) in whom we find evidence of slow rate of learning, difficulty in comprehending complex ideas, limited ability to generalize from one experience to another, and poor academic achievement. If this group were included, as suggested by the American Psychiatric Association (*Diagnostic and Statistical Manual of Mental Disorders,* 1968), the incidence of mental retardation would be in excess of 35 million, or 16 percent of the population. However, the 1973 AAMD definition specifically deleted the borderline category because it was impractical and potentially damaging to label so many people mentally retarded, and because a large number of persons classified in this group are able to make adequate adjustments within the community. It is for this reason that we shall restrict our discussion to the consideration of those persons who meet the intellectual and adaptive criteria of the AAMD definition (IQ scores that are two standard deviations or below the mean IQ score).

Most studies show that mental retardation is higher in males than females, in black children than white, in lower socioeconomic levels as contrasted with middle and upper classes, and in different geographical areas of the country—where there are striking variations in the availability of facilities and services for the retarded (Robinson and Robinson, 1965, 1976; Smith, 1971). In addition, approximately 10 percent of the mentally retarded population have IQs below 50, while about 90 percent have IQs between 50 and 70 (Dingman and Tarjan, 1960; *The Decisive Decade*, 1970).

LEVELS OF RETARDATION

It is customary to subdivide mental retardation in terms of degree of intellectual and adaptive impairment, although the primary importance of the IQ is reflected in most, if not all, classification systems. The AAMD manual (Grossman, 1973) describes four categories: *Mild, Moderate, Severe,* and *Profound,* and it carefully specifies that intelligence is to be measured by standardized intelligence tests that are administered individually by trained professionals. Each level of mental retardation is expressed by a range of IQ scores corresponding to a standard deviation unit that describes the distribution of IQ scores in the general population on the most widely used tests of intelligence. Because an IQ score is subject to errors of measurement, it can be expected to vary from one time to another. Therefore, it is arbitrary and misleading to regard an IQ near the top of one range as fixed within this level, since it may actually reflect the individual's capacity to function in the lower portion of the next higher category.

Another problem associated with the classification of mental retardation by levels stems from the inclination to use the scores to draw inferences about the child's future behavior, in spite of the fact that test scores (and IQs) reflect only present performance. The danger in inferring future potential lies in the possibility that planning for the child will be limited by his or her presumed capacity, which may preclude opportunities for education and training beyond this predicted level. In the absence of any preconceived notion about a child's limited potential, achievement can reach heights that exceed prior expectations (Birnbrauer et al., 1965). Consequently, scores and levels of retardation must be interpreted as indicative of present functioning rather than as a stereotyped and fixed prediction of the child's future limitations.

Mild Mental Retardation (IQ range of 52 to 67). This is the largest category, accounting for almost 90 percent of all retardates. Although as adults their intellectual level is much like that of children aged eight to eleven, with proper training and special education many of the mildly retarded are able to make an adequate social and vocational adjustment. When employed, they typically hold unskilled jobs that yield a low income. They frequently need supervision in the management of their social and financial affairs, and because of their limited work skills, they are particularly vulnerable to unemployment as the economy fluctuates. Some find employment in sheltered workshops where supervision is provided and where working conditions are uncomplicated and nonstressful. The vast majority show no signs of brain pathology or physical aberrations that would readily distinguish them from normals. In fact, it has been estimated that only about 1 percent of this group is institutionalized (Hobbs, 1964). Many mildly retarded children are unidentified until the academic demands of school make their deficiencies apparent. Once they are diagnosed, the school regards them as *educable* (a descriptive label that corresponds to this IQ range) and as eligible for special education classes (if available). Unfortunately, only one out of three children is placed in a program where the teacher is a specialist, where the classes are small, and where students learn at their own pace without the social stigma of failure (Mackie, 1965).

Moderate Mental Retardation (IQ range of 36 to 51). This is a category that accounts for approximately 6 percent of retardates. Persons who function at this level are very slow to learn, and their conceptualization skills are extremely limited. While they have some command of the spoken language, typically they cannot read or write. With proper training, they are capable of acquiring self-care behaviors and of performing routine chores in the home or in a sheltered workshop. In school they are considered *trainable*, and they are eligible for special education classes that emphasize the development of practical and basic self-help skills in lieu of academic material. Most moderately retarded individuals stand out as different from others in that they have poor motor coordination as well as physical deformities and anomalies. They require close supervision in almost everything they do, and they have few, if any, friends. Institutionalization is dependent on their level of social competence and the extent to which their families are willing and able to care for them in the home.

Severe Mental Retardation (IQ range of 20 to 35). This represents approximately 3.5 percent of the retarded population, most of whom are institutionalized or under constant supervision in the home. Only the upper range are eligible for trainable classes, while the others are not accepted by most school systems. The vast majority of the severely retarded exhibit genetic disorders, brain pathologies, sensory defects, or, in some instances, severe emotional disturbances. Their learning capacity is very limited, to the extent that they require prolonged training in order to acquire minimal self-help skills. Their motor, speech, and social development are severely retarded.

Profound Mental Retardation (IQ under 20). This is the rarest and most extreme category, accounting for about 1.5 percent of all retardates. Ordinarily individuals in this group are institutionalized and require constant supervision and frequent medical care. Many are confined to a bed or are unable to move about unaided because of central nervous system disorders, sensory and motor disturbances, metabolic aberrations, and other physical disabilities. As a group, their life expectancy is short, with death often occurring during the childhood years. They show little evidence of learning, although some manage to learn to walk, to speak one or two simple phrases, or to acquire partial self-care in feeding and in going to the toilet.

CAUSAL FACTORS AND RELATED CLINICAL DISORDERS

It should be apparent from what has been said that mental retardation is not a unitary entity that appears in the same form, to the same degree, at the same time. It is not always produced by the same causal factors, and it can result either from one circumstance or from the interaction among a number of circumstances that may occur before, during, or after birth. Moreover, the condition varies in severity and in the behavioral characteristics of those affected. It has been estimated that there are more than 300 known or suspected causes of mental retardation, yet these account for not more than 25 percent of all the cases (Love, 1973). A more recent retrospective study in Sweden of children with mild retardation who were born between 1959 and 1970 showed that the etiology was unknown in 43 percent of the cases (Blomquist et al.,

Sidelight 11-1: Idiot Savant

Yoshihiki Yamamoto is a famous and gifted Japanese artist, although he has never obtained an IQ score above 47. When he was six months old, it was learned that he had hydrocephalus (a condition that involves an abnormal accumulation of fluid on the brain) and that in all likelihood he would be mentally retarded. His retardation was more apparent when he was old enough to start school; he had a moderate hearing loss, could not talk, and was not toilet trained. Because special education was not available, his parents were forced to place him in the regular elementary school, from which he graduated at age twelve at the very bottom of the class. On an evaluation before entering junior high, he obtained an IQ of 23 (or a mental age of three), indicating that he was unable to continue in the regular school program. It was Yamamoto's good fortune to be placed in a special class with a teacher, Takashi Kawasaki, who patiently developed a special curriculum around Yamamoto's artistic talent, promoted and sold his art work in order to purchase additional art supplies, and helped his student maintain a rigid and intensive daily work schedule.

Two illustrations of Yamamoto's work are included here to reflect the unbelievable quality and beauty of his artistic talent. Yet Yamamoto may be referred to as an *idiot savant,* a retardate with some highly developed skill that is grossly discrepant with his level of functioning in other areas. Stories similar to Yamamoto's (but probably concerning less gifted children) have appeared in the literature, albeit infrequently. There is no satisfactory explanation for the rare appearance of specific superior skills in these mentally retarded individuals, although Yamamoto's story provides the optimistic suggestion that with special care, interest, program construction, and supervision, some retardates may achieve unexpected levels of performance.

Figures 11-1 and 11-2 (From Morishima, 1975, p. 72 and 73 and reprinted with permission of the Ziff-Davis Publishing Co.).

1981). In approximately 75 percent of all retarded individuals, there is no evidence of brain pathology. These cases are usually referred to as the cultural-familial defectives, in whom incompletely understood sociocultural, psychological, and hereditary factors are implicated as etiological variables.

We turn now to the consideration of the major biological and environmental factors leading to mental retardation, and to the description of some of the distinguishable clinical types of retardation associated with known biological causes. At the same time we note that our efforts to separate biological and environmental forces are intended for convenience and ease of exposition, and not to deny or ignore the important interplay that exists among them. The baby who is born with the rare hereditary milk sugar disease known as *galactosemia* will suffer permanent brain damage and will eventually die if fed with milk that contains lactose. However, with early identification and proper environmental changes in diet, the baby may develop normally. Thus, the interaction of both biological and environmental factors contributes significantly to the critical questions of whether and how the infant survives.

Hereditary and Chromosomal Abnormalities

There is a long-standing popular view that heredity plays a primary causative role in mental retardation. Stimulated by Darwin's theory of natural selection, Galton studied the family trees of certain distinguished British families and arrived at the conclusion that genius is inherited (Hunt, 1961). In this country Goddard in 1912 published the results of his well-known study of the Kallikak family, in which he argued that feeblemindedness and certain other undesirable traits are genetically transmitted. The pioneer constructors of intelligence tests (Simon, Binet, Stern, and Goddard) were influenced by this view and to varying degrees regarded intelligence as fixed and genetically predetermined (Sattler, 1974). Subsequent research evidence indicating that (1) the IQ is constant from one age level to another, (2) Binet-type intelligence tests are highly intercorrelated, and (3) the tests results are good predictors of general academic achievement led many to believe that intellect is a fixed and genetically determined characteristic. Further support came from animal studies in which Coghill demonstrated that development proceeds on an orderly basis and is rarely affected by exigencies of the external environment (Coghill, 1929), and from infant studies showing that the emergence of a fundamental skill such as walking is virtually unaffected by the deprivation of practice opportunities (Dennis and Dennis, 1940). Thus, there seemed to be strong evidence to support the view that development is genetically regulated and relatively uninfluenced by experiential factors.

But soon the weight of research support shifted to the importance of prior experiences in determining whether or not certain patterns of behavior would be exhibited. The effects of early stimulation on both the rate and quality of development, and the influence of many environmental factors on such primary areas as learning, memory, thinking, perception, and personality formation, were considered increasingly important. The battle between hereditarians and environmentalists over the nature-nurture problem continues even today without resolution. Most contemporary students of behavior regard it as an insoluble problem, principally because it begins with an erroneous assumption and asks the wrong questions. Heredity and experiential factors interact, and both contribute to human development and behavior. Instead of pitting one set of variables against another, it is more appropriate to attempt to study the effects of one factor while the other is held constant, and to determine the specific conditions under which both heredity and environment may influence behavior (Hebb, 1965).

While it is true that many forms of mental retardation tend to run in families, known hereditary diseases or chromosomal abnormalities are evident in only a small number of these cases. A recent study of 727 retarded individuals found that 16 percent of the cases could be linked to genetic causes (Thoene et al., 1981). The most prevalent of the retarded are the cultural-familial type, who fall within the mildly retarded category, and who best exemplify the interactive effects of both genetic and environmental factors. We shall consider this group when we discuss environmental factors, since little is known about the specific genetic defect or mode of transmission for this population. In the meantime we shall look at those already-identified genetic conditions that lead to mental retardation. Obviously, only a selected sample of these disorders can be included here to provide the reader with some better understanding of the variety of genetic effects and the resulting types of clinical symptoms.

Recessive Genetic Disorders. Within recent years technical advances in laboratory methods in the field of genetics have made possible significant contributions to our understanding of the etiology of mental retardation. At present most of the genetically determined syndromes involve recessive genes that alter in some way the development of an enzyme essential for normal metabolism, or that impair metabolic processes.

1. Abnormalities of amino acid metabolism. Although recessive disorders affect the metabolic processes in different ways, the largest number of known syndromes is associated with faulty metabolism of amino acids (Robinson and Robinson, 1970). Donohue (1967) noted that there are at least eighteen different types of amino acid metabolic disturbances associated with mental retardation and neurological dysfunction. While these account for approximately 3 percent of the institutionalized retardates, about one-third of this group are affected by a disorder known as *phenylketonuria,* or *PKU* (Holmes et al., 1972; Robinson and Robinson, 1976).

Phenylketonuria is an autosomal recessive metabolic disorder in which the affected infant lacks a liver enzyme needed to oxidize phenylalanine (an amino acid found in protein food) to tyrosine. As a result, phenylalanine is improperly utilized by the body, and its accumulation in the bloodstream causes brain damage and mental retardation. Large amounts of phenylpyruvic acid are excreted in the urine, which gives the urine a characteristic musty odor. As a matter of fact, this odor led to the identification of PKU by Folling in 1934, after mothers of retarded children called it to his attention. Although it is a rare disorder occurring in 1 in 10,000 to 1 in 20,000 Caucasian births, PKU has received a good deal of public attention because it illustrates a form of mental retardation that can be prevented by early detection and low phenylalanine diets (Bakwin and Bakwin, 1972; Reed, 1975).

Evidence of mental retardation may appear within the first few months of life, and almost certainly between six and twelve months after birth. Behaviorally, PKU is characterized by hyperactivity, bizarre body movements, severe temper outbursts, and retardation that is most often severe (although moderate cases can occur). There are reports of rare instances in which intelligence is normal or even superior in persons whose phenylpyruvic acid is high (Perry, 1970). Some victims exhibit eczema, vomiting, and convulsions. Hair, skin, and eye color is usually lighter than that of the unaffected members of the family (Gellis and Feingold, 1968).

The diagnosis may be made by adding a few drops of ferric chloride to an infant's urine and observing the subsequent color stain. A green or greenish-blue color indicates the presence of PKU. However, the absence of a green color obtained within six weeks of birth may not be a true indication of normality, because an excess of phenylalanine may be absorbed in the mother's blood during fetal life. A blood test measuring the level of phenylalanine and tyrosine is a more reliable method of identifying PKU early, and this is now required in most states as a means of prevention (Berman et al., 1969). Treatment by controlled intake of phenylalanine is ordinarily effective if initiated prior to the age of three months and continued to middle childhood; otherwise, the resultant brain damage is irreversible, and mental retardation cannot be arrested. Some infants are damaged by an elevated level of phenylalanine in their mothers, a condition that can be prevented if the mother's phenylalanine intake is controlled during pregnancy (Holmes et al., 1972).

Other amino acid metabolic disorders leading to mental retardation include Menkes's syndrome, or Maple-Syrup disease; Hartnup's disease; Citrillinuria; and Homocystinuria, all of which are extremely rare and are best treated early by special diets.

2. *Amaurotic family idiocy: Abnormalities of lipid metabolism.* In general, these disorders are transmitted genetically as autosomal recessive traits, and they result in the faulty metabolism of fatty compounds needed for the development of the central nervous system. They are characterized by progressive mental and physical deterioration that almost always results in early death.

Tay-Sachs disease is probably the best known of this group of disorders. It is found most frequently among children of Eastern European Jewish ancestry, who represent some 50 to 60 percent of these cases (Carter, 1970). Affected infants appear normal at birth and only begin to show gradual signs between four and eight months of age, when they display sensitivity to noise, tremors of the extremities, listlessness, and retarded motor development. The disorder is progressive, and the child exhibits signs of muscular spasticity, muscular degeneration, blindness, convulsions, and accentuation of hearing as well as of the startle reflex. The child's head and abdomen enlarge, and typically a cherry red spot on the eyegrounds is present. Death usually occurs before the age of four years. There is no known treatment for this disorder.

Prospective parents of Eastern European Jewish ancestry can be tested for the presence of the recessive gene (blood is analyzed for the level of the enzyme produced by normal genes). If both the father and mother carry the gene, amniocentesis can determine whether the fetus has inherited the fatal double dose. If only one member of the couple carries the recessive gene, the child may also be a carrier, but he or she will not have the disease. In other words, this could really be eliminated from the population through genetic testing and abortion of fetuses found to have the disease.

While *Niemann-Picks' disease* is rarer, it is quite similar to Tay-Sachs disease in that it also affects primarily Jewish children, has an early and gradual onset of common symptoms, and results in early fatality (Carter, 1970). Distinction between the two conditions is made by the absence of the eyeground sign characteristic of Tay-Sachs disease. If there is a family history of the disease, a skin biopsy of prospective parents will reveal the presence or absence of the recessive gene.

In two other types of Amaurotic Idiocy, the clinical picture is somewhat the same as already described, but the onset occurs either in young children between the ages of six and eight (*Early Juvenile Cerebral Lipoidosis*) or later in life, between the ages of twenty and thirty (*Early Adult Amaurotic Idiocy or Kuf's disease*).

3. *Abnormalities of carbohydrate metabolism.* The best-known form of these disorders is *Galactosemia* (referred to earlier), another autosomal recessive metabolic condition, which in this case impairs the infant's ability to metabolize galactose. The disorder appears immediately after birth or as soon as the child begins to ingest milk. Symptoms include vomiting, diarrhea, colic, weight loss (or failure to gain weight), and cataracts, which may later be followed by jaundice and cirrhosis of the liver (Carter, 1970). Although the disorder usually produces mental retardation, it can be prevented by early detection (through a test of the urine) and treated by the elimination of lactose in the diet, probably for the duration of the child's life.

4. *Abnormalities of endocrine function.*

The labels *hypothyroidism* and *cretinism* are used to designate several aberrant conditions of the thyroid that may be associated with mental retardation. Hypothyroidism could result from thyroid or iodine deficiency in the mother during pregnancy, from an absence of the thyroid gland, or less frequently from a genetically determined enzyme defect that interferes with the proper synthesis of thyroxine (Heber, 1970). According to Holmes and colleagues (1972), instances of congenital hypothyroidism resulting from different causes are clinically indistinguishable except for the presence of a goiter early in life in nongenetic cases, in contrast to a later appearance of this symptom (between the ages of five and ten) in genetically caused cases. Children who are cretins have a characteristic appearance that includes puffy eyelids, flat nasal bridge, open mouth with a thick protruding tongue, short and thick neck, enlarged abdomen, dry and mottled skin, short stature, stubby fingers, and, if untreated, delayed or no sexual maturation. In addition, their motor and mental development is retarded, the degree of retardation being proportional to the severity of the thyroid deficiency and the age at which it occurred. Thyroid extract is often successfully used to reverse the symptoms of congenital hypothyroidism, although evidence suggests that only 50 percent of infants treated before six months of age had average or better IQ scores (Wilkins, 1965).

Chromosomal Abnormalities. It is estimated that the prevalence of chromosomal abnormalities in live-born infants is about 1 in 20,000. This estimate is even higher if fetuses are considered, since 90 percent of fetuses carrying such an abnormality are spontaneously aborted (Holmes et al., 1972). In general, infants born with chromosomal abnormalities are equally divided between those with autosomal abnormalities and those with sex chromosomal abnormalities. We shall consider an example of each type of chromosomal abnormality.

1. *Down's syndrome,* or *Mongolism,* is a disorder that was described clinically well over a hundred years ago, although its identification as an autosomal syndrome associated with an extra Group-G chromosome (trisomy 21) was discovered in 1959 by Lejeune, Gautier, and Turpin (1963). Mongolism occurs more frequently in boys than in girls, and it is seen in all racial, ethnic, and socioeconomic groups. It has been estimated that approximately 1 out of every 600 live births and about 10 to 15 percent of all institutionalized retardates are mongoloid (Heber, 1970). A decrease in the occurrence of Down's syndrome was reported in New York State after the legislature liberalized the abortion law; women at high risk (over thirty-five years of age) sought termination of their pregnancies more frequently than young women (Hansen, 1978). Mongoloid children typically fall within the moderate to severe categories of mental retardation, and they are characterized by distinctive physical features, deficient muscle tone (hypotonia), congenital heart defects, and feeblemindedness.

> The mongoloid has almond-shaped, slanting eyes, with the skin of the eyelids very thick. The lips are thin and appear fissured and dry, with the tongue also showing deep fissures. The teeth are usually small and misshapen; the nose is flat; hair is generally sparse, fine and straight. Hands and feet are broad and clumsy, and the mongoloid is awkward in both gross and fine motor coordination. He has fingerprints with L-shaped loops rather than the usual whorls. One other outstanding characteristic of the mongoloid is his deep voice, which is often helpful in making a diagnosis. (Love, 1973, p. 59)

Mongolism is a chromosomal aberration that does not follow simple Mendelian genetic transmission. Most instances of Down's syndrome are attributable to the presence of extra genetic material for the chromosome number 21. This material does not originate exclusively in the mother; research has shown that it originates in the sperm in about 20 to 25 percent of the cases. Moreover, the high risk commonly associated with advancing maternal age is also now found for fathers forty-one years of age or older. This finding is apparently quite independent of the mothers' age, and it indicates that the extra chromosome can originate in either the egg or the sperm (Abroms and Bennett, 1983). Research into the factors that cause the chromosomal aberration has failed to yield definitive results. Reported correlations with viral hepatitis and with fluoride in the drinking water have been soundly criticized and seem unpromising at present. However, it is well established that older mothers run a high risk of bearing mongoloid children (Somasundarum and Papakumari, 1981); more than half these youngsters are produced by mothers who are in their late thirties and forties. Moreover, the approximate risk per pregnancy in mothers under twenty-nine years of age is 1 in 3,000, contrasted to a risk of 1 in 55 for mothers in their forties (Koch, Fishler, and Melnyk, 1971). Faulty intrauterine conditions that are more likely to occur in older pregnant women have been thought to produce the chromosomal abnormality, although the specific factors have not as yet been identified.

At present, Down's syndrome is irreversible and not amenable to treatment, although chromosomal analysis of the mother after conception helps in estimating risk and in preventing the disorder in most instances. Mongoloid children have been described in the literature as less intense, less persistent, and more placid than normal control subjects, and they are depicted as having a lower threshold for stimulation. However, mothers' ratings of the temperament of their mongoloid children have failed to support these stereotyped characteristics (Bridges and Cicchetti, 1982). IQ scores obtained from the Stanford-Binet given to 180 children with Down's syndrome showed that the average IQ was 44.3, with 40 percent of these children above the score of 50 (Connolly, 1978). Connolly concludes that the abilities of these children may not be as limited as previously thought, and it may be possible for them to make some developmental gains through a stimulating environment. Piper and Ramsay (1980) showed through a biweekly program designed to stimulate normal development that such factors as maternal involvement, opportunities for a variety of daily stimulation, and the organization of the physical and temporal environment are important for the personal and social development of mongoloid children. The authors further suggested that these factors may prevent a major decrease in the mental functioning of these children.

Greenwald and Leonard (1979) studied the development of communicative and sensorimotor skills among Down's syndrome children and found, as in normal children, that those mongoloid youngsters who had a higher sensorimotor level also had more advanced communication skills than those at a lower level. On the basis of this observed relationship, the authors optimistically suggested that increased training in motor skills for Down's syndrome children may very well facilitate the improvement of their communicative skills. However, when a neurodevelopmental remediation program designed to improve postural tone and reflexes, equilibrium, and movement patterns was given to Down's syndrome babies between the ages of two months and twenty-one months, no significant change occurred in either their overall motor performance or overall mental performance (Harris, 1981).

2. *Klinefelter's syndrome* (47/XXY) illustrates a group of disorders associated with chromosomal abnormalities of the sex chromosome. In this condition, which affects only males, there is an extra X chromosome. The disorder is characterized by a tall and effeminate body build, sterility, small testes, breast enlargement (in adolescents and adults), and diminished facial and body hair. Although the frequency of mental deficiency among those with Klinefelter's syndrome is higher than in the general population (about 25 percent), in a large number of the cases intelligence is either unaffected or slightly lower than average.

The most common anomaly of the sex chromosome in females is *Turner's syndrome* (XO), in which approximately 20 percent of those affected are mentally retarded. Sexual infantilism, short stature, webbing of the neck, flat nasal bridge, epicanthal folds, and protruding and/or low-set ears are common features associated with this disorder. Hormonal treatment given at the proper time for both Klinefelter's and Turner's syndromes helps increase the maturation of secondary sexual characteristics (Gellis and Feingold, 1968).

Other Biological Factors. In this section we shall consider a number of other biological determinants of mental retardation that may occur before, during, or after birth.

1. *Infections and toxins.* Obviously, not all infections give rise to brain damage and mental deficiency, although some that are contracted by the mother during pregnancy, and others that occur in the child postnatally, are known to produce neurological and intellectual deficits. For example, mothers who have rubella (German measles) during the first trimester of pregnancy give birth to offspring who show an array of congenital anomalies, including sensory defects (deafness and cataracts), heart lesions, and mental retardation. However, the discovery of a vaccine to protect youngsters against rubella has radically reduced the serious consequences of this infectious disorder. During the twenty-year period between 1935 and 1955, the danger of fetal infection from mothers infected with syphilis decreased as this venereal disease declined. Within recent years the frequency of syphilis has increased, making this form of transplacental infection more likely (Heber, 1970). Congenital syphilis is associated with premature births, copper-colored or red spots on the buttocks, saddlenose deformity, seizures, brain damage, and mental deficiency. The greatest risk of fetal infection occurs after the first four months of pregnancy in mothers who have recently contracted syphilis (Holmes et al., 1972). Postnatally, encephalitis (viral infections of the brain) and infections of the meninges (membrane cover of the brain) result in brain damage and mental retardation in about 10 to 20 percent of the children affected (Koch, 1971; Telford and Sawrey, 1977). Early symptoms of fever, stiff neck and back, and headache are usually exhibited. Fortunately, these infections are rare in this country.

Toxic substances such as lead and carbon monoxide also can produce brain damage and mental retardation. Lead ingestion (from old paint) interferes with brain-cell metabolism and may result not only in severe retardation but possibly also in death. Jaundice occurring after twenty-four hours in the newborn is a sign of possible incompatibility of blood types between the mother and the fetus. If untreated by proper blood-exchange transfusions, it usually leads to kernicterus (a yellow bilirubin staining of brain areas) and mental retardation. The two most common types of blood incompatibility are Rh-factor and ABO.

2. *Trauma, injury, or physical agent.* The potentially harmful effects of irradiation and nuclear fallout have been well known since the atomic bombing of Hiroshima and Nagasaki at the close of World War II. Pregnant women who have been exposed to large amounts of irradiation of the uterus run the risk of giving birth to offspring who are microcephalic (small head), mentally retarded, and structurally deformed in the eyes and the limbs. Birth is a physically demanding and traumatic event for the newborn, and precipitous or prolonged labor, the fetal position, the baby's head size, uterine and pelvic anomalies, and hazards associated with the umbilical cord can lead to either intracranial hemorrhage or anoxia. Either condition may produce brain damage and mental retardation, although medical advances have substantially reduced the probability of mental deficiency occurring from birth trauma (*Infant Care,* 1968). Unconsciousness, persistent vomiting, and possible mental confusion are common symptoms of trauma to the brain. Head injuries caused by household or automobile accidents also may result in brain damage and impaired cognitive functioning. Nylander and Nylander (1964) made the interesting observa-

Sidelight 11-2: Fetal Alcohol Syndrome

At a recent conference on birth defects, Dr. Sterling Clarren reported that he could smell alcohol on the breath of a baby he had delivered. The child's mother was a heavy drinker who had continued to imbibe during the course of the pregnancy. At birth "the child's eyes were small. His nose and cheekbones were flat. The child's growth was stunted—he weighed in at under five pounds—and the joints got stuck. He couldn't move his fingers."

First identified as *fetal alcohol syndrome* by Dr. David Smith, the problem is said to occur in 1 out of every 4,000 births, and possibly more frequently. Clarren estimates that the disorder ranks as the third leading cause of mental retardation.

Apparently, alcohol is particularly damaging to the early development of the fetus during the first eighty-five days of pregnancy, although the specific manner by which the damage occurs is not now known. The extent of the impairment is said to be dependent on the amount of alcohol used by the pregnant mother. Unfortunately, the defect cannot be detected before birth and in time for a therapeutic abortion. Of course, the disorder would be prevented entirely if pregnant mothers would abstain from drinking. (From "Baby Born Deformed with Alcohol on Breath." UPI, January 5, 1977, p. 9B)

tion that head injuries are more likely to occur in retarded than in normal youngsters, and that most head injuries are too mild to be regarded as a cause of mental retardation.

3. *Premature birth.* Follow-up studies of premature infants with birth weights less than three pounds five ounces indicate a high incidence of physical and mental disorders, including mental deficiency. However, many of these studies have been criticized for their failure to account for the relationship between social class and birth weight, and for their tendency to ignore the fact that the expected distribution of intelligence for premature infants is below the normal mean. Nevertheless, the results of the more carefully controlled studies consistently show that prematurity is associated with a higher rate of mental retardation in both white and nonwhite populations (Pasamanick and Lilienfeld, 1955; Masland, 1960; McDonald, 1964).

4. *Nutritional deprivation.* Malnutrition, especially deficiencies of certain vitamins during early development, can cause physical and intellectual deterioration (Cravioto, De Licardie, and Birch, 1966). Moreover, vitamin deficiency, particularly of Vitamins A and E, in the mother during pregnancy has been associated with prematurity, congenital malformations of the central nervous system, and mental retardation (Carter, 1970). Several experimental studies involving both humans and animals have demonstrated that protein deprivation reduces appetite and adversely affects brain growth and mental performance (Barnes et al., 1967; Winick 1968; Zamenhof, van Marthens, and Margolis, 1968; Das and Pivato, 1976; Zeskind and Ramey, 1981). Although comparable evidence for humans is not available, it is interesting to note that animals deprived of proper nutrition over successive generations are less efficient in both reproduction and mothering, and they tend to have smaller litters with lower birth weights and higher mortality (Stein and Kassab, 1970). At present the social and preventive implications of these animal studies for those people who live under poverty conditions from one generation to another are striking, although tentative.

Environmental Factors and Cultural-Familial Retardation. In the absence of demonstrable evidence of genetic and/or biological factors causing more than 75 percent of all cases of mental retardation, there is a strong inclination to turn to environmental influences as a viable alternative. In this light the importance of the environment in shaping behavior is secondary to biological considerations, and instances of unknown (organic) etiology become attributed to psychosocial determinants. The issue is not which of the two classes of variables is of primary significance, but the implication that the absence of one set of conditions can be taken as supportive evidence for the other. Obviously, in order to consider a variable as a causal agent, its influential effects must be demonstrated empirically. Therefore, we shall examine the sociocultural forces that appear to play a significant role in determining mental retardation.

Cultural-Familial Mental Retardation. Although the current AAMD definition of mental retardation avoids etiological considerations, it is generally accepted that the cultural-familial type of mental deficiency refers to those mildly retarded individuals in whom no biological or genetic abnormality can be found, and who have a retarded parent or sibling. This implies that both heredity and environment play a causal role—and yet almost without exception, discussions take the form of heredity versus environment, where the two are in opposition to each other. Girardeau (1971), after an extensive and critical review of the literature, concluded that there appears to be no scientific evidence at present to confirm either heredity or environment as a major causative factor in cultural-familial retardation. The question of how these factors interact "could be approached more appropriately in terms of specific experimental questions rather than as a gross generalization" (p. 341). Nevertheless, it is interesting to note that seven pathogenic factors were found which tend to be significantly more common for the cultural-familial type of retardate than for the genetically determined type (Costeff et al., 1981). These include the following, which tend also to be highly related to low socioeconomic status: (1) a history of maternal insufficiency in reproduction, (2) bleeding during pregnancy, (3) toxemia during pregnancy, (4) signs of perinatal stress, (5) neonatal anoxia, (6) neonatal jaundice, and (7) seizures during the first year of life (especially related to severe retardation).

It is well established that mental retardation is essentially a lower-class phenomenon for those cases (primarily falling between IQs of 50 to 75) in which there is no evidence of neurological and/or genetic abnormalities (Hardy, 1965; Kushlick, 1966). Persons of low socioeconomic status often have incomes that do not permit adequate nutrition, medical care, housing and living conditions, or social and intellectual enrichment. Children in this group tend to be less supervised during the day, having either working parents or one parent who has been left with the full responsibility of managing the household. Their schools are apt to have poor facilities and educational programs, while the availability of academic, verbal, and intellectual materials is likely to be extremely limited in both the schools and the home. Therefore, poverty may indirectly or directly lead to some of the biological determinants of mental deficiency already discussed, such as prematurity, infections and toxins, birth injuries, and malnutrition.

Support for the influence of social and economic deprivation on brain weight, learning, and intellectual development is derived from a variety of sources. Tests show that animals reared in enriched environments with bright lights and with conditions that facilitate play and exploration have heavier cerebral cortices and greater cortical activity than those reared in a sensory-deprived environment (Bennett et al., 1964). Restricted environments impair the learning performance of preadult rodents. However, as Meier points out: "Primate studies indicate that any laboratory rearing procedure leads to defective behavior, especially of connotative rather than cognitive behavior, when these animals are compared with feral or socially reared controls" (1970, p. 291). Thus, there is a disparity in results between the two animal species, which Meier believes is attributable to a failure to understand differences among species and among the variables that affect their behavior. More importantly, he criticizes the categorical generalization of findings based on animal data to rearing practices in humans. Nevertheless, longitudinal studies with humans have shown that lower-class children, as compared to those of the middle class, receive from their mothers significantly fewer vocalizations, smiles, rewards for developmental progress, or prolonged periods of play (Kagan, 1969). Kagan argues that deprivation of these early experiences has a deleterious effect on mental development, which is reflected in lower IQ scores.

We know that the usual outcome of socioeconomic deprivation is academic failure and restricted employment potential after school. The academic progress of many lower-class children may be impaired both because of their bilingualism and because of the negative attitude that disadvantaged communities hold toward education as well as toward their prospect of social and economic upward mobility. Data on the effects of early sensory and maternal deprivation largely derived from animal studies are provocative, but too tenuous to extend to humans without much more research. It is entirely possible that the atypical social histories associated with members of low social and economic classes have a greater deleterious influence on emotional and motivational factors than on cognition.

As a matter of fact, there is ample evidence that the mentally retarded (due to a history of repeated experiences of failure) expect little success, set low goals for themselves, accept levels of success that are much below their cognitive abilities, and tend to exhibit avoidance behavior under conditions of heightened expectations of failure (MacMillan, 1969; Zigler, 1971). Zigler (1971) also notes that social deprivation largely contributes to an array of overdependent behaviors often observed in retardates (especially the institutionalized familial retardate), such as seeking attention and affection. He suggests that their perseverative behavior can be more properly attributed to their heightened motivation for adult support than to inherent cognitive rigidity. Moreover, Zigler convincingly argues that observed changes in IQ scores following some environmental intervention reflects motivational changes and is not attributable to the influence of intellectual stimulation.

One of the most impressive and convincing demonstrations of the potent influence of environmental factors on later intellectual and social functioning is Skeels's follow-up study of infants evaluated some thirty years earlier (Skeels, 1966). Skeels studied two groups of children, mostly from poor family backgrounds, many of whom had mentally retarded mothers and were illegitimate. After evaluation the two groups received different treatments. One group was transferred before age three from an overcrowded and unstimulating orphanage to an institution for the mentally retarded, where the environment was regarded as more enriched in interpersonal relationships, and where there were mother-surrogates and a greater amount of developmental stimulation. The second group, known as the contrast group, was confined for a prolonged period of time to the nonstimulating orphanage environment. Children in the experimental group remained in the institution for the retarded until they had received maximum benefit, and then they were either placed in adoptive homes or returned to the orphanage for transfer to an adoptive home. The length of stay in the institution for the retarded ranged from 5.7 to 52.1 months. Children in the contrast group remained in the orphanage until placement, for periods of time ranging from 21.4 to 43.1 months.

Over the first two years of the study, the experimental group showed a dramatic average gain of 28.5 IQ points, while the contrast group, which was initially higher in intelligence, showed an average decline of 26.2 IQ points. After twenty-one years all subjects were located and further studied. Essentially, the divergent patterns noted earlier for the two groups persisted into adulthood. All the experimental subjects were self-supporting, and all had completed an average of twelve grades in school. Eleven were married, and nine had children whose IQs ranged from 86 to 125. In the contrast group one member had died in adolescence, and four were still institutionalized. The contrast group completed, on the average, less than three grades of school; only 64 percent were employed, and those who were employed held menial and unskilled jobs. Only two members of this group were married, and one was subsequently divorced.

Skeels's findings suggest that nurturance and cognitive stimulation early in childhood are important determinants of intellectual, personality, and social development through adulthood.

REMEDIAL APPROACHES

In the early 1960s the president's panel on mental retardation sent missions to several European countries in order to learn more about their progress in the care, education, and rehabilitation of the mentally retarded. The initial task of identifying those promising aspects of facilities and programs for later replication in this country was relatively easy. But as is the case with most transplants, the ultimate success largely depends on the extent to which the donor and the recipient are compatible. Compatibility here refers to the attitudes and values held by different societies toward mental retardation, which greatly influence the basic policies and programs selected and how they are implemented. Lippman (1972) contends that the advances he observed in Scandinavia as compared to the United States primarily are attributable to attitudinal differences between the countries. He identified the following three fundamental attitudes in Scandinavia that seemed to be responsible for its successful programs and services:

1. Mentally retarded people are human beings. They should therefore be treated with respect for their individual dignity.
2. We do not always know what capabilities a retarded person may have, but we must do all we can to help each one achieve his (or her) fullest potential.
3. It is society's responsibility to help the retarded, as it must help others who are handicapped or dependent; and society works most effectively through the state. (1972, p. 7)

In Scandinavia comprehensive health services, special education, sheltered workshops, hostels for community living, and residential facilities are provided when needed for all citizens, whereas in the United States a full range of these services is not uniformly available. Scandinavian residential programs are state operated or sponsored, and they are designed to provide for a smaller number of clients than most state institutions for the retarded in this country. Living conditions are rarely crowded and overpopulated, as they are here, because privacy and individuality are highly regarded, and because the Scandinavians hold different attitudes toward the retarded than Americans do. Consequently, the Scandinavian countries typically design their facilities to provide clean, colorful, and well-furnished surroundings with space for personal belongings, attractive pictures hanging on the walls, an absence of locks, and strict adherence to the simple amenity of knocking on closed doors before entering a room. In contrast, many of our institutions are drab, sterile, and impersonal, and they are operated on the premise that the retarded are just as personally insensitive and unaware of the environment as they are intellectually limited. Inactivity is uncommon in Scandinavian residences, even for those who are severely retarded. All are encouraged to participate in some productive activity and to utilize their resources to the fullest. Most Scandinavian retardates live in the community, where a large proportion find employment without resistance or prejudice. Apparently, they are judged by the same criterion of productivity that other employees are expected to meet.

While little, if any, data are available to assess public attitudes toward mental retardation in this country, inferences can be drawn from an examination of the institutional environment in which some retardates are required to live. The deplorable living conditions in institutions for the retarded, together with an analysis of the political and social forces that interfere with improvement, have been candidly described elsewhere (Blatt and Kaplan, 1966; Blatt, 1970).

A severe indictment of institutions for the mentally retarded is voiced by Braginsky and Braginsky (1971), who argue that many children have been institutionalized because they were rejected and unwanted by their families and not because of mental retardation per se. They claim that residential facilities and labels such as "mental retardation" are used primarily by society and parents as ways to justify their acts of abandonment and to alleviate the guilt that accompanies these actions. It is not unusual for the retardate to be rejected by his or her family, shunned by employers, ostracized by peers, denied heterosexual relationships, and ignored by the community (Love, 1973).

As unpleasant as these revelations may be, it is necessary to understand our attitudes toward the retarded as we consider the kinds of programs and services offered in this country.

Overcoming Parental Resistance

All prospective parents hope for a "normal and healthy child." While any abnormality is disappointing, emotionally disturbing, and difficult to accept, the diagnosis of mental retardation is particularly shocking and troublesome for most affected parents. Perhaps this is attributable to the pessimistic assumptions commonly held in our society that imply that the retarded child's potential and future outlook are dismal and hopeless. It may be that such a diagnosis is threatening and guilt provoking to parents because it reflects uncomfortably on the family "line" in terms of either inheritance or some biological defect. The fear that the child either will have to be banished permanently to an institution or, if kept at home, will become the object of ridicule and embarrassment to members of the family are real possibilities and problems. Moreover, the sudden prospect of having to cope with and manage a poorly understood condition is sufficient in itself to arouse a great deal of anxiety in most parents.

There is general agreement that parental attitudes and reactions to their mentally retarded child are important influences in shaping the life of both the family and the handicapped child. It has been found that parents of retarded children are quite anxious about the future and are especially concerned about what will happen to the child when they are no longer able to care for him or her (Condell, 1966). In fact, when American and Danish families with recently born retarded children were compared to families with nonhandicapped children, the families with the retarded children were more negative about both the child and themselves. Moreover, the supportive services for the families in Denmark did not have a greater impact in the adjustment of the parents than did the support provided in this country (Waisbren, 1980). Other research data are interpreted as indicating that parents of retarded children are more rejecting than those of average youngsters, and that fathers have more difficulty in accepting retarded sons than daughters (Worchel and Worchel, 1961; Paymer, 1965; Levine, 1966). Parental guilt, ambivalence, anger, shame, and grief are some of the other parental reactions that are likely to disturb the relationship between parents, affect child-rearing practices, and have a significant impact on the adjustment of normal children in the family.

In dealing with the problem of mental

retardation, the clinician cannot function merely as a thorough diagnostician, since parents are neither unaffected by the clinical findings nor knowledgeable and omnipotent enough to manage the situation without any further professional assistance. Counseling over a period of time is necessary; parents may have specific questions about the diagnosis, etiology, prognosis, and immediate and long-range therapeutic plans for their child (Kanner, 1961, pp. 453–461). In addition, the clinician must be prepared to deal with the emotional reactions of parents and to help them work through their feelings to the point where they can be comfortable with themselves and the limitations of the child. Toward these ends participation in group sessions with other parents who are experiencing similar difficulties, and availability of counseling services at various stages of the child's life, may be very beneficial.

Programs for the Institutionalized Retarded

No type of retardation in itself indicates the need for residential care, although most institutionalized retardates are classed as severe or profound and require almost constant and specialized management. There is general agreement that the retarded child should remain in the home and function in the community for as long as possible. However, the extent to which this can be accomplished will depend on the adequacy and stability of the family, its economic resources, and its capacity to cope with the special needs and problems of the child. In addition, the child's placement is influenced by the availability and strength of the educational programs, the vocational training and placement opportunities, and other resources in the community. Thus, a mildly or moderately retarded child from a broken home may require institutionalization or foster home placement because the remaining working parent is unable to provide proper supervision and care. In circumstances where the community fails to provide the necessary program or service, residential care may be the most desirable placement for the child.

Privately supported residential facilities are available throughout the country, but the cost is usually prohibitive for most families from middle and lower socioeconomic groups. Publicly supported state institutions typically are overcrowded, with waiting periods that may be longer than a year before admission is possible. With increasing frequency state institutions are occupied by the more severely and profoundly retarded, who evidence a higher incidence of multiple problems that cannot be readily managed on the outside. Medical advances have significantly increased the life expectancy for some of these children, which, in effect, has unexpectedly decreased the turnover rate in most state institutions.

Residential facilities offer such varied services as nursing, medical and dental care, special education, vocational training, and recreational activities. However, institutions have been criticized on the grounds that they tend to process patients in a depersonalized way, shifting them from service to service rather than using existing resources flexibly (Kirman, 1972; Gunzburg, 1973). Moreover, many severely retarded, institutionalized individuals spend between one-third to one-half of their waking day doing absolutely nothing, and up to one-fifth of their time engaging in autistic behaviors (Klaber, 1969).

However, in recent years dramatic changes have been taking place in the institutional programs, in the attitudes of the staff, and in the behavior of the residents. These changes can be attributed largely to the systematic application of learning principles known as *behavior modification*. This approach is essentially positive in nature, since it assumes that retardates can learn, can do things for themselves, can function more effectively, and can profit from and enjoy a wider range of experiences. As Bigelow (1977) so aptly stated:

> The focus is always upon improvement. No limit is set on what an individual can learn, other

> than the limits of his own rate of progress. Some individuals may progress quickly, others more slowly, but all are capable of learning. This positive approach of focusing upon teaching specific skills can drastically alter one's view of retardation. Frustration and pessimism is minimized once we see the residents learning. (p. 18)

Illustrations of behavior modification with the mentally retarded are numerous, demonstrating that new behaviors can be acquired and maintained, and that old unwanted behaviors can be eliminated. Beginning with Fuller's (1949) interest in showing that through operant conditioning an eighteen-year-old vegetative idiot (who was thought hopelessly unable to learn) could learn the simple response of moving his arm in order to receive a food reinforcer, behavior modification has been used with increasing frequency and effectiveness to alter the behavior of retardates. Since that time a variety of self-help behaviors have been taught successfully to the severely retarded, such as bowel and bladder control, tying shoes, fastening buttons, and washing. In addition, language acquisition, speech correction, increased social competence in the acquisition of table manners, conversational skills, and mending and sewing skills have been taught through behavior modification, and it has been used to eliminate fighting, suppress chronic drooling, and reduce self-stimulatory behaviors (Weisberg, 1971; Thompson and Grabowski, 1972; Kelly, Furman et al., 1979; Kelly, Wildman et al., 1979; Cronin and Cuvo, 1979; Drabman et al., 1979; Denny, 1980).

The ease with which behavior modification can be taught to the nonprofessional staff makes possible and economically feasible the involvement of a larger number of caretakers in teaching new behaviors to the retarded. Those using this approach must first select target behaviors for improvement that are both useful to the resident in normal living and in keeping with his or her limitations. Errors that ordinarily slow the learning process are lessened by breaking the target behavior into a series of small steps. Thus, learning to name colors may be approached by learning to name one color at a time and even by dividing this task into specific, simple components; for example, looking at the stimulus, saying the name, and then saying the correct name when the stimulus is presented. Of course, the learning of each step is accomplished primarily through the careful arrangement of the consequences of the behavior—that is, giving a reward immediately following the correct response, while incorrect responses are unrewarded. At present the use of behavior modification extends beyond institutional programs to community-based special education and vocational activities.

Programs for the Community-Based Retarded

In this section we look mainly at the mildly retarded and the two major programs—special education and vocational training and placement—that seem to play the most significant role in their future adjustment.

Special Education. Programs in special education are neither uniform from state to state nor necessarily uniform among cities and counties of a given state. Some communities are entirely without special eduation programs for the educable retarded, while others differ with regard to either the maintenance of a separate facility apart from the regular public schools or the segregation by classes within the regular school of programs that service the mentally retarded. The community special school is designed to meet the needs of those children who are unable to cope with and profit from a normal school situation, and who presumably require a specialized environment that is too costly for decentralization (Cruickshank, 1967). Youngsters who are isolated in such an environment may or may not have their special educational needs met there, but all are deprived of opportunities to learn to socially interact with normal children, with whom they must successfully relate if they are to make an adequate adjustment as adults. This concern is also raised by some educators who prefer not to have separate self-contained classes for the retarded as part of the regular school program, but rather would handle retarded students through *mainstreaming,* where the retarded could participate at some time during the school day in normal classes and activities. The effectiveness of mainstreaming has not yet been evaluated systematically, although some studies are in progress with regard to preschool and school-aged children (Ingram, 1976; Cooke, Appolloni, and Cooke, 1977; Levitt, 1977). A review of the literature indicates that the results are inconsistent with regard to the effect of mainstreaming on academic achievement. Most studies have found that mainstreaming does not improve the social acceptance of retarded children, although the integration of retarded children into the school program enhances the attitude of these children to school (Corman and Gottlieb, 1978; Cavallaro and Porter, 1980). Another special education technique is use of a resource teacher, who provides special assistance to students in areas where they require additional help, such as reading, braille for blind students, speech correction, or arithmetic.

Unfortunately, special classes for the mentally retarded service only about 20 percent of those who need it (*The Decisive Decade,* 1970). Even where they are available, there may not be enough classes to accommodate all those who should be placed there. In addition, some schools attempt to move disruptive but otherwise normal children from the regular program into special classes, but in most instances, the special teacher can resist such efforts by adhering to the standards of eligibility established by the school system (IQ scores below a certain cut-off point).

At the elementary level special education curricula for the mentally retarded generally include information that will help the retardate function in the normal environment, and skills that will enable the retarded to achieve social, personal, and vocational self-sufficiency. These programs seek to maintain adequate levels of performance for appropriate interaction with the environment (Smith, 1971). Class size should be small enough so that the teacher can provide each student with individual attention to facilitate maximum growth. Ample opportunities for successful experiences are needed to build self-confidence and to motivate students to make additional progress. At the secondary level the curriculum is ordinarily structured to continue the efforts of the elementary school program and to teach social and vocational skills that will maximize the retardate's personal adjustment and employment potential.

Vocational Training and Placement. Among the mildly retarded, training and personality rather than intellectual ability appear to be the most influential determinants of employment success. Inadequate performance, and difficulties in interpersonal relationships, are the chief reasons for their adjustment failures (Shawn, 1964; Gorelick, 1966). Schools and sheltered workshops have been the primary vocational training grounds for the mentally retarded. After observing school programs across the country, Gold (1973) drew the following conclusions:

1. Little connection exists between classroom activities and work activities.
2. Where work experience is part of the program, training is left to the student's job supervisors.
3. Criteria for success are poorly defined.
4. Subjective evaluation of student performance by the job supervisor is often the only measure by which the student is judged.
5. There is a reliance on the creativity and enthusiasm of staff in the absence of a technology of systematic training. (pp. 101–102)

Workshops may be either transitional or permanent, and students may prepare for later placement or work for indefinite periods of time, because they are incapable of competitive work assignments. Work contracts are obtained from the business world to provide vocational training and actual paid work experience for the trainees. Research has shown that work performance can be increased by using a token reinforcement system, giving a bonus, or isolating the student from other trainees if work production fails to meet a certain level (Campbell, 1971). The relatively recent development and success of autoinstructional techniques to teach new work skills to the retarded is extremely promising, having increased both the employability of the retarded and the willingness of industry to contract with sheltered workshops.

PREVENTION

Although some progress has been made in preventing mental retardation, it is curious and deplorable that in a society such as ours, preventive measures and programs have not kept pace with our knowledge of the etiological factors involved in this disorder. Not all states require that newborns be tested for known metabolic disorders, such as phenylketonuria or galactosemia, or that babies whose mothers are group O be given routine tests for red-cell ABO antibodies in the cord blood. Genetic counseling based on laboratory evaluation of chromosomal numbers and types occasionally is available to assist parents in planning future pregnancies. However, most states and communities throughout the country do not have a premature-infant program, which experts believe would significantly reduce the incidence of multiple handicaps, mental retardation, and fatalities. Rh-blood testing of pregnant mothers prior to delivery should be routinely performed, and standard nursery provisions should be established in all hospitals handling newborns, in order to reduce the problem of infection and crowding. We need to make available to more expectant mothers adequate nutritional and medical care throughout the entire period of pregnancy, not just near the time of delivery, because it is now apparent that many of the etiological factors of mental retardation are related to intrauterine conditions.

More attention needs to be given to postnatal environmental forces, primarily those associated with poverty and low socioeconomic status. Variables known to affect intellectual and social development, such as nutritional deficiencies, deprivation of sensory, intellectual, and social stimulation, infections and poisonings, and family disorganization, are frequently found in slum environments.

Sex education and family planning, including measures to reduce venereal disease and prevent unwanted pregnancies, are of particular importance to the cultural-familial group of retardates. There is a segment of society that advocates sterilization and eugenics in order to significantly reduce mental retardation; but a discussion of the moral, ethical, and social implications of this view is beyond the scope of this presentation.

Increased support for research in the areas of etiology and prevention is, of course, necessary, even though we lag behind in the development of preventive programs commensurate with our current knowledge.

SUMMARY

Mental retardation is a heterogenous condition involving many different patterns of assets and liabilities, and a diversity of etiologies. It may be associated with or mimic the symptoms of a variety of abnormal behaviors, thus making discrimination between the two conditions difficult. The current definition of mental retardation specifies two concurrent criteria: sub-average intellectual functioning, as measured by standardized individual intelligence tests (IQ scores); and deficits in adaptive behavior, for which assessment is less refined and available. Based on an IQ score of 70 or below, more than 6 million Americans, or 3 percent of the population, are retarded.

Approximately 90 percent of the mentally retarded population have IQs between 50 and 70, while about 10 percent have IQs that fall below 50. The following four levels of mental retardation have been used to describe the degree of intellectual and adaptive impairment:

Mild	IQs between 52 and 67
Moderate	IQs between 36 and 51
Severe	IQs between 20 and 35
Profound	IQs below 20

These categories are arbitrary, inasmuch as an IQ score is subject to errors of measurement and can be expected to vary from one time to another.

More than 300 known or suspected biological causes account for approximately 25 percent of all cases of retardation, whereas there is no evidence of brain pathology for the vast majority of the cases (75 percent). Members of this group are usually called *cultural-familial retardates,* for whom incompletely understood sociocultural, psychological, and hereditary factors are implicated as etiological variables. Recessive genetic disorders affecting amino acid, lipid, and carbohydrate metabolism and endocrine functioning were discussed, and they were illustrated with such specific conditions as PKU, Tay-Sachs disease, galactosemia, and cretinism.[1]

Approximately 1 in 20,000 live-born infants have chromosomal abnormalities of either the autosomal or sex chromosome type. Down's syndrome, or mongolism, is the best known and most frequent of the autosomal abnormalities (trisomy 21). It occurs more often in boys than in girls, and in babies of older pregnant women. Although specific causal factors have not yet been identified, it is thought that faulty intrauterine conditions produce the chromosomal anomaly. Klinefelter's and Turner's syndromes were described as disorders associated with chromosomal abnormalities of the sex chromosome. Other biological factors, such as infections and toxins, trauma, injury, irradiation, prematurity, and nutritional deprivation, were also considered.

There is evidence that sociocultural forces play a significant role in mental retardation, especially the cultural-familial type, which is essentially a lower-class phenomenon. Poverty environments are characterized by poor nutrition, poor medical care, and deprivation of the sociocultural stimulation needed for normal growth and development. These early and continued deprivations not only have a deleterious effect on cognitive development but perhaps exercise an even greater influence on the individual's emotional and motivational structure.

Management and remedial programs for the retarded in the Scandinavian countries were contrasted to the programs offered in the United States.

In general, most authorities agree that retarded youngsters should live at home and function in the community for as long as possible. Residential facilities are occupied by the more severely and profoundly retarded, although some mild and moderate retardates are also institutionalized. The use of behavior modification has dramatically changed institutional programs, staff attitudes, and the behavior of the residents.

Special education classes for the retarded serve only about 20 percent of those who need it. At the elementary school level, the program strives to provide the retardate with information that will help him or her function in the normal environment, and with skills that will facilitate social, personal, and vocational self-sufficiency. Sheltered workshops are either transitional or permanent; they prepare retardates for later placement or provide them with opportunities to work for indefinite periods of time. Token reinforcement systems, work for pay, financial bonuses, or social punishment are among the various behavior modification techniques used successfully in vocational training and placement.

Preventive programs have failed to keep pace with our current knowledge of the etiological factors involved in mental retarda-

[1] These disorders, with the exception of Tay-Sachs disease, can be successfully treated by special diets or hormones if treatment is started early.

tion. Laboratory tests for the early detection of known metabolic disorders, for red-cell ABO antibodies, and for Rh-blood testing of pregnant mothers should be routinely required. Genetic counseling to assist parents in making decisions about future pregnancies and to ensure the maintenance of adequate prenatal medical and nutritional care, and premature infant programs, should be available in or near all communities. Postnatal environmental factors, particularly those associated with low socioeconomic status, need more attention, so that we may reduce their adverse effect on intellectual and social development.

EPILOGUE

Regina's parents found it difficult to accept the diagnosis of mental retardation, even though (or perhaps because) it confirmed their worst fear. It took several sessions with the psychologist to explore their feelings and concerns about Regina and her condition. As they became more open and willing to discuss the situation, they agreed to participate in group sessions with other parents of retarded children, and to begin to make short-, and long-term plans for Regina. Discussions between the school authorities, the parents, and the psychologist were initiated, continuing until Regina was properly placed in a special class. At home the parents were more accepting of Regina in terms of both her assets and her limitations. They all worked hard to increase Regina's social competence, to give her support and positive reinforcement for her accomplishments, and her gradual, independent functioning in certain areas. Regina's small successes delighted her parents, who—in turn—spontaneously showed their pleasure with appropriate rewards. Two years later Regina shows definite but slow signs of learning in school. She also shows better social skills in greeting people, in her eating behavior, and in her personal hygiene and appearance. She is a happy child at school and at home with both parents and teachers—all of whom are working together to provide her with understanding and the assistance she needs to make the most use of her resources.

REFERENCES

Abroms, K. I., and Bennett, J. W. Current Findings in Down Syndrome. *Exceptional Children,* 1983, *49,* 449–450.

American Psychiatric Association. DSM-II: *Diagnostic and Statistical Manual of Mental Disorders,* 2nd ed. Washington, D.C.: American Psychiatric Association, 1968.

Baby Born Deformed with Alcohol on Breath. *Atlanta Journal,* January 5, 1977, p. 9B.

Bakwin, H., and Bakwin, R. M. *Behavior Disorders in Children,* 4th ed. Philadelphia: Saunders, 1972.

Barnes, R. H., Moore, A. U., Reid, I. M., and Pond, W. G. Learning Behavior Following Nutritional Deprivations in Early Life. *Journal of the American Dieticians Association,* 1967, *51,* 34–39.

Bennett, E. L., Diamond, M. C., Krech, D., and Rosenzweig, M. R. Chemical and Anatomical Plasticity of the Brain. *Science,* 1964, *146,* 610–619.

Benton, A. L. Psychological Assessment and Differential Diagnosis. In H. A. Stevens and R. F. Heber (eds.), *Mental Retardation: A Review of Research,* 1st ed. Chicago: University of Chicago Press, 1964, pp. 16–56.

Benton, A. L. Interactive Determinants of Mental Deficiency. In H. A. Stevens and R. F. Heber (eds.), *Mental Retardation: A Review of Research,* 1st ed. Chicago: University of Chicago Press, 1970, pp. 661–671.

Bialer, I. Relationship of Mental Retardation to Emotional Disturbance and Physical Disability. In H. C. Haywood (ed.), *Social-Cultural Aspects of Mental Retardation.* New York: Appleton-Century-Crofts, 1970, pp. 607–660.

Berman, J. L., Cunningham, G. C., Day, R. W., Ford, R., and Hsia, D. Y. Y. Causes of High Phenylalanine with Normal Tyrosine in Newborn Screening Programs. *American Journal of Diseases of Children,* 1969, *117,* 54–65.

Bigelow, G. The Behavioral Approach to Retardation. In T. I. Thompson and J. Grabowski (eds.), *Behavior Modification of the Mentally Retarded,* 2nd ed. New York: Oxford University Press, 1977, pp. 17–45.

Birnbrauer, J. S., Wolf, M. M., Kidder, J. D., and Tague, C. E. Classroom Behavior of Retarded Pupils with Token Reinforcement. *Journal of Experimental Child Psychology,* 1965, *2,* 219–235.

Blatt, B. *Exodus from Pandemonium: Human Abuse and a Reformation of Public Policy.* Boston: Allyn and Bacon, 1970.

Blatt, B., and Kaplan, F. *Christmas in Purgatory:* A

Photographic Essay on Mental Retardation. Boston: Allyn and Bacon, 1966.

Blomquist, H., Son, K., Gustavson, K. H., and Holmgren, G. Mild Mental Retardation in Children in a Northern Swedish County. *Journal of Mental Deficiency Research,* 1981, *25,* 169–186.

Braginsky, D. D., and Braginsky, R. M. *Hansels and Gretels: Studies of Children in Institutions for the Mentally Retarded.* New York: Holt, Rinehart and Winston, 1971.

Bridges, F. A., and Cicchetti, D. Mothers' Ratings of the Temperament Characteristics of Down Syndrome Infants. *Developmental Psychology,* 1982, *18,* 238–244.

Campbell, N. Techniques of Behavior Modification. *Journal of Rehabilitation,* 1971, *37,* 28–31.

Carter, C. H. *Handbook of Mental Retardation Syndromes,* 2nd ed. Springfield, Ill.: Chas. C Thomas, 1970.

Cavallaro, S. A., and Porter, R. H. Peer Preferences of At-Risk and Normally Developing Children in a Preschool Mainstream Classroom. *American Journal of Mental Deficiency,* 1980, *84,* 357–366.

Coghill, G. E. *Anatomy and the Problem of Behavior.* New York: Macmillan, 1929.

Condell, J. F. Parental Attitudes Toward Mental Retardation. *American Journal of Mental Deficiency,* 1966, *71,* 85–92.

Connolly, J. A. Intelligence Levels of Down's Syndrome Children. *American Journal of Mental Deficiency,* 1978, *83,* 193–196.

Cooke, T. P., Appolloni, T., and Cooke, S. A. Normal Preschool Children as Behavioral Models for Retarded Peers. *Exceptional Children,* 1977, *43,* 531–532.

Corman, L., and Gottlieb, J. Mainstreaming Mentally Retarded Children: A Review of Research. In N. R. Ellis (ed.), *International Review of Research in Mental Retardation,* Vol. 9. New York: Academic Press, 1978, pp. 251–275.

Costeff, H., Cohen, B. E., Weller, L., and Kleckner, H. Pathogenic Factors in Idiopathic Retardation. *Developmental Medicine and Child Neurology,* 1981, *23,* 484–493.

Cravioto, J., DeLicardie, E. R., and Birch, H. G. Nutrition, Growth and Neurointegrative Development: An Experimental and Ecologic Study. *Pediatrics,* 1966, *38,* 319–372.

Cronin, K. A., and Cuvo, A. J. Teaching Mending Skills to Mentally Retarded Adolescents. *Journal of Applied Behavior Analysis,* 1979, *12,* 401–406.

Cruickshank, W. M. Current Educational Practices with Exceptional Children. In W. M. Cruickshank and G. O. Johnson (eds.), *Education of Exceptional Children and Youth,* 2nd ed. Englewood Cliffs, N.J.: Prentice-Hall, 1967, pp. 43–93.

Das, J. P., and Pivato, E. Malnutrition and Cognitive Functioning. In N. R. Ellis (ed.), *International Review of Research in Mental Retardation.* Vol. 8. New York: Academic Press, 1976, pp. 195–223.

The Decisive Decade. President's Committee on Mental Retardation. Washington, D.C.: Government Printing Office, 1970.

Dennis, W., and Dennis, M. G. The Effect of Cradling Practice upon the Onset of Walking in Hopi Children. *Journal of Genetic Psychology,* 1940, *56,* 77–86.

Denny, M. Reducing Self-stimulatory Behavior of Mentally Retarded Persons by Alternative Positive Practice. *American Journal of Mental Deficiency,* 1980, *84,* 610–615.

Dingman, H. F., and Tarjan, G. Mental Retardation and the Normal Distribution Curve. *American Journal of Mental Deficiency,* 1960, *64,* 991–994.

Donohue, W. L. Lesions in the Central Nervous System Associated with Inborn Errors of Amino Acid Metabolism. *Acta Paediatrica,* 1967, *56,* 116–117.

Drabman, R. S., Cruz, G., Ross, J., and Lynd, S. Suppression of Chronic Drooling in Mentally Retarded Children and Adolescents: Effectiveness of a Behavioral Treatment Package. *Behavior Therapy,* 1979, *10,* 46–56.

The First Report to the President on the Nation's Progress and Remaining Great Needs to the Campaign to Combat Mental Retardation. President's Committee on Mental Retardation. MR 67. Washington, D.C.: U.S. Government Printing Office, 1962.

Fuller, P. R. Operant Conditioning of a Vegetative Human Organism. *American Journal of Psychology,* 1949, *62,* 587–590.

Gellis, S. S., and Feingold, M. *Atlas of Mental Retardation Syndromes.* U.S. Department of Health, Education and Welfare. Washington, D.C.: U.S. Government Printing Office, 1968.

Girardeau, F. L. Cultural–Familial Retardation. In N. R. Ellis (ed.), *International Review of Research in Mental Retardation,* Vol. 5. New York: Academic Press, 1971, pp. 303–348.

Gold, M. W. Research on the Vocational Habilitation of the Retarded: The Present, the Future. In N. R. Ellis (ed.), *International Review of Research in Mental Retardation,* Vol. 6. New York: Academic Press, 1973, pp. 97–147.

Gorelick, M. C. *An Assessment of Vocational Realism of High School and Post–High School Educable Mentally Retarded Adolescents.* Los Angeles: Exceptional Children's Foundation, 1966.

Greenwald, C. A., and Leonard, L. B. Communicative and Sensorimotor Development of Down's Syndrome Children. *American Journal of Mental Deficiency,* 1979, *84,* 296–303.

Grossman, H. J. (ed.). *Manual on Terminology and Classification in Mental Retardation: 1973 Revision.* Special publication of the American Association on Mental Deficiency, 1973.

Gunzburg, H. C. The Role of the Psychologist in Manipulating the Institutional Environment. In A. D. B. Clark, and A. M. Clarke (eds.), *Mental Retardation and Behavioral Research. Study Group # 4.* Baltimore, Md.: Williams and Wilkins, 1973, pp. 57–67.

Hallahan, D. L., and Kauffman, J. M. *Exceptional*

Children: Introduction to Special Education. Englewood Cliffs, N. J.: Prentice-Hall, 1978.

Hansen, H. Decline of Down's Syndrome after Abortion Reform in New York State. *American Journal of Mental Deficiency,* 1978, *83,* 185–188.

Hardy, J. B. Perinatal Factors and Intelligence. In S. F. Osler, and R. E. Cooke (eds.), *The Biosocial Basis of Mental Retardation.* Baltimore, Md.: Johns Hopkins Press, 1965, pp. 35–60.

Harris, S. R. Effects of Neurodevelopmental Therapy on Motor Performance of Infants with Down's Syndrome. *Developmental Medicine and Child Neurology,* 1981, *23,* 477–483.

Hebb, D. O, Heredity and Environment in Mammalian Behavior. In A. Anastasi (ed.), *Individual Differences.* New York: John Wiley, 1965, pp. 160–170.

Heber, R. *Epidemiology of Mental Retardation.* Springfield, Ill.: Chas. C Thomas, 1970.

Hobbs, M. T. A Comparison of Institutionalized and Noninstitutionalized Mentally Retarded. *American Journal of Mental Deficiency,* 1964, *69,* 206–210.

Holmes, L. B., Moser, H. W., Halldorsson, S., Mack, C., Pant, S. S., and Matzilevich, B. *Mental Retardation: An Atlas of Diseases with Associated Physical Abnormalities.* New York: Macmillan, 1972.

Hunt, J. McV. *Intelligence and Experience.* New York: Ronald Press, 1961.

Infant Care, U.S. Government, Washington, D.C.: Universal Publishing and Distributing Corporation, 1968.

Ingram, S. H. An Assessment of Regular Classroom Teachers' Attitude Toward Exceptional Children Subsequent to Training on Mainstreaming. *Dissertation Abstracts International,* 1976, 37 (3–A), 1307.

Kagan, J. Inadequate Evidence and Illogical Conclusions. *Harvard Educational Review,* 1969, 39, 126–129.

Kanner, L. Parent Counseling. In H. Rothstein (ed.), *Mental Retardation.* New York: Holt, Rinehart and Winston, 1961, pp. 453–461.

Kelly, J. A., Furman, W., Phillips, J., Hathorn, S., and Wilson, T. Teaching Conversational Skills to Retarded Adolescents. *Child Behavior Therapy,* 1979, *1,* 85–97.

Kelly, J. A., Wildman, B. G., Urey, J. R., and Thurman, C. Group Skills Training to Increase the Conversational Repertoire of Retarded Adolescents. *Child Behavior Therapy,* 1979, *1,* 323–336.

Kirman, B. H. *The Mentally Handicapped Child.* London: Thomas Nelson, Ltd., 1972.

Klaber, M. M. The Retarded and Institutions for the Retarded—A Preliminary Research Report. In S. B. Sarason and J. Doris (eds.), *Psychological Problems in Mental Deficiency.* New York: Harper and Row, 1969, pp. 148–185.

Koch, R. Postnatal Factors in Causation. In R. Koch and J. C. Dobson (eds.), *The Mentally Retarded Child and His Family: A Multi-disciplinary Handbook.* New York: Brunner/Mazel, 1971, pp. 87–94.

Koch, R., Fishler, K., and Melnyk, J. Chromosomal Anomalies in Causation: Down's Syndrome. In R. Koch and J. C. Dobson (eds.), *The Mentally Retarded Child and His Family: A Multi-disciplinary Handbook.* New York: Brunner/Mazel, 1971, pp. 111–137.

Kushlick, A. Assessing the Size of the Problem of Subnormality. In J. E. Meade and A. S. Parkes (eds.), *Genetic and Environmental Factors in Human Ability.* A symposium held by the Eugenics Society in September–October, 1965. New York: Plenum, 1966, pp. 121–147.

Lejeune, J., Gautier, M., and Turpin, R. Study of the Somatic Chromosomes of Nine Mongoloid Idiot Children. In S. H. Boyer (ed.), *Papers on Human Genetics.* Englewood Cliffs, N.J.: Prentice-Hall, 1963, pp. 238–240.

Lemkau, P. V., and Imre, P. D. Results of a Field Epidemiologic Study. *American Journal of Mental Deficiency,* 1969, *74,* 858–863.

Levine, S. Sex-Role Identification and Parental Perceptions of Social Competence. *American Journal of Mental Deficiency,* 1966, *70,* 822–824.

Levitt, M. L. Former Special Education Pupils in the Mainstream: A Descriptive Follow-up Study. *Dissertation Abstracts International,* 1977, 37 (8–A), 5039.

Lippman, L. D. *Attitudes toward the Handicapped: A Comparison Between Europe and the United States.* Springfield, Ill.: Chas. C Thomas, 1972.

Love, H. D. *The Mentally Retarded Child and His Family.* Springfield, Ill.: Chas. C Thomas, 1973.

MacMillan, D. L. Motivational Differences: Cultural-Familial Retardates vs. Normal Subjects on Expectancy for Failure. *American Journal of Mental Deficiency,* 1969, *74,* 254–258.

MacMillan D. L. *Mental Retardation in School and Society.* Boston: Little, Brown, 1977.

McDonald, A. D. Intelligence in Children of Very Low Birth Weight. *British Journal of Preventative Social Medicine,* 1964, *18,* 59–74.

Mackie, R. P. Spotlighting Advances in Special Education. *Exceptional Children,* 1965, 32, 77–81.

Masland, R. L. Current Knowledge Regarding the Prenatal and Environmental Factors in Mental Deficiency. *Proceedings of the London Conference on the Scientific Study of Mental Deficiency,* 1960, *Part 1,* 55–76.

Meier, G. W. Mental Retardation in Animals. In N. R. Ellis (ed.), *International Review of Research in Mental Retardation,* Vol. 4. New York: Academic Press, 1970, pp. 263–309.

Morishima, A. His Spirit Raises the Ante for Retardates. *Psychology Today.* 1975, 9, 72–73.

Nylander, B. H., and Nylander, I. Acute Head Injuries in Children: Traumatology, Therapy and Prognosis. *Acta Paediatrica,* 1964, *152–157* (Suppl.), 1–34.

Pasamanick, B., and Lilienfeld, A. M. Association of Maternal and Fetal Factors with Development of Mental Deficiency. *Journal of American Medical Association,* 1955, *159,* 155–160.

Paymer, S. S. Reciprocal Role Expectations and Role Relationships: The Adjustment of the Mentally Retarded. *American Journal of Mental Deficiency*, 1965, *70*, 382–388.

PERRY, T. The Enigma of PKU. *The Sciences*, 1970, *10*, 12–16.

PIPER, M. C., and RAMSAY, M. K. Effects of Early Home Environment on the Mental Development of Down Syndrome Infants. *American Journal of Mental Deficiency*, 1980, *85*, 39–44.

REED, E. Genetic Anomalies in Development. In F. D. Horowitz (ed.), *Review of Child Development Research.* Chicago: University of Chicago Press, 1975, pp. 50–99.

ROBINSON, H. B., and ROBINSON, N. M. *The Mentally Retarded Child: A Psychological Approach.* New York: McGraw-Hill, 1965.

ROBINSON, H. B., and ROBINSON, N. M. Mental Retardation. In P. H. Mussen (ed.), *Carmichael's Manual of Child Psychology*, Vol. 2, 3rd ed. New York: John Wiley, 1970, pp. 615–666.

ROBINSON, N. M., and ROBINSON, H. B. *The Mentally Retarded Child: A Psychological Approach*, 2nd ed. New York: McGraw-Hill, 1976.

SATTLER, J. M. *Assessment of Children's Intelligence.* Philadelphia: Saunders, 1974.

SHAWN, B. Review of a Work Experience Program. *Mental Retardation*, 1964, *2*, 360–364.

SKEELS, H. M. Adult Status of Children with Contrasting Early Life Experiences: A Follow-up Study. *Monographs of the Society for Research in Child Development*, 1966, *31*, Serial No. 105.

SMITH, R. M. *An Introduction to Mental Retardation*, New York: McGraw-Hill, 1971.

SOMASUNDARUM, O., and PAPAKUMARI, M. A Study on Down's Anomaly. *Child Psychiatry Quarterly*, 1981, *14*, 85–94.

STEIN, Z. A., and KASSAB, H. H. Nutrition. In J. Wortis, (ed.), *Mental Retardation: An Annual Review, II.* New York: Grune and Stratton, 1970, pp. 92–116.

TELFORD, C. W., and SAWREY, J. M. *The Exceptional Individual*, 3rd ed. Englewood Cliffs, N.J.: Prentice-Hall, 1977.

THOENE, J., HIGGINS, J., KRIEGER, I., SCHMICKEL, R., and WEISS, L. Genetic Screening for Mental Retardation in Michigan. *American Journal of Mental Deficiency*, 1981, *85*, 335–340.

THOMPSON, T. I., and GRABOWSKI, J. (eds.). *Behavior Modification of the Mentally Retarded.* New York: Oxford University Press, 1972.

WAISBREN, S. E. Parents' Reactions after the Birth of a Developmentally Disabled Child. *American Journal of Mental Deficiency*, 1980, *84*, 345–351.

WEISBERG, P. Operant Procedures with the Retardate: An Overview of Laboratory Research. In N. R. Ellis (ed.), *International Review of Research in Mental Retardation*, Vol. 5. New York: Academic Press, 1971, pp. 113–145.

WILKINS, L. *The Diagnosis and Treatment of Endocrine Disorders in Childhood and Adolescence*, 3rd ed. Springfield, Ill.: Chas. C Thomas, 1965.

WINICK, M. Changes in Nucleic Acid and Protein Content of Human Brain During Growth. *Pediatric Research*, 1968, *2*, 352–355.

WORCHEL, T., and WORCHEL, P. The Parental Concept of the Mentally Retarded Child. *American Journal of Mental Deficiency*, 1961, *65*, 782–788.

WORTIS, J. Introduction: What is Mental Retardation? In J. Wortis (ed.), *Mental Retardation. An Annual Review, II.* New York: Grune and Stratton, 1970, pp. 1–6.

ZAMENHOF, S., VANMARTHENS, E., and MARGOLIS, F. L. DNA (Cell Number) and Protein in Neonatal Brain: Alteration by Maternal Dietary Protein Restriction. *Science*, 1968, *160*, 322–323.

ZESKIND, P. S., and RAMEY, C. T. Preventing Intellectual and Interactional Sequelae of Fetal Malnutrition: A Longitudinal, Transactional, and Synergistic Approach to Development. *Child Development*, 1981, *52*, 213–218.

ZIGLER, E. Familial Mental Retardation: A Continuing Dilemma. *Science*, 1967, *155*, 292–298.

ZIGLER, E. Motivational Aspects of Mental Retardation. In R. Koch and J. C. Dobson (eds.), *The Mentally Retarded Child and His Family: A Multi-disciplinary Handbook.* New York: Brunner/Mazel, 1971, pp. 369–385.

12

NEUROSES AND PSYCHOPHYSIOLOGICAL DISORDERS

PROLOGUE

Billy was an eight-year-old who was referred to a psychiatrist for symptoms of increasing anxiety, extreme fearfulness, night terrors, and phobias that had prevented him from attending school for a period of about eight months. He spent most of the time at home either playing or reading alone in his room, although on occasion he went out into the yard to play with a friend in the clubhouse they had made. For the most part, he was an active boy who liked to make things with his hands and who seldom was bored because of his capacity to be inventive and imaginative. However, daily (at least once) attacks of panic and apprehension disrupted his state of tranquility. These attacks occurred especially in the evening when father came home or at bedtime. At times, Billy would lie awake in crippling terror as he imagined the presence of strange creatures in the closet, or the movement of shadows in his darkened room. He would hold his breath out of fear of being heard, and sometimes, after a long period of silence and rigid immobility, he would jump out of his bed and run into his parents' bedroom. In addition, Billy had phobias about dirt, germs, and bugs that interfered with his daily living. He meticulously washed his hands before each meal or whenever he touched anything he considered dirty. He had numerous somatic complaints that took the form of a headache, stomachache, fatigue, or merely "I feel bad all over."

Billy's birth and early development were normal, except that during the first year of life he had severe colic that continued far beyond the usual three-month period. He screamed almost constantly during this first year and was unable to sleep longer than two or three hours at a time. His language developed precociously as did his sense of humor, sensitivity, empathy, and personal charm. He was well liked by adults, but he never seemed comfortable with peers. He was quite content and felt safe being alone in his room with a book, and when he was seven he confessed that people had hurt him or disappointed him so often that he felt better off staying away from them. He did well in school but seldom performed at a level commensurate with his ability. His teachers noted that he was often preoccupied, unwilling or incapable of applying himself, and incomplete with assignments. He tended to be late to school and late getting home, and his inclination to be slow in almost everything exasperated both his teachers and parents.

Billy was an only child, although his mother was previously married and had a son sixteen years older than Billy. Mother was an outgoing person but tense, emotional, and given to occasional episodes of "nervous exhaustion," and to periods of incapacitation (each winter) from severe bronchial asthma. Father was a stoic, apathetic, but quick-tempered man who worked as a laborer, had few interests, limited ambition, and who led a routine life that consisted of working, eating, reading the evening paper, and sleeping. He was virtually a stranger to Billy as he sat silently in his chair for hours while at home, only to break the silence with an occasional unpredictable outburst of anger. Billy lived in fear of his father and could only relax when father was absent from the home. When it came time for father to return from work each day, Billy became tense.

There was a very close bond between Billy and his mother. She recognized that she was overprotective and that their relationship was abnormally close. The overinvolvement between them was further enhanced by the mother's asthmatic condition. During her severe attacks both she and Billy feared that she would die, and he would sit by her bedside for hours on end in a kind of deathwatch. The onset of his severe symptoms and his refusal to attend school occurred at the time of her worst asthma attack eight months prior to his psychiatric evaluation (excerpts from a clinical case from Shaw, 1966. Courtesy of Appleton-Century-Crofts, Publishing Division of Prentice-Hall, Inc.)

The diagnosis of psychoneurosis used to classify Billy's condition illustrates only one neurotic reaction we shall discuss in this chapter. In addition, we shall consider other types of childhood neuroses and psychophysiological disorders—describing the clinical picture, the frequency of occurrence, the etiological considerations, and the therapeutic approaches that are popular or promising for both forms of abnormal behavior.

NEUROSES

Psychoanalytic and Learning Views

Although neurotic disorders can take many forms, according to psychoanalytic theory, all of them display the common ingredients of intense feelings of anxiety, personal suffering and discomfort, and self-directed or internalized reactions to the stress of intrapsychic conflicts (Kessler, 1972). There can be little doubt that Billy's anxiety was severe and progressive. He suffered painfully from the fear of imagined creatures and moving shadows as he lay awake in his darkened room. He also suffered from his phobias of germs and dirt and from his many somatic ailments. His behavioral symptoms were self-directed or internalized (washing hands or having a headache) rather than externalized (expressing anger toward his father or acting out his ambivalent feelings toward his mother). Similarly, a learning-oriented view of neuroses emphasizes the presence of an uncomfortable level of anxiety as a chief component of these disorders. The anxiety is accompanied by personal discomfort and the persistence of coping responses that are inappropriate and ineffective for the situation.

The differences between these theoretical positions center largely on the nature of the conflicts or the anxiety-producing stimuli, the manner by which the coping responses are established, and the purpose these responses serve.

Psychoanalytic thinking regards neuroses as a fundamental outgrowth of unconscious conflicts over the handling of sexual and aggressive impulses. In its mediating role the ego struggles to maintain equilibrium between the expression of id impulses and the censorship of these responses by the superego. The ego expends a great deal of energy in dealing with the intrapsychic conflict and in attempting to maintain some semblance of harmony between these warring personality factions. In the process ego functioning is often impaired, and the resulting behavioral patterns (symptoms) symbolize the unconscious conflict as well as the ego's efforts to reduce the anxiety level. When the conflict is unresolved, two forms of neurotic disturbance tend to occur. One type is restricted to the stage of psychosexual development of the current conflict and is indicative of a favorable prognosis. Children with this type usually have an uneventful premorbid history with no significant parental problems or contributing constitutional factors. The second type occurs more frequently and is usually evident as a multisymptom blend of two or more neurotic reactions, as illustrated in Billy's clinical picture. In these instances there is evidence of family pathology, constitutional predisposing factors, prior history of neurotic behaviors, and primitive defense mechanisms.

In contrast, a *learning view* neither restricts the anxiety-producing stimuli to specific kinds of impulses nor postulates separate and combative components of the personality. Rather, it states that the child, in the face of high anxiety, will seek ways to reduce it to more tolerable levels. Any response of the child that promptly decreases the anxiety (even responses not appropriate to demands of the situation) will be reinforced and will be more likely to occur again in response to the same or similar anxiety-arousing stimuli. Thus, through learning paradigms such as classical conditioning and phenomena such as generalization and reinforcement, the child establishes complex associations between the anxiety-producing stimuli (that is, any stimulus that arouses anxiety) and the responses he or she uses to cope with that anxiety.

As a point of departure, it matters little which of these views is more persuasive; there are several important *areas of agreement* that may further our understanding of neurotic disorders. Clearly, these abnormal behaviors involve severe anxiety that prompts responses, albeit inappropriate or inefficient, aimed at allaying tension. These responses form a persistent behavioral pattern as the child's energies increasingly become tied up in trying to deal with high-anxiety levels. The resultant neurotic child is painfully uncomfortable, grossly unhappy, and noticeably impaired in functioning, since he or she is occupied in playing out the repetitious cycle of high anxiety and attempts to reduce it.

Therefore, anxiety plays a key role in the development of neuroses, and it is responsible for the emergence of a variety of counterreactions. In some instances the child may experience diffuse (free-floating) but intense anxiety that is not attached to an object or event, while in others the anxiety is displaced onto some symbolic object or even converted into somatic symptoms. In still other instances anxiety may be counteracted by ritualistic and repetitious behaviors, or it may be dissipated by self-deprecation. These various ways of dealing with the central problem of high anxiety represent the diverse forms of neurotic reactions seen clinically. Some Freudians also have given the affective state of depression a similar place of conceptual importance as an arousing state in which the child defends himself or herself against it by various neurotic reactions (Anthony, 1972). The question of why the child chooses a particular technique (set of symptoms) and not another is one that has been especially troublesome for both psychoanalytic and learning theories to answer.

DSM-III's View

In a dramatic and controversial break with past tradition and practice, DSM-III has omitted Neuroses as a major category, although many of the neurotic disorders are included under other categories within the system (APA, 1980). In the area of psychopathology, Freud's greatest impact was in the neuroses—a term which he and his followers used in two ways: (1) to describe a set of symptoms and (2) to indicate an underlying causal process. Since there is little consensus about the etiology of neuroses, and considerable ambiguity as to how the term is used, DSM-III made the decision only to descriptively define neurotic disorders, classifying them with conditions that are similar in symptoms. The neuroses, therefore, are scattered throughout DSM-III and cannot be found collectively in any one major category. For example, there is only one category under children's disorders (Anxiety Disorders of Childhood or Adolescence) that may be regarded as paralleling neuroses. To further complicate matters, this category includes the following disorders: Separation Anxiety Disorder; Avoidant Disorder of Childhood or Adolescence; and Overanxious Disorder (see Chapter 2 and Table 2–2 for a description of these disorders). Moreover, within the adult categories of DSM-III there are two conditions that also resemble Anxiety Neurosis (Panic Disorder and Generalized Anxiety Disorder).

For pedagogical reasons it makes for greater ease of presentation to keep the major neurotic disorders together, and not to follow the organizational arrangement of DSM-III. Therefore, we turn now to a more detailed description and discussion of the following neurotic disorders: Anxiety Reaction, Phobic Reaction, Obsessive-Compulsive Reaction, Conversion Reaction, Depressive Reaction, and Mixed Reaction.

Anxiety Reaction

Children who are given this diagnosis experience intense anxiety as vague, undifferentiated, and free-floating (not anchored to a particular object or event) feelings that carry the dreadful expectation of impending doom or catastrophe. Their anxiety is the central symptom, and it goes beyond the apprehensions and fears experienced by almost all children. It is more severe and usually unrelated to external reality, although it may be triggered by a variety of events ranging from the innocuous experience of being called in for dinner to the more serious happenings of failing in school, falling ill, or losing a pet. Irritability, bodily and health concerns, and sudden and severe attacks of anxiety are also present. Physical symptoms become prominent especially during an acute anxiety attack, where the child often manifests shortness of breath, palpitations, profuse sweating, faintness, dizziness, nausea, abdominal pain, and diarrhea. Many of these youngsters have anxiety attacks at bedtime, possibly because their sleep pattern is frequently interrupted by nightmares and night terrors, or because their fantasies involve fear of potential threats. In almost all instances their symptoms bring secondary gain from the special concern and attention that parents usually show. For some of these youngsters the anxiety level may be chronically high and persistent to the point that their self-preoccupation results in indecisiveness, excessive worrying, and impaired attention. The uneasiness and distress that come with chronic anxiety also encourage timidity and withdrawal from people and outside activities.

Phobic Reaction

This form of neurosis consists of persistent, severe, and irrational fear, of which the child is aware but from which he or she cannot free himself or herself. Some observers regard the irrational nature of the fear as the important element in distinguishing phobias from ordinary fears, while others contend that the experience of fear is the same whether its origin is real or imagined (Jersild, 1968; Kessler, 1972). The ingredient of severity is probably more important, since a phobia is usually so debilitating that it interferes with the child's daily functioning. In addition, a phobia has an obsessional quality; the child ruminates about it and cannot completely free his or her thoughts from it. Persistence and maladaptiveness are additional characteristics that have been used to distinguish fears and phobias (Morris and Kratochwill, 1983).

In young children fears and phobias are particularly difficult to distinguish, because fears occur with regularity during the course of normal development. Table 12-1 notes the so-called normal fears children frequently have at various ages.

All infants show a startle response (freeze reaction) to loss of support or to any sudden and loud noise. Later, during the first year of life (between five and ten months), babies evidence a fear of strangers, in which they react with fearlike panic to unfamiliar people, objects, or situations (see Chapter 4). Between the ages of two and three, fear of animals tends to appear, while beginning in the third year of life, children become fearful of the dark, perhaps because they feel alone and vulnerable to outside forces they can't control. Animal fears increase during the preschool years as animals become part of frightening dreams and as children become more aware of the powerful and dangerous aspects of animals. Frequently, animal fears are learned and heightened by contagion—that is, through parents, siblings, and others in the environment transferring their own anxiety and fear of animals. "Don't get too close to the dog, he may bite," or "Be careful, the cat may scratch," or "My God! There's a mouse in the room . . . somebody quick do something and catch it!" are only a few illustrations of people communicating fear and arousing it in others who may not have been previously affected.

A recent review of the literature indicates that the fears of young children between the ages of two and three seem to decline with age up to five or six years, except for the fear of snakes, which apparently persists (see Morris and Kratochwill, 1983, for an excellent discussion of fears and phobias in children). The review also shows that in general, girls have more fears than boys, boys tend to have more fears about the future, and adolescent youngsters from high socioeconomic levels have more fears than those from low socioeconomic levels. A survey of behavior therapists in the northeastern United States found that approximately 6 percent of all their child referrals were cases of fears and phobias (Gra-

Table 12-1 Common Fears of Children at Various Ages

0-6 months:	Loss of support, loud noises
7-12 months:	Fear of strangers, fear of sudden, unexpected, and looming objects
1 year:	Separation from parent, toilet, injury, strangers
2 years:	A multitude of fears including loud noises (vacuum cleaners, sirens/alarms, trucks, and thunder), animals (e.g., large dog), dark room, separation from parent, large objects/machines, change in personal environment
3 years:	Masks, dark, animals, separation from parent
4 years:	Parent separation, animals, dark, noises (including at night)
5 years:	Animals, "bad" people, dark, separation from parent, bodily harm
6 years:	Supernatural beings (e.g., ghosts, witches, "Darth Vader"), bodily injuries, thunder and lightning, dark, sleeping or staying alone, separation from parent
7-8 years:	Supernatural beings, dark, fears based on media events, staying alone, bodily injury
9-12 years:	Tests and examinations in school, school performance, bodily injury, physical appearance, thunder and lightning, death, dark (low percentage)

Source: Ilg & Ames, 1955; Jersild & Holmes, 1935a; Kellerman, 1981, Lapouse & Monk, 1959; Scarr & Salapatek, 1970. Reproduced from Morris, R. J. & Kratochwill, T. R. *Treating Children's Fears and Phobias: A Behavioral Approach.* Elmsford, N. Y.: Pergamon, 1983, p. 2.

ziano and deGiovanni, 1979). In England the prevalence figure for children with clinical fears and phobias was estimated at about 7 percent (Rutter, Tizzard, and Whitmore, 1970). While prevalence data vary with each study, Morris and Kratochwill (1983) note that the estimate is consistently under 8 percent for children who require treatment for intense fears and phobias.

In the last three decades there have been many attempts to classify childhood fears, some of which were derived before or without statistical analysis, while others were based primarily on factor-analytic findings (Angelino, Dollins, and Mech, 1956; Bandura and Menlove, 1968; Kennedy, 1965; Miller et al., 1972; Scherer and Nakamura, 1968). However, Morris and Kratochwill (1983) caution against drawing any firm conclusions from the fear classification literature because (1) no system has, as yet, been firmly based on extensive empirical findings, (2) most systems (even the factor-analytic ones) are arbitrary and were derived from initial self-report data which have not been validated, and (3) most systems classify the feared object while assuming (without empirical support) that children who have the same kind of fear are homogeneous with regard to what they fear and how the fear was acquired and is maintained. Morris and Kratochwill (1983) also discuss the development of behavior classification systems as alternatives for classifying children's fears; but they caution that the possible conceptual advantage of these systems is offset by the lack of research data.

School phobia is of special significance, representing (when present) a difficult management problem in school-aged children, especially during the middle years. It is a disruptive condition characterized by acute anxiety, refusal to go to school or leave the home, and numerous somatic complaints (such as hyperventilation, diarrhea, nausea, stomachache, headache, and sleep disturbance). The onset may be quite sudden and unexpected, although it can usually be traced to some significant precipitating event such as the change of school or classes; the prospect of returning to school following an illness, hospitalization, or serious illness of a parent (especially the mother); an embarrassing incident at school; academic or social failure; and death or fear of death (one's own or that of another) (Leventhal and Sills, 1964; Tietz, 1970).

It is difficult to obtain an accurate estimate of the frequency of occurrence of school phobia, although the available literature (with its methodological shortcomings) cites estimates ranging from less than 1 percent to approximately 3 percent (Kennedy, 1965; Miller, Barrett, and Hampe, 1974; Smith, 1970). The disorder may occur at any age, although it tends to be evident more often in the first four or five grades of school, and to appear equally as often in both boys and girls in this age group. However, it seems to occur more frequently in girls during the secondary school years (Leton, 1962; Chapman, 1974). There seems to be a positive relationship between age and the severity of the underlying disturbance, and between age and prognosis. Children with school phobia are good academic performers; they tend to like school and are no different in intelligence from children in the general population (Nichols and Berg, 1970; Hampe et al., 1973). These children are distinguishable from truants by their acute anxiety, somatic symptoms, overattachment to home and family, refusal to leave the home, good academic performance, and absence of antisocial behaviors.

Although it is generally considered to be a neurotic reaction, there are those who regard school phobia as a complicated entity that may reflect different disorders, causes, and, in turn, require different treatments (Shapiro and Jegede, 1973). For example, in a seven-year-old, refusal to go to school may reflect separation anxiety and the thwarting of dependency needs, whereas in an older adolescent this behavior may represent a more serious withdrawal pattern that is part of a schizophrenic reaction. Nevertheless, the most frequent cause of school phobia is thought to be a specific form of separation anxiety in which fear of separation is mutually shared by mother and child (Johnson et al., 1941; Kelly, 1973; APA, 1980). For the child a school phobia occurs when this anxiety is repressed and is displaced onto the school environment. Mothers of school-phobic children are viewed as overprotective, ambivalent, fearful of aggression, and inconsistent in their child-rearing practices, while these children evidence immaturity and excessive dependency on their mothers (Davidson, 1961; Nichols and Berg, 1970; Berg and McGuire, 1974).

Evidence of separation anxiety, dependency, and depression was found more frequently in school-phobic children than in controls (Waldron et al., 1975). Moreover, other data indicate that mothers of school-phobic children tend to be older, since these youngsters appeared late in the birth order of the family, and that these mothers preferred excessively dependent children (Berg and McGuire, 1974; Veltkamp, 1975). Taken collectively, the studies suggest that separation anxiety exists for both mother and child, and that these relatively older mothers are more apt to encourage and nurture dependency in their young offspring as a way of prolonging motherhood and of holding on to their youth. In these cases the mutual dependency tie is so strong that the school phobia may serve to maintain this attachment for both the mother and child.

Leventhal and Sills (1964) present a somewhat different viewpoint, holding that phobic children tend to overvalue themselves and their achievements. As they try to maintain their unrealistic self-image, they invariably suffer anxiety when their overestimated self-perception is threatened in the school situation. They avoid the threatening situation by withdrawing from it and by using helplessness. This, in turn, stimulates the mother to act as the child's protector, enabling the child to seek refuge in the home where the mother can repair the damaged self-image. These children vigorously resist attempts to return them to school, since they are oriented toward maintaining their unrealistic self-image or power beliefs.

Another way of explaining school phobia has been through learning principles, especially classical conditioning. According to this view, the school environment acquires the capacity to elicit anxiety or fear through repeated pairings of the neutral stimulus (school) with the fear-arousing one (separation from the mother). In the presence of situations in which the loss of the mother is either real or imagined, fear is intensified and the phobia is formed. In a similar manner, a fear reaction to some specific aspect of school (a punitive teacher or a bully) can generalize to the total school situation, making it a highly anxious place that must be avoided.

Obsessive-Compulsive Reaction

In this particular, rare type of neurotic reaction, the anxiety is isolated from its origin (the unacceptable impulse) through recurrent thoughts (obsessions) or acts (compulsions), or both, that the child must perform in spite of the fact that the ideas or the behaviors seem silly or unreasonable. Although the child is unaware of the original source of the anxiety, it is very much tied to the maintenance of obsessions and compulsions; the child experiences marked apprehension when something or someone interferes with their completion. Minor obsessions and compulsions occur in all children and in many different forms, such as bedtime or feeding rituals that must be played out in proper sequence, walking on the sidewalks without stepping on the cracks, the reverberation of a tune or a jingle in one's thoughts, or the ritualistic behaviors performed by the young baseball batter or the basketball player at the foul line. These reactions are distinguishable from neurotic reactions in severity and in the degree to which they affect functioning.

Obsessive-compulsive reactions occur in less than 2 percent of child referrals. They appear with equal frequency in both boys and girls, and they are found in children of above-average intelligence (Judd, 1965; Templer, 1972; Adams, 1973; Hollingsworth et al., 1980). The onset may be either sudden or gradual, but in either case the symptoms often put the child in conflict with the environment and produce guilt feelings. One recent study showed no differences between parents of obsessive children and their middle-class, white, Anglo-Saxon, Protestant counterparts, although it has long been maintained that these youngsters come from obsessional parents (Adams, 1972; Anthony, 1972). Adams (1973) found that these children were very unhappy, unspontaneous, verbose, and given to obsessions and compulsions, while their parental models tended also to be very verbal, unemotional, socially distant, and economically thrifty. It has also been shown that obsessions and compulsions occur together as variations of the same disorder and that children with this condition evidence guilt, a rich fantasy life, and considerable aggression toward their parents. Also, we find unusually high rates of psychopathology and physical illness in their parents (Judd, 1965; Adams, 1973; Carr, 1974).

Conversion Reaction

The psychoanalytic view of this neurotic reaction posits that the original anxiety is transformed into a dysfunction of body parts that are under the voluntary control of the central nervous system. The symptoms symbolically express the underlying conflict and decrease the anxiety generated from it to the extent that the child appears to be relatively indifferent to the physical dysfunction. This has been referred to as *la belle indifférence,* reflecting the absence of marked anxiety that one would ordinarily expect to be associated with impaired bodily functioning. The physical symptomatology in conversion reactions can mimic almost any organic disease, although it can be influenced by suggestion, and it ordinarily does not follow anatomical lines. Frequent symptoms involving motor disturbances include paralysis, tics, and tremors, while those involving sensory difficulties include loss of sensation (anesthesia), a peculiar skin sensation without objective cause (paresthesia), and extreme sensitivity (hyperesthesia).

Conversion reactions are as common among boys as among girls, although they are more frequent in female adolescents and adults and in black children (Proctor, 1967). Clinicians tend to think that this disorder is relatively rare in children and that it is not usually evident before five years of age (Goodyer, 1981). However, recent estimates range from 3 to 13 percent of children who have come to the attention of pediatric and psychiatric facilities (Rae, 1977). Intellectually, these children tend to be rated average or higher, although in general, they evidence a history of psychological disturbance, poor academic performance, and poor interpersonal relationships with peers. They manifest despondency and dependency and are likely to have overprotective mothers and inadequate fathers (Goodyer, 1981; Rock, 1971). Proctor indicates that these youngsters tend to be older than others who come to clinics for abnormal behaviors. He notes, however, that this may reflect his observation that many conversion reactions are seen more frequently and given symptom relief by pediatricians and other physicians. Thus, he contends that earlier instances are both unrecognized and unrecorded as conversion reactions. A number of observers (Proctor, 1967; Anthony, 1972; Kessler, 1972) note that conversion reactions have declined, especially in the middle and upper social classes. They are now largely confined to working-class and educationally unsophisticated people. The facts that there have been cultural changes from strict to permissive tendencies in childrearing practices and sexual attitudes, and that people are more knowledgeable than ever before about their biological functioning, suggest a decrease in the superego's need to use repression, and a decline in the influence of suggestion in the formation of neurotic reactions.

Depressive Reaction

Children with depressive reactions internalize their original conflict through self-depreciation and despondency. These youngsters experience guilt, loss of self-esteem, ambivalent feelings toward significant people in their environment, helplessness, and loneliness. But because we don't expect children to be depressed, and because they are frequently unable to verbalize or describe their feelings, these reactions often go undetected by parents and professionals alike. In fact, some clinicians say that depressive reactions make up about 25 percent of their caseload, and that almost all of these reactions are associated with real-life events affecting the child and involving the parents (Clark, 1977). Other estimates range widely from less than 3 percent to as high as 60 percent, although it is likely that the high estimates have included instances of depressive symptoms as well (Pearce, 1977; Kashani and Simonds, 1979). In fact, in their study of prevalence rates of depressive symptoms, depressive syndrome, and depressive disorders that meet the DSM-III criteria, Carlson and Cantwell (1980) found that about 60 percent of the children studied showed depressive symptoms, 49 percent evidenced a depressive syndrome (as measured by the Beck Depression Inventory), and 27 percent met the DSM-III criteria for a depressive disorder (under the Affective Disorder category). A recent study found that depressed children do not differ from nondepressed youngsters in age, sex, grade level, academic achievement, or IQ, but that there is a very high rate of psychiatric disturbance in the family history of the depressed children (Brumback, Jackoway, and Weinberg, 1980). Retrospectively, female neurotic depressives recalled their mothers and fathers as being rejecting and depriving more often than did a comparable group of anxiety neurotics. Mothers of the neurotic depressives were also remembered as being more controlling and difficult to please (Lamont, Fischoff, and Gottlieb, 1976).

Depressive symptoms in children may be masked by apathy, social withdrawal, somatic complaints (headache or abdominal pain), and even by a display of aggressive behaviors such as vandalism, sexual acting-out, or truancy, especially in older children. Poor appetite, weight loss, and disturbed sleep patterns—characteristic of severe depressions in adults—may be present, although some youngsters have been known to increase their intake of food and gain weight during bouts of depression.

In addition to the difficulties already noted in recognizing depressive reactions in children, the diagnosis is further complicated by the fact that depression may be present as a symptom associated with some other disorder—as an acute grief reaction to loss of a loved one, as a temporary state of a developmental crisis, or as a separate psychotic condition.

Most professionals agree that children can and do experience depression, although there is considerable controversy about whether they evidence a depressive disorder and whether the concept of a depressive disorder in childhood is useful. Pearce (1977) argues for the existence of such a disorder and spells out specific symptom and behavioral criteria that must be met for the diagnosis to be given. Brumback and Weinberg (1977) and Birleson (1981) hold a similar position, which is bolstered by the findings that there are disturbed vegetative functions in 85 percent of depressed children (with 8 percent showing sleep disturbance), and that depressed children are differentiated from controls by the following items: show pessimism about the future; appear sad; are tearful; demonstrate retarded activity; are withdrawn and quiet; show inhibition in play; are preoccupied with morbid thoughts; evidence low self-esteem; and say they feel unwanted. In contrast, Lefkowitz and Burton (1978) hold that depressive symptoms are quite common in children and therefore cannot be regarded as evidence of abnormality. They contend (although not very convincingly) that depression in childhood is part of development; it dissipates over time and is not a distinct clinical entity.

Moreover, Cytryn and associates (1980), using a variety of criteria to diagnose depression in children, found that the disorder is not unique in childhood and that DSM-III (under Affective Disorder) is the most valid system for diagnosing the condition. Finally, Klerman and associates (1979) question the utility of the term *neurotic depression*, which is vague and has multiple meanings. They propose more specific terms for each of the four types of depressive neurosis they identified.

Mixed Reaction

This is probably one of the most frequently seen forms of neurosis in children, because it provides for the occurrence of a combination of symptoms that are characteristic of the other reaction types. It is particularly common in children, since they are immature and ever-changing organisms whose personality traits and neurotic character structure are much less defined than those of adults. Consequently, the neurotic symptoms of children typically do not follow the classical form noted in adults; instead, their symptoms may occur in isolation or in combination with other symptoms that may be unrelated in origin (Freud, 1965). Changes in parental behaviors or family circumstances, or even fortuitous events in school or outside of the home, may be sufficient to reduce unconscious conflicts and the necessity for neurotic behaviors. In addition, the mixed reaction is a catch-all category that tends to be abused by clinicians who are uncertain about what specific neurotic reaction to use as a diagnostic entity. Nevertheless, the category serves a useful function for cases such as Billy's, where the symptom picture is truly a blend of several neurotic behaviors such as anxiety attacks, phobias, compulsions, and possibly conversion reactions.

Incidence

Estimates of the incidence of neuroses have been hindered by the paucity of data based on large samples and adequately controlled studies. To make matters worse, these estimates seem to vary with the theoretical orientation of the clinician, the willingness of the clinician to use a psychiatric label that may stigmatize the child and influence how others react to him or her, and the type of clinical setting to which the child is referred. One would expect fewer hospitalized cases, since the rather drastic measure of removal from the home often implies a serious disturbance such as a psychosis. In contrast, outpatient cases should be greater in number, although these services may be more inclined to focus on situational factors and not on intrapsychic conflict as a source of the child's difficulties. Moreover, neurotic reactions in children frequently are masked by the presence of somatic complaints that are likely to be evaluated and symptomatically treated by pediatricians. If pediatricians find no organic basis for the complaint, the reassured parents may very well be less inclinded to attend to the child's symptoms. It is also true that neurotic behaviors in young children are difficult to distinguish from behaviors that occur with normal development. Therefore, it is almost impossible to determine how many of these instances go undetected and unrecorded as neurotic reactions.

In light of these limitations, it is not surprising to find that incidence estimates of neurotic reactions vary considerably. One report noted that children under eighteen comprised slightly more than one-half of the patients serviced at community mental health clinics throughout the country in 1961, and that 10 percent of these children were diagnosed as neurotic (Rosen, Barn, and Cramer, 1964). As might be expected, a slightly lower incidence of neuroses (8 percent) was found when hospitalized youngsters under the age of fifteen were tallied. The data also suggested a significant interaction between the variables of sex and age, indicating that boys between the ages of nine and fourteen years have a higher incidence of neurotic reactions than girls of the same age, while there is a reversal of this sex trend between the ages of fourteen and sixteen. At age ten there were twice the number of boys classified as neurotic as there were girls; but by age twenty, girls outnumbered boys by the same ratio. Perhaps the highest incidence estimate comes from data involving children referred to a child guidance clinic, where between 25 and 50 percent of them were diagnosed as neurotic (Kurlander and Colodny, 1965; Hollingsworth et al., 1980). Findings based on the GAP classification but consisting of different populations of outpatient children showed the incidence of neurotic reactions to be approximately 6 to 11 percent, a figure that is more conservative and in line with earlier estimates (Sabot, Peck, and Raskin, 1969; Bemporad, Pfeiffer, and Bloom, 1970; Christozev, Bozhanov, and Youchev, 1975–76).

Etiological Considerations

Biological Views. In the course of contemporary history, two major views, psychoanalytic theory and learning theory, have received unparalleled acceptance as etiological models of neurotic reactions to the extent that biological causative factors have been virtually ignored. In fact, thus far the weight of the meager evidence that could implicate central nervous system dysfunction has been negative, adding further credence to the psychogenic position. Indeed, studies based on the comparison of EEG tracings and neurological signs have shown less frequent abnormalities in neurotic children than in either psychotic or hyperkinetic children (Ellingson, 1954; Kennard, 1960; White, DeMyer, and DeMyer, 1964). Moreover, it has been argued that even when autonomic and central nervous system differences are present, they cannot be considered as causal factors, since they are more likely the result of neurosis (Cohen, 1974).

As early as 1951 Hans Eysenck, one of the leading proponents of genetic involvement in neurosis, statistically isolated a dimension related to emotional instability and a poorly integrated personality that successfully predicted scores on several objective personality tests. He labeled this factor *neuroticism* and demonstrated a higher concordance for neuroticism with monozygotic (identical) twins than with dizygotic (fraternal) twins (Eysenck and Prell, 1951). However, the conclusion that neurotic behavior is largely determined by genetic factors must be tempered by the fact that only normal subjects were used in the study. In later studies concordance rates of neuroses for monozygotic twins were found to range from one-and-a-half to almost two times greater than that for dizygotic pairs (Shields and Slater, 1961; Pollin et al., 1969; Schepank, 1971). But in considering their data, Pollin and his colleagues concluded that heredity is implicated only minimally as a cause of neuroses. Despite the resurgence of interest in the relationship between heredity and a variety of abnormal behaviors, there is a dearth of unequivocal evidence that would warrant any other conclusion at this time.

Psychogenic Views.

Psychoanalytic theory. By all scientific yardsticks the enormous popularity enjoyed by psychoanalytic theory as an explanation of neurotic reactions is truly remarkable. The voluminous psychoanalytic literature is replete with pronouncements and untested hypotheses that were drawn from either the clinical experiences of various writers or their analyses of the psychodynamics of small samples (sometimes a single case) of illustrative clinical cases. Restatements of Freud's position and neo-Freudian interpretations of the development of one or several neurotic reactions have been plentiful. The obvious limitations of these reports, and the absence of empirical studies designed to test the theory, have made it virtually impossible to evaluate it. Yet the theory's widespread acceptance has given it an aura of validity that is a tribute to Freud's personal persuasiveness, the innovativeness and completeness of his system, and his clinical genius in carefully analyzing a small number of neurotic cases.

According to this view, the distinguishing cornerstone of psychoneuroses is intrapsychic conflict arising from the battle over the expression of unconscious impulses (sex and aggression) on the one hand, and the repression of these libidinal forces on the other. The conflict between the id and the superego produces anxiety that is allayed by the ego's attempts to mediate between these two rather unyielding components of the personality. While the measures taken by the ego to counteract the anxiety do not effectively resolve the intrapsychic conflict, they do reduce the tension. Consequently, neurotic behaviors are maintained because they allay anxiety, and they can be eliminated only when the basic intrapsychic conflict is resolved.

How do intrapsychic conflicts arise? Freud believed that they stem from environmental stimuli and events that take on particular significance during a given stage of psychosexual development. For example, the horse phobia manifested by Hans, a five-year-old boy whose analysis Freud supervised, occurred during the Oedipal stage, when boys allegedly have incestuous wishes for the mother, death wishes for the father (or at least a wish for his absence), and the fear of castration as retaliation by the father should he find out about these wishes. Hans was terrified of being harmed or bitten by horses, and of their falling. He also feared things associated with horses, such as carts and vans (Freud, 1955). Apparently, Hans's fear of horses followed a specific frightening event in which he saw a horse fall and thought it was dead. At about this time Hans was very sexually aroused by sleeping with his mother whenever his father was away from home. He masturbated nightly, but he was apprehensive that his sexual actions would lead to the disappearance of his penis, since he noted that his mother did not have one. The fact that his sexual fantasies were gratified when his father was absent, and that he was not the primary object of his mother's affection when his father was home, fostered rivalry, resentment, and the inevitable conclusion that he was better off without his father. But how could Hans get rid of a father he also loved, whom he had enjoyed as a playmate, and who had cared for him throughout his lifetime? Thus, according to Freud, Hans's sexual impulses resulted in death wishes for his father, which were banished from consciousness through repression. Hans handled the fear that was generated from his aggressive impulses (death wishes) by projection; that is, by turning them into fears that he would be harmed by external forces. Horses became the specific object of the fear because of his one frightening experience (trauma) and because they served as a symbolic substitute for his father, with whom he had played "horsey" on many prior occasions.

As for the other forms of psychoneuroses, Freud suggested that each is distinguishable by the primary defense mechanisms the child uses to reduce the anxiety generated by intrapsychic conflicts. As we have already seen, Hans displaced his projected fear of being harmed by his father onto horses, whereas hysterical youngsters allay their anxiety by converting it into some somatic disturbance. Obsessive-compulsive children set standards for themselves that are impossible to reach, and they often are guilt-ridden because their superegos tend to be strict and stern (Kessler, 1972). They behaviorally express their banished impulses through excessive virtue (reaction formation); and they defend themselves against intrapsychic anxiety primarily through the mechanism of undoing. The defense of undoing serves the superego, providing for repetitious acts that appease or alleviate guilt, such as seen in the symbolic cleansing of the compulsive handwasher who is extremely guilty about forbidden sexual thoughts or acts. Similarly, depressive reactions reflect rigid and strict superego development in which the intrapsychic anxiety (often over hostile impulses) is internalized in the form of self-depreciation, self-condemnation, and guilt feelings.

Learning theory. Actually, there is no single theory that can systematically explain neuroses, although various learning theorists as well as data from learning studies have contributed to our understanding of it. The first direct attempt to relate learning to neurotic-like behavior came in the early 1900s. Classical conditioning was used to demonstrate that an eleven-month-old child, Albert, could learn to be afraid of a white rat and subsequently of other small furry animals (Watson and Rayner, 1920). Watson and Rayner paired the previously neutral white rat with a noxious sound that was frightening to Albert, in order to establish the conditioned fear. Unfortunately, Albert and his family moved away before the experimenters could use learning principles to eliminate the specific and generalized fear. However, several years later Mary Carver Jones (1924) successfully treated a boy by the name of Peter (aged two years and ten months), who was afraid of a white rabbit and other small, furry animals by pairing pleasurable experiences with the feared stimulus and using social imitation. Jones paired the pleasurable activity of eating with the incompatible fear-evoking presentation of the rabbit, which initially was introduced in a cage at a distance far enough away from Peter so as not to interfere with his eating. Gradually, the rabbit was brought closer to Peter, and eventually the animal was released from the cage. In addition, Jones periodically brought children who were unafraid of the rabbit into the experimental session as social models for Peter.

In 1938 a conditioning technique was introduced as a treatment for enuresis (Mowrer and Mowrer, 1938). The technique consisted of placing an electric pad in the child's bed that activated a bell when the child wet the pad. The purpose of the bell was to both waken the child and inhibit urination. Successive pairings of the bell with the sphincter contraction that results in the cessation of urination proved to be successful in eliminating nocturnal enuresis in all the children studied, although some relapses occurred later.

As noted in Chapter 3, Dollard and Miller (1950) were the first to attempt to translate psychoanalytic postulates into a more systematic and testable drive-reduction model of learning. Their reinterpretation of Freudian concepts into learning terms corresponded closely with psychoanalytic assumptions about unconscious conflicts and the conditions under which specific symptoms develop. Although their work brought more scientific respectability to psychoanalytic theory and underscored the importance of learning in the etiology of abnormal behaviors—especially neurotic reactions—it did little to stimulate innovations or to discourage clinicians from using their own experience rather than empirical tests to validate psychoanalytic theory (Bandura and Walters, 1963).

Since it was first reported in Pavlov's laboratory, there have been ample demonstrations showing that conflict situations can produce experimental neuroses or a behavioral breakdown that simulates neurotic symptoms (Pavlov, 1928; Masserman, 1950; Wolpe, 1958, 1973). These studies have shown that anxiety can be induced by certain (external) environmental conditions that, in turn, give rise to abnormal behaviors. We now know that when two valued goals conflict, the choice of either alternative leads to the frustration of the other. The choice may be between two positive goals (approach-approach), two negative ones (avoidance-avoidance), or the positive and negative aspects of the same goal (approach-avoidance). Approach-approach conflicts are readily resolved without creating any significant disruption in most individuals—they simply choose one of the desirable alternatives. Blocking and failing to respond is ordinarily the reaction to avoidance-avoidance conflicts, while approach-avoidance conflicts tend to produce vascillation and are usually the most difficult conflicts to resolve.

Based on research in which neurotic-like behaviors were experimentally produced, Wolpe (1958, 1973) formulated a view of the disorder in which anxiety plays a primary role in the acquisition and maintenance of these maladaptive habits. He proposed that anxiety responses can be conditioned either by specific noxious stimuli that evoke anxiety or by ambivalent ones that heighten anxiety levels. Noxious stimuli include those producing pain or discomfort, such as loud sounds, and those thwarting pleasure; while ambivalent stimuli involve situations in which the organism is required to make a fine choice between opposing responses, such as the situation in which Pavlov's dog had to make a discrimination (between a circle and an ellipse) that exceeded its sensory capacity. However, Wolpe's major contribution was in the development of a treatment strategy, called *reciprocal inhibition* (discussed in Chapter 6), designed to eliminate neurotic symptoms by inhibiting anxiety responses through the conditioning of new and more adaptive responses to the same conditions that give rise to the original anxiety. More specifically, anxiety is reduced by introducing responses that are either incompatible or antagonistic to those produced by the original situation. Typically, Wolpe teaches his patients deep relaxation, because he believes that it is antagonistic to anxiety responses, and because it provides a method for its *systematic desensitization*.

The work of Skinner and his followers in operant conditioning (instrumental learning) and of Bandura and others in modeling (imitation learning) was discussed more fully in Chapter 4. These studies have shown that these learning paradigms also can account for the acquisition of abnormal behaviors much like those evident in neurotic reactions. Accordingly, neurotic behaviors increase in their probability of occurrence as a function of either reinforcement or imitation of a model. Unlike psychoanalysis, learning approaches typically are less concerned with diagnosis and traditional classification; they prefer to focus on the symptom or deviant behavior, in order to construct a treatment strategy for its elimination or modification. In addition, learning-oriented clinicians differ from their psychoanalytic counterparts with respect to the goal of treatment—the latter seek to discover or resolve underlying unconscious conflicts, and the former direct their efforts toward modifying or alleviating neurotic behaviors in situations where they were previously manifested. There will be more about treatment in the next section.

Therapeutic Approaches

Somatic Therapies. In light of the minimal role played by biological factors in the etiology of psychoneuroses, it is not surprising that somatic therapies similarly are unimportant in the treatment of these reactions. Although tranquilizing drugs such as Benadryl and Thorazine sometimes are used by pediatricians to make children experiencing anxiety attacks feel more comfortable and less anxious, chemotherapy is rarely, if ever, effective as a long-term remedy by itself (Bakwin and Bakwin, 1972; Solomon and Hart, 1978). Antidepressant drugs sometimes are used for severe depressive reactions with "marked and persistent lowering of vitality, with associated sleep and appetite disturbance, reduced mobility and verbal retardation" (Graham, 1976, p. 104). Drugs in combination with other treatment procedures reportedly have been used, for example, with school-phobic children (Gittelman-Klein and Klein, 1973). Interestingly, imipramine was more effective than a placebo in returning these youngsters to school. However, since the drug was used in conjunction with parent and child counseling and a desensitization program, it was impossible to identify which of the several treatment approaches was responsible for the improvement. Confounding of treatment effects has been noted in many of the therapy studies reported in the literature. In addition, the frequency with which single cases are used as a measure of therapeutic effectiveness prohibits an adequate appraisal of the various treatment approaches to neuroses. Yet it seems safe to say that at present there is a consensus suggesting that psychological therapies, and not somatic ones, are the primary remedial measures to be used to successfully treat neurotic reactions.

Psychological Therapies. In one form or another, psychoanalytically oriented therapy has for years been the primary treatment approach for neuroses, probably because of its widespread popularity among clinicians with regard to normal and abnormal personality development. The object of this treatment is to uncover the underlying intrapsychic conflict that gives rise to the neurosis and to provide the child with an opportunity to resolve it. Although overt symptoms give much-needed information about the conflict, the defenses, and the character structure, they are not the chief targets of treatment. In fact, Freudians contend that removing symptoms without resolving the basic conflict leads to symptom substitution; that is, other and different symptoms soon appear. This assumption has been the subject of much controversy, since learning-oriented therapists argue that neurotic behaviors—and not their conjectured causes—should be the object of treatment. They argue further that symptom substitution will not occur if the child learns new behaviors in the place of unwanted ones (Spiegel, 1967; Cahoon, 1968; Blanchard and Hersen, 1976).

Dynamic therapy with children involves the establishment of a relationship between therapist and child; therapy with one parent—usually the mother; play activities along with conversation, ventilation, and acceptance of feelings; and interpretations by the therapist (Kessler, 1972). Traditionally, the child is seen weekly or biweekly by a therapist, while the mother is seen by another collaborating therapist, who helps her deal with her feelings and reactions to the child, with any changes that occur, and with day-to-day events. Play is used, especially for young children, as a natural medium through which (1) the therapist can understand the child's conflicts and feelings, (2) the child can express unacceptable feelings without disapproval, and (3) the therapist can interpret the child's unconscious conflicts. Within recent years therapy involving the entire family (parents, child, and siblings) or the parents and the child has received increased attention as a promising technique for treating neuroses and other forms of abnormal behavior. Family therapy is thought to be useful when the child's symptoms are viewed as expressions of a disturbed family, when the child is old enough to comprehend the verbalizations of the therapy session, when no improvement has been noted in individual psychotherapy, and when individual therapy results in stress for other family members (Glick and Kessler, 1974; Hafner et al., 1981). In contrast, it is not considered useful when the family is in the actual throes of a breakup, and when the child's problems are either intrapsychic or stem from specific stressors outside of the family, such as school.

Behavior therapies are now the chief rival of psychodynamic therapies in treating neurotic behaviors, especially phobic reactions. We have already described the basic characteristics of Wolpe's theory of reciprocal inhibition and his technique of systematic desensitization. Having reviewed studies using desensitization for phobias, we can conclude that the treatment was effective in the majority of the cases, and that the successes were achieved without recurrence of the symptoms and without symptom substitution (Rachman, 1967; Danquah, 1974; Pomerantz et al., 1977; Le Unes and Siesgluz, 1977; Prout and Harvey, 1978; Johnson and Melamud, 1979; DiNardo and DiNardo, 1981).

Because deep relaxation is difficult to teach children, Lazarus (1971) has used emotive imagery. He presents children with increasingly fearful stimuli that are "woven into progressively more enjoyable fantasies" (Lazarus, 1971, p. 211). Several studies have demonstrated that desensitization in combination with operant conditioning techniques has been quite successful in treating school-phobic youngsters (Lazarus, Davison, and Polefka, 1965; Garvey and Hegrenes, 1966). For example, Garvey and Hegrenes (1966) constructed an anxiety hierarchy that consisted of a graded series of twelve steps ranging from proximity to the school to actually attending classes. The therapist met with the child, Jimmy, each school morning to take him through each step until the point where Jimmy reported anxiety or fear. The therapist then terminated the session and positively reinforced Jimmy's behavior with both praise and candy. After twenty sessions Jimmy was able to resume normal school attendance, and after a two-year follow-up he remained free of any adjustment difficulties.

Modeling also has been effective in eliminating phobic reactions (Windheuser, 1977; Dash, 1981). This was illustrated in a study that treated youngsters with a dog phobia by exposing them to a fearless peer model who comfortably approached a dog (Bandura, Grusec, and Menlove, 1967). The mere viewing of the unafraid peer model with the dog reduced the avoidance responses noted in the previously phobic children. Another behavior therapy, *implosive therapy*, stems from the proposition that anxiety or fear responses will be extinguished when high-anxiety–evoking stimuli are presented in the absence of the primary aversive stimulus. This technique was used successfully to treat a school phobia: Vivid descriptions of intense anxiety-arousing scenes related to school were constructed and then presented to a boy to extinguish his fear of attending school (Smith and Sharpe, 1970). The improvement in the boy's adjustment to school remained unchanged after a thirteen-week follow-up.

In general, the literature on psychological therapies abounds with testimonials, descriptions of successfully treated single cases, or otherwise uncontrolled reports about their effectiveness. Frequently it is difficult to assess any given therapy, since in practice, therapists employ a mixture of methods and introduce—in some unknown way—their own special orientation and skills. Fortunately, most neurotic children have a favorable prognosis, with the expectation that one-third of the cases will be completely "cured," one-third improved, and one-third unimproved, regardless of the treatment method used. Indirect support for this conclusion comes from a review of studies designed to assess the effectiveness of group therapy in children (Abramowitz, 1976). One-third of the studies yielded positive treatment results, one-third mixed results, and another third negative results. Moreover, there were no apparent differences between types of therapy, although there seemed to be more behavior modification techniques than other therapies represented in the positive and mixed-outcome results.

Some data, although meager, are now available that bear on the question of long-term prognosis. One study showed that the symptoms of indecision, fear of thunder, headaches, and insomnia could be predicted in adult women by their presence in childhood, while another found that neurotic adults had significantly more school phobias during childhood than a matched group of orthopedic and dental patients (Abe, 1972; Tyrer and Tyrer, 1974). Finally, recent data suggest that the prognosis for child neurotics may not be as favorable as we had once thought. Waldron (1976) compared forty-two young adults who had neurosis in childhood with twenty controls on various aspects of their functioning. The results indicated that 75 percent of the former patients were at least "mildly ill" at follow-up, in contrast to only 15 percent of the controls. While these data suggest a pessimistic outlook for neurotic children, at this point they can only be regarded as tentative. The findings need to be replicated with larger and more completely defined samples.

PSYCHOPHYSIOLOGICAL DISORDERS

Unlike most of the previously discussed clinical conditions—where behavioral maladjustment is the chief problem—*psychophysiological disorders* are characterized by physical symptoms arising from dysfunctioning of and structural damage to a single organ system usually innervated by the autonomic nervous system. Typically these disorders involve a significant interplay between physiological and psychological forces, since the physical changes are to a great extent caused by prolonged psychological and social stress. They have also been referred to as *psychosomatic* and *somatization reactions*, although the specific label *psychophysiological disorders* is preferred, to avoid confusion with the more general term *psychosomatic*, which refers to an orientation and approach common to medical practice today. In addition, this label circumvents the implication of somatization reactions wherein psychophysiological disorders would be classified as merely another form of neurosis (GAP Report No. 62, 1966). While somatic complaints are evident in neurotic reactions, the physical symptoms of psychophysiological disorders differ in a number of important ways. They neither serve to allay anxiety—as do the various neurotic counterreactions—nor do they characteristically affect those bodily parts that are under the voluntary control of the central nervous system, as illustrated by the paralysis of the conversion reaction. Instead, psychophysiological disorders are those in which primarily emotional factors cause actual changes and even damage to a single organ system (respiratory, digestive, genitourinary, cardiovascular) that is regulated by the involuntary portion of the nervous system. The idea that psychological and social stress may trigger off or contribute to physical symptoms should not be taken to imply that these disorders are imagined, contrived, or trivial. In fact, they are very real and important, since they involve irreversible damage to bodily tissues that may prove fatal, or at least may require a good deal of medical attention.

The term *psychosomatic* or *psychophysiological disorder* has been excluded from DSM-III because it was used infrequently in prior classification systems, and because of growing objections to the mind-body dichotomy and to the view that only a special group of physical disorders are multiply determined. Lipowski (1977) contends that we now think of all diseases as caused by the interaction of biological and psychosocial variables, and not in terms that would favor one over the other or fail to consider both sets of determinants. DSM-III, therefore, diagnoses physical illnesses such as asthma, ulcerative colitis, hypertension, and so forth on a separate axis (III) intended to record the physical-medical condition, and allows for the acknowledgment of psychological factors (if present), that are associated with the physical condition on axis I. Nevertheless, many clinicians would argue that a special category of psychophysiological disorders is meaningful and useful, since these disorders represent the substantial impact of psychosocial factors in the production of physiological changes and in the formation of disease.

Stress and Psychophysiological Disorders

The pioneering work of Hans Selye in constructing a theory that involves the endocrine system in relation to bodily or psychological stress is particularly pertinent to the study of psychophysiological disorders (Selye, 1956, 1969). Selye identified the pattern of reactions to prolonged stress as the general adaptation syndrome (GAS), which consists of three temporal phases repeated in sequence: the *alarm reaction*, the *stage of resistance*, and the *stage of exhaustion*. When a stressor exists for a prolonged period of time, it serves initially (alarm reaction) to stimulate the production of corticosteroids throughout the body. In the second stage of resistance, the body's defensive response becomes more localized and confined to the specific body area of stress. As the stress continues, these localized defensive reactions become exhausted (stage of exhaustion), while at the same time the body is stimulated to produce certain corticosteroids that inhibit these localized reactions. Under conditions of severe stress and prolonged exhaustion, death is likely to occur.

We have known for a long time from both human and animal studies that a variety of psychological stressors—such as war, maternal separation and inadequate stimulation, and conflict—can bring about physiological changes in the function and structure of bodily organs. The effect on English civilians of the prolonged stress of almost constant enemy bombings during World War II was associated with a precipitous rise in the incidence of perforated peptic ulcers (Stewart and Winser, 1942). Other and more recent reports indicate that increases in the number of psychiatric casualties are associated with either the prolonged stress of military operations, the prolonged stress of work requirements without rest or sleep, or the accumulated effect of a number of life stressors (Selye, 1969; Myers, Lindenthal, and Pepper, 1971; Birley, 1972). Pediatricians are quite aware of a condition known as *marasmus*, in which infants evidence progressive emaciation and possible death as a result of malnutrition. A similar condition was identified by Spitz (Spitz, 1945; Spitz and Wolf, 1946), who described the wasting away of marasmus, along with the sadness, immobility, apathy, and poor appetite and sleep patterns of what he called *anaclitic depression* in infants who were subjected to the stress of prolonged maternal separation and inadequate stimulation.

Studies with human subjects have indicated that conflict tends to produce physiological changes, especially in the autonomic nervous system, such as increases in vasoconstriction levels under conditions of competing instructions, and increases in heart rate and galvanic skin responses (GSR) when discrimination between two stimuli is difficult (Johnson, 1963; Moss and Edwards, 1964). Even more dramatic physiological changes have been brought about in animals under conflict situations. When hungry and thirsty rats were placed in a chronic approach-avoidance conflict requiring them to live for about two weeks in a chamber in which strong electric shock was given whenever they approached food or water, many of the experimental animals developed gastric ulcers, and some died from intestinal bleeding—the controls showed none of these effects (Sawrey and Weisz, 1956; Sawrey, Conger, and Turrell, 1956).

Theoretical Models of Psychophysiological Disorders

Most theories dealing with these disorders begin with the premise that psychological stress can bring about physiological malfunctioning and actual tissue change. This proposition gives rise to several important questions for which theorists with different orientations have sought answers. The first question asks, Who are the people likely to develop a psychophysiological disorder, and why are they affected by stress in this way while others are not? The second question focuses on the factors that determine why a particular organ system is affected and another is not. And finally, an acceptable theory must grapple with the issue of how, or by what mechanisms, psychological stressors become translated into physical symptoms (Purcell, Weiss, and Hahn, 1972). Let us consider some of the major theoretical models, although as we shall see, they tend to be general and not sufficiently specific or comprehensive to adequately explain or predict psychophysiological disorders.

1. Two biological views have aroused considerable interest: the ideas of *genetic vulnerability* or *somatic weakness*, and of *innate specific autonomic response patterns*. The premise of genetic vulnerability or somatic weakness attributable to constitutional factors, prior illness, toxic substances, and the like is neither new nor specific to psychophysiological disorders, since we have seen a similar model proposed for other disorders, especially childhood psychoses. Here these factors are believed to predispose or weaken a particular bodily system, leaving it more susceptible to damage from stress. The vulnerable or weakened somatic area is selected as

the affected organ system when noxious psychological stress conditions occur and persist: It is as if a rubber band flawed by a pinhold eventually breaks at that vulnerable point under the stress of stretching.

The specific response theory holds that people differ in their physiological reactions to stress, and that these specific patterns are probably of genetic origin. Autonomic reactivity to stress is regarded as idiosyncratic (Lacey and Lacey, 1958), although the individual pattern tends to be quite consistent and similar from one stressor to another. Thus, on the basis of their specific autonomic response patterns to stress, people may be considered as primarily "stomach reactors," "heart reactors," "skin reactors," and so forth (Wolff, 1950; Coleman, 1972). "Stomach reactors" are persons who are likely to respond to stress with increased secretion of stomach acid that would, in turn, make them more vulnerable to stomach ulcers.

2. One of the earliest *psychological views* suggested a relationship between certain personality traits and intrapsychic conflicts on the one hand, and psychosomatic disorders and organ choice on the other (Dunbar, 1943; Alexander, 1950). Alexander suggested that unresolved dependency conflicts are involved intimately in the production of ulcers. He believed that the stomach and food are symbolically equated with parental love, and that the thwarting of longstanding childhood dependency wishes results in autonomic overactivity of the stomach and eventually ulcers. However, the weight of subsequent research has failed to support the claim that there are specific personality types for each psychophysiological disorder (Hamilton, 1955). More recent work along similar lines argued for a relationship between people's characteristic attitudes toward stress and the particular psychophysiological disorder they are likely to evidence (Graham, 1962). Graham found, along with other relationships, that hypertension patients feel endangered and are on constant guard to ward off the threat of danger, while ulcer patients seek to get even with people or situations that have injured or deprived them of something promised.

Ever since Pavlov demonstrated that autonomic changes in heart and respiration rate could be conditioned, there has been ample evidence not only to support this finding but also to foster the belief that physiological symptoms mediated by the autonomic nervous system can be learned only through classical conditioning. However, Miller and his colleagues (DiCara and Miller, 1968; Miller and Banuazizi, 1968; Miller, 1969) have opened up the real possibility that physical changes in visceral and glandular responses (heart rate and rate of intestinal contraction) can be produced by operant conditioning procedures, and that these learned alterations can be maintained for several months in the absence of additional practice. Miller (1969) argues that children may learn certain psychophysiological patterns as a function of parental concern and parental reinforcement of specific behaviors. Thus, when a child evidences several physiological responses to a stressful situation, the parent may inadvertently reinforce one, such as gastric distress, by permitting the child to avoid the stress as a result of the intestinal symptoms. Although this work has been impressive and has led others to a behavioral interpretation of all psychophysiological disorders, replication of these findings along with new data are needed before the theory can be confirmed (Lachman, 1972).

Psychophysiological disorders are subcategorized by types according to the particular organ system affected. The GAP classification system lists eleven different types that include all the major bodily systems and reflect the enormous variety of diseases thought to be influenced by psychogenic factors (GAP, 1966). For our purposes it is neither possible nor necessary to cover all these disorders. We can obtain a reasonable grasp of them by limiting our discussion to the most common psychophysiological disorder in children, bronchial asthma, and an intriguing adolescent condition known as anorexia nervosa.

Bronchial Asthma in Children

This is a disorder of the respiratory system found more commonly in children than in adults, and in boys more than in girls, by a ratio of about 2:1 (Apley and McKeith, 1962; Graham et al., 1967; Purcell, Weiss, and Hahn, 1972). While the incidence of asthma falls somewhere between 2 and 5 percent for the general population, the vast majority of the cases (approximately 60 percent) consists of children under the age of seventeen who are sufficiently debilitated so that they are responsible for nearly 25 percent of the total school days missed by all children (Purcell, Weiss, and Hahn, 1972; Melamed and Johnson, 1981). The seriousness of the disorder is further reflected in the fact that there are approximately 1.5 deaths per 1000 each year directly attributable to asthma (Mustacchi, Lucia, and Jassy, 1962). Yet the long-term prognosis for many children in whom asthma began before the age of thirteen seems favorable: Data from a twenty-year follow-up study indicates that over 70 percent improved during or shortly after adolescence and continued to do well through the early adult years (Rackeman and Edwards, 1952).

Bronchial asthma involves an episodic contraction of the muscles of the bronchial tubes, thus restricting air exchange—especially in expiration—and producing the frightening physical symptoms of convulsive coughing, wheezing, labored respiration (dyspnea), difficulty in drawing deep breaths, and tightness in the chest. Asthmatic attacks may range from the mild form to the severe form in which the child has a great deal of difficulty getting air in and out of the lungs and experiences the fear of suffocation. Repeated serious attacks can result in progressive deterioration of the bronchial system. Air exchange then becomes even more difficult: The bronchial muscles lose their elasticity, the bronchial tissues swell, and mucous accumulates. Asthmatic attacks also vary in duration from a few minutes to several hours, and they are accompanied by feelings of anxiety, irritability, and depression. Obviously, things go better for these youngsters between attacks, although the children understandably experience apprehension about future episodes and the stimuli that trigger them off. The physical symptoms can be a painful source of embarrassment to youngsters who face a sudden eruption at almost any time and under a variety of circumstances. These children often feel "different," frustrated, and inadequate, because the disorder impairs their social ability for normal peer interactions, especially in physical activities. Asthmatic children also affect others, who become frightened when they witness an attack and feel helpless to alleviate it. Many parents feel guilty because they believe that they are in some way responsible for producing a damaged child, and because they periodically resent the additional expenditure of time and money these children frequently require. According to Purcell and Weiss: "This guilt appears to be one of the antecedents of the commonly observed overprotective maternal attitude toward the asthmatic child, with reciprocal overdependence of the child on the mother" (Purcell and Weiss, 1970, pp. 601–602).

Etiological Views. The etiology of asthma may be caused by the primary influence of a single factor, or more frequently by the complex interaction of a number of contributing variables. The widespread belief that heredity plays a role in the disorder is supported by data indicating a much higher incidence of asthma in the families of these patients than in nonasthmatic families (Criep, 1962; Jones, 1976). However, just how and where the genetic factor is implicated remains uncertain, although it is likely that it causes the respiratory apparatus to be more responsive to a variety of stimuli (genetic vulnerability)

Sidelight 12-1

Knapp writes of a patient whose asthma began at age nine while he and his father were walking in the woods. Although his condition worsened over the next several years, he was symptom-free between the ages of thirteen and twenty-three. From that time on, his asthma became progressively more severe and chronic until his death at age fifty-two.

Abundant data from this patient's life suggest the importance of emotional factors in precipitating exacerbations of his asthma. He gives a graphic description of developing wheezing and shortness of breath upon separation from his mother. Once, while away on a trip with either her or his grandmother (it is not clear which), in a strange hotel, separated from his companion by a wall, he suffered through the night, having the feeling that his wheezes might be loud enough to be heard and bring her in to rescue him.

He described clearly the relationship of his symptoms to odors. His response to the scent of flowers may have had an allergic basis. That seems less likely in the case of the scent of "lovely ladies," which he stated also gave him asthma. So did certain "bad" smells, of asparagus and cigar smoke. . . . He had many conflicts around weeping, frequently described being dissolved in tears, but always with the implication that he never really was exhausting the reservoir of "sobbing." Less conspicuous was the role of excitement, which at times appeared to provoke his attacks. Some of his written associations lead from sexualized recollections directly to descriptions of asthma. Underneath the excitement were not only forbidden sexual impulses but also deep hostile ones. At the time of his brother's marriage, the patient was jealous; he managed to forget to mail the 150 invitations to the ceremony that had been entrusted to him. In the church he was almost more prominent than the bride, walking down the aisle just before the ceremony, gasping for breath, and wearing a fur coat, although the month was July. (P. H. Knapp, "The Asthmatic and His Environment," *Journal of Nervous and Mental Diseases,* © 1969 The Williams and Wilkins Co., Baltimore, Md.)

which, in turn, can precipitate an attack (Purcell, Weiss, and Hahn, 1972). At present three classes of stimuli (*infections* such as whooping cough, pneumonia, or tonsillitis; *allergens* such as pollen, foods, and dust; and *emotional factors*) have been identified as causative agents that either act alone (in relatively few cases) or in combination with each other (Rees, 1964). Our discussion focuses on emotional factors, since the diagnosis of psychophysiological disorders applies to those conditions that are caused primarily by psychological variables. It is presumed that the disorder is most often determined by the interaction of a number of etiological agents.

Through the years studies have shown that various emotional stressors can either induce an asthmatic attack or produce some of the physiological changes associated with the disorder. Experimenters have brought these alterations about by using, among other tactics, stressful interviews, emotional stimuli selected from the patient's history, the arousal of resentment and anxiety, and even the radical measure of confining a patient in a locked but allergen-free chamber (Treuting and Ripley, 1948; Dekker and Groen, 1956; Stein, 1962; Dudley, Martin, and Holmes, 1964). In addition, there have been many reports suggesting that asthmatic attacks in humans, or symptoms resembling the labored breathing of asthmatics in animals, can be conditioned classically. While much of these data implicate learning as an important contributor to asthma in some people, the findings by no means prove that asthma is acquired through conditioning—the subjects either failed to show all the important physiological signs of the disorder or the findings were not replicated. After critically reviewing the literature, Purcell and his colleagues concluded: "It appears accurate to state that with either animals or human beings, the successful conditioning of asthma remains to be demonstrated, even in the opinion of those investigators whose original positive reports on conditioning are cited frequently" (Purcell, Weiss, and Hahn, 1972, p. 715).

Researchers also have pursued the psychoanalytically influenced notion that asthmatics have a common personality profile with a particular type of unresolved intrapsychic conflict (heightened dependency on mother). Some regard this as the causative agent of the disorder, while others view the conflict as developing from the disorder. Working from a different premise, namely, that asthmatics are heterogeneous, Purcell and his associates identified two subgroups of asthmatic children: (1) those who showed rapid remission of their symptoms when they were separated from their families and admitted to a hospital setting shortly after (RR) and (2) those who required continued steroid medication after they were separated and institutionalized (SD). The RR youngsters reported more frequently than did the SD children that emotions, such as anger, anxiety, and depression, precipitated their asthma attacks while at home (Purcell, 1963). More recently differential predictions were made successfully for two groups of carefully evaluated asthmatic children who were separated from their families while their physical surroundings were kept relatively constant (Purcell et al., 1969). The family of each asthmatic child lived in a motel for two weeks and had no contact with the child, who was cared for in the home by a surrogate parental figure. All the measures of asthma used in the study significantly improved during the separation period—and then declined when the family and the child were once again united—for the group of children who were predicted to be affected by family interactions. The predicted nonresponders showed no difference during or after separation, except for one measure.

In addition, parents of RR children hold stronger authoritarian and punitive attitudes than their SD counterparts, raising the possibility that neurotic conflict and emotional states are primary causes of asthma in the RR group, while allergens and infections are more important etiological factors in the SD youngsters (Purcell, Bernstein, and Burkantz, 1961; Purcell, 1975). Subgroupings of this sort seem to be a promising line of inquiry, since they tend to reduce the variability of an otherwise heterogenous and multiply determined disorder and to enable more specific assessment of the relative contributions each class of stimuli makes in triggering asthmatic attacks in certain children.

Therapeutic Considerations. Almost every form of treatment has been tried with asthmatics, including drugs; suggestion and hypnosis; relaxation; behavior therapies; individual, group, and family therapy; long-term psychoanalysis; and institutionalization (separation from family) (Knapp, Mathé, and Vachon, 1976). Rapid or immediate symptomatic relief or recovery usually can be brought about by the administration of a number of drugs, primarily corticosteroids and sympathomimetic amines, depending on the severity of the attack and the status of the child. Preventive measures typically are suggested where allergens are involved. They may take the form either of environmental manipulation, as in the removal of rugs that tend to collect dust, or of prescribing medicines that tend to bolster the body's tolerance to the allergen.

The array of psychological treatments used for asthmatic children is particularly difficult to assess, since too few studies are available; and more often than not, these studies are flawed by methodological errors. However, the literatures does suggest that individual, group, and family therapy may be instrumental in aiding asthmatic children to deal more effectively with the emotional stimuli that may trigger their attacks, and to cope more effectively with their symptoms. For example, Alexander (1972) showed that systematic relaxation is successful in reducing the severity of symptoms for those asthmatic children in whom emotional factors play a prominent role in precipitating asthma attacks. In addition, a recent review of the literature suggests that relaxation training and systematic desensitization are the most effective behavioral treatments for asthma (Knapp and Wells, 1978). Another possible benefit of these therapies may be that some parents learn to modify those attitudes and behaviors that seem to contribute to the child's illness. Weekly family therapy sessions aimed at discovering—and then changing—those family and emotional situations that excite and maintain asthmatic symptoms did prove helpful in several cases in which acute attacks leading to hospitalization were almost totally eliminated (Liebman, Minuchin, and Baker, 1974).

A relatively new therapeutic approach, called *biofeedback,* seems to hold particular promise for psychophysiological disorders. Biofeedback monitors the physiological responses of the patient and provides information to the patient about the performance of various physiological functions that he or she could then learn to control with the aid of positive reinforcement. Ordinarily, the subject is provided with an electronic signal that varies with some aspect of a physiological response and is told to try to control the electronic signal. For example, one recent study showed that muscle relaxation associated with pulmonary function can be learned through biofeedback with and without the use of reinforcement (Kostes et al., 1976). Using operantly manipulated levels of muscle tension, these investigators are actively studying the relationship between muscular and respiratory events that seem applicable to the control of asthma in children (Glaus, 1976; Kostes et al., 1976; Kostes et al., 1977). They have found that tension levels in or around the frontalis muscle (forehead) significantly influence measures of lung airway resistance, that frontalis tension is inversely related to peak expiratory flow rate, that this relationship holds for both asthmatic and nonasthmatic subjects, and that the effects of frontalis tension changes on airway resistance are immediate, being observable after a single training session. Working on the premise that asthmatic attacks are based on operant events (in which the child's separation from the mother is prevented by the attack), Khan (1977) demonstrated that significant improvement could be brought about in asthmatic children through a combination of biofeedback and counterconditioning. Experiments are now underway to evaluate a self-management program in which the child learns behaviors through biofeedback that will decrease the symptoms of bronchial asthma (Glaus, private communication). In evaluating biofeedback techniques, it is important to be sure what component of airflow is being measured and to decrease the effects of suggestion and possible hidden reinforcers (Feldman, 1976).

ANOREXIA NERVOSA

Anorexia nervosa refers to the most extreme form of refusal to eat; persistent aversion to food continues for long periods of time, resulting in marked weight loss and emaciation (Bruch, 1973). It is a physiological disorder that affects mostly females (9 or 10 : 1) during early adolescence and through the teenage years, and it is fatal in about 10 to 15 percent of all cases (Crisp and Toms, 1972; Minuchin, Rosman, and Baker, 1978). Most often anorexic youngsters come from middle-class and upper-class families, where both family closeness and ambition are valued (Jones et al., 1980). The disorder seems to be on the increase, especially in youngsters between fifteen and twenty-four years of age. Characterized by average or better intelligence, perfectionist tendencies, and high achievement needs, these children are morbidly preoccupied with dieting and concerned about being overweight. Their pursuit of thinness results in self-starvation and a loss of as much as 25 to 50 percent of their body weight; in 80 to 100 percent of the women, it results in cessation of menstruation (Rollins and Piazza, 1978).

Dieting reflects the disturbed self-perception of anorexics: They continue to see themselves as too fat even when they are quite emaciated. Their energy is rigidly and almost totally tied up in a self-imposed regimen of restricted caloric intake to the extent that they are likely to induce vomiting if and when any increase in eating takes place. In fact, their refusal to eat inevitably brings them into a severe battle with their families, since they will do anything to resist eating. They will gag and vomit, empty their plates into the trash when not watched, and pad themselves with a pillow or extra clothing before stepping onto a scale to prove that they haven't lost weight. Many of these youngsters eventually require hospitalization in order to bring their food intake under careful regulation and to begin psychotherapy.

Observations of anorexic youngsters have led to the widely accepted view that the disorder represents an attempt to cope with the frightening demands and responsibilities of approaching maturity (Thoma, 1967; Dally, 1969). Anorexic girls fear their own sexuality and the prospect of functioning as women (Rampling, 1978; Beumont, Abraham, and Simson, 1981). The disorder appears at a time when they begin to show signs of sexual maturation and when interest in boys and dating occur. By reducing their body weight, they restore themselves to childlike physical characteristics, make themselves unattractive to boys, and become amenorrheic—safe from the anxiety and threat of mature heterosexual relationships. Disturbed mother-daughter relationships in which the youngster has been both overly dependent on and rebellious against maternal domination, or the fear of oral impregnation (the association of fatness with being pregnant) also have been proposed as etiological factors (Warren, 1968).

Several writers contend that anorexia nervosa is the result of hypothalamic dysfunction, pointing to the lower production and reactivity of lutinizing hormone (LH) in these emaciated women, as contrasted to the rise of LH levels often found in women who experience famine conditions (Bemis, 1978; Jeuniewic et al., 1978). However, there is not much evidence to support this view at this time. The involvement of neurotransmitters in anorexia nervosa has been posited as a result of observations indicating low levels of noradrenaline and seratonin and a high level of tyrosine B hydrosylase which, in turn, has led to the use of psychoactive drugs for the treatment of this condition (Redmond, Swann, and Henninger, 1976; Plantey, 1977; Neeleman and Waber, 1976; Kendler, 1978).

As interesting as these hypotheses are, the psychological and physiological aspects of anorexia nervosa are still poorly understood. In fact, there is considerable uncertainty and disagreement among clinicians as to the diagnostic category in which anorexia nervosa properly belongs.

The treatment of anorexics is often difficult, and it requires a combination of medical and psychotherapeutic procedures. Many of these youngsters are best treated in a hospital, where special feedings (liquid diet, intravenous or tube feeding) and close nursing supervision can be readily obtained. Feedings must be observed until everything is eaten, in order to guard against the possibility of food being concealed, disposed of, or vomited by the youngster. Sometimes medical management includes the administration of drugs to reduce anxiety and to stimulate the appetite, but stimulating appetite and introducing weight gain may create as many problems in the management of anorexic clients as it solves (Goldberg et al., 1979; Kendler, 1978).

While most clinicians tend to focus on the prompt stabilization of the anorexic's physical state by whatever measures necessary, at least one group makes no attempt to coerce or control food intake beyond the wishes of the client (Reinhart, Kenna, and Succop, 1972). Because these workers believe that the disorder is psychological, they emphasize psychological, and not physiological, factors. Consequently, they maintain that outpatient treatment is preferable to hospitalization, and that psychotherapy should begin promptly. They give the responsibility for eating to the child to foster her independence and bolster her attempts to separate from highly anxious parents. Frequent goals of psychotherapy include understanding and resolving fears of becoming fat and of growing up, and working out ambivalent (dependent and angry) feelings toward the mother. Treatment aimed at restoring food intake without relapse can be achieved in a variety of ways in about one-half to two-thirds of the cases, whereas treatment intended to remove the underlying psychopathology is only successful with a few of these youngsters (Tolstrup, 1975).

An attempt to understand anorexia nervosa from a systems model approach has led to descriptions of the influence of family members on each other, beginning early in the life of the anorexic family member. The systems model regards the disorder as a consequence of a dysfunctional family group and tries to discern the faulty family structure, gain the trust of the family, and find ways to reconstruct the roles of family members (Minuchin, Rosman, and Baker, 1978; Caille et al., 1977; Rosman et al., 1977). Although proponents of family therapy claim that this treatment approach is effective, at this time we can only suggest that this approach appears to have promise—much too little data are available from which to draw definitive conclusions. Somewhat more research is available on behavioral approaches in which primarily reinforcement has been used to produce weight gains in anorexics (Erwin, 1977; Hauserman and Lavin, 1977; Geller et al., 1978; Poole, Sanson-Fischer, and Young, 1978; Pertschuk, Edwards, and Pomerleau, 1978; Eckert et al., 1979; Ollendick, 1979). Many of these studies report improvement (mostly in single case studies), although one follow-up study of sixteen years, and a study which compares forty anorexics who received behavior therapy to forty-one cases who received milieu therapy, showed that the behavioral treatment was not effective (Erwin, 1977; Eckert et al., 1979). However, any treatment approach that focuses entirely on inducing weight gains in these women is likely to be doomed to failure.

BULIMIA

This disorder is characterized by episodic binge eating, occurring predominantly in adolescent or young adult females. DSM-III (APA, 1980) notes that the course of the disorder is often chronic, and it appears periodically over many years along with alternate periods of normal eating and sometimes fasting. It is seldom an incapacitating condition, although it is almost always accompanied by excessive concern about appropriate body weight and persistent and repeated attempts to control one's weight with dieting. For many, binge eating is followed by vomiting, and/or the use of laxatives and/or diuretics, and fasting in order to lose weight and to purge oneself from the effects of the binges. Individuals who are bulimic recognize the abnormality of their behavior, and consequently, they binge eat as inconspicuously as possible—sometimes they eat quickly and secretly. Foods eaten during a binge often are high in calories. They are likely to be sweet, such as chocolate, and they are consumed in large quantities until abdominal pain, sleep, induced vomiting, or something of this sort terminates the eating.

The diagnostic criteria listed in DSM-III (pp. 70–71) for bulimia are as follows:

Diagnostic Criteria for Bulimia

A. Recurrent episodes of binge eating (rapid consumption of a large amount of food in a discrete period of time, usually less than two hours).
B. At least three of the following:
   (1) consumption of high-caloric, easily ingested food during a binge
   (2) inconspicuous eating during a binge
   (3) termination of such eating episodes by abdominal pain, sleep, social interruption, or self-induced vomiting
   (4) repeated attempts to lose weight by severely restrictive diets, self-induced vomiting, or use of cathartics or diuretics

(5) frequent weight fluctuations greater than ten pounds due to alternating binges and fasts

C. Awareness that the eating pattern is abnormal and fear of not being able to stop eating voluntarily.

D. Depressed mood and self-deprecating thoughts following eating binges.

E. The bulimic episodes are not due to Anorexia Nervosa or any known physical disorder.

SUMMARY

In this chapter two sets of disorders, neuroses and psychophysiological disorders, were discussed. All types of neurotic reactions display the common ingredients of intense anxiety, personal discomfort, persistence of coping responses that are inappropriate or ineffective for the situation, and self-directed or internalized reactions to anxiety-producing stimuli. Although similarities and differences between a psychoanalytic and a learning view of neuroses were described, there is agreement that anxiety plays a key role in the development of these reactions and is responsible for the emergence of the variety of counterreactions seen clinically. A summary of the primary descriptive characteristics of each type of neurotic reaction follows.

Anxiety Reaction:	Intense free-floating anxiety with feelings of impending doom, usually unrelated to external reality, that may be triggered off by a variety of events. Sudden and severe attacks (either acute or chronic) are often accompanied by physical symptoms of shortness of breath, palpitations, sweating, faintness, dizziness, nausea, abdominal pain, and diarrhea.
Phobic Reaction:	Persistent, severe, and irrational fear that usually interferes with the child's daily functioning. *School phobia* represents a frequent problem of school-aged children. It is characterized by acute anxiety, refusal to go to school, and numerous somatic complaints. It is distinguished from truancy by the presence of acute anxiety, somatic symptoms, overattachment to home and family, good academic performance, and the absence of antisocial behaviors. Separation anxiety mutually shared by mother and child is often viewed as its cause.
Obsessive-Compulsive Reaction:	Characterized by recurrent thoughts, acts, or both, which the child must perform although the ideas or the behaviors seem silly and unreasonable. Although the child is unaware of the original source of the anxiety, anxiety is responsible for the maintenance of these behaviors, since the child experiences marked apprehension when their completion is interfered with.
Conversion Reaction:	Dysfunction of body parts that are under the voluntary control of the central nervous system. Anxiety is converted into symptoms that symbolically express the basic conflict and reduce the anxiety generated from it. The symptomatology can mimic almost any organic disease, but it ordinarily does not follow anatomical lines. These reactions have declined and are now seen in older children of working class and educationally unsophisticated families.
Depressive Reaction:	Internalization of the original conflict through self-depreciation and despondency manifested in guilt, loss of self-esteem, helplessness, and loneliness, which may be masked by apathy, withdrawal, somatic complaints, and acting-out behaviors. The diagnosis is difficult to make, because children are not expected to be depressed, and they are unable to verbalize their feelings. Further, depression is often a symptom associated with other disorders.
Mixed Reaction:	Characterized by a combination of symptoms manifested in other reaction types. The category is often a catch-all for clinicians who are uncertain about what specific diagnostic entity to use.

Etiological considerations of psychogenic variables primarily derived from psychoanalytic and learning theories were presented and were critically evaluated as the most likely origin of these reactions. There is both a lack of interest and evidence reflected in the literature supporting biological causes. Data from experimental studies using both humans and animals indicate that various learning models (classical and instrumental conditioning, modeling, and reciprocal inhibition) play a major role in the formation of neuroses. Such studies also have contributed to the development of specific treatment strategies.

Except for the use of drugs to reduce the symptoms associated with anxiety or to alleviate the discomforting aspects of depression, somatic therapies have been relatively unimportant as a remedial approach for neurotic reactions. Psychological therapies comprised the major thrust of the discussion, which focused on the description and evaluation of psychodynamic individual therapy, group and family therapy, systematic desensitization, conditioning, modeling, and implosive therapy.

Psychophysiological disorders are characterized by physical symptoms that arise from dysfunctioning of and structural damage to a single organ system innervated by the autonomic nervous system. They involve a significant interaction between physiological and psychological forces, since the physical changes are primarily caused by psychological and social stress. These disorders differ from neuroses in that the physical symptoms neither serve to allay anxiety nor affect those bodily parts that are under the voluntary control of the central nervous system. The importance of stress to psychophysiological disorders was noted in Selye's general adaptation syndrome as well as in experimental studies involving a variety of psychological stressors, such as war, maternal separation and inadequate stimulation, and conflict. Theoretical models of genetic vulnerability, somatic weakness, specific autonomic response patterns, specific personality types and conflicts, and learning views were discussed, although none was considered sufficiently specific or comprehensive to adequately explain or predict psychophysiological disorders.

Finally, bronchial asthma, the most common of these disorders in children, and anorexia nervosa, an adolescent condition, were selected for discussion with regard to their clinical picture, incidence, etiological considerations (especially emotional factors), and therapeutic approaches. Another adolescent eating disorder, bulimia, was also described.

EPILOGUE

As is so often the case, decisions about a treatment plan for youngsters like Billy are influenced by a variety of interacting factors that usually differ in importance from one situation to another. While the nature of the child's difficulties and needs must be the overriding consideration, the treatment choice also depends (1) on the extent to which a full range of treatment options are available and (2) on whether the child's support systems (family and community) are both capable and willing to help. In Billy's case the treatment program was dictated primarily by his mother's poor health (her asthmatic condition had worsened), by her inability to manage him any longer at home, and by his persistent school refusal. Moreover, the positive decision to admit Billy to a hospital (residential treatment center) was possible only because the family was both able and willing to pay for the costly services, and such a treatment center was available nearby. While most neurotic children are treated as outpatients, Billy's story provides us with an opportunity to see how the controlled environment and multitherapeutic approaches of a hospital setting were used to bring about significant changes in his personal, academic, and social adjustment.

On admission, Billy was homesick and despondent, although he slept comfortably and without interruption that night. His night terrors promptly disappeared, and he slept better throughout his nine months of hospitalization than he ever did at home. From the first day he attended the inpatient school, where he participated readily and performed at a superior level. These early signs of improvement can be attributed to environmental changes, in which he moved from a home situation that was charged with anxiety to one that was orderly, controlled, comforting, attentive, and less threatening and conflictual. In addition to the day-school program, the hospital setting also provided Billy with recreational activities and opportunities to socialize with peers. He had his own therapist who saw him on a regular basis and on occasions when he needed more help. Hospital personnel and his cottage parent were also available for daily interactions, as sources of support, and as sensitive people who could observe and deal with his progress and setbacks.

Billy's academic gains were outstanding—he easily caught up with his grade level in all areas and was very well prepared to resume his regular class by the end of his hospitalization. Although not as substantial, his social gains were impressive as well. He participated in many games and peer activities and was more comfortable relating to others than before, although he never became close friends with any of the other children. He tended to avoid the overt expression of aggression but enjoyed it vicariously as he watched other youngsters fight; and he listened to their verbal outbursts of profanity with a grin of pleasure on his face. However, if Billy could not allow his language to become "dirty," the same could not be said of his person. His prior meticulousness and compulsive attention to cleanliness gave way to the other extreme, in which he seemed to take delight in wallowing in "dirt" and in becoming the filthiest kid at the hospital. Finally, and apparently after his messiness was sufficiently gratified, his personal cleanliness shifted to a middle position between these two extremes.

During the first four-and-one half months of psychotherapy, Billy was friendly but distant, preferring to talk about his symptoms rather than play games or draw (as many youngsters of his age seem to prefer). He thought that play was a waste of time when he could be talking about his problems and trying to understand them. He wanted to go straight to the heart of the matter so that he would learn how to make his symptoms "disappear." He avoided any digression, not even wanting to take time to talk about his friends back home, his family, his daily activities in the hospital, or his roommate in the cottage. In fact, Billy was dissatisfied with therapy when he was not talking about his symptoms. All else made him feel cheated and put off by his therapist.

After six months of hospitalization, Billy's treatment took a dramatic turn one morning. He had been in bed for three days with a severe cold and was supposed to return to school that morning. However, after breakfast he was found sitting alone on his bed crying. His therapist went to see him. When asked what was wrong, Billy burst into tears and said, "Everything has gone wrong." They talked for a while, and Billy began to cheer up. When the therapist suggested that he might go to school rather than sit around in the cottage, he again burst into tears, saying, "That's what the trouble was before I came here. When my nerves were like this, I didn't feel like going to school, but they made me go and then I would feel worse." Sensing that Billy wanted desperately to relate, the therapist suggested that Billy might like to come to his office and talk. He readily accepted the invitation, and in a period longer than two hours he poured out all the feelings and thoughts he had kept to himself for so long. He told of the fears that he had felt, especially toward his father—fears that his father might kidnap him and do terrible things to him. He had fantasies while driving in a car with his father that his father was a member of a bandit gang who intended to deliver him to the gang for some sort of harm. He felt that his mother wanted to protect him, but that she had to give in to the father's will. He resented her for this weakness and felt that she had failed him. He also talked about fears that went back to memories of early childhood.

Billy also talked of his great need to tell somebody about his fear and of his awful feeling that he could never be close enough to other persons to confide in them, that nobody could really understand or accept his feelings, and that if he told somebody, that person would laugh at him or reject him. He used the word *trust* often, prompting the therapist to ask, "Do you trust me?"—to which Billy replied, "Not completely." When the therapist reflected, "But you are telling me about many things," he said, "Yes, and you're the only person I could tell these things to. I couldn't tell them to my mother or dad, or any other doctor or any other counselors, or anybody." The therapist acknowledged that being able to tell him these things was a very good sign. Billy looked thoughtful, then smiled and said, "Maybe I can get to trust you, then it will spread to other people and then I will get better."

Indeed, Billy did get better. He returned home and to school, managing both very well. There were a few occasions when his old fears returned, but he mastered them. He continued in therapy as an outpatient for about a year until his family moved away, primarily because of his mother's health. Annual letters from his mother revealed that Billy continued to do well in school, was maturing normally, and was well liked by his peers (adapted from Shaw, 1966, pp. 123–126).

REFERENCES

ABE, K. Phobias and Nervous Symptoms in Childhood and Maturity: Persistence and Associations. *British Journal of Psychiatry*, 1972, *120*, 275–283.

ABRAMOWITZ, C. V. The Effectiveness of Group Psychotherapy with Children. *Archives of General Psychiatry*, 1976, *33*, 320–326.

ADAMS, P. Family Characteristics of Obsessive Children. *American Journal of Psychiatry*, 1972, *128*, 1414–1417.

ADAMS, P. *Obsessive Children*. New York: Brunner/Mazel, 1973.

ALEXANDER, B. A. Systematic Relaxation and Flow Rates in Asthmatic Children: Relationship to Emotional Precipitants and Anxiety. *Journal of Psychosomatic Research*, 1972, *16*, 405–410.

ALEXANDER, F. *Psychosomatic Medicine: Its Principles and Application*. New York: W. W. Norton and Co., 1950.

American Psychiatric Association. DSM-III: *Diagnostic and Statistical Manual of Mental Disorders*, 3rd ed. Washington, D.C.: American Psychiatric Association, 1980.

ANGELINO, H., DOLLINS, J., and MECH, E. V. Trends in the "Fears and Worries" of School Children as Related to Socio-economic Status and Age. *Journal of Genetic Psychology*, 1956, *89*, 263–276.

ANTHONY, E. J. Neurosis of Children. In A. M. Freedman, and H. I. Kaplan (eds.), *The Child: His Psychological and Cultural Development*, Vol. 2. New York: Atheneum, 1972, pp. 105–143.

APLEY, J., and MCKEITH, R. C. *The Child and His Symptoms: A Psychosomatic Approach*. Philadelphia: Davis, 1962.

BAKWIN, H., and BAKWIN, R. M. *Behavior Disorders in Children*, 4th ed. Philadelphia: Saunders, 1972.

BANDURA, A., GRUSEC, J. E., and MENLOVE, F. L. Vicarious Extinction of Avoidance Behavior. *Journal of Personality and Social Psychology*, 1967, *5*, 16–23.

BANDURA, A., and MENLOVE, F. L. Factors Determining Vicarious Extinction of Avoidance Behavior Through Symbolic Modeling. *Journal of Personality and Social Psychology*, 1968, *8*, 99–108.

BANDURA, A., and WALTERS, R. H. *Social Learning and Personality Development*. New York: Holt, Rinehart and Winston, 1963.

BEMIS, K. M. Current Approaches to the Etiology and Treatment of Anorexia Nervosa. *Psychological Bulletin*, 1978, *85*, 593–617.

BEMPORAD, J., PFEIFFER, C., and BLOOM, W. Twelve Months' Experience with the GAP Classification of Childhood Disorders. *American Journal of Psychiatry*, 1970, *127*, 658–664.

BERG, I., and MCGUIRE, R. Are Mothers of School Phobic Adolescents Overprotective? *British Journal of Psychiatry*, 1974, *124*, 10–13.

BEUMONT, P. J., ABRAHAM, S. F., and SIMSON, K. G. The Psychosexual Histories of Adolescent Girls and Young Women with Anorexia Nervosa. *Psychological Medicine*, 1981, *11*, 131–140.

BIRLESON, P. The Validity of Depressive Disorder in Childhood and the Development of a Self-rating Scale: A Research Report. *Journal of Child Psychology and Psychiatry*, 1981, *22*, 73–88.

BIRLEY, J. L. Stress and Disease. *Journal of Psychosomatic Research*, 1972, *16*, 235–240.

BLANCHARD, E. B., and HERSEN, M. Behavioral Treatment of Hysterical Neurosis: Symptom Substitution and Symptom Return Reconsidered. *Psychiatry*, 1976, *39*, 118–129.

BRADY, J. V., PORTER, R. W., CONRAD, D. G., and MASON, J. W. Avoidance Behavior and the Development of Gastroduodenal Ulcers. *Journal of Experimental Analysis of Behavior*, 1958, *1*, 69–72.

BRUCH, H. *Eating Disorders: Obesity, Anorexia Nervosa, and the Person Within*. New York: Basic Books, 1973.

BRUMBACK, R. A., JACKOWAY, M. K., and WEINBERG, W. A. Relation of Intelligence to Childhood Depression in Children Referred to an Educational Diagnostic Center. *Perceptual and Motor Skills,* 1980, *50,* 11–17.

BRUMBACK, R. A., and WEINBERG, W. A. Childhood Depression: An Explanation of a Behavior Disorder of Children. *Perceptual and Motor Skills,* 1977, *44,* 911–916.

CAHOON, D. D. Symptom Substitution and the Behavior Therapies: A Reappraisal. *Psychological Bulletin.* 1968, *69,* 149–156.

CAILLE, P., ABRAHAMSEN, P., GIROLAMI, C., and SØRBYE, B. A Systems Theory Approach to a Case of Anorexia Nervosa. *Family Process,* 1977, *16,* 455–465.

CARLSON, G. A., and CANTWELL, D. P. A Survey of Depressive Symptoms, Syndrome and Disorder in a Child Psychiatric Population. *Journal of Child Psychology and Psychiatry,* 1980, *21,* 19–25.

CARR, A. T. Compulsive Neurosis: A Review of the Literature. *Psychological Bulletin,* 1974, *81,* 311–318.

CHAPMAN, A. H. *Management of Emotional Problems of Children and Adolescents,* 2nd ed. Philadelphia: Lippincott, 1974.

CHRISTOZEV, C., BOZHANOV, A., and YOUCHEV, V. Neuroses and Neurotic Development in School-Age Children. *International Journal of Mental Health,* 1975–76, *4,* 64–82.

CLARIZIO, H. F., and MCCOY, G. F. *Behavior Disorders in School-Aged Children.* Scranton: Chandler, 1970.

CLARK, M. Troubled Children: The Quest for Help. In *Annual Editions, Reading in Human Development 77/78.* Guilford, Conn.: Dushkin Publishing Group, 1977, pp. 167–171.

COHEN, D. B. On the Etiology of Neurosis. *Journal of Abnormal Psychology,* 1974, *83,* 473–479.

COLEMAN, J. C. *Abnormal Psychology and Modern Life,* 4th ed. Glenview, Ill.: Scott, Foresman, 1972.

CRIEP, L. H. *Clinical Immunology and Allergy.* New York: Grune and Stratton, 1962.

CRISP, A. H., and TOMS, D. A. Primary Anorexia Nervosa or Weight Phobia in the Male: Report on 13 cases. *British Medical Journal,* 1972, *1,* 334–338.

CYTRYN, L., MCKNEW, D. H., and BUNNEY, W. E. Diagnosis of Depression in Children: A Reassessment. *American Journal of Psychiatry,* 1980, *137,* 22–25.

DALLY, P. *Anorexia Nervosa.* New York: Grune and Stratton, 1969.

DANQUAH, S. A. The Treatment of Monosymptomatic Phobia by Systematic Desensitization. *Psychopathologie Africaine,* 1974, *10,* 115–120.

DASH, J. Rapid Hypno-behavioral Treatment of a Needle Phobia in a 5-Year-Old Cardiac Patient. *Journal of Pediatric Psychology,* 1981, *6,* 37–42.

DAVIDSON, S. School Phobia as a Manifestation of Family Disturbance: Its Structure and Treatment. *Journal of Child Psychology and Psychiatry,* 1961, *1,* 270–287.

DEKKER, E., and GROEN, J. Reproducible Psychogenic Attacks of Asthma. *Journal of Psychosomatic Research,* 1956, *1,* 58–67.

DICARA, L. V., and MILLER, N. E. Changes in Heart Rate Instrumentally Learned by Curarized Rats as Avoidance Responses. *Journal of Comparative and Physiological Psychology,* 1968, *65,* 8–12.

DINARDO, P. A., and DINARDO, P. G. Self-control Desensitization in the Treatment of a Childhood Phobia. *Behavior Therapist,* 1981, *4,* 15–16.

DOLLARD, J., and MILLER, N. E. *Personality and Psychotherapy.* New York: McGraw-Hill, 1950.

DUDLEY, D. L., MARTIN, C. J., and HOLMES, T. H. Psychophysiologic Studies of Pulmonary Ventilation. *Psychosomatic Medicine,* 1964, *26,* 645–660.

DUNBAR, H. F. *Psychosomatic Diagnosis.* New York: Hoeber, 1943.

ECKERT, E. D., GOLDBERG, S. C., HALMI, K. A., CASPER, R. C., and DAVIS, J. M. Behavior Therapy in Anorexia Nervosa. *British Journal of Psychiatry,* 1979, *134,* 55–59.

ELLINGSON, R. The Incidence of EEG Abnormality Among Patients with Mental Disorders of Apparently Nonorganic Orgin: A Critical Review. *American Journal of Psychiatry,* 1954, *111,* 263–275.

ERWIN, W. J. A 16-Year Follow-up of a Case of Severe Anorexia Nervosa. *Journal of Behavior Therapy and Experimental Psychiatry,* 1977, *8,* 157–160.

EYSENCK, H. J., and PRELL, D. B. The Inheritance of Neuroticism: An Experimental Study. *Journal of Mental Science,* 1951, *97,* 441–465.

FELDMAN, G. M. The Effect of Biofeedback Training on Respiratory Resistance of Asthmatic Children. *Psychosomatic Medicine,* 1976, *38,* 27–34.

FREUD, A. *Normality and Pathology in Childhood.* New York: International Universities Press, 1965.

FREUD, S. *Analysis of a Phobia in a Five-Year-Old Boy (1909),* standard ed., Vol. X. London: Hogarth Press, 1955.

GAP Report No. 62. Group for the Advancement of Psychiatry, Committee on Child Psychiatry. *Psychopathological Disorders in Childhood: Theoretical Consideration and a Proposed Classification.* New York, June 1966.

GARVEY, W. P., and HEGRENES, J. R. Desensitization Techniques in the Treatment of School Phobia. *American Journal of Orthopsychiatry,* 1966, *36,* 147–152.

GELLER, M. I., KELLEY, J. A., TRAXLER, W. T., and MARONE, F. J. Behavioral Treatment of an Adolescent Female's Bulimic Anorexia: Modification of Immediate Consequences and Antecedent Conditions. *Journal of Clinical Child Psychology,* 1978, *7,* 138–142.

GITTELMAN-KLEIN, R., and KLEIN, D. F. School Phobia: Diagnosis Considerations in the Light of Imipramine Effects. *Journal of Nervous and Mental Diseases,* 1973, *156,* 199–215.

GLAUS, K. D. The Effects of Conditioned Muscle Tension Changes on Respiration. Unpublished doctoral dissertation, Ohio University, 1976.

GLICK, I. D., and KESSLER, D. R. *Marital and Family Therapy.* New York: Grune and Stratton, 1974.

GOLDBERG, S. C., HALMI, K. A., ECKERT, E. D., CASPER,

R. C. and DAVIS, J. M. Cyproheptadine in Anorexia Nervosa. *British Journal of Psychiatry*, 1979, *134*, 67–70.

GOODYER, I. Hysterical Conversion Reactions in Childhood. *Journal of Child Psychology and Psychiatry*, 1981, *22*, 179–188.

GRAHAM, D. T. Some Research on Psychophysiologic Specificity and Its Relation to Psychosomatic Disease. In R. Roessler, and N. S. Greenfield (eds.), *Physiological Correlates of Psychological Disorder*. Madison, Wisc.: University of Wisconsin Press, 1962, pp. 232–238.

GRAHAM, P. Management in Child Psychiatry: Recent Trends. *British Journal of Psychiatry*, 1976, *129*, 97–108.

GRAHAM, P., RUTTER, M., YULE, W., and PLESS, I. Childhood Asthma: A Psychosomatic Disorder? Some Epidemiological Considerations. *British Journal of Preventive and Social Medicine*, 1967, *21*, 78–85.

GRAZIANO, A. M., and DEGIOVANNI, I. S. The Clinical Significance of Childhood Phobias: A Note on the Proportion of Child-Clinical Referrals for the Treatment of Children's Fears. *Behaviour Research and Therapy*, 1979, *17*, 161–162.

HAMILTON, M. *Psychosomatics*. New York: John Wiley, 1955.

HAMPE, E., MILLER, L., BARRET, C., and NOBLE, H. Intelligence and School Phobia. *Journal of School Psychology*, 1973, *11*, 66–70.

HAUSERMAN, N., and LAVIN, P. Post-hospitalization Continuation Treatment of Anorexia Nervosa. *Journal of Behavior Therapy and Experimental Psychiatry*, 1977, *8*, 309–313.

HAFNER, R. J., GILCHRIST, P., BOWLING, J., and KALUCY, R. The Treatment of Obsessional Neurosis in a Family Setting. *Australian and New Zealand Journal of Psychiatry*, 1981, *15*, 145–151.

HOLLINGSWORTH, C. E., TANGUAY, P. E., GROSSMAN, L., and PABST, P. Long-Term Outcome of Obsessive-Compulsive Disorder in Childhood. *Journal of the American Academy of Child Psychiatry*, 1980, *19*, 134–144.

JERSILD, A. T. *Child Psychology*. Englewood Cliffs, N. J.: Prentice-Hall, 1968.

JEUNIEWIC, N., BROWN, G. M., GARFINKEL, P. E., and MOLDOFSKY, H. Hypothalamic Function as Related to Body Weight and Body Fat in Anorexia Nervosa. *Psychosomatic Medicine*, 1978, *40*, 187–198.

JOHNSON, A. M., FALSTEIN, E. I., SZUREK, S. A., and SVENDSEN, M. School Phobia. *American Journal of Orthopsychiatry*, 1941, *11*, 702–711.

JOHNSON, H. J. Decision Making, Conflict, and Physiological Arousal. *Journal of Abnormal and Social Psychology*, 1963, *67*, 114–124.

JOHNSON, S. B., and MELAMED, B. G. The Assessment and Treatment of Children's Fears. In B. B. Lahey and A. E. Kazdin (eds.), *Advances in Clinical Child Psychology*, Vol. 2. New York: Plenum, 1979, pp. 108–139.

JONES, D. J., FOX, M. M., BABIGAN, H. M., and HUTTON, H. E. Epidemiology of Anorexia Nervosa in Monroe County, New York: 1960–1976. *Psychosomatic Medicine*, 1980, *42*, 551–558.

JONES, M. C. The Elimination of Children's Fears. *Journal of Experimental Psychology*, 1924, *7*, 383–390.

JONES, R. S. *Asthma in Children*. Acton, Mass.: Publishing Sciences Group, 1976.

JUDD, L. L. Obsessive Compulsive Neurosis in Children. *Archives of General Psychiatry*, 1965, *12*, 136–143.

KASHANI, J., and SIMONDS, J. F. The Incidence of Depression in Children. *American Journal of Psychiatry*, 1979, *136*, 1203–1205.

KELLY, E. School Phobia: A Review of Theory and Treatment. *Psychology in the Schools*, 1973, *10*, 33–42.

KENDLER, K. S. Amitriptyline-Induced Obesity in Anorexia Nervosa: A Case Report. *American Journal of Psychiatry*, 1978, *135*, 1107–1108.

KENNARD, M. A. Value of Equivocal Signs in Neurologic Diagnosis. *Neurology*, 1960, *10*, 753–764.

KENNEDY, W. A. School Phobia: Rapid Treatment of Fifty Cases. *Journal of Abnormal Psychology*, 1965, *70*, 285–289.

KESSLER, J. W. Neurosis in Childhood. In B. B. Wolman (ed.), *Manual of Child Psychopathology*. New York: McGraw-Hill, 1972, pp. 387–435.

KHAN, A. U. Effectiveness of Biofeedback and Counter-conditioning in the Treatment of Bronchial Asthma. *Journal of Psychosomatic Research*, 1977, *21*, 97–104.

KLERMAN, G. L., ENDICOTT, J., SPITZER, R., and HIRSCHFELD, R. M. Neurotic Depressions: A Systematic Analysis of Multiple Criteria and Meanings. *American Journal of Psychiatry*, 1979, *136*, 57–61.

KNAPP, P. H. The Asthmatic and His Environment. *Journal of Nervous and Mental Diseases*, 1969, *149*, 133–151.

KNAPP, P., MATHÉ, S. A., and VACHON, L. Psychosomatic Aspects of Bronchial Asthma. In E. Weiss and M. Segal (eds.), *Bronchial Asthma: Mechanisms and Therapeutics*. Boston: Little, Brown, 1976, pp. 1055–1080.

KNAPP, T. J., and WELLS, L. A. Behavior Therapy for Asthma: A Review. *Behaviour Research and Therapy*, 1978, *16*, 103–115.

KOSTES, H., GLAUS, K. D., BRICEL, S. K., CRAWFORD, P. L., and EDWARDS, J. E. *Muscle Relaxation Effects on Peak Expiratory Flow Rate in Asthmatic Children*. Paper presented at annual meeting of the Biofeedback Society, Orlando, March 1977.

KOSTES, H., GLAUS, K. D., CRAWFORD, P. L., EDWARDS, J. E., and SCHERR, M. S. Operant Reduction of Frontalis EMG Activity in the Treatment of Asthma in Children. *Journal of Psychosomatic Research*, 1976, *20*, 453–459.

KURLANDER, L. F., and COLODNY, D. Pseudoneurosis in the Neurologically Handicapped Child. *American Journal of Orthopsychiatry*, 1965, *35*, 733–738.

LACEY, J. F., and LACEY, B. C. Verification and Extension of the Principle of Autonomic Response-Stereotypy. *American Journal of Psychology*, 1958, *71*, 50–73.

LACHMAN, S. J. *Psychosomatic Disorders: A Behavioristic Interpretation*. New York: John Wiley, 1972.

LAMONT, J., FISCHOFF, S., and GOTTLIEB, H. Recall of Parental Behaviors in Female Neurotic Depressives. *Journal of Clinical Psychology*, 1976, *32*, 762–765.

LAZARUS, A. A. *Behavior Therapy and Beyond*. New York: McGraw-Hill, 1971.

LAZARUS, A. A., DAVISON, G. C., and POLEFKA, D. A. Classical and Operant Factors in the Treatment of a School Phobia. *Journal of Abnormal Psychology*, 1965, *70*, 225–229.

LEFKOWITZ, M. M., and BURTON, N. Childhood Depression: A Critique of the Concept. *Psychological Bulletin*, 1978, *85*, 716–726.

LETON, D. A. Assessment of School Phobia. *Mental Hygiene*, 1962, *46*, 256–264.

LE UNES, A., and SIESGLUZ, S. Paraprofessional Treatment of School Phobia in a Young Adolescent Girl. *Adolescence*, 1977, *12*, 115–121.

LEVENTHAL, T., and SILLS, M. Self-image in School Phobia. *American Journal of Orthopsychiatry*, 1964, *34*, 685–695.

LIEBMAN, R., MINUCHIN, S., and BAKER, L. The Use of Structural Family Therapy in the Treatment of Intractable Asthma. *American Journal of Psychiatry*, 1974, *131*, 535–540.

LIPOWSKI, Z. J. Psychosomatic Medicine in the Seventies. An Overview. *American Journal of Psychiatry*, 1977, *134*, 233–244.

MASSERMAN, J. H. Experimental Neuroses. *Scientific American*, 1950, *182*, 38–43.

MELAMED, B., and JOHNSON, S. B. Behavioral Assessment of Chronic Illness: Asthma and Juvenile Diabetes. In E. Marsh and L. Terdal (eds.), *Behavioral Assessment of Childhood Disorders*. New York: Guilford Press, 1981, pp. 529–572.

MILLER, L. C., BARRETT, C. L., HAMPE, E., and NOBLE, H. Factor Structure of Childhood Fears. *Journal of Consulting and Clinical Psychology*, 1972, *39*, 264–268.

MILLER, L. C., BARRETT, C. L., and HAMPE, E. Phobias of Childhood in a Prescientific Era. In A. Davids (ed.), *Child Personality and Psychopathology: Current Topics*, Vol. 1. New York: John Wiley, 1974, pp. 89–134.

MILLER, N. E. Learning of Visceral and Glandular Responses. *Science*, 1969, *163*, 434–445.

MILLER, N. E., and BANUAZIZI, A. Instrumental Learning by Curarized Rats of a Specific Visceral Response, Intestinal or Cardiac. *Journal of Comparative and Physiological Psychology*, 1968, *65*, 1–7.

MINUCHIN, S., ROSMAN, B. L., and BAKER, L. *Psychosomatic Families: Anorexia Nervosa in Context*. Cambridge, Mass.: Harvard University Press, 1978.

MORRIS, R. J., and KRATOCHWILL, T. R. *Treating Children's Fears and Phobias*. New York: Pergamon Press, 1983.

MOSS, T., and EDWARDS, A. E. Conflict vs. Conditioning: Effects upon Peripheral Vascular Activity. *Psychosomatic Medicine*, 1964, *26*, 267–273.

MOWRER, O. H., and MOWRER, W. M. Enuresis: A Method for Its Study and Treatment. *American Journal of Orthopsychiatry*, 1938, *8*, 436–459.

MUSTACCHI, P., LUCIA, S. P., and JASSY, L. Bronchial Asthma: Patterns of Morbidity and Mortality in the United States; 1951–1959. *California Medicine*, 1962, *96*, 196–200.

MYERS, J. K., LINDENTHAL, J. J., and PEPPER, M. P. Life Events and Psychiatric Impairment. *Journal of Nervous and Mental Diseases*, 1971, *152*, 149–157.

NEEDLEMAN, H. L., and WABER, D. Amitryptyline Therapy in Patients with Anorexia Nervosa. *Lancet*, 1976, *2*, 580.

NICHOLS, K. A., and BERG, I. School Phobia and Self-evaluation. *Journal of Child Psychology and Psychiatry and Allied Disciplines*, 1970, *11*, 133–141.

OLLENDICK, T. H. Behavioral Treatment of Anorexia Nervosa: A 5-Year Study. *Behavior Modification*, 1979, *3*, 124–135.

PAVLOV, I. P. *Lectures on Conditioned Reflexes*, Vol. 1, trans. W. H. Gantt. London: Lawrence and Wishart, 1928.

PEARCE, J. Depressive Disorder in Childhood. *Journal of Child Psychology and Psychiatry*, 1977, *18*, 79–82.

PERTSCHUK, M. J., EDWARDS, N., and POMERLEAU, O. F. A Multiple-Baseline Approach to Behavioral Intervention in Anorexia Nervosa. *Behavior Therapy*, 1978, *9*, 368–376.

PLANTEY, F. Pinozide in Treatment of Anorexia Nervosa. *Lancet*, 1977, *1*, 1105.

POLLIN, W., ALLEN, M. G., HOFFER, A., STABENAU, J. R., and HRUBEC, Z. Psychopathology in 15,909 Pairs of Veteran Twins. Evidence for a Genetic Factor in the Pathogenesis of Schizophrenia and Its Relative Absence in Psychoneurosis. *American Journal of Psychiatry*, 1969, *126*, 597–609.

POMERANTZ, P. B., PETERSON, N. T., MARHOLIN, D., and STERN, S. The In Vivo Elimination of a Child's Water Phobia by a Paraprofessional at Home. *Journal of Behavior Therapy and Experimental Psychiatry*, 1977, *8*, 417–421.

POOLE, A. D., SANSON-FISCHER, R. W., and YOUNG, P. A Behavioural Programme for the Management of Anorexia Nervosa. *Australian and New Zealand Journal of Psychiatry*, 1978, *12*, 49–53.

PROCTOR, J. T. The Treatment of Hysteria in Childhood. In M. Hammer and A. M. Kaplan (eds.), *The Practice of Psychotherapy with Children*. Homewood, Ill.: Dorsey Press, 1967, pp. 121–150.

PROUT, H. T., and HARVEY, J. R. Applications of Desensitization Procedures for School Related Problems: A Review. *Psychology in the Schools*, 1978, *15*, 533–541.

PURCELL, K. Distinctions Between Subgroups of Asthmatic Children: Children's Perceptions of Events Associated with Asthma. *Pediatrics*, 1963, *31*, 486–495.

PURCELL, K. Childhood Asthma: The Role of Family Relationships, Personality, and Emotions. In A. Davids (ed.), *Child Personality and Psychopathology: Current*

Topics, Vol. 2. New York: John Wiley, 1975, pp. 1010–1035.

PURCELL, K., BERNSTEIN, L., and BURKANTZ, S. C. A Preliminary Comparison of Rapidly Remitting and Persistently "Steroid Dependent" Asthmatic Children. *Psychosomatic Medicine*, 1961, *23*, 305–310.

PURCELL, K., BRADY, K., CHAI, H., MASER, J., MOLK, K., GORDON, N., and MEANS, J. The Effect on Asthma in Children of Experimental Separation from the Family. *Psychosomatic Medicine*, 1969, *31*, 144–164.

PURCELL, K., and WEISS, J. H. Asthma. In C. G. Costello (ed.), *Symptoms of Psychopathology*. New York: John Wiley, 1970, pp. 601–602.

PURCELL, K., WEISS, J., and HAHN, W. Certain Psychosomatic Disorders. In B. B. Wolman (ed.), *Manual of Child Psychopathology*. New York: McGraw-Hill, 1972, pp. 706–740.

RACHMAN, S. Systematic Desensitization. *Psychological Bulletin*, 1967 67, 93–104.

RACKEMAN, F. H., and EDWARDS, M. D. Medical Progress: Asthma in Children: Follow-up Study of 688 Patients After 20 Years. *New England Journal of Medicine*, 1952, *246*, 815–858.

RAE, W. W. Childhood Conversion Reactions: A Review of Incidence in Pediatric Settings. *Journal of Clinical Child Psychology*, 1977, *6*, 66–72.

RAMPLING, D. Anorexia Nervosa: Reflections on Theory and Practice. *Psychiatry*, 1978, *41*, 296–301.

REDMOND, D. E., SWANN, A., and HENNINGER, G. R. Phenoxybenzamine in Anorexia Nervosa. *Lancet*, 1976, *2*, 307.

REES, L. The Importance of Psychological, Allergic, and Infective Factors in Childhood Asthma. *Journal of Psychosomatic Research*, 1964, *7*, 253–262.

REINHART, J. B., KENNA, M. D., and SUCCOP, R. A. Anorexia Nervosa in Children. *Journal of the American Academy of Child Psychiatry*, 1972, *11*, 114–131.

ROCK, N. L. Conversion Reactions in Childhood: A Clinical Study on Childhood Neuroses. *Journal of the American Academy of Child Psychiatry*, 1971, *10*, 65–93.

ROLLINS, N., and PIAZZA, E. Diagnosis of Anorexia Nervosa. *Journal of the American Academy of Child Psychiatry*, 1978, *17*, 126–137.

ROSEN, B. M., BARN, A. K., and CRAMER, M. Demographic and Diagnostic Characteristics of Psychiatric Clinic Outpatients in the U.S.A., 1961. *American Journal of Orthopsychiatry*, 1964, *34*, 455–468.

ROSMAN, B. L., MINUCHIN, S., BAKER, L., and LIEBMAN, R. A Family Approach to Anorexia Nervosa: Study, Treatment, and Outcome. In R. A. Vigersky (ed.), *Anorexia Nervosa*. New York: Raven Press, 1977, pp. 341–348.

RUTTER, M., TIZZARD, J., and WHITMORE, K. *Education, Health and Behaviour: Psychological and Medical Study of Childhood Development*. New York: John Wiley, 1970.

SABOT, L. M., PECK, R., and Raskin, J. The Waiting Room Society: A Study of Families and Children Applying to a Child Psychiatric Clinic. *Archives of General Psychiatry*, 1969, *21*, 25–32.

SAWREY, W. L., CONGER, J. J., and TURRELL, E. S. An Experimental Investigation of the Role of Psychological Factors in the Production of Gastric Ulcers in Rats. *Journal of Comparative and Physiological Psychology*, 1956, *49*, 457–461.

SAWREY, W. L., and WEISZ, J. D. An Experimental Method of Producing Gastric Ulcers. *Journal of Comparative and Physiological Psychology*, 1956, *49*, 269–270.

SCHEPANK, H. Hereditary and Environmental Influences in 50 Neurotic Pairs of Twins (English summary). *Zeitschrift fur Psychotherapie und Medizinische Psychologie*, 1971, *21*, 41–50.

SCHERER, M. W., and NAKAMURA, C. Y. A Fear Survey Schedule for Children (FSS-FC): A Factor Analytic Comparison with Manifest Anxiety (CMAS). *Behaviour Research and Therapy*, 1968, *6*, 173–182.

SELYE, H. *The Stress of Life*. New York: McGraw-Hill, 1956.

SELYE, H. Stress: It's a G.A.S. *Psychology Today*, 1969, 3(4), 24–26.

SHAPIRO, T., and JEGEDE, R. O. School Phobia: A Babel of Tongues. *Journal of Autism and Childhood Schizophrenia*, 1973, 3, 168–186.

SHAW, C. R. *The Psychiatric Disorders of Childhood*. New York: Appleton-Century Crofts, 1966, pp. 121–126.

SHIELDS, J., and SLATER, E. Heredity and Psychological Abnormality. In H. J. Eysenck (ed.), *Handbook of Abnormal Psychology*. New York: Basic Books, 1961, pp. 298–343.

SMITH, R. E., and SHARPE, T. M. Treatment of a School Phobia with Implosive Therapy. *Journal of Consulting and Clinical Psychology*, 1970, 35, 239–243.

SMITH, S. L. School Refusal with Anxiety: A Review of 63 Cases. *Canadian Psychiatric Association Journal*, 1970, *15*, 257–264.

SOLOMON, K., and HART, R. Pitfalls and Prospects in Clinical Research on Antianxiety Drugs: Benzodiazepines and Placebo–a Research Review. *Journal of Clinical Psychiatry*, 1978, 39, 823–831.

SPIEGEL, H. Is Symptom Removal Dangerous? *American Journal of Psychiatry*, 1967, *123*, 1279–1282.

SPITZ, R. A. Hospitalism: An Inquiry into the Genesis of Psychiatric Conditions in Early Childhood. *Psychoanalytic Study of the Child*, 1945, *1*, 53–74.

SPITZ, R. A., and WOLF, K. M. Anaclitic Depression: An Inquiry into the Genesis of Psychiatric Conditions in Early Childhood. *Psychoanalytic Study of the Child*, 1946, 2, 113–117.

STEIN, M. Etiology and Mechanisms in the Development of Asthma. In the First Hahnemann Symposium on Psychosomatic Medicine. Philadelphia: Lea and Febiger, 1962.

STEWART, D. N., and WINSER, D. M. Incidence of Perforated Peptic Ulcer: Effect of Heavy Air-raids. *Lancet*, 1942, *1*, 259–261.

TEMPLER, D. The Obsessive-Compulsive Neurosis:

Review of Research Findings. *Comprehensive Psychiatry,* 1972, *13,* 375–398.
THOMA, H. *Anorexia Nervosa.* New York: International Universities Press, 1967.
TIETZ, W. School Phobia and the Fear of Death. *Mental Hygiene,* 1970, *54,* 565–568.
TOLSTRUP, K. Treatment of Anorexia Nervosa in Childhood and Adolescence. *Journal of Child Psychology, Psychiatry, and Allied Disciplines,* 1975, *16,* 75–78.
TREUTING, T. F., and RIPLEY, H. S. Life Situations, Emotions and Bronchial Asthma. *Journal of Nervous and Mental Diseases,* 1948, *108,* 380–389.
TYRER, P., and TYRER, S. School Refusal, Truancy, and Adult Neurotic Illness. *Psychological Medicine,* 1974, *4,* 416–421.
VELTKAMP, L. *School Phobia. Journal of Family Counseling,* 1975, *3,* 47–51.
WALDRON, S. The Significance of Childhood Neurosis for Adult Mental Health: A Follow-up Study. *American Journal of Psychiatry,* 1976, *133,* 532–538.
WALDRON, S., SHRIER, D. K., STONE, B., and TOBIN, F. School Phobia and Other Childhood Neuroses: A Systematic Study of the Children and Their Families. *American Journal of Psychiatry,* 1975, *132,* 802–808.
WARREN, W. A Study of Anorexia Nervosa in Young Girls. *Journal of Child Psychology and Psychiatry,* 1968, *9,* 27–40.
WATSON, J. B., and RAYNER, R. Conditioned Emotional Reactions. *Journal of Experimental Psychology,* 1920, *3,* 1–14.
WHITE, R. T., DEMYER, W., and DEMYER, M. EEG Abnormalities in Early Childhood Schizophrenia: A Double-Blind Study of Psychiatrically Disturbed and Normal Children During Promazine Sedation. *American Journal of Psychiatry,* 1964, *120,* 950–958.
WINDHEUSER, H. J. Anxious Mothers as Models for Coping with Anxiety. *Behavioral Analysis and Modification,* 1977, *2,* 39–58.
WOLFF, H. G. Life Stress and Cardiovascular Disorders. *Circulation,* 1950, *1,* 187–203.
WOLPE, J. *Psychotherapy by Reciprocal Inhibition.* Stanford: Stanford University Press, 1958.
WOLPE, J. *The Practice of Behavior Therapy,* 2nd ed. New York: Pergamon Press, 1973.

Part 5 CLINICAL SYNDROMES OF ADOLESCENCE AND YOUTH

13

ABNORMALITIES OF ADOLESCENCE AND YOUTH

Delinquency, Drug Abuse, and Suicide

PROLOGUE

Gather ye rosebuds while ye may,
Old time is still a-flying;
And this same flower that smiles today
Tomorrow will be dying.

The glorious lamp of heaven, the sun,
The higher he's a-getting,
The sooner will his race be run
And nearer he's to setting.

That age is best which is the first,
When youth and blood are warmer;
But being spent, the worse, and worst
Times still succeed the former.

Then be not coy, but use your time,
And, while ye may, go marry;
For, having lost but once your prime,
You may forever tarry.

Robert Herrick

The poet's admonition to fully enjoy one's youth while it lasts is echoed by our cultural expectations that this developmental period be used fruitfully to produce adults who will be responsible and productive citizens. But adolescence is also a period when young people are placed in limbo; they are not regarded as children, yet they are not quite ready to assume the responsibilities of adulthood. It is a stage of life that is not the same in all cultures. In some societies adolescence is characterized by an uneventful and untroubled transition from childhood to adulthood, while in our society, it is a very stressful and tumultuous period. The time span can be very brief, or it may even be omitted in societies that are well organized around the family and tightly controlled by their elders. Under these circumstances the role of the adolescent in the family and in the community is relatively fixed, leaving little room for experimentation or mobility (Cavan and Cavan, 1968). The rite of passage into adulthood usually occurs at the time of physical maturity and, in some instances, after a ritualistic period of formal initiation. In fact, before the twentieth century adolescence was almost nonexistent in our culture as a separate stage of development. However, later advances in technology, and industrialization, have lengthened the period of adolescence considerably to meet the demands of training for vocational specialization.

Prolongation of adolescence has kept many young people dependent on their families (at least financially) not only during high school but through most of the college years as well. Our society provides no well-structured role for its adolescents, and none that recognizes them either as useful citizens or as contributors to the community. Instead, a nagging public uneasiness exists about the activities of young people, which periodically focuses on a particular issue. Some years ago this was reflected in the results of a Gallup Poll (June 1970) in which "campus unrest" aroused such intense reactions that it was considered our country's major problem (Keniston, 1975). Although this no longer is an issue, young people of each generation express dissatisfaction and disenchantment with some aspects of the adult world, and many are quite hesitant to join it. "Far from seeking adult prerogatives of their parents, they vehemently demand a virtually indefinite prolongation of their nonadult state" (Keniston, 1975, p. 8).

With its rapid and dramatic physical changes, especially in the development of adult sexual characteristics, puberty marks the beginning of adolescence. However, before this period is over, profound social and psychological changes occur that can affect the young person's self-perception, relationships with peers and others, self-control, autonomy and independence, academic and vocational competence, and sexual adjustment. Conflicts between parents and the adolescent are common, particularly conflicts involving the relinquishing of parental authority as the youngster tries to assume more freedom and adult privileges. The specific battle may be over the choice of friends, over clothes and appearance, or over such restrictions as those pertaining to dating, curfew, and the use of the family car. Inevitably, the power struggle generates resentment, resistance, and sometimes rebellion. In addition, there are internal conflicts that are concerned with impulse control, shifting moral standards, self-acceptance and inadequacy, and the uncertainty of goals and directions. From all indications, more than enough turmoil and volatility exist during this transitional period to produce a variety of serious behavioral problems.

In this chapter we shall focus on *delinquency, drug abuse,* and *suicide* as major problems of adolescence and youth that appear to have reached growing proportions in both frequency and severity.

DELINQUENCY

Tom, a sixteen-year-old high schooler, was sent to a state hospital by the juvenile court after being charged with illegal possession of a pistol that was used in the fatal shooting of a child. Tom told several versions of what happened, although it was clear that he had found an old German Luger and a box of bullets while rummaging through closets of a neighbor's home. Pleased with his find and eager to show them off, Tom took them to the school playground where he met a little girl who lived in the neighborhood. The child did not believe that the gun was real, so Tom loaded it. At this point the story becomes confused, although there is no doubt that the gun went off, hitting her in the temple and killing her instantaneously. When she fell to the ground, Tom became frightened and fled the scene on his bicycle. He threw the pistol and bullets away in a deserted lot, and then returned to the playground to see if he could help the wounded child. By this time the police had arrived after being summoned by people who had heard the shot and saw Tom riding away. Apparently no one had witnessed the shooting. Initially Tom accused another boy of the crime and calmly maintained that he had just arrived for the first time. He later admitted that he did the shooting, although he insisted that it was accidental. He took the police to the abandoned gun and said that he was too frightened to tell the truth earlier.

Tom had a checkered history of attending many schools and of being a behavior problem in each. He was disrespectful to teachers, restless, very active, and involved in frequent fights and truancy. Outside of school he was also given to fighting and destructiveness. He lied and blamed others for any of his misbehaviors, even when he stole things and was apprehended with the objects in his possession. He was born out of wedlock and abandoned by his mother at birth. For the first seven years of his life, he was brought up in a large orphanage that provided minimal care. Prior to his legal adoption, he was placed twice but returned on each occasion because he had difficulties adjusting to siblings and other children in the neighborhood or because the foster parents did not like him. His adoptive parents worked and moved frequently, so that he was left at the homes of either relatives or neighbors and was enrolled in numerous new schools. For a long time Tom did not feel that he really belonged to them. (Reprinted with permission of Macmillan Publishing Co., Inc., from *Patterns of Psychopathology* by M. Zax and G. Stricker. Copyright © 1963 by Macmillan Publishing Co., Inc.)

Tom's present difficulties, along with his chronic history of acting-out behaviors, represent a familiar pattern to most juvenile jurists, although the details of the story may differ from one youngster to another. As an abandoned and unloved child, Tom only gained attention when he responded in aggressive and antisocial ways. He did not have the benefit of parental models who could show him socially acceptable behaviors or who could provide him with a sense of belonging and security. He was a delinquent, but strictly speaking, delinquency, much like the word *insanity*, is a legal and not a psychological term. It refers to the commission of an act by a minor that otherwise would be regarded as criminal if committed by an adult. Delinquent behavior also may include acts that are illegal specifically for minors (such as running away). In popular usage *delinquency* is an ambiguous and catch-all label that may well suggest different meanings to different people. For some it may refer to young men with long hair and beards, or describe a wide range of mischievous acts (such as egging a car on Halloween), while to others it may mean teenagers who rob, steal, or murder. Even a legal definition lacks precision in light of the fact that statutory provisions differ widely among the states, and enforcement procedures and practices are noticeably heterogeneous. The tendency of different agencies and disciplines to formulate their own views of delinquent conduct further complicates the definitional problem (Eldefonso, 1972). For example, law enforcers may classify delinquents into two groups: those impulsive and/or immature youngsters who commit a delinquent act for the first time and respond to corrective measures; and those incorrigible recidivists who have failed to respond to many previous remedial efforts. Educators may view delinquency as academic underachievement as well as disruptive and unmanageable behavior in the classroom, while many psychologists may be inclined to think of delinquency as a manifestation of some abnormal condition.

Problems with Incidence Data

It is apparent from the above discussion that the incidence of delinquency should vary with its definition; that is, estimates should differ depending on whether we view delinquents as minors committing illegal acts, as academic underachievers, or as youngsters repeatedly convicted for antisocial behaviors. Almost all youngsters at one time or another are guilty of some unlawful behavior, whether it be shoplifting, engaging in sex with a minor, vandalism, or smoking pot. However, there are fewer who are underachievers in a school population, and probably even a smaller number who are incorrigible recidivists. Incidence data also will be affected by differences in state laws with respect to the type of offenses and the age criterion used to define a minor over whom the juvenile court has jurisdiction. In addition, communities differ in the availability of child-related service agencies that function as alternatives to the court and that are equipped to deal with cases of delinquency. Unfortunately, juvenile offenders who are handled by agencies other than the police or the courts are not included in the primary data that describe the problem. Thus, it is important to note that we have no precise measure of either crime or delinquency, although we do have estimates that are based on records maintained by law enforcement agencies and the juvenile courts.

The Magnitude and Seriousness of Delinquency[1]

In 1973 slightly more than 1 million youngsters under eighteen were arrested and came before our nation's juvenile courts for a variety of criminal acts excluding traffic offenses. Eight years later, in 1981, the number of juvenile arrests dramatically increased to just over 2 million cases, which represents 20 percent of all recorded arrests for that year. Table 13–1 gives a further breakdown of arrests in 1981 by age and by criminal act. Estimates of arrests of youngsters under eighteen are even higher if one includes cases of delinquency that never appear on arrest and court records because they have been handled discreetly by the police and the family. The fact that the rate of delinquency continues to rise sharply with each passing year is alarming. It increased 106 percent between 1960 and 1970, a considerably faster rate than the growth (28 percent) in the number of children falling into this age group during the same period of time. In the thirteen-year period between 1960 and 1973, crime increased for all ages some 35 percent, whereas the increase for youngsters under eighteen was an astronomical 144 percent. A breakdown of arrests by type of offense and age for this period is provided in Table 13–2, which shows that almost all offenses increased more rapidly for youngsters under eighteen than for adults. The most recent figures (1981) shown in Table 13–1 indicate an additional increase between 1973 and 1981 of just under 50 percent.

Does the increase in delinquency over the years merely reflect a sharp rise in minor offenses? If we could answer yes to this question, we would be consoled by the fact that things are not as grave as they might seem. Unfortunately, the data do not support this conjecture but instead provide ample justification for serious public concern about delinquency and crime in this country. While all types of offenses (combined) more than doubled between 1960 and 1970, and doubled again between 1973 and 1981, serious acts such as criminal homicide, forcible rape, burglary, robbery, aggravated assault, larceny, and auto theft together increased some 95 percent between 1960 and 1970, and another 61 percent between 1973 and 1981. Major crimes against persons and property have increased substantially in the past two decades, as have less serious crimes such as forgery and

[1]Information reported in this section is based primarily on three publications: *Juvenile Court Statistical Series*, 1970; *Uniform Crime Reports*, 1973; and *Crime in the United States: Uniform Crime Reports*, 1981.

Table 13-1 Total Arrests, Distribution by Age, 1981

[12,811 agencies; 1981 estimated population 214,369,000]

Offense charged	*Total all ages*	*Ages under 15*	*Ages under 18*	*Ages 18 and over*	*Age*						
					Under 10	*10–12*	*13–14*	*15*	*16*	*17*	*18*
TOTAL	10,293,575	623,018	2,035,748	8,257,827	53,931	153,993	415,094	375,216	483,674	553,840	596,937
Percent distribution	100.0	6.1	19.8	80.2	.5	1.5	4.0	3.6	4.7	5.4	5.8
Murder and non-negligent manslaughter	20,432	205	1,858	18,574	8	27	170	305	533	815	1,024
Forcible rape	30,050	1,193	4,449	25,601	56	213	924	857	1,115	1,284	1,499
Robbery	147,396	10,250	42,214	105,182	271	2,016	7,963	8,563	11,228	12,173	12,264
Aggravated assault	266,948	10,458	37,332	229,616	826	2,542	7,090	6,529	9,202	11,143	12,028
Burglary	489,533	71,782	208,650	280,883	5,874	18,581	47,327	40,591	47,639	48,638	42,453
Larceny-theft	1,197,845	172,064	417,346	780,499	16,870	51,020	104,174	74,135	84,078	87,069	79,402
Motor vehicle theft	122,188	11,913	49,449	72,739	244	1,585	10,084	11,552	13,413	12,571	9,861
Arson	19,632	5,014	8,210	11,152	1,422	1,533	2,059	1,062	1,051	1,083	928
Violent crime	464,826	22,106	85,853	378,973	1,161	4,798	16,147	16,254	22,078	25,415	26,815
Percent distribution	100.0	4.8	18.5	81.5	.2	1.0	3.5	3.5	4.7	5.5	5.8
Property crime	1,828,928	260,773	683,655	1,145,273	24,410	72,719	163,644	127,340	146,181	149,361	132,644
Percent distribution	100.0	14.3	37.4	62.6	1.3	4.0	8.9	7.0	8.0	8.2	7.3
Crime Index total	2,293,754	282,879	769,508	1,524,246	25,571	77,517	179,791	143,594	168,259	174,776	159,459
Percent distribution	100.0	12.3	33.5	66.5	1.1	3.4	7.8	6.3	7.3	7.6	7.0

Other assaults	466,359	28,163	79,259	387,100	2,464	7,473	18,226	14,366	16,803	19,927	20,486
Forgery and counterfeiting	81,429	1,468	8,625	72,804	47	318	1,103	1,534	2,204	3,419	4,215
Fraud	272,900	4,639	14,158	258,742	87	741	3,811	4,599	1,854	3,066	6,324
Embezzlement	8,170	162	824	7,346	7	38	117	95	217	350	411
Stolen property; buying, receiving, possessing	122,452	9,074	33,003	89,449	387	1,864	6,823	6,449	8,241	9,239	9,506
Vandalism	228,849	53,908	108,555	120,294	8,884	17,722	27,302	17,419	18,791	18,437	14,700
Weapons; carrying, possessing, etc.	170,660	6,294	25,422	145,238	278	1,271	4,745	4,654	6,419	8,055	9,334
Prostitution and commercialized vice	103,134	311	3,030	100,104	13	48	250	409	765	1,545	4,789
Sex offenses (except forcible rape and prostitution)	68,365	4,386	11,291	57,074	341	1,051	2,994	1,994	2,377	2,534	2,668
Drug abuse violations	586,646	13,812	96,231	490,415	179	1,436	12,197	16,880	27,854	37,685	45,809
Gambling	40,959	160	1,371	39,588	5	14	141	204	393	614	828
Offenses against family and children	51,908	1,378	2,399	49,509	875	203	300	282	375	364	1,630
Driving under the influence	1,422,342	552	28,602	1,393,740	146	71	335	925	6,888	20,237	47,317
Liquor laws	453,356	9,469	138,503	314,853	143	701	8,625	18,148	42,519	68,367	74,199
Drunkenness	1,088,875	3,295	37,748	1,051,127	183	311	2,801	4,994	10,160	19,299	38,784
Disorderly conduct	748,603	30,603	115,803	632,800	2,363	7,524	20,716	20,240	27,374	37,586	47,029
Vagrancy	31,706	899	3,590	28,116	38	181	680	677	928	1,086	1,838
All other offenses (except traffic)	1,801,740	90,106	318,752	1,482,988	8,431	20,638	61,037	59,513	80,988	88,145	106,586
Suspicion	15,468	880	3,174	12,294	96	178	606	616	748	930	1,025
Curfew and loitering law violations	90,599	21,519	90,599	....	634	3,825	17,060	18,937	27,203	22,940	....
Runaways	145,301	59,061	145,301	....	2,759	10,868	45,434	38,687	32,314	15,239	....

Adapted from *Crime in the United States: Uniform Crime Reports,* 1981, p. 171.

Table 13-2 Total Arrest Trends, 1960-1973—2,378 agencies; 1973 [population 94,251,000[1]]

Offense charged	*Number of persons arrested*								
	Total all ages			*Under 18 years of age*			*18 years of age and over*		
	1960	*1973*	*Percent Change*	*1960*	*1973*	*Percent Change*	*1960*	*1973*	*Percent Change*
TOTAL	3,242,574	4,381,968	+ 35.1	466,174	1,138,046	+ 144.1	2,776,400	3,243,922	+ 16.0
Criminal homicide:									
Murder and nonnegligent manslaughter	4,541	10,629	+134.1	337	1,197	+ 255.2	4,204	9,432	+124.4
Manslaughter by negligence	1,766	1,660	− 6.0	132	216	+ 63.6	1,634	1,444	− 11.6
Forcible rape	6,857	13,823	+101.6	1,185	2,753	+ 132.3	5,672	11,070	+ 95.2
Robbery	31,197	83,012	+166.1	7,352	29,336	+ 299.0	23,845	53,676	+125.1
Aggravated assault	50,402	108,076	+114.4	6,306	19,306	+ 206.2	44,096	88,770	+101.3
Burglary—breaking or entering	117,084	211,029	+ 80.2	55,149	112,606	+ 104.2	61,935	98,423	+ 58.9
Larceny—theft	190,443	431,506	+126.6	91,375	204,913	+ 124.3	99,068	226,593	+128.7
Auto theft	54,202	87,975	+ 62.3	32,939	49,747	+ 51.0	21,263	38,228	+ 79.8
Violent crime [2]	92,997	215,540	+131.8	15,180	52,592	+ 246.5	77,817	162,948	+109.4
Property crime [3]	361,729	730,510	+101.9	179,463	367,266	+ 104.6	182,266	363,244	+ 99.3
Subtotal for above offenses	456,492	947,710	+107.6	194,775	420,074	+ 115.7	261,717	527,636	+101.6

Other assaults	115,156	182,985	+ 58.9	11,938	36,287	+ 204.0	103,218	146,698	+ 42.1
Forgery and counterfeiting	21,329	28,175	+ 32.1	1,502	3,081	+ 105.1	19,827	25,094	+ 26.6
Fraud and embezzlement	30,551	56,208	+ 84.0	779	2,376	+ 205.0	29,772	53,832	+ 80.8
Stolen property; buying, receiving, possessing	9,147	48,141	+426.3	2,531	15,925	+ 529.2	6,616	32,216	+386.9
Weapons; carrying, possessing, etc.	30,865	85,749	+177.8	6,353	13,950	+ 119.6	24,512	71,799	+192.9
Prostitution and commercialized vice	24,331	40,354	+ 65.9	413	1,595	+ 286.2	23,918	38,759	+ 62.0
Sex offenses (except forcible rape and prostitution)	39,582	35,693	− 9.8	8,738	7,078	− 19.0	30,844	28,615	− 7.2
Narcotic drug laws	29,889	328,670	+999.6	1,725	82,340	+4673.3	28,164	246,330	+774.6
Gambling	105,607	43,983	− 58.4	1,230	1,239	+ .7	104,377	42,744	− 59.0
Offenses against family and children	35,906	24,063	− 33.0	697	523	− 25.0	35,209	23,540	− 33.1
Driving under the influence	142,698	413,837	+190.0	1,125	5,640	+ 401.3	141,573	408,197	+188.3
Liquor laws	81,735	109,392	+ 33.8	17,207	43,329	+ 151.8	64,528	66,063	+ 2.4
Drunkenness	1,215,555	837,551	− 31.1	12,209	22,959	+ 88.0	1,203,346	814,592	− 32.3
Disorderly conduct	364,289	317,531	− 12.8	46,271	69,864	+ 51.0	318,018	247,667	− 22.1
Vagrancy	127,643	40,508	− 68.3	7,151	4,089	− 42.8	120,492	36,419	− 69.8
All other offenses (except traffic)	411,799	841,418	+104.3	151,530	407,697	+ 169.1	260,269	433,721	+ 66.6
Suspicion (not included in totals)	123,196	30,876	− 74.9	22,651	9,430	− 58.4	100,545	21,446	− 78.7

1 Based on comparable reports from 1,854 cities representing 79,540,000 population and 524 counties representing 14,711,000 population.

2 Violent crime is offenses of murder, forcible rape, robbery, and aggravated assault.

3 Property crime is offenses of burglary, larceny, and auto theft.

* *Uniform Crime Reports,* 1973, p. 124–125.

counterfeiting; fraud and embezzlement; buying, receiving, or possessing stolen property; prostitution and other sex offenses (except forcible rape); violation of narcotic drug and liquor laws; drunkenness, and disorderly conduct.

When we think of crime and delinquency, we tend to regard them as almost the exclusive property of urban centers, and especially of the inner cities. To some extent this view is supported by the data, which shows that delinquency is between two and three times greater in cities than in other areas. However, rural areas are no longer as safe and secure as they once were. In 1969 there was a 16 percent increase in delinquency in rural areas, and rural juvenile courts were busier than ever, showing a higher percent increase in such cases than either urban or semiurban courts. If there once was a haven from this problem there is now no area of the country that is unaffected. The rise in delinquency continues everywhere, and it seems to be spreading rapidly to our rural areas.

Over the years delinquency has been predominantly a male problem by a ratio of about 4:1, although the incidence of girls' delinquency has sharply increased—by 1970 the ratio was reduced to approximately 3:1. Between 1969 and 1970 arrests for girls under eighteen increased more than twice as much as did arrests for boys (10 percent as compared to 5 percent), and this increase was equally evident in urban, semiurban, and rural courts. Figures obtained in 1981 indicate that young men under eighteen account for approximately 19 percent of all male arrests, while young women under eighteen represent 25 percent of all female arrests. These data support the idea that young women (under eighteen) proportionally account for more of the female crimes than do young men for male arrests, and that the rate of crime is increasing more rapidly for young women than for young men. In fact, since 1965 delinquency cases involving girls have increased by 78 percent, as compared to a 44 percent increase for boys. Moreover, the rise in arrests of girls under eighteen was considerably higher than for boys for both *violent* and *property* crimes. Perhaps this is a reflection of society's changing attitude toward females, who no longer are expected to assume passive, dependent, and compliant roles and functions.

Types of Delinquency

Through the years investigators have recognized delinquency as a diverse and broad category that could be better studied, understood, and controlled if more specific and homogeneous subgroups could be identified. Attempts to grapple with the problem have failed to yield uniform results because of the differences in research purposes, procedures, and kinds of data gathered. For example, the classification of delinquent behavior in terms of statutory violations necessarily must result in typologies that are different from those designed to classify delinquency on the basis of the social factors, or those that search for its hereditary and physical characteristics (Reed and Baali, 1972).

For more than thirty years Jenkins and his collaborators have studied the clinical case records of large samples of delinquents who were either seen as outpatients of child guidance clinics or as residents of a training school (Jenkins and Hewitt, 1944); Jenkins and Boyer, 1968; Jenkins, 1973). Influenced by a Freudian view of personality development, Jenkins hypothesized three types of delinquency that he considered to be the products of different early family-child relationships. He clinically judged data from the case records and later intercorrelated them for clusters of associated personality traits and family backgrounds. This procedure led to the identification of the following three major clusters for both boys and girls.

Type I. *The Socialized Delinquent* (or cooperative delinquent, pseudosocial delinquent, or gang delinquent) refers to children of normal personality structure and function who are not different in this regard from matched nondelinquent youngsters. Their inclination toward antisocial behavior is part of their socialization within a delinquent group to which they are extremely loyal, while they hold no sense of obligation toward members of any other group. These youngsters are the product of inadequate parental supervision, discipline, and control, and of families in which there is little cohesion, involvement, or loyalty.

Type II. *The Unsocialized Delinquent* (or psychopathic personality or unsocialized-aggressive type) refers to those who have inadequate internal control over their impulses and who are likely to display open hostility toward others. They are selfish, boastful, defiant, self-indulgent, and inclined to act out without feelings of guilt or remorse. Their hostilities and bitterness are attributable to early and continued parental rejection (especially by the mother), and to an atmosphere of disharmony and instability in the home, where parents are unaffectionate, hot-tempered, and abusive. In a few cases there is evidence of brain damage or neurological impairment.

Type III. *The Overinhibited Delinquent* (or neurotic delinquent) is a child characterized by internal conflict and anxiety stemming from an overly developed tendency to inhibit the expression of feelings and impulses. Their antisocial behaviors are considered to be manifestations of severe internal conflicts, although it is not at all clear why delinquent behavior appears in some and neurosis is evident in others. These youngsters come from cold, rigid, socially disciplined, and excessively repressed home environments in which they can gain approval only by being very good and inhibited. Neurotic symptoms such as sleep disturbances, fears, shyness, and seclusiveness are likely to be evident in early childhood, while later these youngsters are apt to have night terrors, anxiety attacks, or in some instances conversion symptoms.

Quay, both in collaboration with Peterson and Tiffany and independently, employed a different methodology (factor analysis) to identify distinguishing personality characteristics among delinquents (Peterson, Quay, and Tiffany, 1961; Quay, 1964, 1966). The results of this work revealed three broad personality types that are quite similar to those reported by Jenkins, although the labels attached to the types are different. However, there is general agreement among these researchers as to the personality descriptions that are associated with each type of delinquent behavior. Table 13–3 summarizes the major personality traits and family characteristics for each of the three types of delinquency.

Factors Related to Delinquent Behaviors

Attempts to investigate the relationship between delinquent behavior and a host of sociological, psychological, biological, and legal variables have been voluminous. Yet the literature is not without its share of methodological limitations, thus producing contradictory results and erroneous or overstated conclusions. In considering the summary of the major findings, we should bear in mind that these data reflect associational, and not causal, evidence.

Socioeconomic Level. Studies done in England, Germany, and the United States consistently indicate an inverse relationship between socioeconomic level and delinquency (especially as reported for boys) (McDonald, 1969; Remschmidt et al., 1977; Achenbach and Edelbrock, 1981). While delinquency appears to be highly related to a background of socioeconomic deprivation, there are noteworthy qualifications that tend to reduce both the potency and clarity of this factor (*The Challenge of Crime in a Free Society*, 1967). To begin with, the relationship may be restricted to populations of delinquent youngsters drawn from large cities, inasmuch as studies conducted in small cities

Table 13-3 Personality and Family Characteristics of Delinquency Types

Gang Delinquent	*Psychopathic*	*Neurotic*
Stable lower-class homes in communities that sanction delinquent conduct.	Lack of guilt or remorse for acts.	Behavior is prompted by prolonged internal conflicts and anxieties.
Basically of normal personality, except for antisocial acts.	Defective moral development.	Parents are often middle class, but cold, rigid, disciplined, and repressive.
Select undesirable models with whom to identify.	Impulsivity and acting out without internal controls. Often in trouble in school and with police.	Homes are hostile and unloving, and sometimes delinquency is unconsciously encouraged by parents.
Steadfast loyalty to their group, with no sense of loyalty to others.	Rebellious and defiant of authority.	Delinquent acts are ordinarily committed alone.
Most crimes committed in groups.	Make favorable impression as outgoing, gregarious, and manipulative.	
Values are high for duping others, physical prowess, defiance, excitement and thrills, and taking chances.	Self-centered, selfish, and self-serving.	
Their patterns reflect those of the lower-class culture in which they were reared.	Unable to postpone or delay pleasure or gratification.	
	Disharmony and instability in the home. Parents are unaffectionate and apt to be hot-tempered and abusive. Parental rejection is frequent and longstanding.	

Table based on findings in Jenkins, 1973. Courtesy of Chas. C Thomas, Publisher, Springfield, Illinois.

and in local communities failed to support the notion that delinquency is largely a phenomenon of lower socioeconomic groups (Clark and Wenninger, 1962; Erickson and Empey, 1965). In addition, the urban relationship may simply reflect differing law enforcement practices and the availability of nonjudicial community agencies in dealing with lower-middle and lower-class offenders. Middle- and upper-class youngsters are more likely to be the beneficiaries of more liberal enforcement policies, and they have greater access to alternative forms of intervention than inner-city impoverished children. In fact, several studies have shown that there is no difference in socioeconomic levels when unrecorded instances of delinquent behavior are obtained through an anonymous questionnaire procedure (Empey and Erickson, 1966; Haney and Gold, 1973; Empey, 1978).

Family and Home Environment. Substantially more delinquent than nondelinquent children come from broken homes in which one parent is absent through death, separation, divorce, or desertion (Anderson, 1968; Glueck and Glueck, 1968; Cortes and Gatti, 1972). This is particularly true within families of low socioeconomic status. It is interesting to note that many of the delinquent youngsters were between the ages of four and seven when the break occurred, suggesting that family instability may be more damaging to personality development in early childhood than in the later years. Obviously, not every broken home is the same, nor is it necessarily one in which disorganization, tension, discord, or unhappiness exists. However, the fact remains that children reared in homes that are stable, cohesive, warm, loving, and happy are not likely to become involved in delinquent behavior (*The Challenge of Crime in a Free Society*, 1967).

Several forms of parental discipline have been found to be related to delinquency (McCord, McCord, and Zola, 1969; Glueck and Glueck, 1968; Trojanowicz, 1973; Hetherington, and Martin, 1979). Permissiveness provides the child with an early opportunity to establish independent patterns of action without parental interference or restrictions. When the child's freedom is challenged or threatened by the demands of authority figures outside of the home, the child, being accustomed to behaving in terms of his or her own rules, tends to react with resentment, hostility, and open defiance. Extreme strictness, in which physical punishment is used more than verbal discussion, may produce negative attitudes toward parents, which, in turn, will reduce the child's desire to conform to parental wishes and to behave in ways that will please parents. However, parental control that lacks consistency appears to be the most damaging factor: It is the most frequent parental pattern found in delinquent children. When parents vacillate, the child may lose respect for parental authority and control, lack consistent guidelines for behaving in a socially acceptable manner, and assume that he or she can avoid the consequences of his or her acts because it is unlikely that parents will respond in any consistent way (Aichhorn, 1969).

But more important than discipline as a correlate of delinquency is the affective quality of the parent-child relationship. As succinctly stated by Gibbons: "Scientific candor compels us to conclude that the link between parental rejection and aggressive conduct is one of the more firmly established generalizations concerning delinquency" (Gibbons, 1970, p. 202). The failure of the delinquent boy to gain the favor and affection of his father appears to be a particularly significant background factor. Fathers of delinquent boys are rejecting and prone to be physically punitive to the extent that they arouse in their sons feelings of bitterness and hostility and aggressive antisocial behaviors as a means of retaliation (Hetherington and Martin, 1979).

Rejecting and abusive fathers are difficult to model or identify with, not only because of their poor relationships with their sons but also because they often are unemployed, alcoholic, or otherwise ineffective "heads" of their families. Glueck and Glueck (1968) observed that fewer than two out of ten of the delinquents they studied regarded their fathers as the sort of men they would like to emulate, as contrasted to more than half of the nondelinquents, who viewed their fathers as positive models.

A relationship between delinquency and emotional instability of parents has also been reported (Glueck and Glueck, 1968; Aichhorn, 1969; Freeman and Savastona, 1970). Parental personality problems are likely to interfere with family relationships and with child-rearing practices in diverse ways. Especially in times of stress, the probability is high that psychotic, neurotic, alcoholic, retarded, or other seriously disturbed parents will be inconsistent, neglectful, and rejecting in both attitude and behavior toward their children. They may unconsciously encourage acting-out behaviors, or they may fail to provide the necessary sanctions and prohibitions that help to distinguish acceptable from unacceptable actions, or that serve as models for antisocial responses. Emotional instability in one or both parents is not only a frequent background finding of delinquent youngsters but also a characteristic that can be traced to the previous generation of parents (Aichhorn, 1969).

School Performance. Delinquent youngsters are generally recognized as poor academic performers in school, although as a group they do not differ from nondelinquents in intelligence or achievement test scores (Hathaway and Monachesi, 1963; Elliott, 1966; Elliott, Voss, and Wendling, 1966). There is a consistently reported relationship between school dropout rate and delinquency; the delinquency rate for dropouts is estimated to be ten times higher than the rate obtained for the total youth population (Schreiber, 1963; Jeffrey and Jeffrey, 1970). Lack of interest, carelessness, restlessness, tardiness, truancy, misconduct in school, and avoidance of anticipated failure are some of the reasons offered to explain delinquents' academic retardation. It is interesting to note that in a large-scale study of urban schoolchildren, early adolescents (between twelve and thirteen years of age) exhibited more self-consciousness, increased instability of self-image, lower self-esteem, and less favorable reactions by other people than did younger children (Simmons, Rosenberg, and Rosenberg, 1973). In addition, these findings were more pronounced for those early adolescents who entered junior high school as compared to those who continued on in elementary school (through the eighth grade) until entering high school.

Because of the poor school performance, and the high dropout rate associated with delinquent youngsters, it has been conjectured that their delinquent behavior is etiologically linked to learning disabilities. A recent study compared institutionalized delinquent boys between the ages of fifteen and eighteen with a matched group of nondelinquents on a battery of tests designed to assess neuropsychological functioning (on the grounds that certain deficits in functioning are associated with specific learning disabilities) (Berman and Siegal, 1976). Differences in test scores were found between the two groups of boys; more specifically, the delinquents were poorer in verbal intelligence, perceptual organization, and comprehension than the matched nondelinquent controls. In addition, twice as many delinquents as controls were found to have a specific learning disability. Largely on the basis of follow-up data and findings from retrospective studies, a relationship between hyperactivity, especially in childhood, and antisocial behavior in late adolescence or adulthood has been reported (Cantwell, 1978). While this finding may hold for some delinquent youngsters, especially those who are neurophysiologically underaroused, it is quite apparent that there are other hyperactive youngsters who evidence no antisocial behavior and who do not become delinquents. In addition, there are many delinquent adolescents for whom no earlier history of hyperactivity is apparent.

Biological Factors. As early as 1949 Sheldon, Hartl, and McDermott (1949) found a significant relationship between the mesomorphic (muscular) body type and delinquency. While Sheldon's findings were soundly criticized on methodological grounds, the Gluecks (1956) and others (Gibbens, 1963; Cortes and Gatti, 1972) have consistently obtained the same results, in spite of the fact that these studies used different criteria and methods to measure body type. Moreover, mesomorphs describe themselves as aggressive, active, adventurous, and impulsive, which are temperamental traits that have been found to be associated with delinquency (Cortes and Gatti, 1972).

Recent studies have shown that the presence of an extra Y chromosome is related to the increased probability of some psychological disorder in males, although little agreement exists as to the specific type of personality aberration (Hook, 1973; Dalgard and

Kringlen, 1976). In spite of the fact that criminal behavior was found in many of these males, more research is needed to clarify the relationship. The current evidence is not sufficient to support the view that chromosomal abnormality plays a significant role in delinquent behavior.

Abnormal brain waves (EEG), especially positive spike patterns that occur at fourteen and six waves per second, have been observed in youngsters who manifest aggressive antisocial behaviors. However, inasmuch as this pattern occurs in approximately 50 percent of normal adolescents, its meaning and significance are greatly obscured (Solomon, 1967).

ETIOLOGICAL CONSIDERATIONS

From what has been said thus far, it should be apparent that there is no simple, single causal explanation of delinquency. Behaviors that are so inclusive, diverse, and intricately related to so many other variables must, in all likelihood, have multiple origins. At present there are three prominent approaches to the etiology of delinquent behavior that reflect a sociological, psychological, or multidiscipline view. As we summarize the major positions within each approach, it is important to note that these explanations should be considered not as oppositional approaches but rather as alternative and supplementary ways of looking at the same problem.

Sociological Views

While only several of these formulations can be reviewed here, they all emphasize (although different in details) the contributions of the external environment as the primary cause of delinquency. While this approach deals effectively with the questions of how and why crime occurs in a society, it offers little explanation about how a particular individual becomes delinquent.

Thrasher (1936) suggested that delinquent gangs arise from playgroups during adolescence as a result of conflict with other groups, and as an organized means of banding individuals together to protect their rights and to satisfy needs that are not being met by their environments. Gangs fester in permissive and poorly controlled settings and in environments where adult crime is sanctioned. Thrasher also noted that members of the gang studied were involved in nondelinquent and normal teenage activities much of the time.

Other theorists have focused on lower-class youngsters and their difficulties in successfully achieving highly valued middle-class goals as the basis of gang delinquency. Cohen (1955), for example, believed that working-class boys are poorly prepared to cope with such demands of middle-class institutions as delay of gratification and pressures for achievement and success. Failure brings frustration, loss of status and deep resentment over rejection by middle-class society. Affiliation with a gang subculture provides an important sense of belonging as well as performance and status criteria that these youngsters can meet. "The hallmark of the delinquent subculture is the explicit and wholesale repudiation of middle-class standards and the adoption of their very antithesis" (Cohen, 1955, p. 130). Delinquent activity within the confines and sanctions of the gang makes aggression against middle-class institutions legitimate, while it bolsters and enhances self-esteem by group membership.

Taking a somewhat different tack, Ohlin and Cloward (1960) emphasized the very limited opportunity provided in the social order for lower-class youngsters to satisfy their needs. Under these conditions the stress of failure results in alienation and the use of illegitimate alternatives as possible routes to the successful fulfillment of goals. Ohlin and Cloward identified three different types of delinquent subcultures with which lower-class urban males affiliate in an attempt to adapt to the pressure created by the limited accessibility of middle-class channels to satisfy their aspirations. One is called the *criminal subculture,* in which there is a strong tie to adult criminal circles, and where the youngsters learn patterns of criminal behavior through a sort of apprenticeship program. A second group is referred to as the *conflict subculture,* in which there is no direct connection with adult criminals, but where the gang aggresses against others and uses physical violence to acquire status for itself and for its members. The third group is the *retreatist subculture,* in which members have reservations about committing criminal acts against persons or property, and instead engage in the use of drugs, sexual promiscuity, or other self-indulgent pleasurable experiences.

While most theorists have attended to delinquency in lower-class boys, Vaz (1967) is among the few who have made a major effort to deal with middle-class delinquency. He suggested that middle-class delinquency represents a gradual outgrowth of normal group activities in which deviant explorations for fun and excitement such as shoplifting or vandalism become, in time, the expected standard for the group. Similarly, England (1972) proposed that hedonistic pursuits are fast becoming the articulated role of middle-class adolescents, because in the prolongation of this age period there are few opportunities to perform productive functions. Play and the seeking of fun and excitement are gratifying, especially if they are supported and condoned by the group norms. Hedonistic behavior is readily maintained by the strong motivation of teenagers to share with and gain approval from their peers, even though the standards of behavior are discrepant with adult norms.

In the main, sociological views of delinquency are difficult to test empirically. Not only are they broad and general, but also they make assumptions about the responses of youngsters to the stress of the environment's social structure. In addition, these formulations fail to account for the large number of youngsters who do not become delinquent. Nevertheless, the sociological approach has been useful in identifying the social conditions "under which the psychological factors conducive to the development of antisocial behavior may more readily operate" (Bandura and Walters, 1959, p. 4).

Psychological Views

The psychological approach to delinquent or antisocial behavior can be characterized by attempts to account for its occurrence either through the psychodynamic development of basic personality structure in early childhood or through the acquisition of related behavioral traits by different learning paradigms.

Influenced by Freudian theory, various writers have assumed that delinquent youngsters are emotionally troubled (an erroneous assumption, since there is a large number of delinquents who manifest no psychological disorder), and that the roots of these youngsters' psychological disturbance can be found in unresolved and unconscious conflicts arising in early family relationships and in the management of sexual and aggressive impulses. Much of this work appeared in the literature during the 1940s and 1950s, and much was couched in Freudian language and concepts, particularly those studies dealing with the three components of personality—the *id, ego,* and *superego.* Personality problems of delinquents are most likely to be in ego and superego functions, inasmuch as delinquent behavior often involves the uncontrolled and outwardly directed expression of aggression without guilt, remorse, or pangs of conscience.

The best-known explanation of faulty superego function was formulated by Adelaide Johnson (1949), who referred to the deficiency as *superego lacunae,* thus connoting an absence of the superego rather than its weakness or ineffectiveness. Specific lacunae in certain areas of the child's behavior are similarly found in the parent's super-ego. Although unconscious and subtle, parental lacunae serve to sanction the child's behavior, since the parents experience vicarious pleasure when the behavior occurs. For example, excessive warnings and admonitions not to misbehave are interpreted as a parental invitation for misconduct. In this instance either the wish or the fear that the child will get into trouble is likely to be realized. Superego lacunae are also apparent in the father who is told by his teenage son that the son has impregnated the girl next door. While the father expresses strong disapproval and concern, he also flashes a quick and faint smile as a reflection of pride and admiration for his son's sexual prowess. This illustration can be further extended to the girl's parents, who may have encouraged her to act out sexually by displaying anxiety and excessive attention to what they suspect is going on when she is out with a boy. Under these conditions both sets of parents derive vicarious pleasure from their children's sexual activities, which were either unconsciously condoned or even encouraged by them. The acting-out behavior serves the dual purpose of gratifying forbidden parental wishes and of expressing hostility to the child for doing what he or she should not have done.

While these psychoanalytically inspired formulations have been interesting to and popular with clinicians, they remain difficult to test and verify. Another approach that has a more empirical basis has involved the systematic study of aggression and imitation, behaviors that are directly related to antisocial and delinquent conduct.

Contemporary research on the determinants of aggressive behavior began with the formulation by Dollard and associates, who postulated that aggression is always elicited by frustration (Dollard et al., 1939). They defined "aggression" as behavior that is intended to injure the person toward whom it is directed, and "frustration" as the blocking or thwarting of ongoing goal-directed activity. In addition, their frustration-aggression hypothesis consisted of a number of specific propositions beyond the major formulation that aggression is always a response to frustration. These theorists regarded the social conditions of low socioeconomic and educational status, and marital instability, as sources of frustration that provoke aggressive behavior where the fear of punishment (prison) is relatively weak.

However, subsequent research has uncovered some flaws in this theoretical formulation. Block and Martin (1955) demonstrated that frustration does not always lead to aggression, and it is now apparent that the instigator of aggression need not always be frustration. Moreover, the proposition that an act of aggression reduces the strength of other aggressive impulses has not been supported by the research data. Mallick and McCandless (1966) showed that children given the opportunity to engage in aggressive play after they were experimentally frustrated were no less aggressive than controls who were not permitted to play aggressively. Similar results were obtained by Kahn (1966), who found that college students, when compared to controls, expressed more aggression toward their frustrators if aggression was permitted following frustration. Thus, it seems clear that aggressive acts do not reduce the strength of subsequent aggressive behavior.

Buss (1966) took a different view of aggression, regarding it as an operant response that is maintained if it is instrumental in fulfilling the person's wants, or if it removes a noxious stimulus. In a nicely designed study he demonstrated that aggression increased when it had instrumental value, but did not increase as a result of frustration. With respect to delinquent and antisocial aggressive behaviors, this view of aggression seems fruitful. It suggests that the aggressive behaviors of delinquents are maintained by reinforcements that are readily available in their environment. In fact, Patterson and Cobb (1971) observed and identified a number of such reinforcements for aggression in their studies involving institutionalized delinquents and families of aggressive children. These children obtain peer approval and recognition for delinquent acts, and their aggression often is reinforced as a response that is instrumental in limiting or terminating aggression from others (peers, family members, and authority figures).

Although first proposed more than thirty years ago (Miller and Dollard, 1941), the more recent work of Bandura (Bandura and Walters, 1959; Bandura, Ross, and Ross, 1963; Bandura, 1969a, b, 1977) emphasizes *imitation* as an instrumental response in the acquisition of aggressive and other behaviors. Preferring the term *modeling* to *imitation,* he showed that young children in an experimentally controlled situation model the aggressive behavior of both live and filmed adults (models) who act aggressively. Furthermore, parents of aggressive boys encourage more aggression and more often serve as aggressive models for their youngsters than parents of nonaggressive children.

Modeling of aggressive behavior by young children who watch numerous television programs showing violence and crime has been a source of public concern and controversy. There is some evidence that early viewing of TV shows containing violence (in third grade) is positively related to measured aggression in nineteen-year-old males (Eron et al., 1972). Follow-up data show that preference for television violence predicts later aggression in boys (Eron, 1980). In addition, it has been shown that experimental exposure to TV violence increases aggressive behavior in children, and that watching a lot of violence on TV results in serious aggressive acts, especially of the type that is easily imitated from television (Murray, 1973; Belson, 1978). While the jury is still out on the relationship between aggression and TV, there are mounting data which consistently implicate the viewing of violence on television as one of the many factors in the development of aggression, particularly in boys.

Multifactor Views

Although this approach has been criticized as "a grab bag of superficial generalizations" (Trojanowicz, 1973, p. 54), it nevertheless attends to the many and diverse variables that seem to be implicated in the complicated problem of delinquency. The best-known example of this approach stems from the long and extensive work of Sheldon and Eleanor Glueck (Glueck, 1950; Glueck and Glueck, 1968), who studied 500 delinquent and nondelinquent boys over a period of years in terms of a number of sociological, psychological, and constitutional (physique) variables. On the bases of their initial sample of boys—who ranged in age from nine to seventeen—they found an excess of mesomorphic (muscular) body builds in delinquents with corresponding personality traits of aggressiveness, adventurousness, and acquisitiveness. They also characterized delinquent youngsters by scholastic retardation (although no difference in intelligence was found between the two groups of boys), dislike for school, pugnaciousness toward schoolmates, truancy, and misconduct occurring at an earlier age than in those few nondelinquents who also misbehaved. The Gluecks found that delinquents tend to keep late hours, smoke and drink earlier, and run away from home more frequently than nondelinquents. Further, delinquent youngsters gravitate toward gangs and are inclined to make friends with other delinquents. They live in overcrowded homes and come from families with a higher incidence of intellectual and emotional abnormalities, including alcoholism and criminality, and that are more often physically and/or psychologically broken. Delinquent boys, as compared to the controls, have fewer positive and warm relationships with their fathers and are inclined to reject fathers as desirable models to emulate.

In what they refer to as a "biopsychosocial" approach, Cortes and Gatti (1972) studied 100 delinquent and 100 nondelinquent boys who ranged in age from 16.5 to 18.5 years. Their findings were similar to those obtained by the Gluecks with respect to physique and personality traits. In addition, they found that delinquents have a high need for achievement, which was interpreted as a potential for successful entrepreneurship if such energies could be constructively channeled. They also found that delinquents are less religious and less supervised, but more rejected by parents. As in the Gluecks' sample, more delinquents came from broken homes and had disrupted father-son relationships than do the controls.

Therapeutic Considerations

The values, attitudes, and practices of our society toward antisocial acts are predicated on the Judeo-Christian ethic that dictates "an eye for an eye," or punishment to fit the crime. Our society's position with respect to the misbehavior of minors is somewhat more lenient, flexible, and influenced by a desire to remediate and rehabilitate. The judge may sentence a guilty child to a training or detention facility for a designated period of time, or may place the child on probation, where he or she will be supervised or guided by a case worker or probation officer. The judge may also refer the child to his or her family or to some community agency for remedial measures. Many more delinquents are dealt with by the courts along the lines of the last two options than are accorded the more stringent one of incarceration.

Even when institutionalization occurs, most facilities are open, in the sense that they are not designed to prevent escape (an event that happens frequently). Minimally funded and poorly conceived and implemented programs of educational and vocational training are often provided, and sometimes psychological help is offered in the form of counseling, group therapy (especially oriented around the misuse of alcohol and drugs), and individual psychotherapy. In the main, young inmates removed from undesirable environments are placed in a setting that is possibly more corrupt and conducive to further criminal behavior than the conditions under which they previously lived. Most juvenile judges are reluctant to use incarceration as a remedial approach, because they are aware of the evidence that no more than 20 or 30 percent of delinquent boys improve after institutionalization to the extent that they have no subsequent arrest record (Gibbons, 1970; Cohen and Filipczak, 1971). Nevertheless, one study showed significant improvement in institutionalized delinquents in reading level, IQ, and social behaviors such as trust and relations to others—especially authority figures—and control of aggression (Kahn and McFarland, 1973).

Unfortunately, it appears that a community-based remedial program involving individual and group psychotherapy, vocational counseling and supervision by a probation officer was no more effective in reducing recidivism than incarceration (Gibbons, 1970). Yet the results are not all negative. Nir and Cutler (1973) suggest that community-based psychotherapy can work and be effective in treating delinquent youngsters if the court authorizes treatment as a condition of probation for as long as it is necessary. Most delinquent youngsters are resistant and reluctant to enter into psychotherapy, and it is generally agreed that most will terminate treatment as early as possible unless some authority or dire consequence requires them to continue. Unless there is an enforceable requirement for the delinquent's continuance in psychotherapy, this treatment form is difficult to implement, and is often doomed to failure (Kaplan et al., 1969). Project CREST, which began in 1972, is an example of a counseling (individual, family, and group) program jointly operated by the University of Florida and the Florida Youth Services Program for delinquency-prone adolescents, families of delinquents, and juveniles on probation who are referred by their probation officers (DeJong and Stewart, 1980). The program also provides consulting assistance to schools in the community. Preliminary findings after two years indicate that youngsters who had received counseling in the CREST program were charged with fewer criminal offenses and showed significant improvement in their school attendance and grades as compared to control subjects.

Special community-based residential facilities that have used a variety of so-called therapeutic milieu programs have been reported in the literature. Most of these programs emphasize group interaction to improve socialization, but they differ in the manner in which they are operated, ranging from staff control to inmate self-government. Counseling, individual and group psychotherapy, recreation, vocational training, and supervised work experiences are frequently offered. While programs of this sort usually arose a good deal of public and professional interest, few can claim unequivocal success, and even fewer can muster sufficient evidence to justify their higher cost as compared to existing training schools.

A recent study demonstrated the effectiveness of training in role-taking skills with chronically delinquent boys (Chandler, 1973). Training consisted of writing, acting, and videotaping brief, lifelike skits about people their own age. These three-hour sessions enabled the subjects to see themselves as others do and to learn to overcome their deficient role-taking skills. As compared to controls, delinquents who received the experimental training improved significantly in assuming roles that facilitated their social competence and cooperation. Moreover, follow-up data after eighteen months indicated that these improvements were associated with decreases in delinquent behavior. Another program involving a twenty-seven-day course in survival training claimed to be effective in reducing recidivism for as long as one year after parole of delinquent males (Kelly, 1971). The rationale for the program stemmed from the observation that delinquent boys prefer motoric over verbal expression. In addition, it was thought that giving boys a severe physical test in which they could achieve beyond their expectations would increase the likelihood of their tackling heretofore unachieved goals (like going "straight").

One of the most promising treatment approaches is behavior modification, in which positive reinforcement, punishment (especially withholding rewards), and token systems are employed to alter antisocial behavior and to improve educational levels of delinquent youngsters. Schwitzgebel (1964) paid delinquent youngsters to talk to him about delinquency on the assumption that they would talk about their own delinquent acts and thus gain insight into themselves. In the process he found that either they were tardy for appointments or they did not arrive at all. He then used the payment to effect behavioral changes that could be carried over to daily living, such as being on time and performing well in a talk session.

Cognitive behavior modification has been applied to delinquents with reported success in the form of role playing, modeling, and talks about how to deal with life situations to improve their social skills (Freedman et al., 1978; Sarason, 1978). In addition, tokens as reinforcers have been used effectively by behaviorally trained house parents to bring about socially desirable behaviors in small groups of delinquent adolescents who live together as a family; however, the long-term effects are not yet known (Quay, 1979).

The National Training School Project, which was implemented for one year as a pilot and demonstration program to alter delinquent behavior, is illustrative of the application of a token economy system. Points (each equal to one cent) that the student could use to purchase comfort and luxury items, such as snacks and clothing, were used to reinforce successful academic performance. Students were not required to study or work for points, although at the end of the year most of them had increased their achievement scores by several grades.

Parsons and Alexander (1973) significantly altered the destructive communication patterns of delinquent families in a short-term family therapy study. They formulated a token economy system on the basis of how each family member wanted to be rewarded by the others. They employed social reinforcement and modeling in the training of each family member in solution-oriented communication patterns, and they used a behavior modification primer to familiarize family members with the concepts and language of the treatment program. Families were trained over a three-week period of time, and then they began the four-week therapy program. At the end of therapy, family interaction patterns were significantly modified in the direction of communicative patterns characteristic of normal families.

In spite of the promising findings, it is too early to render a final verdict regarding the effectiveness of behavior modification with delinquent children. To date, most studies have failed to include either no-treatment controls or reversal designs, leaving open the possibility of spontaneous improvement, especially since adolescents are at a point in their lives where maturation often produces change. More research, especially studies to determine the long-term effects of this treatment approach, is needed (Davidson and Seidman, 1974).

DRUG ABUSE

We would be remiss if we didn't follow up the discussion of delinquency with the consideration of drug abuse in adolescence, inasmuch as the toll of deaths, addiction, and crime related to drugs has reached alarming proportions. Just in the thirteen years between 1960 and 1973 (see Table 13–2), arrests for drug offenses increased by a staggering 4,673.3 percent for youngsters under eighteen as compared to an increase of 774.6 percent for persons over eighteen. Figures shown in Table 13–1 for 1981 indicate that adolescent and youth arrests involving alcohol abuse are approximately twice as frequent as those for other drug violations. Taken together, these figures represent almost 15 percent of arrests for all youngsters under eighteen during 1981. It is also estimated that about one-ninth of our total population, or some 24 million Americans (over eleven years of age), have experimented with marijuana (*Marijuana: A Signal of Misunderstanding,* 1972). Among college students sampled in 1971, 51 percent admitted having tried marijuana at least once, 18 percent experimented with amphetamines, 15 percent tried barbituates, 7 percent had experience with cocaine, and 2 percent admitted to using heroin (*Current Views of College Students on Politics and Drugs,* 1972). Except for the reported use of heroin (which was about the same), somewhat lower incidence figures were obtained from high school youngsters in that 20 percent had experience with marijuana, 10 percent with amphetamines, and about 6 percent with barbiturates (Johnston, 1973). Self-report data obtained from about 5,000 high school seniors from a county near San Francisco indicated that between 1968 and 1974, marijuana use (smoked at least one time each year) rose from 38 percent to 60 and from 22 percent to 43 percent (smoked ten times or more each year) (Blackford, 1974). The results also showed that the use of hallucinogens (LSD) did not decline but rather remained stable at about 17 percent over this six-year period.

Males typically have had a higher incidence of drug abuse than females by a ratio of about 2:1, although the ratio declined during the early 1970s as greater numbers of girls became involved with drugs. Adolescent drug users are inclined to use more than one drug, with the most likely combination being amphetamines, barbiturates, and hallucinogens (Johnston, 1973). In a sample of 100 adolescent marijuana users, Halikas and Rimmer (1974) found that all used one other drug, and 52 percent used more than two other drugs. In addition, the factors of use of illicit drugs at an early age, poor high school socialization, poor adolescent adjustment, antisocial behavior, homosexual experiences, and numerous parental conflicts were found to predict multiple drug abuse. It is also true that experiences with marijuana were found in more than 96 percent of herion and cocaine users, and in 85 percent of the users of stimulants and depressants (Gergen, Gergen, and Morse, 1972). However, these data cannot be interpreted to support the popular belief that marijuana leads to the use of more serious drugs, because correlational evidence cannot be taken to reflect a causal relationship. As a matter of fact, Johnston's data indicate that more than 50 percent of marijuana users failed to become involved with any of the more serious drugs after one year had elapsed.

It is entirely possible that estimates of the scope of the problem reflect only the tip of an iceberg that is very difficult to accurately and completely measure. Arrest data do not include the incidence with which prescription and over-the-counter drugs are used, such as alcohol, glue, lighter fluid, aerosols, caffein, and diet pills. In addition, they do not reflect the differences in law enforcement practices or availability of alternative community services, or the many instances of illegal drug abuse that are undetected and unreported. Self-report questionnaire data are influenced greatly by the willingness of the respondent to admit to illegal drug abuse, and by the nature and extent of the questions that deal with legal and over-the-counter substances. The patterns of drug use change over time, making it almost impossible for researchers to keep pace with current trends. Nevertheless, most observers would agree that drug abuse is a sizeable and serious problem occurring at all levels of the social scale, in all environments, and at all ages (some neonates are born addicted).

Types of Mood-Altering Drugs

Drug abuse refers to an excessive use of one or more chemical substances that are illegal and/or considered harmful to the person's health, to social and personal adjustment, or to society. These agents ordinarily are taken to achieve an unusual mood or state, or to obliterate unpleasurable and uncomfortable feelings. The list of substances that may be categorized as *mood-* or *mind-altering drugs* is quite extensive and diverse.

Heroin is the most frequently used narcotic or "hard" drug, claiming approximately 250,000 active addicts, who live primarily in the economically impoverished areas of our country's urban centers. Users are predominately male (about 85 percent), and about two-thirds of them are either black, Puerto Rican, or Mexican-American (Wald and Hutt, 1972). Because they are members of minority groups and come from broken and/or disrupted homes and poverty conditions, they are apt to have low self-esteem, low frustration and anxiety tolerance, and inadequate defenses to cope with the stress and strain of daily living. Baer and Corrado (1974) confirmed the importance of parent-child relationships as predisposing factors in heroin addiction. They found that addicts were more likely to have experienced an unhappy childhood, harsh physical punishment, and little parental concern for their schoolwork, sexual conduct, careers, or choice of friends. Heroin users have low academic achievement and low self-esteem, and they tend to lack warmth and discipline (Gandossy et al., 1980). They are only capable of forming tentative and weak relationships, and they tend to cope with anxiety by means of repression and withdrawal (Milkman and Frosch, 1973). They are not likely to be gang delinquents or to be overtly and physically aggressive. They lack security and a sense of belonging somewhere or to someone, and they use heroin as a solitary habit to escape the unpleasantness of the real world (Chapel and Taylor, 1972). Narcotic users are physically dependent on the drug and have habits that range in cost from as little as \$10 to as much as \$150 daily. Of course, this means that much of their waking energy is tied up in raising the necessary funds and in making a connection with a "pusher" to obtain a "fix." Most addicts are unable to accomplish this through legal channels and are forced to resort to criminal activities to satisfy their physical and psychological dependence. There is a high incidence of hepatitis, tetanus, endocarditis (from bacterial infection of the heart), and suicide among heroin users (Eldefonso, 1972). Moreover, death from heroin usage occurs in 25 percent of these addicts. Cure in terms of long-term abstinence is expected to occur in only about 1 percent of the heroin users (Walker, 1973).

Heroin is the preferred drug for most narcotics addicts primarily because of its capacity to produce euphoric feelings quickly and to maintain the "high" over a prolonged period of time. Users rapidly develop a tolerance for heroin that requires them to continually increase the dosage to obtain the desired effect. Overdoses (ODs) resulting in fatalities can and do occur, because the quality of the drug is often so poorly controlled by the illegal seller. Although it is difficult to separate the physical from the psychological effects of heroin, withdrawal from the drug typically produces severe reactions that include cramps, muscle twitching, profuse sweating, nausea, anxiety, agitation, and sleep disruption (Bates and Crowther, 1973).

Data indicate that heroin use has sharply declined since the almost epidemic peak reached in this country in 1970, suggesting that stricter law enforcement, more treatment facilities, and increased public awareness of its dangers may have played an important role in stemming the tide for the time being (DuPont and Greene, 1973).

Marijuana is a wild plant that produces an active ingredient known as resin, which is found in the leaves at the top of the plant. It is the preferred drug of high school and college-aged youngsters, and compared to most other drugs, it is probably the cheapest. Marijuana is readily available, and unlike the narcotics, its users often become suppliers. It is a drug that is often taken in a group or social setting in order to "share" experiences and to instruct the novice. Participants experience rapport and closeness with each other, although verbal interactions are often minimal (Chapel and Taylor, 1972). As might be expected, suburban high school marijuana users are more likely to over-estimate the percentage of peers using the drug, to believe that friends would not react negatively to marijuana use, to view its use as a positive expression rather than as a response to group pressure or personal difficulties, and to ascribe a positive rather than a harmful effect to the drug (Tec, 1972).

Adolescents use marijuana as a means of being accepted by peers, as an act of rebellion against society and/or parents, as a way of coping with personality problems, and/or as a release and form of pleasurable relaxation. Peer relationships are extremely important during adolescence, giving the youngster a sense of belonging and feelings of adequacy and self-worth. It is difficult for many adolescents to resist peer pressure and deny themselves the great satisfaction that comes from peer acceptance. Rebellion may be part of the group theme that is tacitly accepted by all its members, or it may be a manifestation of family and personal adjustment problems. There are those who would suggest that the use of marijuana to deal with personality difficulties identifies the persons who are most likely to graduate to more serious and addictive drugs (Stanton, 1966). The recent results of a survey of middle school and high school children showed that heavier consumers of alcohol reported more illicit drug use, delinquent activities, and alienation from their parents, and more frequent personal problems with their peers and school performance (Wechsler and Thum, 1973). There is also evidence supporting the relationship between maternal ideology and child-rearing practices and the adolescent's involvement in problem behaviors. Jessor and Jessor (1974) found that the more traditional the mother's ideology (nonpermissive), the less likely it would be that the adolescent would use alcohol and marijuana, behave promiscuously, or hold radical political beliefs. Some support was also found in the relationship between high maternal nurturance and control and the low incidence of these behavior problems.

As far as we know, marijuana is neither addictive nor physically harmful, although more study is needed—especially with respect to long-term effects—before we can reach a definitive conclusion. "The real issue over marijuana appears to be not whether it causes mild physical damage but whether its use has already spread so widely that, as is true of alcohol, the social costs of efforts to prohibit it exceed the physical costs that would be incurred by eliminating criminal penalties for, or even legalizing, its use" (Wald and Hutt, 1972, p. 7).

LSD, or lysergic acid diethylamide, was first synthesized in 1938, but it wasn't until five years later that a chemist by the name of Albert Hofmann discovered its potent hallucinogenic properties. Hofmann tested the drug on himself and experienced vivid fantasies of a bizarre and grotesque nature; visual hallucinations and illusions; vertigo; and uncontrollable, incoherent speech, among other effects. During the 1950s LSD was used experimentally by researchers who variously regarded it as a substance that produced psychosis (psychotogenic), mimicked psychosis (psychotomimetic), or expanded the mind (psychedelic). But LSD became popular as a psychedelic drug in the mid- and late 1960s at the time of the hippie movement, when it was faddish for young people to seek new pleasure experiences and to rebel against the Establishment under the guise of "doing one's own thing."

LSD is tasteless and odorless; it can be injected, or else it can be ingested in pill, powder, or liquid form (commonly a small drop is placed on a sugar cube). Small doses are capable of producing autonomic changes, vivid visual hallucinations, illusions, sensory distortions, and feelings of estrangement, depersonalization, and alterations of mood. It is nonaddictive, but because a tolerance for the drug builds up rapidly, it cannot be taken more than several times a week without losing the potency of its effects. The reaction of users to the drug is quite varied, depending on the personality of the person, the setting in which LSD is taken, and prior experience with the drug. Especially in those with preexisting psychopathological conditions, psychotic reactions that require hospitalization have been reported, in which the user is overwhelmed by fear, uncontrolled violent impulses, and intense auditory hallucinations.

During the height of its popularity, when almost 2 million Americans had taken an LSD "trip," there were numerous frightening reports that suggested persistent and even irreversible adverse effects from LSD use (McGlothlin and Arnold, 1971). However, adequate support for the claims of brain damage, chromosomal abnormalities, cancer, suicide, or enduring personality and behavioral changes simply has not been presented as yet. Indeed, the results of the relatively few well-controlled studies on LSD indicate that when the drug was administered to psychologically normal subjects under secure circumstances, lasting adverse behavioral effects did not occur (McWilliams and Tuttle, 1973).

Amphetamines, popularly known as "pep pills," "speed," and "bennies," are drugs that stimulate the central nervous system. Often they are used to produce a state of euphoria, increase alertness, reduce fatigue and depression, and curb the appetite. They are taken orally in pill form, but they may also be injected to produce a quicker and more pronounced "high." Heavy doses can produce irritability, thought disturbances, and psychotic reactions. There is an increasing tolerance for amphetamines that requires the user to increase the dose to get the desired effect, but withdrawal of the drug produces profound depressive states and sometimes suicidal tendencies. Amphetamines are readily available either through the "black market" or through medical prescriptions, where they are plentiful—12 billion pills are legally produced by pharmaceutical houses each year in this country (Grinspoon and Hedblom, 1975). The heaviest abusers of amphetamines are adolescents, who initially may take the drug to stay awake to complete an academic assignment or to aid in weight control. Although physical dependence is not known to occur, the user may develop the psychological need to be stimulated to the extent that he or she turns to the drug to achieve that effect. The personality style of amphetamine users has been found to be different from that of heroin addicts in that the addict reduces anxiety by means of withdrawal and repression, while the amphetamine user tries to maintain a posture of active confrontation with the environment (Milkman and Frosch, 1973).

The most extreme and disastrous abuse of amphetamines takes the form of intravenous injections or large doses of the drug where the user ("speed freak") administers the drug for several consecutive days. During this period (sometimes referred to as a "run") the user experiences an intense "high" and euphoria, hyperactivity, tenseness, and paranoid ideas. Often users go without eating or sleeping for two or three days before they "crash" in exhaustion and sleep without interruption for as many as two days.

Cocaine is a central nervous system stimulant derived from a coca shrub, which is grown primarily in the mountains of Peru and Bolivia. It was known centuries ago as the drug of the privileged, the kings, the high priests, and the aristocrats. Later it fell out of favor and came to be associated with the lowest forms of human life (Gay et al., 1975). In the 1970s and early 1980s cocaine became very popular again, especially with middle-class and affluent adults. The drug is typically snorted, rather quickly producing a "high" or a state of euphoria which is characterized by increased mental agility and physical endurance (Post, 1975). Physiological effects include increased energy, heart rate, and blood pressure; dilated pupils; constriction of peripheral blood vessels; and a rise in body temperature and in metabolic rate. Long-term use of cocaine can seriously damage the mucous membrane of the nose and produce the following chronic effects: headaches, nausea, abdominal pain, convulsions, confusion, disruption of sleep and eating, irritability, impaired concentration, paranoia, and serious psychological dependence (Grinspoon and Bakalar, 1981; Schnoll, 1979). High doses of cocaine, usually taken by habitual users, may produce a psychotic reaction much like that noted with high doses of amphetamines, although this reaction is shorter. In rare cases it also may result in death from respiratory or cardiac arrest (Grinspoon and Bakalar, 1981).

Barbiturates are sedatives that act as central nervous system depressants to aid relaxation and sleep. They cause drowsiness, impaired motor coordination, mental confusion, slurred speech, irritability, and poor emotional control. Users develop a tolerance to the sedative effects of barbiturates, and some continue to take the drug until they ingest lethal doses. Overdoses can occur readily; the drug tends to blur time perception and produce mental confusion to the point where the user may erroneously take more than is intended. Consequently, the drug appears to be one of the most frequent causes of either suicide or accidental death (Eldefonso, 1972). The drug is physically addictive, and its withdrawal is particularly difficult and hazardous. Initially the body becomes tremulous—followed by hypotension, fever, vomiting, uncontrolled tremors, and sometimes grand mal convulsions and delirium. Medical supervision is essential, since withdrawal from barbiturates represents a real threat to life itself. Heavy doses of barbiturates may be fatal, and even more moderate doses are dangerous when used in combination with amphetamines, heroin, and alcohol.

Barbiturates, much like amphetamines, are easy to obtain either through medical prescriptions or on the illegal drug market, with as many as thirty-four doses for each person over ten years of age being supplied each year by both legal and illegal channels (Bates and Crowther, 1973). Because they are relatively inexpensive and are so accessible, adolescents of all socioeconomic levels find them useful as "downers" to reduce "uptightness" quickly and facilitate relaxation and sleep.

Alcohol is a psychoactive drug that has a depressant effect on the central nervous system. Generally the drinker feels relaxed and less inhibited. He or she becomes more talkative (sometimes with slurred speech), impulsive, clumsy, and poorly coordinated with relatively small concentrations of alcohol in the blood. With increasing concentrations of alcohol, unsteadiness of gait, sensory distortions, impaired and disjointed speech, cognitive difficulties, drowsiness, and even stupor are apt to appear. Loss of consciousness and even death can occur with a large intake of alcohol in a brief period of time.

The consumption of alcohol is so prevalent in our society that we often tend to disregard it as a potentially dangerous drug. Because alcohol is readily available in a variety of beverages and strengths, and because individuals differ greatly in alcohol tolerance and drinking patterns, its use and abuse are difficult to assess. Nevertheless, professionals who work with adolescents believe that alcohol consumption represents a serious and probably increasing problem for this age group.

During the 1960s, when adolescents seemed extremely fascinated with illicit drugs, there appeared to be little concern about their drinking behavior. But apparently, young people have rediscovered alcohol as a cheaper, more accessible, and more socially sanctioned remedy for their discontent, or for their pleasure. A recent survey of the drinking patterns of seventh to ninth, and tenth through twelfth graders in lower-middle-, middle-, and upper-middle-class students living in a semi-industrial city and in a residential town showed the following: (1) There were no sex differences in drinking patterns between socioeconomic classes or places of residence, although in the lower grades (seventh through ninth), more boys were heavier drinkers (defined as distilled-spirit users who reported having been drunk) than girls; (2) 33 percent of the lower graders from the city were heavy drinkers, while only 18 percent from the town were so classified; and (3) among the upper grades (tenth through twelfth), 66 percent from the city were heavy drinkers in contrast to 44 percent from the town (Wechsler and Thum, 1973). In addition to these alarmingly high estimates of excessive drinking, the survey found that heavy users also admitted to more illicit drug use, delinquent actions, alienation from their parents, interpersonal problems with peers, and poorer academic performance. It seems that alcohol is not a substitute for illicit drugs; but for many youngsters it is an important companion in a combination of drugs (Freed, 1973). As a matter of fact, one study indicated that alcoholic beverages are almost always the first stage of adolescent involvement in illicit-drug use (Kandel, 1975). Kandel found four stages of involvement with drugs that were consistent for most of the high school youngsters sampled. They went from beer and/or wine, to cigarettes and/or hard liquor, to marijuana, and finally to other illicit drugs. During the six-month period of the study, 36 percent of non–drug users progressed to legal drugs (alcohol and tobacco) and then to marijuana, while 26 percent escalated to other illicit drugs.

Unfortunately, we do not have an accurate estimate of how many adolescent drinkers go on to become alcoholics, but we do know that uncontrollable alcohol consumption in adults is a major problem. It represents 25 percent of all admissions in a given year to state and county mental institutions, and it is a primary contributing factor to poor health (and even early death), unemployment, broken families, and delinquency and crime (Page, 1975).

ETIOLOGICAL CONSIDERATIONS

Genetic and Biological Views

With the exception of alcoholism, at present there is no clear-cut evidence implicating either genetic or biological factors as causes of drug abuse. The fact that alcoholism runs in families is interpreted by some as favoring a genetic view, although others contend that the evidence is reflective of social learning or imitation rather than of hereditary influences

(Winokur et al., 1970; Goodwin et al., 1973; Tolor and Tamerin, 1973). Recent findings show that a family history of heavy-drinking parents, especially fathers, is a good predictor of problem drinking in adult males (Calahan and Room, 1974).

These data could be used to argue for the importance of social learning in the etiology of alcoholism. However, Goodwin and associates (1973) found that sons of alcoholics who were placed in foster homes early in their lives were much more likely (almost four times as much) to become alcoholics than were controls. Further analysis of these data showed high, but not different, rates of alcoholism between sons of alcoholics removed from the home in infancy and their brothers who remained at home (Goodwin et al., 1974). These authors conclude that genetic factors play an etiological role in alcoholism, since their study controlled for environmental forces and the impact of the family in social learning. The fact that the majority of sons did not turn out to be alcoholics (regardless of home placement) was interpreted to mean that there is a genetic predisposition for severe alcoholism but that psychogenic factors are more likely to be significant both for heavy drinking and for all other degrees of drinking. Even if we assume that genetic factors contribute to the development of alcoholism, the large percentage (82 percent) of high-risk children who do not become alcoholics suggests that there is ample room for environmental and experiential influences to operate.

Biochemical factors also have been explored with respect to alcohol intake, but the results have been contradictory (Segovia-Riquelme, Varela, and Mardones, 1971). Various biochemical differences have been found between nonalcoholic and alcoholic individuals, although it has been virtually impossible to determine whether these differences are attributable to the drinking behavior or the biochemistry of the individuals prior to alcohol addiction.

It has been known for a long time that sociocultural factors play a role in determining the extent, the incidence, and the patterns of drug use, especially with alcohol (Bates, 1946). In cultures where alcohol is prohibited, such as among the Moslems, the incidence of drinking is low. On the other hand, the incidence of opiate use is high in a culture such as China where its use is sanctioned. Both Italy and France have high rates of alcohol consumption, but they differ in their rate of alcoholism. Alcoholism is low in Italy, where drinking other than at mealtime is frowned upon; while the relatively high rate of alcoholism in France corresponds to its more permissive attitude toward drinking. Other sociocultural variables, such as religious preference, socioeconomic status, and geographical area, also are known to be related to alcohol consumption and patterns.

But beyond these broad variables, much has been written (especially about alcoholism) about the psychological forces that produce drug abuse. For many years the literature has reflected a strong psychoanalytic influence that views addiction as an attempt to resolve stress or conflict, by which the addict gains pleasure from the drug and relief from intrapsychic pain and anxiety (Blum, 1966). For example, the alcoholic is viewed as an immature, dependent, and orally fixated person who substitutes "booze for boobs" (infantile feeding) and who derives pleasure from being taken care of and nurtured. Drug abusers, like other disturbed personalities, are viewed by psychoanalysts as wrestling with conflicts that are sexual or aggressive in nature. More specifically, alcoholics are seen as using alcohol as a maladaptive way of dealing with latent homosexual impulses or coping with internalized hostility and depression.

A more parsimonious and empirically based view of alcoholism and drug abuse centers on a tension-reduction model of learning that was extremely popular during the late 1940s and in the 1950s. Simply stated, the model assumes that life stresses produce tension and that alcohol and other drugs are potent alleviators of the discomfort generated by the stress. In a matter of a few trials under stress conditions, drug use is reinforced, because it promptly reduces the heightened tension state of the individual. In addition, the pleasurable effects of the drug increase its chances of occurring (in the presence of stress) and persisting, since immediate gratification tends to be more powerful than the long-term negative effects of drug abuse. With continued use, and as the person becomes physically addicted to the drug, the drug response will become even stronger, because its use will enable the person to avoid the very unpleasant reactions that come with withdrawal.

The evidence for this view came largely from several animal studies that are now classic. Masserman and Yum (1946) used an unsolvable approach-avoidance conflict situation wherein electric shock was given whenever hungry cats approached the food box. The animals reacted to this stressful condition by fear-related behaviors, which were referred to as *experimental neuroses*. After the neuroticlike reaction was established, the experimenters gave the animals a choice between plain milk and a solution of alcohol and milk. Under the stressful shock condition, cats who previously preferred the nonalcoholic fluid showed a greater preference for alcohol than did the controls. In addition, their neurotic behaviors decreased while under the influence of alcohol. Similarly, it has been found that monkeys increase their alcohol consumption under stress and decrease it under normal conditions (Clark and Polish, 1960).

In 1951 Conger did two experiments showing that rats are less affected by the stress of an approach-avoidance conflict when given an injection of alcohol as compared to control rats given a placebo. More specifically, rats under the influence of alcohol make more approach responses than their controls in the shock stress situation. In addition, Conger demonstrated that alcohol inhibits or reduces the avoidance responses of the animals, while their approach tendency is not affected. More recent and similar experimental work found that rats in an approach-avoidance conflict increase their alcohol consumption, but only while they are in the conflict situation (von-Wright, Pekanmäki, and Malin, 1971). An increase in alcohol intake was also noted for rats subjected to shock not contingent on their behavior, although under these conditions the increase occurs only after the stress periods. These findings imply that it is noncontingent stress that is more potent in producing a permanent increase in alcohol intake than specific conflict situations, although conflict seems to be responsible for a temporary increase in alcohol consumption.

Research with human subjects confirms the relationship between an increase in alcohol intake and stress, particularly when the nature of the stress concerns social frustrations and anxieties—that is, when subjects are angered and cannot express their feelings, or when the subjects are being evaluated on personal attractiveness by peers of the opposite sex (Higgins and Marlatt, 1973, 1975; Marlatt, Demming, and Reid, 1973).

The idea that drug use reduces tension and is a way for the individual to cope with interpersonal frustrations and anxieties (stressful situations) is certainly viable, although other possibilities exist. It may be that factors such as modeling of parental drug abuse, peer membership, and reinforcement for drinking or pill popping, and the opportunity to behave without inhibition while under the influence, operate in the acquisition of drug abuse. As a matter of fact, a review of the literature showed that parents of drug abusers as compared to controls tend to have a higher incidence of broken marriages, more evidence of emotional disturbance, and a higher frequency of drug abuse (Harbin and Maziar, 1975). In addition, student reports of their parents' use of drugs is positively related to their own frequency of drug use, suggesting the effects of modeling in the development of drug-use patterns (Smart and Fejer, 1972). The jury may still be out with regard to the specific etiological factors involved in drug abuse, but as the evidence mounts, it clearly suggests that the answer will be found in social learning variables.

THERAPEUTIC CONSIDERATIONS

Before discussing the diverse treatment forms that have been used for alcoholism and drug abuse, it is important to note that while these forms of abnormal behavior may be regarded as homogeneous, the population manifesting them is, in fact, quite heterogeneous. Indeed, drug abusers are very different, although their common behavior and diagnostic label lead us to talk about them as if they were the same. Studies that have attempted to identify a distinctive alcoholic personality, for example, have failed, although the results generally show that there are more indications of maladjustment in alcoholics than there are in normal people (Goss and Morosko, 1969). Alcoholics and other drug abusers may be neurotic, psychotic, or even representative of a variety of personality disorders. The fact that we are dealing with such a diverse clinical population makes the choice and the evaluation of treatment methods much more difficult.

Biological Approaches

Hardly any professional working with alcoholics and other drug abusers would rely on a single remedial measure as an effective and total treatment program. Instead, favorable outcomes (and there are far too few) most often occur when a combination of remedies is used. This is especially true of the biological approaches that attempt both to restore some sort of physiological balance and to provide some effect that makes the drug use either unnecessary or undesirable.

Almost all alcoholics and addicts (hard drug users) need a *detoxification program* as a beginning phase of intervention and rehabilitation. Detoxification involves withdrawal from the addictive drug under medical management and the treatment of the unpleasant and severe behavioral and physiological reactions of withdrawal by means of tranquilizers and other drugs. In addition, vitamins and a high carbohydrate diet are given, especially to alcoholics, who are often poorly nourished. The "drying out" process requires a minimum of several days before the abuser can proceed with further treatment. At this point some detoxification facilities begin alcoholics on daily doses of an emetic drug such as Antabuse, which makes the person extremely nauseous and violently ill if alcohol is consumed. The object of giving Antabuse is to prevent the alcoholic from further drinking (aversive conditioning), but its effectiveness depends on the willingness and the ability of the abuser to take the drug daily.

A synthetic narcotic drug, called methadone, which was developed accidently in 1965; is now frequently used as a substitute for heroin in the treatment of these addicts (Dole and Nyswander, 1965). Methadone maintenance programs in which abusers are regularly given doses of methadone proportionate to their heroin habit have become so widespread that more than 60 percent of the estimated narcotic users in 1974 were coming to centers daily to take the drug (McGlothlin, 1975). Methadone has a number of advantages: It can be taken orally, it has a longer action than heroin, and it is less expensive and legally available. However, in a curative sense it does no more than shift the addiction from one drug to another, and in the end the abuser is still addicted to a narcotic. In fact, as long as a person is on methadone maintenance, there is no motivation or need to "kick the habit" (Lennard, Epstein, and Rosenthal, 1972).

Psychotherapeutic Approaches

Psychoanalytically oriented and other forms of individual psychotherapy designed to provide insight and bring about changes in basic personality have been widely used for drug abusers without much success (Hill and Blane, 1967). The method may have failed because it depends largely on ingredients that are not usually present in drug abusers—that is, motivation to change and an ability to develop a mutually trusting relationship with the therapist. Moreover, psychotherapy on a once-a-week or even biweekly basis is severely hampered without strict drug control, since the immediate, rewarding aspects of the addiction and the avoidance of the pain of withdrawal are both more potent than any talk sessions can be.

In contrast, group therapy, especially as one part of an overall treatment program, has enjoyed more success (Thomas, 1968; Zucker and Waksman, 1970/73). It provides abusers with an opportunity to recognize that others have the same problem, and to gain a better view of themselves by group affiliation and acceptance. With group support the abuser can admit the truth about his or her problem and can gain the courage to practice abstinence. During recent years family therapy also has been used in the treatment of alcoholics and other drug abusers, but there are too few studies available to adequately assess this approach (Meeks and Kelly, 1970). While the assumption that drug abuse is a manifestation of or involves a family problem is unchallenged at present, one must question the feasibility of this approach with the chronic alcoholic or addict, who frequently is irreparably separated from the family. However, family therapy seems more promising for adolescent drug abusers, whose relationships with their families are likely to be strained but not irreconcilable.

While a number of behavioral treatment approaches to drug abuse have been reported in the literature, most have been based on individual case reports in hospital settings, and they provide either no follow-up or inadequate follow-up measures (Callner, 1975). When long-term data are available, we find, for example, that aversive conditioning in which the abused drug is paired with some noxious stimulus such as a nausea-inducing chemical or a strong electric shock results in only temporary abstinence in alcoholics and drug addicts (Droppa, 1973; Miller and Barlow, 1973). However, the ineffectiveness of behavioral methods in producing enduring changes should not be the basis for discarding this approach—perhaps therapists might include it in a multiform treatment regime.

Self-Help Organizations

Alcoholics Anonymous is probably the best-known and most far-reaching organization in the world for helping any alcoholic who wishes to stop drinking. There are more than 0.5 million members who maintain sobriety through their participation in A.A., and there are more than 16,000 A.A. groups in this country alone to which alcoholics can belong (Goldenberg, 1977). Membership is on a voluntary basis, and A.A. has no fees or complicated structure. The program was founded by laymen, and it continues to be run by laymen even today. Its twelve guiding principles include a heavy religious emphasis, in which the individual is asked to believe in a greater Power who could restore sanity, to admit to God the nature of his or her wrongdoings, to gain a better understanding of God through prayer and meditation, and to turn his or her will and life over to God. Alcoholics are encouraged to admit their impotence with regard to alcohol and to recognize that they can never drink again. Regular meetings are held in which members publicly confess, and recovered alcoholics speak about their experiences. Each new member is paired with an ex-alcoholic who is available night and day to help the novice with the struggle over abstinence, and to provide strength and understanding when needed. Inasmuch as A.A. is not a research-oriented organization, there is little data concerning its effectiveness. However, its continued growth and popularity provide indirect evidence that it is a useful program for a substantial number of alcoholics.

A parallel self-help group for drug addicts is Synanon, which was founded by a former alcoholic who developed a problem with hard drugs. Synanon is a residential center staffed by former addicts, which provides a tightly controlled live-in environment. New members are required to carry out assigned jobs within the residence, although jobs get progressively better as the person complies with the expectations of the community, behaves maturely, and abstains from drug use. Members are encouraged to find new friends and lifestyles that are quite different from their previous drug subculture. Participation in group therapy several times a week is required, in which frank and sometimes painful verbal confrontations take place among the members. The idea behind these verbal attacks is to penetrate and strip away the common tendency of addicts to deceive themselves and rationalize their drug abuse. Other residential centers representing some variant of Synanon have since opened and are operating in various parts of the country. The effectiveness of these programs has been difficult to evaluate, since few outcome studies are available. However, what little data we have indicate that relatively few addicts have been reached this way—the most favorable result has been obtained with those addicts who continue to live at Synanon and who are employed by the residence (Volkmann and Cressey, 1963; Yablonsky, 1967).

Prognosis

The overall outlook for drug abusers, especially chronic alcoholics and long-term narcotic addicts, is very poor. However, the extreme diversity in personality characteristics and in the type, duration, extent, and degree of drug abuse makes the issue of outcome virtually impossible to evaluate more specifically. In general, most observers agree that young drinkers and drug abusers who continue to function within their families and maintain employment have the most favorable prognosis. In contrast, chronic alcoholics of the Skid Row type, and long-term narcotic addicts, have the poorest chance of attaining total abstinence and of achieving a good social adjustment. Moreover, outcome tends to vary with the type and degree of personality disorganization—that is, the more severe the disorganization, the poorer the prognosis. The evaluation of outcome is also complicated by the criteria employed: The percentage of recoveries will depend on the definition one uses. For example, it stands to reason that one can obtain a higher rate of recovery for alcoholics if a sobriety period of three months is used as the criterion rather than a period of two years. The matter becomes even more complex and pessimistic with regard to favorable outcomes when vocational, marital, and other aspects of social adjustment are included as criteria for recovery.

SUICIDE

Problems of adolescents and college students that have been discussed so far, plus many others, may all play a role in the grim matter of suicide. There is always grief and tragedy surrounding death, but no death is so devastating, so puzzling, and so lamentable as that of the child who willingly takes his or her own life. For most of us, life is precious and worth living, yet every half hour one American intentionally commits suicide. Self-destruction is the seventh leading cause of death among people of all ages in this country. But even more striking is the fact that it ranks fourth among adolescents between the ages of fifteen and nineteen, and it is assuming greater importance as deaths from other causes decline (Knott, 1973; McAnarney, 1975). In this age group suicide is exceeded as a cause of death only by accidents, malignant neoplasms, and homicide, whereas among college students it is second to accidents and two times higher than in the same-aged youngsters who are not attending college (Knott, 1973; McAnarney, 1975). Moreover, studies have shown that students enrolled in the most prestigious universities (Yale, Harvard, Oxford, and Cambridge) have higher suicide rates than those attending lower-ranked schools, although those who take their own lives tend to have better academic records than their peers (Ross, 1969; Seiden, 1969; McCulloch and Philip, 1972).

In 1972 the rate of suicides for those between the ages of fifteen and twenty-four was 10 per 100,000, less than 1 per 100,000 for ten- to fourteen-year-olds, and almost nonexistent in children under ten (*Monthly Vital Statistics Report: Annual Summary for the United States, 1972*, published 1973). At all ages more males take their own lives than females by a ratio of almost 3:1, although females greatly outnumber males in terms of suicide attempts (Toolan, 1968). Self-destruction is not the exclusive behavior of any particular socioeconomic or educational level, religion, or occupation. However, the suicide rate seems to be higher in middle and upper classes than in the lower socioeconomic class, in urban than in rural dwellers, in Caucasians than in blacks, in the higher educated professional and student populations, and among Protestants as compared to Jews and Catholics. However, there is some recent indication that suicide is on the increase for young black males and females living in large urban centers as well as for divorced persons of both sexes (Morris et al., 1974; Schneer, Perstein, and Brozovsky, 1975). Suicide among children between the ages of eight and seventeen tends to occur most frequently during the spring, although this seasonal relationship is independent of temperature, humidity, wind, or weather conditions (Mulcock, 1955; Porkorny, Davis, and Harberson, 1963).

For children between the ages of ten and fourteen, the preferred method of suicide is hanging and strangulation, while fifteen- to nineteen-year-olds most often use firearms and explosives, followed in frequency by poisoning and strangulation. More girls than boys in the older group use poison (Bakwin and Bakwin, 1972), and this may, in part, explain the reversal of the sex ratio in attempted and actual suicides. Boys, who are more successful than girls in killing themselves, are inclined to use the more masculine weapon—firearms—as their means of suicide. Consequently, they have less chance of survival or of being found before death occurs; whereas girls may have a higher attempted suicide rate than boys because they prefer poisons, which act slower and increase the possibility of survival.

Most observers agree that suicide figures, particularly among children, are underestimated because the criteria used by coroners in reporting the official cause of death differ widely, and because families and others involved tend to protect the living (and the dead child) from the guilt and social stigma that such an event usually brings. In addition, self-destructive behavior may be expressed in ways that are not easily categorized as suicidal, as may be the case with some car accidents by reckless drivers, overdose of drugs, or those homicides where victims precipitate and provoke their own murder (Schuyler, 1973). When instances of attempted suicide are considered, the magnitude of the problem is even greater. It has been estimated that for every successful adult suicide, there are approximately eight to ten unsuccessful attempts, while the ratio dramatically jumps to as high as 1:120 for teenagers (Finch, and Poznanski, 1971; Kreitman, 1972).

Apart from the essential condition of life or death, the difference between attempted and actual suicide is often a fortuitous matter that is dependent on the subject's lethal intent and the care with which the self-destruction is planned and carried out. The act of suicide is not as much a wish to die as it is a desperate response to the utter futility of life and its unalterable and intolerable circumstances. Were it only possible to find a solution to their problems, many would readily choose to live rather than die. Coleman (1972) refers to an unpublished report by Farberow and Litman (1970) in which the following three types of suicidal behavior are described:

1. Those who use suicide as a way of communicating their distress to others, but not as an actual wish to die. This behavior represents about two-thirds of the suicide population in which suicidal attempts are minor and arranged to be

interrupted (although sometimes the plan backfires).

2. This group comprises another 30 percent of the suicide population, and it represents those who are ambivalent about death and who rely on chance or fate to determine the final outcome of their suicidal behavior. Dangerous but slow-acting methods of suicide are characteristically used by these individuals.
3. This is the smallest group, consisting of about 3 to 5 percent of the suicide population and involving individuals who are intent on killing themselves. Little or no opportunity for interruption is left open, and the most certain and instant means of death are chosen, such as shooting or jumping from tall buildings.

It is clear from Farberow and Litman's descriptive account that better than 95 percent of suicidal acts are committed with some wish to live. Many attempts are either interrupted or aborted, but among those who have attempted suicide, approximately 10 percent eventually are successful (*prevention of Suicide*, 1968).

Suicide and Abnormal Behavior

While it is true that suicide is more prevalent in those who manifest abnormal behavior, it should be noted that the two are separate and distinct entities (Wolfe and Cotler, 1973; Schneer, Perstein, and Brozovsky, 1975). Suicides can and do occur in persons who otherwise show no evidence of classifiable psychopathology, and it is also apparent that not all those who have a diagnosable abnormal disorder evidence suicidal inclinations. Nevertheless, most of us are apt to consider suicide irrational, seemingly the product of a disordered and troubled mind.

For adults, the evidence indicates that former inmates of mental hospitals have a far greater risk of suicide than that expected in the population at large, and that 15 percent of those diagnosed as manifesting one of the affective psychoses die by their own hand. Higher rates (but not as high as the affective disorders) are also found in schizophrenics, organics, alcoholics, sociopaths, and psychoneurotics (Osmond and Hoffer, 1967; *Prevention of Suicide*, 1968; Lester and Lester, 1971; Goodwin, 1973). As many as 50 percent of all actual suicides are committed by persons suffering from some form of depression (Choron, 1972). As a general rule, suicide attempts are more likely to occur in neurotics, while completed suicides are more apt to be found among psychotic individuals (Lester and Lester, 1971).

The relationship between suicide and abnormal disorders is less clear among children and adolescents than among adults. Except for psychotic youngsters, most adolescents who attempt suicide do not evidence discernible changes in behavior that would serve as a reliable warning to those around them (Otto, 1964; Sanborn, Sanborn, and Cimbolic, 1973). For that matter, there is nothing especially significant about the events or circumstances that precipitate the adolescent's suicide: These are often stressors that are common during this age period, such as a quarrel with a parent, sibling, or friend, or the sudden dissolving of a romantic relationship. In addition, as noted in Chapter 12, depression in children and adolescents tends to be overlooked or undiagnosed because it represents a disorder that many do not expect to find in young people, and because the clinical picture is less clear than it is with adults. The sharp and sudden mood swings and the emotional lability that characterize the adolescent often serve to mask depressive episodes: Only instances of the most profound symptoms, such as loss of appetite, sleep difficulties, and social withdrawal, are readily recognized. Behavioral equivalents of depression in teenagers may be truancy, somatic preoccupation, restlessness, and antisocial acting out. Among those adolescents who have attempted suicide, approximately 40 percent showed depressive symptoms (Mattsson, Seese, and Hawkins, 1969). Psychotic youngsters who attempt suicide are more apt to give no warning, use more serious lethal methods, and show the greatest risk during the first year of their disorder or during an acute psychotic episode. Probably the largest group of teenagers manifesting suicidal behavior are those impulse-ridden, angry, and vengeful youngsters who are unable to adequately cope with a variety of psychological and social problems. They often are manipulative, and when angry they threaten either homicide and/or suicide (Finch and Poznanski, 1971).

Etiological Considerations

Suicidal behavior is puzzling and difficult to explain. As noted above, some emphasize psychopathology as the primary and underlying cause, but surely this is not a sufficient explanation—it neither accounts for those emotionally disturbed individuals who do not try to kill themselves nor for those who are not disordered but who do attempt suicide. The popular idea that genetic factors are implicated in suicide has not been empirically supported (Kallmann et al., 1949), while the only biological variable found to be positively related to suicidal behavior, premenstrual and menstrual cycle, fails to provide an unequivocal interpretation (Mandell and Mandell, 1967; Tonks, Rack, and Rose, 1968). The relationship may be viewed either as implicating hormonal factors or as supporting a psychogenic position in which premenstrual and menstrual tensions serve to heighten emotional stress.

In the main, investigators have focused on psychological and social variables in their search to understand the etiology of suicide. Many psychological studies and clinical reports have been influenced by the Freudian notion that suicide represents repressed aggression that is turned inward either because of the death instinct (thanatos) or due to the loss of a love object for whom there are ambivalent feelings. To be sure, it can be argued that suicide is an act of aggression against oneself, but to do so in psychoanalytic terms is to make inferences about the unconscious motivation of the victim. This is not easily tested or demonstrated; data cannot be obtained from those who have been successful, and there is an inherent difficulty in uncovering information that is presumed to be out of the awareness of the subject. Nevertheless, it is not surprising that studies have been undertaken within the psychoanalytic, and later within a learning, orientation that attend to the relationship between early childhood experiences and suicidal behavior. Loss of a parent—either through death, separation, divorce, or desertion—and how it relates to attempted and completed suicide, has yielded conflicting results. However, the data from recent studies of college students and adolescents strongly suggest that parental loss by age sixteen is an important factor in the development of suicidal tendencies and is a very important variable in producing suicide (Jacobs and Teicher, 1967; Jacobs, 1971; Lester, 1972; Wolfe and Cotler, 1973. Adams, Lohrenz, and Harper, 1973; Knott, 1973). Families of adolescent boys of low socioeconomic status who had attempted suicide were clinically studied by Margolin and Teicher (1968), who found that the boys were unwanted babies and that their mothers were angry, depressed, and withdrawn before and after pregnancy. Moreover, the boys were deprived of maternal affection and attention during the first year of life and experienced loss of the father sometime before the age of four or five. Frequently the boys acted as heads of their households and as husbands to their mothers, but maternal love was not reciprocated. Attempts at suicide often came at a time when the mother was depressed and withdrawn, and when the boy experienced maternal rejection or loss of her love. However, we must keep in mind that these findings exemplify much of the clinical literature where impressions are reported in the absence of adequate control groups and data analysis.

Another line of psychological research has consisted of attempts to determine personality correlates of suicidal behavior. Studies have shown that adolescents who attempt suicide are more irritable and impulsive, more negative about themselves, and more apt to be rigid thinkers, to be involved in conflict situations, and to have communication problems than their nonsuicidal counterparts (Jacobs, 1971; Lester and Lester, 1971; Levenson, 1974). In addition, these youngsters characteristically tend to use sleep as an escape from problems, although insomnia frequently appears as a presuicidal symptom (Lester and Lester, 1971).

Toolan (1968) studied a sample of 102 children (mostly adolescents) who were admitted to Bellevue Hospital in New York City for either suicide attempts or threats. He found that most were immature and impulsive, and were diagnosed as having behavioral and character disorders. On the basis of his clinical examination of these records, he arrived at the following five categories of causes: (1) internalized anger at another, (2) manipulative attempts either to gain love or to punish others, (3) a cry for help and a distress signal, (4) a psychoticlike reaction to inner disintegration, and (5) a wish to join a dead relative. More recently Jacobs (1971) postulated a sequence of etiological steps regarding adolescent suicide, which includes a chronic history of problems throughout childhood to the beginning of adolescence, an increase in problems beyond that which is normally associated with the period of adolescence, progressive failure of the coping mechanisms to deal with the rise in problems, withdrawal and feelings of despair prior to the suicide attempt, and finally the rationalization (justification) of suicide to narrow the discrepancy between the suicidal thought and action.

Among college students suicidal behavior has been attributed to a number of stressors that are particularly prominent during these years of schooling. Knight (1968) described fear of homosexuality, identity confusion, separation anxiety (resolving dependency while thrust into independent functioning), depression, fear of academic failure, and conflicts over the expression of aggressive feelings as potential determinants of suicidal acts in students. Knott (1973) found that students who attempted suicide reported feelings of rejection, hopelessness, and self-blame; and they evidenced more somatic complaints related to their emotional discomfort (headaches) than did control subjects. Suicidal students, more frequently than nonsuicidal ones, come from families in which there are a greater number of divorces, separations during childhood, and death of a parent. Further, their families are highly educated—suggesting the possibility that they are under more pressure to achieve academically (Blaine and Carmen, 1968; Adams, Lohrenz, and Harper, 1973). In addition, more suicide attempts are made by freshmen than by older students, and certain aspects of the college environment, such as "impoverished interpersonal relationships, and intense, competitive atmosphere," are related to suicidal gestures (Wolfe and Cotler, 1973; Knott, 1973, p. 68).

Studies of the social variables involved in suicidal behavior have been influenced greatly by Durkheim's sociological view of suicide (Durkheim, 1951). After analyzing suicide records obtained in different countries, Durkheim posited that suicidal behavior is common in societies where there is a high and a low degree of social integration and social regulation. Societies with a moderate degree of both social integration and regulation have the lowest incidence of suicide. For example, suicide is higher among the divorced, widowed, and single individuals, and lower among those who are married—that is, higher for those who have a low degree of social integration than for those who have maintained group ties. However, a high degree of group identification, such as evidenced by the Japanese during World War II and the Buddhist monks of Vietnam, is likely to heighten the suicide rate, as in the case of hari-kari and of monks burning themselves to protest against the policies of the Vietnamese government. In addition, when group standards or norms decline in their social regulatory influence (anomie), such as in periods of economic depression or social revolution, the incidence of suicide is likely to be high. Using data from a sample of fifty-five societies, Rootman (1973) found that social integration may be more important than social regulation as a determinant of suicide rates.

The major problem with Durkheim's theory is similar to the one encountered with other sociological views; namely, it does not account for the different behaviors of individuals who have been exposed to the same demands and conditions of a given society. Nevertheless, the research dealing with the realtionship between social variables and suicidal acts has shown that when group condemnation of suicide is high, the incidence is low (Catholics have a very low rate of suicidal behavior). Moreover, unemployment carries a greater risk of completed suicides, and both low and high occupational status have a high incidence of suicide (Farber, 1968; Tuckman and Youngman, 1968; Ravensborg and Foss, 1969; Stengel, 1970). In addition, suicide seems to be negatively related to the state of the economy, and positively correlated to social disorganization as reflected in the instability introduced into the social system of a mental hospital by an influx of new patients and staff (Kahne, 1968; Simon, 1968).

As research continues, it is clear that the data currently available do not provide any systematic or satisfactory answer to the perplexing question of why people try to kill themselves. Much emphasis is now placed on the matter of prevention.

Prevention Approaches

One obvious approach to prevention is to devise a method whereby individuals who are suicide risks can be successfully identified. Psychologists have, in fact, addressed themselves to this issue, using either existing tests such as the MMPI, the Rorschach, and the TAT, or constructing new instruments specifically designed for this purpose. Lester (1970) provides us with a good review of the literature, in which he notes that many studies have methodological limitations in addition to the more obvious problem of finding individuals to test prior to, rather than following, their suicidal acts. There is also the problem of securing adequate data from those who have been successful in their suicide attempts. Lester concludes that the TAT, Bender-Gestalt, Semantic Differential, and Rosenzweig Picture-Frustration Test were of little or no value in identifying suicide risks, whereas the use of the sign approach with the Rorschach and profile analysis with the MMPI showed promise. New and specially designed tests have not proved useful in identifying suicide risks or in discriminating those who have threatened from those who have attempted suicide. A more recent study by Resnick and Kendra (1973) found that the Scale for Assessing Suicidal Risk failed to identify suicide risk potential among hospitalized patients who attempted suicide.

The second major preventive thrust, the crisis intervention approach, is probably well known among laypersons: Almost every major community in the country operates such a program. In general, crisis intervention is not intended to provide long-term treatment for problems. Rather, its central focus is on intervention and referral. Crisis centers never close, and individuals may make contact either by phone or in person at any hour of the day or night, seven days a week. They usually are staffed by medical personnel who provide emergency medical treatment, as well as by other trained personnel who deal with psychological problems. Counselors attempt to establish rapport with the client, to maintain contact, and to obtain information about the specific nature of the current problem. At the same time they assess the potential suicide risk and the strengths of the client, as well as other resources. To the extent possible, counselors and other members of the staff help formulate a constructive plan of action for the client, as well as try to mobilize the client to follow their recommendations.

Although there is both public and professional support for the value and effectiveness of crisis intervention centers, there is, in fact, little evaluative data available to date. The few studies that have attempted to compare suicide rates in communities with and without crisis programs have produced conflicting and not overly supportive results; and studies that have tried to evaluate the effectiveness of some centers in reducing suicide have shown increases in suicide or additional suicidal attempts in 20 percent of those treated intensively (Weiner, 1969; Bagley, 1971).

SUMMARY

Several major problems of adolescence and youth were considered in this chapter—*delinquency, drug abuse,* and *suicide.*

Information about the incidence, and a description of the types, of delinquent behaviors were provided in Tables 13–1, 13–2, and 13–3. A summary of the factors known to be related to delinquency, as well as its etiological considerations and therapeutic approaches, is also given in Table 13–4.

Drug abuse (arrests for drug offenses) has increased by a staggering 4,673.3 percent for youngsters under eighteen, as compared to an increase of 774.6 percent for persons over eighteen, between 1960 and 1970. Experimenting with drugs and the use of multiple drugs are common among high school and college students, with males showing a higher incidence than females by a ratio of about 2:1. For adolescents and college-aged youngsters, the problem is sizeable and serious at all levels of the social scale. Excessive consumption of alcohol by adolescents was also discussed as an area of growing concern.

Other than some inconclusive evidence about alcoholism, there are no clear-cut data implicating either genetic or biological factors as causes of drug abuse. The weight of the present evidence points to cultural and social learning variables as playing the most significant role in the etiology of alcoholism and drug abuse. Psychoanalytic and tension-reduction models of learning were discussed—along with modeling, peer affiliation, and the opportunity to behave without inhibition while under the influence—as possible etiological factors operating in the development of drug abuse.

Various therapeutic measures were presented, but it was noted that alcoholism and drug abuse represent very heterogeneous populations that one may erroneously view as homogeneous because of the way these common behaviors are classified. Biological approaches attempt to restore some sort of physiological balance and provide some effect that renders using the drug either unnecessary or undesirable. Such approaches include detoxification programs, the use of Antabuse to make drinking aversive, and the substitution of maintenance doses of methadone for heroin. Individual psychotherapy, group and family therapy, and behavior therapies were discussed and evaluated in light of the available literature. Self-help organizations such as Alcoholics Anonymous and Synanon were described as widely known and popular treatment programs for alcoholism and drug abuse. Issues complicating the evaluation of outcome were also discussed.

Suicide ranks fourth as a cause of death for adolescents between the ages of fifteen and nineteen, and only second to accidents among college students. It seems to be higher in the middle and upper classes, in urban dwellers, in Caucasians, in educated professional and student populations, and among Protestants. For children between ten and fourteen, the preferred method of suicide is hanging and strangulation, while fifteen- to nineteen-year-olds prefer guns. Boys have a higher incidence of completed suicides, and girls have a higher attempted suicide rate.

Suicide is not always attributable to abnormal conditions, but in fact these are two separate and distinct entities. The relationship between suicide and abnormal disorders is less clear among children and adolescents

Table 13-4 Delinquency

Related Factors	*Etiological Considerations*	*Therapeutic Approaches*
Delinquency is related to low socioeconomic background, especially in urban areas. When unrecorded instances of delinquency are obtained, there is no difference in socioeconomic levels.	1. Gangs arise from playgroups as a result of conflict with other groups and as a means of banding individuals together. 2. Out of difficulties in successfully achieving middle-class goals, lower-class boys affiliate to legitimatize their aggression against middle-class institutions and to bolster self-esteem. 3. Different types of delinquent subcultures are formed by lower class urban males as attempts to adapt to pressures created by the limited accessibility of middle-class channels. 4. Middle-class delinquency is a gradual outgrowth of normal group activities, in which deviant explorations become the group standard.	Juvenile judge may sentence to training or detention facilities, place on probation, or refer elsewhere for remedial measures.
More delinquents come from broken than from unbroken homes. Both extreme permissiveness and extreme strictness are associated with delinquency, although inconsistent discipline is most damaging. Parental rejection is also related.	Psychological-personality problems are likely to be found in deficiencies of the ego or of the superego.	Institutionalization offers poor programs, and no more than 20 to 30 percent improve from them.
Delinquents are poor academic performers and have high dropout rates from school.	Systematic research on aggression as an operant response shows that it is maintained by reinforcements that are readily available in the environment.	Community-based programs involving individual and group therapy, vocational counseling, and supervision by probation officer are no more effective in reducing recidivism than incarceration.
Mesomorphic body type is related to delinquency, and positive EEG spike patterns are frequently noted.	Aggressive behavior is acquired through imitation or modeling.	Psychotherapy under court authority may be useful. Milieu-residential programs where group interaction and socialization are emphasized have been tried, but without adequate evaluation.
	Multifactor views relate mesomorphic body build with personality traits of aggressiveness, adventurousness, and acquisitiveness were found in delinquent youngsters. Also, they disliked school, were scholastically retarded, were pugnacious toward schoolmates, were truant, and misbehaved at an earlier age than nondelinquents.	Behavior modification in which positive reinforcement, punishment, and token systems were used to alter antisocial behavior and improve level of education have been successful.
		However, more research to determine the long-term effects of behavior modification is necessary before a final verdict can be rendered about this treatment approach.

than among adults. There is nothing discernible about the precipitating events and circumstances of adolescent suicide, and depression in youngsters tends to be overlooked and undiagnosed.

Genetic factors are not implicated as a cause of suicide, and other than a relationship between menstrual cycle and suicide, there are no significant biological variables as yet uncovered. In the search to understand the etiology of suicide, the major emphasis has been on psychological and social variables.

Preventive approaches to suicide have taken two major courses: the construction of psychometric devices to identify those individuals who are suicide risks, and the crisis intervention programs that aim to prevent suicide by providing support and assistance during times of personal crisis. Neither approach has, as yet, demonstrated effectiveness.

EPILOGUE

In Defense of Youth

We call them wrong! God pity us, the blind,
Imputing evil as our grandsires did,
When we explored new realms with feet and mind,
Uncovering what old fogies damned and hid!
The dreams, the wanton fantasies are there,
As you and I once knew them loved them, till
We came to staleness and to foolish fear
Lest something change, be different, jolt our will!
'Tis life they seek, not sin, no sordid thing,
But joy in health and beauty, and in all
The urge of thrilling bodies that would sing
And freely dance with laughter at earth's call.
Let's laugh with them, full knowing that when tried
By Truth and Duty, Youth is on God's side!

Barstow

REFERENCES

Achenbach, T. M., and Edelbrock, C. S. Behavioral Problems and Competencies Reported by Parents of Normal and Disturbed Children Aged Four Through Sixteen. *Monographs of the Society for Research in Child Development,* 1981, *46,* Serial No. 188.

Adams, K. S., Lohrenz, J. G., and Harper, D. Suicidal Ideation and Parental Loss: A Preliminary Research Report. *Canadian Psychiatric Association Journal,* 1973, *18,* 95–100.

Aichhorn, A. *Delinquency and Child Guidance.* New York: International Universities Press, 1969.

Anderson, R. E. Where's Dad? Paternal Deprivation and Delinquency. *Archives of General Psychiatry,* 1968, *18,* 641–649.

Baer, D. J., and Corrado, J. J. Heroin Addict Relationships with Parents during Childhood and Early Adolescent Years. *Journal of Geriatric Psychology,* 1974, *124,* 99–103.

Bagley, C. An Evaluation of Suicide Prevention Agencies. *Life Threatening Behavior,* 1971, *1,* 245–259.

Bakwin, H., and Bakwin, R. M. *Behavior Disorders in Children,* 4th ed. Philadelphia: Saunders, 1972.

Bandura, A. *Principles of Behavior Modification.* New York: Holt, Rinehart and Winston, 1969a.

Bandura, A. Social-Learning Theory of Identifactory Processes. In D. A. Goslin (eds), *Handbook of Socialization Theory and Research.* Chicago: Rand McNally, 1969b, pp. 213–262.

Bandura, A. *Social Learning Theory.* Englewood Cliffs, N. J.: Prentice-Hall, 1977.

Bandura, A., Ross, D., and Ross, S. A. Imitation of Film-Moderated Aggressive Models. *Journal of Abnormal and Social Psychology,* 1963, *66,* 3–11.

Bandura, A., and Walters, R. H. *Adolescent Aggression: A Study of the Influence of Child-Training Practices and Family Interrelationships.* New York: Ronald Press, 1959.

Barstow, R. W. "In Defense of Youth." In T. C. Clar, and E. A. Gillespie (eds.), *1000 Quotable Poems: An Anthology of Modern Verse.* New York: Willett, Clark, 1937, pp. 290–291.

Bates, R. F. Cultural Differences in Rates of Alcoholism. *Quarterly Journal of Studies on Alcohol,* 1946, *6,* 480–499.

Bates, W., and Crowther, B. *Drugs: Causes, Circumstances, and Effects of Their Use.* Morristown, N. J.: General Learning Press, 1973.

Belson, W. A. *Television Violence and the Adolescent Boy.* Farnborough, England: Saxon House, 1978.

Berman, A., and Siegal, A. A Neuropsychological Approach to the Etiology, Prevention, and Treatment of Juvenile Delinquency. In A. Davids (ed.), *Child Personality and Psychopathology,* Vol. 3. New York: John Wiley, 1976, pp. 259–294.

Blackford, L. *Student Drug Use Surveys, San Mateo County, California.* Preliminary Report, County Department of Health and Welfare, San Mateo, 1974.

Blaine, G. B., Jr., and Carmen, C. R. Causal Factors in Suicidal Attempts by Male and Female College Students. *American Journal of Psychiatry*, 1968, *125*, 834–837.

Block, J. and Martin, B. Predicting the Behavior of Children Under Frustration. *Journal of Abnormal and Social Psychology*, 1955, *51*, 281–285.

Blum, E. M. Psychoanalytic Views of Alcoholism: A Review. *Quarterly Journal of Studies on Alcohol*, 1966, *27*, 259–299.

Buss, A. H. Instrumentality of Aggression, Feedback, and Frustration as Determinants of Physical Aggression. *Journal of Personality and Social Psychology*, 1966, 3, 153–162.

Calahan, D., and Room, R. *Problem Drinking among American Men*. New Haven, Conn.: College and University Press, 1974.

Callner, D. A. Behavioral Treatment Approaches to Drug Abuse: A Critical Review of the Research. *Psychological Bulletin*, 1975, 82, 143–164.

Cantwell, D. P. Hyperactivity and Antisocial Behavior. *Journal of the American Academy of Child Psychiatry*, 1978, *17*, 252–262.

Cavan, R. S., and Cavan, J. T. *Delinquency and Crime: Cross-Cultural Perspectives*. Philadelphia: Lippincott, 1968.

The Challenge of Crime in a Free Society. A Report by the President's Commission on Law Enforcement and Administration of Justice. Washington, D.C.: U.S. Government Printing Office, 1967.

Chandler, M. J. Egocentrism and Antisocial Behavior: The Assessment and Training of Social Perspective-taking Skills. *Developmental Psychology*, 1973, 9, 326–332.

Chapel, J. L., and Taylor, D. W. Drugs for Kicks. In J. P. Reed, and F. Baali (eds.), *Faces of Delinquency*. Englewood Cliffs, N.J.: Prentice-Hall, 1972, pp. 64–65.

Choron, J. *Suicide*. New York: Scribner's, 1972.

Clark, J., and Wenninger, E. Socioeconomic Class and Area as Correlates of Illegal Behavior among Juveniles. *American Sociological Review*, 1962, *27*, 826–834.

Clark, R., and Polish, E. Avoidance Conditioning and Alcohol Consumption in Rhesus Monkeys. *Science*, 1960, *132*, 223–224.

Cohen, A. K. *Delinquent Boys, the Culture of the Gang*. Glencoe, Ill.: The Free Press, 1955.

Cohen, H. L., and Filipczak, J. *A New Learning Environment*. San Francisco: Jossey-Bass, 1971.

Coleman, J. C. *Abnormal Psychology and Modern Life*, 4th ed. Chicago: Scott, Foresman, 1972.

Conger, J. J. The Effects of Alcohol on Conflict Behavior in the Albino Rat. *Quarterly Journal of Studies on Alcohol*, 1951, *12*, 1–29.

Cortes, J. B., and Gatti, F. M. *Delinquency and Crime: A Biopsychosocial Approach: Empirical, Theoretical, and Practical Aspects of Clinical Behavior*. New York: Seminar Press, 1972.

Crime in the United States: Uniform Crime Reports. Federal Bureau of Investigation. Washington, D.C.: U.S. Government Printing Office, 1981.

Current Views of College Students on Politics and Drugs. *Gallup Opinion Index*, Report No. 80, Princeton, N.J.: Gallup International, February 1972.

Dalgard, O. J., and Kringlen, E. A Norwegian Twin Study of Criminality. *British Journal of Criminology*, 1976, *16*, 213–232.

Davidson, W. S., and Seidman, E. Studies of Behavior Modification and Juvenile Delinquency: A Review, Methodological Critique, and Social Perspective. *Psychological Bulletin*, 1974, *81*, 998–1011.

DeJong, W., and Stewart, C. *Project CREST Gainesville, Florida*. U.S. Department of Justice, National Institute of Justice, Office of Development, Testing and Dissemination, July 1980.

Dole, V. P., and Nyswander, M. A Medical Treatment for Diacetylmorphine (Heroin) Addiction: A Clinical Trial with Methadone Hydrochloride. *Journal of the American Medical Association*, 1965, *193*, 646–650.

Dollard, J., Doob, L. W., Miller, N. E., Mowrer, O. H., and Sears, R. R. *Frustration and Aggression*. New Haven, Conn.: Yale University Press, 1939.

Droppa, D. C. Behavioral Treatment of Drug Addiction: A Review and Analysis. *International Journal of the Addictions*, 1973, *8*, 143–161.

Dupont, R. L., and Greene, M. H. The Dynamics of a Heroin Addiction Epidemic. *Science*, 1973, *181*, 716–722.

Durkheim, E. *Le Suicide*. Paris: Librarie Felix Alcan (1897) Trans. J. A. Spaulding and G. Simpson. Glencoe, Ill.: Free Press, 1951.

Eldefonso, E. *Youth Problems and Law Enforcement*. Englewood Cliffs, N. J.: Prentice-Hall, 1972.

Elliott, D. S. Delinquency, School Attendance and Dropout. *Social Problems*, 1966, *13*, 307–314.

Elliott, D. S., Voss, H. L., and Wendling, A. Capable Dropouts and the Social Milieu of the High School. *Journal of Educational Research*, 1966, *60*, 180–186.

Empey, L. T. *American Delinquency: Its Meaning and Construction*. Homewood, Ill.: Dorsey Press, 1978.

Empey, L. T., and Erickson, M. L. Hidden Delinquency and Social Status. *Social Forces*, 1966, *44*, 546–554.

England, R. W., Jr. A Theory of Middle-class Juvenile Delinquency. In J. P. Reed and F. Baali (eds.), *Faces of Delinquency*. Englewood Cliffs, N. J.: Prentice-Hall, 1972, pp. 270–277.

Erickson, M. L., and Empey, L. T. Class Position, Peers, and Delinquency. *Sociology and Social Research*, 1965, *49*, 268–282.

Eron, L. D. Prescription for Reduction of Aggression. *American Psychologist*, 1980, *35*, 244–252.

Eron, L. D., Husemann, L. R., Lefkowitz, M. M., and Walder, L. O. Does Television Violence Cause Aggression? *American Psychologist*, 1972, *27*, 253–263.

Farber, M. L. *Theory of Suicide*. New York: Funk and Wagnalls, 1968.

Farberow, N. L., and Litman, R. E. *A Comprehensive*

Suicide Prevention Program. Suicide Prevention Center of Los Angeles, 1958–1969. Unpublished final report, Department of Health, Education and Welfare, NIMH Grants No. MH 14946 and MH 00128, Los Angeles, 1970.

FINCH, S. M., and POZNANSKI, E. O. *Adolescent Suicide*. Springfield, Ill.: Chas. C Thomas, 1971.

FREED, E. X. Drug Abuse by Alcoholics: A Review. *International Journal of the Addictions*, 1973, 8, 451–473.

FREEDMAN, B. J., ROSENTHAL, L., DONAHOE, C. P., SCHLUNDT, D. G., and MCFALL, R. M. A Social-Behavioral Analysis of Skill Deficits in Delinquent and Nondelinquent Adolescent Boys. *Journal of Consulting and Clinical Psychology*, 1978, *46*, 1448–1462.

FREEMAN, B., and SAVASTONA, G. The Affluent Youthful Offender. *Crime and Delinquency*, 1970, *16*, 264–272.

GANDOSSY, R. P., WILLIAMS, J. R., COHEN, J., and HARWOOD, H. J. *Drugs and Crime: A Survey and Analysis of the Literature*. U. S. Department of Justice, National Institute of Justice, May 1980.

GAY, G. R., INABA, D. S., SHEPPARD, C. W., NEWMEYER, J. A., and RAPPOLT, R. T. Cocaine: History, Epidemiology, Human Pharmacology, and Treatment. A Perspective on a New Debut for an Old Girl. *Clinical Toxicology*, 1975, 8, 149–178.

GERGEN, M. K., GERGEN, K. J., and MORSE, S. J. *Journal of Applied Social Psychology*, 1972, *2*, 1–16.

GIBBENS, T. C. N. *Psychiatric Studies of Borstal Lads*. London and New York: Oxford University Press, 1963.

GIBBONS, D. C. *Delinquent Behavior*. Englewood Cliffs, N. J.: Prentice-Hall, 1970.

GLUECK, E. *Unraveling Juvenile Delinquency*. New York: Commonwealth Fund, 1950.

GLUECK, S., and GLUECK, E. *Physique and Delinquency*. New York: Harper and Row, 1956.

GLUECK, S., and GLUECK, E. *Delinquents and Nondelinquents in Perspective*. Cambridge, Mass. Harvard University Press, 1968.

GOLDENBERG, H. *Abnormal Psychology: A Social/Community Approach*. Monterey, Calif.: Brooks/Cole, 1977.

GOODWIN, D. W. Alcohol in Suicide and Homicide. *Quarterly Journal of Studies on Alcohol*, 1973, *34*, 144–156.

GOODWIN, D. W., SCHULSINGER, F., HERMANSEN, L., GUZE, S. B., and WINOKUR, G. Alcohol Problems in Adoptees Raised Apart from Alcoholic Biological Parents. *Archives of General Psychiatry*, 1973, *28*, 238–243.

GOODWIN, D. W., SCHULSINGER, F., MOLLER, N., HERMANSEN, L., WINOKUR, G., and GUZE, S. B. Drinking Problems in Adopted and Nonadopted Sons of Alcoholics. *Archives of General Psychiatry*, 1974, *31*, 164–169.

GOSS, A., and MOROSKO, T. E. Alcoholism and Clinical Symptoms. *Journal of Abnormal and Social Psychology*, 1969, *74*, 682–684.

GRINSPOON, L., and HEDBLOM, P. *The Speed Culture: Amphetamine Use and Abuse in America*. Cambridge, Mass.: Harvard University Press, 1975.

GRINSPOON, L., and BAKALAR, J. B. Adverse Effects of Cocaine: Selected Issues. *Annals of the New York Academy of Sciences*, 1981, *362*, 125–131.

HALIKAS, J. A., and RIMMER, J. D. Predictions of Multiple Drug Abuse. *Archives of General Psychiatry*, 1974, *31*, 414–418.

HANEY, B., and GOLD, M. The Juvenile Delinquent Nobody Knows. *Psychology Today*, 1973, 7, 49–55.

HARBIN, H. T., and MAZAIR, H. M. The Families of Drug Abusers: A Literature Review. *Family Process*, 1975, *14*, 411–432.

HATHAWAY, S. R., and MONACHESI, E. D., *Adolescent Personality and Behavior: MMPI Patterns of Normal, Delinquent, Dropout, and other Outcomes*. Minneapolis: University of Minnesota Press, 1963.

HETHERINGTON, E. M., and MARTIN, B. Family Interaction. In H. C. Quay and J. S. Werry (eds.), *Psychopathological Disorders of Childhood*, 2nd ed. New York: John Wiley, 1979, pp. 247–302.

HERRICK, R. To the Virgins, to Make Much of Time. In A. W. Allison, H. Barrows, C. R. Blake, A. J. Carr, A. M. Eastman, and H. M. English, Jr. (eds.), *The Norton Anthology of Poetry*. New York: W. W. Norton and Co., 1975, p. 111.

HIGGINS, R. L., and MARLATT, G. A. The Effect of Anxiety Arousal on the Consumption of Alcohol by Alcoholics and Social Drinkers. *Journal of Consulting and Clinical Psychology*, 1973, *41*, 426–433.

HIGGINS, R. L., and MARLATT, G. A. Fear of Interpersonal Evaluation as a Determinant of Alcohol Consumption in Male Social Drinkers. *Journal of Abnormal Psychology*, 1975, *84*, 644–651.

HILL, M. J., and BLANE, H. T. Evaluation of Psychotherapy with Alcoholics: A Critical Review. *Quarterly Journal of Studies on Alcohol*, 1967, *28*, 76–104.

HOOK, E. B. Behavioral Implications of the Human XYY Genotype. *Science*, 1973, *179*, 139–150.

JACOBS, J. *Adolescent Suicide*. New York: Wiley-Interscience, 1971.

JACOBS, J., and TEICHER, J. D. Broken Homes and Social Isolation in Attempted Suicides of Adolescents. *International Journal of Social Psychiatry*, 1967, *13*, 139–149.

JEFFREY, C. R., and JEFFREY, I. A. Delinquents and Dropouts. An Experimental Program in Behavior Change. *Canadian Journal of Corrections*, 1970, *12*, 47–58.

JENKINS, R. L. *Behavior Disorders of Childhood and Adolescence*. Springfield, Ill.: Chas. C Thomas, 1973.

JENKINS, R. L., and BOYER, A. Types of Delinquent Behavior and Background Factors. *International Journal of Social Psychiatry*, 1968, *14*, 65–76.

JENKINS, R. L., and HEWITT, L. Types of Personality Structure Encountered in Child-Guidance Clinics. *American Journal of Orthopsychiatry*, 1944, *14*, 84–94.

JESSOR, S. L., and JESSOR, R. Maternal Ideology and Adolescent Problem Behavior. *Developmental Psychology*, 1974, *10*, 246–254.

JOHNSON, A. M. Sanctions for Superego Lacunae of Adolescents. In K. R. Eissler, (ed.), *Searchlights on*

Delinquency. New York: International Universities Press, 1949, pp. 225–245.

JOHNSTON, L. Drugs and American Youth: A Report from the Youth in Transition Project. Ann Arbor, Mich.: Institute for Social Research, University of Michigan, 1973.

Juvenile Court Statistical Series. U.S. Department of Health, Education and Welfare. Washington, D.C.: U.S. Government Printing Office, 1970, p. 10.

KAHN, M. The Physiology of Catharsis. *Journal of Personality and Social Psychology*, 1966, *3*, 278–286.

KAHN, M. W., and MCFARLAND, J. A Demographic and Treatment Evaluation Study of Institutionalized Juvenile Offenders. *Journal of Community Psychology*, 1973, *1*, 282–284.

KAHNE, M. J. Suicides in Mental Hospitals: A Study of the Effects of Personnel and Patient Turnover. *Journal of Health and Social Behavior*, 1968, *9*, 255–266.

KALLMANN, F. J., DEPORTE, J., DEPORTE, E., and FEINGOLD, L., Suicide in Twins and Only Children. *American Journal of Human Genetics*, 1949, *1*, 113–126.

KANDEL, D. Stages in Adolescent Involvement in Drug Use. *Science*, 1975, *190*, 912–914.

KAPLAN, M., RYAN, J. F., NATHAN, E., and BAIROS, M. The Control of Acting-out in the Psychotherapy of Delinquents. In S. A. Szurek and I. N. Berlin (eds.), *The Antisocial Child: His Family and His Community*. Palo Alto, Calif.: Science and Behavior Books, 1969, pp. 93–104.

KELLY, F. J. The Effectiveness of Survival Camp Training with Delinquents. *American Journal of Orthopsychiatry*, 1971, *41*, 305–306.

KENISTON, K. Prologue: Youth as a Stage of Life. In R. J. Havighurst and P. H. Dreyer (eds.), *Youth*. The 74th Yearbook of the National Society for the Study of Education. Chicago: The University of Chicago Press, 1975, pp. 3–26.

KNIGHT, J. A. Suicide among Students. In H. L. P. Resnik, (ed.), *Suicidal Behaviors: Diagnosis and Management*. Boston: Little, Brown, 1968, pp. 228–240.

KNOTT, J. E. Campus Suicide in America. *Omega: Journal of Death and Dying*, 1973, *4*, 65–71.

KREITMAN, N. Aspects of the Epidemiology of Suicide and "Attempted Suicide" (Parasuicide). In J. Wadenstrom, T. Larsson, and N. Ljungstedt (eds.), *Suicide and Attempted Suicide*. Stockholm: Nordiska Bokhandelns Forlag, 1972, pp. 45–46.

LENNARD, H. L., EPSTEIN, L. J., and ROSENTHAL, M. S., The Methadone Illusion. *Science*, 1972, *176*, 881–884.

LESTER, D. Attempts to Predict Suicidal Risk Using Psychological Tests. *Psychological Bulletin*, 1970, *74*, 1–17.

LESTER, D. *Why People Kill Themselves: A Summary of Research Findings on Suicidal Behavior*. Springfield, Ill.: Chas. C Thomas, 1972.

LESTER, G., and LESTER, D. *Suicide: The Gamble with Death*. Englewood Cliffs, N. J.: Prentice-Hall, 1971.

LEVENSON, M. Cognitive Correlates of Suicidal Risk. In C. Neuringer, (ed.), *Psychological Assessment of Suicidal Risk*. Springfield, Ill.: Chas. C Thomas, 1974, pp. 150–163.

MALLICK, S. K., and MCCANDLESS, B. R. A Study of Catharsis of Aggression. *Journal of Personality and Social Psychology*, 1966, *4*, 591–596.

MANDELL, A. J., and MANDELL, M. P. Suicide and the Menstrual Cycle. *Journal of the American Medical Association*, 1967, *200*, 792–793.

MARGOLIN, N. L., and TEICHER, J. D. Thirteen Adolescent Male Suicide Attemptors. *Journal of the American Academy of Child Psychiatry*, 1968, *7*, 296–315.

Marijuana: A Signal of Misunderstanding. National Commission on Marijuana and Drug Abuse. New York: Signet, 1972.

MARLATT, G. A., DEMMING, B., and REID, J. B. Loss of Control Drinking in Alcoholics: An Experimental Analogue. *Journal of Abnormal Psychology*, 1973, *81*, 233–241.

MASSERMAN, J. H., and YUM, K. S. An Analysis of the Influence of Alcohol on Experimental Neurosis in Cats. *Psychomatic Medicine*, 1946, *8*, 36–52.

MATTSSON, A., SEESE, L. R., and HAWKINS, J. W. Suicidal Behavior as a Child Psychiatric Emergency: Clinical Characteristics and Follow-up Results. *Archives of General Psychiatry*, 1969, *20*, 100–109.

MCANARNEY, E. R. Suicidal Behavior of Children and Youth. *The Pediatric Clinics of North America*, 1975, *22*, 595–604.

MCCORD, W. M., MCCORD, J., and ZOLA, I. K. *Origins of Crime: A New Evaluation of the Cambridge-Somerville Youth Study*. Montclair, N. J.: Patterson, Smith, 1969.

MCCULLOCH, J. W., and PHILIP, A. E. *Suicidal Behavior*. Oxford: Pergamon Press, 1972.

MCDONALD, L. *Social Class and Delinquency*. London: Faber and Faber, 1969.

MCGLOTHLIN, W. D. Drug Use and Abuse. In M. F. Rosenzweig and L. W. Porter (eds.), *Annual Review of Psychology*, Vol. 26. Palo Alto, Calif.: Annual Reviews, 1975, pp. 45–64.

MCGLOTHLIN, W. H., and ARNOLD, D. O. LSD Revisited: A Ten-Year Follow-up of Medical LSD Use. *Archives of General Psychiatry*, 1971, *24*, 35–49.

MCWILLIAMS, S., and TUTTLE, R. J. Long-Term Psychological Effects of LSD. *Psychological Bulletin*, 1973, *79*, 341–351.

MEEKS, D. E., and KELLY, C. Family Therapy with the Families of Recovering Alcoholics. *Quarterly Journal of Studies on Alcohol*, 1970, *31*, 399–413.

MILKMAN, H., and FROSCH, W. A. On the Preferential Abuse of Heroin and Amphetamine. *Journal of Nervous and Mental Diseases*, 1973, *156*, 242–248.

MILLER, N. E., and DOLLARD, J. *Social Learning and Imitation*. New Haven, Conn.: Yale University Press, 1941.

MILLER, P. M., and BARLOW, D. H. Behavioral Approaches to the Treatment of Alcoholism. *Journal of Nervous and Mental Diseases*, 1973, *157*, 10–20.

Monthly Vital Statistics Reports: Annual Summary for the United States, 1972. Washington, D.C.: U.S. Department of Health, *21,* June 1973.

MORRIS, J. B., KOVACS, M., BECK, A. T., and WOLFFE, A. Notes Toward an Epidemiology of Urban Suicide. *Comprehensive Psychiatry,* 1974, *15,* 537–547.

MULCOCK, D. Juvenile Suicide. *Medical Officer,* 1955, *94,* 155–160.

MURRAY, J. P. Television and Violence: Implications of the Surgeon General's Research Program. *American Psychologist,* 1973, *28,* 472–478.

NIR, Y., and CUTLER, R. The Therapeutic Utilization of the Juvenile Court. *American Journal of Psychiatry,* 1973, *130,* 1112–1117.

OHLIN, L. E., and CLOWARD, R. A. *Delinquency and Opportunity, A Theory of Delinquent Gangs.* Glencoe, Ill.: Free Press, 1960.

OSMOND, H., and HOFFER, A. Schizophrenia and Suicide. *Journal of Schizophrenia,* 1967, *1,* 54–64.

OTTO, U. Changes in the Behavior of Children and Adolescents Preceding Suicidal Attempts. *Acta Psychiatric Scandinavia,* 1964, *40,* 386–400.

PAGE, J. D. *Psychopathology: The Science of Understanding Deviance.* Chicago: Aldine Publishing Co., 1975.

PARSONS, B. V., JR., and ALEXANDER, J. F. Short-Term Family Intervention: A Therapy Outcome Study. *Journal of Consulting and Clinical Psychology,* 1973, *41,* 195–201.

PATTERSON, G. R., and COBB, J. A. A Dyadic Analysis of "Aggressive Behaviors". In J. P. Hill (ed.), *Minnesota Symposia on Child Psychology,* Vol. 5. Minneapolis: University of Minnesota Press, 1971, pp. 72–129.

PETERSON, D. R., QUAY, H. C., and TIFFANY, T. L. Personality Factors Related to Juvenile Delinquency. *Child Development,* 1961, *32,* 355–372.

POKORNY, A. D., DAVIS, F., and HARBERSON, W. Suicide, Suicide Attempts and Weather. *American Journal of Psychiatry,* 1963, *120,* 377–381.

POST, R. M. Cocaine Psychoses: A Continuum Model. *American Journal of Psychiatry,* 1975, *132,* 255–231.

Prevention of Suicide. World Health Organization. Public Health Paper No. 35, Geneva, WHO, 1968.

QUAY, H. C. Dimensions of Personality in Delinquent Boys as Inferred from the Factor Analysis of Case History Data. *Child Development,* 1964, *35,* 479–484.

QUAY, H. C. Personality Dimensions in Preadolescent Delinquent Boys. *Educational and Psychological Measurement,* 1966, *26,* 99–110.

QUAY, H. C. Residential Treatment. In H. C. Quay and J. S. Werry (eds.), *Psychopathological Disorders of Childhood,* 2nd ed. New York: John Wiley, 1979, pp. 387–410.

RAVENSBORG, M. R., and FOSS, A. Suicide and Natural Death in a State Hospital Population: A Comparison of Admission Complaints, MMPI Profiles, and Social Competence Factors. *Journal of Consulting and Clinical Psychology,* 1969, *33,* 466–471.

REED, J. P., and BAALI, F. (eds.). *Faces of Delinquency.* Englewood Cliffs, N. J.: Prentice-Hall, 1972.

REMSCHMIDT, H., HOHNER, G., MERSCHMANN, W., and WALTER, R. *Epidemiological Approaches in Child Psychiatry.* New York: Academic Press, 1977.

RESNICK, J. H., and KENDRA, J. M. Predictive Value of the "Scale for Assessing Suicide Risk" (SASR) with Hospitalized Psychiatric Patients. *Journal of Clinical Psychology,* 1973, *29,* 187–190.

ROOTMAN, I. A Cross-cultural Note on Durkheim's Theory of Suicide. *Life Threatening Behavior,* 1973, *3,* 83–94.

ROSS, M. Suicide among College Students. *American Journal of Psychiatry,* 1969, *126,* 220–225.

SANBORN, D. E., III, SANBORN, C. J., and CIMBOLIC, P. Two Years of Suicide: A Study of Adolescent Suicide in New Hampshire. *Child Psychiatry and Human Development,* 1973, *3,* 234–242.

SARASON, I. G. A Cognitive Social Learning Approach to Juvenile Delinquency. In R. D. Hare and D. Schalling (eds.), *Psychopathic Behavior: Approaches to Research.* New York: John Wiley, 1978, pp. 229–317.

SCHNOLL, S. H. Pharmacological Aspects of Youth Drug Abuse. In G. M. Geschner and A. S. Friedman (eds.), *Youth Drug Abuse. Problems, Issues, and Treatment.* Lexington, Mass.: Heath, 1979, pp. 255–275.

SCHNEER, H. I., PERSTEIN, A., and BROZOVSKY, M. Hospitalized Suicidal Adolescents: Two Generations. *Journal of the American Academy of Child Psychiatry,* 1975, *14,* 268–280.

SCHREIBER, D. Juvenile Delinquency and the School Dropout Problem. *Federal Probation,* 1963, *27,* 15–19.

SCHUYLER, D. When Was the Last Time You Took a Suicidal Child to Lunch? *Journal of School Health,* 1973, *43,* 504–506.

SCHWITZGEBEL, R. K. *Streetcorner Research: An Experimental Approach to the Juvenile Delinquent.* Cambridge, Mass.: Harvard University Press, 1964.

SEGOVIA-RIQUELME, N., VARELA, A., and MARDONES, J. Appetite for Alcohol. In Y. Israel and J. Mardones (eds.), *Biological Basis for Alcoholism.* New York: Wiley-Interscience, 1971, pp. 299–334.

SEIDEN, R. H. *Suicide among Youth.* Bulletin of Suicidology Supplement. Washington, D.C.: U.S. Government Printing Office, 1969.

SHELDON, W. H., HARTL, E. M., and MCDERMOTT, E. Varieties of Delinquent Youth: An Introduction to Constitutional Psychiatry. New York: Harper and Row, 1949.

SIMMONS, R. G., ROSENBERG, F., and ROSENBERG, M. Disturbance in the Self-image at Adolescence. *American Sociological Review,* 1973, *38,* 553–568.

SIMON, J. L. The Effect of Income on the Suicide Rate: A Paradox Resolved. *American Journal of Sociology,* 1968, *74,* 302–303.

SMART, R. G., and FEJER, D. Drug Use among Adolescents and Their Parents: Closing the Generation Gap in Mood Modification. *Journal of Abnormal Psychology,* 1972, *79,* 153–160.

SOLOMON, S. The Neurological Evaluation. In A. M. Freedman and H. I. Kaplan (eds.), *Comprehensive Text-*

book of Psychiatry. Baltimore, Md.: Williams and Wilkins, 1967, pp. 420–443.

STANTON, A. H. Drug Use among Adolescents. *American Journal of Psychiatry*, 1966, *122*, 1282–1283.

STENGEL, E. *Suicide and Attempted Suicide*. Baltimore, Md.: Penguin Books, rev. ed., 1970.

TEC, N. Differential Involvement with Marijuana and Its Sociocultural Context: A Study of Suburban Youths. *International Journal of the Addictions*, 1972, *7*, 655–669.

THOMAS, M. The Group Therapies. In R. J. Catanzaro, (ed.), *Alcoholism: The Total Treatment Approach*. Springfield, Ill.: Chas. C Thomas, 1968, pp. 127–145.

THRASHER, F. M. *The Gang*. Chicago: University of Chicago Press, 1936.

TOLOR, A., and TAMERIN, J. S. The Question of a Genetic Basis for Alcoholism: Comment on the Study by Goodwin et al., and a Response. *Quarterly Journal of Studies on Alcohol*, 1973, *34*, 1341–1345.

TONKS, C. M., RACK, P. H., and ROSE, M. J. Attempted Suicide and the Menstrual Cycle. *Journal of Psychosomatic Research*, 1968, *11*, 319–323.

TOOLAN, J. M., Suicide in Childhood and Adolescence. In H. L. P. Resnik (ed.), *Suicidal Behaviors: Diagnosis and Management*. Boston: Little, Brown, 1968, pp. 220–227.

TROJANOWICZ, R. C. *Juvenile Delinquency: Concepts and Control*. Englewood Cliffs, N. J.: Prentice-Hall, 1973.

TUCKMAN, J., and YOUNGMAN, W. F. A Scale for Assessing Suicide Risk of Attempted Suicides. *Journal of Clinical Psychology*, 1968, *24*, 17–19.

Uniform Crime Reports: 1968–1971. U.S. Department of Justice, Federal Bureau of Investigation. Washington, D.C.: U.S. Government Printing Office, 1972.

Uniform Crime Reports. Federal Bureau of Investigation. Washington, D.C.: U.S. Government Printing Office, 1973, pp. 124–125.

VAZ, E. W. *Middle-Class Juvenile Delinquency*. New York: Harper and Row, 1967.

VOLKMANN, R., and CRESSEY, D. R. Differential Association and the Rehabilitation of Drug Addicts. *American Journal of Sociology*, 1963, *64*, 129–142.

VONWRIGHT, J. M., PEKANMÄKI, L., and MALIN, S. Effects of Conflict and Stress on Alcohol Intake in Rats. *Quarterly Journal of Studies on Alcohol*, 1971, 32, 420–433.

WALD, P. M., and HUTT, P. B. *Dealing with Drug Abuse: A Report to the Ford Foundation*. New York: Praeger, 1972.

WALKER, R. N. *Psychology of the Youthful Offender*, 2nd ed. Springfield, Ill.: Chas. C Thomas, 1973.

WECHSLER, H., and THUM, D. Teen-age Drinking, Drug Use, and Social Correlates. *Quarterly Journal of Studies on Alcohol*, 1973, *34*, 1220–1227.

WEINER, I. W. The Effectiveness of a Suicide Prevention Program. *Mental Hygiene*, 1969, *53*, 357–363.

WINOKUR, G., REICH, T., RIMMER, J., and PITTS, F. N. Alcoholism III: Diagnosis and Familial Psychiatric Illness in 259 Alcoholic Probands. *Archives of General Psychiatry*, 1970, *23*, 104–111.

WOLFE, R., and COTLER, S. Undergraduates Who Attempt Suicide Compared with Normal and Psychiatric Controls. *Omega: Journal of Death and Dying*, 1973, *4*, 305–312.

YABLONSKY, L. *The Tunnel Back: Synanon*. Baltimore, Md.: Penguin Books, 1967.

ZUCKER, A. H., and WAKSMAN, S. Results of Group Therapy with Young Drug Addicts. *The International Journal of Social Psychiatry*, 1970/73, *17–18*, 267–279.

Part 6 FUTURE CONSIDERATIONS

14

OUTCOME IMPLICATIONS AND PREVENTION

PROLOGUE

I am the Child.
All the world waits for my coming.
All the earth watches with interest to see
what I shall become.
Civilization hangs in the balance,
For what I am, the world of tomorrow will be.

I am the Child.
I have come into your world, about which
I know nothing.
Why I came I know not;
How I came I know not.
I am curious; I am interested.

I am the Child
You hold in your hand my destiny.
You determine, largely, whether I shall
succeed or fail.
Give me, I pray you, those things that make
for happiness.
Train me, I beg you, that I may be a blessing
to the world.

COLE

Most Americans readily accept, in principle at least, the rather simple plea of the poet for the right of every child to succeed, to be happy, and to be a credit to society. In this land of opportunity, freedom, and vast riches, who among us would deny an innocent child his or her heritage? Because in a real sense children represent our future, we fondly think of them as our most treasured national resource, although in practice we have treated this valuable resource rather badly (Zigler, 1974; Keniston, 1975; Gordon, 1977). The infant mortality rate in the United States is almost twice as great for nonwhite as for white infants, and it is higher than in thirteen other countries in the world. Each year approximately 1 million children are physically abused by their parents to the extent that in excess of 1,000 die and 100,000 require hospitalization. We continue to rely on a foster care system that shifts children in and out of many different homes, while we espouse the contradictory belief that every child has a right to a stable home, and "when we know that continuity, affection and solidity are what make for normal development" (Zigler, 1974, p. 25). There are more than 100,000 emotionally disturbed, handicapped, and minority children circulating in the foster care market, whom nobody seems to want or who cannot be permanently adopted because our laws place more importance on the rights of biological parents than on the basic needs of the child. Thousands more of our children are abandoned in public institutions for the retarded or in back wards of mental hospitals, with minimum care, stimulation, or hope for a better tomorrow.

Current statements on child advocacy affirm "the rights of children to be wanted, to be born healthy, to live in a healthy environment, to receive basic need satisfaction and continuous loving care, to acquire optimal intellectual and emotional skills and appropriate treatment when required" (Williams, 1974, p. 45). To this, Williams adds the following commentary:

> On the surface, child advocacy seems to fall within the limbo of those vacuously idealistic, hopelessly consensually validated concepts reflexly accepted by the zeitgeist. In actuality, however, advocacy refers to a radical social process which requires tremendous courage to implement and incisive examination to implement wisely. Child advocacy in action would challenge and work to change existing institutions which are inharmonious with the fullest development of the child. Implicit in the concept is recognition of the serious damage produced in children by many obsolete but entrenched social and political structures and of the necessity to oppose these structures. Without active intervention, child advocacy becomes dogooder lip service and the envisioned Child Development Councils little more than sites for grant hustlers. (1974, pp. 45–46)

In the spirit of child advocacy, it is only fitting that our last chapter discuss prevention of abnormal behaviors in children. Almost all discussions of this topic follow the public health model, in which three levels of prevention are identified: (1) *primary prevention,* referring to measures taken to ensure that abnormal behaviors will not occur in the first place, (2) *secondary prevention,* dealing with the early identification of vulnerable or risk populations for the purpose of applying intervention measures (treatment) to abbreviate the duration and decrease the seriousness of the psychological disorder, and—when all else fails, (3) *tertiary prevention,* referring to the rehabilitation of those who are emotionally disturbed and for whom treatment would increase their chances of a more satisfactory adjustment. For the most part we shall focus on primary prevention, since the other levels have already been touched on in earlier chapters, and since these are measures with the greatest potential payoff for the elimination of childhood psychopathology. But first let us put the matter of prevention into perspective by reviewing some research findings concerning the size of the current problem and some of the variables associated with psychopathology that are relevant to prevention.

RELEVANT RESEARCH FINDINGS

Current Incidence Estimates

Although noted in Chapter 2, it bears repeating that childhood psychological disorders represent a sizeable problem in our society, where approximately 10 percent of all children enrolled in our public schools are affected (Bower, 1969). Other estimates indicate that there are more than 2.5 million mentally retarded children, 3 million with speech impairments, and between 5 and 10 million who are considered emotionally disturbed (Cowen, 1973; Huntington, 1974).

Incidence figures obtained either from longitudinal data on normal children studied from infancy to fourteen years or from middle childhood samples randomly selected from birth records reflect fewer instances of abnormal behavior and less frequent hospitalizations in children than in adults (Macfarlane, Allen, and Honzik, 1954; Hagnell, 1966; Jonsson, 1967). These findings suggest that adjustment in childhood is not a good predictor of adult psychopathology, inasmuch as there are relatively more emotionally disturbed adults who were normal as children than maladjusted children who later are classified as disturbed adults (Clarizio and McCoy, 1976). Moreover, these hospitalization figures suggest that children's disorders are less severe than adults', since we know that families are more able to care for their emotionally disturbed youngsters at home and that fewer psychiatric hospital beds are needed for children than for adults. In fact, research data on the duration of childhood disorders indicate that most children are affected temporarily and that less than one-third continue to be emotionally disturbed after a four-year follow-up (Glavin, 1967). However, for the specific conditions of delinquency, drug abuse, antisocial sociopathy, and psychosis, the estimates of persistence are considerably higher. For example, Glueck and Glueck (1940) followed up a group of 1,000 juvenile delinquents in three 5-year periods and found that after the first five years, as many as 80 percent were rearrested, while Roberts (1967) found a similarly high (82 percent) recidivist rate for adolescent drug offenders. Other data indicate a poor prognosis for antisocial adolescents, no recovery in psychotic children after a five-year follow-up, but recovery in 91 percent of children classified as neurotic (Masterson, 1967). However, a recent study involving the follow up of 255 male delinquents provided a much lower recidivist rate (only 28 percent); but it found that those with subsequent criminal records were twice as likely to require psychiatric care as those without further convictions (Koenigsberg, Balla, and Lewis, 1977). Thus, it seems clear that certain childhood disorders have the poorest prospects for the future and bear the greatest social and economic costs over the long haul unless effective preventive measures are implemented. It is important to note that these duration estimates do not include those youngsters who are more or less permanently disabled by mental retardation and brain damage, and for whom prevention is even more urgently needed.

The most recent report of nationwide data gathered on the use of psychiatric services by children and youth estimated that approximately 441,000 persons under the age of eighteen were either admitted to or discharged from private or public hospitals and outpatient services during 1975 (Sowder et al., 1981)[1]. These data do not include youngsters served by the schools, special demonstration programs, substance abuse centers, private practitioners, and certain kinds of federally funded hospitals and community mental health centers. Consequently, they are serious underestimates of incidence or prevalence data and are quite limited in estimating the extent of the problem, the need for services, and the types of services needed. Never-

[1] The information provided in this section is based on the 1981 report by Sowder and associates.

theless, the report provides us with some interesting data, showing that about three-quarters of the total population were between ten and seventeen years of age and were Caucasian, while about 60 percent were males. Further, 43 percent of the total population received the DSM-III diagnosis of Adjustment Reaction. Moreover, as one would expect, the vast number of these youngsters (81 percent) were serviced as outpatients, while a smaller number (19 percent) were inpatients. The substantial use of an Adjustment Reaction diagnosis is somewhat unexpected, but it may very well reflect the inclination of clinicians to avoid stigmatizing children with labels that have more serious and negative connotations. For two-thirds of the population, there was no record of prior psychiatric care, although increasing age (over ten years old) increased the likelihood of previous psychiatric help. Interestingly, about 2 percent of the inpatients and one-third of the outpatients were given no psychiatric treatment beyond an intake and/or diagnostic evaluation session. Individual psychotherapy was by far the most favored treatment (given to about 80 percent of the inpatients and one-third of the outpatients), followed by family therapy, group therapy, and drug therapy. There was a negative correlation between length of hospitalization and the age of the child, so that younger children stayed longer (especially those under ten years of age), while the largest number of outpatients (especially under fifteen years of age) had between two and five visits. The report emphasizes that at this time, the need for services for children and youth far surpasses our society's ability to provide them. For example, 14 percent of the catchment areas in 1914 were without psychiatric services of any kind for their residents; there is a shortage of professional personnel to meet the current needs for services; there are far less funds available than are needed; and current services are not maximally utilized because there is poor coordination between and among the available service agencies.

An earlier study estimated that for 1975, 655,000 children and youths under eighteen, or almost 1 percent of all the children in the United States, were admitted to an organized mental health facility (Rosen, 1979). Moreover, this report indicates that 8 percent of the inpatient admissions were children, while youngsters comprised 25 percent of the outpatients. As had been found previously, the outpatient admission rate for boys was 67 percent higher than for girls; but the inpatient rate was only 9 percent higher.

Some Variables Related to Childhood Psychopathology

Research data tell us that low socioeconomic level is related to delinquency, to disruptive behaviors in school, and to poor academic achievement (Douglas, 1964, 1966). But even more powerful than socioeconomic status is the variable of parental influence, because antisocial parents or grandparents (regardless of socioeconomic condition) will have significantly more male offspring who drop out of school or who have police records than comparable groups of more adequate and stable parents (Robins and Lewis, 1966). In addition, a survey of the literature by Robins (1972) revealed that the presence of psychological disorders in parents increased the likelihood of their children having either the same or some other disturbance. The question arises as to whether the inadequate parenting reflects a genetic component or whether it represents faulty environmental influences, or some combination of both. No definitive answer is available at this time; although in a pragmatic sense, either interpretation would have similar implications for primary prevention, at least with respect to the advisability of psychiatrically disordered adults having children. In this connection it has been found that child abuse leads to serious psychological and physical problems in the abused children, and that those youngsters who are removed from the home show significant physical and intellectual gains over those children who remain with their abusive parents (Elmer and Gregg, 1967). More recently suggestive findings from a study of ten infants who came from homes with poor mothering and who were placed into a day care program showed a subsequent salutary effect on IQ scores at age three (Resch et al., 1977).

Children of families in which one or both parents have serious psychopathology such as schizophrenia are themselves at high risk for manifesting a mental disorder. In reviewing the literature on high-risk children, Goodman (1983) concludes that these youngsters show deficits and delays on psychophysiological and neurological variables (such as hyperlabile and hypersensitive autonomic functioning, right-left orientation, auditory-visual integration), and that the likely occurrence of these findings increases with the greater severity of disturbance in the mother. It is also more likely where child rearing is more urban than rural, and in cases involving school-age children rather than those who are younger. In addition, Goodman reports that there are generally no differences across high-risk groups in IQ, except that children of both schizophrenic and depressive parents have lower academic achievement than control subjects, and children of schizophrenic and chronically ill mothers evidence dysfunction in sustained attention. She also found that high-risk children have more social-interpersonal problems than controls, and that they show more evidence of emotional disturbance and poor adjustment than do controls.

In general, abnormal behaviors of children tend to be age specific and are not likely to be evident some years later, although certain behaviors such as destructiveness, somberness, shyness, jealousy, and the demanding of attention tend to persist into the teens if they appear at age six or seven (Robins, 1972). Prior to that age symptoms of psychological disorder are not good predictors of the child's later adjustment; but after that time more consistency and better forecasting can be expected. For example, children with many symptoms are likely to manifest multiple symptoms later, and those who are poor academic performers, rebellious in school, and disliked by their peers are likely to be future delinquents in adolescence (Macfarlane, Allen, and Honzik, 1954; Mulligan et al., 1963; Rutter et al., 1964; Conger and Miller, 1966; Robins, 1972).

From the viewpoint of prevention, it is tempting to interpret these findings to support the idea that intervention should begin in the early years before certain behavioral patterns become more stable and difficult to modify (prior to age six or seven). However, as logical and appropriate as early intervention may be, the data cannot be interpreted beyond their forecasting value. The fact that early childhood problems tend to be age specific does no more than emphasize the particular importance of developmental factors during early childhood. At present we know little about the frequency with which these young children develop new symptoms later on, and not enough about whether the behavioral signs of early problems are obscured by very limited response repertoires and restricted opportunities to perform outside of the home.

PREVENTION

Ideally, everyone favors prevention, but as a society we have invested little of our resources and energies in actively working toward this end, especially in the area of childhood psychopathology. We resist understanding prevention and its implementation because the task is so enormous and extremely complex, and because it potentially involves alterations in our basic attitudes and values—and perhaps the restructuring of our society (Broskowski and Baker, 1974).

Eugenic Measures

The most obvious—but controversial—forms of primary prevention involve the control of procreation in certain at-risk individuals through sterilization, birth control practices, and therapeutic abortion. Involuntary sterilization for the improvement of the human race is quite unacceptable to Americans, because it strikes a fatal blow to our fundamental beliefs and our societal institutions. In a society such as ours, where freedom and individual rights are highly regarded and protected, the idea of "others" determining who should or should not reproduce is repugnant and outrageous. However, we find voluntary measures of limiting conception or of aborting damaged or high-risk fetuses more palatable, and therefore more realistic, approaches to prevention, since both individual and societal rights are more readily safeguarded by these methods.

Family Planning

Simplified surgical procedures for sterilization, the availability of new methods of contraception, and statutory changes in our abortion practices have helped promote the idea of family planning as an approach that aids parents in limiting and adequately spacing their families, and reducing the number of defective children born. However, it has been estimated that of the more than 5 million indigent women who have sought assistance in family planning, only about one in ten actually received help, because of the limited number of available programs (*Crisis in Child Mental Health,* 1969). These women represent an important target population for family planning and prevention because of their high incidence of various types of morbidity, including offspring with mental retardation, neurological and sensory handicaps, learning disabilities, and emotional disorders.

For example, Goodman (1983) reports that about 50 percent of children of one schizophrenic parent are likely to be emotionally disturbed, and consequently it would be appropriate to target schizophrenic parents for family planning. In a recent paper Gordon (1977) noted that we live in an age in which it is acceptable for mature and healthy couples to decide not to have children, and in which it is no longer necessary or highly valued for married women to bear large numbers of children. According to Gordon, the time is also right for an active national campaign to dispel the idea that every adult should be a parent and to discourage procreation for persons who are unable to take care of themselves, since "no couple has a right to bring a child into this world whom they cannot love and nurture" (1977, p. 8). Increased public focus on family planning, and greater availability of these programs to target populations, would be a large step forward in the prevention of childhood disorders.

Genetic Counseling

As substantial informational and technical gains are made in the field of genetics, and since an increasing number of pediatric disorders (20 percent) are now thought to be genetically based, genetic counseling is rapidly becoming a promising prevention measure (Day and Holmes, 1973). The process involves assessing the degree of genetic risk as well as the social and psychological consequences of birth, followed by a discussion of this information with a couple to aid them in making their decision about conception (Headings, 1975; Nitowsky, 1976). Genetic risk is determined by family pedigree and chromosomal analysis in which the karyotype (arrangement of chromosome pairs by their length and other features of their appearance) made from one individual is compared to a standardized normal karyotype. In addition, statistical techniques are used to calculate and estimate probable genetic risk. While the effectiveness of genetic counseling services has not been adequately evaluated other than through subjective positive impressions, one group of investigators has suggested the following as factors that influence people's responses to counseling: (1) severity of the abnormal condition at-risk, (2) the existence of an effective therapy for the condition, (3) the statistical degree of risk, (4) the religious attitudes of the couple,

(5) the socioeconomic level of the couple, and (6) the educational level of the couple (Leonard, Chase, and Childs, 1972; Coldwell, Say, and Jones, 1975).

Genetic counseling also includes *prenatal genetic diagnosis*, involving the use of a number of laboratory tests to detect chromosomal disorders, inherited metabolic disorders, X-linked disorders, as well as other fetal abnormalities (Littlefield, 1972; Goodner, 1976). The primary diagnostic tool for chromosomal problems is *amniocentesis*, a technique by which amniotic fluid is withdrawn for the purpose of examining through a chromosomal analysis those cells that grow on the culture medium. A relatively new radiologic procedure, called *ultrasonography*, uses ultrasound to diagnose neural tube defects and other congenital malformations. Golbus (1976) and Young, Matson, and Jones (1976) emphasized that amniocentesis should be done only after careful recording of the family pedigree and appropriate genetic counseling, since the procedure itself is serious, and many women who request it do so for poor reasons. Apparently, the probability of fetal loss by this procedure is no greater than the expected abortion rate in the general population, and its effectiveness is extremely good—as many as 97 percent of the women obtained the information they sought from the test (Young, Matson, and Jones, 1976; Golbus, 1976). One group of investigators has warned of a high incidence of depression (92 percent among women and 82 percent among men) following abortion of the fetus for genetic reasons rather than after psychosocial abortions or the birth of stillborns, although most of these families indicated that they would make the same decision again given the same circumstances (Blumberg, Golbus, and Hanson, 1975).

As might be expected, considerable concern has been expressed in the literature about the legal and ethical issues associated with genetic counseling, diagnosis, and therapeutic abortions. These measures have raised many questions for which there are no clear-cut answers, although the need for adequate standards is more apparent than ever. For example:

1. When does a couple have enough information to be able to decide on conception or to give their consent to an abortion?
2. Is having children a right or a privilege?
3. Which member of a couple should have the final say when the mother and father disagree about an abortion?
4. When does the fetus become a living human who has a right to live?
5. Should the counselor be primarily concerned with the survival of the individual or the survival of the species?
6. What are the prospects of a "cure" becoming available in the near future?
7. Do counselors reflect their bias and thus influence the facts and the eventual decisions?
8. Should the heterozygote carrier have the privilege of confidentiality, or should close relatives who may be at-risk have this information? (Kaback, 1972; Baumiller, 1974; Murray, 1974; Milunsky and Reilly, 1975; Hinman, 1976; Tormey, 1976)

Prenatal Care

Adequate medical, dietary, and emotional care can reduce birth complications and prematurity, which are conditions long known to be associated with neurological impairment resulting in intellectual and behavioral deficits in newborns (Birch, 1974). More specifically, a number of noxious factors that may be present during the course of pregnancy have been identified as contributing to miscarriages, congenital anomalies, premature births, and the subsequent abnormal development of the child. These stress-agents include maternal infectious diseases (rubella, syphilis, diabetes), maternal malnutrition, large doses of radiation, ingestion of drugs (barbiturates, thalidomide, narcotics), blood-type incompatibility between mother and fetus, and possibly maternal emotional stress (Herbert, 1974). In addition to these sources of prenatal complications, we also know that premature birth is associated more frequently with congenital malformations, as well as with neurological, sensory, and behavioral disorders, than are full-term births (Baumgartner, 1962; Pasamanick and Knobloch, 1966).

Complications during pregnancy and at delivery, and premature births, are all much more common in mothers of lower socioeconomic status and in socially disadvantaged mothers, in whom poor diet, physical status, and health—and lack of or inadequate obstetrical care—are prevalent (Thomson and Billewicz, 1963; Donnelly et al., 1964; Drillien, 1964; Goodman, 1983). It has been estimated that more than 40 percent of medically indigent pregnant women deliver their babies either without any prenatal care or with only one visit sometime in the last trimester before birth. Mothers who received no prenatal care have fetal deaths at a rate four times greater than that of women who have one or more prenatal care visits (Hartman and Sayles, 1965). Although we know that comprehensive health care and adequate medical services significantly reduce infant mortality and premature births, especially for nonwhite females (Birch, 1974), we have been reluctant to make the social and economic commitment necessary for this form of prevention. In light of this paradox, the Joint Commission on Mental Health of Children (*Crisis in Child Mental Health*, 1969) strongly recommended programs of "early and systematic prenatal care for all pregnant women," together with "... reduced working hours, paid maternity leave, homemaking services, nutritional supplements, prepregnancy immunizations, extensive testing and strict control of drugs, and education aimed at teen-agers and young adults to emphasize the importance of good health and suitable timing of pregnancies" (p. 32).

Neonatal Assessment and Care

Most hospitals routinely do an early evaluation of the neonate within minutes after birth as a means of alerting the pediatrician to potential problems of the infant that could lead to serious developmental problems later on. The Apgar method is regarded as the best way to quantitatively evaluate the infant's condition at birth (Tooley and Phibbs, 1975). A score of 0, 1, or 2 is given to the infant on each of five parameters, which include heart rate, respiratory effort, muscle tone, reflex irritability, and color. If the total score (sum of each score on each area) is between eight and ten within the first five minutes after the infant's birth, the baby is considered all right and not in need of special attention such as active resuscitation (which might prevent anoxia). Babies who receive scores of five or less require additional and immediate medical attention. In addition, pediatric neurologists have described the advantages of an early but thorough neurological assessment of the infant in order to detect possible signs of central nervous system dysfunction (Volpe, 1975). This type of evaluation can provide early indications of later neurological disorders, as well as early intervention that can lessen the child's impairment and subsequent adjustment.

Several pediatricians are in the process of constructing a system that will both record and analyze mother-infant interactions primarily for the purpose of assessing the mother's capacity to attend to the needs of her infant and also to evaluate the degree of pathology that might characterize their future relationship (Brazleton, Koslowski, and Main, 1974).

Child-Care Programs

These are interventions aimed at supplementing deficiencies in the child's environment of factors that are regarded as essential for normal and healthy development. Programs of this sort typically focus on providing infants and preschool children of working or disabled families with adequate nutrition, health care, intellectual and social stimulation, and affection that otherwise may be absent—especially in homes of low-socioeconomic status. For example, some of the consequences of faulty diet were noted in a recent study that found intellectual impairment, higher frequency of infections, and less social responsiveness in a group of chronically malnourished Philippine children ranging in age from six to thirty-six months (Guthrie, Masangkay, and Guthrie, 1976). The fear of interfering with and perhaps weakening the mother-infant bond by separating the infant from the mother for long periods of time each day has kept many programs from accepting infants younger than six months of age. However, several carefully done studies have dispelled this concern by showing that the mother-child relationship is not adversely affected by attendance in an infant-care program (Caldwell et al., 1970; Keister, 1970).

Carolyn Goodman (1980) described an interesting program intended to assist emotionally disturbed mothers in finding better and more effective solutions to their problems, as well as to teach them how to better meet their needs. The program, referred to as PACE (Parent and Child Education), offered four-day-per-week partial hospitalization for the mothers along with enrollment for their children (ranging in age from three months to five years) in a closely associated nursery school program. The program also provided posthospitalization transition lasting an average of nine months for about 60 percent of the mothers. It was found that children's cognitive functioning was better and more likely to be at age level at discharge than at entry into the program. Further, parental competency was judged by agency workers to have improved with participation in the program. However, methodological shortcomings, including the absence of a control group, makes Goodman's project and its presumed effectiveness difficult to evaluate.

The Vermont Child Development Project (Rolf and Harig, 1974; Rolf and Hasazi, 1977; Rolf et al., 1981) was designed to assess the effectiveness of a therapeutic day care program for high-risk children (children with demonstrated behavioral disturbances, serious developmental lags, or seriously disturbed parents). The prevention efforts were aimed at reducing the probability of later disorders in these children through interventions intended to minimize their existing dysfunctions and maximize their coping competencies. Three intervention conditions were used: home care, day care, and enriched day care, with children in the latter condition considered as the target population. The findings showed that target children improved in competencies such as verbal communication and motor skills more than controls, although this success must be interpreted cautiously; 84 percent of the intervention subjects left the program before the intervention was completed, and the project failed to involve the parents in significant ways.

The Mauritius Project initiated in 1972 by Mednick and Schulsinger and their associates in Mauritius (an island in the Indian Ocean off the coast of Southern Africa) is essentially an enriched nursery school intervention program (Mednick, Schulsinger, and Schulsinger, 1975; Mednick and Witkin-Lanvil, 1977; Schulsinger, 1976; Schulsinger and Mednick, 1981). Residents of the island generally speak both French and English and include a number of groups: Hindus, Tamils, Moslems, and Creoles. The project was undertaken to test whether or not certain psychophysiological measures (fast autonomic nervous system recovery) found in earlier studies completed in Copenhagen would be useful for early detection and then selection of subjects for the intervention program. Two groups of children (high-risk–fast recoverers and low-risk–average and slow recoverers) were identified and placed in a nursery school program for two years. The first year was used to gather baseline observational data, and the second year was used for the intervention program, which included behavior training and systematic compensations for disruptions at home. Mednick and his associates found that on entering the nursery school, the fast autonomic recoverers were more aggressive and emotionally disturbed than the average or slow recoverers, but that these behaviors quickly decreased in the nursery school and were replaced by spontaneity in play as well as an active interest in people and objects. Long-term follow-up studies are underway: Since the island has a very stable population, researchers have high hopes of succeeding in data gathering.

Infant day care programs vary in terms of such variables as the program director's preferences, the service needs of the infants and mothers, the funds available, and the legal constraints (some states do not permit infant care outside of the home) (Honig, 1974). Honig described the advantages and disadvantages of tutorial programs where a trained specialist comes to the home to enhance the development and competence of the infant; of home-visit programs in which a specialist provides low-income mothers aid with the nutrition as well as with the total development of the child; and of parent-group programs where parents are taught in a group ways to foster the development of older preschool children. She also noted that day care center programs to which young children are brought for such services as baby sitting, proper nutrition, and pediatric care have demonstrated their effectiveness in producing significant developmental gains during the time the children were in attendance. While day care centers outside of the home provide youngsters with the benefits of pleasurable activities, adequate nutrition, good health, and the enhancement of their cognitive, social, and emotional development, they also bear the burden of high financial cost and the risk of decreasing already low parental involvement in the daily care of their children. With more than 4 million children below the age of six having working mothers, and with every prospect that this number will increase in the years ahead as more women choose careers outside of the home, the need for more well-planned and competently staffed day care and preschool programs is obvious and urgent (*Crisis in Child Mental Health*, 1969).

Early Identification (after birth)

Essentially, these programs involve the assessment of children at critical transition times (such as when they leave the home to begin kindergarten, or when they are about to enter first grade) for the purpose of determining in advance which children are likely to have difficulties and what might be done to help them cope with the demands of the new situation more effectively. For example, one approach is to develop ways to screen preschool children who are about to enter kindergarten. The Sumter Child Study Project (Newton and Brown, 1967) used psychological testing, structured observations, and interview data as the basis for dividing the children into two groups—the adjusted and the maladjusted. Significant differences between the two groups were later found in such areas as absenteeism, initiative, number of completed reading assignments, and self-concept. The study also provided unverified clinical reports suggesting that specific remedial efforts by the professional staff successfully aided the subsequent adjustment of the children who were not then ready to enter school. Speech problems were helped through parent education and speech-skills programs, while children who needed peer experiences and the development of school-related skills were either sent to a summer camp or directed to a community recreational program.

An interesting and consistent research finding concerning the optimal age at which children should be admitted to first grade has prevention implications that most school systems tend to ignore. Apparently, children who are younger than the mean age of their first-grade classmates are more likely to achieve less throughout all twelve years of schooling, to be viewed as emotionally disturbed, and to be referred more frequently for professional help than their older counterparts (Weinstein, 1968–1969). However, it was found that differences between entering younger and older first graders dissipated by the end of their second school year in a school program that grouped new students for the first four grades on criteria that included maturity level (Miller and Norris, 1967). In spite of the finding that it is inadvisable for children to begin first grade early, or (if this is done) to ignore maturity levels as a basis of assigning them to classes, school systems have not changed their admission or programming policies. Bower (1974) attributes the schools' unresponsiveness partly to the "inertia of social institutions and all sorts of legislative and pseudolegislative (I'm sorry, Mrs. Einstein, but since your son Albert was born at 11 P.M. on December 31, he will have to start school this September, not next September) fol-derol" (p. 237). He optimistically maintains that appropriate changes can be brought about, although it would require enormous efforts from both parents and schools to alter legislative and administrative regulations.

Other attempts at early identification have focused on the development of screening programs for specific learning disabilities, which typically consisted of the administration of a large battery of tests to kindergarten children. One such program failed to distinguish test patterns for high-risk learning disabled children (Haring and Rideway, 1967), while several others effectively identified children with learning problems, particularly with reading failures (DeHirsch, Jansky, and Langford, 1966; Ferinden and Jacobson, 1970; Feshbach, Adelman, and Fuller, 1974). Interestingly, it was found that the subjective ratings of teachers proved surprisingly effective in identifying learning disabled children, and that a combination of teacher ratings and scores on the Metropolitan Readiness Test yielded an extremely high degree of accuracy (about 90 percent) (Maitland, Nadeau, and Nadeau, 1974).

In recent years considerable attention has been focused on the health of children from poor families and from culturally disadvantaged minorities. In 1967 the Early and Periodic Screening, Diagnosis, and Treatment Program (EPSDT) became a provision under the Medicaid Act, offering eligible children (which represented approximately 12,000,000 children, from birth to twenty-one years of age) a variety of services for early detection, assessment, and treatment of physical and mental defects (Moore, 1978). This program is still in the process of evaluation; so far the data on the "developmental assessment component" (the assessment of mental defects) suggest that the EPSDT cannot adequately meet the urgency of the developmental needs of these children. The American Orthopsychiatric Association (Developmental Assessment in EPSDT, 1978) proposed a series of regional, experimental pilot programs prior to implementation of EPSDT on a national level. These programs should be "aimed at determining and enhancing individual children's strengths to help offset developmental weaknesses and at defining structures of service useful to the Medicaid population" (p. 19).

In general, early identification programs are expensive and, as yet, unproven as a way of predicting later periods of poor adjustment, particularly in young children such as five- and six-year-olds (Bower, 1969; Bradley and Caldwell, 1978). Moreover, the belief that early identification readily results in the placement of the child into an effective remediation program is more mythical than real: Most school systems are not geared toward the special handling of emotional or learning problems, and most communities do not have the mental health resources to provide the needed services.

Educational Programs

Some investigators have been concerned about the paradox whereby our schools avow their interest in fostering the intellectual, social, and emotional development of children, but construct programs that primarily are designed for the restricted purpose of intellectual development. According to Dinkmeyer (1974), schools "are not as willing or ready to deal with the child's social immaturity, feelings of inadequacy, anger, joy, and excitement. They would really, in many instances, prefer to deal with 'an intellectual receptacle' in which they could place knowledge to be withdrawn and inspected at regular intervals" (p. 252). A number of innovative programs have been introduced into the schools for the purpose of enhancing the total development of the child. They maintain that this goal can be realized by educational programs aimed at teaching children and their teachers the motivational basis of human behavior, mental health principles, the understanding of self and others, and the like (Ojemann, 1967; Bessell and Palomares, 1967).

Special courses have been developed to teach school children basic behavioral science concepts such as learning theory, intelligence, and Erikson's psychosocial stages of development, among others, and to teach them about emotional problems and mental health (described in Clarizio and McCoy, 1976). However, we do not know whether these courses have had a positive effect on the subsequent adjustment of the youngsters who were exposed to them. In contrast, Ojemann (1967) reported that the educational program developed by him and his colleagues produced favorable changes in his elementary school students. Unfortunately, the findings are open to criticism on a number of methodological issues. Essentially, Ojemann's approach was founded on the idea that early instruction in the underlying motivational components of situations and behaviors beyond their surface meaning lays the groundwork for children to be more sensitive to others and more effective in coping with their own problems. In many ways Ojemann's program is too imprecise, and therefore difficult for teachers to learn—perhaps so unspecific and cumbersome that it has not been widely used even though it has been known to educators since the early 1940s.

Sex education is one of the most controversial instructional programs a school can offer, although its potential for decreasing ignorance about sex and reducing anxieties, unwanted pregnancies, venereal disease, and sexual hangups is apparent to many. Opponents of sex education in the school curriculum argue that it might lead to an increase in promiscuity, illegitimate births, homosexuality, rape, and venereal disease. They also hold that some teachers are not trained or are not sufficiently stable to offer such a course. Some claim that sex is a natural phenomenon requiring no prior instruction, and that factual discussions will decrease its mystery and enjoyment later in life. While the opposition is usually vocal and sufficiently troublesome to create unnecessary problems for school administrators, the vast majority of American parents (about 70 percent) apparently favor sex education in the schools (Breasted, 1970). Perhaps this tells us something about the reluctance of many parents to assume the responsibility for educating their own children. Nevertheless, in spite of the fact that most youngsters prefer receiving sex instruction from their parents, friends rather than parents seem to be the primary source of their sexual information (Gagnon, 1965). Inasmuch as peers provide much of a youngster's sex education, it seems only reasonable that measures be taken to assure that what children learn and later communicate to others is sound and accurate.

Gordon (1974) suggests that sex education broadly conceived as encompassing biological and reproductive information as well as the interpersonal aspects associated with sexuality cannot be effectively taught as a separate course in the regular school curriculum. Instead, he favors the integration of human reproduction into an existing biology course where the topic of reproduction is ordinarily covered, and the inclusion of information about venereal disease in health classes that typically discuss other communicable diseases. Additional sex education should ideally come from the parents, but since this is not likely to occur often enough, he advocates the development and utilization of community resources for sex information, counseling, birth planning, and so forth. At present, sex education programs in the schools vary considerably with respect to their goals and content, to the extent that, their effect is extremely difficult to evaluate. Although much more systematic evaluation of its impact is sorely needed, "the contention is indisputable that the failure to receive a timely sex education makes children's and adolescents' growth into adequately functioning sexual adults considerably more difficult" (McCary, 1973, p. 22).

Educational programs outside of the school curriculum and aimed at young adults, expectant parents, or parents of young children have also enjoyed a measure of popularity as a prevention approach. Books, pamphlets, lectures, TV shows, magazine articles, and newspaper series are among the techniques used with the intent of increasing the sophistication level of the general population about such varied topics as birth control, prenatal care, proper nutrition, factors affecting normal and abnormal development, parent-child interactions, enhancing normal personality development, the effect of drugs on the developing child, family interactions, and a host of other pertinent topics. The fact that these efforts are frequently lucrative is but one indication of their large public appeal and the interest of so many in increasing their effectiveness as parents. However, too little is known about the impact of these mass communication approaches for bringing about enduring changes in behavior. Since these techniques are usually brief, general and superficial, easily misinterpreted to suit ones needs, and relatively unsupervised, it would seem doubtful that they alone could be powerful enough to alter existing habits and patterns.

Parent Effectiveness Training (PET) is an illustration of a more formal educational program designed to teach parents how to shift from either an authoritative or permissive stance to one of mutuality with the child in dealing with parent-child interactions and problems (Gordon, 1970). The idea is to eliminate power struggles between parent and child, to provide both opportunities for self-esteem, and to increase effective communication between parents and child. Lectures, group discussions, and role playing are used to train parents to be more effective, but evaluative data are needed to determine the benefits (if any) of the PET program.

Recently a government-created Follow-Through program has been developed for first and second graders to bolster and maintain the academic and social gains made in the Head Start program (O'Leary and O'Leary, 1977). Workshops provide training to parents in behavioral methods aimed at maintaining and increasing desirable behaviors. According to O'Leary and O'Leary: "If teachers and parents are not taught to follow-through by reinforcing desired academic and social behaviors, the newly acquired academic and social behaviors will die" (1977, p. 45).

Changing Roles of Female and Male Parents

From the beginning of recorded history, women have occupied a subservient, secondary, and devalued position in society. Their position has been tied to cultural, political, and economic influences and curiously enough, to their unique biological ability to bear children. In primitive days, when paternity was often unknown and men were free to gather food without additional responsibilities, the burden of child care and survival fell almost entirely on women. The status of women and their children varied in terms of the economic conditions of the times, but it almost always worsened when food was scarce and children (whom women brought into the world) were seen as unwanted competitors for these resources (Horton, 1974). The die was cast for centuries as generation after generation expected women to function primarily as child bearers and caretakers, and later as wives and homemakers.

Within recent years dramatic changes have taken place in the roles, functions, and status of women: Old economic circumstances no longer apply, and more and more women refuse to live vicariously through their children and husbands. Today women represent 38 percent of the labor force, and an increasing number are preparing for vocational careers—although many are still exploited in salary and restricted in job opportunities and promotions (Horton, 1974). More than ever before, women are exercising reproductive control and are gaining society's sanction for legal abortions. Women also have markedly changed their sexual attitudes and practices, reaching a parity with men and a sense of independence that carries with it implications for the joint sharing of child care. Motherhood, with all its nurturant and homemaking functions, will in the future become even more obsolete as an exclusive responsibility of women.

Changes in the status of women and in their roles and functions also require alterations and new roles for men. The old role of "breadwinner," and the historical idea of "fatherhood," are rapidly vanishing, giving way to *parenting* and the sharing of household jobs within the family that formerly were sex typed (Pickett, 1974). The importance of the male parent in fostering the normal development of the child was noted in Chapter 3. In making this transition, men will have to deal with and change their notions of masculinity to include as acceptable the performance of roles and functions that have traditionally been assigned to women. Male parents and female parents will share in daily chores of homemaking, and provide warmth, nurturance and affection, as well as discipline to their children, without regard for one's biological gender—but with consideration of the family's needs and particular circumstances. Whoever (male or female) is available to cook, take the child to school, listen to problems, run the vacuum cleaner, change the baby, or mow the yard will perform the function free of the exploitation that formerly characterized our male-oriented society. As Pickett so aptly stated:

> Women have been the truly conservative force in society in that they have traditionally tended the hearth and nurtured the child while men have gone forth to procure food and make war. It is abundantly clear that these historic functions are in a state of rapid change, and that the social being known as the father will not return to past ways any more than the mother. If he would truly remove himself from the category of obsolescence, planned or otherwise, the man called Father, or the parent who happens to be male, will have to operate in future times as a conserving yet generative force in society.
>
> To do so will mean to cease lamenting for lost glories and to seize the challenge of the hours and days ahead. The sole alternative is oblivion. (1974, pp. 441–442)

Professional workers have recognized these changes and have tended to place increasing importance on joint parenting to enhance the child's development and to strengthen the family unit. In addition, the erosion of traditional sex-typed roles has not only brought the sexes into closer parity, but more importantly, it has increased the opportunities for both boys and girls to develop and utilize fully their abilities and resources. In fact, Horton optimistically notes:

> The liberation of women guarantees that each child will be wanted, not an accident; that every child will be cared for by two parents that love him/her, not by one in absentia and the other full of resentment; that every child can grow up to his/her fullest potential, not artificially stunted by inappropriate expectations; and that every child will have the chance to become a unique individual, and to be appreciated for what is, not what "should" be. When women are liberated, children can be liberated too. (1974, p. 436)

REFERENCES

Baumgartner, L. The Public Health Significance of Low Birth Weight in the U.S.A.: With Special Reference to Varying Practices in Providing Special Care to Infants of Low Birth Weights. *Bulletin of the World Health Organization*, 1962, *26*, 175–182.

Baumiller, R. C. Ethical Issues in Genetics. *Birth Defects*, 1974, *10*, 297–299.

Bessell, H., and Palomares, U. *Methods in Human Development.* San Diego: Human Development Training Institute, 1967.

Birch, H. G. Health and the Education of Socially Disadvantaged Children. In G. J. Williams and S. Gordon (eds.), *Clinical Child Psychology: Current Practices and Future Perspectives.* New York: Behavioral Publications, 1974, pp. 266–291.

Blumberg, B. D., Golbus, M. S., and Hanson, K. H. The Psychological Sequelae of Abortion Performed for a Genetic Indication. *American Journal of Obstetrics and Gynecology*, 1975, *122*, 799–808.

Bower, E. M. *The Early Identification of Emotionally Handicapped Children in School.* Springfield, Ill.: Chas. C Thomas, 1969.

Bower, E. M. Mental Health. In R. Ebel (ed.), *Encyclopedia of Educational Research*, 4th ed. New York: Macmillan, 1969, pp. 811–828.

Bower, E. M. The Three-Pipe Problem: Promotion of Competent Human Beings Through a Preschool Kindergarten Program and Sundry Other Elementary Matters. In G. T. Williams and S. Gordon (eds.), *Clinical Child Psychology: Current Practices and Future Perspectives.* New York: Behavioral Publications, 1974. pp. 224–241.

Bradley, R. H., and Caldwell, B. M. Screening the Environment. *American Journal of Orthopsychiatry*, 1978, *48*, 114–130.

Brazleton, T. B., Koslowski, B., and Main, M. The Origins of Reciprocity: The Early Mother-Infant Interaction. In M. Lewis and L. A. Rosenblum (eds.), *The Effect of the Infant on its Caregiver.* New York: John Wiley, 1974, pp. 49–79.

Breasted, M. *Oh! Sex Education!* New York: Praeger, 1970.

Broskowski, A., and Baker, F. Professional, Organizational, and Social Barriers to Primary Prevention. *American Journal of Orthopsychiatry*, 1974, *44*, 707–719.

Caldwell, B. M., Wright, C. M., Honig, A. S., and Tannenbaum, J. Infant Day Care and Attachment. *American Journal of Orthopsychiatry*, 1970, *40*, 397–412.

Clarizio, H. F., and McCoy, G. F. *Behavior Disorders in Children.* New York: Thomas Y. Crowell, 1976.

Coldwell, J. G., Say, B., and Jones, K. Community Genetics I. *Journal of the Oklahoma State Medical Association*, 1975, *68*, 299–302.

Cole, M. G. The Child's Appeal. In T. C. Clark and R. S. Gillespie (eds.), *1000 Quotable Poems.* Chicago: Willett, Clark, 1937, pp. 161–162.

Conger, J. J., and Miller, W. C. *Personality, Social Class, and Delinquency.* New York: John Wiley, 1966.

Cowen, E. L. Social and Community Interventions. *Annual Review of Psychology*, 1973, *24*, 423–472.

Crisis in Child Mental Health: Challenge for the 1970s. *Report of the Joint Commission on Mental Health.* New York: Harper and Row, 1969.

Day, N., and Holmes, L. B. The Incidence of Genetic Disease in a University Hospital Population. *American Journal of Human Genetics*, 1973, *25*, 237–246.

DeHirsch, K., Jansky, J. J., and Langford, W. S. *Predicting Reading Failure.* New York: Harper and Row, 1966.

Developmental Assessment in EPSDT. *American Journal of Orthopsychiatry*, 1978, *48*, 7–21.

Dinkmeyer, D. Developing Understanding of Self and Others Is Central to the Educational Process. In G. J. Williams and S. Gordon (eds.), *Clinical Child Psychology: Current Practices and Future Perspectives.* New York: Behavioral Publications, 1974, 252–257.

Donnelly, J. F., FLowers, C. E., Creadick, R. N., Wells, H. B., Greenberg, B. G., and Surles, K. B. Maternal, Fetal and Environmental Factors in Prematurity. *American Journal of Obstetrics and Gynecology*, 1964, *88*, 918–931.

Douglas, J. W. B. *The Home and the School.* London: Macgibbon and Kee, 1964.

Douglas, J. W. B. The School Progress of Nervous and Troublesome Children. *The British Journal of Psychiatry*, 1966, *112*, 1115–1116.

Drillien, C. M. *The Growth and Development of Prematurely Born Children.* Baltimore, Md.: Williams and Wilkins, 1964.

Elmer, E., and Gregg, G. S. Developmental Characteristics of Abused Children. *Pediatrics*, 1967, *40*, 595–602.

Ferinden, W. E., and Jacobson, S. Early Identification of Learning Disabilities. *Journal of Learning Disabilities*, 1970, *3*, 589–593.

Feshbach, S., Adelman, H., and Fuller, W. W. Early Identification of Children with High Risk of Failure. *Journal of Learning Disabilities*, 1974, *7*, 639–644.

Gagnon, J. H. Sexuality and Sexual Learning in the Child. *Psychiatry*, 1965, *28*, 212–228.

Glavin, J. P. *"Spontaneous" Improvement in Emotionally Disturbed Children.* Geroge Peabody College for Teachers, doctoral dissertation, August 1967.

Glueck, S., and Glueck, E. *Juvenile Delinquents Grown Up.* New York: The Commonwealth Fund, 1940.

Golbus, M. S. The Antenatal Detection of Genetic Disorders: Current Status and Future Prospects. *Obstetrics and Gynecology*, 1976, *48*, 497–506.

Goodman, C. A Treatment and Education Program for Emotionally Disturbed Women and Their Young Children. *Hospital and Community Psychiatry*, 1980, *31*, 687–689.

Goodman, S. H. Children of Disturbed Parents: An Integrative Review of the Findings from the High Risk Studies. Unpublished paper, 1983.

Goodner, D. M. Prenatal Genetic Diagnosis: Present and Future. *Clinical Obstetrics and Gynecology*, 1976, *19*, 973–980.

Gordon, S. Second Thoughts about Sex Education in the Schools. In G. J. Williams and S. Gordon (eds.), *Clinical Child Psychology: Current Practices and Future Perspectives*. New York: Behavioral Publications, 1974, pp. 453–460.

Gordon, S. Is Parenting for Everybody? *The Exceptional Parent*, 1977, 7, M8-M10.

Gordon, T. *Parent Effectiveness Training*. New York: Wyden Press, 1970.

Guthrie, G. M., Masangkay, Z., and Guthrie, H. A., Behavior, Malnutrition, and Mental Development. *Journal of Cross-Cultural Psychology*, 1976, 7, 169–180.

Hagnell, O. A *Prospective Study of the Incidence of Mental Disorders*. Stockholm: Svenska Bokforlaget, 1966.

Haring, N. G., and Rideway, R. W. Early Identification of Children with Learning Disabilities. *Exceptional Children*, 1967, 33, 387–395.

Hartman, E. E., and Sayles, E. B. Some Reflections on Births and Infant Deaths among the Low Socio-Economic Groups. *Minnesota Medicine*, 1965, *48*, 1711–1718.

Headings, V. E. Alternative Models of Counseling for Genetic Disorders. *Social Biology*, 1975, 22, 297–303.

Herbert, M. *Emotional Problems of Development in Children*. London: Academic Press, 1974.

Hinman, L. F. Legal Considerations and Prenatal Genetic Diagnosis. *Clinical Obstetrics and Gynecology*, 1976, *19*, 965–972.

Honig, A. S. Infant Development Projects: Problems in Intervention. In G. J. Williams and S. Gordon (eds.), *Clinical Child Psychology: Current Practices and Future Perspectives*. New York: Behavioral Publications, 1974, pp. 142–167.

Horton, M. M. Liberated Women = Liberated Children. In G. J. Williams and S. Gordon (eds.), *Clinical Child Psychology: Current Practices and Future Perspectives*. New York: Behavioral Publications, 1974, pp. 425–436.

Huntington, D. S. Programs of Child Care: The United States Need and What Should Be Done. In G. J. Williams and S. Gordon (eds.), *Clinical Child Psychology: Current Practices and Future Perspectives*. New York: Behavioral Publications, 1974, pp. 168–178.

Jonsson, G. Delinquent Boys, Their Parents and Grandparents. *Acta Psychiatrica Scandinavia*, 1967, *43*, (Suppl. 195), 264.

Kaback, M. M. Perspectives in the Control of Human Genetic Disease. In *Genetics and the Perinatal Patient: Mead Johnson Symposium on Perinatal and Developmental Medicine*, 1972, *1*, 51–57.

Keister, M. E. *The Good Life for Infants and Toddlers: Group Care of Infants*. Washington, D.C.: National Association for the Education of Young Children, 1970.

Keniston, K. *Do Americans Really Like Children?* Paper presented at the meeting of the 52nd Annual meeting of the American Orthopsychiatric Association, Washington, D.C., March 21–25, 1975. (Summary of Meeting published in The State of the Child: Highlights from the 52nd Annual Meeting of the American Orthopsychiatric Association, *Hospital and Community Psychiatry*, 1975, *26*, 518–527.)

Koenigsberg, D., Balla, D. A., and Lewis, D. O. Juvenile Delinquent, Adult Criminality, and Adult Psychiatric Treatment: An Epidemiological Study. *Child Psychiatry and Human Development*, 1977, 7, 141–146.

Leonard, C. O., Chase, G. A., and Childs, B. Genetic Counseling: A Consumer's View. *New England Journal of Medicine*, 1972, 287, 433–439.

Littlefield, J. W. Recent Experience with Prenatal Genetic Diagnosis. In *Genetics and the Perinatal Patient*. Mead Johnson Symposium on Perinatal and Developmental Medicine, 1972, No. 1, pp. 25–27.

Macfarlane, J. W., Allen, L., and Honzik, M. P. *A Developmental Study of the Behavior Problems of Normal Children between Twenty-one Months and Fourteen Years*. Berkeley, Calif.: University of California Press, 1954.

Maitland, S., Nadeau, J. B., and Nadeau, G. Early Screening Practices. *Journal of Learning Disabilities*, 1974, 7, 645–649.

Masterson, J. F., Jr. The Symptomatic Adolescent Five Years Later: He Didn't Grow Out of It. *American Journal of Psychiatry*, 1967, *123*, 1338–1345.

McCary, J. L. *Human Sexuality*. New York: Van Nostrand, 1973.

Mednick, S., Schulsinger, F., and Schulsinger, H. Schizophrenia in Children of Schizophrenic Mothers. In A. Davids (ed.), *Child Personality and Psychopathology: Current Topics*, Vol. II. New York: John Wiley, 1975, pp. 221–252.

Mednick, S., and Witkin-Lanvil, G. H. Intervention in Children at High Risk for Schizophrenia. In G. W. Albee and J. M. Joffe (eds.), *Primary Prevention of Psychopathology. Vol. I: The Issues*. Hanover, N. H.: University Press of New England, 1977, pp. 153–163.

Miller, W. D., and Norris, R. C. Entrance Age and School Success. *Journal of School Psychology*, 1967, 6, 47–60.

Milunsky, A., and Reilly. P. The "New" Genetics: Emerging Medicolegal Issues in the Prenatal Diagnosis of Hereditary Disorders. *American Journal of Law and Medicine*, 1975, *1*, 71–88.

Moore, B. D. Implementing the Developmental Assessment Component of the EPSDT Program. *American Journal of Orthopsychiatry*, 1978, 48, 22–31.

Mulligan, G., Douglas, J. W. B., Hammond, W. A., and Tizard, J. Delinquency and Symptoms of Maladjustment: The Findings of a Longitudinal Study. *Proceedings of the Royal Society of Medicine*, 1963, 56, 1083–1086.

Murray, R. F. The Practitioner's View of the Values Involved in Genetic Screening and Counseling: Individual vs. Societal Imperatives. *Birth Defects,* 1974, *10,* 185–199.

NEWTON, R., and BROWN, R. A. A Preventive Approach to Developmental Problems in School Children. In E. M. Bower and W. G. Hollister (eds.), *Behavioral Science Frontiers in Education.* New York: John Wiley, 1967, pp. 499–528.

NITOWSKY, H. M. Genetic Counseling: Objectives, Principles, and Procedures. *Clinical Obstetrics and Gynecology,* 1976, *19,* 919–940.

OJEMANN, R. H. Incorporating Psychological Concepts in the School Curriculum. *Journal of School Psychology,* 1967, *5,* 195–204.

O'LEARY, K. D., and O'LEARY, S. G. Behavior Modification in Children. In K. D. O'Leary and S. G. O'Leary (eds.), *Classroom Management: The Successful Use of Behavior Modification,* 2nd ed. New York: Pergamon Press, 1977, pp. 1–56.

PASAMANICK, B., and KNOBLOCH, H. Retrospective Studies on the Epidemiology of Reproductive Causality: Old and New. *Merrill-Palmer Quarterly,* 1966, *12,* 7–26.

PICKETT, R. S. Children and Fathers. In G. J. Williams and S. Gordon (eds.), *Clinical Child Psychology: Current Practices and Future Perspectives.* New York: Behavioral Publications, 1974, pp. 437–442.

RESCH, R. C., LILLESKO, R. K., SCHEER, H. M., and MIHALOV, T. Infant Day Care as a Treatment Intervention: A Follow-up Comparison Study. *Child Psychiatry and Human Development,* 1977, *7,* 147–155.

ROBERTS, C. F., JR. *A Follow-up Study of the Juvenile Drug Offender.* Institute for the Study of Crime and Delinquency, Sacramento, California, October 1967.

ROBINS, L. N. Follow-up Studies of Behavior Disorders in Children. In H. C. Quay and J. S. Werry (eds.), *Psychopathological Disorders of Childhood.* New York: John Wiley, 1972, pp. 414–450.

ROBINS, L. N., and LEWIS, R. G. The Role of the Antisocial Family in School Completion and Delinquency: A Three-Generation Study. *Sociological Quarterly,* 1966, *7,* 500–514.

ROLF, J. E., BEVINS, S., HASAZI, J., CROWTHER, J., and JOHNSON, J. Prospective Research with Vulnerable Children and the Risky Arts of Prevention Intervention. *Journal of Prevention in the Human Services,* 1981, pp. 107–122.

ROLF, J. E., and HARIG, P. T. Etiological Research in Schizophrenia and the Rationale for Primary Intervention. *American Journal of Orthopsychiatry,* 1974, *44,* 538–554.

ROLF, J. E., and HASAZI, J. Identification of Preschool Children At Risk and Some Guidelines for Primary Intervention. In G. W. Albee and J. M. Joffe (eds.), *Primary Prevention of Psychopathology, Vol. I: The Issues.* Hanover, N. H.: The University Press of New England, 1977, pp. 121–152.

ROSEN, B. M. Distribution of Child Psychiatric Services. In J. Noshpity, I. N. Berlin, and L. Stone (eds.), *Basic Handbook of Child Psychiatry: Prevention and Current Issues.* New York: Basic Books, 1979, pp. 485–500.

RUTTER, M., BIRCH, H. G., THOMAS, A., and CHESS, S., Temperamental Characteristics in Infancy and the Later Development of Behavioural Disorders. *British Journal of Psychiatry,* 1964, *110,* 651–661.

SCHULSINGER, F., and MEDNICK, S. A. Implications from the First 18 Years of Prospective Study on Children at High Risk for Schizophrenia. In Huber Ged. Schizophrenie: *Stand under Entwicklungstendinzen der Forschung.* Stuttgart: Schlatlauer Verlag, 1981.

SCHULSINGER, H. A Ten-Year Follow-up of Children of Schizophrenic Mothers: Clinical Assessment. *Acta Psychiatrica Scandinavica,* 1976, *53,* 371–386.

SOWDER, R. J., BURT, M. R., ROSENSTEIN, M. J., and MILAZZO-SAYRE, L. J. *Use of Psychiatric Facilities by Children and Youth, United States 1975.* Mental Health Service System Reports, No. 6. Washington, D.C.: U.S. Government Printing Office, 1981.

THOMSON, A. M., and BILLEWICZ, W. Z. Nutritional Status, Maternal Physique and Reproductive Efficiency. *Proceedings of the Nutritional Society,* 1963, *22,* 55–60.

TOOLEY, W. H., and PHIBBS, R. H. Delivery Room Management of the Newborn. In G. B. Avery (ed.), *Neonatology.* Philadelphia: Lippincott, 1975, 111–126.

TORMEY, J. F. Ethical Considerations of Prenatal Genetic Diagnosis. *Clinical Obstetrics and Gynecology,* 1976, *19,* 957–963.

VOLPE, J. J. Neurological Disorders. In G. B. Avery (ed.), *Neonatology.* Philadelphia: Lippincott, 1975, pp. 729–795.

WEINSTEIN, L. School Entrance Age and Adjustment. *Journal of School Psychology,* 1968–69, *7,* 20–28.

WILLIAMS, G. J. The Psychologist as Child Advocate: Reflections of a Devil's Advocate. In G. J. Williams and S. Gordon (eds.), *Clinical Child Psychology; Current Practices and Future Perspectives.* New York: Behavioral Publications, 1974, pp. 45–49.

YOUNG, P. E., MATSON, M. R., and JONES, O. W. Amniocentesis for Antenatal Diagnosis: Review of Problems and Outcomes in a Large Series. *American Journal of Obstetrics and Gynecology,* 1976, *125,* 495–501.

ZIGLER, E. F. Children's Needs in the Seventies: A Federal Perspective. In G. J. Williams and S. Gordon (eds.), *Clinical Child Psychology: Current Practices and Future Perspectives.* New York: Behavioral Publications, 1974, pp. 24–34.

GLOSSARY

Activity therapy. Group therapy designed for prepubescent youngsters, in which play activities that are functionally related to the clinical needs of the children are used separately or as a group project.

Amniocentesis. Diagnostic tool for chromosomal problems, in which amniotic fluid from a pregnant mother is drawn to permit a chromosomal analysis.

Anal stage. Second phase of psychosexual development, in which the anus becomes the site of sexual stimulation and gratification. The period extends from about eighteen months to approximately three years, during which time the child seems to derive sensual pleasure from both retention and expulsion of fecal matter.

Animal magnetism. Mesmer's belief that the stars influence people through magnetic forces and that an imbalance of them within an individual could cause illness.

Anomie. Concept referring to a breakdown of society's regulatory machinery, wherein the socially defined standards of conduct no longer serve as effective guidelines for behavior.

Anorexia. Refusal to eat, varying in severity from fussy appetites to rare, life-endangering self-starvation.

Anterograde amnesia. Loss of memory for those matters that have occurred after the precipitant event.

Aphasia. Term used to designate an impairment of symbolic language (involving reception and/or expressive deficits) and in the comprehension of language.

Asynchronous growth. Principle of development holding that different parts and subsystems of the human organism develop at different rates and times, and that the various parts of the organism do not grow equally or all at once.

Battered child syndrome (child abuse). Term referring to regular physical assaults of the child by the parents (usually one) with harmful objects, which often result in serious injury and sometimes death to the child.

Behavior therapy. General term used to refer to treatment of abnormal behaviors by methods and techniques that have been derived from experimental psychology and the principles of learning.

Behavioral assessment. Procedures that grew out of behavior therapy; they measure target behaviors and the person's behavioral repertoire for the purpose of effecting behavior change in some desired direction.

Biofeedback. Therapeutic approach in which the client's physiological responses are monitored and fed back so that the client can learn to control them (sometimes with the aid of positive reinforcement).

Bronchial asthma. Psychophysiological disorder of the respiratory system in which the bronchial tube is restricted in air exchange, producing frightening symptoms of wheezing and labored breathing.

Cephalocaudal development. Directional flow of physical development in which growth and motor development generally proceed from the head to the tail end of the human body.

Child welfare. Social and legislative movement that began late in the nineteenth century as a response to excessive child abuse, and which produced regulatory legislation and the creation of special social agencies for the protection of children.

Classical conditioning (respondent conditioning). Learning paradigm first introduced by Pavlov, in which a neutral stimulus (CS), when repeatedly paired with a stimulus (UCS) that naturally elicits a response (UCR), will come to elicit by itself a response (CR) that is similar to the original one.

Client-centered therapy. Treatment strategy introduced by Carl Rogers, in which the therapist provides the client with complete acceptance and warmth while being reflective of what the client says.

Colic. Condition that occurs within the first few weeks of life; characterized by loud and persistent crying.

Conceptual model. Frame of reference that provides a broad but cohesive way of understanding and explaining abnormal behavior.

Concordance rate. Percent of cases in which both members of monozygotic and dizygotic twin pairs manifest the trait in question.

Conflict. Competing or opposing responses that tend to block or inhibit overt behavior.

Contingency contract. Agreement reached by the therapist and the client concerning the behavioral goals of treatment and the reinforcement to be received when the goals are successfully met.

The contingency or family-risk method. Use of large samples of relatives of index cases (known carriers of the trait under investigation) to assess the degree to which the trait is related to blood ties and to hereditary factors.

Contingent negative variation (CNV). Type of cortical response that has been associated with attention; characterized by a slow rise in negative potential when the subject anticipated the presentation of a stimulus.

Cretinism (hypothyroidism). Term used to designate several aberrant conditions of the thyroid that may be associated with mental retardation.

Criterion. Standard of functioning against which an assessment or treatment technique can be evaluated.

Cross-fostering method. Research approach that reflects the relative potency of hereditary and environmental factors. It provides for a comparison between children from biologically "normal" parents who are placed in foster homes in which one or both of the adopted parents are affected by a disorder, and children with at least one biological parent evidencing the disorder, who are placed in "normal" foster homes.

Cultural norms. Approved standards and expectations set by society for the behavior of its members.

Defense mechanisms. Set of coping methods used to deal with conflict and anxiety that are unconscious but relatively fixed.

Delayed speech. Failure to talk by the age of 30 months, or very slow progress in the acquisition of new words and in the formation of sentences.

Delusion. Fixed belief that is based on a false premise and is discrepant with the person's cultural training.

Dementia praecox. Obsolete term for schizophrenia, originally used to describe a psychotic condition in adults that was characterized by unalterable and progressive deterioration of mental functioning beginning in adolescence.

Demonology. Ancient view holding that abnormal behaviors are caused by evil spirits that inhabit people.

Denial. Unconscious act of simply denying the existence of painful facts or feelings.

Detoxification. Procedure involving withdrawal from an addictive drug under medical management.

Developmental norms. Expected age (expressed in range and average) for growth and behavioral patterns based on data obtained from large samples of normal children.

Diagnosis. Process of accumulating and discriminating data for the purpose of identifying (labeling) a pathological state.

Displacement. Transfer of instinctual emotions from one object to another, which permits the release of tensions in a manner that is less anxiety producing.

Dissociation. Phenomenon described by Janet to reflect a separation between the systems of the personality—(normal personality consists of systems of organized ideas and actions that interact with each other)—and the isolation of certain systems from the rest of the personality.

DNA (deoxyribonucleic acid). Complex chemical substance of genes responsible for genetic replication from one generation to another and for transferring genetic information.

Down's syndrome (mongolism). Autosomal syndrome associated with an extra Group-G chromosome, resulting in distinctive physical features and mental retardation.

Drive. Motivational state that impels or energizes the organism to respond (without specific direction).

DSM-I, DSM-II, DSM-III. Diagnostic and Statistical Manual of Mental Disorder (and revisions), representing the diagnostic classification system officially adopted by the American Psychiatric Association.

Dyslexia. Term used to label those children of average intelligence who have a reading disability not attributable to deprived educational opportunities or to gross sensory or neurological impairment.

Echopraxia. Unsolicited repetition and imitation of motor acts performed by another person.

Ego. Component of the personality postulated by Freud; it emerges from the id to facilitate the aims of the id by acquiring skills that enable the child to achieve pleasure in ways that are within the bounds of objective reality. The ego controls cognitive and intellectual functioning and acts as a mediator between id impulses and the demands of reality, and between the id and the superego.

Electroencephalogram (EEG). Instrument used to record electrical activity of the brain by means of electrodes attached to the scalp.

Emotive imagery. Modification of systematic desensitization that pairs imagery of pleasurable scenes (instead of relaxation) with a graded series of anxiety stimuli.

Encopresis. Involuntary defecation and withholding of feces not directly caused by physical disease, occurring in children beyond the age of 3 years.

Enuresis. Involuntary passage of urine during sleep (nocturnal) or more infrequently during the day (diurnal) in children past the age of 3 or 4, in which the cause is not linked to any demonstrable organic pathology.

Evoked potential. Cerebral reponses evoked by sensory stimuation such as flashes of light or auditory clicks.

Expectancy measure. Probability that a person will fall into a specific category of abnormal behavior sometime during his or her lifetime.

Extinction. Elimination of a learned response through the discontinuance of reinforcement.

Factor analysis. Statistical method used to isolate empirically clusters of traits or characteristics derived from a series of intracorrelations of test scores.

Family therapy. Therapeutic approach in which family members interact with each other and with the therapist, and which is based on the idea that abnormal behaviors of a child represent expressions of family transactions and pathology.

Feeblemindedness (mental deficiency and mental retardation). Terms used interchangeably to characterize subnormal intelligence and retarded social development in individuals who have not been culturally or educationally deprived.

Filial therapy. Variant of play therapy in which parents are trained to conduct nondirective play with their emotionally troubled children.

Free association. Technique developed by Freud

for releasing suppressed emotions and for revealing unconscious problems; the individual is asked to say whatever comes to mind without censuring his or her throughts.

Galactosemia. Autosomal recessive metabolic condition which impairs the metabolism of galactose and usually results in mental retardation if not treated early.

Galvanic skin response (GSR). Measure of the change in skin resistance due to alterations in sweat gland activity, which is thought to indicate arousal or emotionality.

General paresis. Disease caused by syphilitic infection, which involves irreversible and severe damage to the brain and produces the clinical picture involving loss of contact with reality, personality disorganization, delirium, paralysis, tremors, and locomotor ataxia.

Genital stage. Last psychosexual stage of development, occurring during adolescence and at a time when the sexual drive is heightened—the opposite sex becomes the sexual object for those who have developed normally.

Group therapy. Therapeutic approach in which a number of unrelated clients are brought together at regular intervals to engage in psychologically planned interactions with each other and one or more therapists.

Hallucination. Sensory misperception experienced while awake and in the absence of any corresponding external stimuli.

Higher-order conditioning. Successful pairing of a conditioned stimulus with a new conditioned stimulus which will elicit the same conditioned response as that produced from the initial classical conditioning.

High-risk children. Youngsters who have one biological parent manifesting the disorder but who have not themselves shown signs of the disturbance at the time of the initial study.

Homonculus. Ancient view of children in which a child was perceived as a little adult without a personality of his or her own.

Hyperamnesia. Unusual ability to recall minute and sometimes insignificant details learned in the distant past.

Hyperesthesia. Sensory difficulty characterized by heightened or extreme sensitivity.

Id. Inherited and original energy system of the personality posited by Freud as present at birth, from which the other two components of the personality (the ego and superego) are later energized and differentiated. The id represents the world of subjective reality, and its activities are governed by the seeking of pleasure and the avoiding of pain.

Implosive therapy (flooding). Therapy based on maximal anxiety arousal; exposes the client to highly threatening stimuli to extinguish aversive reactions.

Incidence. Total number of new cases of a disorder that occur within a specified population and a period of time.

Instincts. Inborn energy states and unconscious drives of the id that give rise to tension and which are reducible to the two fundamental drives of sex and aggression.

Intellectualization. Process of concealing threatening feelings by discussing them in an abstract, intellectual manner.

Intelligence quotient (IQ). Quantitative term of intelligence reflecting the relationship between the child's mental age and chronological age.

Intelligence tests. Standardized techniques for measuring intellectual functioning.

Intermittent reinforcement. Schedule of reinforcement in which the wanted response is not always followed by a reinforcer.

Karyotype. Pictures pairs of normal chromosomes arranged in a prescribed order, by which comparisons can be made in identifying chromosomal abnormalities.

Klinefelter's syndrome. Disorder associated with an extra X chromosome in males; it produces feminine secondary sex characteristics and sometimes mental retardation.

Latency stage. Longest psychosexual stage of development, extending from about 6 years of age through preadolescence. It is a stage where sexual tensions and activities are dormant, where the child can recover from the turmoil of the Oedipal phase, and where further identification with the same-sex parent occurs.

Learning. Process by which environmental forces bring about lasting changes in behavior through practice.

Libido. Psychoanalytic term used to reflect the energy of the sex drive.

Manic depressive psychosis. Affective disorder manifested in either alterations of emotional excitement and euphoria (mania) with periods of melancholia and depression, or episodes of mania or depression, or both.

Marasmus. Condition in which infants evidence progressive emaciation and possible death as a result of malnutrition or prolonged maternal separation and deprivation.

Maturation. Physical alterations in size, and qualitative changes in tissues or in anatomical and physiological organization, that occur in the course of human development.

Mental age. Measure of mental development derived from test results that have been standardized according to chronological age.

Mental retardation (mental deficiency, feeblemindeness). Significantly subaverage intellectual functioning, existing concurrently with deficits in adaptive behavior, that is manifested during the developmental period prior to adulthood.

Milieu therapy. Term used to refer to treatment methods involving ongoing experiences in which the daily environment is ordered, arranged, and planned as a therapeutic program.

Modeling (imitation learning). Learning that takes place by observing another person or a model making a response or a set of responses.

Negative reinforcement. Strengthening of behavior through the removal of an unpleasant or aversive consequence.

Neologism. Coining of a new word.

Neuroticism. Statistically isolated dimension that is related to emotional instability and a poorly integrated personality.

Neurotransmitters. Chemical mediators of neural communication in the central nervous system.

Nightmare. Common fright reaction that occurs during the last third of the night in Stage 1–REM sleep.

Night terror. Relatively rare fright reaction that occurs within the first two hours of the night in Stage 4–non REM sleep.

Oedipal stage. Psychosexual stage of development between the ages of 4 and 6, in which the opposite sex parent becomes the object of libidinal pleasure; also known as the phallic stage.

Operant conditioning (instrumental learning). Learning paradigm in which S-R bonds are strengthened by making reinforcement contingent on the emission of the proper response.

Oral stage. First stage of psychosexual development, occurring during the initial eighteen to twenty-four months of the infant's life, in which stimulation of the erogeneous zones of the lips and mouth provide pleasure and relieve libidinal tension.

Paresthesia. Peculiar skin sensation without objective cause.

Pedigree method. Research method that consists of tracing the incidence of a trait in all family members over several generations in order to make inferences about the genetic principle involved.

Perseveration. Repetition of one's prior response.

Phallic stage. See Oedipal Stage.

Phenyketonuria (PKU). Autosomal recessive metabolic disorder in which phenylalanine is improperly utilized by the body. Its accumulation in the bloodstream causes brain damage and mental retardation.

Phobia. Persistent and irrational fear of an object or situation that the person is unable to dispel; usually leads to the avoidance of the object or situation.

Phrenology. Theory proposed by Gall, holding that character traits are localized in 37 different areas of the brain and that abnormal behavior is tied to the overdevelopment of these areas (which can be felt as bumps on the skull).

Pica. Craving and consumption of substances not ordinarily considered edible.

Play therapy. Therapeutic approach for preadolescent children, in which play activities are used to establish rapport and to facilitate communication.

Pleasure principle. Psychoanalytic principle by which the id seeks immediate gratification of drives and desires and the avoidance of pain without regard for the consequences.

Positive reinforcement. Strengthening of behavior through rewards; it meets either the biological requirements or the learned needs of the individual.

Prevalence. Total number of cases (old and new) present in a given population during a specified time interval.

Principle of differentiation. Structural and

functional development that progresses from the general to the specific or from the simple to the complex in patterns.

Projection. Unconscious act of blaming others or attributing one's faults to others.

Projective tests. Class of personality tests consisting of a set of unstructured and ambiguous stimuli to which it is assumed the respondent will reveal his/her basic personality.

Proximodistal development. Directional flow of physical development in which growth and motor development proceed from the central axis to the periphery of the human body.

Psychic determinism. Belief that every human act occurs as a function of prior mental events and not as a matter of happenstance. Previous events and experiences determine all facets of a person's behavior.

Psychoneuroses. Set of psychological disorders characterized by intense feelings of anxiety, personal discomfort and distress, and self-directed reactions to the stress of conflicts.

Psychopathology. Abnormal behavior attributable to psychological and/or biological causes.

Psychophysiological disorders. Psychopathological conditions characterized by physical symptoms that arise from dysfunctioning and structural damage to a single organ system usually innervated by the autonomic nervous system, which is primarily caused by prolonged psychological and social stress.

Psychosexual stages of development. Series of sequential and crucial developmental stages postulated by Freud that are associated with libidinal impulses (sexual) that play an important role in later personality formation.

Psychosocial stages of development. Sequential series of developmental stages postulated by Erikson that focus on important socialization conflicts at various points in a person's life.

Psychosurgery. Removal or destruction of brain tissue as a therapeutic intervention for the elimination of abnormal behaviors.

Psychotherapy. Psychologically planned and ongoing interaction between a trained person—the therapist—and a client who has adjustment problems.

Punishment. Condition or event that is presented after a response occurs, which will decrease the probability that the response will be emitted (weaken the S-R association).

Rationalization. Process of avoiding anxiety by finding justifiable excuses for doing something unacceptable.

Reaction Formation. Process by which the ego substitutes actions and feelings directly opposite to those that might be produced by sexual or aggressive impulses.

Reality principle. Psychoanalytic principle governing the ego, by which gratification of pleasure is deferred through the consideration of the demands of objective reality.

Reality therapy. Therapeutic approach which focuses on the present and encourages the client to make value judgments about his or her behaviors, to make a plan that would achieve the desired goal, and to be commited to the plan.

Regression. Method of dealing with external or internal conflicts by retreating to an immature stage of development or by resorting to earlier modes of responding.

Reinforcement. Any event or condition which leads to the strengthening of a stimulus-response connection or to the increased probability that a response will be emitted.

Reliability. Extent to which a measure (test or rating) yields the same results each time it is used. The consistency of results may be derived from agreement between two or more observers (observer agreement), agreement between the same measure over points in time (consistency agreement), or agreement between two or more samples of the same population with regard to the expected frequency of occurrence of the measure (frequency agreement).

Repression. Basic and primary defense mechanism which actively banishes from consciousness unacceptable or anxiety-arousing impulses, thoughts, or wishes.

Resistance. Psychoanalytic term that depicts the individual's opposition to therapeutic attempts to bring unconscious material to consciousness.

Retrograde amnesia. Loss of memory for matters that took place prior to the precipitant event.

RNA (ribonucleic acid). A single-strand molecule that receives the coded information in a DNA molecule. It acts as a messenger and initiates certain chemical reactions that eventually determine bodily structure and function.

Schizophrenia. Adult psychosis characterized by

loss of contact with reality, ambivalence, disordered thinking, attentional deficits, and affective impairment.

Self-actualization. Realization of one's inherent potentials.

Shaping. Technique used by operant conditioners: Approximations of the wanted behavior is reinforced, followed by the reinforcement of responses that are increasingly similar to it, until only the appropriate response is reinforced.

Shock therapy. Somatic therapy in which drugs (Metrazol) or electricity are used to produce a convulsive reaction.

Somnambulism. Disruption of sleep characterized by sleepwalking, and occurring during the first two hours of the night in non-REM sleep.

Spontaneous remission. Improvement that occurs over time without planned treatment intervention.

Stuttering. Term used to refer to a particular breakdown in speech fluency; characterized by blocking, repetition, and prolongation of speech sounds.

Sublimation. Way of expressing unacceptable impulses in an acceptable manner by channeling ego-threatening drives into constructive outlets such as art and science.

Superego. Postulated by Freud as the moral and conscience component of the personality, it is recognized by its judicial functions in rendering judgments about right and wrong and in its strivings for perfection and the ideal.

Symptom. Biological, psychological, or behavioral manifestation of a disorder or illness.

Systematic desensitization (counterconditioning). Behavioral treatment method introduced by Wolpe, in which the incompatible response of relaxation is paired with a graded series of anxiety stimuli to prevent the occurrence of a fear response and to allow anxiety to be extinguished.

Tay-Sachs disease. Recessive disorder of lipid metabolism found predominantly among children of Eastern European Jewish ancestry. The disorder is progressive, and death usually occurs before the age of 4.

Temperament. Concept referring to individual differences in inborn potentials for action. Characterized by particular behavioral styles, temperament is significantly affected by the interplay of environmental forces.

Thought disorder. Gross disruption and impairment of normal thought processes and content; characterized by incoherence, disorganization, and inappropriate or bizarre content.

Tic. Involuntary spasmodic muscle twitching of the face or body parts that is repeated at frequent intervals.

Turner's syndrome. Anomaly of the sex chromosome in females (XO); results in sexual infantilism, distinctive physical features, and mental retardation in about 20 percent of the cases.

Twin study method. Research method in which monozygotic twins and dizygotic twins are studied with respect to a particular trait to determine the influence of genetic factors.

Unconscious. Primarily but not exclusively a Freudian concept, it refers to a state of unawareness in which certain unacceptable mental contents are inaccessible to consciousness under ordinary circumstances. Mental material banished from consciousness is stored in the unconscious.

Validity. Extent to which a measure or a hypothesis verifies what it purports to measure or say.

Name Index

Note: References to persons as subjects appear in the Subject Index.

Subject Index